ALSO BY PAUL FREEDMAN

Out of the East: Spices and the Medieval Imagination
Food: The History of Taste (Editor)
Images of the Medieval Peasant

Ten Restaurants That Changed America

PAUL FREEDMAN

INTRODUCTION BY DANNY MEYER

LIVERIGHT PUBLISHING CORPORATION

A DIVISION OF W. W. NORTON & COMPANY

Independent Publishers Since 1923

NEW YORK   LONDON

For information about permission to reproduce selections from this book,
write to Permissions, Liveright Publishing Corporation,
a division of W. W. Norton & Company, Inc.,
500 Fifth Avenue, New York, NY 10110

For information about special discounts for bulk purchases, please contact W. W. Norton Special
Sales at specialsales@wwnorton.com or 800-233-4830

Manufacturing by RR Donnelley, Crawfordsville
Book design by JAM Design
Production manager: Louise Mattarelliano

Library of Congress Cataloging-in-Publication Data

Names: Freedman, Paul, 1949– author.
Title: Ten restaurants that changed America / Paul Freedman ; introduction by Danny Meyer.
Description: First edition. | New York : Liveright Publishing Corporation, a division of W.W.
Norton & Company, [2016] | Includes bibliographical references and index.
Identifiers: LCCN 2016029340 | ISBN 9780871406804 (hardcover)
Subjects: LCSH: Restaurants—United States—History.
Classification: LCC TX909 .F697 2016 | DDC 647.9573—dc23 LC record available at
https://lccn.loc.gov/2016029340

Liveright Publishing Corporation
500 Fifth Avenue, New York, N.Y. 10110
www.wwnorton.com

W. W. Norton & Company Ltd.
15 Carlisle Street, London W1D 3BS

1 2 3 4 5 6 7 8 9 0

This book is dedicated to
my brother Dan Freedman
and to his family

CONTENTS

LIST OF ILLUSTRATIONS

TEN RESTAURANTS AND AMERICAN CUISINE

Fig. 1:   Delmonico's menu for a dinner in honor of Grand Duke Alexis of Russia. (*Menu for the 'Diner de 100 Couverts En l'Honeur de S. M. le Grand Duk Alexis, Decembre 1871', Delmonico's,* from Charles Ranhofer, *The Epicurean* [New York: C. Ranhofer, 1894], p. 1092. Schlesinger Library, Radcliffe Institute, Harvard University, RSMJ8K.)

Fig. 2:   Medieval "street food." (Woodcut with hand coloring, in Ulrich von Richenthal, Concillium zu Constencz [Augsburg, 1483], Technische Universität Darmstadt, Universität- und Landesbibliothek Darmstadt, Inc III 55.)

DELMONICO'S

Fig. 3:   A page from the 1838 Delmonico's menu. (*Menu, Carte du Restaurant Français des Frères Delmonico,* 1838. Collection of the Museum of the City of New York, 34.295.2.ALT3.)

Fig. 4:   Cover of the 1838 Delmonico's menu. (*Menu, Carte du Restaurant Français des Frères Delmonico,* 1838. Collection of the Museum of the City of New York, 34.295.2.)

Fig. 5:   Photograph of "The Citadel," Delmonico's at Beaver and S. William Street. (Baxter St. [Baxter Street to Broad Street], photograph, J. Clarence Davies Street Views Scrapbook. Collection of the Museum of the City of New York, X2012.61.2.3.)

Fig. 6:   Watercolor of the exterior of Delmonico's Fourteenth Street at Fifth Avenue. (Unknown, *Delmonico's,* 1875, watercolor on board, 15.5 x 10.25 in. Collection of the Museum of the City of New York, 29.100.2082.)

Fig. 7:   Confectionary Department at Delmonico's. (*Delmonico's, Confectionary Dept., 1902,* photograph, Byron Company [New York, N.Y.]. Collection of the Museum of the City of New York, 93.1.1.6151.)

EPILOGUE

Ten Restaurants That Changed America is a chronicle of inventive food, creative chefs, and the joys and perils of running a restaurant. This is a completely new kind of American history, as well as a revelation about restaurants and society.

This book cracks open a window that allows us to view the larger history of the United States as seen through dining out. As Paul Freedman demonstrates, restaurants are more than a leisure activity or a more colorful alternative to dining at home: they channel the broad currents of political and social trends—the effects of immigration, the American love of convenience, the role of women as consumers, or the influence that the Great Migration of African Americans from South to North played in shaping American food culture.

Beginning with my first restaurant, Union Square Café, and with each subsequent restaurant I've opened, I have been interested in historical restaurant models and ideals: the Italian trattoria, the colonial tavern, the hamburger stand, the Southern barbecue joint, the iconic luxe restaurant, even the New York coffee shop. I tried to think what it might be like to transform these models by providing the best possible food and warm hospitality—not always the primary goal for the antecedents—and making them relevant to their moment in time. *Ten Restaurants* shows how the most successful and influential types of restaurants are always rooted in some particular time and place. It reveals not only the myriad options for dining out but also the societal trends that shape American restaurants and their customers.

Reading about the ten different restaurants gives me a sense of American diversity, and how these individual experiments expressed a sense of love that is the basic ingredient of any major endeavor. Each one of them ultimately found a profitable model, although it is surprising that some, such as the Four Seasons and Chez Panisse, had to wait such a long time before making any money. The impressive thing about the chefs and entrepreneurs who founded these establishments is their love for providing good food and hospitality—even greater than their passion for making a profit. Some successful restaurants were created by coldly calculating managerial geniuses, such as Howard Deering Johnson, or the arrogant and eccentrically irascible, such as Henri Soulé of Le Pavillon. Yet even these men put the pleasure of their customers at the center of their mission (although Soulé was famous for his "cafeteria hospitality," selectively choosing which clients would, and would not, benefit from his largesse). Nevertheless, people—the chefs and proprietors featured here—who recall Le Pavillon and the other restaurants refer to their experiences with affection, even with some longing, because each establishment offered something that couldn't be found elsewhere. It might have been a particular dish, such as Howard Johnson's fried clams and unusually rich ice cream, or the secret recipe for Oysters Rockefeller at Antoine's. But the unique feature is often something less tangible: the gracious but efficient organization of Schrafft's, the meticulous splendor of Delmonico's, or the festive nightly scene at Mamma Leone's.

What is particularly noteworthy about *Ten Restaurants* is the way Freedman examines restaurants from the point of view of managers and chefs, communicating the vigilance and anxiety involved in making sure the experience of diners is consistently delightful. The personality types that have been successful appear to be, like the indomitable Cecilia Chiang or the restlessly creative Joe Baum, fanatically on top of every aspect of the customer's experience. Just as Freedman analyzes the challenges faced by the management, he also sees things through the guests' eyes. The efforts of restaurant staff may not often be directly noted or appreciated by patrons, but this book emphasizes their crucial role in providing pleasure. These emotions—more than just culinary impressions—are at the heart of many reminiscences: Greil Marcus's account of opening night at Chez Panisse, where discontent about the long wait between courses gave way to rapture when the food arrived; or Adam Gopnik's memory of the "optimism" that surrounded childhood visits to Howard Johnson's; or Gael Greene's surprise at being hugged by Sylvia Woods on her first adventurous visit uptown to Sylvia's.

I was also fascinated by the variety of ingredients and dishes that we no longer see—and by just how many things from our own past now only rarely grace American menus (game, terrapin, pigs' feet, organ meat, French sauces). The taste of the past is a legacy, an unseen presence, and an inspiration. More than anything else, this is a book about food and taste. It shows why American cuisine has so frequently been led in the direction of convenience, quantity, and special effects at the expense of pure quality.

Ten Restaurants is also about continuity and change: Why did French food dominate the high end for 150 years and then decline? How was seasonality reintroduced as a priority? Why has Italian food today attained high-end status, but not Chinese? Amid the tide of change, these ten stories reveal a remarkable continuity that provides some answers to the surprisingly difficult question: "What is American cuisine?" The importance of pleasure is a permanent feature—more important even than novelty, efficiency, convenience, and luxury.

These insights convince me that Freedman is onto something new. He demonstrates that our nation's restaurants are anything but ephemeral. Here is a book that can be savored by both history readers and food lovers, an American culinary chronicle that convinces us, if we know where to look, that restaurants are a key feature of our variegated American history. So much life is lived in restaurants, by workers and patrons alike, that it would be irresponsible to ignore what they say about us, as mirrors of our social wants and needs.

DANNY MEYER

NEW YORK, NEW YORK

TEN RESTAURANTS
AND AMERICAN CUISINE

An exploration of American cuisine, *Ten Restaurants That Changed America* is as much a history of American eating habits as it is a chronicle of ten restaurants over three different centuries. Our journey takes us from the 1830s, when Delmonico's, the first real restaurant in the United States, was established, right on to the present. Of this list Antoine's, Sylvia's, and Chez Panisse are still going concerns, while the Four Seasons has just been ejected from its landmark modernist home of over fifty years. Delmonico's closed in 1923, but there is now a successor Delmonico's at one of the restaurant's original locations.

This book is not about the ten *best* restaurants that ever existed in the United States. Some of the establishments on our list have served marvelous food; others changed how we eat, even if in retrospect their innovations don't seem so wonderful or their food fails to satisfy today's tastes. The selection is based on influence and exemplification: the importance of each restaurant for setting or reflecting trends in what Americans think about food and particularly dining out. Culinary fashions, as social history shows us, are determined not just by the upper classes who pride themselves on discernment but by the enthusiasms of less pretentious people for modest but ubiquitous places to eat, such as coffee shops, ice-cream parlors, or highway restaurants.

What we eat today is the result of the innovations of these ten restaurants. The restaurant itself as a particular place to dine out was reproduced along the model set by Delmonico's, but varying customers and wildly different ambitions steered restaurants in many directions: the tourist destination typified by Antoine's and Mamma Leone's, the inexpensive middle-class chain restaurant by Schrafft's and Howard Johnson's, and restaurants presenting the cuisine of another country, here represented by Mamma Leone's and the Mandarin. Distinctly American ways of eating include roadside restaurants developed by Howard Johnson's and the late-twentieth-century shift toward offering seasonal menus as pioneered by the Four Seasons and Chez Panisse.

If we take a long historical view, we find that American taste has been molded by the country's natural environment and the origins and traditions of the diverse people who settled it. How Americans eat has been influenced by cultural forces such as the international reach of French haute-cuisine, the history and legacy of slavery and immigration, and the drive toward an affluent but uniform consumer society. These ten restaurant histories show, however, beyond such generalities, the power of particular restaurant visions: Delmonico's determination to reproduce French fine dining and elegant service; Schrafft's efforts to cater to women; and the mission of Chez Panisse to change how America thinks about where its food comes from and how it might be improved both socially and aesthetically.

At the outset it's worth asking: Is there such a thing as American cuisine? In many countries the very idea provokes amusement because Americans are assumed to be uninterested in any food that doesn't come from McDonald's. More knowledgeable foreign observers admire the variety of

American "ethnic" restaurants but are mystified about what, if anything, native to the United States underlies this diversity. Even in a country like Germany, with a multitude of Italian, Greek, Turkish, and Thai restaurants, there is a strong sense of regional and national ingredients and recipes—something missing from the modern United States.

In the nineteenth century, the United States presented considerable regional culinary variety, from Chesapeake Bay terrapin (turtles) to New Orleans gumbo; from Low Country (South Carolina) perlou (a rice dish) to Western bison and other game. The twentieth century witnessed the erosion of regional distinction caused by a decline in the number of farms and the rural population; the degradation of the environment, thus endangering local specialties; and the proliferation of burgers, pizza, doughnuts, and other fast-food items that are the same from one end of the country to the other. In addition to its long history and French influence, one of the reasons for selecting Antoine's as one of the restaurants featured here is that it exemplifies the most robust of American regional food traditions—that of Louisiana and particularly New Orleans. Apart from isolated areas of the country, however, there are few other places that have preserved their culinary legacies except in an artificial and commercialized sense, as found in Texas chili cook-offs, Maine lobster festivals, and the like.[1]

Dividing the country into culinary regions is too weak to support a unified concept of American cuisine, however, and so dining out in the United States might better be considered in terms of an eclectic collection of options, particularly with the availability of dozens of different ethnic restaurant types. As early as 1873, the indefatigable and celebrated French writer Alexandre Dumas observed that, after Paris, San Francisco had the most restaurants and that unlike Paris, there were restaurants representing the cuisine of every country, even China.[2] Twenty years later, L. J. Vance, writing in *Frank Leslie's Popular Monthly*, could boast of New York's culinary internationalism, where it was possible to "breakfast in London, lunch in Berlin, dine in Paris and have supper in Vienna." In 1892 San

Francisco was again singled out for its variety. A reporter named Charles Greene, writing in *The Overland Monthly*, said that San Francisco provided the gastronomic equivalent of a grand tour, and he was a little more adventurous than his New York colleague in including Chinese, Italian, Jewish, and Mexican possibilities.[3]

A correspondent for a magazine called *The Steward* in 1909 declared that with regard to food, as with much else, "Europe lives on tradition, America lives on variety," a perceptive remark that shows a fundamental difference between what Americans look for in food in contrast to the approach of almost everywhere else.[4] To take just one example: Lucknow, India, has a local specialty called shirmal—a flat, leavened bread flavored with saffron. Derived from Persian influence, this bread is found elsewhere in northern India but is associated particularly with Lucknow, where, in fact, there is a street whose shirmal makers are renowned. On that single lane crammed with shirmal vendors, one stand is generally regarded as producing the best example (in terms of taste and texture) of something that can be found everywhere on this street, in the city, and throughout this part of Uttar Pradesh. The shirmal has only a few ingredients, but it requires skill in preparing, resting, and baking the dough. Factors affecting the quality of the shirmal include the difficult process of incorporating the ghee (clarified butter) into the dough, where to place the dough in the tandoor oven, when to splash on the saffron milk, oven temperature, timing, and so forth.[5]

This fanatical attention to basic products is not what built the culinary world of the United States. True, there are examples of local competition for a specific dish. In New Haven, Connecticut, the rivalry between Pepe's and Sally's for thin-crusted, charred pizza is legendary, and aficionados line up on either side. Generally, however, the United States has been about choice, not craft. Even in this special pizza sector, Pepe's now has branches outside of New Haven, and New Haven–style pizza is available in New York and elsewhere.

The erosion of regionalism and the standardization of food supply and preparation have tended to promote variety rather than comparison among different kinds of the same thing. Instead of discussions over who can best make tortellini in Bologna, or dosas in Chennai or rice pilaf in Isfahan, the American scene has offered mass-produced products in many flavors. The yogurt might not be very good, since it is produced in a factory and consumed hundreds of miles from where it was prepared, and weeks afterward, but it is available in dozens of flavors; the orange juice in the market comes to processing plants in trucks and then is sealed in plastic-coated paperboard cartons, but it can be purchased with pulp, added calcium, without pulp, or mixed with grapefruit juice. Providing options is a way of diverting the subject away from quality.

Rice-A-Roni, a product popular in my childhood, exemplifies some of the basic trends in American taste: the adaptation of recipes by immigrants, industrial production, mass-market promotion, flavor options, and obsolescence.[6] An Italian immigrant of the 1890s named Domenico DeDomenico opened a pasta factory in San Francisco. In the 1950s, his son Vince tasted a rice pilaf made by an Armenian neighbor who cooked the rice with pasta before adding chicken broth. Vince DeDomenico imitated this pilaf by mixing dry chicken soup mix with rice and vermicelli and dubbed it "Rice-A-Roni" because it combined rice and macaroni. Beginning in 1962 a memorable jingle advertised Rice-A-Roni as "the San Francisco treat."[7] The announcer pointed out how San Francisco was famous for its food, and a cable car bell clanged through the entire commercial. The advertisement thus merged the inventor's coincidental home with the cuisine of a city that did not, in fact, specialize in rice and pasta mixtures. Rice-A-Roni was neither Italian, Armenian, nor San Franciscan, but so what?

At first available only in chicken flavor, Rice-A-Roni soon came in "four fabulous flavors": chicken, Spanish, fried (that is, Chinese), and beef. There are now nineteen varieties of just the "original" Rice-A-Roni. In the 1960s it occupied a niche as a convenient side dish. Rice-A-Roni was unlikely to be put in front of upper-middle class dinner guests, and in its advertising it modestly claimed a role as a substitute for potatoes. Nevertheless, Rice-A-Roni had a creative, even gourmet, image, and the product was advertised on San Francisco's actual cable cars to lend verisimilitude to its local origins. Tourists would see that it was a local product. It eventually lost favor to the extent that it ceased to be an item every shopper or television-watcher knew about since it was neither as convenient as microwaving nor as interesting as more sophisticated prepared or take-out food.

The American food industry's emphasis on choice is exemplified by Rice-A-Roni's multiple flavors. The proliferation of what are commonly referred to as "ethnic" restaurants is another manifestation of the American passion for options as opposed to authenticity. This is not to dismiss international restaurants as simply polyglot mediocrity. They really are distinctive of American restaurant dining. Nevertheless, how authentically they represent Chinese, Thai, Italian, or whatever cuisine they purport to serve remains a source of legitimate anxiety to many diners. As will be seen, chop suey and spaghetti with meatballs were wildly popular among American diners and later became discredited as inauthentic, only to be replaced by other dubious favorites such as General Tso's chicken or tiramisu. Authenticity may not be important to everyone and may often be beside the point. Chinese food in the United States bears only a tangential relation to what people in China eat, but it has a claim as a culinary style nonetheless. It is also worth bearing in mind that any transfer of a cuisine over a distance means that native fish, spices, vegetables, and methods of preparation are likely to be unavailable or inconvenient in the new place, so any discussion of "authenticity" is already complicated by this fact.

Given the prevalence of processed food, the lack of regional variety, and the adaptations made by ethnic restaurants to American tastes, perhaps the United States in the end doesn't have a real cuisine. Sidney Mintz, an anthropologist who pioneered the study of food as a vital part of human culture, defined a true cuisine as more than a set of elite preferences, but rather something that ordinary people care about and discuss.

This sort of discussion has not been common in the food culture of the modern United States.[8]

There was a more sweeping and far-reaching dismissal of the idea of American cuisine that dates as far back as the winter of 1871–1872, when the Russian Grand Duke Alexis, fifth child of Tsar Alexander II, visited the United States. The duke called on President Ulysses Grant, hunted buffalo on the Great Plains, and attended Mardi Gras in New Orleans. Having been fêted all over the country, including at Delmonico's, the most famous restaurant of the time, he stated that although there was elegant food in the United States, all of it was French—there was no such thing as American cuisine, he opined flatly. Alexis probably considered his statement self-evident and not especially controversial or even harsh. After all, the Russian elite, like their American counterparts, subsisted on French dishes.

A series of indignant and patriotic protests resulted from this casual but well-publicized statement. James Parkinson, the owner of one of the best restaurants in Philadelphia, denied that American high-end offerings depended on France and pointed especially to game, fish, and other native products. Parkinson extolled canvasback duck (a large wild duck) and terrapin, the two most prestigious dishes in the United States. American shad, sturgeon, trout, lobsters, and oysters were unmatched. Parkinson included not just ingredients but prepared dishes such as New England chowders and baked pork and beans, and what about buckwheat pancakes and New Jersey sausage, he asked? Parkinson reserved his most fulsome encomium for American ice cream but, given that he had started as a confectioner, this is not surprising.[9]

A look at the splendid and seemingly endless meal offered to the Russian duke by Delmonico's supports both opinions. Charles Ranhofer, the chef at Delmonico's, was from Alsace and trained in French cuisine. The twelve-course menu (in French) included such haute-cuisine classics as woodcocks in pie crust and aspic (*Chaudfroid de bécasses en croustade à la gelée*) and partridge filets à l'Aquitaine (with an Espagnole sauce flavored with Madeira and cinnamon). Ranhofer even invented a "consommé au Grand Duc" for the occasion, but the recipe does not survive. In addition to these French-inspired delicacies, however, the banquet menu presented American terrapin à la Maryland and canvasback duck along with California salmon (albeit with a French red-wine Genevoise sauce).[10]

At the time when Parkinson and Ranhofer were cooking, America could be said to possess regional culinary styles. In 1880, Mark Twain published a travel book, *A Tramp Abroad*, which included an expression of homesickness as evoked by a list of eighty American specialties he missed. These included Philadelphia terrapin soup, canvasback ducks, Boston baked beans, and many Southern items from fried chicken to hoecakes.[11] Without intending to write a response to Grand Duke Alexis, Twain assumed that there was not just one but many regional tendencies in American food.

In later years, the same question about whether there was a real culinary tradition in America would periodically come up. In 1937 the mystery writer Rex Stout had his gourmand detective Nero Wolfe answer a European chef who is contemptuous of what people eat in America by asking him if he had ever tasted terrapin stewed with butter and chicken broth and sherry? Or planked Porterhouse steak with parsley, limes, mashed potatoes and slightly undercooked mushrooms? Creole tripe of New Orleans? The list goes on: Tennessee opossum, Philadelphia snapper soup, and chicken in curdled egg sauce.[12] Despite Nero Wolfe's defense of "the American contribution to *la haute cuisine*," the regional traditions that had developed in the United States were virtually obliterated during the twentieth century.

FROM FRENCH FOOD TO FAST FOOD

What didn't change until quite recently, though, was the complementary part of Grand Duke Alexis's statement about American cuisine: the pres-

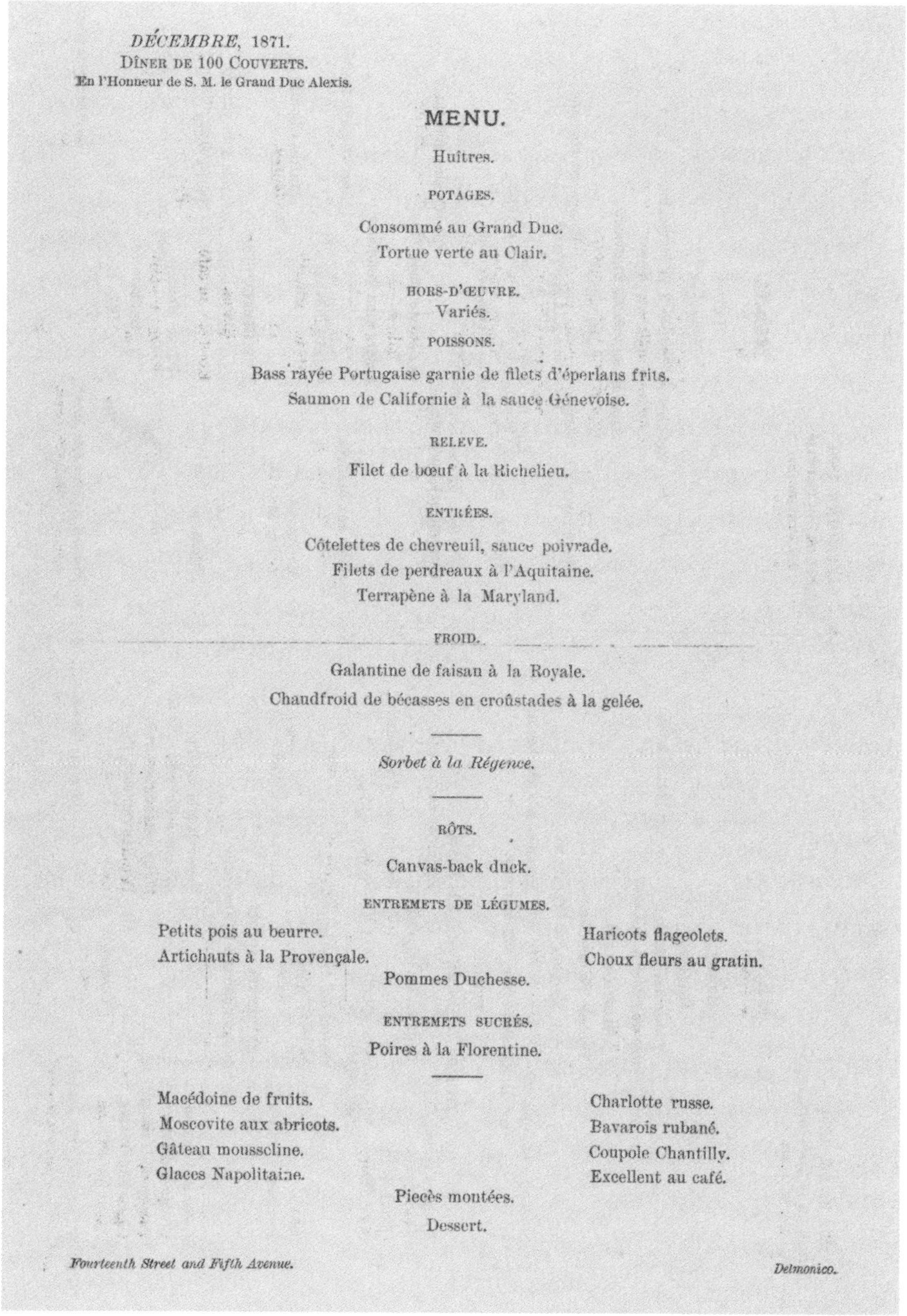

DÉCEMBRE, 1871.
DÎNER DE 100 COUVERTS.
En l'Honneur de S. M. le Grand Duc Alexis.

MENU.

Huîtres.

POTAGES.

Consommé au Grand Duc.
Tortue verte au Clair.

HORS-D'ŒUVRE.
Variés.

POISSONS.

Bass rayée Portugaise garnie de filets d'éperlans frits.
Saumon de Californie à la sauce Génevoise.

RELEVE.

Filet de bœuf à la Richelieu.

ENTRÉES.

Côtelettes de chevreuil, sauce poivrade.
Filets de perdreaux à l'Aquitaine.
Terrapène à la Maryland.

FROID.

Galantine de faisan à la Royale.
Chaudfroid de bécasses en croûstades à la gelée.

Sorbet à la Régence.

RÔTS.

Canvas-back duck.

ENTREMETS DE LÉGUMES.

Petits pois au beurre.
Artichauts à la Provençale.
Haricots flageolets.
Choux fleurs au gratin.
Pommes Duchesse.

ENTREMETS SUCRÉS.

Poires à la Florentine.

Macédoine de fruits.
Moscovite aux abricots.
Gâteau mousseline.
Glaces Napolitaine.
Charlotte russe.
Bavarois rubané.
Coupole Chantilly.
Excellent au café.
Piecès montées.
Dessert.

Fourteenth Street and Fifth Avenue.

Delmonico.

Fig. 1. Delmonico's menu for a dinner
in honor of Grand Duke Alexis of Russia, December 1871.

tige of French food that defines upper-class gastronomy. Of the restaurants discussed in this book, Le Pavillon, which epitomized the high end of mid-twentieth-century dining out, was unabashedly, even exaggeratedly French in the way it presented itself. Delmonico's referred to its cuisine as French, and although it featured American delicacies, as already observed, its preparations and overall aesthetic were consistently French. Antoine's, until recently, billed itself as a French restaurant and its menu is still in French even though its offerings are a Creole variation of French-inflected cuisine.

The last of the restaurants we explore in terms of chronology, Chez Panisse, pioneered the development of a new American cuisine beginning in the 1980s, but as its name implies, it too was originally inspired by France. The Four Seasons was established in 1959 as an unusual attempt to create an elegant, as we would now say "world-class," restaurant in New York that was *not* French—a daring experiment in global eclecticism allied to a precocious attention to place and season. Thus, half of the restaurants named here as the most important in the culinary history of the United States were either French, aspired to be French, or reacted against French domination.

One of the main stories of world cuisine over the last fifty years is the waning of the once-hegemonic influence of France. To get a sense of how France's domination was taken for granted, consider a 1969 interview with French food critics Henri Gault and Christian Millau, who were asked by the glossy American travel journal *Holiday* what the best restaurant in the world was. Before deciding on two restaurants in France to share the honor (Paul Bocuse and La Maison Troisgros), they quickly dismissed the United States and Canada: there were, of course, fine restaurants there, but they were all staffed by French chefs.[13] A reiteration of Grand Duke Alexis's opinion precisely, but in the late 1960s, as opposed to the 1870s, no one claimed to refute these arrogant foreigners and assert that America had a glorious, native haute cuisine.

In addition to the long-lasting upper-class infatuation with France, two major driving forces behind American dining have been convenience and a variety of "ethnic" restaurants that offer the food of the diverse populations that have come to America. Convenience has been related to predictability. Rather than having to consider the look, menu offerings, or even cleanliness of individual establishments, the customer finds a consistent experience. Having been to one, you know what to expect at others. I have concentrated on Howard Johnson's rather than McDonald's or other fast-food chains because its orientation toward middle-class families, highway driving, and uniformity made Howard Johnson's the pioneer in coast-to-coast standardization of dining experiences. An emphasis on predictability did not grow just out of cost-cutting or an obsession with organization, but was designed to create a predictable meal and so accustom people to thinking of the restaurant as a routine, hence frequently repeatable, part of their lives.

Also included in our discussion is Schrafft's, a restaurant group founded at the end of the nineteenth century, long before Howard Johnson's. Beginning as a candy and ice cream store, Schrafft's developed into a small chain in the Northeast that never had the numbers or geographical range of Howard Johnson's, let alone McDonald's. Nevertheless, it pioneered the middle-class restaurant experience, carving out a space between the fancy places like Delmonico's or Antoine's on the one hand, and workingmen's cafés, taverns, and hash houses on the other. Serving ice-cream treats, but also whole meals, Schrafft's offered a reasonably gracious, efficient, and moderately priced option that was particularly appealing to women. It wasn't that restaurants were off limits to women in the nineteenth century, but there were few establishments that women could patronize without a male escort, something many twenty-first-century readers may have a hard time imagining. There were few restaurants in which women alone or with other women would have felt safe. Schrafft's did not serve beer, wine, or liquor, and in company with teahouses, department-store restaurants, cafeterias, and Automats, Schrafft's provided a welcoming place for women. Notions of respectability clearly rendered it impossible for most women to enter bars, grills, and other clearly male haunts. High-end restaurants differed in that they welcomed couples and flattered well-dressed and bejeweled women in the company of their husbands. At the same time, however, the managers of fancy restaurants regarded women as trespassers on a male space during lunch. In the evening, unless they came with a man, they might be suspected of being prostitutes.

The other pillar of middle-class dining is the ethnic restaurant. As early as the turn of the nineteenth century, American food writers boasted about the variety of foreign cuisines available in cities such as New York that had attracted a large number of immigrants. The "chop suey craze" that began in 1896 was the first example of the mass-market appeal of dining out on foreign cuisine and proof of China's place in the American restaurant firmament. The Mandarin, a higher-end Chinese restaurant in San Francisco, will be considered as an important example of the trend away from chop suey toward a more sophisticated understanding of Chinese food.

Along with China, Italy has provided the most popular foreign cuisine. Italian restaurateurs initially catered to their immigrant compatriots, but quickly, by 1890, turned their attention toward the limitless generic American market, tailoring their food to American tastes while keeping a distinct flavor and atmosphere. The Italian example we offer here is Mamma Leone's, which began in 1906 as a small place with Mamma literally in the kitchen and expanded to become an immense, festive, and touristy monument of New York's Theatre District. In the course of its history it exemplified the movement of Italian restaurants from small, hip, "Bohemian" places in New York's Greenwich Village or San Francisco's North Beach to an amazingly popular cuisine that, to use John Mariani's formulation, conquered the world.[14]

Sylvia's in New York's Harlem exemplifies African American cuisine that originated in the South. This is not exactly an ethnic restaurant for two reasons: (1) the ancestors of most black people came to the United States and its colonial predecessors not as immigrants but as slaves, and (2) because their food, developed in many settings and over centuries, has been so influential, it is hard to divide something called American food from African American food. This is most obvious in the South, where fried chicken, barbecue, rice, and greens have been eaten by blacks and whites, but it extends also to a large number of dishes thought of as typically American that have African American origins.

The ten restaurants listed in this book are intended to present not only a historical narrative from 1830 but also an exploration of the archetypes outlined just now: French high-end, regional, ethnic, African American, and New American. More than such cuisine categories, the restaurants' histories show the erosion and survival of American regional cooking, the role of women as customers and restaurateurs (the Mandarin, Mamma Leone's, Sylvia's, and Chez Panisse were created by women), the pressures of efficiency and standardization in American history, and the various obfuscations as well as explorations of what it might mean to talk about "American cuisine."

The list includes ten very different establishments, each with its peculiar story. Part of what I hope will seem attractive about the book is the variety of these separate colorful histories. Various, but they form a unified narrative about American taste and how it has been molded by such factors as class differences, variety of cuisines, modernity (especially standardization), and resistance to the aesthetic and environmental costs of that very modernity.

It is worth focusing for a moment on class as well as racial and gender differences because these affect the image of American food. Class often determines food preferences, not necessarily on the basis of taste in the physical sense but rather in terms of prestige. In the Middle Ages the aristocracy ate game, fresh fish, highly spiced sauces, and medicinal sugar candies. Peasants were thought to subsist on lowly foods such as gruels and porridges, root vegetables, and dairy products. Spices, epitomizing medieval luxury gastronomy, were expelled from most European dishes except for a few desserts by the eighteenth century. In nineteenth-century Britain and America, the upper classes admired and served French food so that elite dining in London resembled that of far-away San Francisco. The middle and working classes were more tied to regional cooking traditions, but with the technological and business innovations of the second part of the nineteenth century, such distinctions gave way in the face of national brands of processed bread, meat, canned produce, and the like.

Such tendencies toward culinary homogenization notwithstanding, racial minorities, women, and immigrants came to be associated with certain foods and taste preferences, so what people ate was a mark of distinction or opprobrium. African Americans were egregiously depicted as favoring entrails such as chitterlings, or having an exaggerated affection for fried chicken and other dishes thought of as standard fare among all sorts of people. In the nineteenth century women came to be seen as particularly fond of ice cream and other childish treats, but at the same time were depicted as diet conscious and eager to partake of salads and other lighter fare. Immigrants were admired for their restaurants at the same time that they were condemned for using garlic, or having "complicated" food, or simply for paying too much attention to food, an un-American preoccupation, since a combination of Protestant austerity and the cult of efficiency exalted blandness and speed over sensuous food and time-consuming preparation.

The picture is complicated, however, by the attractiveness of the way other people dined, including other people who were considered socially inferior according to the standard hierarchy. Maybe African Americans had a greater culinary skill and a more interesting cuisine than whites; maybe Chinese food was more fun than meat and potatoes. Among our restaurants are upper-class places such as Delmonico's or Le Pavillon but also modest establishments catering to the middle social level. Class is important, but tastes are not irrevocably fixed by status. Living as we do in the age of $35 foie-gras-infused hamburgers or sustainable gourmet pizzas, the movement of dishes up and down the ladder of social hierarchy should be familiar.

THE RISE OF THE RESTAURANT

There was a time when there were simply no restaurants in the United States. Although restaurants might seem an inevitable part of urban civilization, most prosperous, commercial societies in the past managed quite well without them. It has always been necessary to have food available outside the home, of course. Travelers were served by inns, and drinkers could have snacks or simple meals at taverns. Take-out food has always been a feature of markets, festivals, or any activity that gathers people together in public. In the ruins of Pompeii, destroyed in the eruption of Mount Vesuvius in 79 CE, something on the order of 128 of the buildings that have been excavated were found to have had counters facing the street, and served food.[15] The great international church council that met between 1414 and 1417 in the small city of Constance in what is now southern Germany on the Swiss border attracted food vendors from all over the region. Ulrich von Richental's illustrated chronicle of the council, which resolved a conflict that divided the Church among three rival popes, shows a mobile oven mounted on a wheeled cart that could make pies or other hot dishes. In the London of 1850 there were 4,000 people selling ready-to-eat food.[16]

Take-out spots and other necessary conveniences aren't restaurants, however. A restaurant is based on choice more than speed or necessity. Unlike inns or boardinghouses, which served meals at a single stated time, restaurants offered a range of times when patrons could show up and expect food. Rather than having to accept a set meal, the restaurant-goer could choose from a menu, and in place of the single communal table, cus-

Fig. 2. Medieval "street food." Mobile ovens depicted in a
chronicle of the Church Council of Constance, 1414–1417.

tomers ate with their own group in a public setting, but set off from other
parties.

Defined this way, most dining out in the past took place as an accompaniment to drinking, or a requisite for a journey or attending a market.
Unlike the restaurant, the inn or take-out stand was not a culinary destination. The contemporary fast-food stop is therefore only partially a restaurant since more patrons eat in their cars than at tables, there is a limited

menu, and the establishment is a convenience more than a designated place for dining and conversation. When McDonald's or Kentucky Fried Chicken first opened in new markets such as Russia or China, they *were* effectively restaurants, as they functioned as places to be seen; to patronize in groups; and to try an unfamiliar, relatively expensive but internationally prestigious set of offerings. Once they proliferated and became easily affordable, however, fast-food places in newly opened economies became more like their counterparts in the United States. Almost half the meals eaten in the United States take place outside the home, and a majority of those are consumed in fast-food chains.[17] The origins and expansion of fast-service dining will be considered in the chapter on Howard Johnson's, but all of the establishments discussed in the pages that follow are properly thought of as restaurants, and these have only existed as such in the United States since the 1830s.

Restaurants, according to this definition, may have existed in the United States only since 1830, but there are much older historical precedents elsewhere for this kind of eating establishment. At ancient Pompeii on the eve of its destruction there were dining rooms upstairs at forty-six of the take-out places and a variety of food (reconstructed from the contents of drains and containers) was offered. These rooms above the kitchen functioned as what we would consider restaurants, where customers reclined on couches and could choose from a menu. Often restaurants feature dishes hard to prepare at home, and at Pompeii such exotic fare as dormice, sea urchins, and even in one case giraffe was on offer.[18]

Another early civilization that developed restaurants was imperial China. Beginning in about 1000 CE, frequent mention is made in descriptions of cities and in literary texts of elaborate teahouses and taverns that offered a wide choice of food as well as musical and sexual entertainment. Marco Polo, writing around 1300, described the passion of the people of "Quinsai" (modern Hangzhou) for fish, and mentions large banqueting palaces on islands in the nearby West Lake. Chinese accounts of the same period show that there were restaurants in Hangzhou specializing in regional cuisines of distant parts of China such as Hopei and Sichuan.[19]

In its modern Western form, the restaurant first took shape in Paris before the French Revolution of 1789 at the dawning of an age of accelerated urbanization.[20] The restaurant developed out of the café, which was open more or less all day and had separate tables for conversation, or for individuals to read the newspapers or otherwise occupy their leisure time. Cafés might serve pastries or other small items, but nothing like actual meals. The "restaurant" takes its name from the French *restauration*, meaning a kind of reviving hot drink such as broth or consommé taken for health. The first Parisian restaurants catered to people of a fragile or hypochondriacal constitution who would drink bouillon as a restorative. Because they might need this tonic at any time of day, restaurants remained open to serve them. Very soon such establishments started adding other delicate but complicated-to-prepare foods, such as stewed chicken or preserved fruit

This seems a rather feeble beginning for such an important institution, but the idea of obtaining a choice of food in gracious surroundings at different times of day was so appealing that by 1770 diners with hearty appetites were shoving aside the sickly and restaurants responded by expanding their options and preparing hundreds of different dishes. By 1800, even in the midst of the political upheavals following the Revolution and the ascent of Napoleon, Parisian restaurants were a major tourist draw for people from the rest of Europe, where such institutions were unknown. Véry's, Au Rocher de Cancale, and Les Trois Frères Provençaux were among the dozens of famous places at first clustered around the Palais Royale and rue de Rivoli and later dispersed throughout Paris.[21]

The fact that patrons could choose what to eat from a large number of possibilities required the invention of the menu virtually simultaneously with the appearance of the first restaurants. Once competition became lively, restaurant reviews by self-described experts began to appear. As early as 1804 one guidebook estimated that there were 2,000 restaurants in Paris. A more credible English observer in 1837 gave the number at 927.[22] Restaurant ratings and commentary began in 1803 with the publication of the first edition of the *Almanach des gourmands*, a guide for natives, not just an orientation for tourists. The author, the opinionated Alexandre Baltha-zar Laurent Grimod de la Reynière, addressed a reader of taste who was looking for gastronomic pleasure rather than convenience or value.

The restaurant, the menu, and the gastronomic guidebook were all created at a particular place and time: Paris, 1760–1810. Large cities in the rest of the world were surprisingly slow to imitate Paris. By way of public dining, London had little more than glorified chophouses until the Café Royale opened in 1865. An "Epicure's Almanac" for London was published in 1815, but the hypothetical epicure was going to have to be satisfied with eating houses and taverns serving plain English fare in unprepossessing surroundings.[23] In high Victorian London, men's clubs had the best dining facilities—the curries at the Oriental and East India Clubs were famous, and the first celebrity chef of Britain, Alexis Soyer, earned his reputation at the Reform Club.[24]

As early as 1828, a New York guidebook claimed that New York sur-passed Paris in the abundance of places suitable for "cultivating the noble science of gastronomy," but this was laughable puffery, not an accurate evaluation of the boardinghouses, oyster stands, hotels, and chophouses that made up the culinary offerings of the American metropolis. A more realistic "stranger's guide" to New York in 1817 listed hotels and board-inghouses as places to eat, but nothing resembling a restaurant.[25] Already in the early nineteenth century, however, New York's commercial district was large enough to make walking home impractical for many business-men, and so they took lunch at eating houses (or refectories as they were sometimes termed) where price and speed were more important than actual dining. An establishment called Clark and Brown's on Maiden Lane consisted of a bar and some booths and tables where a shilling would buy sliced roast beef or steak with plum pudding, bread, pickles, and ale or brandy. The Bank Coffee House was fancier, offering soup, game, and fish, but all of it was prepared and served in a slipshod manner, with everything laid out on the table haphazardly.[26]

More gracious were pastry shops and confectioneries that sold ice cream or flavored shaved ice. French and Italian entrepreneurs brought over recipes, techniques, and knowledge of how to create a pleasant atmosphere that would appeal to ladies and men with some leisure time. Guerin's, opened in 1815, sold candies, chocolate, and liqueurs in addition to pastries. Another Frenchman, John Contoit, created an ice-cream and coffee shop in 1799 and expanded it into what he called the New York Garden on Broadway. The "garden" was a rather scrawny collection of trees around wooden booths, where one could obtain lemonade, pound cake, and ice cream. Contoit and Guerin were soon joined by an Italian spot, Palmo's Garden, and the Café Français.[27]

All these were the predecessors to Delmonico's. The leading restaurant in America during the entire nineteenth century, Delmonico's was the creation of the two Delmonico brothers, John and Peter, from the Italian part of Switzerland. When it opened in 1827, Delmonico's seemed to be just another pastry shop and café—a rather "primitive" affair, according to Abram C. Dayton, an early patron. There was a pastry counter and a few tables where you could have a cup of coffee or glass of brandy with your pastry. Another early visitor, the banker Samuel Ward, was more favorably impressed than Dayton, later recalling that he had "reveled in the coffee, the chocolate, the bavaroises, the orgeats, and petits gateaux and bonsbons." From the start, Delmonico's offered a polite, considerate, and well-cared-for environment that delighted Ward and assured its quick success. The Delmonicos were eager to expand and willing to borrow money and undertake risks that their competitors weren't interested in imitating. By 1830, there was a restaurant next to the pastry shop, an attractive alternative to the ample but indifferent food of the eating houses. Delmonico's provided an extensive menu, French cuisine, an excellent wine list, and served food throughout the afternoon and evening. The kitchen could prepare a wide range of vegetables, something of a novelty in dining out.[28]

Unusual attention to quality, mastery of French cooking, and a gracious ambience set Delmonico's apart so that it was already a celebrated institution by the end of the 1830s. It may not have been the very first establishment to fit at least some of the attributes of a restaurant, but it was the first famous restaurant in America, and its influence and importance lasted into the next century.

Before we begin with Delmonico's, one more introductory facet of this book needs to be mentioned. The selection of restaurants is heavily weighted to New York and to the East and West Coasts. Five of the restaurants considered here operated in New York City, two in the San Francisco Bay Area. Two (Schrafft's and Howard Johnson's) were chains, the former confined to the East Coast, the latter started in New England but eventually becoming a cross-country operation. The only restaurant in the middle of the United States, though also in a coastal city, is Antoine's in New Orleans.

The orientation toward New York and San Francisco is not intentional. Like New Orleans these two cities were ports, and many of the influences on American food, from French food to immigration, passed through them. New Orleans is exceptional because it developed its own cuisine that people would travel long distances to sample. New York was, and remains, a restaurant tourism destination, but not because of anything that could be considered "New York cuisine." The same is true for San Francisco, the claims of Rice-A-Roni notwithstanding. People came to New York in the nineteenth century to dine at Delmonico's, later at Mamma Leone's, Le Pavillon, and the Four Seasons. In the case of Sylvia's, eventually a tourist restaurant as well, it was the cooking of South Carolina and not New York that was on offer.

New York and other large cities developed their own restaurant types and personalities. Within New York City, Brooklyn today has an identifiable set of restaurant trends and characteristics distinct from those of Manhattan, whereas Philadelphia restaurants differ considerably from those of both boroughs. The most influential restaurants were themselves the product of foreign and domestic trends and ideas that tended to coalesce in cities that were centers of gastronomic consumption and tastemaking, not of native culinary talent. The interest in such restaurants, therefore, is to find out not just what New Yorkers considered fashionable but rather what ideas seized the imagination of the entire country and affected what people ate—then and now.

Ten Restaurants
That Changed
America

ENTRÉES DE BŒUF.	s.	d.	BEEF.
Beef-steak aux cornichons	1		Beef-steak with pickles
" au beurre d'anchoix	1		" with anchovy sauce
" à la sauce tomate	1		" with tomata sauce
" à la Montigny	1		" Montigny fashion
" aux légumes	1		" with vegetables
Beef-steak Américain	1	6	American beef-steak
Filet de bœuf, sauté	1	6	Tender-loin with sauce
" " aux olives	1	6	" with olives
" " aux tomates	1	6	" with tomata sauce
" " aux champignons	2	6	" with mushrooms
" " au vin de Madère	2	6	" with Madeira sauce
Entre côte de bœuf à la sauce	1	6	
Langue de bœuf à la sauce	1		Beef's tongue with sauce

ENTRÉES DE VEAU.	s.	d.	VEAL.
Filet de veau	1		Fillet of veal
Poitrine de veau à la sauce	1		Breast of veal with sauce
" " farcie	1		" " stuffed
Tendon de veau aux légumes	1		Tendon of veal with vegetables
Veau à l'Impériale	1	6	Veal dressed Imperial fashion
" à l'Impératrice	1	6	" " Empress fashion
" à la bourgeoise	1	6	" " family fashion
Cotelette de veau panée	1		Veal cutlet, breaded
" " aux truffes	3		" " with truffles
" " aux champignons	1	6	" " with mushrooms
" " en papillote	1	6	" " in paper
" " à la sauce Robert	1	6	" " with Robert sauce
" " sauté dans sa glace	1	6	" " with gravy
Blanquette de veau	1	6	Veal with white sauce
" " à la Perigueux	1	6	" Perigueux fashion
Escalope de veau	1		Veal scolloped
Fricandeau au jus	1		Fricando of veal with gravy
" aux épinards	1	6	" " with spinage
" à l'oseille	1	6	" " with sorrel
Carbonade de veau	1		Carbonade of veal
" aux petits pois	1	6	" with green peas
" aux fines herbes	1	6	" with herbs
Ris de veau piqués	1	6	Veal sweetbread, larded
" " à l'oseille	2	6	" " with sorrel
" " à la financière	2	6	" " financier fashion
" " aux champagnons	2	6	" " with mushrooms
" " aux truffes	4		" " with truffles

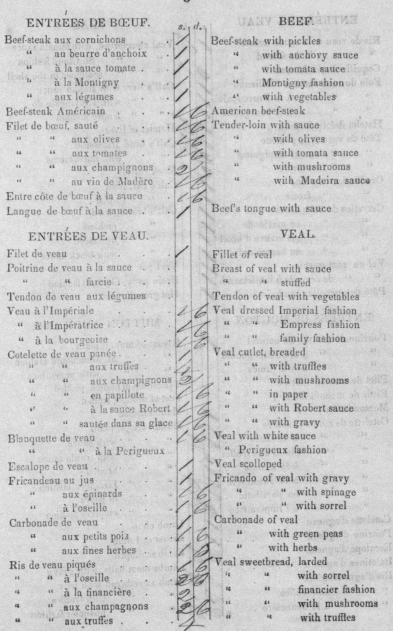

Fig. 3. A page from the 1838 Delmonico's menu.

DELMONICO'S
AMERICA'S FIRST RESTAURANT

efore Delmonico's opened in New York City there were already restaurants . . . of a rudimentary sort. Although no one knows for sure,
the first American restaurant might have been Julien's Restarator,
established in Boston in 1794 and modeled on what was offered in Paris, the
world's gastronomic capital.[1] But in the United States there was very little
dining out, apart from taverns, lodging houses, and stands selling street
food such as oysters. What was available was hardly luxurious. European
travelers were often taken aback by the crudeness of the new country's
culinary offerings, the slipshod rapidity of dining, and the absence of leisurely conversation imposed by the emphasis on speed and quantity rather
than enjoyment and quality. An English visitor in the 1820s sniffily recalled
the spectacle of fifty to a hundred hotel guests sitting down to breakfast
and consuming a motley array of dishes in less than ten minutes. The main
midday meal usually required no more than twenty minutes, and while
the food was being voraciously gulped down, no conversation took place.
Another traveler describes the atmosphere of one eating house as that of

a funeral in its absence of conviviality, and otherwise as a contest to see how quickly one could finish what seemed to be regarded as an unpleasant task.[2] Edward Henry Durell, briefly mayor of New Orleans during the Civil War, wrote in 1845 that American businessmen (as opposed to the more leisurely French Creoles) took a mere five minutes to devour dinner. The Anglo-Saxon race might be generally superior, he opined, but not in matters involving the delicate perception of taste.[3]

With its fine French food, immense menu, efficient service, and gracious atmosphere, Delmonico's seemed a revelation. It began as a simple pastry shop, opened in 1827 by two brothers from the Alpine canton of Ticino, the Italian part of Switzerland. By 1830, the success of what was already considered a delightful oasis in the bustle of New York induced John (originally Giovanni) and Peter (Pietro) Delmonico (originally Del-Monico) to expand their establishment into a restaurant that would offer impeccable French cuisine worthy of Paris. Neither brother had restaurant training, although Peter had experience as a pastry chef. Nevertheless, they were successful, not only with pastry but with hundreds of sophisticated dishes. The oldest surviving menu from the "Restaurant Français des Frères Delmonico," an eleven-page document from 1838, shows an astonishing mastery of French gastronomy: forty veal dishes ranging from sweetbreads to blanquette de veau; no fewer than eight preparations of partridge; and four styles of venison. The ubiquity of imported French truffles on the menu is remarkable. Truffles accompanied meat dishes but were also available by themselves *en croute* or sautéed in Champagne. There were vegetables such as artichokes, endive, sorrel, and eggplant, which had rarely if ever before been seen in America.[4]

That the menu was not simply an inflated pretense is evident from the response of the restaurant's patrons. Louis Napoleon, the future president and then emperor of France from 1849 to 1870, visited New York in 1837 and dined regularly at Delmonico's.[5] Among the most devoted early clients of Delmonico's was Samuel Ward (1814–1884), the son of a prominent

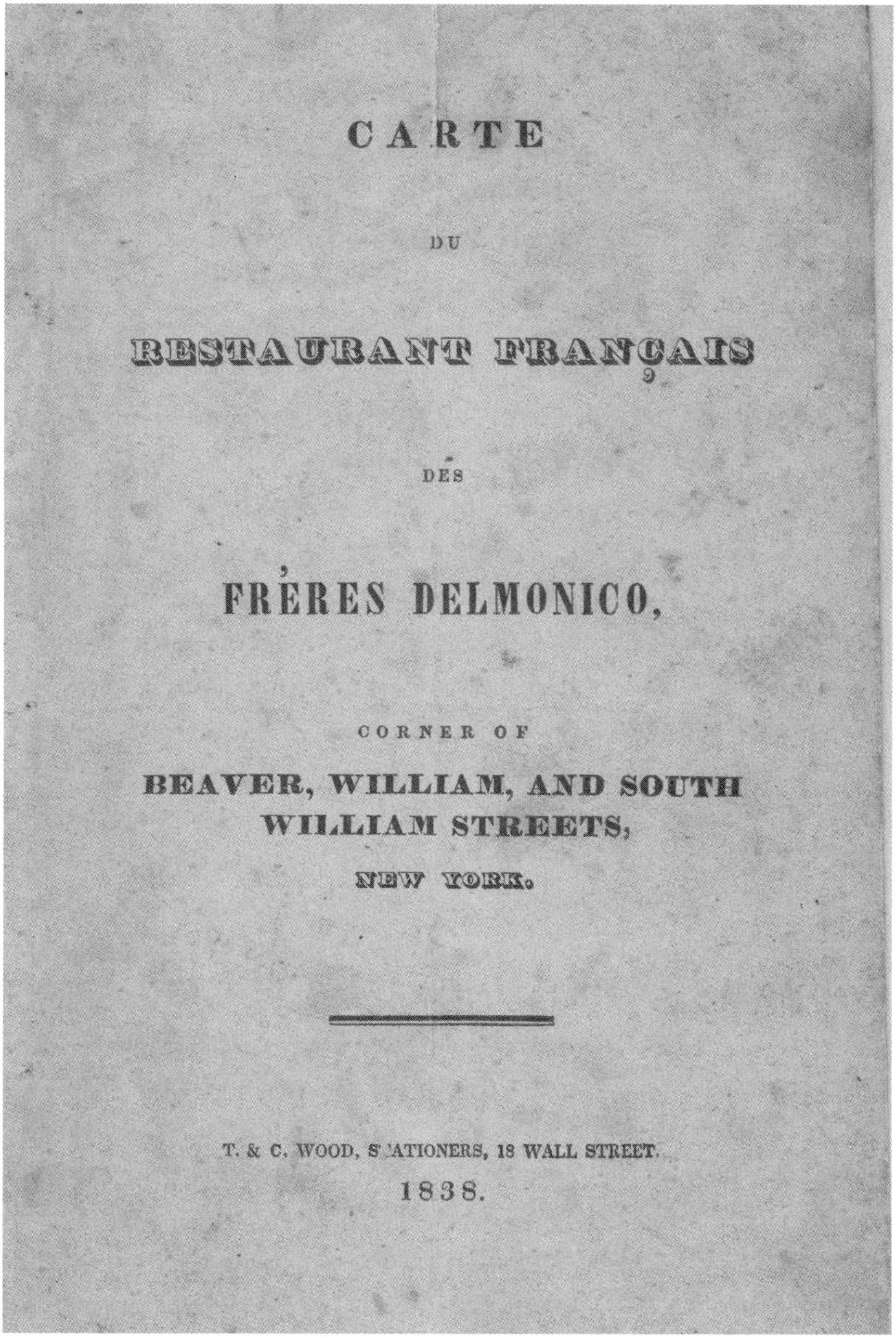

CARTE

DU

RESTAURANT FRANÇAIS

DES

FRÈRES DELMONICO,

CORNER OF

BEAVER, WILLIAM, AND SOUTH WILLIAM STREETS,

NEW YORK.

———

T. & C. WOOD, STATIONERS, 18 WALL STREET.

1838.

Fig. 4. Cover of the 1838 Delmonico's menu.

banker. Ward made and lost more than one fortune in speculation and in the California Gold Rush but found his true vocation in Washington, perfecting the modern form of congressional lobbying in the Gilded Age following the conclusion of the Civil War. Ward first discovered Delmonico's when it was still a pastry shop, and he was struck by its "prompt and deferential" service, so different from the "democratic nonchalance" of eating houses. Ward wrote an unpublished and unfinished history of Delmonico's in which he particularly praised the variety of its food. Besides presenting a definitive French repertoire, the restaurant's culinary range encompassed "the Caviare of Archangel, the Polenta of Naples, the Olla Podrida of Madrid, the Bouillabuise [sic] of Marseilles, the Cassola of Santiago de Chili [sic] and the Buffalo Hump of Fort Laramie."[6] In fact, Archangel is in northern Russia, far from the Caspian Sea where caviar comes from, polenta is a northern Italian rather than Neapolitan staple, but no matter—the distinction of Delmonico's, Ward's statement notwithstanding, was not so much international variety as a combination of reliable service and elegant French cuisine.

SETTING THE STANDARD

It is hard to exaggerate Delmonico's influence. It set a pattern for what fine dining meant for the nineteenth century and had many worthy and successful imitators, maintaining its reputation until it was killed off in 1923 by the effects of Prohibition. In 1890, as in 1840, everyone agreed that the greatest restaurant in the United States was Delmonico's. It was admired despite an enduring American tradition of mistrusting gourmandise and exalting rugged simplicity and democratic values.

Disdain for gastronomic pretentiousness has often influenced politics.[7] During the 1840 presidential campaign, the incumbent Martin Van Buren was portrayed as routinely eating fricandeau de veau and omelette soufflé, or in another attack, enjoying pâté de foie gras from a silver plate followed by soupe à la Reine sipped from a golden spoon. His opponent, William Henry Harrison, an aging hero of the War of 1812, was extolled for his simple tastes, by contrast, favoring raw beef without salt, and he adopted a campaign image of a "hard cider man." In fact, Van Buren was the son of a tavern keeper, while Harrison was a member of the privileged class, but mere facts are often unimportant in politics. Harrison deftly exploited American anxiety about luxury and snobbery and won the election, though he would die within a month of taking office, the raw beef and hard cider perhaps having taken a toll.[8] American history evolves, but it repeats certain patterns and prejudicial inclinations in such a way that more than 160 years later, George W. Bush's presidential campaign mocked John Kerry's fluent French while the wealthy, dynastic president's man-of-the-people image was carefully nurtured by publicizing his love of pork rinds.

A concern for fine food has often been seen as unbusinesslike or unmasculine. Women were supposed to enjoy fripperies and delicate cooking. Yet not only does it turn out that men often like well-made food, but restaurants attracted them by offering an elegant setting conducive to strengthening business ties and affirming status. Within just a few years of its founding, Delmonico's fulfilled social as well as gastronomic functions seemingly effortlessly. Writing in 1884, a contributor to *Harper's Weekly* recollected the howling wilderness of pre-Delmonico's dining, remarking, "We shall not think it extravagant to call Delmonico's an agency of civilization." Delmonico's taught those who assumed it frivolous to give attention to dining that "dinner was not merely an ingestion, but an observance."[9]

A year after the *Harper's* article, Oscar Wilde, who had visited America in 1882–1883, wrote a similar paean to Delmonico's. Reviewing a book entitled *Dinners and Dishes*, Wilde took the author to task for underestimating American cuisine. How could he ignore the nation's marvelous soft-shell crabs, canvasback ducks, bluefish, and pompano, especially as served by Delmonico's? In fact, Wilde continued, the two most impressive sights in the United States were Delmonico's and Yosemite Valley, the restaurant having "done more to promote good feelings between England and America than anything else has in this century."[10]

The New York that received Delmonico's with such éclat in the 1830s was a metropolis that was neither the capital of national government nor a seat of learning on the order of Boston or Philadelphia. It was given over to business, and its size and population were expanding rapidly. The completion of the Erie Canal in 1825 had opened the port of New York to the agricultural wealth of the Midwest. The development of the railroads in the following decades made New York into an international manufacturing and distribution center, the headquarters of the financial world, and a magnet for immigration. Its population of 60,000 in 1800 had more than quintupled to 312,000 by 1840.

In 1831, the year after the Delmonico brothers created their restaurant, Alexis de Tocqueville visited the United States, and his famously perceptive account probes Americans' manners, desires, and outlook. *Democracy in America* remains among the most thoughtful descriptions of the young nation. Although de Tocqueville doesn't devote any space to American gustatory habits, he describes the ways in which democratic mistrust of snobbery, luxury, and other Old World vices was undermined by an individualistic desire to compete and to achieve status in a society without formal titles, orders, or guilds. America might be businesslike and its pace hurried, but its prominent citizens did not altogether ignore the pleasures of the table. Thomas Jefferson, for example, was a serious gourmand, kept records of French recipes, and insisted that his slaves learn how to cook authentic French food. He had a distinguished wine cellar and had pasta shipped from Italy along with a "maccarony machine" to make his own. His good taste was not universally acclaimed: Patrick Henry said that Jefferson "came home from France so Frenchified that he abjured his native victuals."[11]

Neither the advent of Jacksonian democracy in the 1830s and its appeal to rural values nor the widespread mistrust of the eastern seaboard and its upper classes did anything to hinder the success of Delmonico's. The "great march of the suddenly rich upon the social capitals of the nation," as one observer looking back from the vantage point of 1911 called it, created opportunities for all manner of elegant restaurants. All of these were modeled after Delmonico's. The much-imitated restaurant guarded its preeminence, managing to retain old-money clients while drawing in the flood of new wealth. Though one Gilded Age observer described Delmonico's as "a salon of Saracenic splendor," the restaurant was by no means inaccessible or frozen in a particular moment of elite culinary style.[12] As New York's Theatre District and social center moved uptown, first to Fourteenth Street after the Civil War, then to Madison Square, and finally to Times Square in the waning years of the nineteenth century, Delmonico's followed without abandoning its original branches in the downtown business center.

Delmonico's always claimed to be a French restaurant, but it was especially known for American specialties such as oysters, diamondback terrapin, and canvasback duck. The bays and inlets around New York once produced oysters of immense size, fine quality, and staggeringly large quantities before pollution and reckless harvesting destroyed their banks. While in France oysters were usually eaten raw, in America they were served raw at the beginning of the meal and then appeared baked, broiled, in soups and stews, or cut up and made into patties. The best canvasback ducks were from around the Chesapeake Bay, where they fed on wild celery. Usually they were roasted or broiled fairly simply and served with celery sauce, hominy, or samp (a kind of dried and pounded corn kernel). Terrapin was complicated to cook, to say nothing of the preliminary necessity of killing the turtle by scalding it and then separating out the edible from inedible parts. The finest terrapins were also thought to be from the Chesapeake region, although people in New Orleans disputed this.

The Victorian novelist Anthony Trollope visited Baltimore during his North American tour at the opening of the Civil War, and he called canvasback ducks and terrapin the city's twin glories.[13] Americans boasted about these two dishes; Gen. Winfield Scott, a hero of the Mexican War and the best-known antebellum gourmet, observed that canvasbacks and Maryland terrapin were the "supreme native delicacies."[14] In Edith Wharton's *The Age of Innocence*, written about the 1870s, the Lovell Mingotts serve canvasbacks, terrapin, and vintage wines and the Newland Archers' first festive entertainment as a married couple features a hired chef and gilded menus that indicated either terrapin or canvasbacks would be presented.[15]

It was not just the quality of the food but also the refined and delightful atmosphere of Delmonico's that was renowned. In *The Bostonians*, published in 1886, Henry James's narrator describes Verena Tarrant's anticipatory pleasure at the prospect of a meal at Delmonico's, "a bright consciousness, sufficient for the moment, that one was . . . to dine at Delmonico's . . . There was enough of the epicurean in Verena's composition to make it easy for her in certain conditions to live only for the hour." Verena is escorted by the wealthy Henry Burrage, who seemed to "preside in the brilliant public room of the establishment, where French waiters flitted about on deep carpets and parties at neighboring tables excited curiosity and conjecture."[16] The spectacle was both gastronomic and social. Henry James depicts Delmonico's as a splendid but sterile space for Burrage to perform in, opposing to it a sedate French restaurant favored by Verena's more serious (and priggish) suitor, Basil Ransom, that offers wonderful food in a more quietly luxurious space than ostentatious Delmonico's. For James, no fan of New York's aggressive materialism, Delmonico's fame was taken as obvious.

ORIGINS

The Delmonico brothers were adaptable, quick learners. Before coming to America, Giovanni had gone from the mountainous Swiss canton of Ticino to become a sailor and he was rapidly promoted to captain. He commanded a schooner that traded in Cadiz, Havana, and New York. Pietro, of a less adventurous temperament, opened a pastry shop in Berne. Giovanni decided to give up his ship to settle in New York and, after a brief stint as a wine merchant, he convinced his brother to help him establish a pastry shop in the prosperous but gastronomically impoverished new metropolis. John and Peter, as they now styled themselves, had substantial capital. They immediately distinguished themselves by the quality of the basic products the offered: excellent coffee, thick and deep-flavored hot chocolate, and luxurious pastries. The brothers exemplified the entrepreneurial virtues of constant innovation and the practice of reinvesting profits in one's business. Delmonico's became distinguished, as already stated, by the range of its menu, punctilious but friendly service, and most of all by the care lavished on cooking even the simplest dishes. Delmonico's did not invent fine food but rather refined it and the manner in which it was served.[17]

The Delmonicos paid high wages and attracted European chefs. Not satisfied with the quality of produce they could procure in the markets of New York, the brothers bought a 220-acre farm in Williamsburg, Brooklyn, in 1834. That same year they acquired a hotel on Broad Street, which proved fortunate because the great fire of December 16, 1835, destroyed Delmonico's restaurant, along with most of lower Manhattan. The hotel was intact, however, and immediately became the site of a temporary restaurant while a new one was constructed at Beaver and South William Streets. It opened in 1837, a year marred by another sort of disaster: a financial panic that wiped out fortunes and led to many business failures. The new building was three and a half stories and it featured novelties for New York such as private dining rooms and wooden parquet floors. Its immense wine cellars held a veritable city of 16,000 bottles. In later years, as other Delmonico's locations were established in the city, the old Beaver and South William Street branch was known as the Citadel.[18] It was henceforth the spiritual home of the enterprise, and although the building was later reconstructed in 1891 as an eight-story edifice, the original entrance portico of marble

Fig. 5. Photograph of "The Citadel," Delmonico's
at Beaver and South William Street, early twentieth century.

Corinthian columns still stands, taken (supposedly) from the ruins of
Pompeii. That grandiose portal still invites diners into a restaurant that,
although not directly descended from the original, is called Delmonico's.

LORENZO THE MAGNIFICENT

As it turned out, the most important event in perpetuating the reign of
the Delmonico brothers was the arrival in 1831 of their young nephew
Lorenzo, who would mold the restaurant into an unrivaled temple to gastronomy and a shrine to upper-class social status. He did not do this alone;

his younger brothers Siro, François, and Constant joined him, and along with his nephew Charles (son of François) they would be instrumental in running the business. From the 1840s until his death in 1881, however, Lorenzo was clearly in charge.

Unlike his uncles, Lorenzo did not Americanize his name. Although he had been brought on as a distinctly junior partner, Lorenzo became the animating force of the restaurant considerably before John's death in 1842 from a stroke while hunting and Peter's subsequent retirement. Lorenzo's retention of his Italian name might seem to indicate a certain flamboyance, but he was in fact quiet and retiring, to the point of asceticism. Earnest and unpretentious, his strengths were conscientiousness and imperturbability rather than charisma.

Under Lorenzo's management, Delmonico's became the first restaurant to serve as a gathering place for an elite that had previously dined and entertained at home. As with other high-end restaurants in the century to come, such as Le Pavillon or the Four Seasons, the constant presence of the owner or maître d'hôtel and his skill at managing as well as welcoming guests were indispensable for the restaurant's social distinction. Lorenzo could be firm with clients who failed to obey the clear, if unwritten, laws. Two basic rules were to pay your bills on time (regulars were given lines of credit rather than being presented with a check after each meal), and not to become obviously drunk or rowdy. Offenders would find that after some disorderly incident or in response to failure to pay their debt within a certain grace period that the next time they would suffer a quiet but public humiliation. Arriving at the restaurant, the offender would be warmly welcomed and shown to his usual table. His order would be taken with dispatch, but no food would follow. The waiter would apologize and promise to see what could be causing the delay in the kitchen, but still nothing would come forth. Apologies and promises would go on until the miscreant realized he was never going to be served anything unless restitution were made.[19]

According to legend, an even harsher penalty was meted out to one Ben Wenberg, a sea captain who in 1876 supposedly showed Lorenzo and Charles how to cook lobster tableside in a chafing dish. The name of this new and popular preparation, Lobster à la Wenberg, was allegedly changed to Lobster à la Newberg after Wenberg started a brawl in the restaurant. This is hard to verify, as no such dish as Lobster à la Wenberg is found on any surviving Delmonico's menu. Terrapines à la Wenberg appears on a menu dated May 2, 1873, and there is a Terrapin à la Newberg in the 1893 cookbook of Charles Ranhofer, Delmonico's chef, so perhaps the story originally was about terrapin, or the name was changed without dramatic motive.[20]

Like all brilliant restaurateurs, Lorenzo was a restless innovator, not just a manager. He was ceaselessly altering the business to maximize profits, but also to serve a varied clientele in a rapidly changing New York City. He gave up the Williamsburg farm as the food-supply infrastructure improved, and he personally supervised the purchase of meat and produce from the Washington Market downtown (destroyed for development projects in 1962), near where One World Trade Center now stands. Often accompanied by his brother Siro, Lorenzo was a favored customer at the market, where he would arrive at dawn. He would return to the Citadel and await his orders' arrival by delivery vehicles. He would drink a cup of strong coffee, smoke a cigar or two (made in Havana to his specifications), and look over the accounts and reservations lists. After a nap he would go to the front of the house to supervise the coming and going of diners.[21]

EXPANSION

Lorenzo was more than a restaurateur devoted to protecting one perfect establishment. He was a pioneer in expanding his brand. The restaurant moved with the changing geography of New York's social life, but without vacating all its former locations. It could not be described in any sense as a "chain" in that each Delmonico's was different in layout, staffing, and menu. There were ten sites in the history of Delmonico's from 1830 to 1923, but never more than four restaurants were in operation at one time. The different Delmonico's restaurants served a varied clientele, from simple clerks to arriviste magnates and old-money plutocrats, but in different rooms and at different sites. By offering a number of options under one name, Lorenzo was able to preserve an aura of refined exclusivity and at the same time prosper financially. A stable of reliable relatives under his employ obviated some of the problem of supervision.

Running several restaurants in the same city under one management differs from guarding one unique location, as is the practice at other famous restaurants such as Antoine's, the Four Seasons, or Chez Panisse. Neither does it resemble the international growth pursued by today by chef-entrepreneurs such as Alain Ducasse or Jean-Georges Vongerichten. As a strategy, it has something in common with Danny Meyer's group of distinguished restaurants in one city (Union Square Café, Gramercy Tavern, Maialino, and others), but Meyer's restaurants emphasize different cuisines while Delmonico's consistently followed the only recognized haute-cuisine type, French, albeit with some admixture of American methods of preparing local foods.

Lorenzo's first expansionist innovation was to open a second Delmonico's restaurant in 1846 as part of a hotel run by Delmonico's at 25 Broadway near the southern tip of Manhattan. Along with the New York Hotel farther uptown, this establishment was among the first in the United States to charge meals separately from rooms, making it less like an inn or boarding house and more like a pair of distinct enterprises. An equally dramatic development was that a substantial bar was installed that attracted more customers than a small, more leisurely, pastry-oriented café. Not only was the appeal of strong drink irresistible, but one could stand at the bar to obtain solid as well as liquid refreshment quickly and depart.[22]

For a time, the hotel was a stunning success. Jenny Lind, the world-renowned Swedish opera singer, stayed there in 1850 and 1851. With tickets to her concerts in Castle Garden at the Battery auctioned by scalpers, she sang arias in front of the hotel to crowds that thronged Bowling Green. Probably among the first women to be able to command a table on her own, Jenny Lind dined at Delmonico's after her performances. The fastidious epicure Gen. Winfield Scott often dined with Lorenzo. William Tecumseh Sherman, the future Union general, brought to the hotel the first news received in New York of the 1849 California gold discovery. The Hungarian patriot Louis Kossuth stayed there, as well, as did the renowned English author of *Vanity Fair*, William Makepeace Thackeray.[23]

The hotel's success notwithstanding, Lorenzo was restless and unhindered by emotional investment in any particular property. A mere ten years after it had opened, the hotel was closed and a restaurant (only) was opened a bit farther uptown, near City Hall, at Chambers Street and Broadway. The new establishment, which would last from 1856 to 1876, was advantageously located around the corner from A. T. Stewart's splendid dry-goods store on Broadway. Stewart's sold fabric, trim, clothes, and furs in a setting commonly described as a "marble palace." In the 1850s it became the largest store in the world and attracted multitudes of female shoppers. As we will see in our discussion of Schrafft's in a later chapter, these women would patronize restaurants called "ice-cream saloons" set up for their custom in the neighborhood of Stewart's.

Delmonico's at this point did not encourage trade from women unescorted by men, but the Chambers Street branch attracted a lunch crowd of male retail and legal clerks from the neighborhood along with the more distinguished clients. Samuel Ward recollected that the outer ground-floor room was for the clerks, along with lesser politicians and contractors. A more formal dining room on the same floor catered to small-business owners, while "men of distinction," including A. T. Stewart himself, dined in a grand second-floor room. At night a less business-oriented and more purely social elite monopolized the premises, where, Ward remembered, the laughter of young ladies filled the air.[24] Lorenzo continued to devote most of his time to the Citadel, assisted by his brother Constant. Chambers Street was supervised by Siro and Lorenzo's precocious nephew Charles.

MOVING UPTOWN (1862–1881)

In the seemingly inauspicious war year of 1862, a mere six years after establishing the location at Chambers Street, Lorenzo opened a third Delmonico's on Fourteenth Street in the new theatre district just west of Union Square. Under the care of Charles Delmonico, despite the economic woes associated with the Civil War, the restaurant became the center of New York society. While it was condemned by some as a meeting place for Confederate sympathizers, who were surprisingly numerous in New York, and though its rival, the Maison Dorée, was more staunchly Unionist, political divisions did no significant damage to Delmonico's reputation or profits.

The chef at this new establishment was an indefatigable Frenchman, Charles Ranhofer. He was the greatest cook of his generation in America, and he would serve the Delmonicos for thirty years. The prominent families of New York, who had previously held their receptions, balls, and celebrations at their homes, now found it more pleasant and convenient to have their refined, if ostentatious, events at a restaurant. Opening-night dinner at Fourteenth Street consisted of a modest eight courses and included French classics such as Timbales à la Monglas (meat, mushroom and truffle timbales) and Filets de Volaille à l'Imperiale (chicken filets with cream sauce and forcemeat tarts). There were also trout from Long Island and canvasback ducks from the Chesapeake.

The Fourteenth Street restaurant flourished even before the disruptions of the Civil War came to an end, and it became the scene of some of the grandest meals of the Gilded Age of postwar prosperity and tax-free

Fig. 6. Watercolor of the exterior of Delmonico's
Fourteenth Street at Fifth Avenue, ca. 1875.

excess. The Russian fleet's visit in November of 1863 provided one of many occasions for a grand banquet. Russia was the only European power to unequivocally favor the Northern cause in the Civil War, and so there was a strong effort to publicize the diplomatic and military implications of this gesture of support.

Whatever its reputation for harboring a pro-Confederate element among its clientele, Delmonico's went all out on behalf of the Unionist hosts of the banquet. Thirty-one dishes made up the first four courses, followed by no fewer than twenty desserts and then fifteen *pièces montées*—sugar-sculpted tableaux and effigies. These depicted the Hermitage Palace, the Parisian Arc de Triomphe, George Washington, Abraham Lincoln, a horn of plenty, and similar inspirational and historical themes. Game birds were ubiquitous in this meal, so that—in addition to a canvasback duck pâté—snipe, woodcock, pheasants (in two varieties), and ortolans also appeared. Just a year later (when it was clear that the North was winning the war), a visit from the French Navy occasioned a meal with only a few courses served to a mere twenty-six guests.[25]

In late 1865, with the Civil War concluded, the British railroad magnate Sir Morton Peto hosted a dinner notable in the long annals of banqueting excess. At the cost of a mere $50,000, equivalent to more than $700,000 today, 250 men in the tea and coffee business were treated to a nine-course meal that included seven *pièces montées*, twelve desserts, Salmon à la Rothschild (whole salmon stuffed with whiting, covered with decorated fish-based crusts, and served with Champagne sauce, sole filets, and skewers of smelts); Pheasants à la Londonderry (breasts of pheasants with truffles, tongue slices, and a meat ragout); saddle of venison; ducks; game; eels, beef . . . The wines included an 1815 sherry, Imperial Tokay, and Napoleon brandy. The menus were printed in gold leaf on satin, and each guest was given a silk cushion embroidered with his initials.[26]

Fig. 7. Confectionery Department at Delmonico's, ca. 1900.

Three years later, in April of 1868, Charles Dickens, the world-famous author of *David Copperfield* and *A Christmas Carol*, was honored by the New York Press Club on his second voyage to the United States. Although there were eleven courses, this meal was restrained compared to the grotesquely large, tedious, and rather plain dinner given at the City Hotel in New York during the author's first American trip in 1842, a meal that Dickens recalled with contempt. The Delmonico's menu was imaginative and reflected the literary tastes of New York's upper class: timbales à la Dickens, stuffed lamb à la Walter Scott, grouse cutlets à la Fennimore Cooper. Dickens used this occasion to retract criticisms of Americans made after his previous visit, when he characterized them as rude, vulgar, and uncivilized. In an after-dinner speech, he remarked how touched he was by the courtesy and consideration received during this second voyage.

These extravaganzas took place at what was considered "the most palatial [restaurant] on the continent," located along the East-West thoroughfare of Fourteenth Street, center of nightlife and the theatre.[27] In the decade after the Civil War, there were four Delmonico's locations. In 1865, Lorenzo opened an additional downtown venue on Broad Street right by the New York Stock Exchange, welcoming stockbrokers and investors during one of America's many eras of speculative exuberance. Chambers Street catered to Boss Tweed when Tammany Hall ran the city government. Fourteenth Street was thronged with members of high society and notables of the entertainment world. Apart from the venerable Citadel, however, no branch of Delmonico's had a particularly long heyday. In 1876, with Manhattan's social center continuing its march uptown, Lorenzo closed Fourteenth Street in favor of exploiting the new social hub at Madison Square and shuttered Chambers Street, reestablishing a second downtown presence on Pine Street in the Equitable skyscraper, where 1,000 diners could be accommodated daily. These changes show Lorenzo's attempts to cater to the social elite while making money from a well-heeled but essentially mass-market clientele.

The Delmonico's restaurants managed to profit from the excess of the times without being tarnished by it, perhaps because of a certain unerring good taste behind the spectacles or else because of the self-effacing if ambitious personality of Lorenzo. He satisfied the whims of the nouveaux riches without alienating what passed for old money in New York. Beginning in the 1870s, under the patronage of Mrs. William Astor (née Schermerhorn), the social elite was marked out by Samuel Ward McAllister, a cousin of Samuel Ward and equally devoted to Delmonico's.

Aghast at the effect of new money and the consequent erosion of exclusivity, McAllister identified "the 400," who, by virtue of their background (roughly four generations of distinction) and quiet wealth, were entitled to deference and consideration. An inner circle of 25 of the original 400 organized the first "Patriarchs' Ball" in 1872. The restricted but glittering event was replete with Astors, Schermerhorns, Rutherfords, and Livingstons, and invitations were rigorously vetted by McAllister. Subsequently, these events would take place several times a year during the social season. Although considered something of an odd character (and financially dependent on his wife's family wealth), McAllister's decisions were nevertheless accepted by the press and public as authoritative demarcations of social distinction.[28]

By 1876 the grand hotels and restaurants were concentrated around Madison Square, where Broadway met Fifth Avenue at Twenty-Third Street. In 1879 the first Madison Square Garden was built at Madison Avenue and Twenty-Sixth Street. The new Delmonico's was a block away, at Twenty-Sixth Street and Fifth Avenue. The wealthy public, distressed by the closing of the Fourteenth Street Delmonico's, nevertheless trusted Lorenzo's judgment. The *Herald* expressed confidence that "the new quarters and the magnificence of the surroundings will atone for the loss of the old."[29] Customers were pleased with the mirrors, silver chandeliers, a flower-banked central fountain, and the frescoed ceiling of the main dining room. Upper floors had private rooms, a banquet hall, and a ballroom. The

Patriarchs' Balls were held in the ballroom and adjacent supper rooms, but the new aristocracy of Vanderbilts and other industrial magnate families also hosted sumptuous dinners and parties there.[30]

The pioneer at Madison Square was the venerable Fifth Avenue Hotel, established in 1859. Not long after the hotel opened, the social observer Reuben Vose wrote that within its precincts pass "more of the real beauty and wealth of the nation than in any other spot in the city."[31] Other elegant establishments on the square were the Café Brunswick, nearly as celebrated as Delmonico's; the St. James Hotel; and Gilsey House, the latter of which was popular with theatre people. The devastating Panic of 1873, resulting clashes between the police and New York's unemployed in 1874, and the Great Railroad Strike of 1877 did nothing to discourage the hordes of socially prominent gourmands from thronging Delmonico's. Perhaps the perceived need grew for the wealthy to separate themselves from the nouveaux riches and expanding upper middle class.

Lorenzo himself was given little time to enjoy this latest example of his prescience and success. He suffered from gout and from what medical opinion at the time considered nicotine poisoning, brought about, it was said, by his habit of consuming thirty or more of his custom-made cigars daily. His death at the age of sixty-eight on September 4, 1881, provoked consternation in New York comparable to that greeting the news of the assassination of President Garfield just two months earlier. The *Sun* credited Lorenzo Delmonico with improving the standards of cookery throughout America and for making New York second only to Paris as the city with the greatest restaurants. The *Times* remarked that the Delmonico name was everywhere understood to be synonymous with gastronomic perfection.

The encyclopedic *American National Biography* series echoes the obituaries of 1881 in giving Lorenzo credit for running restaurants that were "the equal of the best in the civilized world." The modern author of the entry, Jerome Mushkat, goes on to say that Lorenzo "turned eating into a form of entertainment."[32] This is true to the extent that the restaurant became a setting for the rituals of social prominence. Only later, at the end of the nineteenth century, would fine restaurants embrace music, dancing, themed décor, and other distractions. For Lorenzo and for Delmonico's, the paramount distinction was always the food. How food was served and in what setting were important as far back as the pastry-shop days, but it was the gastronomic experience that was most important and uniquely delightful.[33]

Lorenzo's demise was followed in 1884 by the bizarre death of his nephew and close collaborator Charles Delmonico at the age of forty-four. Considerably younger than Lorenzo, Charles was afflicted by what appears to have been a bipolar disorder that left him increasingly listless, morose, and irritable. Although he was able to supervise the restaurants, he went through periods of inactivity and his appearance and affect deteriorated. In the fall of 1883 he was taken to Long Branch on the New Jersey Shore to undergo a "rest cure" at the house of a friend. During a bitter cold spell after New Year's Day, 1884, Charles disappeared. After three days some torn letters, telegram vouchers, and gloves belonging to him were found by boys playing near railroad tracks passing through the Jersey Meadows near Newark. More than a week passed before Charles's body was found in a ravine between the towns of Orange and Montclair, New Jersey. It was frozen, covered with ice from a stream at the bottom of a gully. Later it was revealed that Charles had escaped from what amounted to involuntary confinement, boarded a train, and was overheard to have said he was going to visit the famous but disgraced General McClellan of Civil War fame who lived near Montclair.

Contrary to what one might have expected, the two deaths in the family did not set back the fortunes of Delmonico's. Charles's nephew Charles Crist, son of his sister Rosa, took over, changed his name to Charles Delmonico, and was known as "Young Charley" to distinguish him from his unfortunate uncle. He had trained as a stockbroker, but took easily to managing the business from Madison Square, though toward the end of his life he moved to the new Forty-Fourth Street location. Although not completely unrivaled, Delmonico's continued throughout the 1880s to dominate the New York and national dining horizon.

CHEF CHARLES RANHOFER

The food style of Delmonico's, French with American accents and ingredients, was in place long before the arrival of Chef Charles Ranhofer in 1862, but his reign in the kitchens until the 1890s coincided with the height of the restaurant's prosperity and distinction. We know a lot about what was served at Delmonico's because of Ranhofer's massive cookbook, *The Epicurean*, published in 1893, an unrivalled reflection of high-end gastronomic taste during America's version of the French Belle Époque.[34] Its 3,700 recipes allow us to understand what kind of French and American food was prepared. The cuisine reflected the classic French repertoire of its time, but many of the signature dishes will be unfamiliar to the twenty-first-century reader: salmis (game in small pieces in sauce, often prepared at the table), chartreuse (an elaborate arrangement of meat and vegetables cooked in a mold), tiny birds such as woodcock or ortolan, or haunches of meat such as saddle of mutton or venison. The same degree of unfamiliarity applies to American specialties requiring ingredients that are now so endangered as to be virtually unknown—canvasback ducks, terrapin, prairie hens, shad, and Atlantic Ocean or Maine river salmon.

As with almost all famous chefs at American restaurants well into the twentieth century, Charles Ranhofer was European; not only that, but he was actually French. Born in 1836 in St. Denis just north of Paris, cooking was in his blood, as both his father and grandfather were chefs. At the age of twelve he was apprenticed to a pastry chef in Paris. He had a number of short-term positions and developed a high reputation very quickly. While

Fig. 8. Chef Charles Ranhofer in 1902.

still a teenager, he became the chef de cuisine for the count of Alsace, senior representative of the distinguished noble family of Hénin-Liétard. He then moved back to Paris to work at a caterer's establishment, and then cooked for two prominent aristocrats of the Second Empire, the Duke of Noailles and the Baron Rothschild. His arrival in New York in 1856 was to take a position in the household of the Russian consul, but he soon moved to Washington, DC, and subsequently New Orleans.[35]

Ranhofer briefly returned to France in 1860, but was in America again in 1861 to become chef at the Maison Dorée, a magnificent restaurant in New York that had opened in 1860. He didn't last long there either, and finally settled down at Delmonico's in 1862. There was a hiatus from 1876 to 1879, when Ranhofer ran the Hotel Américain at Enghien-les-Bains, a resort in the Paris suburbs, but otherwise he spent the rest of his career in New York at Delmonico's.

Maison Dorée on Union Square had set out to rival Delmonico's, and some regarded it as more authentically Parisian. It only lasted four years, however, and Lorenzo profited from its demise by buying up its wine cellar. The Civil War had undermined Maison Dorée, as did the establishment of Delmonico's Fourteenth Street branch just around the corner the year after Maison Dorée opened. Luxury restaurants abounded in New York by this time, but the Maison Dorée tried deliberately and most obviously to usurp Delmonico's preeminence. Charles Ranhofer may have seen the proverbial writing on the wall, or perhaps he was simply enticed by Lorenzo and the fame of Delmonico's, but whatever the reasons, in 1862 he became the chef at the new Fourteenth Street restaurant.

Ranhofer's *Epicurean* records menus, meals, and dishes offered during his direction of Delmonico's kitchens. The recipes are brief and daunting. No one would mistake this compendium for a user-friendly, step-by-step guide for housewives. As was the case at most fancy restaurants, the Delmonico's cooking staff were exclusively men, and there was a firm division in this era between the male chef as restaurant professional and the female household cook. Many chefs, such as Ranhofer's colleague at Delmonico's, Alexander Filippini, did write instructional cookbooks for home use, marketed on the basis of the author's professional credentials.[36] This should not be taken to imply that cookbooks addressed to housewives were simple or assumed lack of prior knowledge. By current standards, the meals that middle-class women were expected to prepare seem elaborate and sophisticated, involving much more in the way of roasting and baking than is in evidence in today's cookbooks, to say nothing of the necessity of cutting up and preparing poultry, meat, and fish to make them ready for cooking—plastic-wrapped boneless chicken breasts or frozen fish filets were unknown in the nineteenth century. Nevertheless, such women, assisted by one or two servants in the kitchen, were not cooking on the level of the grandest restaurant in the country. *The Epicurean* is not so much an aspirational cookbook (on the order of books composed by celebrity chefs today, with lovely illustrations and seemingly impossible recipes), as a professional reference work and an exhaustive career summary.

The book had what the French call a *succès d'estime*—it was acclaimed but did not immediately sell many copies and is now a great rarity. It has nevertheless always had a high reputation among chefs. Ranhofer expected the cook who followed these recipes to have on hand such basics as chicken forcemeat (like stuffing, but with other uses) or sauce Lucullus (an elaborate sauce requiring partridge and truffles) in order to make such dishes as timbales (soft preparations of meat or fish, in this era cooked in a mold). There are thirty timbale recipes in *The Epicurean*, and the timbales are supposed to emerge from their molds in dazzling patterns: for example, "à la Dumas," with oblong domino-like shapes made from truffle slices and beef tongue; and "harlequin timbales," which involve a suprême sauce (a white sauce with chicken consommé), a salpicon of artichoke bottoms and quenelle forcemeat decorated with a multicolor lozenge pattern of tongue, truffles, and sauce royale (white sauce of chicken stock, cream, butter, truffles, and sherry).[37]

❖ MENU ❖

—

Huîtres

(HAUT SAUTERNES)

Potages

Consommé Châtelaine   Bisque d'écrevisses

(AMONTILLADO, '34)

Hors d'oeubre

Variés   Timbales, milanaise   Variés

Relebes

Bass à la régence   Eperlans, dauphine

(JOHANNISBERGER RED SEAL)

Filet de boeuf à la Florentine   Selle de mouton à l'anglaise

(POMMERY SEC)

Entrees

Côtelettes de pigeonneaux à l'Albufera

Ris de veau à la Toulouse   Terrapin à l'Indiana

(LATOUR, '68)

Froid

Aspic de foie-gras   Bastion de gibier

(CHATEAU YQUEM)

Sorbet

Young America

Rotis

Dindonneaux truffés   Canvas-back

(CHAMBERTIN)

Entremets

Petits pois   Artichauts   Haricots verts

Sucres

Plum pudding, St. George

Gelée Orientale   Charlotte Victoria   Sicilien

Strawberries

Bombe japonaise   Fruits à la crême

Fruits & dessert

Le 11 Fevrier, 1881   *DELMONICO*

Fig. 9. Delmonico's menu, 1881.

It might now seem perverse, but Ranhofer claimed to have simplified the recipes, but his audience would have been chefs rather than home cooks. He gave extended information on matters such as selecting, cutting up, and cooking terrapin—instructions unlikely to be of use for amateurs. He lists tables of price, proportions of wastage versus useful meat depending on turtle size, and other data needed to calculate the best way of buying and serving this expensive treat. The basic terrapin cooking instructions seem to require techniques drawn from surgery and the construction trades. There follow ten recipes for classics such as Terrapin à la Maryland—cut-up terrapin cooked in butter and Madeira to which cream and mashed hard-boiled eggs-yolks were added—but there is also an unusual combination of terrapin cutlets and croquettes in a cream sauce.[38]

Ranhofer includes a table of produce and their seasons, illustrations of sculpted-sugar desserts (*pièces montées*), and describes forms of table service. Notwithstanding the elaborate courses and dishes at Delmonico's, Ranhofer accommodated the American desire for speed. He expected a fourteen-course meal to be served in a mere two hours and twenty minutes (ten minutes per course) but was happy, upon request, to accelerate the pace to eight minutes per course so that the meal might conclude in less than two hours.

Fourteen courses! We know how they were made not only from Ranhofer's cookbook but also from descriptions of his efficient kitchen. An article in the *Sun* describes Ranhofer supervising forty cooks, "perfectly trained and drilled as a regiment of soldiers" from his office in the middle of the kitchen.[39] But who could have eaten such meals routinely? Even ordinary, everyday menus of the period assume separate services of soup, fish, boiled meat, cold platters, roast meat, a choice among several entrées (delicate and complicated dishes with sauces), vegetable accompaniments, and perhaps a spot of game such as wild duck just before the dessert to renew the appetite. To be sure, there were different concepts of body image then

Fig. 10. Dinner given at Delmonico's by the New York Chamber of Commerce, 1890.

and now. Thinness signaled ill humor and bad digestion; women were expected to be plump, ideally of Rubenesque proportions, while men were given considerable license for girth. Nevertheless, gross obesity was not approved of. The people who enjoyed these meals seem in retrospect to have been either unusually fortunate or uniquely ravenous. Unless they possessed extraordinarily rapid and strong digestion or routinely indulged in extreme sports, it's hard to come up with a convincing explanation for how such quantities of rich food were put away.

A premium was placed on ostentation and excess. It was expected that at an elegant meal too much would be served; Delmonico's did not offer doggie bags. Perhaps one could take small bites of a number of dishes, or ignore the plethora of what was set out in favor of a few selections, but there is no indication that restraint was normal practice. Wasteful as these meals must have been, they show a degree of enchantment and enjoyment that should challenge common assumptions that our current age is unique in its food obsession, or that we eat far better than people did in the past.

The Epicurean includes a complete repertoire of grand French cuisine, although almost nothing of the provincial or bourgeois traditions that were becoming popular in France at the same time—for example Occitan cassoulet or Burgundian coq au vin. Ranhofer also has an extensive selection of American food, and not just the high-end game and fish such as the aforementioned canvasback ducks or shad. One hundred and sixteen sumptuous breakfast menus go well beyond the skimpy "continental breakfast" of bread, butter, and jam to include American corned-beef hash, pancakes, Saratoga potatoes, and cream pies. Elsewhere we can find instructions for making pumpkin pie, succotash, curried oysters, and clam chowder.

There is a recipe for a cream of corn soup "à la Mendocino" that would have a curious afterlife at Chez Panisse in the 1970s, where its rediscovery by Chef Jeremiah Tower would be regarded as the beginning of the new American regional cuisine.[40] Whatever its later importance (and as we'll see, its importance is exaggerated), the Mendocino soup is one of a handful of American regional dishes presented by Ranhofer. How he ever heard of the remote Northern California county of Mendocino is unknown. He expresses appreciation for the bounty of American farms and landscape, but for all his time in New Orleans, Ranhofer offers little in the way of Creole cuisine (two gumbo recipes), while New England and the South are completely neglected.

Rather surprisingly, Ranhofer has a recipe for Chinese bird's nest soup, but although the cookbook was published at a time of increasing American curiosity about the food of immigrants, Ranhofer was not interested in anything approaching a global food culture. This is in contrast to the other Delmonico's veteran, Filippini, who described meals from Hong

Kong, Korea, Japan, and Hawaii, and provided an early recipe for chop suey, defined here as "bits of pork."[41]

By contrast, *The Epicurean* reflects the elaborate, complicated, heavily garnished French grande cuisine of the nineteenth century. Butter, truffles, cream, and an intimidating variety of rich sauces were the basis of a cooking style with more game and mutton than we are familiar with; perhaps a bit less beef; many more fish species; and softer, thicker food— quite the opposite of our current preference for lightly grilled meat, *al dente* pasta, and crisp, lightly cooked vegetables. Meat and fish were served with elaborate garnishes, and not just any frippery but according to a French code of what "edible decorations" belonged with what dishes. The 1961 *Larousse Gastronomique* lists about 200 "simple" garnishes and 150 "composite" garnishes involving quenelles, truffles, shaped vegetables, mushrooms, potato nests, and all manner of delightful, difficult, and now-forgotten ornaments.

More than a mere imitator of Parisian culinary fashions, Ranhofer was inventive. Lobster Newberg first appeared under his command, and if he wasn't the first to develop the method of preparing ice cream in a hot meringue surrounding, he did give the name "Baked Alaska" to this confection in honor of Secretary of State Seward's extravagant purchase of Alaska from Russia in 1867.[42]

With 3,700 recipes, 500 suggested bills of fare, and 85 complete banquet menus, it would seem as if *The Epicurean* had revealed to all and sundry Delmonico's proprietary information. The retired Delmonico's manager Leopold Rimmer said that Ranhofer "gave away all the secrets of the house" to every "Tom, Dick and Harry who calls himself a chief cook" and blamed him for causing a decline in the restaurant's business.[43] Yet the book's front matter includes a handwritten note of endorsement from young Charles Delmonico, which seemed a pretty clear indicator it was not perceived as undermining the restaurant but rather as assuring the perpetuation of its fame.

Despite Leopold Rimmer's complaints, Ranhofer's cookbook did not adversely affect Delmonico's—perhaps because its recipes were so hard to duplicate even for well-equipped kitchens, or perhaps because those recipes were already rather old-fashioned by 1893. There were some more turbulent waters to be navigated in the closing decades of the nineteenth and opening of the twentieth century, but at first these were mere ripples in the changing fashionable surface. In 1881, the year of Lorenzo Delmonico's death, Louis Sherry, the son of a carpenter from Vermont, opened a confectionery and catering establishment. The enterprise flourished as Sherry received contracts for galas at the Metropolitan Opera beginning in 1883 and in 1885 devised delicate Japanese décor for parties during the wildly successful run of Gilbert and Sullivan's *Mikado*. Sherry opened a restaurant, Sherry's, in 1889 on Fifth Avenue and Thirty-Seventh Street, farther uptown than Delmonico's had yet ventured.

Sherry's was a more successful and enduring rival to Delmonico's than the Maison Dorée had been thirty years earlier. It offered distinguished, more-or-less French food in a splendid atmosphere designed to evoke the palace at Versailles. In 1891, a reporter for the *Herald* complained about waiting around at Delmonico's because Young Charley wouldn't accept reservations for anytime after six thirty. The writer lamented that with all its irritating inconveniences, Delmonico's was still preeminent— "You can say what you please, that other places are as good; they may be. Delmonico's is by no means superlatively excellent these days. But people won't go to other places." This was not quite true, for as another *Herald* writer noted, there were other options. For the season of balls, the young flocked to Sherry's while the "wall flowers, old timers and patricians" clung to Delmonico's.[44]

Sherry's was flashier than Delmonico's and accommodated itself to the increasingly showy tastes of a new wave of parvenus. In December 1896,

Sherry's was raided by the police, who had received a tip about a bachelor party for a flamboyant character named Herbert Barnum Seeley, nephew of circus impresario P. T. Barnum, at which the dancer known as "Little Egypt" was preparing to perform in the nude.[45] If anything, Sherry's profited from the scandal, which increased its reputation for providing an amusing rather than stuffy atmosphere.

In Theodore Dreiser's novel *Sister Carrie*, which itself created a scandal when it appeared in 1900, the young, ambitious protagonist has heard from newspapers about Sherry's, "the luxuriousness and gorgeousness of this temple of gastronomy." As with Henry James observing Verena's love for Delmonico's, the Hoosier-born Dreiser rather more acidulously disapproved of the ostentation, waste, and cost of a meal at a New York luxury restaurant. His heroine is still a working-class girl at this point, and so it is more likely she would be taken to Sherry's than to Delmonico's.

Another rival to Delmonico's was the Waldorf Hotel, opened on Park Avenue in 1893 and soon merged with the adjoining Astoria. The restaurant at the Waldorf was under the direction of Oscar Tschirky, a Swiss immigrant who had worked at Delmonico's as a waiter and then manager of private rooms and catering. Tschirky had a knack for providing a splashier kind of publicity than that afforded by Delmonico's. For wealthy people who did not figure in Ward McAllister's 400, publicity was not something to be avoided. The velvet rope, still today a mark of distinction and discrimination, was designed by Tschirky to allow ordinary people to congregate in the hotel lobby to gape at A-list arrivals while clearing a path for these luminaries.

In the waning years of the nineteenth century, as the Gilded Age was transformed without losing any of its vulgarity, the Bradley Martin Ball of February 1897 at the Waldorf was a well-publicized riot of excess. Not that it differed so much from the run of common showing off, but it did have roses, clematis, "flirtation bowers," myriad orchids, and a virtual forest landscaping the ballroom and adjacent corridors. The 700 bejeweled guests were dressed in historical costumes. Their hostess, Cornelia (Mrs. Bradley) Martin, wore $50,000 worth of jewelry adorning her Elizabethan-period outfit. We don't hear much about the food, but the event galvanized resentment against the turn-of-the-century plutocracy and the Martins shortly thereafter felt it prudent to leave for Europe permanently.[46] Here again, the venue in which the affair was held did not bear any opprobrium; Tschirky had demonstrated his ability to host an event no matter what the scale or expense. He would rule for forty years at the Waldorf.

As the twentieth century approached, Delmonico's was no longer alone at the summit of American gastronomy, but its glittering reputation was untarnished. A glowing portrait of the restaurant and its food in 1896 is provided in *The Alienist* (written in 1994), Caleb Carr's historical novel of suspense and abnormal psychology. The team trying to figure out the identity of a serial killer has dinner in a private room at Delmonico's. They are greeted by Young Charley Delmonico, described as "suave, dapper and eternally tactful." The party of five dines on oysters, green-turtle soup, bass with Mornay sauce, saddle of lamb Colbert, Maryland terrapin, canvasback duck with hominy and currant jelly, foie gras in aspic, fried pears marinated in wine with apricot sauce, and petits fours. A "sorbet Elsinore" midway during the meal is a refreshing interval. Two kinds of sherry, a Riesling (Hochheimer), a red Bordeaux (Chateau Lagrange), and a red Burgundy (Chambertin) accompany the meal. In setting the scene of this chapter, the author depicts the still-magical reputation of Delmonico's for extraordinary food, elegance, and its apparent openness and lack of exacting social discrimination.[47]

In 1897, Young Charley established what was to be the last Delmonico's, on Forty-Fourth Street and Fifth Avenue, close to Times Square, the newest location of the city's migratory entertainment center. Smoking was for the first time permitted in the public rooms and an orchestra played, although it was discreet. Complaints about the relatively cramped and awkward space at Forty-Fourth Street became louder when the beloved but now not very busy Madison Square Delmonico's closed in 1899. That left but two Delmonico's, the new branch and the old Citadel.

A novel challenge to Delmonico's came from restaurants designed for entertainment. While Sherry's or the Waldorf allowed guests to create their own festivities, their public restaurants were conventionally restrained in manner, heavily decorated in Louis XV or XVI style, and somnolent. For a fancy restaurant to be fun in itself was new. Rector's, a restaurant that originated in Chicago, became the proverbial talk of the town when it opened in Times Square in 1899.[48] Rector's was the most famous of what were known as "lobster palaces"—venues with large rooms and luxurious but garish décor, where Champagne flowed freely and every meal was a loud celebration. An orchestra accompanied the diners, playing excerpts from Offenbach operettas and other light music, and dancing for patrons was added in 1910. The restaurant was ornate in a style of traditional excess, but it also featured the first revolving-door entrance.

Rector's was an ideal place for men with money to entertain chorus girls (*chorines* as they were known) without fear of making an inappropriate social statement. According to George Rector himself, the restaurant was "the supreme court of triviality" and "the cathedral of froth." A hit from the 1913 Ziegfeld Follies was "If a Table at Rector's Could Talk" and people lined up on Broadway to see a musical farce entitled *The Girl from Rector's*.

The concepts of "froth" and "triviality" generally meant fun in an opulent and socially undiscriminating setting. "Frivolity" or "lack of seriousness" in this context meant a chance for men to indulge in sexual license of a sort that was less obviously sordid than consorting with prostitutes but hardly to be confused with respectable courtship. Chorines or dancers at the Follies were talented entertainers and amusing if not socially presentable. New York was now full of young, unattached women of unconventional temperament who might eventually settle down with a middle-class husband but who meanwhile took part, like Sister Carrie, in the night-

Fig. 11. Menu cover from Rector's, 1917.

life of the city. William Glackens's painting *Chez Mouquin* (1905) shows a middle-aged man dining with a young woman at Mouquin's, a French restaurant on Sixth Avenue and Twenty-Eighth Street. The gentleman was readily identifiable to contemporaries as James B. Moore, a well-known

Fig. 12. William Glackens, *Chez Mouquin*, 1905.

Fig. 13. The main dining room at Rector's, ca. 1920.

man about town. Although the picture was extensively noticed, his anonymous, beautifully dressed, slightly bored companion was not of such low or obviously "professional" status as to cause a scandal. Mouquin's, one of several rivals to Rector's, aspired to haute cuisine, but, as one regular patron recalled, "one entered Mouquin's to shed all forms of seriousness."[49]

Given the fervid atmosphere, the food at Rector's seems to have been surprisingly good and the menus were large and varied, offering considerably more than just lobsters. A menu from May 1900 lists 378 dishes. You could eat canvasback ducks, redhead ducks, partridges, or terrapin (the most expensive items on a 1904 menu). Although there was lots of foie gras, the food was not meticulously French. Many dishes were on the order of "lamb kidneys, sautés échalottes" (sautéed with shallots)—not really more French than the deviled lamb kidneys, salmon sauce verte, or oyster cocktail.[50]

Fig. 14. Rector's menu, 1902.

By 1900, Delmonico's, its atmosphere still more "serious" and soigné than the likes of Rector's, had given in to changing times by offering food that was less French and more American than had been the case in its grandest years. A 1900 menu from the Citadel lists French items such as Vol-au-Vent Financière (pastry shells with a rich, complex sauce of which truffles was only one ingredient), beef tournedos (beef with foie gras), and sweetbreads, but the ensemble of dishes is comparatively plain—roast turkey, mushrooms on toast, glazed ham, pigeon with peas. American specialties are featured, not just the de rigueur canvasbacks and terrapin but shad roe, pompano from the Gulf of Mexico, and local bluefish.[51]

More dangerous than competition from the likes of Rector's or Sherry's was the manifestation of long-term problems in Delmonico's management and finances. After sixteen years in charge, "Young Charley" died of tuberculosis in 1901 at the age of forty-one. He was succeeded by his mother, Rosa Delmonico, affectionately known as "Aunt Rosa," who died soon afterward, in 1904, leaving the restaurant to her niece, Josephine Crist Delmonico Otard, and Josephine's brother, Lorenzo Crist Delmonico.

Day-to-day management was in the hands of Eugène Garnier, who had been employed at Delmonico's for more than thirty years. Garnier was a fine host but a poor manager, and it became obvious that the restaurants, although busy and popular, were losing money. In 1906–1907, legal proceedings were launched by Lorenzo Delmonico and Albert Thieriot, an executor of the will of Rosa Delmonico, to take over and exclude Josephine, who was allied with Garnier. The restaurant was shown to be losing money as a result of multiple mortgages and various other forms of borrowing, as well as mismanagement, thus Lorenzo and Thieriot asked to have it placed in receivership. Ultimately this effort was unsuccessful, but new management was agreed upon and this move salvaged the restaurant's financial position for the time being. The public airing of Delmonico's divisions and financial fragility did not help its fortunes. Long-term problems were competition with other luxury restaurants that prevented it from raising its prices, and difficulties of staffing and maintenance.

The Great War had an adverse effect on Delmonico's, exacerbated by changes in dining habits in favor of lighter and less elaborate meals and dishes, as well as the growing clamor of the Temperance movement. When cracks in the structure of the building housing the Citadel were discovered in 1917, it was simply closed. Lorenzo filed for bankruptcy in 1919. Even the presiding judge in the insolvency proceedings hoped the restaurant could be reborn if it were sold. In his ruling, Judge Julius Mayer lauded Delmonico's credo of consideration for guests, quiet and dignified rooms, deferential and polished waiters, and comforting familiarity.[52] The judge's statement reads like a modern lament for one of New York's gracious French restaurants such as La Caravelle or Lutèce that have met their demise in recent decades.

By this time one begins to see from the disappointing menus that the restaurant, whatever its distinguished atmosphere, was no longer French but rather conformed to a vaguely English, American, or what would later be called "Continental" ersatz style. Caviar was available, but the featured entrées are banal: lamb curry, breaded veal cutlets with noodles, English mutton chops with sweet potatoes, even, sad to say, turkey hash with fried bananas.[53] The Delmonico family had the good fortune to sell the sole remaining restaurant on Forty-Fourth Street on January 17, 1920, the precise day that Prohibition took effect.

The inability to serve wine and liquor legally doomed the elegant restaurant model that Delmonico's had established. Not only was it difficult to imagine classic French cuisine served without wine, but alcoholic beverages have always been a lucrative aspect of the business, as the markup is great, prices are easy to set in relation to costs, and people like to drink. Federal agents raided Delmonico's in April 1921, and on May 21, 1923, the last meal was served, accompanied by mineral water. Verses by Arthur

DELMONICOS

FOUNDED 1827

Lobster cocktail 80 — Crab meat cocktail 70

Canapé, *Marietta* 60 — Canapé, *Allumini* 80

BELUGA CAVIAR (own importation, per person) 1 75
Little Neck clams 35 — Cherrystone clams 40
Blue Points 40 — Cape Cods 40
Cocktail sauce 10

RELISHES

Celery 35 — Supreme of grape fruit *with Maraschino* 75
Olives 35 — Stuffed *or* ripe olives 40 — Anchovies *on toast* 55 — Lyon sausage 50
Sardines 50 — Tomato, surprise 60 — Salted almonds 45
Smoked salmon *in oil* 50 — Assorted relishes 75

SOUPS

Consommé 45 — Chicken broth 50 — Clam broth 40 — Tomato *with rice* 45
Essence of tomato, *Excelsior* 45 — Green turtle, Madeira 75 — Chicken gombo 50
Cream of celery, quenelles of marrow 45

FISH

Filet of lemon, sole, Cardinal 85 — Fried smelts, sauce Remoulade 75
Fried oystercrabs, Tartar sauce 90 — Scallops, Boston style 90 — Crabmeat, Florentine 85
Stuffed deviled lobster 80 — Long Island trout, Meunière 90

EGGS

Poached, Blanchard 60 — Sur-le-Plat, Bercy 55 — Omelette, Chasseur 80

ENTREES

CURRY OF LAMB, RICE BORDURE 85 — VEAL CUTLET BREADED,CREAMED NOODLES 1 25
Turkey hash, fried bananas 1 25 — English mutton chop, sweet potatoes 1 15
Croquette of capon, French peas 85 — Bouchée of sweetbreads, mushrooms 80
Breast of chicken, Jardinière 1 50

ROASTS

Roast ribs of prime beef au jus 90
Stuffed young turkey, Americaine 1 25 — Loin *of* lamb 90
Squab chicken 1 50 — Whole chicken (2 pers.) 2.50 — Whole large chicken (3 pers.) 3.25

VEGETABLES

Oyster Bay asparagus 80 — Artichoke 65 — Egg plant, *any style* 50
Spaghetti *or* Macaroni 50 — Brussels sprouts with chestnuts 65 — New green peas 65
Young carrots *in cream* 55 — Spinach 55 — New string beans 65
New succotash 60 — New Lima beans 65
POTATOES: French fried 40 — Stewed 40 — Gratinée, *Delmonicos* 45
Mashed 40 — Sautées 40 — Hashed, *in cream* 40 — Sweet 40 — Bermuda boiled 40

SALADS

Endive 60 — Celery 45 — (With French dressing) — Tomato 50 — Lorenzo 60
Cucumbers 45 — Heart of lettuce or Romaine 50 — Escarole 45
Watercress 40 — Chiffonnade 55 — Chicory 45 — Alligator pear 75
(Any other dressing 20 cents)
LOBSTER or CHICKEN Mayonnaise 1 25 — Crab flakes, *Mayonnaise* 1 00

DESSERTS

PASTRY: English apple tart with whipped cream 50 — Cabinet *or* Rice pudding 40
French pastry 20 — Caramel custard 40 — Assorted cakes 40 — Peach *flambée* 50
Peach short cake 50 — Rum cake 40 — Apple, pumpkin or cocanut pie 25
Compote of fresh pear 40 — Orange or grapefruit marmelade 30 — Bar-le-Duc 40
Currant jelly 25, Guava 30 — Eclairs 20 — Assorted bonbons 40
ICE CREAMS: Chocolate 40 — Vanilla 40 — Coffee 40 — Strawberry 50 — Pistaches 40
Hazelnut 50
WATER ICES: Raspberry 40 — Orange 40 — Lemon 40
CHEESE: *(Individual service)* — Cream Gervais 25 — *with* Bar-le-Duc 60
Camembert 35 — Roquefort 50 — Swiss 40 — Liederkranz 30 — Port-du-Salut 40
FRUITS: Grape fruit *half* 40 — Pear 25 — Bananas 20 — Pineapple 30 — Apple 20 — Orange 20
Grapes 50
Honey Dew or Casaba melon 60
Coffee and milk 25 w. cream 35 — Brandied pineapple, peaches *or* figs 50

LUNCHEON — Thursday, October 25, 1917

BUY YOUR LIBERTY BOND AT BOOTH IN MAIN OFFICE

Fig. 15. Delmonico's menu, 1917.

Nies mourned the death of Delmonico's at the hands of Prohibition and the triumph of mediocrity in its place:

> No more the grape with fire divine
> Shall light the torch of pleasure gay,
> And where the gourmand paused to dine
> Hot dog and fudge shops have their day.[54]

The mystique of Delmonico's has nevertheless survived the ninety years since the closing of the original business. In 1929 a restaurateur named Oscar Tucci reopened the Citadel on South William Street (the address is now officially 56 Beaver Street), and the establishment was popularly known as "Oscar's Delmonico." It tried to restore some of the glamour of the original Delmonico's, but was never considered one of the finer restaurants of New York. It lasted until 1977. Another family ran it as "Delmonico's Restaurant" until 1992. An Italian business venture, the Bice Group, bought the vacant premises in 1998 and restored the restaurant to something resembling its late-nineteenth-century look. Bice then sold it to a partnership led by Milan Licul, who has since made an ambitious effort to recapture the luster of America's first grand restaurant.

LEGACY AND INFLUENCE

Delmonico's unequivocally established an American standard for elegance and refinement and inspired many imitators. Restaurants in New Orleans and San Francisco called themselves "Delmonico's" without authorization (the New Orleans establishment, founded in 1895, is now run by Emeril Lagasse); a New York Chinese restaurant called Mon Lay Won referred to itself as "the Chinese Delmonico."[55] In 1863, a North Carolina writer described an African American–owned boardinghouse as "the Delmonico's of New Bern."[56] Owen Wister's *The Virginian*, a classic novel of the Old West, mockingly describes a place in Omaha claiming to serve "Frogs Legs à la Delmonico's."[57] Even comical imitations were tributes to Delmonico's preeminence.

In its long era of distinction, Delmonico's inspired the American luxury restaurant. We have seen that Delmonico's was never so purely

Fig. 16. Menu cover from Mon Lay Won, "the Chinese Delmonico," ca. 1910.

French that it did not offer distinctly American dishes such as terrapin or shad. Looking at other celebrated restaurants of the nineteenth century shows that while their menus were often written in French and they had a number of French-inspired dishes such as Chicken à la Marengo, or fricandeau of veal or fish with Hollandaise sauce, they tended to favor a vaguely international style rather than strictly French cuisine. A particularly hard-to-explain phenomenon is a passion for baked macaroni, a seeming anomaly, since no other Italian dishes were popular at fancy restaurants until well into the twentieth century. At the elegant Revere House Hotel in Boston, a series of 706 daily menus between 1862 and 1865 shows that the most popular entrées were, in descending order:

Macaroni au gratin
Escalloped oysters
Oysters baked in their shells
Oyster patties
Chicken fricassee
Macaroni and cheese [similar to, if not the same as, Macaroni au gratin]
Salmis of duck
Baked macaroni
Macaroni au Parmesan
Beef à la mode
Baked beans with pork
Apple fritters[58]

Beef à la mode (larded and braised beef), chicken fricassee, and the salmis of duck are more-or-less French. Although obviously Italian in origin, macaroni made in a rich, soupy sauce was also popular in nineteenth-century Paris. Nevertheless, the overall impression is that even at the Revere House, considered a gastronomic temple, the most popular dishes were thrifty rather than magnificent.

A survey of eighty-four other US restaurant menus from between 1840 and 1865, comprising about 1,000 entrées, gives similar results for the most popular entrées:

Macaroni au gratin
Chicken fricassee
Baked beans and pork
Macaroni à l'Italienne
Oyster patties
Escalloped oysters
Apple fritters
Beef à la mode
Salmis of duck with olives
Currie of lobster [sic]
Oysters baked in shell
Fillet of beef with mushrooms[59]

Even before the advent of Sherry's and others of its type, there were some more impressive rivals to Delmonico's than this prosaic list might lead one to believe. The first grand hotel in the United States, Tremont House in Boston, opened in 1829 and although no menus survive from its earliest days, an 1844 menu in French includes sweetbreads in sorrel sauce, jellied venison with currant sauce, larded beef filets with Champagne sauce, and other dishes from the French repertoire.[60] As we will see in the next chapter, Antoine's in New Orleans began in 1840 with a French-trained chef as owner and in a city with a particular but, in its fashion, authoritative, take on French cuisine.

In 1851 there was even a contest between Delmonico's and a restaurant in Philadelphia with the retrospectively unfortunate name "Parkinson's" and, contrary to all expectations, Delmonico's lost. We only know what was served by James Parkinson, the victor, who presented a meal in seventeen courses lasting from six p.m. until the blush of dawn twelve hours later. Even at Parkinson's, however, the food was only inconsistently French: sweetbreads with tomato sauce; mutton cutlets, chicken croquettes, Vol-au-Vent à la Financière. What was impressive was the ability to transport food from far away (reed birds from South Carolina; salmon from the Kennebec River in Maine), an unusual sorbet made from very old Tokay, and the sheer number of courses including terrapin (of course) and wild game birds.[61]

Most striking about Delmonico's and its imitators is how unfamiliar the food seems to us today. The French dishes represent a vanished grande cuisine based on sauces, truffles, elaborate garnishes, and a veritable stampede of game. Salmis and timbales have not disappeared in France but are not at the center of attention anymore. The American dishes are, for the most part, equally strange, either because they are based on now-endangered species (terrapin, game birds), or items we don't seem to like anymore—organ meat, timbales, pig's feet, mutton, calf's head, fritters, croquettes.

Looking at ten specific restaurants, we are trying to fathom the mystery of what American cuisine really is. With Delmonico's, arguably the most famous restaurant in American history, we are at an early stage of the investigation into what makes American cuisine, but already we can see how mysterious and unfamiliar the process of finding an answer can be.

ANTOINE'S[1]

HAUTE CREOLE

W hile not quite the oldest restaurant in the United States, a distinction enjoyed by Boston's Union Oyster House founded in 1826, Antoine's is by far the oldest grand restaurant in continuous existence. Over its long history, the restaurant has been run by a single family, descendants of founder Antoine Alciatore. Established in 1840 in the French Quarter of New Orleans, close to its present location on St. Louis Street, Antoine's exemplifies the magnificent but endangered regional culinary heritage of America. It has described itself as a French restaurant for almost all of its history, but has actually created dozens of original dishes and made use of the unique ingredients and cooking style of New Orleans.

With fifteen dining rooms, Antoine's size is surpassed in our list of ten restaurants only by that of Mamma Leone's and the Rockefeller Center branch of Schrafft's. Its décor and culinary style are historically evocative, and the restaurant occupies a conspicuous and striking four-story edifice, the oldest part built in 1790. Thin columns support an ornate wrought-iron fronted balcony in what we think of as typical French Louisiana style,

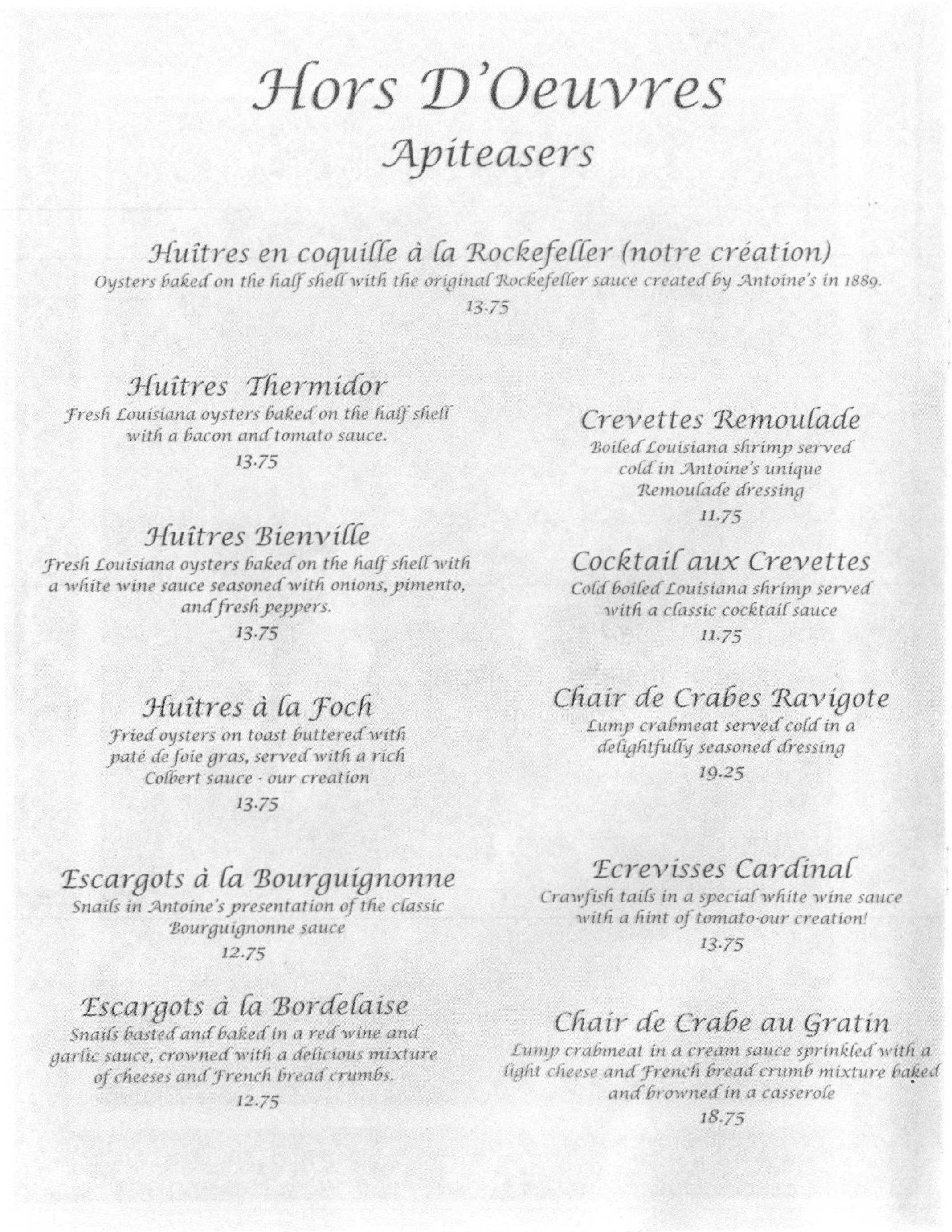

Hors D'Oeuvres
Apiteasers

Huîtres en coquille à la Rockefeller (notre création)
Oysters baked on the half shell with the original Rockefeller sauce created by Antoine's in 1889.
13.75

Huîtres Thermidor
Fresh Louisiana oysters baked on the half shell
with a bacon and tomato sauce.
13.75

Crevettes Remoulade
Boiled Louisiana shrimp served
cold in Antoine's unique
Remoulade dressing
11.75

Huîtres Bienville
Fresh Louisiana oysters baked on the half shell with
a white wine sauce seasoned with onions, pimento,
and fresh peppers.
13.75

Cocktail aux Crevettes
Cold boiled Louisiana shrimp served
with a classic cocktail sauce
11.75

Huîtres à la Foch
Fried oysters on toast buttered with
paté de foie gras, served with a rich
Colbert sauce - our creation
13.75

Chair de Crabes Ravigote
Lump crabmeat served cold in a
delightfully seasoned dressing
19.25

Escargots à la Bourguignonne
Snails in Antoine's presentation of the classic
Bourguignonne sauce
12.75

Ecrevisses Cardinal
Crawfish tails in a special white wine sauce
with a hint of tomato-our creation!
13.75

Escargots à la Bordelaise
Snails basted and baked in a red wine and
garlic sauce, crowned with a delicious mixture
of cheeses and French bread crumbs.
12.75

Chair de Crabe au Gratin
Lump crabmeat in a cream sauce sprinkled with a
light cheese and French bread crumb mixture baked
and browned in a casserole
18.75

Fig. 17. Antoine's menu, 2009: Hors d'oeuvres.

which is actually much more Spanish. Large glass windows in wooden door-frames run along the front of the building which is considerably more deep than it is wide. Although it extends quite some distance along St. Louis Street between Royal and Bourbon Streets, Antoine's doesn't immediately look as if it could house so many dining rooms and seat more than 700 people. Over 175 years, the public and private spaces of Antoine's have witnessed a multitude of New Orleans celebrations, but it has also played a part in tragic aspects of the city's always intriguing history.

CHEF ALCIATORE

Only eighteen when he opened his restaurant, Antoine Alciatore was already a successful chef. Born in 1822 at Alassio in Liguria, he began work at the Hôtel de Noailles in Marseilles.[2] Like Chef Ranhofer of Delmonico's, Antoine was a kitchen apprentice whose precocious talents were quickly recognized. Prince Talleyrand, the great courtier, diplomat, and gourmand, was so impressed with Antoine's marinated beef tenderloin, cooked rare enough to be slightly bloody, served with a sauce of beef stock, sweetbreads, and chicken livers, that he summoned the cook. Recovering quickly from his surprise at

Fig. 18. Antoine Alciatore, 1822–1877.

the chef's youth, Talleyrand praised his skill and asked what the dish was called. Antoine had not thought of naming it, but in a gruesomely comic bit of quick thinking, he told the prince "Beef Robespierre," thinking of his father's eyewitness recollection of the execution of the French revolutionary leader Maximilien Robespierre in 1793. Beef Robespierre would be listed on the Antoine's menu as a specialty until the 1960s.[3]

Arriving in America in 1838, Antoine Alciatore spent two years amidst the crowded labyrinth of downtown Manhattan. It would be nice to think that he crossed paths with the Delmonicos and became acquainted with their restaurant, but nothing is known about his time in New York except that, as was the case for most off-the-boat immigrants, it was frustrating. Antoine set out for New Orleans, a booming city with a substantial French cultural influence. He worked briefly at the new St. Charles Hotel, one of the most luxurious in the United States, but soon tired of the huge establishment and decided to start a boardinghouse and restaurant (what is known in French as a *pension*) in the old colonial French and Spanish district of New Orleans.

The initial fame of his restaurant was based on Dinde à la Talleyrand, turkey à la Talleyrand, an invention of Antoine's that he brought over from France and named after the astute statesman, the first of many celebrity clients. Word of this apparently marvelous dish spread rapidly in the Crescent City, and Antoine started making it available to the public from a take-out window. Alas, we have no idea what made Dinde à la Talleyrand special, because the recipe somehow disappeared into the mists of culinary history and legend sometime after 1914.[4] What is significant is that the early success of Beef Robespierre and Dinde à la Talleyrand, along with puffed potatoes (*pommes de terres soufflés*—still on the menu), induced Antoine to turn the *pension* into a public restaurant.

Antoine Alciatore established a dynamic for the restaurant that would endure for about 100 years: innovative new dishes against a background of traditional French cuisine. As a chef, Antoine was resplendently inventive. In addition to the specialties just mentioned, he created Toast St. Antoine (crabmeat in wine and Béchamel sauce, breaded and served on toast with anchovies); Toast Balthazar, named after a now forgotten French painter (oysters and cheese on toast with pimentos); and Pompano Montgolfier, a predecessor of his son Jules's famed Pompano en Papillote. This latter fish entrée was baked and brought to the table in a parchment paper bag whose balloon shape led Antoine to name the dish after the Montgolfier brothers, developers of the first functioning hot-air balloons shortly before the French Revolution.[5]

All this creativity notwithstanding, Antoine's, like Delmonico's, was a resolutely French restaurant and described itself this way rather than claiming to provide "Creole," or "New Orleans" cuisine. Until the 1990s the menu was in French without English translation or explanation, as if the hauteur of Paris had been transmitted to Louisiana. In its early decades, the style of food was international French rather than being particularly identifiable with New Orleans in terms of either basic ingredients or cooking methods. The menu featured dishes that would have been perfectly at home at Delmonico's: Filet of Sole Joinville (poached sole with a white-wine sauce with mushrooms, truffles, and shrimp); Filet of Beef Périgueux (with truffles); Bouchées à la Reine (a puff-pastry shell like a vol-au-vent, filled with diced meat, usually sweetbreads, and a white cream sauce); and Becassine sur Canapé (snipe, a small game bird, on toast). By the 1880s, Antoine's had become more regional, offering turtle, pompano, redfish, shellfish, and other natural bounty of the Gulf of Mexico and its shores, but the manner of preparation continued to reflect a French aesthetic, especially with regard to sauces.[6] The only cookbook ever issued with the Antoine's imprimatur, written in 1980 by its then owner and chef Roy F. Guste Jr., follows the Byzantine demands of old-fashioned French cookbooks for complex, time-consuming, interdependent sauces: one makes Bordelaise sauce, for example, by heating butter; then sautéing green onions, garlic, and parsley; and then adding Marchand de Vin sauce, which itself requires cooking a purée of mushrooms, onion, and garlic in butter and then adding Espagnole sauce, a complicated master-sauce that involves beef or chicken stock and tomato sauce.[7]

The owners of Antoine's did not propose to serve what we think of as typical Louisiana cuisine, such as jambalaya or crawfish étoufée. In fact, its menus barely mentioned gumbo among the soup options. For much of its history, Antoine's has presented itself first as a French restaurant and second as a place that served hundreds of its own unique dishes. It was not alone in asserting a French identity: on a 1954 menu from Brennan's, another New Orleans institution, the establishment is typified as "Brennan's French Restaurant," and the only two explicitly Creole dishes mentioned are gumbo and cheesecake. A menu from about 1948 for another well-known eatery, La Louisiane, describes it as "One of the Oldest World Famous French Restaurants."[8] To understand the complicated nature of the French heritage and Creole cuisine requires some account of the history of New Orleans and the setting of Antoine's in its early years.

THE ASCENDANT CRESCENT CITY

When Antoine Alciatore arrived in 1840, New Orleans was in the midst of a heady expansion comparable to, and if anything more powerful than, that experienced by New York. In 1815, three years after Louisiana became a state, only 25,000 people lived in New Orleans, yet in 1840 there were 102,192 inhabitants, making it the fourth largest city in the United States (at something around 400,000, it is currently ranked fiftieth by population). Its port, the major Gulf Coast entrepôt for exports and imports, was as large as that of New York, exporting the agricultural products of the Mississippi River valley such as wheat, salt pork, and animal hides, along with Southern cotton. It received Caribbean imports such as rum, coffee, and sugar. The amount of banking capital and the per-capita wealth of New Orleans were probably greater than New York's in 1840. New Orleans was a center of the slave trade and, much more than New York, its economy was directly dependent on slavery, although a substantial free black population also lived in the city.

Fig. 19. Antoine's Restaurant exterior, ca. 1925.

The French had recognized the strategic position of New Orleans once they found it was possible to navigate, just barely, the shallow and debris-choked mouth of the Mississippi. Its establishment in 1717 on (it seems ironic to say this) relatively high ground allowed the French to control territories along the Gulf of Mexico and the lower Mississippi against threats from the English and Spanish colonies. Explorations of the Great Lakes and Mississippi valley by Samuel de Champlain, Jean Nicolet, and Robert de la Salle also made the French aware of the promising future economic significance of an axis of productive land along the great river.

In the early eighteenth century, however, Louisiana was a speculative venture. Its brief moment of notoriety was from 1718 to 1720, when John Law's Mississippi Company took over virtually all French colonial trade, offering a grossly inaccurate prospectus of Louisiana as a land rich in gold and silver, when in fact its hinterland was mostly desolate swamp. The company's stock was run up to astronomical levels, producing what came to be known as the "Mississippi Bubble." The ensuing crash destroyed many fortunes and did not help the image of the French colonial enterprise.

The real financial engine of the French New World empire was not Louisiana but rather Saint-Domingue, the future Haiti. For much of the eighteenth century New Orleans was but a satellite of the sugar industry, the economic beneficiary of slave labor on the Caribbean plantations. A slow trickle of settlement from France was augmented by the influx of French refugees from Canada between 1755 and 1764, violently forced by the British to leave their homes in what was known as Acadia—the maritime provinces of Nova Scotia, Prince Edward Island, and New Brunswick. The Acadians populated the countryside west of New Orleans and are the ancestors of today's Cajuns (the word "Cajun" itself is derived from "Acadian").

In 1763, the Spanish, still powerful in the Caribbean, wrested New Orleans and Louisiana west of the Mississippi from the French, returning it to Napoleon in 1801 as part of a deal over Italy. The jewel in the French New World crown, Saint-Domingue, rebelled in 1791, and two years later, the revolutionary French regime abolished slavery. Saint-Domingue's colonial wealth was in sugar plantations, and the end of slavery meant the collapse of the sugar-based economy. The end of French rule came in 1804, and even before that date New Orleans was receiving new waves of French Caribbean immigrants. With the eclipse of the Saint-Domingue sugar industry, the entire French presence in the Caribbean and the Gulf of Mexico became less valuable politically as well as economically to the embattled French state. Napoleon's ambition to expand was directed to southern and central Europe as well as Egypt, not in the New World, and so he was quite willing to cede Greater Louisiana for a bargain price to the fledgling United States. Thus in 1803, at a price of $11 million (estimated as the equivalent of 4 cents an acre), French Louisiana was sold to the United States along with territories extending as far north and west as Montana.

Thomas Jefferson, the architect of the Louisiana Purchase, declared, "The position of New Orleans certainly destines it to be the greatest city the world has ever seen." It would be the great channel for America's wealth, "brought from more than a thousand rivers, leaving the emporia of the Eastern world far behind." At the time of the purchase, the only outlet for the products of what was to be the American Midwest was by way of the Mississippi River. "Kick a barrel of flour at Minneapolis, and it will roll to the Gulf," as one contemporary observer put it. The difficulty, however, was sending barrels of West Indian rum or coffee upstream to Minneapolis, a difficulty solved by coal-fired steam engines and the consequent creation of substantial and constant riverboat traffic.[9]

What Jefferson did not foresee was that New Orleans would have commercial competition. The Erie Canal, first proposed in 1808 and finished in 1825, linked Buffalo and the Great Lakes with the Hudson River and the port of New York, allowing for a rival eastward, rather than southbound, water route for the transport of agricultural products from the Midwest. The spread of railroad networks in the 1830s and 1840s created even more alternatives to the Mississippi River and ultimately New Orleans. But before the Civil War, the settlement of territories in the Mississippi valley and the expansion of cotton in the South more than made up for the diversion of Midwestern crops to the canals and railroads of the East.

With cotton and sugar came slavery; New Orleans had the greatest slave market in the United States. The literature of the period, including one of the most powerful sections of *Uncle Tom's Cabin* in which Tom is sold in New Orleans to the evil Simon Legree, reveals the tragic stories of the victims of the nineteenth-century slave trade. But because it was home to a Catholic rather than Protestant elite, a substantial free African American population, and a diverse array of immigrants, New Orleans was never exactly a Southern city in character. It was somewhat Caribbean and still partly French. If its culture was diverse, New Orleans and its economic fortunes were nevertheless singularly tied to the Southern cotton trade, and at the opening of the Civil War, the white population of the city firmly supported the Confederacy. New Orleans was occupied more quickly than other Southern cities by federal troops brought in by a naval invasion in 1862. Although not substantially damaged by war in the way that Richmond and Atlanta were, New Orleans never recovered the position it had held in the mid-nineteenth century, yet paradoxically, a catastrophic Yellow Fever epidemic in 1878 ushered in an economic and cultural revival. The regional rail network expanded, the city's port was restored with the deepening of the Mississippi estuary, and other river projects increased barge traffic.

The large black presence gave both pre– and post–Civil War New Orleans a different character from New York, but both cities were enriched by successive waves of immigration, in the case of New Orleans from Spain (especially the Canary Islands) during the period of Spanish governance; from Germany (Alsace and the Rhineland) beginning in the Mississippi Company years, but particularly after 1848; and from Italy between 1885 and 1915 (especially from Sicily). Americans from other parts of the United States also moved to the prospering city, and their relations with the old French Creole elite were sufficiently uneasy that they created new settlements (called the "American sectors") to the west of Canal Street and east of Esplanade, thus defining what came to be known as the French Quarter, or Vieux Carré, nestled between American neighborhoods. The result was a metropolis with a uniquely varied and alluring character that, like New York, was regarded as not really American and thereby earned both admiration and mistrust from the people of the heartland.

The cuisine of New Orleans was affected by the new arrivals, but in a way that was different from New York, where immigrant groups kept a version of their cuisine without merging into a larger whole. In New Orleans, the local cuisine incorporated elements of cooking from the voluntary and involuntary immigrants: Mediterranean spices and rice dishes from the Spanish; sausages from the Germans; spices, okra, gumbo, and braising styles from the Africans; and tomato-based sauces, pasta, and po'boy sandwiches adapted from Sicilian cuisine. These are not segmented, but rather they overlap—rice was brought by Africans as well as the Spanish; the style of bread and bakery products is an amalgam of French, German, and Italian influences.

Louisiana's climate and French colonial history, combined with the absorption of immigrant foodways, produced what is known as Creole cuisine. Antoine's extensive and slowly changing menu has tended to avoid direct reference to Creole tradition in favor of two basic culinary practices: (1) a self-consciously French cuisine, and (2) a large set of dishes invented by chefs and members of the Alciatore family. Only in the unacknowledged background was its food identified with an elegant and subtle Creole tradition. Following a French model did not mean any lack of innovation. Particularly during the time of Jules Alciatore, who directed Antoine's from 1887 until 1934, new dishes were constantly invented, some of them, such as Oysters Rockefeller, achieving international fame. Roy Alciatore, who ran the restaurant from 1934 until 1972, revealed to a reporter in 1930 that they had 560 recipes just for making eggs, and that altogether they knew how to prepare more than 1,000 dishes, many of these found nowhere else.[10]

In addition to traditional French cuisine and the breadth of the Alciatores' culinary innovations, the third aspect—the sophisticated Creole cooking of New Orleans—deserves some explanation and comment because, whether acknowledged or not, it is what Antoine's has come to represent over the course of its long history. The current owner, Rick Blount, describes the food at Antoine's as "Haute Creole," a term that might be applied to describe the food served during most of the restaurant's entire 175-year history, even if its previous owners avoided the world "Creole" for about 150 of those years.

It is now agreed that Creole cuisine emerged from a mix of people, ingredients, and cooking techniques, but this consensus disguises a long and tendentious history of the term "Creole." While it now denotes the French culture of New Orleans, at times "Creole" has implied racial intermarriage that was painful if not intolerable for a substantial segment of the white population to acknowledge in their own background. The narrow colonial definition of Creole was a person of European ancestry born in the New World; thus someone born in Mexico of Spanish parents, or in Brazil of Portuguese parents, would fit the definition. As time went on, the reference point changed from geography (whether you were born in Europe or the New World) to race, but with some ambiguity. Creole could refer to the white descendants of European colonists, but also to people of mixed racial background. In New Orleans, as in all of the United States, any African ancestry rendered one legally black, and because of slavery and its legacy there was a perceived urgency to assert entirely white ancestry, and so to avoid using words like "Creole" that might be understood as conveying racially mixed heritage.

Until the late nineteenth century, the term was used more by outsiders than by people in New Orleans to describe the French population. A travelogue by a self-described "Yankee" published in 1835 tells of a misunderstanding by a Massachusetts father who, when his son informed him that he was marrying a Creole girl from New Orleans, assumed this meant a mixed-race "mulatto," and at first refused to have anything to do with the couple.[11] The author of this account says that in the North it was commonly but mistakenly assumed that Creole meant "coloured," and that because of the diffusion of this notion, French Louisianans avoided using the word. Insistence on pure French identity refuted the supposed taint of racial intermarriage.

Creole as a cooking term has a parallel history. What we think of as

Creole food took shape long before local people started using the word to describe their cuisine. This was partly carried over from a reluctance to evoke a racially ambiguous background but also because the cooking of the elite was supposedly French, or at least French modified to local conditions.

In fact, Creole cuisine is quite distinctive. Basic elements include:

1. roux (flour and butter, lard, or oil cooked together—in France the flour is browned separately) to make sauces and soups[12]
2. celery, onions, and bell peppers (often referred to as "the Holy Trinity"), added to the roux base for sauces and other dishes
3. a spicier flavor than what is called for in French food
4. more use of tomatoes than in France
5. reliance on certain ingredients of the region such as *filé* (powdered sassafras used to flavor and thicken gumbo); hominy grits; mirlitons (a Caribbean squash, also known by its Spanish name, *chayote*); fish such as pompano, speckled trout (a saltwater fish), and redfish; shellfish such as Gulf oysters and shrimp; and game such as wild duck
6. reliance on originally non-native ingredients, such as okra or sausage, brought over by different populations; or regionally distinctive adaptations of standard American items, such as coffee mixed with chicory, or Creole cream cheese, which is more like curds in liquid than the smooth, glossy supermarket product

All these are placed within a basically French aesthetic, which emphasizes complex sauces and slow cooking.

Among the signature dishes of Creole cuisine, gumbo—a moderately thick spiced soup made with seafood, meat, or just vegetables—is both the most famous and the first to have become known to a larger public. It is a dish with uncertain origins whose variations reflect the influence of different migrant groups. Mention of gumbo can be found as far back as 1764, and by the early nineteenth century it was regarded as the quintessential specialty of New Orleans.[13] Pierre de Lassa, the last French administrator of Louisiana, presented twenty-four different gumbos, including several based on turtle soup, at a banquet for the outgoing Spanish representative as part of the complicated handover of the territory to the United States in 1804.[14]

In the nineteenth century, gumbo was served even in the American sections of New Orleans where Creole food was otherwise avoided. The basement-level bar of the St. Charles Hotel was famous for its gumbo, while the hotel's magnificent mirrored and vaulted second-floor dining room featured standard restaurant items on the order of macaroni Italian-style, oyster patties, calf's head with brain sauce, or beef à la mode.[15] Until about 1880, then, the French population of the Vieux Carré ate food they thought of as French. The American population of the new city appropriated a few of these dishes, but their fine restaurants offered the same quasi-French things served at other grand restaurants around the nation.

The word "Creole" was shunned by locals but employed as an occasional culinary term by outsiders. Dishes named "à la Creole" were not intended to refer to New Orleans, but the term was deployed in the vague way the French might name a sauce "Espagnole" or "Béarnaise" without its origin having much to do with either Spain or the Pyrenean region of Béarn. French cooks used "à la Créole" to refer to something served over rice.[16] Marie-Antoine (Antonin) Carême, the most renowned chef of the nineteenth century, developed a recipe for "fresh herrings à la Créole" which comes out as herring cooked in white wine with minced vegetables and herbs, accompanied by rice. Odd though this seems (herring being very much a northern European fish), Herring à la Créole was popular in the English-speaking world, and a recipe appears, for example, in an 1866 guide to the East Anglian fishing towns of Yarmouth and Lowestoft.[17]

In the United States generally, "Creole" as a culinary term referred to a sauce with tomatoes and peppers. Menus from Boston and New York mention "soft shell crabs à la Creole" or "stuffed crabs à la Creole." A Jacksonville, Florida, restaurant lists "chicken sauté à la Creole" in 1882. Chef Charles Ranhofer of Delmonico's had a dessert recipe in his *The Epicurean* for "fruits à la Creole," but here we're back to rice as the giveaway: pineapple and peaches with rice in vanilla syrup, apricot, and maraschino sauce.[18]

Suddenly in the 1880s, New Orleans embraced "Creole" as descriptive of its cookery in order to market local quaintness to tourists. The New Orleans World's Fair in 1884, commemorating the first exportation of cotton from the United States, provided an opportunity to market the city to hundreds of thousands of visitors. A guidebook issued in connection with this "Cotton and Industrial Centennial Fair" boasts that nothing "tickles the palate, satisfies the appetite, is so nutritious or costs so little as the Creole gumbo."[19] In addition to this commercial promotion, the discovery of Creole cuisine accompanied a revival of interest in the romantic history of French New Orleans, which appealed to a local as well as out-of-town audience. The Vieux Carré, previously regarded as merely run-down, was fixed up a bit to attract visitors, but not too much for its picturesque look and slightly decadent reputation to be spoiled by excessive modernization. The romanticized image was still flourishing in 1947, when Tennessee Williams's play *A Streetcar Named Desire* opened.[20] French Quarter restaurants, previously quiet redoubts of local society, became in the late-nineteenth and early-twentieth century destinations for visitors eager to try what was now generally called Creole cuisine.

A third factor promoting local cuisine was the publication in 1885 of two cookbooks: *La Cuisine Créole* by Lafcadio Hearn, and *The Creole Cookery Book*, put out to raise money for the Christian Woman's Exchange, a charitable organization of Protestant ladies. Even though the cookbooks were written by outsiders, they became authoritative guides to New Orleans gastronomy. Hearn was born on a Greek island, raised in Ireland, and came to New Orleans in 1877. He attained fame as a writer about the romantic passions and intrigues of old French Louisiana. Eventually he tired of New

Orleans and in 1887 moved first to Martinique in the West Indies and then to Japan, becoming a passionate interpreter of Japanese culture and taking the name Koizumi Yakumo. Hearn was thus in New Orleans for only ten years, but he greatly influenced the image of the city and its food.

The Christian Woman's Exchange ladies were Protestant, thus also alien to the French Quarter population, which was, naturally, Catholic. The fact that Protestant women, few of them French in origin, would offer a recipe book on Creole food is perhaps due to their enterprising attitude toward what was, after all, a fund-raising activity, but also to the coming together of New Orleans as a city with a curious semi-French heritage, a tradition that could be marketed by those who, strictly speaking, weren't originally representative of it.

The version of Creole cuisine constructed in the late-nineteenth century was that of a French-influenced style that had many contributors, but was essentially the cooking of the white elite of New Orleans. African Americans were not so much excluded from this story as firmly subordinated to it. Cooks of African origin were misrepresented as having relied exclusively on what their French or Spanish mistresses taught them, and so they were pictured as resourceful but essentially passive guardians of a culinary tradition. The first edition of *The Picayune's Creole Cook Book* in 1900 lamented the passing of the "old Creole negro cooks," and the second edition a year later elaborated on this: "The bandana and tignon [*a type of head-scarf*] are fast disappearing from our kitchens. Soon the last of the olden negro cooks of ante-bellum days will have passed away and their places will not be supplied . . ." In fact, one of the stated purposes of *The Picayune's Creole Cook Book* was to teach white housewives, now without kitchen servants, how to make what had been provided for their mothers by African American cooks who, even in the hard years after the Civil War, could prepare "for their 'ole Miss' table a 'ragout' from a piece of neck meat, or a 'pot-au-poivre' from many mixtures that might grace the dining room of a king."[21]

For much of the twentieth century, however, white New Orleanians attempted to suppress any notion that the word "Creole" had anything to do with black people. In the 1922 edition of *The Picayune's Creole Cook Book* and subsequently, all direct reference to the role of African Americans was eliminated. Thirty years later, a 1951 guidebook, insisted "A Creole is ALL WHITE . . . The capitalized noun, referring to a person . . . definitely and without exception refers to the descendants of those noble-blooded . . . Spanish and French colonists."[22] However, this attitude was impossible to maintain consistently with regard to food. Even the later editions of *The Picayune's Creole Cook Book* retained a frontispiece illustration of an African American woman in front of a hearth with a pot. The famous black Creole chef and cookbook author Lena Richard taught classes in Creole cooking, and a 1938 article noted with amazement: "That a negro woman should undertake to teach white folks about Creole cooking seems eminently sensible to Lena." The author considered this notable, but not unthinkable.[23] Beginning in 1947, Richard hosted what for many years was the only regularly scheduled television show starring a black chef.

In fact, there has always been a flourishing black Creole culinary tradition, which has become better known to a wider public in recent years through such figures as Leah Chase, owner of the restaurant Dooky Chase's, and Louis Bluestein, who ran the kitchen at Brennan's for many years.[24] Black and white cooks have mastered a similar repertoire of dishes. Black versions may start with a darker roux, or use different spices, but it is hard to formulate a set of rules separating black from white Creole recipes.

Meanwhile, there is a difference between the Creole cuisine of New Orleans and the Cajun cuisine of the southwestern Louisiana countryside. No one would have confused these before 1979, when Paul Prudhomme opened K-Paul's Louisiana Kitchen in New Orleans. Prudhomme, who died in 2015, an ebullient, larger-than-life character who flourished on television, retailed Cajun-influenced food in Creole New Orleans, thereby obscuring the distinction between the two styles and putting genteel Francophile Creole cuisine in the shade.

Creole and Cajun are actually quite distinct. Although they are both of French origin, they were produced by different French colonial and immigrant populations. Many of the same ingredients are used, but Cajun food is especially partial to sausage and crawfish, uses corn as well as rice, and its definition of game includes not only wild duck but alligator. Both cuisines feature gumbo, but jambalaya is more Cajun than Creole. New Orleans relies more on shrimp than crawfish, on braised domestic meat (to produce beef "grillades," for example), and less on game. The essential distinction has been rural versus urban: one-pot Cajun dishes, as opposed to the separately prepared dishes of the Creoles. New Orleans composes sauces that are richer, less spicy, and more French than Cajun ones: ravigote, remoulade, cardinale, and Hollandaise are typical of the city.

Until the 1970s, the Creole cooking of New Orleans was celebrated while the spicier and heartier fare of the French Acadians was little known outside the region. The network of bayous and rivers of southwestern Louisiana seemed to outsiders inhospitable, but were nevertheless teeming with wildlife that provided the basis for a varied and creative cuisine.

If Antoine's and other older, well-known New Orleans restaurants have made few gestures toward Creole cuisine, they have completely ignored Cajun cuisine—even now, neither blackened redfish nor white boudin sausage nor alligator appear on their menus. Both traditions are threatened by the loss of the French language and the general homogenization of culture, but the Cajun way of life has proven more resistant to erosion from mass-market America than the culture of the Creole population of New Orleans. Cajun cuisine fits with the American enthusiasm for cooking-show characters and culinary heartiness, while Creole food has suffered as a result of the overall decline of French and French-inspired cuisine in the United States.

The Creole story is complicated furthermore because it is positioned between several interpretations of French tradition, and because it has been adversely affected both by its own mythologies and the pressures of homogenization to an American standard. Nevertheless, even though it may be inconsistently acknowledged, this is the cuisine that stands out most prominently in the history of Antoine's.

JULES ALCIATORE

The 1880s were a turning point in Creole self-consciousness and the development of the New Orleans tourist industry. Antoine's regarded itself as above such trends, but in the last decades of the nineteenth century Antoine's grew to national prominence. Afflicted with tuberculosis, Antoine Alciatore gave up the direction of his restaurant in 1875, returning to France to die two years later at the age of fifty-five. Older histories of the restaurant put out by Antoine's say that Antoine's son Jules immediately took over, but he was only fourteen when his father died. The restaurant was in fact run by Antoine's wife, Julie Freyss Alciatore, from 1875 until 1887. She had seven children, six boys and a girl, but Jules seemed best suited to the job of managing the restaurant. Jules's mother sent him to France for four years of training, and on his return to New Orleans he worked in the kitchen of the Pickwick Club until in 1887, when his mother ceded control of Antoine's.[25]

We know virtually nothing about the years of Mme. Alciatore's direction, except that she must have supervised the move in 1877 to Antoine's present quarters farther up St. Louis Street. Both Antoine's long success and later difficulties are related to this location's unusually large size. Antoine's has two stories of dining rooms and groups together what were originally a few separate buildings. Although there have been changes and additions since 1877, the main dining room, with its elegant but austere white walls, wooden floor, and brass and glass light fixtures, is a magnificent and understated monument of the age. There are two large rooms to the left of the main dining room, and one of them, now referred to as the Large Annex, seats more than twice as many people as the front room. The other, which fronts the street, was formerly a dining room but since 2009 has housed the Hermes Bar, named after one of the Mardi Gras associations, called "krewes," that hold parades during Carnival. The Hermes Bar serves food from a small menu in a casual atmosphere. The convivial bar is popular with a younger demographic than the usual crowd at Antoine's, and the bar's success is part of the restaurant's revitalization.

The twelve other dining rooms range in size, from the tiny Tabasco Room that can hold no more than 6 people to the Japanese Room with a capacity of 200. The Rex and Proteus rooms, in addition to the Hermes Bar, are named after Carnival krewes. Rex is one of the most socially prominent krewes, and has always been closely associated with Antoine's.

The rooms have been shaped and re-formed so that, for example, the Mystery Room, now a private dining room that seats thirty people, was originally part of the kitchens converted during Prohibition to serve liquor on the sly. Customers would enter through the back of what purported to be a ladies' room, holding some innocuous crockery such as a coffee cup, and return to the dining room with their drink. The Escargot Room is a very small dining room carved out of a larger space, and is named for a now-defunct society of gastronomes who were particularly fond of escargots à la Bordelaise (snails with red-wine sauce and cheese), one of the Antoine's many specialties.

Despite its size and prominence, Antoine's at the turn of the century was not the most famous restaurant in the city. That distinction went to Madame Bégué's, a modest establishment next to the French Market on what is now Decatur Street. Mme. Bégué herself can be credited with inadvertently inventing brunch. Her "breakfast," served late at eleven a.m., was a full meal, with Creole, French, and American main courses.[26] Butchers in the French Market ended their morning's work at eleven, and were eager to have what the Germans still call "second breakfast"—something

Fig. 20. The "1840 Room" at Antoine's.

more substantial than the early morning coffee and bread, but served earlier than the normal afternoon dinner. Mme. Bégué was born Elizabeth Kettenring, a German from a family of butchers. Her brother was a butcher in New Orleans and she married a Creole butcher named Louis Dutreuil. Together they opened a restaurant that catered especially to the market trade. Dutreuil died in 1875, and in 1880 Elizabeth Dutreuil took another French husband with experience in the meat industry. Hippolyte Bégué tended bar while Mme. Bégué, as she now was, ruled the kitchen and the upstairs dining room.

The 1884 World's Fair, coinciding with the discovery of New Orleans as a romantic tourist site, transformed what had been a small market café into a celebrated, if still small, restaurant. In 1898, the *New York Sun* reported that 9 out of 10 visitors to New Orleans had heard of Bégué's, and in order to handle reservation requests one of the first restaurant telephones had been installed. The butchers were displaced by throngs of outsiders infatuated with the "Bohemian Breakfasts," as local reporters and social observers termed the late-morning meals at Bégué's.[27] These featured, indeed before noon, five or six dishes, usually including an omelet (of sweetbreads, veal, or bread, for example); well-known Creole dishes such as court-bouillon (a fish stew, probably in this instance served on toast); jambalaya (with chicken and ham or shrimp); and a few French classics, such as blanquette de veau (veal and carrots in a cream ragout). Wednesday was the most important day of the week, for that was when Liver à la Bégué was served, the most famous offering of the house, something people of the era rhapsodized about and didn't mind waiting in long lines to taste. The recipe seems to be a not-particularly-imaginative preparation of calves' liver—sautéed in butter with bacon and onions—but perhaps Mme. Bégué originated this manner of cooking liver. Her death in 1906 merited a full obituary notice in the *New York Times*. Hippolyte remarried, and for a time Bégué's continued to flourish, but it closed after his death in 1917 and the restaurant Tujague's now occupies the site.

Antoine's and Bégué's weren't really competitors, because the latter was inexpensive, informal, and seated only thirty, whereas Antoine's was an immense, pricey restaurant. It competed with elegant places like Galatoire's, Commander's Palace (outside the French Quarter, in the Garden District), and Arnaud's. Like Antoine's, these restaurants were diffident about describing their food as "Creole." As late as 1958, Arnaud's used the evasive phrase "La Cuisine Classique" to describe what it served.[28]

Not all restaurants, however, were so timid about using the world "Creole." A 1908 menu from the Grunewald Hotel (renamed the Roosevelt in 1923) mentions not only Creole gumbo but lake shrimp Creole, Creole snipe Anglaise, and such readily identifiable local preparations as court-bouillon. In 1911, the Grunewald published a booklet in connection with

Fig. 21. Bégué's Restaurant, before 1917.

what proved to be an unsuccessful attempt to secure the 1915 Panama Canal Exposition for New Orleans. It provided recipes for "famous Creole dishes" served at a meal for congressional representatives. Fabacher's New Rathskeller in 1910 had a large menu that included canvasback ducks (roasted with oyster dressing, or served on toast), and broiled squirrel (also presented on toast), but also five kinds of gumbo and twenty varieties of oysters, and it used the word "Creole" liberally.[29]

After the death of Mme. Bégué, Antoine's became the best-known restaurant in New Orleans. It developed an extensive menu that was fixed in place in about 1910 and changed very little until 1940.[30] Jules Alciatore was, if anything, even more creative at coming up with new dishes than his father. His supervision lasted until 1934, although his son Roy assumed most of the day-to-day responsibilities in the late 1920s. Jules was both a personable manager and talented chef.

Antoine's in the era of Jules was not just another fancy French Quarter restaurant, but it was also large, severely formal, and yet quirky. It hosted political leaders such as presidents Theodore Roosevelt, William Howard Taft, Calvin Coolidge, and Herbert Hoover; performers such as the opera tenor Enrico Caruso and the celebrated and notorious actress Sarah Bernhardt; as well as stars of sports and entertainment—Babe Ruth, Rudy Vallee, and Theda Bara, for example.[31] Unlike other restaurants that became identified with international celebrities, Antoine's always maintained its status within New Orleans society. It developed an unusual style of service for regular customers by providing them with the same waiter every night rather than, as at virtually every other restaurant, apportioning "stations" among waiters with a responsibility for a contiguous group of tables. On an average night there would be a combination of regulars and tourists, the latter served by waiters according to a conventional station system. With an assigned waiter, a client could actually make a reservation. Otherwise it was necessary to await a free table. Having your own waiter was therefore a real convenience, and also, more important, a mark of social distinction, and it is typical of Antoine's success that it managed to make a form of exclusivity well known in such a way as to attract even more visitors who weren't actually going to have this privilege.[32] As late as the 1980s, to say of someone that he had his own waiter at Antoine's was to identify him unquestionably as a member of the New Orleans social elite.

Local notables and tourists alike enjoyed classic dishes such as Boeuf Robespierre or puffed potatoes, which dated from the founding of Antoine's, but also innovations, none of which rivaled the success of Jules Alciatore's "Oysters Rockefeller," first served in 1899. This dish consists of oysters broiled in their shells and covered with a green sauce whose ingredients remain a secret, known only to the proprietor and one or two other members of the family. Supposedly the creation of Oysters Rockefeller was prompted by a shortage of imported snails, inducing Jules Alciatore to develop a sauce appropriate to cooked oysters. The result was so rich in flavor that he named the dish after the richest man in the country at that time.

Clementine Paddleford, a well-known food columnist for the *New York Herald Tribune*, gave a recipe for Oysters Rockefeller in 1948, along with ten other "closely-guarded" secrets of Antoine's. She had been able to convince Roy Alciatore to share the recipes with her readers, leaving out the exact formula for the oysters. Paddleford acknowledged that her version of Oysters Rockefeller, an adequate home-cook approximation, could not match and therefore subvert the uniqueness of what the restaurant served. Her instructions call for a sauce made with butter, minced spinach, celery, onions, and cooked lettuce, along with herbs, bread crumbs, and anchovy paste.[33] In his 1980 cookbook, Antoine's proprietor Roy F. Guste Jr., mentions the oysters without giving the recipe, asserting that one thing the sauce for Oysters Rockefeller definitely does *not* contain is spinach.[34]

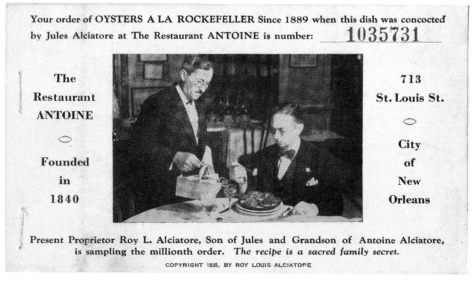

Fig. 22. Certificate accompanying an order of Oysters Rockefeller: Serving #1,035,731.

Several other cooked-oyster recipes were developed by Jules: Oysters Bienville (broiled in their shells with a béchamel, pimento, and cheese sauce); Oysters à la Ellis (named after a prominent New Orleanian—poached oysters simmered in a tomato sauce with caramelized sugar, vinegar, and anchovy paste, served on toast); and Oysters à la Foch (fried oysters in sauce Colbert, which combines tomato with Hollandaise sauce), named for the French general of the First World War, who visited Antoine's.

Jules also perfected pompano baked in a paper container. As with his father's Pompano Montgolfier, pompano en papillote honored (without in this case naming him) a famous balloonist, the Brazilian Alberto Santos-Dumont. His airship won a prize in 1901 for traversing the 6.8 kilometers between the Parc Saint-Cloud and the Eiffel Tower, and he visited New Orleans that same year.

Along with Charles Ranhofer of Delmonico's, Jules was an early adopter of avocados among American chefs. Jules filled halved avocados with shrimp in a ravigote sauce (mayonnaise with pepper, onions, anchovies, and pimentos) and then covered them with vinaigrette. This dish was named after the Italian patriot and leader of the unification Giuseppe Garibaldi. Another cold stuffed-vegetable recipe was christened "Tomates à la Jules César" in honor of the birth of a son, Jules César Alciatore. To prepare this dish, the tomatoes are chilled, scooped out, stuffed with crabmeat ravigote, and served in a vinaigrette. The elder Jules Alciatore intended for his son to succeed him, but Jules César lacked interest in the business and devoted himself instead to the academic study of French literature, becoming a well-regarded authority on Stendhal. All of these dishes of Jules's, however, remained on the menu into the 1980s, and some are still there.

Although the history of Antoine's can be divided according to which member of the family ran it, in fact the stability of the menus defines the phases of its long chronology. From about 1910 until the restaurant's centennial in 1940, the menu, like an impregnable fortress, did not change, save for price responses to inflation, and neither did it alter with the seasons of the year. A menu cover from 1910 or shortly after shows a man mooring his boat after a successful fishing trip on a lake, and to his right, two nymphs, or nude female mortals, also fishing. The legend reads, "Allons Chez Antoine" (Let's go to Antoine's).[35] Somewhat later, probably in the late 1920s, the menu cover with the same "Allons Chez Antoine" motto shows a well-dressed couple sitting across from each other. On the table is a bucket with (presumably) Champagne, but their meal has not yet been served. A violinist leans over the table—odd, since Antoine's own publicity called attention to the absence of music, which the restaurateurs regarded as a distraction from food and conversation.[36]

Except for a notice about the minimum charge and a heading for Antoine's specialties at the top of the first page, the 1910–1940 menu was entirely in French. In the earlier period there was a roast fowl course, including duck, snipe, partridge, and teal ducks (*sarcelles*), but this category later was dropped while salads were added.[37] The menu always featured pâté de foie gras as the single entry under "Relevé," an archaic intermediate course that originally marked the clearing of dishes and their replacement. According to the earlier menus, the pâté was made by the restaurant, but it was later imported from Strasbourg.

The menus from the 1910s and 1920s listed appetizers such as oysters and canapés on toast as particular specialties. All the soups were seafood bisques, except for Gumbo Créole and a consommé on the 1910 version. The fish course was particularly impressive, and included French classics such as Sole Marguery and trout meunière, as well as local soft-shell crabs and busters (smaller soft shells), pompano en papillote or simply grilled, and terrapin. The 1930s menus of this type list Eggs Sardou, yet another dish invented by Jules Alciatore (poached eggs with spinach, artichoke bottoms, and Hollandaise sauce—the original version also calls for anchovies). Eggs Sardou is so marvelously rich as to make Oysters Rockefeller seem like raw kale salad by comparison. It was invented in 1908 and named after

Fig. 23. Menu cover from Antoine's, before 1930.

the French writer Victorien Sardou, author of many successful plays in which Sarah Bernhardt starred.

The entrées formed the most classically French category—lamb cutlets prepared in various ways, sweetbreads financière or Montpensier (garnished with artichoke bottoms filled with asparagus tips, noisette potatoes, and a julienne of truffles), or beef with Marchand de Vin sauce. No one could mistake this menu for that of a Parisian restaurant—not only do the French not cook oysters, but the presence of pompano, gumbo, and Jules's own creations shows the anchoring of Antoine's cuisine in New Orleans. Nevertheless, identification with France and fame for its own unique dishes defined Antoine's, at least in the restaurant's own corporate imagination.

During the time of Jules's leadership Antoine's achieved its preeminence among New Orleans restaurants. It is a mark of his almost peerless success that Prohibition did not significantly damage business. Perhaps this was because of the relatively lax local enforcement of the laws, which, after all, overlooked a comically transparent subterfuge such as the "Mystery Room." While business at Delmonico's and other New York fine restaurants was wrecked by the restrictions imposed by Prohibition, in New Orleans elegant new restaurants such as Arnaud's, founded in 1918, managed to achieve fame and fortune despite the constricting regulations placed on liquor. It may indicate how different Creole culture was from the norms of French cuisine and its standard American imitations that New Orleans restaurants could flourish on bootleg liquor rather than the civilized delectation of fine wines.

ROY ALCIATORE

Antoine's reached the height of its fame under Roy Alciatore, Jules's second son, who took complete control after Jules died in 1934 and partially relinquished responsibility in the mid-1960s when his nephews (sons of his sister Marie Louise Alciatore Guste) assumed some of the administration. Roy was not a chef, although some dishes were added in his era, notably Bouillabaisse à la Marseillaise, listed on the menu under "Fish" rather than "Soup." It consisted of pompano, crawfish, shrimp, tiny soft-shell crabs, and other local seafood served on a plate and surrounded by a tomato and saffron sauce.[38]

Roy Alciatore, who died in 1972, was a famous host, and welcomed virtually every celebrity of the 1930s through 1960s to Antoine's. Many of these guests were willing to have their words of praise quoted. H. L. Mencken, the renowned journalist, gourmet, and curmudgeon, said after a visit: "Mr. Alciatore: like every other visitor who has been in your restaurant, I remember it with pleasure." A renowned business columnist, George Sokolsky, lavished a somewhat non-sequitur compliment: "The very best dinner I have eaten east of Shanghai, and then equal to the Lung Foo Soo, which to epicures is heaven."[39] Unlike his predecessors, Roy Alciatore, never one to be provincial, visited many other famous restaurants in the United States, from Don the Beachcomber in Los Angeles, the progenitor of the pseudo-Polynesian "tiki" restaurant, to the London Chop House in Detroit. His curiosity not satisfied by limiting himself to America, Roy traveled frequently to France and collected menus from the restaurants he dined in.[40]

His charm and activity notwithstanding, Roy Alciatore was rather diffident and often felt crushed by the responsibilities of running Antoine's.[41] Nevertheless, or perhaps because of his conscientiousness, Antoine's was never more successful than it was during his era. Neither the Depression nor the Second World War adversely affected the popularity of Antoine's; it drew ever-larger crowds of tourists while remaining a mainstay of the New Orleans establishment and its entertainments.

A sense of Antoine's status can be obtained from *Dinner at Antoine's*, a once-famous novel by the once-famous novelist Frances Parkinson Keyes. It was published in 1948 and became a bestseller, coming in at number 6 on the *New York Times* annual fiction list for 1949.[42] A murder mystery set in an exotic city of aristocratic Creole passion, honor, and betrayal, its opening tableau is a dinner party in the 1840 Room at Antoine's. While tourists are lined up waiting for tables, the restaurant's habitués are swept in ahead of the mob. So familiar was the restaurant to the general public that it did not need to be further identified—the title conveyed that the plot would unfold in New Orleans.

In honor of the publication of the book, Roy Alciatore held a private party on November 18, 1948, closing Antoine's to the public for only the third time in its history. The meal featured Lake Ponchartrain shrimp in aspic, onion soup, mallard ducks, and puffed potatoes, and concluded with Cherries Jubilee (cherries flambéed in Kirsch, served over vanilla ice cream) and Café Brûlot Diabolique (coffee flambéed with brandy and other flavorings).[43]

The real restaurant's atmosphere at the time of the fictionalized *Dinner with Antoine's* is portrayed from the employees' side through recollections contained in interviews by Erin Greenwald, conducted in the 1990s, with waiters who began work at Antoine's as far back as the 1940s.[44] At that time apprenticeship took up to ten years, and most waiters and staff generally had decades of experience.

Wiley Smith, for example, started as a busboy in 1946 and recalled that there were always long lines along St. Louis Street north to Bourbon Street and South to Royal Street—every room was filled for both lunch and dinner. Waiters had to memorize orders and were not allowed to write anything down.

George LeBlanc had started in 1944 when business was booming, the Second World War notwithstanding, though the Japanese Room, identified with America's enemy, had to be closed at the outbreak of the conflict and wouldn't be restored to use until the 1980s.[45] LeBlanc, as it happened, was one of the first Antoine's waiters not to know French. Until then, ability to read and understand spoken French was a requirement for employment. Still, he seems to have managed with skill and aplomb. The most frequently ordered dishes in LeBlanc's early career were pompano, both en papillote and grilled, and Chicken Rochambeau (baked chicken, boned, with ham in a sweet-and-sour brown sauce).

Equally significant, if less evocative than *Dinner at Antoine's*, is a Bugs Bunny cartoon of 1951 entitled *French Rarebit*. Bugs Bunny finds himself in Paris, a particularly dangerous place for a rabbit, and two chefs immediately capture him. They both want to serve him up at their competing restaurants and fall to arguing over who gets to cook him. The ever-resourceful carrot lover escapes, beginning his complicated getaway by offering a recipe for "Louisiana Back-Bay Bunny Bordelaise," according to the famous recipe from Antoine's: "Antoine's of New Orleans?" one of the French chefs asks, obviously impressed. "I don't mean Antoine's of Flatbush," is the retort. Even in our food-besotted age, it's hard to imagine any restaurant so well known that children (or for that matter adults) watching a cartoon could be assumed to have some point of reference for it.

It is an irony of Antoine's history that the height of its fame coincided with the period from the 1920s to the 1970s, decades otherwise regarded as the nadir of American cooking and cuisine. This half century is considered, not without justification, to be the Dark Ages of American tastes— the unfortunate era of cottage cheese, canned fruit, Jell-O as a cooking ingredient, and mayonnaise and marshmallows as salad decorations. Even elegant restaurants with plush carpeting, candlelight, and tuxedoed waiters featured Yankee pot roast, Salisbury steak, pork passed off as veal, and thawed-out shrimp scampi. Yet New Orleans was a gastronomic destination, and tourists, seeking a break from the prevailing blandness, continued to line up outside Antoine's.

Recognition of the special cuisine of New Orleans coincided with a sense that, alone among American regions, the city offered fine food that was widely available and not just restricted to one or two elite shrines. It was, in the words of a 1903 culinary guidebook, "the one place in the country where the inner man could be made comfortable by reason of the many varied and appetizing dishes made by the accomplished chefs of the French or Creole restaurants . . ."[46] A more general guide from just after the First World War observed: "From the standpoint of the epicure, New Orleans is the one bright spot on American soil. Her cooks, descended of the best of their kind from France and Spain, and taking on the added art of the Creole, produce viands which have created for this city a reputation at home and abroad."[47]

Antoine's was constantly singled out as a bastion of fine dining. In 1913, an observer from Harvard University called it "the last frontier of the palate, the last blockhouse standing before the advance of the stream-lined hamburger."[48] Forty years later, the arch-snob, private railroad-car owner, and gourmand Lucius Beebe dubbed his article, which appeared in the travel and lifestyle magazine *Holiday*, "The Miracle at Antoine's." The miracle was really a three-part phenomenon: that the restaurant could be so good despite the large number of customers, the Philistinism of the masses, and local competition. Beebe offers grudging acknowledgment of Antoine's fame as he remarks that the horde of visitors may not know whether they will like Oysters Rockefeller, but they can't go home without having tried them. Antoine's is a victim of its "universal fame," but while sacrificing some of its grand manner, it has been able nevertheless to maintain standards. Beebe notes with approval Roy Alciatore's decision to keep the menu entirely in French—it forces customers unfamiliar with the restaurant to ask their waiter for advice, thus preventing them from just ordering a T-bone steak and French fries.[49]

The menu in Roy Alciatore's era finally reached its maximum size and complexity. The centenary of the restaurant in 1940 provided a perhaps welcome excuse to change the menu, including the design of its cover. From 1940 until today, the cover has been a lively painting of two gallant-looking gentlemen standing on some fanciful flowered Mediterranean patio, toasting each other and pledging friendship while others look on

Fig. 24. Antoine's menu cover, 2009. The same cover in use since 1940.

with amusement. The 1940 menu, which continued in its essential form until the end of the twentieth century, is immense. Even if it doesn't quite list all the 1,000 original dishes that Roy claimed the restaurant had in its files, the menu contains about 140 items. The earlier menu listed a mere dozen or so specialties, but there were 24 under the heading "Nous Recommandons" in 1940 and 34 in 1980.[50] The recommendations are all for first-course dishes, including many of Antoine and Jules Alciatore's creations—canapés on toast, the iced tomatoes Jules César, and of course Oysters Rockefeller. All eight oyster dishes and most of the shrimp dishes are recommended. Five crab dishes are specialties, while eight main-course crab dishes (grilled soft-shell crabs and crabmeat au gratin, for example) are listed under "Poissons." All five pompano entrées are written in italic, but there are many other "signature" items that are not highlighted: Eggs Sardou, bouillabaisse, and Beef Robespierre (at $5.00 in the 1940s, the second-most expensive possibility after Châteaubriand). Beef Robespierre had been dropped by 1970, but almost nothing else.

One of the chief differences between the 1910 and 1940 menus is that the later decades saw the addition of classic French continental dishes that had little to do with the blending of influences characteristic of Creole cuisine. Besides the bouillabaisse there is onion soup gratinée, ray (what would later be called skate) in black butter, Tripes à la mode de Caen, and various kinds of tournedos, all of which one would expect in Paris. Some of this rediscovery of France may have been due to Roy Alciatore's visits there, but perhaps also to the postwar revival of French cuisine as the standard for American restaurants, a theme we will revisit in chapter 8 with regard to Le Pavillon. This wave of Francophilia played out oddly in New Orleans, which had already claimed an elevated if peculiar status in a French provincial culinary universe. Among other things, renewed interest in French cuisine in New Orleans encouraged a fierce devotion to sauces, and the affectation of continental French provincial specialties (bouillabaisse from Marseille; tripe from Normandy).[51]

By the 1950s, Antoine's was set in a kind of unbreakable image and tradition. There was little in the way of newly invented dishes, and neither did the restaurant wish to attract a new clientele. It had been successful for so long with unchanging menus, a certain look, and a highly reliable service that the vicissitudes, not only of American society but of culinary tastes in New Orleans itself, seemed to pass it by—"seemed to" being the operative phrase. Restaurants are not permanent monuments, and Antoine's had long since beaten its normal life expectancy. Threats to its complacent well-being first surfaced after Roy Alciatore's death in 1972, but it took until the first years of the twenty-first century for its fragility to become obvious and its survival uncertain.

ÇA PASSE VITE, LE TEMPS

Without exactly intending to, Antoine's waged a campaign in the last quarter of the twentieth century to maintain a standard that everywhere else had been transformed or discarded. Attributes and features that had made Antoine's great became imperiled: gracious service provided by experienced waiters; nineteenth-century French and Creole cuisine; and an immense, unchanging, non-seasonal entirely à-la-carte menu but as yet no bar, brunches, or entertainment. Galatoire's, another grand, old-line restaurant with which Antoine's is often compared, faced similar threats but withstood more successfully the ravages brought on by twenty-first-century culture. This is partly because of its smaller size and because of the loyalty exhibited by a local cadre of regulars who refused to abandon it. Friday afternoon at Galatoire's remains, even now, an all-day, boisterous, and important social occasion. But even Galatoire's suffered. A restaurant that never took reservations, Galatoire's always had lines outside the door, yet by 2000 it often became possible just to walk right in, even at peak times like noon or seven in the evening. A manager not affiliated with the Galatoire family, appointed in 1997, renovated the restaurant and opened up its second-floor dining rooms, closed since the 1930s. Many regulars rebelled against the modernized look, the fact that the second floor accepted reservations, and even the introduction of ice machines in place of old-fashioned ice blocks hacked up with icepicks. Yet the changes saved Galatoire's, and were actually advantageous to the regulars, who could keep possession of the main downstairs room while random visitors were put in the perfectly nice but less imposing upstairs.[52]

Antoine's failed to effectuate even these mild reforms. Before his death in 1972, Roy Alciatore had already brought in his older sister's sons, William Guste Jr. and Roy Guste. Both were attorneys, and the former had just been elected the attorney general of Louisiana. They were unable to commit their energies full-time to the restaurant and ceded control in 1975 to Roy Guste's son, Roy F. Guste Jr., an accomplished chef in the tradition of Antoine and Jules Alciatore. He was twenty-five and, also in the footsteps of his progenitors, had studied, cooked, and traveled extensively in France. He took the bold step of sharing Antoine's most famous recipes, with the exception of Oysters Rockefeller, in the cookbook that is also an important source of information for the history of Antoine's. In 1984, Guste left Antoine's, however, and has since pursued careers as a writer of cookbooks and nonfiction about New Orleans, a restaurant consultant, and real estate agent. His cousin Bernard "Randy" Guste managed the restaurant from 1985 until 2004.

In the last quarter of the twentieth century, New Orleans remained a radically different kind of city from the American norm. Its economy still depended on shipping, but competition from Houston and ports on the Gulf limited its growth. Petrochemicals form the largest industry in Louisiana, and the wealth and activities of this sector have both built the state's economy and sadly despoiled much of its natural environment. Tourism, the third pillar of the New Orleans economy, has simultaneously benefited and undermined the culture of New Orleans. In theory, the rise of tourism should have helped restaurants such as Antoine's, but the restaurant was built for a different age and for a very different kind of tourist.

Antoine's had also been created for an older form of local society, and served a cuisine that by the late-twentieth century was considered charming but antiquated. Times were changing on the culinary front. The New Orleans World's Fair of 1984 was timed to mark the hundredth anniversary of the Cotton Exposition of 1884. As was the case with its ancestor, the fair brought about an alteration in dining habits and the ambitions of the city with regard to food. After 1984, just as after 1884, the city became suddenly self-conscious of its food culture rather than taking it for granted. Some described this derisively as "going gourmet"—what had previously been a tradition of good food now became a competition for novelty; cooks became chefs; chefs became celebrities; and restaurants emphasized ingredients and inventiveness rather than sauces and tradition.

Even before the 1984 fair, the local restaurant world was being transformed. In 1979, veterans of the New Orleans culinary scene opened two innovative restaurants. The first, Mr. B's Bistro, was established on Royal Street, just three blocks from Antoine's, by Ella and Dick Brennan, owners of Commander's Palace and other grand restaurants. The atmosphere was minimalist and unrefined. Mr. B's had no tablecloths. The kitchen was open to the dining room. There was a wood-burning grill, and the emphasis was on fresh, local ingredients served more simply than was the custom at the old luxury restaurants with their repertoire of sauces. The food was more robust than Creole standbys, which now seemed bland, and featured dishes like chicken-andouille gumbo made with a dark roux and spices, and hickory-grilled fish rather than the traditional version sautéed with sauce. A wave of informal "gourmet Creole bistros" accustomed affluent gourmets to browsing and experimenting with restaurants, as well as reading and following the advice of reviewers rather than well-established loyalties, and so they ceased to be regulars of particular places.[53]

Just after the opening of Mr. B's, Paul Prudhomme, chef for the Brennans at Commander's Palace, opened up his soon-to-be nationally celebrated K-Paul's on Chartres Street. While borrowing the concepts of informality and emphasis on local ingredients from the Brennans, Prudhomme created a revolution that reverberated far beyond New Orleans. The extraordinary success of K-Paul's permanently confused outsiders about the difference between Creole and Cajun cuisine, as defined earlier. Blackened redfish (Prudhomme's invention), andouille sausage, pasta with tasso, and even ersatz spicy preparations such as "Cajun fries" spread nationwide, obscuring the delicate, creamy, buttery cuisine of traditional New Orleans. K-Paul's was a pioneer of the chef-driven restaurant with almost no front-of-the-house graciousness—the food was marvelous and carefully sourced, but the restaurant dispensed with tablecloths and cloth napkins. Its seating was communal and its atmosphere borderline raucous.

For a time, the conventional New Orleans narrative simply created a contrast between old-line institutions like Antoine's and newfangled boites that featured a vigorous and more rustic revival of the best aspects of Creole and Cajun food. Informal restaurants were established in neighborhoods outside the French Quarter too. They were more in tune with a national restaurant culture of novelty, but once New Orleans embraced trendiness and a cult of ever-changing new places, it opened itself up to losing its culinary distinctiveness and identity. What did new fashions such as pork belly or pan-Asian fare have to do with an established local cuisine? As the number of restaurants expanded, those that actually adhered to some sort of recognizably Creole cuisine diminished and became as endangered as redfish and pompano.

The locals were no longer accustomed to patronizing the old restaurants regularly, and the tourists were no longer the well-dressed people of the traditional middle class, eager for an expensive restaurant experience in a legendary setting. Foodie visitors sought out-of-the-way places that seemed more authentic and inexpensive, or new restaurants run by famous chefs like Emeril Lagasse. At any rate, they were no longer attracted by traditional high-end New Orleans. Antoine's had difficulty protecting its patrimony and lost the mutual reinforcement of local social exclusivity and tourist appeal.

In recent decades the French Quarter has become in certain respects more charming and Bohemian than ever—it seems to have more used bookstores than Manhattan—but Bourbon Street, except for Galatoire's, has given way to a rowdy sort of tourism, and the city, despite its diversified economy, has become poorer in terms of individual income and social conditions. It holds a not-undeserved reputation for crime.

Antoine's, however, survived gamely if not unruffled. The fact that it owned its own buildings preserved it from the vagaries of certain market forces, but little investment was expended to upgrade its physical fabric—kitchen, electricity, or plumbing—and all these problems were magnified by the restaurant's now near-fatal flaw: its immense size. It was still well known, of course, but in a different way from how it was perceived in the 1940s and 1950s—latterly as a restaurant everyone seemed to have heard of, but few people, outside an old guard of New Orleans natives, actually went to. In fact, it became the kind of place that people were surprised to learn was still in existence.

Belatedly the family and the board of the restaurant recognized its parlous situation, and in 2005, six months before the onslaught of Hurricane Katrina, they brought in as owner and manager Rick Blount, the son of Yvonne Alciatore Blount, daughter of Roy Alciatore. Blount had experience at the restaurant, but had been passed over when his Guste cousins ran things. He settled in just in time to face a hurricane of biblical proportions that damaged Antoine's more than one might think given that the French Quarter, on what passes locally for high ground, did not directly suffer the nightmarish consequences of the levee failure. Nevertheless, the wind undermined one of the building's attic-level brick walls, which collapsed into the street. Even worse, the walls of the main dining room bulged out dangerously and the ceiling sagged as its supporting structure was weakened. The storm was followed by a heat wave, and consequently the failure of the electrical system doomed the air-conditioned wine cellar. The corks popped out of some of the old bottles, and no fewer than 15,000 bottles were ruined. Insurance paid for a good deal of the damage, but there were many indirect consequences that could not be compensated, from the decline of tourism to many employees' ruined homes.[54]

The storm and subsequent flooding took place at the end of August 2005, and the restaurant reopened in January 2006—a relatively rapid recovery, but the establishment now faced the consequences of decades of deferred maintenance, a large payroll, and a dwindling clientele. The restaurant reviewer Tom Fitzmorris describes a 2008 episode of Anthony Bourdain's *No Reservations* showing the peculiar post-Katrina situation. The fragility of the grand restaurants was overlooked while the actual vitality of the neighborhoods was underestimated. The show's producers thought they should concentrate on humble neighborhood joints when, in fact, more of them were in business in 2008 than before the hurricane. Fitzmorris convinced them that the real story about near-death experiences was that of the big, old, high-end restaurants, and so part of the New Orleans episode took place over lunch at Antoine's. Bourdain and Fitzmorris dined on Oysters Rockefeller, soft-shell crabs with brown butter, Tournedos Marchand de Vin, and Baked Alaska. Bourdain was incredulous that these dishes were being served "for real," not as some sort of ironic gesture or tweaked historical homage. That disbelief shows why it's difficult to protect America's greatest surviving regional cuisine and this particular American culinary treasure despite a food revolution that should have exalted it.[55]

In recent years Rick Blount has managed to renovate the building's infrastructure, attract new and younger customers, and create a business model that seems to assure the restaurant's survival—at least for now. One of the results is a radical reduction in the number of menu offerings. The menu is still in French, but with English explanations. For example, "Escargots à la Bordelaise: Snails basted and baked in a red wine and garlic sauce, crowned with a delicious mixture of cheeses and French bread crumbs." There are approximately fifty dishes and everything remains à la carte. Gone are such classics as pompano en papillote (too much trouble), Trout Marguery (more typical of Galatoire's anyway), and Eggs Sardou (there are no egg dishes at all). On the other hand, the trio of oyster specialties (Rockefeller, Bienville, and Foch) remains, as do traditional sauces such as Marchand de Vin and Bordelaise. Even Chicken Rochambeau survives, while little space has been given to Cajun influence and none to Italian food (pasta, for example), the latter having nearly taken over most other supposedly French restaurants.

The Hermes Bar has a more informal menu and offers a "jazz brunch," among other innovations. The main dining room glitters quietly, and the waiters are courtly and professional. There are other touches of fragile graciousness: Café Brûlot Diabolique and Cherries Jubilee are still flamed at the table. Where else, outside of New Orleans, are you likely to find this easily mocked but profoundly evocative manner of service? The city's restaurants have been slow to get on the locavore and seasonal bandwagon that has swept across the rest of America. With some justice they consider themselves to have been locally oriented long before it became a marketing concept. New Orleans was also confident and prescient in that it preserved the cocktail when it had disappeared elsewhere, keeping Sazerac, sidecars and rye old-fashioneds alive to be revived in the new climate. No one can dispute the unfortunate reality that New Orleans has lost some of its population for the long term as a result of Katrina, and the city remains poor, dilapidated, even abandoned in certain areas. But as a culinary center it is stronger than ever, both for its new and its old establishments. Perhaps it will finally benefit from its status as the American city with the strongest roots and the longest run of culinary traditions.

SCHRAFFT'S
SEEKING OUT THE FEMALE CUSTOMER

Having finished the Blue-plate Special
And reached the coffee stage,
Stirring her cup she sat,
A somewhat shapeless figure
Of indeterminate age
In an undistinguished hat.

From W. H. Auden, "In Schrafft's"
Published in *The New Yorker*, February 12, 1949

It is no accident that Auden chose as his poem's protagonist a female "of indeterminate age," and that she is thinking things over at Schrafft's, a once-famous chain of economical but gracious restaurants. Schrafft's, most of whose branches were in the New York area, catered to ladies who wanted to dine alone or with other women in a pleasing setting. This does not seem like much to ask for, but when the first Schrafft's opened at the beginning of the twentieth century, restaurants still tended to extremes with little in the middle in terms of cuisine, price, or ambience. There were elegant restaurants on the order of Delmonico's with elaborate French menus, and on the lower social level, hash houses, gritty workingmen's

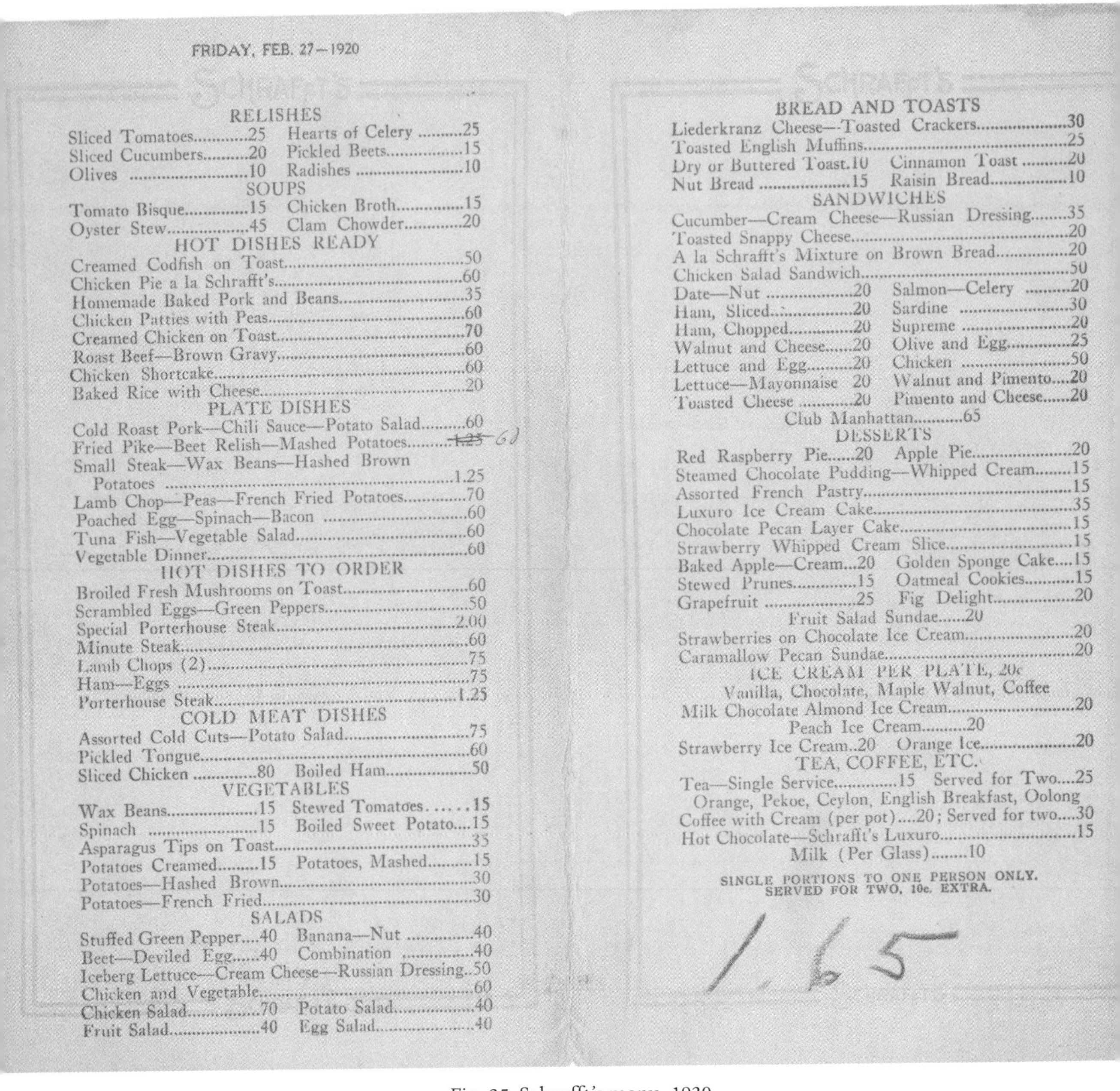

RELISHES

Sliced Tomatoes............25 Hearts of Celery 25
Sliced Cucumbers........20 Pickled Beets................15
Olives ....10 Radishes 10

SOUPS

Tomato Bisque.............15 Chicken Broth............15
Oyster Stew................45 Clam Chowder............20

HOT DISHES READY

Creamed Codfish on Toast..............................50
Chicken Pie a la Schrafft's..............................60
Homemade Baked Pork and Beans................35
Chicken Patties with Peas...............................60
Creamed Chicken on Toast.............................70
Roast Beef—Brown Gravy...............................60
Chicken Shortcake..60
Baked Rice with Cheese...................................20

PLATE DISHES

Cold Roast Pork—Chili Sauce—Potato Salad..........60
Fried Pike—Beet Relish—Mashed Potatoes.........1.25 60
Small Steak—Wax Beans—Hashed Brown
   Potatoes 1.25
Lamb Chop—Peas—French Fried Potatoes............70
Poached Egg—Spinach—Bacon 60
Tuna Fish—Vegetable Salad............................60
Vegetable Dinner..60

HOT DISHES TO ORDER

Broiled Fresh Mushrooms on Toast.................60
Scrambled Eggs—Green Peppers.....................50
Special Porterhouse Steak...............................2.00
Minute Steak...60
Lamb Chops (2)..75
Ham—Eggs 75
Porterhouse Steak..1.25

COLD MEAT DISHES

Assorted Cold Cuts—Potato Salad..................75
Pickled Tongue..60
Sliced Chicken.............80 Boiled Ham..........50

VEGETABLES

Wax Beans..................15 Stewed Tomatoes......15
Spinach ....15 Boiled Sweet Potato....15
Asparagus Tips on Toast.................................35
Potatoes Creamed........15 Potatoes, Mashed.........15
Potatoes—Hashed Brown................................30
Potatoes—French Fried....................................30

SALADS

Stuffed Green Pepper....40 Banana—Nut 40
Beet—Deviled Egg......40 Combination 40
Iceberg Lettuce—Cream Cheese—Russian Dressing..50
Chicken and Vegetable......................................60
Chicken Salad.............70 Potato Salad...........40
Fruit Salad................40 Egg Salad................40

BREAD AND TOASTS

Liederkranz Cheese—Toasted Crackers...................30
Toasted English Muffins.....................................25
Dry or Buttered Toast.10 Cinnamon Toast 20
Nut Bread ....15 Raisin Bread.............10

SANDWICHES

Cucumber—Cream Cheese—Russian Dressing........35
Toasted Snappy Cheese.....................................20
A la Schrafft's Mixture on Brown Bread............20
Chicken Salad Sandwich....................................50
Date—Nut ....20 Salmon—Celery 20
Ham, Sliced..............20 Sardine 30
Ham, Chopped..........20 Supreme 20
Walnut and Cheese......20 Olive and Egg.............25
Lettuce and Egg..........20 Chicken 50
Lettuce—Mayonnaise 20 Walnut and Pimento..20
Toasted Cheese ....20 Pimento and Cheese....20
Club Manhattan............65

DESSERTS

Red Raspberry Pie......20 Apple Pie................20
Steamed Chocolate Pudding—Whipped Cream........15
Assorted French Pastry......................................15
Luxuro Ice Cream Cake......................................35
Chocolate Pecan Layer Cake.............................15
Strawberry Whipped Cream Slice......................15
Baked Apple—Cream..20 Golden Sponge Cake..15
Stewed Prunes.............15 Oatmeal Cookies.......15
Grapefruit ....25 Fig Delight...............20
Fruit Salad Sundae......20
Strawberries on Chocolate Ice Cream.....................20
Caramallow Pecan Sundae....................................20

ICE CREAM PER PLATE, 20c

Vanilla, Chocolate, Maple Walnut, Coffee
Milk Chocolate Almond Ice Cream......................20
Peach Ice Cream............20
Strawberry Ice Cream..20 Orange Ice.............20

TEA, COFFEE, ETC.

Tea—Single Service............15 Served for Two....25
  Orange, Pekoe, Ceylon, English Breakfast, Oolong
Coffee with Cream (per pot)....20; Served for two....30
Hot Chocolate—Schrafft's Luxuro........................15
Milk (Per Glass)........10

**SINGLE PORTIONS TO ONE PERSON ONLY.
SERVED FOR TWO, 10c. EXTRA.**

1.65

Fig. 25. Schrafft's menu, 1920.

bars, and cafés where drinking was as much the point as food, if not more. Both types of eating places were male-dominated, and in neither were middle-class women without male escort likely to feel at ease or be well treated.

Schrafft's, then, represents two crucial and related restaurant trends that took hold at the turn of the twentieth century: marketing to female customers, and the expansion of middle-class dining options. From its very beginning, Schrafft's epitomized the restaurant's role as a decorous but economical refuge, a midday oasis of sorts, where women who were shopping could dine and recuperate, or where women who worked in offices or stores could have a tranquil if more hurried lunch. Schrafft's became not so much a mere convenience but rather a destination, especially for women who wanted to socialize. In the years around 1900, restaurants began to encourage the patronage of women unaccompanied by men in order to augment their revenue. They did this by offering lighter fare, eliminating alcoholic drinks, and providing unintimidating respectability.

The period from 1890 to 1910 saw the proliferation of many types of middle-class restaurants, ranging from those featuring Chinese and other foreign cuisines to tearooms, coffee shops, cafeterias, and other inexpensive but orderly places to have lunch.[1] These were not necessarily intended exclusively for women, but the fact that they did not serve alcohol made them seem appropriate places for unaccompanied women to dine. Schrafft's was neither unique nor even pioneering in offering gentility and affordability in an effort to attract female customers. However, its combination of ice cream, candy, and food, which the founder, Frank G. Shattuck, presented with the slightly nativist encomium as "one hundred per cent quality without any fancy foreign names," gave Schrafft's a lasting success. Schrafft's imagined itself as a place for middle-class ladies, and this image endured even after the restaurants finally closed in the 1980s.[2]

Schrafft's became so closely identified with respectable, thoroughly middle-class women that *The New Yorker* magazine presented dozens of

Fig. 26. Schrafft's on Madison Avenue near Fifty-Ninth Street.

comical snippets from the 1920s until well into the 1960s under the heading "Overheard at Schrafft's," and readers would know immediately what sort of interlocutor to expect. In an issue from 1950, a "thoughtful young lady" arranges to meet a friend who is about to have a baby, suggesting they lunch at Schrafft's. "If anything should happen," the first young lady assures her pregnant companion, "I'm sure Schrafft's would know how to cope with it."[3]

The more typical Schrafft's patron in the pages of *The New Yorker*, as well as in common opinion, was middle-aged and hard to please. Two "plump matrons" entering a midtown Schrafft's at eleven forty-five were surprised to find they had to wait in line to be seated for lunch. "I can't understand this place," one of them remarks to the other, "I *never* come in here but people are eating."[4] *The New Yorker* cartoonist Helen Hokinson built much of her popularity on her portrayal of ladies with little hats and shopping bags relaxing and complaining at Schrafft's.

Men were welcome too, and many dined at Schrafft's for the same reason that women did—gracious convenience and familiar food well prepared, but the familiar food was not the hearty fare supposedly preferred by men. Schrafft's menu featured rather more "ladylike" offerings: salads with fruit and cottage cheese, main courses with Jell-O, and fancy desserts with whipped cream and chocolate sauce. In 1934 a restaurant critic complained that the set luncheons at 50 cents and 75 cents "are useless to any male with an appetite."[5] The ambience was designed for a female clientele, and the food for a supposedly female palate.

WOMEN, RESTAURANTS, AND LUNCH[6]

The desires and demands of female diners in the early twentieth century coincide with women's agitation for the right to vote and campaigns to ban alcohol. The victory of the temperance movement with the passage of Prohibition in 1919 meant the end of bars that served free lunches subsidized by drink as well as the demise of the posh restaurants. At both the high and low end, the sale of wine and liquor at way above cost had been making up for the narrow profit margin from food. For the grand establishments it was hard to entice customers to eat fine French cuisine without wine. In the new environment, less colorful, middle-class dining options flourished, establishments such as coffee shops, luncheonettes, Automats, cafeterias, roadside restaurants, themed restaurants (chuck wagons, tepees), and what would later be called "ethnic" restaurants. All of these were casual and efficient; they didn't rely on alcohol and were relatively accessible to any paying client (the "relatively" here because of the racially discriminatory laws and practices of the period).

Schrafft's restaurants were open all day, serving breakfast, dinner, and even sometimes a late supper, but the meal we are really talking about is *lunch* (or "luncheon" as it was still termed in the early twentieth century). Midday dining presented a challenge for women too busy or too far from home to return there for lunch. They might be in the company of other women or alone, but at any rate not escorted by men who were occupied with work and work-related socializing; men had their own luncheon habits. In the nineteenth-century United States, men made the rules about public dining and admitted women to restaurants on sufferance, according to a complex series of arrangements. Different practices governed the two main meals of the day. Restaurants depended economically on women accompanying men at the evening meal. Ladies were not merely present but were the center of attention for dinner at the St. Charles Hotel in New Orleans, where, according to a description from 1857, they were bejeweled and dazzling.[7] In a survey of New York published ten years later, Junius Browne says that the fancy restaurants on Fourteenth Street and upper Broadway are attended by elegantly attired ladies, "with all the suggestive poetry that night lends to a fine woman."[8]

Lunch, however, was segregated by gender and involved a series of problems, according to the social customs of the nineteenth century. In the grand and even not-so-grand metropolis, men were increasingly likely to work at some distance from home and to stay near their workplace for the midday meal. The point at which women too absented themselves from the house created a demand for their sustenance. The growth of cities and the creation of specialized shopping districts meant that it was often inconvenient for women as well as men to return home for lunch. As early as 1827, Thompson and Sons opened as "the first saloon established in this city [New York] for the accommodation of ladies."[9] In 1833, a restaurant for women also in downtown New York, termed a "ladies' ordinary," stated in an advertisement that:

[The ladies' ordinary] has been opened at the earnest solicitation of several Gentlemen of high standing who have long regretted that such an establishment (so necessary for the accommodation of Ladies from the country, and Ladies from the upper part of the city, who do not wish to return home to dinner), had not long since been opened.[10]

Breakfast and dinner (the latter being taken at midday or early afternoon) were served here, but not evening meals. Beginning in the 1840s, such ladies' ordinaries—segregated dining spaces for women—were features of hotels where female travelers and other women dining without male company could be assured of a socially appropriate environment.

By the time Schrafft's opened, women employed by offices and retail shops supplemented the original clientele of affluent shoppers. Although they possessed neither the leisure nor the financial resources of the women who didn't work, "business girls," as they were sometimes patronizingly called, required lunch, possessed sufficient means to purchase it, and were underserved by the existing options.

Those options provided to women suited the purposes of men. The public rooms at fancy restaurants were usually reserved at lunch for men only, but some of them allowed women to have lunch in private dining spaces. In the era before Prohibition, bars offered free food, which, along with a crowded and boisterous atmosphere, encouraged demand for drink. Free-lunch bars were hopelessly inappropriate spaces for respectable women, as alcohol-driven conviviality was inevitably coarse—the antithesis of what was considered ladylike.

Restaurants and bars afforded opportunities for men to meet and consort with women deemed not respectable. Certain oyster cellars provided private stalls with red curtains and individual gas lamps as well as larger private rooms where, as George Foster describes in *New York by Gaslight* (1850), "men and women enter promiscuously, eat, drink and make merry and disturb the whole neighborhood with their obscene and disgusting revels."[11] New York had a dozen or so "private supper rooms" in the 1840s, and after the Civil War they were understated but ubiquitous in many neighborhoods.[12] These were attached to restaurants that catered to the usual public, but they had their own entrances. Only couples were served; a group of men could not reserve one of these rooms for the sake of mere ordinary privacy. The meal and drink charge were as much as double the stated price on the regular bill of fare. A small room had a set table and adjoined a convenient bedroom, and any sort of food could be ordered at any time of night.

Respectable women had to be isolated from these louche scenes, and were consequently hemmed in by rules concerning their presence in restaurants. An example of the complexities of female dining is provided by the Fourteenth Street branch of Delmonico's, which drew the highest elements of society during its brief reign from 1862 to 1876. Its rules highlight the ambiguity but nevertheless the importance of social boundaries and the attempt to "manage" female patronage. Here ladies were not allowed at all in the first-floor café. They were welcome in the restaurant at dinner, but only in the company of men. At lunch they could dine only in all-female groups and only in private rooms.[13]

Naturally some women took issue with these regulations. When Charles Dickens paid his second visit to the United States in 1868, the New York press corps held a dinner in his honor at the Fourteenth Street Delmonico's.[14] A group of women led by Jane Cunningham Croly, a well-known newspaper writer, had written to the journalists' committee that organized the event asking to purchase tickets. Jane Croly's son, Herbert Croly, would become a leader of the progressive movement and founder of the *New Republic*. In this forward-thinking political dynasty, Jane Croly's husband was managing editor of the *New York World* newspaper, but although possessed of reasonably enlightened opinions and chair of the Dickens committee, he did not offer the women even the courtesy of a response. Croly and her associates enlisted the support of Horace Greeley, editor of the *Tribune*, and the most powerful figure in the newspaper industry. Under Greeley's pressure, the Dickens committee relented to the extent of allowing the women to subscribe as long as they didn't think they would feel "out of place" or "ill at ease." This ungenerous capitulation arrived three days before the dinner and was scorned by the women who by then had other plans.

Croly and her friends had decided to form what would become the first women's literary and artistic club, which they named Sorosis (a botanical term for an agglomeration). Lorenzo and Charles Delmonico offered the new association a private dining room for its monthly lunch meetings, the

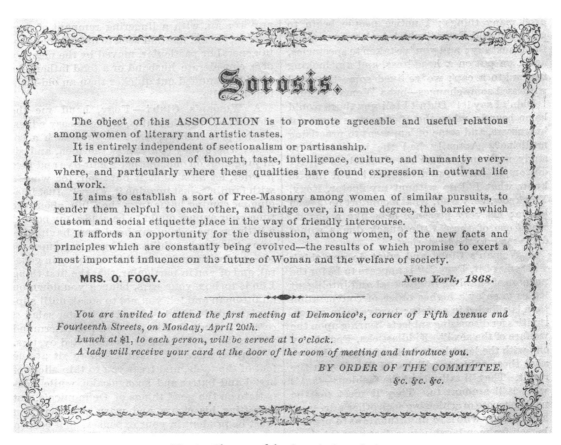

Sorosis.

The object of this ASSOCIATION is to promote agreeable and useful relations among women of literary and artistic tastes.

It is entirely independent of sectionalism or partisanship.

It recognizes women of thought, taste, intelligence, culture, and humanity everywhere, and particularly where these qualities have found expression in outward life and work.

It aims to establish a sort of Free-Masonry among women of similar pursuits, to render them helpful to each other, and bridge over, in some degree, the barrier which custom and social etiquette place in the way of friendly intercourse.

It affords an opportunity for the discussion, among women, of the new facts and principles which are constantly being evolved—the results of which promise to exert a most important influence on the future of Woman and the welfare of society.

MRS. O. FOGY.   *New York, 1868.*

You are invited to attend the first meeting at Delmonico's, corner of Fifth Avenue and Fourteenth Streets, on Monday, April 20th.

Lunch at $1, to each person, will be served at 1 o'clock.

A lady will receive your card at the door of the room of meeting and introduce you.

BY ORDER OF THE COMMITTEE.
&c. &c. &c.

Fig. 27. Charter of the Sorosis Association.

Fig. 28. Luncheon at Delmonico's, 1891.

first of which took place on April 20, 1868, two days after the Charles Dickens dinner. Sorosis Club members invited the famous writer to their meal, but he pleaded another engagement.

A drawing of "Luncheon at Delmonico's" in *Harper's Weekly* in late 1891 shows some degree of change. There are many female diners, although all seem to be accompanied by men. The issue remained having women dine without such escorts.[15] Several well-publicized confrontations took place at the opening of the new century over unescorted women's access to restaurants. In 1900, Rebecca Israel was denied service for dinner at the Café Boulevard, the raffish watering hole of New York's Jewish theater, and she made a public issue of it. In 1907, Harriet Stanton Blatch, the daughter of Elizabeth Cady Stanton, and Hettie Wright Graham, a Quaker active in Appalachian education, were barred from the roof-garden restaurant of the Hoffman House. In response to adverse publicity, the restaurant claimed to be defending respectable women from dining in proximity to non-respectable women. The manager plaintively observed that Blatch and Graham had been offered a table in the indoor ladies' dining room. The women sued and lost, but they had effectively made their point. In response to the assertion that she was being protected from objectionable women, Mrs. Blatch observed that she had never, in fact, been bothered by such women: "When I have been annoyed it has been by men. I do not suppose you make any effort to keep objectionable men out."[16] Her campaign coincided with suffragists' demands not only for the right to vote but that women be considered full public actors in public spaces.

Restaurants' justifications for their policies of discrimination were twofold and contradictory. On the one hand, the Hoffman House defense implied that unescorted women of dubious character were lurking on the premises, and that respectable ladies needed to be isolated from them. Elsewhere, however, women unaccompanied by men might be seated if they were deemed to be "ladies," thus the dining room was reserved for respectable women. Rather than banning unexceptional ladies so as to avoid contact with socially compromised women (lest the former feel "uncomfortable"), some restaurants would admit only women of impeccable credentials. Of course, even on its own dubious terms this policy presented difficulties. When pressed by reporters to define "ladies" in the aftermath of the Hoffman House debacle, the managers of the Waldorf, Delmonico's, and other fine restaurants could come up only with a tautological formulation: a lady was a woman who looked and carried herself like a lady.[17]

Before the last decade of the nineteenth century when Schrafft's and other middle-class, nonalcoholic venues offered women places to dine, two types of establishments catered to female clients: the ladies' ordinaries, as already mentioned, and what were called "ice-cream saloons," which, compared to the ordinaries, were more elegant, public, and less restrictive. In addition to providing a safely respectable ambience, the ice-cream saloons went beyond the practice of the ladies' ordinaries to feature distinctive food that women were thought to favor. The antebellum ladies' ordinaries offered the same kinds of dishes as those served in the men's dining rooms. Until after the Civil War there was little or no sense that women might prefer food of a different sort from what men liked. In some instances we can compare the menus from the ladies' and gentlemen's ordinaries at the same establishment and from the same period. The Pulaski House in Savannah, Georgia, for example, presented six side dishes (the equivalent of entrées) in the main restaurant for April 20, 1857: venison steaks with Port wine sauce, chicken fricasseed, beefsteak and onions, breaded breast of lamb, rice croquettes, and haricot of mutton. We find the same kind of things on a menu for the ladies' ordinary at the Pulaski House on January 31, 1862 (during the war, but before the devastation of Georgia through General Sherman's campaign in late 1864): baked pigeon pies, stewed kidney, veal chops with pickle sauce, breaded breast of mutton, haricot of mutton, and rice cakes.[18]

The term "ladies' ordinary" had disappeared by the end of the Civil War, although hotels and restaurants sometimes retained women's dining rooms. The "ice-cream saloon," was also designed to serve women, but unlike the ladies' ordinary, ice-cream saloons were not explicitly billed as being exclusively for women, but by reason of location, decoration, atmosphere, and eventually the food they served, it was unmistakable whom these establishments were trying to attract. They created spaces for ladies and, beginning with ice cream, offered food women were fond of (or so it was thought), setting themselves apart from the ladies' ordinaries that still conformed to a unisex theory of taste.

Thompson's, the pioneer of ice-cream saloons, was established in 1827, the same year that the Delmonicos opened their pastry shop, and, not surprisingly, it was renowned for its ice cream. Similar restaurants opened in shopping districts shortly before the Civil War. There were five "Saloons Suitable for Ladies" listed in a New York commercial directory for 1859.[19]

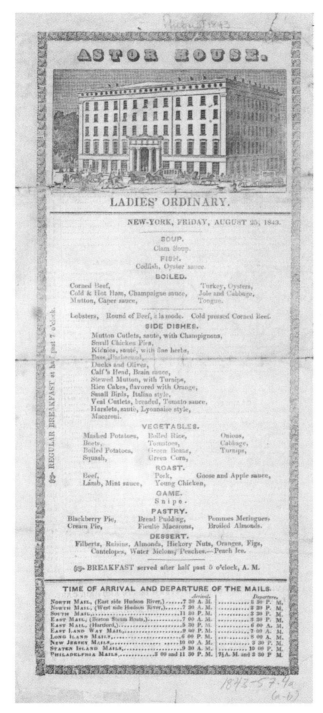

Fig. 29. Astor House Hotel, menu for the ladies' ordinary, August 25, 1843.

The ice-cream saloon was the direct ancestor of Schrafft's, which began as a small group of confectionary and ice-cream stores but later served regular meals. As an article in the *New York Times* observed in 1890:

> The proprietors of the downtown restaurants have come to regard their female patrons as an important element, and special pains are taken in many places to cater to the fair lunchers. While women are not all light eaters, most of them are partial to dainty tid-bits, pastry and ice cream.[20]

Thompson's and Taylor's, both in New York, were the most opulent ice-cream saloons of the antebellum years. The latter was the first eating establishment to have an all-female staff of servers. Both were strategically situated near the splendid dry goods emporium A. T. Stewart on Lower Broadway. Unlike post–Civil War department stores such as Macy's and Wanamaker's, Stewart's did not provide food, and so created an opportunity for a new kind of restaurant enterprise.[21] A popular novel of 1854 mentions Thompson's as a dining venue for women shopping or paying social calls, and Taylor's was equally well known. In the Civil War era, when the great stores moved uptown to what became known as the Ladies' Mile (between Astor Place and Twenty-Third Street along Broadway and Sixth Avenue), Taylor's also moved.[22]

Although they projected an image of dainty luxury, and window shutters protected the ladies from the stares of passersby, the ice-cream saloons were occasionally criticized as being nefarious places for assignations and seductions. After all, men were hardly discouraged from showing up, and in the 1850s popular writers such as George Foster warned that sitting at the tables of such seemingly gracious restaurants were "cautious libertines" who whispered passionate and illicit suggestions to women of purportedly respectable status "whose licentiousness has not yet been discovered."[23]

The ice-cream saloons were lavishly ornamented. Isabella Bird, an English visitor, described Taylor's as "a perfect blaze of decoration . . . a complete maze of frescoes, mirrors, carving, gilding, and marble."[24] Their menus were immense. Menus from Taylor's around 1861–1862 are quarto-size books, the covers made of gutta-percha with inlaid mother-of-pearl decoration. The food listings (in English and French) are interspersed with advertisements for furniture and household items. Women may have been thought partial to sweets—and indeed the menus offer plenty of ice-cream, pastry, and fruit desserts—but as yet there was only a vague sense that women preferred light food. A whole page was given over to game (in one menu a dish of robins is penciled in), another to veal.[25] Until the last decades of the nineteenth century, restaurants did not present an entire menu reflecting the style of cooking that women were thought to prefer.

The luxurious ladies' ice-cream saloons appealed to upper-middle-class women, but the end of the nineteenth and beginning of the twentieth century coincided with important social changes and movements that created demand for more modest restaurants that appealed to women. The growth of office and retail work provided opportunities, or at least jobs, for women who, although less affluent than the leisurely shoppers who patronized the ice-cream saloons, could afford to buy lunch away from the office or store. For their needs, ice-cream saloons were supplanted by plainer, less pretentious places with smaller menus and faster service for those afforded a brief lunch interval. Before 1890, when the *New York Times* article cited earlier appeared, modest lunch spots that appealed to women were spreading beyond the retail districts into the larger commercial and office neighborhoods of American downtowns. Clerical and retail employees might not spend as much money on lunch as bourgeois ladies taking a break from shopping, but there were more of them and they were potentially daily rather than occasional customers. By this time as well, salads, sandwiches, egg dishes, and other light fare was served to the women whose tastes, not just in ambience but in cuisine, for the first time were imagined as being different from those of men.

An additional factor was the increasing political activism of women beginning around the turn of the century, when the right to vote and temperance campaigns gained momentum. The moderately priced restaurants that made their money from lunch and targeted women—coffee shops, department-store restaurants, luncheonettes, Automats, and cafeterias, did not serve alcohol and so created what was considered a safe environment that discouraged boisterous and boorish behavior. The growth of moderately priced, middle-class restaurants extended to the roadside restaurant category as well as to ethnic restaurants, all of which occupied the space between the fancy old-line establishments and raucous men's bars, taverns, or hash houses. Schrafft's was at the higher end of this spectrum of mid-level restaurants, a favorite among female shoppers, but within the reach of working women of modest means.

A SEAT AT SCHRAFFT'S

Part of the novelty of Schrafft's, and the reason it is remembered so fondly by many who, like me, were taken there in the 1950s or '60s by an affectionate, "matronly" aunt or grandmother, is that it balanced efficiency with graciousness. It managed to combine the middle-class anonymity of a cafeteria or Automat with the clubby surroundings of the old ice-cream saloons (more or less extinct by 1900) or of more expensive and sophisticated restaurants.

The original Schrafft's enterprise was a chocolate factory in Boston, owned by William F. Schrafft. Frank Shattuck, a candy salesman for a company called E. Greenfield's Sons, was so impressed with the quality of Schrafft's chocolates that in 1886 he quit his job with Greenfield's to start selling Schrafft's candies outside their New England base of operations. Shattuck's enthusiasm and ambition led him to buy into the business and form a partnership with William Schrafft. Shattuck and his family were

Fig. 30. Window display at Schrafft's, Forty-Second Street near Fifth Avenue.

henceforth the managers and principal owners, and in 1898 Shattuck opened up the first Schrafft's retail candy store in New York City.[26]

Despite Shattuck's later reputation as a marketing genius, the first years of the retail business were difficult, and it took several years for Schrafft's to find a successful formula as something more than a wholesale candy company. The candy store lost money, but Frank's sister Jane came up with the idea of selling ice cream along with candy, and then with offering lunch and finally other meals at the stores. Schrafft's would continue selling its own brand of candies, ice cream, and baked goods, but the business started to turn a profit only when its restaurant aspect became prominent.

The first Schrafft's store to provide lunch was designed as a "Japanese Tea Room" in Syracuse, New York. It opened in 1906, and advertised itself as "the daintiest luncheon spot in all the State."[27] Jane Shattuck introduced meals in New York City at a branch of the establishment located on West

Twenty-Third Street, in the Ladies' Mile shopping district.[28] By 1915 there was a Schrafft's in Boston, one in Syracuse, one in Brooklyn, and nine in Manhattan—all serving lunch. By 1927 there were twenty-five Schrafft's, mostly in New York City, and the *Wall Street Journal* estimated that meal service represented 75 percent of the business. In 1934, there were forty-two locations, and in 1950 there were branches in Boston, Philadelphia, Newark, Syracuse, White Plains, and New Rochelle, as well as the usual preponderance in New York City—a total of more than fifty stores.[29] By the end of the 1950s, Schrafft's not only owned restaurants but sold frozen foods, baked goods, ice cream, and candy; ran a corporate food-service business; and even had "motor inns" (that is, glorified motels).

Although Schrafft's would always be associated with well-off ladies, the restaurants were intended to attract women of all respectable classes,

Fig. 31. "Japanese Tea Room" at Schrafft's, Syracuse, New York, early 1920s.

including those whom Frank Shattuck referred to as "secretaries and stenographers who must watch their pocket books."[30] Shattuck was not the first to target these customers, but was forward-looking in hiring women as cooks and managers, not just as waitresses. He believed that female staff understood what kind of food, service, and ambience would please female customers. A workaholic salesman who believed in get up and go and competition, Frank Shattuck was hardly a self-conscious advocate for women's rights, but he nevertheless implemented unusually generous, or at least considerate, policies to give female employees pregnancy leave and a free layette on the baby's arrival. He also instituted a modest profit-sharing plan.[31]

Shattuck was fanatical about having all of the stores conform to norms of service, cleanliness, and food preparation, but there was no uniform décor. Schrafft's was a chain, but not an innovator in standardization. The Rockefeller Center branch, in the Esso Building, was opened in 1947. It was on four floors and included a huge, streamlined modern dining room; a soda-fountain counter; and a leather-paneled Men's Grill (one of many ultimately futile attempts to change Schrafft's matronly image). It seated 1,283 people and was thought to be the largest restaurant in the world at that time, just edging out Mamma Leone's, which we will visit later in this book. The Schrafft's in the Chrysler Building, by contrast, had a rococo look, with painted inset panels, chandeliers, and a ceiling with elaborate molding. The East Seventy-Ninth Street location, in the fashionable Upper East Side neighborhood once known as the "Silk Stocking District," was neoclassical, but its cool severity was marred, according to the distinguished architectural critic and historian Lewis Mumford, by "decorative mincings and grimacings."[32] All of the New York Schrafft's reflected a repertoire of vaguely historical design coinciding with the apogee of the chain's fortunes and reputation, from 1920 until 1960.

The menu varied less than the décor, tending toward the safe and predictable, but it was not the same everywhere. Surviving menus almost

Fig. 32. Waitresses picking up orders at Schrafft's, Esso Building,
Rockefeller Center branch, 1948.

always include the name of the particular branch, and although one cannot speak of local specialties or menus targeted to particular clientele, the managers had discretion about what they wanted to feature.

Schrafft's became famous, even notorious, as the haunt of bossy, moderately affluent "matrons," but its social position was geared more toward economy and moderate comfort than to any kind of snobbery that would discourage less affluent customers. At the same time, it was fancier than such competitors as Childs, which started in 1889 and began a rapid expansion in 1898. By the 1930s there were more than forty Childs lunchrooms in New York and more than a hundred in the United States and Canada.[33] The Childs brothers were even more obsessed than Frank Shattuck about cleanliness and the perception of cleanliness. Very different from

Fig. 33. Interior of Schrafft's,
Chrysler Building branch, ca. 1962.

the wood-paneled luxury of the typical Schrafft's, Childs restaurants had glazed white tile walls and floors, and the tabletops were white as well. They were popular with female store and office employees, but less so with upper-middle-class shoppers.

Lewis Mumford admired Childs for its "antiseptic elegance," and confident modernity as opposed to the faux historicism of Schrafft's and ladies' tearooms. The look of a typical Childs was reminiscent of a hospital—an impression reinforced by the uniforms of the waitresses, who were dressed in white like nurses, while Schrafft's opted for the English-servant look of dark frocks with white aprons for its waitstaff. There were no surprises at Childs, Mumford admitted, but therefore no disappointments: "The whole structure is as neat, as chaste, and as inevitable as a demonstration in Euclid."[34] Where Schrafft's varied its menus and architecture, Childs adhered to a rigid uniformity. Its concentration on one particular look, as well as constant market research and attention to location, anticipated the practices of the fast-food industry of the later twentieth century.

Childs specialized in pancakes, and its one bit of theatricality was placing the employees who made the griddlecakes in the front windows. The chain featured consistently simple food—eggs, baked beans, milk with toast, hominy, grits, crackers or rice—rather than the composed salads and elaborate desserts of the Schrafft's formula. Childs was a competitor with Schrafft's for the female office worker but had fewer social ambitions and did not make an effort to attract the unhurried ladies of leisure.

The Horn & Hardart Automats were another standardized restaurant form that, even more than Childs, embraced machine-age modernity. Started in 1902 in Philadelphia, the Automat combined a regular cafeteria with mechanical self-service. Hot food was available from a conventional cafeteria line, but small salads, pie slices, sandwiches, and the like were displayed in individual portions behind a wall of small windows. When the proper change was placed into a slot (the amount varying per item), the window could be opened with a handle and the customer could remove the item, which was quickly replaced from behind the Art Deco glass-and-metal wall by means of a turntable. It was magical for children to drop a few nickels in the slot, pull out the dish of pie or Jell-O, and then see an exact duplicate come onto the revolving tray. One had the sensation of being inside a modern but decorative and amusing machine. Like Schrafft's and Childs, the Automat flourished particularly in New York, and although less precisely marketed toward women, it too offered inexpensive food, but not alcoholic drinks, in a modern, safe, and in this case impersonal atmosphere. Appealing though they were, the Automats had no imitators, and represent an intriguing but ultimately unsuccessful road not taken.

Although they emphasized efficiency more than gentility, some inexpensive restaurants and cafeteria chains were able to shift their clientele and atmosphere late at night to become places for an edgier sociability. Childs and the Automats in particular differed from the dowdier Schrafft's

Fig. 34. The Automat.

branches in staying open very late or even all night. The scene changed after the theaters let out, and especially after the bars closed. In the 1920s and 1930s, cafeterias catering to office workers by day were convenient meeting places at night that functioned as inexpensive salons (a "Cafeteria Society" as opposed to the sophisticates' "Café Society," as one wag put it). The police watched certain branches as possible sites of soliciting for prostitution. Others were popular with gay men and women for cruising or socializing. The Automat across the street from Bryant Park on Forty-Second Street was one such venue, but it was Childs that was most favored. It is hard to believe, given the Childs brothers' ultraconventional morality, but in the interwar period the chain was well known among gay people for its tolerant, even welcoming, atmosphere. The Childs in the Paramount Building in Times Square had "a touch of lavender," according to the coded language of the *Vanity Fair* guidebook of 1931. The Columbus Circle branch was so popular with gay men, it was impishly dubbed "Mother Childs," and at another location in Brooklyn a young writer named Parker Tyler, swaddled in a fur coat, was asked by a waiter, "What will you have, gorgeous," and responded, "Nothing you've got, dearie." Tyler only half-derisively concluded from this 1929 banter that Brooklyn was "wide open."[35]

Such goings-on were alien to Schrafft's, whose stores were firmly closed by midnight without fail. Schrafft's aimed at a higher level of service and even pretense than either Childs or the Automat, but not so high that it couldn't survive the Depression, that harsh test of excessive gentility. True, one couldn't go into Schrafft's and make tomato soup out of free self-service ketchup and hot water, a Depression staple at the Automat, but Schrafft's, in the end, was not addressing a truly elite Park Avenue clientele either. Its typical patrons were respectable but not consciously fashionable.

No less a figure than Eleanor Roosevelt, eager to embrace a middle class into which she was not born, admired Schrafft's and sought out the advice of the company to deal with complaints in 1937 about the inferior qual-

Fig. 35. Interior of Schrafft's, Esso Building, 1950s.

ity of food at the White House. Mrs. Roosevelt was neither a gourmand nor a stereotypical Schrafft's patron of the bossy matron sort, but the fact that she'd turned to Schrafft's to organize food service was a mark of the chain's prestige and perceived reliability, and helped to project a demotic image for the popular First Lady.[36]

A great innovation of the 1930s was that, with the end of Prohibition in 1933, Schrafft's started serving cocktails, differentiating it further from other ladies' lunch spots such as Midtown tearooms. Its overall coziness guaranteed that such a seemingly daring move would not be regarded as destroying its core reputation. In any event, the repeal of Prohibition ended the identification of women's social agitation with the anti-alcohol movement. Frank Shattuck recognized that ladies might enjoy an occasional drink too, and that there were few places in the city where a respectable woman could order one. Another "overheard" conversation in *The*

New Yorker, as late as 1966, was supposed to be funny because of the tension between healthfulness and respectability on the one hand and pleasure and drink on the other:

> Conversation in a midtown Schrafft's between a well-turned-out matron
> and a pretty young waitress:
>   "Do you have any buttermilk?"
>   "No, Ma'am, I'm sorry."
>   "Have you yoghurt, perhaps?"
>   "No, Ma'am, I'm sorry."
>   "Oh, well, you might as well bring me a Daiquiri."[37]

DAINTY DECADENCE?

The adjective most commonly used to identify women's food choices before the 1960s was "dainty," and this was the word that was used to describe the first Schrafft's in its advertisements. This was originally considered a compliment and was used by female food writers to praise the sort of dishes women were thought to like, also reflecting their desire for a more sprightly presentation. It was understood that men enjoyed hearty, meaty food and didn't care about colors or garnishes, while women preferred a lighter, more decorative style. "Dainty," however, eventually took on a slightly contemptuous overtone, along with "fussy" or "frilly," in men's cookbooks and in advice and warnings addressed to women about what men liked and disliked. From the 1920s to the early 1960s the male appetite for rich (although simple) and spicy foods, such as steak au poivre, chili, or corned-beef hash was contrasted with women's infatuation with salads, brightly colored gelatin, and whipped cream.[38] Women were supposed to like decorative, bland food and were not expected to show much appetite. Dating advice of the mid-twentieth century counseled young women to have a light meal before a dinner out so that they wouldn't seem hungry at the restaurant.

Schrafft's was widely known for its ladylike food, but this term covered both "dainty" self-denial as well as a somewhat contradictory indulgence. The famous items at Schrafft's were not only salads buttressed with canned fruit or cottage cheese, or its Chicken à la King, but also an array of photogenic ice-cream sundaes and banana splits. The seeming contradiction between light, less-fattening main courses and these irresistible rich desserts constituted Schrafft's particular niche, and was part of the reason for its success. Women might favor relatively low-calorie food in general, but were nevertheless expected to be susceptible to elaborate desserts. The covers of two Schrafft's menus, one from 1919 and one from 1920, show a stylish young waitress bringing a tray on which there are two orders of ice cream, one with what looks like butterscotch sauce, along with a salad.[39] When removed from the company of men, women were expected to enjoy the sensuous side of dining.

The belief that American women are both finicky and self-indulgent about food endures in popular culture today. To take two complementary examples from Nora Ephron scripts, in the 1989 movie *When Harry Met Sally*, Harry demonstrates what he sees as Sally's "high-maintenance" character by imitating her fussy manner of ordering food at a restaurant:

"Waiter, I'll begin with a house salad, but I don't want the regular dressing. I'll have balsamic vinegar and oil, but on the side. And then the salmon with the mustard sauce, but I want the mustard sauce on the side."

"On the side" is a very big thing for you.

Women's contradictory or complementary fondness for desserts is mentioned in passing in *Sleepless in Seattle* (1993), when the bereaved male protagonist is thinking about dating again. His friends go over some of the things that have changed since he courted his late wife. For example, if

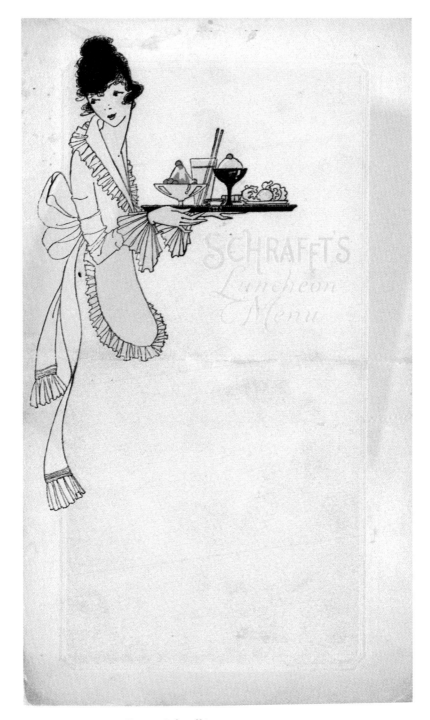

Fig. 36. Schrafft's menu cover, 1920.

he plans to seek out female company, he'd better familiarize himself with tiramisu. Of course, he has never heard of it.[40]

But when did this idea of specifically "female" food start? The ladies' ordinaries did not cater to any theory of women's preferences, and neither did antebellum cookbooks, which, despite their propensity for offering advice, tacitly assumed that women wanted the same things as their families. And even if they didn't, for much of the twentieth century cooking manuals and women's magazines ignored what women might like in favor of preparing food as "the way to a man's heart," the subtitle of the *Settlement House Cookbook*, a perennial bestseller first published in 1903. The common refrain was that women should set aside their own preferences in order to cook what husbands or prospective husbands enjoy. This view implies that women indeed have different tastes, but that female subordination in marriage extends to dining.

Yet despite this impetus to subordination, the development of dining-out options for women was accompanied by a growing sense that women had their own preferences and could, at least in the company of other ladies, indulge them. The obvious advantage of all-female lunches was that women could partake of what they actually liked to eat. An early example of identifying what women enjoy is in the *American Cookery Book* that Jane Croly (here she calls herself "Jennie June") published in 1866. This was the same woman who, two years later, would challenge Delmonico's and the organizers of the Dickens dinner over their exclusion of women. The cookbook gives examples of what women enjoy serving to one another at informal lunches: chicken salad, omelets, poached eggs with boiled ham, rice cakes with cold ham, and broiled lamb chops with diced tomatoes.[41]

So-called women's food was identified, and by women themselves, in the late-nineteenth century. Some of this has to do with friendship. In *Practical Cooking and Dinner Giving* (1876), Mrs. Mary Henderson says that ladies are fond of having luncheon together at home, and that part of the charm of the meal is its informality. Instead of starched white table linens, there is a colored tablecloth; instead of ponderous and constraining table service, the servant should remain in the room only long enough to pass around the first course. Mrs. Henderson offers five menus that show a partiality to chicken salad; mayonnaise of chicken; pastry shells as vehicles for chicken; sweetbreads or oysters; and creamy, chocolaty desserts. The food is in fact not dramatically different from what men prefer, except, Mrs. Henderson remarks, that men like game and wine at late-evening collations. As at Schrafft's, the material and social ambience is as important as the food.[42]

Schrafft's and its imitators quite deliberately offered the same kind of food that women might serve to their friends, but with the addition of ice-cream concoctions and other treats not readily available at home. Tom Wolfe, as astute a social observer as there has ever been, wrote in the 1970s that ladies at Schrafft's typically ordered a cheeseburger, coffee, and a sundae, "but such sundaes . . . of a quality and buttery beauty such as the outside world has never dreamed of!" He then characterized the attraction of the restaurants as affording what he calls "American Comfort," and this is Schrafft's "certain secret beauty."[43] This was written before the term "comfort food" had attained wide circulation, and it referred less to the food than to the skill of the waitresses at cosseting their fussy, vaguely discontented customers. But if Schrafft's represented a certain level of middle-class beauty, it was never a "status lunch" venue for upper-class women who preferred fine restaurants like La Côte Basque, La Grenouille, or Lutèce.

THE MENU AT SCHRAFFT'S

The food offered by Schrafft's becomes significant to a history of American dining for its setting and the debut of fare thought to be attractive to women. Another *New Yorker* observation, from 1933, is particularly reveal-ing: five "West Side boys" (in other words, moderately tough guys) go into Schrafft's for lunch and a lady asks them if they'd like chicken salad with buttered toast and coffee. They say they would prefer corned-beef hash and poached eggs. After twenty minutes with no food in sight, they ask a passing waitress what's going on and she inquires from whom had they ordered. They point to the lady who had originally suggested the chicken salad and are informed that, as a hostess, this lady merely *discusses* food.[44]

Clearly these guys had come to the wrong place, and their error was not merely to misunderstand the restaurant's logistics but to think they were going to get corned-beef hash at all. As it happens, Schrafft's was attempting by 1933 to shed or at least nuance its image of daintiness and attract male customers: it *did* offer corned-beef hash.[45] And compared with today's definition of light food (egg-white omelets, gluten-free or no-fat ingredients) Schrafft's menus, with their preponderance of cream sauces and mayonnaise, seem on the hearty side. "Light" food is often defined in terms of what it is not—not filling, not spicy, not meaty—but its actual positive attributes have changed. Jell-O and mayonnaise, the quintessence of "light" foods sixty years ago or so, have long been out of fashion.

Schrafft's menus were hardly vegetarian, although they sometimes included a "vegetable dinner."[46] In addition to what would have been con-sidered feminine dishes such as creamed chicken on toast or a chicken patty, lunch menus feature calf's liver, lamb chops, spaghetti "à l'Italienne" served with pickle relish and buttered peas, pork and beans, and baked Canadian bacon with Brussels sprouts.[47] A lunch menu from 1956 lists a special sandwich suggestion "for the men": ham and Swiss cheese on pum-pernickel bread with a mustard pickle and sliced tomatoes. The regular, presumably female-friendly, sandwich suggestions are on the order of nut bread supreme, sardine, chicken salad, and chopped egg.[48]

True to Frank Shattuck's dictum about American food, there is almost no hint of foreign influence, except for curried lamb (served with spaghetti) and curried pineapple as an accompaniment to crown roast of lamb.[49] Not that the food represented a folk or regional idea of America—certainly nothing like gumbo, or even crab cakes. The entrées always featured creamed dishes on toast or in pastry shells, cold-cut platters, eggs, and hot sandwiches such as a Monte Cristo (ham, turkey, and Swiss cheese slices served on bread dipped in batter and fried), or plain hot sliced turkey, and other food regarded as attractive to women. What was more distinctive, however, were the salad and dessert categories. Salads included simple varieties such as egg, tomato, and cucumber, but also many varieties of chicken salad, along with other with salad preparations such as stuffed avocados or Waldorf salads (lettuce with celery, walnuts, apples, and mayonnaise). There was not as strong a tendency as one might expect to feature salads that involve fruit, although there was an occasional "avocado pear and orange salad with French dressing" or an orange and grapefruit salad, also with French dressing.[50]

The cakes and ice-cream desserts were varied and elaborate. A 1932 menu lists stewed fruit, baked apples, cakes, and pies (more than twenty to choose from!), and eleven kinds of ice cream, including five types of sundae. The dessert menu is filled with evocative dishes: shadow layer cake was a local specialty of New York kosher bakeries, made with alternating layers of vanilla and chocolate cake and covered with vanilla-cream frosting onto which chocolate is drizzled as a "shadow." There was strawberry shortcake, angel-food cake, and minced pie. Banana splits were a postwar addition. Hot gingerbread à la mode with hot butterscotch sauce combines several dessert attractions. The dessert menu underscores a quip by one of Helen Hokinson's cartoon ladies, who remarks in a 1948 issue of *The New Yorker*, "Sometimes I think Schrafft's doesn't *care* about calories." Or perhaps, more subtly, the Schrafft's menus encouraged a form of caloric calibration—the sundae as a reward for having eaten the ascetic cottage-cheese salad. This was certainly my grandmother's reasoning.

To those of a certain age, the dishes on the Schrafft's menus will seem

"Sometimes I think Schrafft's doesn't care about calories."

Fig. 37. *The New Yorker* cartoon by Helen Hokinson, 1948.

almost boringly familiar. What is interesting is that many of these clichés are all but unavailable today. Once-ubiquitous items such as baked apples, stewed fruit, coconut cream pie, stuffed tomatoes, or pot roast are rare, even at diners whose menus still attempt to offer something for everyone. Just try to find a banana split. It may seem as if many of these endangered foods fall into the Salisbury steak category—dishes that are difficult to find now on menus because they were bad in the first place—but this is not really true even for Salisbury steak. Their fall from favor has more to do with dietary opinions, random fashion, or, more particularly, the demise of a certain kind of genteel dining. The last preserve of genteel dining may have been the South, where cafeterias with a slight claim to social pretension lasted longer than in the rest of the country, and where not only regional specialties such as ham and biscuits or fried chicken were available, but items that might have appeared at Schrafft's as well, like salmon croquettes. Schrafft's fall, as with its rise, had less to do with food than with social change.

A FALL FROM FAVOR

Although Schrafft's actually lasted into the Reagan era of the 1980s, the 1970s marked a precipitous decline in its business and revealed a failure in its attempts to entice new customers—especially young women, but also men of any age. Schrafft's had such a well-established identity that it probably could not under any circumstances have survived the changes in women's roles and self-image that began in the late 1960s. Women were less willing to be identified with bourgeois pursuits like shopping for pleasure, and also eager to avoid anything suggestive of being "matronly." At the same time they eschewed the infantalization implicit in assuming they just wanted to eat ice-cream sundaes and gossip.

Using awkward and occasionally ludicrous strategies, Schrafft's attempted to combat its dowdy image. In 1968 none other than Andy Warhol was hired to make a television commercial centered on the ice-cream sundae. Dubbed the "Underground Sundae," the Schrafft's sundae was presented in a frenzied series of color bursts. The voiceover used hip locutions of the time, notably "groovy" (vanilla ice cream) and "mind-blowing" (chocolate sauce). *Playboy* magazine summarized the commercial as "a long, voluptuous panning shot of a chocolate sundae with all the mistakes TV can make kept in." Another commercial attempted to take on Schrafft's matronly reputation, showing two young women in miniskirts and asking: "Have you seen the little old ladies in Schrafft's lately?"[51]

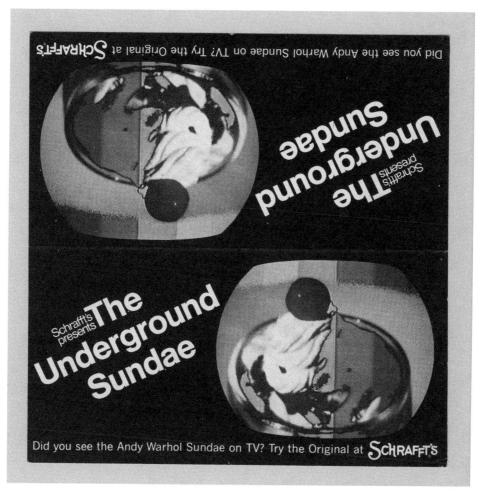

Fig. 38. From Andy Warhol's "Underground Sundae" commercial for Schrafft's, 1968.
© 2016 The Andy Warhol Foundation for the Visual Arts, Inc. / Artists Rights Society (ARS), New York.

Schrafft's wasn't the only restaurant type to fall victim to the youth revolution or the Me Decade. The demand for waitress-served, sit-down lunch places declined, as did the popularity of cafeterias. The 1970s marked the proverbial death knell of the fabled Automat. Before closing for good, these cavernous palaces of modernity had become the haunt of New York's growing homeless population. The urban luncheonette, once as streamlined and seductive as Radio City Music Hall, met its demise at the hands of McDonald's and Burger King. The New York and Los Angeles coffee shops held on a bit longer, but the invasion of cities by fast-food franchises from the suburban highway interchanges provided faster, cheaper lunch options.

Diners are an anomalous holdover, and they continue to offer extensive menus and home-cooked meals, but control of the urban office-lunch market has long since passed to salad bars freighted with bacon bits, baby spinach, and bleu-cheese dressing; so-called delis; and quick-service chains, including those such as Dunkin' Donuts or Tim Horton's that might be regarded primarily as breakfast places.

In 1968, Schrafft's was split up and the candy company was sold to Helme Products, while the large food company Pet, Inc., bought the restaurants. Pet's efforts to reverse decades of image-building aimed at middle-aged women led to the installation of a men-only section on the second floor of the branch on Fifth Avenue between Forty-Fifth and Forty-Sixth Streets. Named "The Male Animal," this short-lived experiment in trying to lure the "Joe Namath crowd" had zebra-striped carpeting and dark paneling.[52] Pet sold most of its New York stores in 1978 to the Riese Organization, which specialized in grouping together fast-food chain operations in urban mini-malls, but Riese sold off the branches of Schrafft's as real-estate parcels in the 1980s when New York began to recover from its near-bankruptcy. A handful of Schrafft's branches survived independently for a few years, but all of them, much like the famous Checker cabs, were gone by the end of the 1980s.

The amount of nostalgia for Schrafft's even now is impressive. The post "When Ladies' Lunched" on Jan Whitaker's *Restaurant-ing Through History* blog in 2008 elicited forty responses, mostly memories of childhood excursions with an elderly female relative. Unexpectedly, sophisticated people mourned the passing of Schrafft's. Andy Warhol described the restaurants as "the beauties of their day." Their attempt to keep up with the times deprived them of their charm, "but if they could just have kept their same look and style, and held on through the lean years when they weren't in style, today they'd be the best thing around."[53]

This evaluation of Warhol's is probably not literally true, but no restaurant discussed in this book evokes more nostalgia than Schrafft's. Its seventy-year history exemplified a certain kind of mass-market graciousness directed particularly to the female customer. Joan Fisher, who worked for many years in theatrical management in New York, recalls dining at Schrafft's, usually happily alone, as a regular from the 1950s to 1970s: "I practically lived at Schrafft's," she says. The chopped-egg sandwich was her favorite, but it was the pleasant atmosphere that was most attractive. Schrafft's was attentive without being intimidating, leisurely but attuned to the needs of women who had a job to go back to, efficient, but at the same time providing a welcome break.[54] Although there are today thousands of restaurants, coffee places, and cafés where one can work or distract oneself, the particular kind of middle-class leisure provided by Schrafft's is impossible to duplicate.

SUNDAES

Hot Fudge .... .20	Cherry Whip............. .25	Coffee Maple M. M. ...... .25
Hot Fudge Pecan .... .25	Cherry Almond Snow ..... .25	Pineapple Whip........... .25
Hot Fudge Walnut........ .25	Chocolate Walnut.......... .20	Pineapple Almond Snow .. .25
Hot Fudge Marshmallow.. .20	Chocolate Marshmallow ... .20	Pineapple Mint .... .20
Coffee Fudge .... .20	Chocolate Noodle......... .20	Banana Royal .... .30
Coffee Fudge Pecan .... .25	Chocolate Almond .... .25	Johnson Special........... .25
Coffee Fudge Walnut ...... .25	Maple Walnut............ .20	Hot Butterscotch .... .20
Coffee Fudge Marshmallow .20	Maple Pecan .... .25	Hot Butterscotch Pecan ... .25
Strawberry (fresh fruit).... .25	Maple Marshmallow .... .20	Hot Butterscotch Almond . .25
Butterscotch Almond	Coffee Maple .... .20	Hot Butterscotch M. M.... .25
Crumble .... .25	Coffee Maple Almond ...... .25	Ginger Snow .... .25

PARFAITS

Chocolate................ .25	Coffee .... .25	Pineapple .... .25
Mocha .... .25	Strawberry .... .25	Ginger .... .25

Ice Cream Sodas	Ice Creams	Sherbets
All Flavors............... .20	Individual Order......... .15	Individual Order.......... .15

ICE CREAM TO TAKE OUT, 80c quart, 40c pint

EGG, MILK AND FRESH FRUIT DRINKS

Milk (individual)......... .10	Frappes (all flavors) .... .20	Egg Lemonade (fresh
Milk Shakes (all flavors)... .15	Egg Shakes .... .20	fruit) .... .25
Floats (all flavors)........ .20	Malted Milks .... .20	Egg Malted Milks .... .25
Orangeade .... .15	Lemonade............... .15	Limeade .... .15

Fresh Fruit Orangeade with Orange Sherbet.............. .25

HOWARD JOHNSON'S
ROADSIDE SHOPPES AND RESTAURANTS
MASSACHUSETTS

Andover	Dorchester	Montello	North Seekonk	Randolph	Waltham
Boston	East Boston	Marshfield	North Weymouth	Revere Beach	Walpole
Huntington Ave.	Framingham	Medford	Nahant	Scituate	West Boylston
Bourne	Grafton	Melrose	Onset	Seekonk	West Roxbury
Brookline	Harwichport	Methuen	Orleans	Salem	Westwood
Cambridge	Hyannis	Nantasket	Oxford	South Weymouth	Whitman
Canton	Lynnfield	Norfolk Downs	Pembroke	South Easton	Wollaston
Cohasset	Middleboro	North Attleboro	Quincy	Wakefield	Wollaston (Blvd.)
Dedham					

CONNECTICUT—Fairfield, Milford   RHODE ISLAND—Hoxie, Cranston, Portsmouth

NEW HAMPSHIRE—Nashua, Seabrook, No. Conway

Fig. 39. 1941 Howard Johnson's menu, sundaes.

HOWARD JOHNSON'S
AS AMERICAN AS FRIED CLAMS

ike Schrafft's, Howard Johnson's began with a single establishment in suburban Boston and a relentless entrepreneur with a plan to expand it. Both restaurant chains were famous for ice cream and bland "American" food, uninflected by ethnic borrowing. Combining informality with respectability, they appealed to a middle-class clientele for whom cleanliness and consistency were all-important. They both offered alcohol-free environments that were welcoming to women and, especially in the case of Howard Johnson's, families with children.

From a business perspective, Howard Johnson's was more aggressive and innovative than Schrafft's: it concentrated on the highways rather than city neighborhoods, and multiplied branches by franchising. In the mid-1970s, Schrafft's was clearly declining while Howard Johnson's still had 929 restaurants and 526 motor lodges coast to coast.[1] In the 1960s, Howard Johnson's served more meals outside the home than any company or organization except for the US Army.[2] Both Schrafft's and Howard Johnson's were undermined, however, by trends that became evident in the 1970s—

above all the expansion of McDonald's and other fast-food establishments that dispensed with waitresses, gentility, and large menus in favor of speed, minimum-wage labor, and hamburgers. Schrafft's and Howard Johnson's were also hampered by transitions in family leadership when the rule of a charismatic founder was succeeded by less capable, or perhaps simply less fanatical, chief executives who tried vainly to refresh the brands' outdated images. Seeing the futility of this effort to stem the tide, they then sold out to haplessly incompetent conglomerates.

Fans of Schrafft's and Howard Johnson's, and they are numerous, are nostalgic for a certain kind of mid-twentieth-century, middlebrow dining. For them chicken croquettes or meatloaf are not "retro" or "comfort" items but simply beloved menu options. It's not that fast food has driven out everything else—plenty of restaurant chains such as Bob Evans or Denny's occupy the inexpensive table-service niche today—but their menus feature post-1950s items like fajitas or Buffalo chicken wings, and offer only a few ice cream flavors.

Unlike the other restaurants featured in this book, Howard Johnson's came up with a plan, what would now be called a "mission statement," early in its history. The founder, Howard Deering Johnson, described his merchandising philosophy in these terms:

> To serve the finest food on the American highways at reasonable prices to a large volume of family and medium-income Americans, and serve it in an attractive atmosphere.[3]

What follows is essentially an elaboration on his statement that, although brief, touches on twentieth-century developments such as automobile culture, the sanctification of the middle-class, mass production, and reproducibility. Howard Johnson's influenced what Americans ate, but even more significantly, the company changed how, where, and in what settings they dined.

Howard Johnson's influence is most apparent in two innovations: its pioneering use of franchising and its adaptation to the American highway. Franchising allows a restaurant chain to expand geographically without investing great sums of its own money, offloading much of the risk and personnel costs on the franchisee, who hopes to profit from an established reputation and supply chain. Success at franchising requires replicability and therefore an executive level of supervision of the type exercised by restaurant entrepreneurs such as Frank Shattuck or the Childs brothers. It also means you need to be able to entice people who are not direct employees to uphold the corporate image in autonomous branches, something more difficult for executives who want total control. Franchising has made the modern fast-food industry possible, but it takes a particular kind of managerial intensity to pull off, a delegation of responsibility that is at odds with the Shattuck- or Childs-type desire for omniscience and meticulous attention to detail.

The need to supervise everything directly is characteristic of the vertical integration perfected by the Ford Motor Company in the 1920s, which made its own raw materials and parts rather than relying on suppliers or outsourcing. Howard Johnson's was hardly a spontaneous collective, and it too tried to limit or control external suppliers. It constructed its own buildings, prepared its own food, and even insisted on being the sole customer of the business that furnished its raw clams. It drew up prototypes for its restaurants that dictated look, color schemes, materials, menu, and service standards. Howard Deering Johnson was famous for his dedication to recipes, rules, and supervision. Max Apple's 1977 short story, "The Oranging of America," pictures Johnson as a fanciful but plausible Flying Dutchman, restlessly crisscrossing America with his secretary and chauffeur, an old man still experimenting with ice-cream flavors and scouting future locations.[4] Nevertheless, despite all this lust for uniformity, Howard Johnson's was built by creating franchises that were not directly staffed with employees from headquarters.

Howard Johnson's expansion was facilitated by the automobile and the network of highways and sprawl of suburbs that followed in its wake. While the modern suburban commercial landscape is considered to be a post-WWII phenomenon, in fact its origins were the auto-crazed 1920s and the increasingly standardized America of the Depression era. Even before the war, Howard Johnson's had pioneered roadside restaurants, taking advantage of easier and cheaper travel conditions and leisure travelers' yearning for predictability. Desire to eliminate surprises might seem to contradict the speed and accessibility to distant places that the automobile provided, but in fact as mobility increased, the taste for adventure along the way declined. The logical outcome of the imperatives of speed and efficiency was the limited-access interstate highway of the late-twentieth century, a

Fig. 40. Howard Deering Johnson and a customer, 1939.

system with the same fast-food chain stops at every exit. As it turned out, Howard Johnson's could not profit from this perfected model of limited choice and uniformity. Rather, in retrospect, the roadside orange-roofed icon was a bridge between the proliferation of intermediate, middle-class restaurants that sprang up in the 1890s and the modern fast-food industry that took off in the 1960s—between Schrafft's and the Automat on the one hand, and McDonald's and KFC on the other.

In the mid-twentieth century Howard Johnson's established a business model, look, atmosphere, and menu that dominated the food-service industry. Its highway locations profited from a much larger customer base than the urban shoppers and office workers who patronized Schrafft's. Combining relatively quick service and uniform appearance, Howard Johnson's defined quality in terms of reliability and hygiene. It created a roadside attraction designed for families and sacrificed other potential customers such as truck drivers or commercial travelers.

FROM QUINCY TO THE OPEN ROAD

Born in 1897, Howard Deering Johnson was raised in an upper-middle-class family in the Wollaston neighborhood of Quincy, Massachusetts, a prosperous shipbuilding center and residential suburb of Boston. His father was a cigar manufacturer. In later life, as the famous founder of a great enterprise, Howard Johnson liked to present himself as a man of simple tastes with no hobbies or interests: "I never played golf. I never played tennis. I never did anything after I left school. I ate, slept, and thought of nothing but the business."[5] In fact, his life was more interesting than his statement implies. He married four times and maintained a yacht, three houses, and an art collection—hardly pastimes associated with the world of Sinclair Lewis's *Main Street* or *Babbitt*. Far from subsisting exclusively on the all-American cuisine promoted by his restaurants, Johnson loved high-end French dining and was a regular at New York's Le Pavillon (which we will visit later on in the book), the epitome of distinguished, not to say snobbish, cuisine and service. Neither was he opposed to living it up after dinner either. Several photographs of Mr. Johnson in Anthony Mitchell Sammarco's *A History of Howard Johnson's* were taken at New York's Stork Club, a haunt of movie stars, playboys, and gossip columnists.[6]

Johnson left school at age sixteen and served with distinction in the American Expeditionary Force in France during the First World War, his military service coming between bouts of attempting to salvage his father's cigar company. This was an uphill struggle because cigars were being undermined by the rise of cigarette smoking. From the start Johnson was a good salesman, even in selling cigars, but his success as a restaurateur was gradual and not the result of latching immediately onto a single brilliant concept.

In his hometown in 1925, Johnson bought a combined drugstore, soda fountain, and newsstand advantageously placed next to a commuter rail station. He soon had hired seventy-five delivery boys for the newspaper side of his business, but after tinkering with recipes and freezer technology, Johnson found ice-cream sales more interesting and profitable than newspapers. He developed a richer product, higher in butterfat content and with a creamier texture. His freezing experiments allowed him to produce ice cream that was smooth (not hard and blocklike) without being too soft. From 1925 to 1929, Johnson perfected most of the twenty-eight flavors that would become identified with the future Howard Johnson's chain, and there would be regular traffic tie-ups in front of his store as people went out of their way to buy his ice cream. In the summer months Johnson opened ice-cream stands on the Quincy shoreline and in other nearby beach communities.[7]

By 1929, Howard Johnson knew he was on to something that amounted to more, perhaps, than an enviable ice-cream business. In that famously inauspicious year he decided to open a restaurant in a new Art Deco office

Fig. 41. Howard Deering Johnson and his wife at the Stork Club, New York.

building on Quincy Square built by the Granite Trust Bank. Newspaper articles reflect what would become a typical pairing of old-fashioned virtue with new technology: the restaurant would feature the New England cooking Johnson learned from his mother, while its all-electric bakery would turn out bread and pastry efficiently "to eliminate the machine taste of [large-scale] cookery."

Just after it opened, the restaurant received a boost when Eugene O'Neill's *Strange Interlude*, which had won the Pulitzer prize for drama in 1928, was banned in Boston largely due to the fact that its lead female character is "promiscuous" and has an abortion. The Quincy of the 1930s, not quite as prudish as its Archdiocese-dominated big neighbor, offered a refuge for putting on the play, benefiting Howard Johnson because the theater was right by his new restaurant. The length of *Strange Interlude*—a staggering four hours plus—required a dinner break. The resulting traffic was an ironic start for Johnson, whose future business success would be based on an ultra-wholesome image closer to Shirley Temple movies than O'Neill's alcohol-infused plays and their tormented protagonists.[8]

Johnson's slow-developing big idea was to expand along the highways and to create an instantly recognizable series of identical establishments that would attract families. It was hardly original to try to capitalize on the growth of automobile ownership and the rise of pleasure driving as roads like the Lincoln Highway and US Route 66 were being put together and as cars were becoming more reliable. If the "American Dream" of postwar America (and later) has been defined as home ownership, the "American Way" of the 1920s was identified with automobile ownership. What was innovative about Howard Johnson's was the combination of family appeal, standardization, and exploitation of the particular setting of the highway.

To be sure, there were already places to eat along the two-lane roads of the prewar United States, but they tended to be ramshackle affairs best adapted to the needs of solitary truckers and other men traveling alone, for whom cleanliness and ambience were unimportant. According to Howard Deering Johnson, the owners of such places felt no incentive to offer good food to customers who were assumed to be unlikely to return.[9] Nevertheless, some effort was made to unearth a few gastronomic diamonds from the sludge. Duncan Hines, whose name is now associated with boxed cake mix and other food products, began as a traveling salesman for a printing firm. He put together a list of 167 reliable restaurants across America that he distributed as a Christmas gift in 1935. This proved so successful that the next year he published *Adventures in Good Eating*, a much larger guide that went through many editions and updates. Despite the use of the word "adventure" in the title, the guide was supposed to make dining on the road predictable, to *prevent* untoward new experiences. Hines's two priorities were cleanliness and what he considered unpretentious "home cooking."

Most of his recommendations were small-town, family-run restaurants in the South and Midwest, but he also extolled Howard Johnson's as an example of safe, wholesome food served in cheerful and spotless surroundings.[10]

Even with Duncan Hines and other serviceable guides, the highway gastronomic scene remained desolate. Bernard DeVoto, an observer of American literature and history, wrote despairingly in 1940 about a cross-country journey punctuated by miserable meals at "Maw's Filling Station" and the like. He concluded that the vigor of Americans was proven by "the fact that by the hundreds of thousands they eat this garbage and survive."[11] DeVoto's opinion was shared by two Soviet comic artists, Ilf and Petrov, who made an automobile trip around the United States in 1935–1936, eating at ordinary places in order to experience the lives of American workers. Everything was clean, well organized, and yet tasteless, they reported. Their assessment was compatible with orthodox Soviet accounts of life in the United States, although this peculiar piece of journalism implies that the Soviet Union, in contrast to the United States, rejoiced in individual, artisanal flavors.[12]

The diner was the closest analogue to the type of restaurant created by Howard Johnson in the 1930s, a long-established institution that has managed to survive the same adversities that led to the eclipse of Howard Johnson's.[13] Diners come out of the horse-drawn lunch wagons set up outside of factories in the late-nineteenth century. These mobile short-order restaurants served workers especially on the night shift (they were sometimes referred to as "night lunch wagons"). Some started to come around during the day for who those wanted food at entry, break, or quitting times. The current vogue for urban food trucks is an atavistic throwback to these humble but homemade offerings, albeit now adapted to a postindustrial schedule. When the wagons were expanded, decorated, and, most important, set up as long-term or permanent restaurants, the diner was born. Suddenly in 1923 and 1924 the term "diner" replaced references to lunch wagons or lunch cars.[14] Modeled on the railroad dining car rather than the trolley, the new diners offered something close to home-cooked food, quick service, low prices, and a kind of neighborly friendliness. They were usually open late or even all hours, appealing to theatergoers and night owls as well as shift workers.

Although enduring, diners were not destined to reap the maximum profit from changes in American transportation and leisure. They were urban rather than highway establishments and retained too much of a "rough" image to attract the self-consciously middle-class family. What is now seen as a picturesque vintage locale of authentic food and conviviality was in the 1930s associated with dreary industrial settings and brash, lower-class patrons, brought to vivid life in the noir films of the 1940s and 1950s. The diner could not make the jump from its workingman's origins to conform to the popular image of the American family enjoying the countryside and the highway as a leisure experience.

The best approximation of roadside gentility in the 1920s was the tearoom, a restaurant genre started at the turn of the century whose light food, temperance beverages, and graciousness were designed to appeal to women. In their automobile-age incarnation, tearooms were located along the roads in picturesque pseudo-colonial houses, sporting names like Ye Ragged Robin or the Sign of the Green Tea Pot. If the idea was to appeal to families traveling for fun, the ability to attract the wife and mother was vital because the assumption was that she made the decisions about where and what to eat. The tearoom was perfect for women alone or in groups, but its tranquility could not withstand the depredations of kids released from the confinement of automobiles. Indeed, a crucial challenge for all roadside restaurants was to figure out how to welcome children without losing other customers. This was something Howard Johnson's perfected. Kids were diverted by the twenty-eight flavors of ice cream and the display of oversize lollipops; the restaurants were spacious and brightly colored. Howard Johnson established a policy of hiring women as waitstaff and even as cooks in order to convey a sense of homey comfort, but eschewed the fragile graciousness of the sort that might discourage family groups with rambunctious children.[15]

To create a successful chain of highway restaurants was therefore not a straightforward proposition; instead it required a combination of elements—none of them completely new, but none of them previously found together: speedy service, cleanliness, family orientation, informality, safety, predictability, and inexpensive food of consistent and (for this genre) high quality. Howard Johnson's was a synthesis of attractive traits borrowed from other types of establishments rather than a revolutionary new idea.

The closest thing to a revolutionary aspect, as it turned out, was the aforementioned innovation of franchising. Unlike Howard Deering Johnson's obsessive management of recipes, service, architecture, and logistics, this experiment in brand leveraging was the result of circumstance and not planning. By the time Johnson decided to embrace the highway, the Great Depression had afflicted retail business and made borrowing money especially difficult. One surprising aspect of the crisis that Johnson noticed was that recreational automobile driving did not decline in the 1930s despite massive unemployment and reduction in overall standards of living.[16]

Franchising was a way of responding to the shortage of capital and what was still a vigorous demand for restaurants, a way of opening them without having to put up much money. The first franchised Howard Johnson's was in Orleans, Massachusetts, just beyond the "elbow" of Cape Cod where it turns north. Johnson was friends with a prominent local family named Sprague who owned a strategically placed property at the junction of Routes 6A and 28. Lacking the funds, or not wanting to develop the restaurant by himself, Johnson convinced young Reginald Sprague to build according to his specifications. Johnson supplied the ice cream, frankfurters, and other food. The Orleans Howard Johnson's opened in May 1935 and quickly became a success. There followed rapidly more than forty other franchised restaurants by 1937.[17]

Fig. 42. Advertisement for Howard Johnson's, 1955.

Another major innovation was to rely on frozen foods sent out to branches from regional commissaries, a system based on how ice cream had been supplied before the chain went into restaurant service. The commissary system reduced costs and assured uniformity. Food prepared and frozen in these central locations was sent out periodically, usually weekly, to franchisees and company-owned restaurants. Pies, clam cakes, shrimp curry, fried chicken, clam chowder, and other soups could be thawed and cooked or reheated.[18] The result was a high degree of predictability, yet, unlike the fast-food formula that replaced Howard Johnson's, a full and varied menu. According to a 1957 report, the commissaries handled 433 different items, an industrial mimicry of the dizzying variety offered at Antoine's.[19]

Uniformity in everything, not just food, was enforced by a manual, a "Bible," of rules and procedures covering kitchen equipment, décor, maintenance, uniforms, and cleaning. Certain items, such as spaghetti or barbecue sauce, could be thawed, heated, and left on steam tables; others, such as fish or mashed potatoes, had to be thawed and then cooked individually to order. There were complicated specifications and protocols for everything from dishwashing to how many small cups of tartar sauce needed to be set out in advance of service to accompany fried clams and scallops (thus saving the time and labor of spooning it out for each order) to how many glasses to have on hand, where to keep them, and how many to fill with water before the customers arrived.[20] Nothing, or at least not much, was left to chance or imagination. In the late 1950s, Howard Johnson's managers energetically debated gas versus electric stoves; technological advances like automatic coffeemakers to replace large urns of rapidly cooling coffee were eagerly anticipated.[21] Replication, predictability, and adherence to an elaborate code of procedures was necessary because in a franchised company, a bad experience at one branch would affect the customer's perception (and word-of-mouth reputation) of the entire system.

That *some* sacrifice of food quality was the price for centralization, frozen food, and cost control was not as obvious before the 1970s as one might think. Perhaps equating bland with homemade allowed predictable food to be perceived as comforting. Uniformity and blandness certainly provided marketing opportunities emphasizing hygiene, reliability, and texture if not flavor. At any rate, Johnson was able to present his restaurants as simultaneously homey and gleamingly ultramodern, offering quality at an inexpensive price. These seemingly contradictory notions were bridged by a mid-twentieth-century consensus that quality *meant* predictability—the variation and imperfection that today signify handmade and "artisanal" in the past denoted food that was poor quality and unreliable. The individuality of the proverbial greasy spoon was unattractive compared to the formulaic, immaculate, white-tiled, orange-roofed "Host of the Highways."

By 1941, Johnson had at least 130 restaurants in twelve eastern states, more than eighty of them franchised. He had also acquired the Red Coach Inn in Wayland, Massachusetts, and created a mini chain called Red Coach Grill—mildly upscale restaurants featuring steak, lobster, and a faux colonial New England look. Another path of expansion was to set up shop along the new state-sponsored toll roads. On October 1, 1940, the initial stretch of the Pennsylvania Turnpike, the nation's first limited-access toll road, opened. The 160-mile highway segment between Irwin and Carlisle traversed the Appalachian Mountains in the western part of the state. Howard Johnson's acted expeditiously and obtained the concession to run eight restaurants along a road that went through nearly empty countryside. The turnpike was built not to link small towns but to serve as a through road. The toll, which had to be paid upon exiting, and the nature of the route through isolated territory, provided a captive audience for the restaurants and guaranteed a substantial business. The war interrupted large-scale civilian construction, and the turnpike wasn't finished until 1956, but Howard Johnson's made plenty of money from its monopoly on this and other, later turnpikes between the 1950s and the late 1970s.[22]

Fig. 43. Howard Johnson's at 165th Street and Northern Boulevard,
Queens, New York, ca. 1940.

The other great event on the eve of war was the opening in January 1940 of the largest Howard Johnson's ever constructed, located on Queens Boulevard in the Rego Park section of Queens, New York. It must have seemed like a neoclassical palazzo in the midst of a sprawling outer borough, with its three floors and grand entrance flanked by Corinthian columns. In winter the restaurant seated seven hundred people and in nice weather an additional three hundred could be accommodated on second-floor terraces. The restaurant was intended to serve visitors to the New York World's Fair, which had opened in 1939. The fair's symbolic colors were blue and orange, taken from the New York state flag—conveniently the same color combination as that of Howard Johnson's.

For this project Mr. Johnson collaborated with Lydia Pinkham Gove, a wealthy investor, intrepid lover of airplanes (she organized the first American transcontinental passenger flight in 1926), and granddaughter of a tremendously successful entrepreneur who'd invented a tonic for "female complaints." The restaurant cost $600,000 to build (the equivalent of $10 million now) and Gove, already a partner in two other Howard Johnson's, paid half the expense.[23]

A CHANGING LANDMARK

Just a few years after opening his first restaurant, Howard Johnson had created a widely recognized brand that deserved the motto: "Landmark for Hungry Americans." The restaurants were designed to be landmarks in the sense of being recognizable from a car going 50 or 60 miles per hour. Johnson routinely placed his establishments on hilltops or extensive flat stretches of land in order to be seen from far away. The normal practice of the pre- and immediate postwar era was to beckon the traveler with billboard advertisements, but Johnson thought these conveyed a cheap image. In the absence of billboards, then, an unmistakable look was essential. The original Howard Johnson's model combined a bright orange porcelain tile roof, not found in any vernacular architecture, with a neo-Georgian base of white clapboard walls with three front-facing dormer windows, shutters, and an octagonal steeple with a weathervane. New England churches, houses, and civic buildings were the point of reference, but here they appeared with assertive, one might even say garish, color trim. The shutters were usually blue-green, and sometimes the cupola roof was as well. The very un-colonial combination of blue and orange was repeated inside, although the basic décor was originally knotty pine. Eclectic though their style might be, the buildings conveyed order and stateliness without being intimidating. The odd juxtaposition of colonial revival house and eye-catching Technicolor roof worked quite well and, as with the food and overall presentation, suggested a reassuring combination of the best aspects of tradition and modernity.

Care was taken with the ornamentation, shrubbery, and even the parking areas, which were paved at a time when most restaurant lots were dirt. The dignified buildings and their surroundings contrasted with the prevailing jerry-built ugliness of roadside businesses. An observation made by

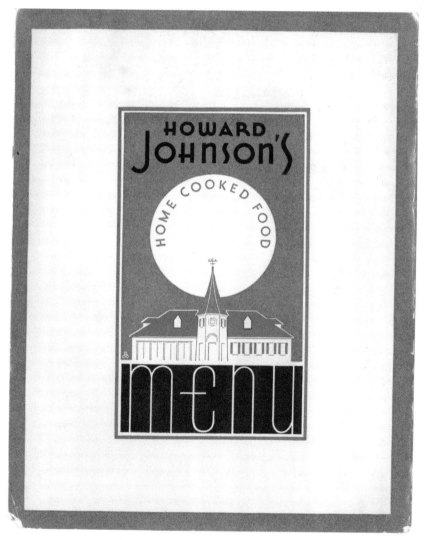

Fig. 44. Howard Johnson's menu cover, 1937.

Curtis Blake, the cofounder of the Friendly Ice Cream Company, could be applied to Howard Johnson's as well: "The crummier the stuff that was around, the better we looked."[24]

The Second World War was disastrous to businesses based on leisure, especially those dependent on drivers who now had to contend with rationed gasoline and the portrayal of pleasure travel as unpatriotic. Besides, millions of men, many of them fathers, had enlisted or been drafted and were far from home. Food was rationed and the controls on sugar made the ice-cream business difficult to impossible. Among the first casualties was the Rego Park Howard Johnson's, opened with so much fanfare just two years before America entered the war. The company nearly went bankrupt, and in late 1944, only twelve restaurants were in operation. Howard Johnson's survived by contracting out its food commissaries to the armed forces, and this proved to be an effective stopgap measure.[25]

After the war, although for some time it remained difficult to acquire construction material and kitchen equipment, economic recovery was rapid. The experience of the sudden drop-off in business followed by a need to rebuild convinced Howard Deering Johnson that the expensive prewar "roadside cathedrals" should not be replicated. A simplified architectural style replaced the earlier combination of colonial pastiche and bright-orange roof. The new model was both relatively inexpensive and confidently modern. The sleek postwar idiom was anticipated in 1938, when the restaurant in Somerville, New Jersey, was decorated by Dorothy Mary Kinnicutt Parish, known as "Sister Parish," who would become one of the leading interior decorators of the twentieth century. Parish decided on aquamarine walls, placemats, and waitress uniforms thus bringing inside the combination of orange and blue that would replace also the colonial architectural style of the early years.[26]

The end of the 1940s and the entire 1950s saw the simultaneous expansion of highways, suburbs, and the number of middle-class restaurant patrons. By 1950, Howard Johnson's locations flanked highways and road stops all over the South and Midwest. The postwar Howard Johnson's merits the overused term "American icon" to the degree that it no longer needed to remind patrons of a colonial past or of anything in particular other than itself. It was famous simply as Howard Johnson's. A new design was first tried out in Miami in 1948 according to plans drawn up by architect Rufus Nims (1913–2005), who spent his life in Florida designing houses intended to break with the prevailing Spanish colonial look. For Howard Johnson's Nims kept the orange tile roof but created a single-story triangular structure with a considerable amount of plate-glass and a radically sloping hip roof. The cupola was retained, but was segmented into rectangular slices so that it could house an exhaust system. The interior changed from rustic to minimalist modern—light with thin curtains, Formica tabletops, and partitions formed out of repeating circles.[27] Although there were in fact many variations, the exterior style became so distinctive that those old enough to remember the heyday of Howard Johnson's will today often drive past what they recognize as a "ghost" Howard Johnson's—structures of an unmistakable shape now abandoned or repurposed.[28]

Fig. 45. Honeyspot Motor Inn, Stratford, Connecticut: a former
Howard Johnson's motor lodge and restaurant.

In addition to the orange-and-aqua color scheme, the restaurants' symbols were a logo taken from the nursery rhyme "Simple Simon" and the particular lettering of "Howard Johnson's" in capitals except for the *n*'s (which were the same size as the other letters to produce a streamlined effect). Classic menu items, such as the fried clam strips and ice cream, also functioned as immediately recognizable brand-identification features.[29] The image of Simple Simon was used on the cupola weathervanes; at the entrance to the restaurants (as a swinging metal sign or attached to the wall); and was repeated on the menus, dishes, napkins, and glassware. The trademark shows a man, a boy, and a dog; the man carrying a teetering stack of pies, the boy pointing eagerly to it, and the dog salivating.

Fig. 46. Howard Johnson's logo, Simple Simon and the Pieman.

The design had been created in 1935 by John Eagles Alcott, who also made up the lettering. This rather complicated image is based on a sobering folktale exemplifying worldly wisdom. Simple Simon has what now would be labeled learning disabilities and is unable to understand how the world works. He asks a pie seller for a pie, but because he hasn't any money, he gets nothing. The harsh moral is that you must pay for what you want. Simon's further adventures involve similarly futile experiments, such as carrying water in a sieve. Fortunately for Howard Johnson's, rather than some pessimistic bit of pre-modern wisdom, the logo communicated the pleasure of eating, and became so familiar that it eventually came to mean simply "You're at Howard Johnson's!"[30]

Fig. 47. Howard Johnson's motor lodge, 1960s, showing Nims-model restaurant.

By 1954, nearly four hundred Howard Johnson's restaurants abounded in thirty-two states. A majority were franchises, run by independent owners but supplied and regulated by the company. The most expansive phase of Howard Johnson's history began at this point with the opening of the company's first motor lodge in Savannah, Georgia, a change in roadside accommodation as Howard Johnson's had previously been designed as an isolated, stand-alone place to eat.[31] Motels in the 1950s often had restaurants in the center of the courtyard formed by the bedroom units. In keeping with its image of comfortable but still democratic travel, Howard Johnson's motor lodges were nicer than most motels, attracting a slightly higher-class clientele by offering lobbies, air conditioning, covered walkways, parking separate from individual rooms, and some effort at décor.[32]

The motor lodges were a logical outgrowth of the restaurants' success and allowed the company to attract business travelers inclined to bypass Howard Johnson's thinking it would be crowded with children slobbering ice cream. The motor-lodge restaurants were attached to the main building, Mr. Johnson said, so that convenience would discourage the guests from seeing their car in the parking area and being tempted to drive and eat somewhere else.[33]

Starting at the end of the 1950s, the Interstate Highway System changed the logistics of where to locate restaurants serving travelers. Funded by the federal government, these highways did not have tolls except when they incorporated existing turnpikes in the eastern states. They followed the routes of the old US highways but bypassed town centers. The new freeways had a greater population density along their routes and more exits than the old state turnpikes. Rather than proprietary concessions for a captive audience, the interstates produced clusters of gas stations, motels, and eateries at their exit cloverleaves. Howard Johnson's motor lodges were well suited to this layout, combining as they did two of the three basics of highway travel (the other being fuel), but no longer did Howard Johnson's stand out in the way it had on the toll roads or rural two-lane highways. The clutter of suburban chain lodging and eating places gave Howard Johnson's competition it had not experienced before.

In 1961, Howard Johnson's became a public company, its stock closing on the first day at $52 per share after being initially priced at $38.[34] In 1960, on the eve of going public, net sales were $95 million, compared to $35.8 million in 1951. At the time of the offering the company owned 265 restaurants outright, another 340 were held by franchisees, and there were 88 motor lodges (all franchised). Howard Johnson's operated in thirty-three states and the Bahamas. There were now also ten Red Coach Grill restaurants.[35]

The corporation was taking over more of its sites from franchisees, and by 1963 the number of company-owned establishments exceeded those of franchisees. An innovator in the world of franchising, Howard Johnson himself nevertheless regarded the practice as an expedient to be used only when money was tight. All things being equal, he preferred to run the units directly. As he told *Forbes* magazine in 1962, doing away with franchises meant "double-barreled profits," both retail and wholesale.[36]

Three years earlier, in 1959, Howard Deering Johnson officially stepped down as head of the company, ceding his position to his son Howard Brennan "Bud" Johnson. The corporation's headquarters was moved to New York's Rockefeller Center, but the elder Johnson continued to come to his old office in Wollaston and remained closely involved with the company's continued expansion. In the mid-1960s, Howard Johnson's became a coast-to-coast chain with the first opening of locations in California.

That Howard Johnson Sr. continued to be in charge is evident from memoirs by Pierre Franey and Jacques Pépin. Authors of well-known cookbooks, Franey and Pépin were French-trained chefs who worked in the 1940s and 1950s at New York's Le Pavillon, universally regarded at that time as the finest restaurant in America. Le Pavillon was the creation of Henri Soulé, obsessive and perfectionistic like Howard Johnson, but more mercurial in temperament. Johnson had tried to lure Franey away from the dictatorial Soulé, promising a high salary, regular hours, generous vacations, and the perquisites of being an executive. In 1960, Soulé attempted to save money by cutting the hours of his kitchen staff and Franey walked out, along with Pépin and a number of other cooks. Franey immediately accepted Howard Johnson's offer and brought Pépin with him.

Aided by Pépin and Albert Kumin, formerly pastry chef of the Four Seasons, Franey tested and revamped the recipes and service practices of Howard Johnson's, keeping the ice cream and clam chowder but changing nearly everything else. Mr. Johnson supported the attempt to make as much improvement as was possible on a vast cooking system that relied on central commissaries. The changes were significant: Instead of supplying masses of frozen materials at one time, smaller shipments were sent to restaurants and these in turn were thawed out in smaller batches. Basics such as precooked chicken or stock for soup were now made at the commissaries, not outsourced. Butter replaced margarine; and fresh vegetables that required chopping replaced those that were industrially cut up, frozen, and ready to use.[37]

This was neither a brief nor symbolic association—Franey and Pépin stayed with Howard Johnson's for ten years, until Bud Johnson effectively took over shortly before his father's death in 1972. Pépin greatly admired the senior Howard Johnson but disapproved of his son, who surrounded himself with well-credentialed but often inexperienced advisers and made cutting food costs a priority. Prime graded steak was replaced by Choice, then Select, and finally by frozen pre-cut portions.[38] Economies of this sort were not invisible, and consumers noticed and commented on a perceived decline in the quality of what was served at Howard Johnson's. A witticism of the 1970s held that "Howard Johnson's ice cream comes in twenty-eight flavors, and its food in one."[39]

AMERICAN FOOD WITH ECCENTRIC TOUCHES

Howard Johnson's has an enduring reputation for wholesome but unimaginative food, but this is not a completely fair characterization. The fried clams, for example, were originally quite unusual and not an easy sell at first. Virtually unknown outside of New England, the clams were promoted by Howard Johnson's at the 1939–1940 New York World's Fair. It took a further concerted campaign to win acceptance—this was not a case of simply providing what people already were accustomed to consuming.

The fact that the clams would become a fondly regarded signature item of Howard Johnson's was an accomplishment, not an accident.

Even food more familiar than clams was prepared and presented with originality. Not only was the ice cream different because of its high butterfat content, but ice-cream sundaes were topped with a cookie embossed with the Howard Johnson's logo, and a special-shaped scoop was used for ice-cream cones, giving the top a distinctive triangular look. "Frankforts" were grilled in butter, served on toasted square buns, and presented in small cardboard troughs.[40] A 1939 booklet put out by the company lists as its "stars" the ice cream, frankforts, fried clams, salads, three-decker sandwiches, bakery products, "sizzling steaks," coffee, and candies. Some offerings, such as the steak, were distinguished in the booklet's promotional language only by the quality of ingredients, others by their preparation in "spotless" surroundings (bakery products, candies). Still others were presented as unique innovations (clams, frankforts, triple-decker sandwiches).[41]

As it grew larger, the company tried to present itself as continuing to be intimately involved in the supply and preparation of what was served. Howard Johnson made much of his personal association with his clam supplier, a small company run by four Greek immigrant brothers named Soffron in Ipswich, Massachusetts.[42] Originally the Soffrons supplied hard-shell clams harvested around Ipswich. Beginning in 1951, however, the restaurant started using strips made from the clam "feet" rather than the soft and more perishable bellies. "Atlantic Surf" clams were preferred over Ipswich hard-shells because they had a relatively large digging foot. Menus after 1951 refer to fried "tendersweet" clams that yielded more uniform and crispy strips than the earlier clams, which had a greater assortment of textures. The Atlantic Surf clams were also easier to freeze and rethaw, as they were tougher than belly clam pieces. By the 1960s, the Soffron Company, whose sole customer was Howard Johnson's, operated clam-processing plants from Maryland to Maine.[43]

Photographs by Paul Davis

CLAMS: "SWEET AS A NUT"

Fig. 48. Advertisement for fried clams, 1950s.

A 1941 menu reveals what the prewar Howard Johnson's offered.[44] Under "Specialties" there are several varieties of steak: club sirloin, cubed steak, minute steak, and an open tenderloin sandwich, ranging in price from 45 cents to $1.25. Two additional daily specials are indicated by pasted labels: a sirloin steak dinner and a broiled chicken dinner. The fried clams are set off in bold type and described as "Howard Johnson's Ipswich Clam Plate with Tartar Sauce" (50 cents). Also in bold type is "Howard Johnson's Grilled Frankforts and Potato Salad" (40 cents). The same idiosyncratic and archaic usage applied to frankfurters/frankforts is given to the hamburger, referred to as "Hamburg Steak." Among the specialties is a "Grilled

Hamburg Plate" and there are three "Hamburg" and "Hamburg Steak" sandwiches.

After the Specialties there follow more than thirty different sundaes, plain ice cream, a few cakes, dessert waffles, and pies. Thirty-five sandwiches are listed, including radically plain offerings, such as a jelly sandwich and some now obsolete varieties: a Western (containing a ham, pepper, and onion omelet), cream cheese and guava jelly, and cube steak. An odd item included in this menu that seems to expire after a brief flare of life is "chop suey roll." It's among the few dishes with even a vague ethnic reference in an otherwise bland smorgasbord of offerings. On menus of the 1950s one finds chili con carne and chow mein. Curried chicken, first served in the 1930s, would become a standard offering . The curry recipe called for an amount of curry powder so small as to put one in mind of a *Mad Men*–era definition of a really dry martini as gin poured into a martini glass with the word "vermouth" whispered over it.[45]

A 1944 menu from Rochester, New York, one of the handful of Howard Johnson's that stayed open during the war, is almost exactly the same as the 1941 menu, but it is supplemented by typewritten inserts indicating specials (several kinds of lobster, for example) and à la carte items for those not wanting to order a complete meal. Somewhat unexpectedly, given war rationing, this is an unusually elaborate Howard Johnson's menu in terms of the sheer number of options presented. The menu cover shows a Howard Johnson's restaurant building and the logo with the red *V* for "victory" springing out of the cupola. The bulk of the space is taken up by a plane, a tank, and naval warships.[46]

Soon after the war ended, the menu expanded and new "traditions" were established. Among the chain's novelties was Welsh rarebit—toast with a savory melted cheese sauce poured over. Here the cheese was served in a casserole dish with bacon and toast points. Other additions to the menu were date-nut bread, fried scallops, fried butterfly shrimp, and griddlecakes. New England origins were evoked by Boston baked beans

Fig. 49. Cover from Howard Johnson's wartime menu, Rochester, 1944.

(now an almost-forgotten regional specialty), which could be had with either brown bread or frankforts. Hamburg steak sandwiches were still available but not highlighted. The frankforts on one menu are listed under salads (frankforts with potato salad and barbecue relish), on another as a "suggestion," served with baked beans *and* brown bread.[47]

Several items on these menus were available to take home. Howard Johnson's dessert sauces (chocolate, fudge, butterscotch, and the like) were sold as to-go items, along with brown bread, date-nut bread, baked beans, French dressing, and Welsh rarebit. Fried clams, onion rings, shrimp, scallops, and potatoes were sold frozen. Howard Johnson's emphasized "take-home" as opposed to "take-out," the idea being that if you enjoyed something at the restaurant, you could serve it at home, but not that you would buy ready-to-eat food in place of sitting down in the restaurant. People in the 1950s and 1960s still cooked at home, and the growing popularity of frozen foods and TV dinners had accustomed them to reheating prepared dishes.

By the early 1960s chicken potpie had been added to the list of Howard Johnson's specialties, and judging from its advertising, the company had accepted the long-established popular abbreviated nickname "Ho-Jo's." It also finally embraced the term "hamburger" in place of "Hamburg steak" and offered several different varieties under this category heading. "Italian spaghetti" and "Italian-style ravioli," seem to represent the limit for imported food ideas. In the ersatz fashion of the period, a special "New Englander" (75 cents) was devised, consisting of barbecued beef on a roll; a choice of a cup of soup, grapefruit juice, or tomato juice; and a beverage.[48]

A DIFFERENT BUSINESS CLIMATE

Howard Johnson's continued to expand rapidly in the 1960s, nominally under the direction of Bud Johnson, but in fact with considerable involvement of his father, whose obsession with quality and standardization offset his son's cost-cutting and desire to diversify. One of the challenges the company dealt with, neither particularly well nor poorly, was the civil rights movement, which targeted restaurants, hotels, and other public accommodations, especially those that had branches in both the segregated South and the integrated North. Desegregation attempts began with the national retailer Woolworth, a chain of stores that carried all manner of small-sized goods and provided lunch-counter restaurants. Peaceful sit-ins began in February 1960 at a Woolworth lunch counter in Greensboro, North Carolina. Integrated groups sat at the counter and ordered apple pie (significantly and deliberately), but were not served. Their attempts to eat at the store's restaurant drew national attention to the injustice of discrimination and led to picketing and boycotts of Woolworths in Northern locations.

A 1957 meeting of Howard Johnson's executives and franchisees at Cornell University, home to a famed school of hotel administration, showed the prevailing attitude of American corporations that the sit-ins challenged. John Sherry, a Cornell Law School professor, discussed the potentially embarrassing necessity of conforming to the segregation practices of Southern states. If local custom or law dictated segregation and a restaurant manager or franchisee was compelled to refuse service to someone on the basis of color, this should be done, he urged, with courtesy and tact. It should be pointed out to the barred patron that the company's overall policy was to provide meals to everyone without discrimination; that the manager himself would much prefer to have his patronage, "but that locally you are up against it." Optimistically, Professor Sherry believed that such a person, courteously denied service, would retain a favorable impression of the experience and so be inclined to visit Howard Johnson's when traveling in the northern United States. He also thought the issues raised by racial discrimination were not likely to be settled within the lifetimes of his audience members.[49]

In 1962, five years after this meeting, Howard Johnson's was targeted by a project called "Freedom Highways" that demanded racial integration at highway facilities in Maryland, Virginia, North Carolina, and Florida:

segregated states regarded as more likely than those of the Deep South to be influenced by such a campaign. In North Carolina some Howard Johnson's units immediately desegregated, but those in Raleigh, Statesville, Durham, and Greensboro, run by franchisees, resisted. The Statesville police dispersed a crowd of six hundred by spraying them with agricultural pesticide vapor. In 1963 demonstrators gathered repeatedly at the Durham Howard Johnson's, demanding that African Americans be given service. The company was embarrassed by the protests, but didn't take any sort of leading position on this issue. The Wollaston office maintained by Howard Deering Johnson was picketed by Harvard and Radcliffe students, along with members of organizations such as CORE (the Congress of Racial Equality).[50] By the end of 1963 the North Carolina state government had enacted legislation to require national chains to desegregate, whether run by franchisees or not, but only the passage of the federal 1964 Civil Rights Act definitively prohibited racial discrimination in public spaces.[51]

National franchised brands, including Howard Johnson's, weathered this crisis and, with varying degrees of enthusiasm, integrated their facilities. After the initial campaigns over the likes of Woolworth and Howard Johnson's, the flash points in the mid-1960s were privately owned restaurants such as the Pancake Pantry in Nashville or Lester Maddox's Pickrick in Atlanta.[52] Maddox, who had never been involved in politics before dramatically barring African Americans from his restaurant, would parlay his resistance to integration into an improbably successful campaign for governor of Georgia in 1966, a reminder that the capitulation of national chains and the passage of the Civil Rights Act did not end the confrontations in the South.

While civil rights was a serious moral challenge, the gravest business challenge to Howard Johnson's in the 1960s was unquestionably that posed by fast food. McDonald's, Burger King, Taco Bell, and Kentucky Fried Chicken trimmed and improved on the Howard Johnson's highway restaurant model by specializing in one or two items and putting into effect a system that allowed patrons to get their food quickly and eat it in a minimally decorated restaurant environment, or even in their cars. Waiters, dishwashers, and experienced cooks were not needed.

The new chains took further the streamlined commissary system of Howard Johnson's, so that each unit's "kitchen" was simply an assembly point and the limited variety of offerings made it possible to hire inexperienced personnel, such as high-school students and others willing to accept low pay. Constant turnover was considered a manageable problem, offset by reduced labor costs and the short training time necessary for a largely automated kitchen.

Fast food took over the American highway interchange and suburban shopping corridors, changing the roadside iconography of America as dramatically as anything in the previous fifty years. In January 1960 there were only 102 McDonald's, and it was still largely a California chain. By 1966 there were 750.[53]

Howard Johnson's slow, agonizing extinction was due more to circumstances than a strategic failure to cope with the fast-food invasion. Fast food and the energy crisis surprisingly did not devastate Howard Johnson's performance in the 1970s, despite the fact that 85 percent of its customers were motorists. Except for 1974 (with the sudden impact of the first fuel crisis), Howard Johnson's surpassed its previous sales and profit records every year through the end of the 1970s. The company responded to the first oil embargo by concentrating more on population centers than on highways, instituting twenty-four-hour service in most of its company-run restaurants, increasing seating, and organizing more special promotions. It also installed cocktail lounges in place of soda fountains in 100 of its branches, a move similar to what Schrafft's was doing in order to change a now excessively wholesome (that is, unprofitable) image.[54]

Howard Johnson's was able to make up for some of the long-term stagnation in its basic restaurant business. The motor inns, appealing to a middle-class family market segment, represented 16 percent of sales in

1978, but 43 percent of earnings. The Red Coach Grill was an early foray into a different dining experience and in the 1960s the group of some thirty-odd branches of this brand were upgraded and featured elaborate menus and cocktails. A casual dining restaurant directed at a younger audience called the Ground Round was inaugurated in 1969, and there were more than sixty of these by the mid-1970s. The Ground Round was something between a simplified Red Coach and more up-to-date Howard Johnson's, combining what was considered a fun adult atmosphere with a family-friendly ambience. Ground Round served beer in pitchers and pop-corn instead of bread; peanuts roasted in their shells were handed out by a mascot called Bingo the Clown. The restaurants could also be rented out for children's parties.[55]

There was, however, a perceptible lack of investment and decline in quality in the core business. Howard Johnson Sr. had been proud of spend-ing a relatively high percentage of his gross revenue on food—48 percent as opposed to the industry standard of 38 percent—because this represented a commitment to quality over adherence to a fixed limit on food expenses. For purposes of comparison with contemporary business metrics, the Chipotle chain, which emphasizes fresh-made or chopped ingredients, is now thought to be in danger of crossing a sustainable frontier by spend-ing 35 percent of its revenue on food costs.[56] Savings to offset relatively high food costs were supposed to come from improving the commissary-kitchen system and monitoring procedures at the units. For a long time this worked quite well.

When he took over in the late 1960s and early 1970s, Howard "Bud" Johnson Jr. fundamentally changed the strategy and practice, reducing the seemingly excessive apportioning of expense to food preparation. Outsourcing food supplies or replacing butter with margarine were not unreasonable from a management perspective, but coupled with under-investment in facilities, such moves opened the way for competing busi-nesses to erode Howard Johnson's basic appeal.

In 1979, when Howard Johnson's was sold to the British company Imperial Group Limited, there were 1,040 restaurants (75 percent company-owned) and 520 motor inns (25 percent company-owned).[57] The price was $630 million, about $28 per share. Imperial inherited a run-down chain of restaurants and lodging places with a cumbersome structure, wherein a franchisee often ran the restaurant attached to a motel owned by the company. Imperial pressured franchisees to refurbish, offering loans as inducements and terminating the franchise arrangements in recalcitrant cases. Its management instituted a central reservation system and corporate discounts for the motels. Restaurants were encouraged to cut costs by buying outside of the commissary system. In 1983, Imperial established a lodging chain dubbed Plaza Hotels, intended for business rather than leisure travelers, which featured meeting and banquet rooms, lounges, and executive floors. The Ground Round restaurant chain was expanded to 210 units (two dozen or so run by franchisees still exist today, mostly in the East and northern Midwest).

None of these measures helped the bottom line. In 1985, Imperial sold the company, except for the Ground Round restaurants, to Marriott Corporation for about half the price it had paid, not accounting for the substantial inflation of this era. Marriott then turned around and sold the franchised Howard Johnson's restaurants, along with the entire motel and hotel chain, to another company, Prime Motor Inns. Marriott now had little inducement to invest in its own Howard Johnson's restaurants, whose name was also that of a competing line of hotels. Company-owned Howard Johnson's restaurants were thus first converted to other brands such as Saga or Big Boy and then sold. By 1991 there were only fifty Howard Johnson's restaurants run by Marriott. Meanwhile Prime had also decided to divest itself of Howard Johnson's restaurants while retaining the inns. In 1986 the franchisees, now cast adrift by Prime, formed a group called Franchise Associates, which obtained the exclusive right to the Howard Johnson's restaurant trademark and acquired the remaining seventeen Marriott units. By the early 1990s only about 100 Howard Johnson's restaurants survived in twenty-six states, a disappearing shadow of a presence when compared with its heyday twenty or thirty years before.

The recession of 1989–1991 forced Prime to sell its Howard Johnson's hotel business to Blackstone Capital Partners, which merged it with Days Inn and took a new hotel chain public, dubbed Hospitality Franchise Systems (later HFS). The hotels have done reasonably well in the past twenty years, mostly run by Cendant Corporation. In 2006 this company split into four pieces and the hotels are now part of Wyndham Worldwide.

The restaurants, on the other hand, have virtually disappeared, a fondly remembered but commercially obsolete recollection of a certain kind of American wholesomeness. The 1991 franchise group attempted to update the design with a more restrained, less quirky look and a menu that featured things like oat-bran muffins, salads, and "garden pizzas." This was the last effort at cooperation. In the 1990s the restaurants were, in effect, vestigial branches without a trunk, and no new ones were established. As franchisees became discouraged with competition, they sold out to chains such as Denny's or simply retired. The perception of a dying brand accelerated. No longer were Howard Johnson's restaurants familiar features of the culinary landscape; they were now curious relics. In 2005 even the New York City landmark Howard Johnson's established near Times Square in 1955 served its last ice-cream cone, and that same year Franchise Associates failed. Cendant reclaimed the right to the Howard Johnson's restaurant name, and then sold it off to a group called La Mancha L.L.C. When plans to relaunch the brand foundered, La Mancha closed up shop. As of late 2015 there are only two Howard Johnson's restaurants left: a stand-alone restaurant in Lake Placid, New York, that is up for sale, and a Howard Johnson's Inn in Bangor, Maine. The latter retains its restaurant, which occupies an original Nims-style space, but the roof is no longer orange.

Howard Johnson's was not done in simply by the rise of fast food. Its own managerial errors and its difficulties repositioning itself as a new-style mid-market restaurant undermined its image and established an enduring impression of mediocrity and obsolescence. On the other hand, as the proliferation of memorializing websites testifies, Howard Johnson's is an object of nostalgia, even more so than Schrafft's. However, it is not something that could ever be revived.

The impression of being permanently stuck in the 1950s is the result of a failure to adapt in the way that other casual dining places have. The innovative, if awful, oat-bran muffins of the 1990s notwithstanding, Howard Johnson's was irremediably identified with famous but no longer popular dishes such as fried clams and potpies. Howard Johnson's began to fail once its founder departed, but it's not clear that even the application of his obsessive ingenuity could have advantageously repositioned the restaurants to survive in a hostile new environment dominated by the fast-food hamburger chain.

In their early incarnations the fast-food businesses were not the impersonal corporate behemoths they have since become. They were usually the creation of an obsessed perfectionist in the mold of Howard Johnson. Colonel Sanders, who at the age of sixty-five peddled his recipe for pressure-cooker fried chicken across the country, was the most colorful of these figures.[58] Ray Kroc, the founder of McDonald's as a national chain, was a less sunny version of Howard Johnson. A fanatic for rules and routines, Kroc was a visionary in the literal sense, who put into effect the idea of an empire after a visit in 1965 to the original San Bernardino hamburger establishment run by the McDonald brothers. Awestruck, Kroc envisioned a business with hordes of happy customers, speedy service, and almost no infrastructure costs.[59] Once he bought out the brothers and was firmly in charge, Kroc made sure that all branches conformed to produce the same product rather than simply making money by selling ingredients or equipment and letting the franchisees run their stores sloppily.[60]

Sanders, Kroc, and others developed what was at its core a take-out business oriented around a single product that could be run by unskilled personnel, for customers who couldn't care less about direct personal contact but who wanted a tasty and convenient meal or snack quickly (Ray Kroc established 50 seconds as the maximum time to deliver an order).[61] These new quick-service restaurants were progeny of Howard Johnson's. They ran according to rigid routines and uniform practices, but these were simpler than at Howard Johnson's restaurants. Burger King, McDonald's, and the like didn't have hundreds of menu items, and with a largely take-out service neither did they require complicated maintenance, service, and cooking procedures.

McDonald's and its imitators eventually returned, partially, to the in-store dining model, redefining the kid-friendly notions developed by Howard Johnson's, by putting in play areas. An important difference, however, was the hamburger. Like tacos and fried chicken, it was a single item with minor variations that could sustain an entire corporation. Howard Johnson's offered different kinds of "Hamburg steak," but these came on a plate with accompaniments and garnishes (gravy, for example), or as a standard sort of sandwich—hardly something to be prepared instantaneously or eaten on the go. The fast-food burger is quite different: it can be eaten with one hand, even while driving. It is a "fun food" for kids, its high fat content—now, of course, criticized—means it is a convenient vehicle for calories that can constitute either a meal or a snack.

Why did the hamburger triumph as opposed to the hot dog? Frankfurters are also easy to eat in the car and historically they were the food item most closely identified with the United States in the late-nineteenth and early-twentieth centuries. This isn't easy to answer, but it's clear from the lack of mammoth national hot-dog chains that even now there is something about the frank that doesn't lend itself to the industry. Like the hamburger, the "frankfurter" or "wiener" shows its Germanic origin by its name. These sausages were brought to the United States by Germans, who, along with the Irish, were the largest segment of immigrants in the mid-nineteenth century. The original Wiener was white and predominantly veal; the Frankfurter spicier and with a greater proportion of beef. They were just another kind of sausage until the moment they started being wrapped in buns. This ingenious invention seems to have been first marketed by Charles Feltman, whose Feltman's German Gardens in Coney Island started as a food cart in 1867. Nathan Handwerker, an employee of Feltman's, opened Nathan's, also on Coney Island, in 1916. The hot dog was popularized by the St. Louis World's Fair of 1904, but so close was the association with its New York birthplace that the name for them in parts of the United States (Michigan, for example) is still "Coney Islands."[62]

As with the hamburger somewhat later, the innovation of putting a ground meat preparation inside a bun made it more convenient. At first this attracted amusement, even mistrustful derision. Because of the resemblance to the (German) dachshund, the frankfurter was dubbed a "hot dog" by the 1890s at the latest. A comical rhyme asked, "How could you be so mean, to grind up all those doggies in your hot-dog machine?"[63] This bit of doggerel also alluded to both the advantage and disadvantage of hamburgers as well as hot dogs: they were produced with ground meat, which made them inexpensive compared to identifiable cuts of meat, but also regarded as dubious in their composition.

Before 1920, hamburgers and hot dogs were essentially novelties like cotton candy or saltwater taffy—eaten at amusement parks, baseball games, state fairs, or from street carts (Sabrett's hot dogs in New York City and Vienna Beef in Chicago are survivors from this era). They were not considered real foods and were thus regarded as lower-class and unhealthful, although certainly tasty and amusing. More than any other purveyor, White Castle, founded in Wichita, Kansas, in 1921, created the modern hamburger.[64] It perfected small, flat hamburgers accompanied by a specially designed square bun with a flat bottom and puffed top that, unlike sliced bread or toast, could absorb the meat juices without becoming soaked. White Castle encouraged people to take the small hamburgers away with them, so that the stores functioned as rudimentary restaurants, but also as, in effect, purveyors of infinitely reproducible, simple, quickly prepared food. The company emphasized the purity of its burgers, using the white image of the crenellated castle exterior while the stainless steel counter gave a hygienic look to the establishments' interior. Standardization was publicized, even boasted about, to demonstrate the quality of a product otherwise viewed with suspicion. Here again, in our age in which individual, artisanal treatment is regarded as superior to robots or freezers for preparing food, it requires an effort to understand the attraction of machine-made, "untouched by human hands" mass production. In 1932, a White Castle brochure instructed the reader:

> When you sit at a White Castle, remember that you are one of several thousands; you are sitting on the same kind of stool; you are being served on the same kind of counter; the coffee you drink is made in accordance with a certain formula; the hamburger you eat is prepared in exactly the same way over a gas flame of the same intensity . . . even the men who serve you are guided by standards of precision which have been thought out from beginning to end.[65]

Standardization is good, according to this set of assumptions, not only because of hygiene but because an exacting and beneficent organization makes sure you are guaranteed a consistent product and experience. The White Castle customer of the 1930s was not flattered into thinking he or she was special or had particular preferences that could be catered to—the reverse of today's Starbucks model of efficiency and predictability combined with individual customization. Starbucks too establishes standards of performance, such as how long customers wait to order, or how fast baristas complete orders, but would never want the public to focus on the mass-production aspects of the enterprise, seeking rather an impression of personal solicitude.

White Castle may not single-handedly have ensured the victory of the hamburger, but it set the path for the postwar fast-food industry. Some later chains, such as Krystal in the South, kept the small-format hamburgers (what would now be called sliders), but most companies made the burger larger than White Castle's dainty squares. The Big Boy, served by a hamburger chain with that name started in 1937, was imitated in the 1960s with McDonald's Big Mac (two 1.6-ounce patties, "special sauce," lettuce, American cheese, pickles, and onions on a three-layered bun) and Burger King's Whopper (4 ounces of grilled beef served on a bun with tomato, onion, lettuce, pickle, mayonnaise, and ketchup). The so-called supersizing of burgers and drinks was the result of this competition to provide lots of calories inexpensively.

The urban hamburger model of White Castle was transformed by highways, suburban roads, and endless yet ubiquitous strip malls. Unlike White Castle, McDonald's embraced franchising, as did other chain restaurants whose expansion had to be rapid. McDonald's may be thought of as combining the White Castle hamburger with Howard Johnson's franchising, close supervision, and roadside orientation.

The durable hot dog remains a staple for backyard barbecues and the like, but in the vast, dreary world of highway commerce, it has for a long time been superseded by the juicier allure and aroma of burgers.[66] With its deliberately quaint "Frankforts" and "Hamburg steaks," Howard Johnson's was able, modestly, to exploit both products. At some point around 1970, the multiplication of signature items (ice cream, clams, chicken potpies, Boston baked beans) stopped being a winning strategy and the fast-food chains raced ahead by having a limited menu and faster service.

Now McDonald's and its peers face some of the same difficulties in assuring quality and protecting identity that once plagued Howard Johnson's in the 1970s. McDonald's is universally recognized, but is regarded as offering a narrow range of low-quality options. Attempts to diversify its menu have led to slower service and diminished attention to its basic products, such as cheeseburgers and French fries. McDonald's core constituency is thus alienated because the chain is no longer reliable in terms of speed or quality (the French fries are sometimes cold), but expanding menu options has not attracted loyal new customers. Members of the millennial generation perceive McDonald's as unhealthful in its offerings, too suburban, and at the same time unappealingly lower-class.[67] The specific complaints against Howard Johnson's in the 1970s and McDonald's in the 2010s might be different, but the perception of blandness, homogeneity, and decline in the core product is similar. What both chains possessed in their best years was the ability to put forward a believable fantasy of ease—a peculiar kind of cheerfulness. When Howard Johnson's lost the image of being a treat, of being fun, it started to lose its way. McDonald's has been able to flourish for a longer time than Howard Johnson's did as a convenience rather than an experience, but it too has lost the sparkling sense of attractive, push-button modernity that the McDonald brothers created in San Bernardino and that Ray Kroc was able to replicate.

Howard Johnson's skillfully exploited this delight in uniformity, efficiency, and cheerfulness, thereby allowing it to endure as a cultural icon, if nothing else. In a recent food memoir, a writer for *The New Yorker*, Adam Gopnik, dreamily recalls the Howard Johnson's of his childhood:

> It was not the deliciousness of the food—my mother made better burgers—but the overcharge of optimism that made the meal matter.[68]

His words are an evocative memorial to an American institution and to consumer preferences that have been swept away by changing tastes and ways of life.

HOWARD JOHNSON'S
TWENTY-EIGHT ICE CREAM FLAVORS
(IN ORDER OF POPULARITY)

1. Vanilla
2. Chocolate
3. Chocolate chip
4. Strawberry
5. Coffee
6. Maple walnut
7. Pistachio
8. Butter crunch
9. Banana
10. Peach
11. Peppermint
12. Burgundy cherry
13. Butter pecan
14. Caramel fudge
15. Frozen pudding
16. Macaroon
17. Orange-pineapple
18. Pecan brittle
19. Butterscotch
20. Black raspberry
21. Pineapple
22. Coconut
23. Fruit salad
24. Lemon
25. Grape nut
26. Peanut brittle
27. Ginger
28. Apple

MAMMA LEONE'S
ITALIAN ENTERTAINMENT

This chapter is centered on Mamma Leone's, an Italian restaurant in New York that flourished for nearly a century, from 1906 until 1994, and the chapter that follows will focus on the Mandarin, a Chinese establishment in San Francisco. These are examples of what are often referred to as "ethnic restaurants," a somewhat recent coinage—its first appearance in the *New York Times* was in Craig Claiborne's 1959 review of an Indonesian restaurant.[1] The concept of a relatively inexpensive place to eat that serves another country's cuisine was long established before this date, however. Italian and Chinese were the most successful of the category, but Mexican, Japanese, Indian, and Thai have also achieved prominence in the United States.

The history of what are often called "ethnic" restaurants reflects America's enthusiastic, if often inaccurate, embrace of foreign cuisines. The term "ethnic" is misleading, as it implies a degree of subordination to a norm set by a complementary "regular" restaurant type. In fact, it is impossible to think about dining out in America without considering these

Fig. 50. Mamma Leone's "Carnevale" menu, 1983.

restaurants established by immigrants who first served their own communities and then found a wider public for their cuisine. They can be thought of as "foreign" restaurants or "immigrant" restaurants, but these are not much better or more accurate descriptors than "ethnic."[2] The restaurants covered by whatever term we are using offer a foreign cuisine, begin and often remain family-run businesses, adapt their food to American tastes, and charge inexpensive prices in a modest setting.

Foreign restaurants are established, it seems almost obvious to say, because people take up residence in another country and wish to offer a new culinary experience to those outside their ethnic community. However, this association of restaurants with immigrants is not always what it seems; most Indian restaurants in the United States and Britain have actually been founded by migrants from Pakistan and Bangladesh, while some Italian restaurants in the United States are now owned by Croatians. Many Japanese restaurants are run by Chinese owners and cooks.

The American colonies and the independent United States were formed by waves of immigration, but it was only in the late nineteenth century that restaurants serving the food of other nations started to attract customers from beyond the immigrant enclaves. All over the world it has been common for entrepreneurs to establish places to eat and drink oriented toward foreign workers or merchants homesick for their own cuisine. What is distinctive about the United States is that foreign restaurants also intrigued customers from the majority culture. Defying nativist, made-in-America sentiment, these diners tend to experiment with cuisines and usually patronize a mix of restaurants rather than simply adding one Italian or one Chinese restaurant to their repertoire. The statement "I don't want to have Thai food tonight; I had it yesterday," or some variation thereof, is routine in the United States but strange, even senseless, in most of the world, not only in Thailand.

The United States has more than 40,000 Chinese and 28,000 Italian restaurants (excluding pizzerias).[3] Few of them cater to an exclusively or even predominantly Chinese or Italian clientele. The adoption of ethnic restaurants by the wider culture was already happening by 1900, when American food was becoming defined less in terms of local or regional traditions but by eclecticism and the availability of restaurants in many categories—so much so that taste preferences eventually shifted toward novelty more than on what Grandma (or Grandma's restaurant) served. As early as 1868, an anonymous San Franciscan assured the "distant reader" that not only was French cookery transplanted to the soil of California, but German, Italian, and Chinese was as well.[4] New York started catching up by 1885, when foreign restaurants were said to be sufficiently numerous (upward of twenty-five) and pleasant that they afforded interesting alternatives to pretentious dining places with exorbitant prices on the one hand, and 15-cent hash houses on the other.

By 1890, New York's and San Francisco's culinary diversity were becoming a defining feature of American taste. A magazine article in 1893 acknowledged that Paris was distinguished for the quality of its restaurants, but touted New York's superior variety.[5]

Of course, as the earlier chapters on Delmonico's and Antoine's showed, the high-end American restaurant was based on French models, but France was a special case. Its culinary sovereignty appealed to an adolescent nation not completely confident in the elite aspects of its cultural identity. On the other hand, older societies from Russia to Great Britain would also acknowledge French culinary supremacy, so American deference was part of an international nineteenth-century phenomenon. French restaurants connected America to the globally authoritative cuisine and thus did not qualify as what later would be considered ethnic or really even foreign, because their food exemplified the highest level of international prestige. Besides, they were usually costly, and the point of ethnic restaurants was to be cheap as well as novel.

Another early culinary import was German cuisine, but this too can only partially be counted as an ethnic cuisine, although not because of prestige as in the French case, but because of the rapid assimilation of German immigrants into American culture, especially their food. Early in the course of European settlement of America, German communities were founded by religious refugees, notably in Pennsylvania. The failed Revolution of 1848 sent another wave of German émigrés to the United States, with a result that in the decade before the American Civil War, German beer gardens, Rathskellers, taverns, and restaurants proliferated. Their moderate prices and *gemütlich* atmosphere also attracted American-born customers. Almost by definition German restaurants served beer, but they did so in what would later be called a "family atmosphere" that encouraged German, and later non-German, women to show up on weekends with children in tow.[6]

These antebellum German establishments were arguably the first foreign restaurants patronized by members of the American middle class, but they were different in effect if not intent from what happened with Italian as well as Chinese restaurant owners a few decades later.[7] The Germans' influence on American dining was so extensive and immediate that the foreignness of their food was forgotten. Lager beer became standard; ketchup and cucumber pickles were introduced by Germans and promptly appropriated and Americanized. Coffee cake was an American adaptation of German sweet yeast breads; chicken-fried steak was a variation on Wiener Schnitzel. Texas barbecue, based on beef brisket and smoked sausages, was perfected by German immigrants. Chopped beef "hamburgers," pork sausage "frankfurters," and potato salad were German imports that soon became all-American products.[8] Restaurants that offered familiar but clearly German dishes such as Hasenpfeffer, Sauerbraten, or Wiener Schnitzel do fit the ethnic restaurant pattern, but because so many aspects of German culinary taste had migrated to American food, German restaurants were less conspicuous than their Italian and Chinese counterparts.

In the twentieth century, ethnic restaurants were essentially those offering the cuisine of another country or people, but not French. The

Fig. 51. Lower East Side restaurants, *The New Yorker*, 1938.

diversity of food offerings was already long-standing for New York City when a cover of *The New Yorker* for April 2, 1938, depicted scenes from eight ethnic restaurants: Japanese, Turkish, Scandinavian, Russian, German, Chinese, Jewish, and Italian. On the left side of each scene are listed several dishes from the respective category. Some are standbys, such as sukiyaki, Risotto Milanese, borshch [*sic*], and Apfelstrudel, but there are many now less-familiar preparations: Turkish eggplant kizartma (here spelled "kezartma"); goma-aye (a Japanese sesame sauce dressing); or Russian kissel (a berry soup or dessert). The Italian section lists Linguine alla Marinara, Ravioli Bolognese, Trippa alla Pomidoro, and some kind of sausage (*salsicia*)—but the rest of the text is obscured by the illustration.

But along with Chinese, Italian has been the most successful cuisine among those consistently perceived and presented as foreign. In the mid-nineteenth century macaroni had already become part of grand French cuisine, and various kinds of macaroni and cheese comprised the most popular restaurant entrées in fancy American restaurants. Macaroni was exceptional, however, and there were almost no other Italian dishes common on elite menus. Beginning with the First World War and voluntary meat rationing, spaghetti became a standard item both at home and dining out for people with no connection to Italy. Beginning in the 1960s, pizza would become among the most commonly consumed foods worldwide, but without entirely losing its Italian origin.

ITALIAN RESTAURANTS

Italian food in America has been an uninterrupted success story. John Mariani's book title *How Italian Food Conquered the World* is only slightly exaggerated.[9] It certainly conquered the United States, although not all at once and not without some changes in style, presentation, and culinary aesthetic. The history of Italian restaurants in the United States falls into three phases. From 1890 to 1920 the typical Italian restaurant was a small, picturesque artists' hangout, popular with urban "Bohemians" who liked wine, informality, and hearty but interesting food. These cozy places gave way in the interwar years to large spaghetti palaces, featuring giant portions and a celebratory, over-the-top Italian atmosphere. These, in turn, beginning in the 1980s, receded in favor of sophisticated and expensive venues serving a regionally inspired, usually Northern Italian, cuisine.

At first, expert opinion opposed this unfamiliar set of food habits and ridiculed Italian immigrants' loyalty to them. At the beginning of the twentieth century, home economists and professional nutritionists viewed Italian food as oily, spicy, garlicky, and too reliant on vegetables. Orthodox nutritional opinion favored milk, meat, and blandness. Italian food was also regarded as too complicated. In 1876 a writer for a magazine entitled *Cook* complained that a pasta and meat sauce recipe offered by a certain Signor Barottoni was difficult, costly, and pretentious as it included three kinds of meat, wine, vegetables and nutmeg.[10] Italians in America stubbornly refused to abandon cooking with expensive imported olive oil and persisted in eating what one social reform leader in 1904 described as an "overstimulating and innutritious diet." A social worker from Columbus, Ohio, around the same time noted after visiting an Italian family that they were "still eating spaghetti, not yet assimilated."[11]

Popular prejudice against Italians as anarchists and gangsters might logically have reinforced the party line on the alien and unhealthful aspects of their diet. Nevertheless, despite the reputation of Italian immigrants first as violent anarchists (as exemplified by the Sacco and Vanzetti trial in 1927) and as members of criminal gangs (the Mafia), the popularity of dining in informal Italian restaurants increased in the 1920s and 1930s. The appeal of these restaurants was their flavorful food, plentiful and inexpensive variety, and wine (also inexpensive)—all combined to produce a pleasantly animated experience. The operatic Italian ambience might have been in itself a performance, but a performative aspect accompanies all ethnic food intended for American consumption because the exact cuisine of the home country cannot be reproduced, nor would it be successful if it could be. Italian restaurants offered a particular flamboyance that played to stereotypes of Italians' love of music, amorous appreciation, spontaneity, and volatile personality. Mamma Leone's combined many of these images, refining them into an early example of a "theme" restaurant, a place where the staged ambience is as important as the food.

Mamma Leone's began life, as it were, in 1906 simply as "Leone's." In its forty-year heyday, 1930 to 1970, it provided staggering portions in a setting that offered huge capacity, strolling musicians, and distracting surroundings. When its founder, Luisa Leone, died in 1944, the restaurant was renamed Mamma Leone's. Her son Gene Leone ran the restaurant until 1959, when he sold it to Restaurant Associates for the then-immense sum of $2 million. That same year RA also opened its high-end flagship, the Four Seasons.

Until it was torn down in 1988, Mamma Leone's always made money. According to Nick Valenti, who once headed Restaurant Associates and is now CEO of Patina Restaurant Group, Mamma Leone's earned the company around $10 million annually in the 1980s.[12] It ceased operations due to rising real-estate values, not cash-flow problems. Comprising a series of five three-story buildings in the theatre district, the restaurant sat on land that could be developed more profitably as a high-rise condominium. During its swan-song years, from 1988 until 1994, Mamma Leone's had a kind of somnambulistic life within the Milford Plaza Hotel near Times Square, and some aspects of its exterior look and décor were retained or reproduced, but the move of a just a few blocks seemed to dampen its spirit and Mamma Leone's finally closed definitively in the mid-1990s, already a souvenir of a bygone era.

New Yorkers may remember Mamma Leone's as a shrine of Italian kitsch that was popular with tourists, and so they might be inclined to dismiss it as the Hard Rock Café equivalent of the 1970s and 1980s. This would be an unfair characterization, because whatever the validity of that image, Mamma Leone's pioneered the Italian restaurant for non-Italians, with appealing food and a seductive if ultimately mass-market atmosphere. The refined, subdued Italian restaurant of the present may seem a far cry from the crowded if not raucous Mamma Leone's model, the up-to-date restaurant eschewing slabs of lasagna and veal Parmesan in favor of artisanal pasta, white truffles, or regional cuisine, but the enduring image and success of Italian restaurants in America would be difficult to imagine without Mamma Leone's and restaurants like it.

This evolution in American expectations about Italian restaurants from Bohemian to middle-class to sophisticated reflects changing attitudes toward class as well as ethnicity. The first Italian restaurants were patronized by an avant-garde of artistically minded cognoscenti. For much of the twentieth century, especially from 1920 to about 1980, Italian food branched out beyond New York's Greenwich Village and San Francisco's North Beach and it became a festive, not-too-foreign part of middle-class restaurant culture. Today, Italian food in America has largely escaped the inexpensive, informal model of the past and displaced French cuisine at the high end. It is now the preferred cuisine of the upper class.

This book, as stated before, is not about the ten best restaurants that America ever produced, but rather the ten that could be considered most influential and exemplary. There is no doubt about the influence of Mamma Leone's, which lasted almost ninety years, served 4,000 people a night for decades, exemplified or perhaps even invented the "theme restaurant," and was a must-visit site in New York as much as Antoine's was in New Orleans.

BOHEMIAN RHAPSODY

In 1890, about 100,000 Italian immigrants lived in New York, and 100 cafés and restaurants served their needs.[13] As the comment on spaghetti-eating from the social worker in Columbus, Ohio, indicates, Italians in America were fiercely loyal to the food of their native country. Unlike eastern European Jews, Poles, or other European immigrants whose children and grandchildren adopted generic American food choices as a form of assimilation, Italians saw to it that succeeding generations continued to cook Italian food. Even being teased in school about what you brought from home for lunch, still today a most powerful inducement to culinary conformity, failed to force Italian kids to reject their parents' cooking.

Nevertheless, the New World was different, and immigrant families made a number of adaptations. Much of the change resulted from the much higher standard of living in the United States. American abundance and the favorable relation between wages and purchasing power meant eating soft white bread, drinking wine, and eating meat—all these rarely affordable in Italy. A miner from Agrigento in Sicily working at a Chicago packing house responded to an anthropologist's question about comparing the food of home to the United States: "Forget it, there's no comparison . . . in America I have all I want to eat," he said. Poor people ate like kings in America, according to Rosa Cavalleri, who couldn't believe the amount of white bread (and butter!) she found being served with an average meal—enough to feed a whole village in Italy. When she returned to Lombardy, her former neighbors had trouble believing that she ate meat every day.[14]

American prosperity allowed those who had eaten meat a few times a year in the old country to consume it at least twice a week here. They ate what were marketed as "Italian sausages," which exemplifies both affluence and modern homogenization, since in Italy every village had a different way of making sausages even if the villagers could rarely afford to eat them. In Italy the average peasant or factory worker rarely could afford sausages of any kind, whereas the American Italian sausages were readily available to people with average income. Macaroni (pasta), consumed by the well-to-do in southern Italy, became the emblem of Italian American cooking both at home and in restaurants. Lasagna, cheesecake, or veal, customarily reserved in Italy for great feast occasions such as Easter, Christmas, or a patron saint's day, now became almost humdrum.[15]

By 1890, Italian restaurants were the most popular foreign restaurants, and, as a *New York Sun* reporter in 1885 observed, a substantial portion of their patronage was from non-Italians.[16] For Italian and other ethnic restaurants, moving out of the enclave of immigrant patrons and catering to the majority population was irresistible, both because there were millions of people of all nations in New York, and because the non-Italians were less critical about the food.

The first American-born patrons of foreign restaurants in the United States, especially patrons of Italian places, were what contemporaries referred to as "Bohemians": unmarried men and women of mildly artistic temperament living in cities, with sophisticated tastes and enough income to spend on small indulgences such as dining out. Without being politically subversive or even interested in politics, Bohemians were unconventional in a way that might encompass cohabitation without marriage or a more-or-less openly gay identity.[17] They were often artists or writers looking for exuberance, informality, and novelty. By 1900, Bohemian neighborhoods such as Greenwich Village and North Beach gained an eclectic, vibrant combination of artistic nonconformists and Italian immigrants. London's Soho also developed Bohemian restaurants in the 1890s, many of them Italian, which served as meeting places for artists and theatre people.[18]

The author of a memoir of pre-earthquake San Francisco defines Bohemianism as "the naturalism of refined people," and a protest against the absurd restrictions of society.[19] Applied to restaurants, this definition exalts authenticity ("naturalism") over ceremony and pretense. The exotic foreign restaurant with simple but intriguing food was therefore preferable to the tediously familiar menu and stifling formality of the grand restaurant. Clarence Edwards's *Bohemian San Francisco* has the subtitle "The Elegant

Art of Dining," but elegance is here artistic and unaffected rather than fancy and formal.

As early as 1860, the celebrated American writer and actress Jane McElhinney, known as "Ada Clare," defined the Bohemian as "a cosmopolite with a general sympathy for the fine arts, and for all things above and beyond convention."[20] The Bohemian is free from the constricting rules of society and its general narrow-mindedness, but is not a self-sacrificing utopian or a political radical. Ada Clare asserted that "principles of good taste and feeling" are a Bohemian's guiding principles for a more joyous as well as authentic life.

The early history of Mamma Leone's was in some ways typical of Italian restaurants in that its first customers were artists, specifically musicians and singers affiliated with New York's Metropolitan Opera. Leone's was originally located on Thirty-Ninth Street and Broadway, right next to the opera house, which would be torn down in the late 1960s when Lincoln Center was built. Girolamo Leone was a wine merchant and his wife, Luisa, was used to making dinners for large numbers of their friends, among them Enrico Caruso, the most celebrated and successful opera star in American and probably world history. At Luisa Leone's thirty-second birthday party in November 1905—a meal she cooked herself on short notice for fifty people—Luisa announced she was opening a restaurant. In fact, according to her son Gene Leone, it was the great Caruso himself who put the matter to Luisa's husband and whose faith in her outstanding cooking convinced Girolamo Leone to go along with the plan to turn their living room into a restaurant dining room. On its first night, April 27, 1906, the menu offered:

Antipasto Supremo
Minestrone
Spaghetti or Ravioli con Ragout di Manzo [meat sauce]
Roast Chicken or Scaloppine [sic] Piccata

Green Salad
Cheese
Spumoni
Caffé Nero[21]

The price for the entire meal was 50 cents and included an inaugural wine supplied by Signor Leone.

Mamma Leone's was one of many intimate restaurants with a table d'hôte menu (minimal choice), plenty of wine, and artsy customers. It differed from most other Italian establishments in that it didn't appeal to a working-class immigrant clientele and was not located in Greenwich Village. Unusual among restaurants in America generally, but not uncommon for Italian places, the creator and undisputed boss of Mamma Leone's was a woman. Three other female-founded restaurants, the Mandarin, Sylvia's, and Chez Panisse, will be discussed later in this book.

Another Italian restaurant that we know Enrico Caruso patronized, although only briefly, was Fior d'Italia in San Francisco, which opened in 1886 and is still in existence. A menu from that first year mentions a special dinner with wine, available for 35 cents, but the courses were not specified. The à-la-carte listings included clam risotto, fritto misto, veal scallopini, and tortellini Bolognese, along with less recognizably Italian items, such as broiled chicken and tenderloin steak.[22] Caruso's last meal at Fior d'Italia took place on April 17, 1906, after which he sang the part of the doomed lover Don José in a performance of *Carmen*. The great earthquake occurred at dawn the next morning, and it touched off a fire that destroyed most of the city. Popular press accounts depicted a panicked Caruso sobbing in the street and running away in a frenzy. This was disputed by the singer, whose departure from the burning city by ferry to Oakland was as orderly as possible under the circumstances. His valet even retrieved his extensive luggage from the sixth floor of the Palace Hotel. At any rate, Caruso never returned.[23]

San Francisco developed a Bohemian, artsy clientele so quickly that by the time Italian restaurants in New York were just being discovered by urban adventurers, certain Italian restaurants in San Francisco were already considered passé. Abandoned by their erstwhile regulars, these restaurants' staged liveliness appealed instead to tourists sent there by hotel guides.[24] This is an early example of a cycle associated with ethnic restaurants whose initial attraction is undiscovered authenticity. A previously hidden gem becomes known to tourists, suburbanites, or bankers, and thus it's "ruined." Perusal of current restaurant-review websites such as Yelp! will confirm that this trajectory from pure to discovered to corrupted continues.

The best-documented example of a first-generation Italian restaurant is Gonfarone's on Macdougal and Eighth Streets in Greenwich Village. We know a lot about the restaurant from the owners' point of view thanks to a memoir by the owner's daughter Maria Sermolino, who worked at her father's establishment from 1900 to 1917.[25] In the 1890s, Gonfarone's had been patronized by Italians and functioned as a kind of boardinghouse, serving only fifteen people at a time. Signora Gonfarone took in Analecto Sermolino as her partner, and they perfected a 50-cent table d'hôte menu and expanded the restaurant's size. Gonfarone's was soon sought out by artists and writers from the neighborhood, and the family deliberately presented what passed for a colorful Italian atmosphere. Sermolino hired an Italian musical trio to play what his daughter recalled as "different sounding noises" to please its Bohemian but actually undiscriminating clientele. A lively tableau featured one of the busboys playing the harmonica, a waiter juggling, and a cook who would emerge from the kitchen brandishing a knife in a picturesque fury as if re-creating in farcical form the violent conclusion of an opera such as I Pagliacci. Maria Sermolino summed up the appeal of Gonfarone's: "a simple, Latin variety of hedonism," a formula of playing at being Italian that would not be extinguished by the social changes of the next hundred years.[26]

As at Leone's, Gonfarone's served minestrone, spaghetti, spumoni, and antipasto (celery hearts, black olives, salami, sardines, anchovies, stewed tomatoes with bread, tuna, and pimento), but the main courses were typically sweetbreads, roast beef, and broiled chicken—more generic American than vividly Italian items. The 50-cent price rose to 60 cents on weekends, but on those days half a lobster with mayonnaise was added to the menu. Gonfarone's was fairly large, packing in as many as 500 customers daily.[27]

Before the First World War, New York and San Francisco boasted dozens of modest, typically small Italian restaurants operating according to a standard model. There were some distinctions—San Francisco already had its Italian American specialty, *cioppino*, a fish soup based on a Genoese recipe, and the restaurants differed as to their entertainment—but they all had inexpensive menus and copious amounts of wine. There might be a back garden, but the restaurant was essentially a private home with a dining room and bar in the front and the kitchen in back. The wife cooked and the husband sold cigars and presided over the dining room. Guffanti's, Maria del Prato's, Renganeschi's, Roversi's, Mori's, Solari's, and Poggi's were some of New York's best-known Italian spots, while Bazzuto's, Fior d'Italia, Coppa's, Campi's, and Sanguinetti's distinguished San Francisco.[28]

A 1912 painting by John Sloan shows diners at Renganeschi's on West Tenth Street in Greenwich Village on a Saturday night. It doesn't look very unconventional, although the presence of a party of three women would have been considered unusual elsewhere. A Renganeschi's menu from 1916 presents a set dinner, but also extensive à-la-carte offerings including veal scallopini, fried brains, and frittata. There is no pasta on the menu.[29]

POST-BOHEMIA

A key moment in the history of Italian and other ethnic restaurants occurred when they grew to be popular not just with an adventure-seeking avant-garde, but also with middle-class patrons able to afford

Fig. 52. John Sloan, *Renganeschi's Saturday Night*, 1912.

dining out, intrigued by "colorful" atmosphere but more concerned with value and mild novelty than social experimentation. Between the artistic core of Bohemia and the vast middle class there have always been cultivated and affluent intermediaries. These include journalists, publishers, commercial artists, designers, and others in creative but moneymaking fields. Just behind them are lawyers, teachers, and other professionals, those living in cities without complicated family obligations or high social position who are thus afforded opportunities for lifestyle and consumption choices. Often held in contempt by the truly creative on the one hand and made fun of as pseudointellectuals by conservative members of the upper class on the other, these intermediaries are nevertheless indispensable to the transmission of culture, including gastronomic culture. Impressionist and abstract paintings went from contemned marginality to valuable objects because of these sorts of people; whole neighborhoods change from impoverished to fashionable (the process known as gentrification) as a result of their preferences. The acceptance of what was previously edgy as hip, and the subsequent movement of hip into the mainstream, are enduring manifestations of American consumer behavior.

As early as the beginning of the twentieth century, restaurants such as San Francisco's Sanguinetti's were largely deemed by the in-crowd to have been tainted by middle-class tourists, but the disapproval of the Bohemians was more than offset by the profits resulting from expanding restaurant size and customer base. In the 1890s, Maria del Prato's on Macdougal Street and then on Twelfth Street hosted writers such as Theodore Dreiser, author of *An American Tragedy* and other dramatic but realistic novels of contemporary life, and Richard Harding Davis, a famed writer and war correspondent. Customers were allowed to mix the salad under Maria's supervision, adding dressing until she approved it. An artistic and literary society called the Pleiades Club, which included Mark Twain and Stephen Crane, met at Maria del Prato's. A member of that circle, the poet Henry Tyrell, wrote in praise of the proprietor:

> How oft Marie, hostess debonair
> Have we, gay wanderers in Bohemia's way,
> Gathered at the closing of a weary day
> To feast on thy minestra beyond compare!
> Thou madest spaghetti and ambrosial fare
> And oh, Thy ravioli! Hence we say
> Salute! And as staunch admirers may
> Pledge Thee in Tuscan rose Chianti rare.[30]

In 1902 Maria moved her restaurant to the nightlife area near Times Square known as the Tenderloin. Regulars complained that the bourgeoisie were invading their restaurant. Julius Chambers of the *New York Tribune* now started to patronize instead the still-picturesque Pensione Livorno on Washington Square. Another (anonymous) reporter for *The Day*, writing in 1904, said that even before the move del Prato's had already been debased by dry-goods clerks and the like. Such disapproval didn't disturb the owners. Defying the predictions of its former core clientele (and the retirement of Maria herself), del Prato's flourished in

Fig. 53. Luisa Leone, 1873–1944.

its large new showcase.[31] Fior d'Italia in San Francisco also expanded after the 1906 earthquake, seating 200 in the 1930s and later as many as 750.[32]

Some newly established Italian restaurants took care to re-create an older Bohemian version of entertaining atmosphere. The Asti on Twelfth Street in Greenwich Village opened in 1923, after the height of the Bohemian table d'hôte, but it continued that tradition, featuring "spontaneous" opera aria performances by waiters and customers. It endured until 2000, carrying on the operatic renditions. More often, by the 1920s, the restaurants had become too big for such intimate diversions and instead literally expanded on the idea of Italianness, offering the same mild hedonism as before but on a larger scale. Over the course of its history, Mamma Leone's would swell from 20 seats to 1,200. As a mega-restaurant it featured marble statues and baroque and Rococo-style art purchased by Gene Leone, huge portions, and comical waiters whose broken English and flirting with the ladies might not have been genuine or sincere but were nevertheless part of the spectacle.[33] The restaurant took on the sobriquet "Mamma's" in addition to "Leone's" not only in honor of Luisa after her death but also to convey a kind of intimacy that no longer existed in reality.

Girolamo Leone died in 1914, and Luisa Leone's sons became involved in running the front of the restaurant and its business side. Mamma had been happy with the original space, but her sons wanted to expand. A move to larger quarters, but still near the opera, took place the same year as Girolamo's death. The 1920s saw a more dramatic move to 239 West Forty-Eighth Street. Mistrusting the change, Luisa Leone asked the composer Victor Herbert, whose endearing operettas enchanted a generation, if he would still patronize her restaurant if it moved uptown to the theatre district. Herbert responded gallantly, "Mother, for you and your wonderful cooking, I'd follow you to the ends of the earth." He was as good as his word and not only showed up but often would play his catchy and lyrical songs for diners at an upright piano.[34]

As we know, Prohibition went into effect in the 1920s and ruined many restaurants. In general, ethnic restaurants weathered the drought because, unlike their competitors at both the high and low ends, they didn't depend on liquor and wine sales for their profit. Middle-class restaurants of the soda-fountain, luncheonette, or roadside type flourished; the Automats, resplendent in their Art Deco look, were at the height of their popularity; Chinese restaurants, which tended not to sell alcoholic drinks anyway, continued their prosperity.

Italian places, whose appeal had included copious servings of Chianti, Lacrima Christi, and other inexpensive wines, did not always fare quite so well. In New York, Italian restaurants seem to have been able to evade the law in many cases by making their own wine, which was not in itself illegal, and serving it in teacups, which *was* illegal, but tolerated when the police were induced to look the other way. The entire category of Greenwich Village Italian places had originally been typified as "red ink" restaurants after the prevailing color of their wine, and to a surprising extent they were able to maintain their earlier practices and reputation.[35] Mamma

Leone's may have been the handiwork of a wine-dealer's wife, but its ability to flourish despite Prohibition is indicated by its move and expansion during that officially abstemious era.

Some West Coast establishments did not enjoy the laxity of law enforcement that characterized both New York and, as seen earlier, New Orleans. In San Francisco, Fior d'Italia had a difficult time under Prohibition, suffering frequent raids by enforcement authorities. The owners also had to deal with gangsters in order to obtain illegal whisky and other alcoholic beverages and engage in various subterfuges in order to keep customers happy.[36]

Outlawing alcohol encouraged a transition from Italian restaurants that were small, picturesque, and popular with artists and their hangers-on to larger, family-oriented places less dependent on wine and dispersed into non-Italian neighborhoods and suburbs. Simone Cinotto describes this evolution as moving "from boardinghouse to Roman gardens." While the small, Bohemian restaurants of Greenwich Village and North Beach survived, a new wave of larger Italian restaurants appealed to the midcentury American masses.[37] They were still colorful, but now focused on generic and reworked Italian symbols of *dolce vita*, sybaritic quantities of food, and an exaggeratedly, if not forced, festive ambience. Even when Prohibition ended, this grandiose model, of which Leone's became the exemplar, triumphed.

CIAO BELLA! MIDCENTURY OPULENCE

The situation facing Italian restaurants in the decades before and after the Second World War is memorably portrayed in the 1996 movie *Big Night*. Set in the 1950s on the New Jersey Shore, the film shows a conflict over culinary authenticity. Primo, the chef of a restaurant called Paradise, whose brother Secundo runs the front of the house, refuses to give in to the uncultivated tastes of his patrons, chastising a customer for ordering a side dish of spaghetti and meatballs to accompany seafood risotto. Her demand is "barbaric" because not only is spaghetti and meatballs an Italian American rather than Italian dish, but also because one ought not consume rice and pasta in the same meal.

Close to the Paradise is Pascal's, a restaurant always filled with diners drawn by the owner's charm and the fun atmosphere he orchestrates. Pascal couldn't care less about dictating what his customers should or should not order. He knows that the food he serves is inferior to that of Paradise, and even tells the Paradise brothers to close their restaurant and join him in order to bring Pascal's cuisine up a notch or two, but from a business standpoint he doesn't need any improvement. Pascal flourishes by providing a welcoming ambience that plays on the popular image of Italians as amorous, musical, spontaneous, and joyful.

Pascal's customers, as the movie makes evident, are hardly artistic Bohemians. They are middle-class suburbanites and mostly not Italian. The trouble for the brothers who run Paradise is that their few customers are equally unadventurous and unconcerned with authenticity. The period from 1920 to 1970 was one of great success and expansion of Italian restaurants, but without much room for variation, least of all when it came to looking at what was actually eaten in Italy.

Visitors from Italy were bemused by what passed for Italian food in the United States. Niccolà de Quattrociochi represented a Sicilian company that produced canned tuna and artichokes. He describes dining at an Italian restaurant in New York in the 1920s and being introduced to two American specialties: spaghetti with meatballs and Cotoletta Parmigiana (chicken parmesan). With disarming sarcasm he remarks that since these and other dishes such as Italian antipasto and beefsteak Milanese were served in every supposedly Italian restaurant, there must be some sort of widely told joke he wasn't aware of. He found them all quite tasty and hoped someone in Italy would invent them for Italian diners.[38] An Italian waiter working at Quo Vadis, a fashionable Italian restaurant in London's

Soho, said the restaurant served food he didn't recognize and that it tended to take French dishes and give them Italian names, so Poulet à la Princesse became Pollo alla Principessa.[39]

This doesn't mean that the food at places like Pascal's was completely made-up or non-Italian. In fact, it was menus of the earlier, Bohemian, Italian restaurants that were less obviously Italian. A limited repertoire of antipasto, a few pasta varieties, Italian ice cream, and minestrone soup comprised the identifiably Italian dishes at the tables d'hôtes. The main courses were usually American items such as roast beef, broiled chicken, or calf's liver.

On menus of the 1920s and 1930s, one starts to find the sort of food that would later be dismissed as "red-sauce Italian" (in other words, everything inauthentically swimming in tomato sauce), but recognizably Italian-style nonetheless. Certain dishes were invented by Italian American restaurateurs: Clams Posilippo and Clams Casino, or Veal Marsala. "Scampi" is a Venetian dialect word for a certain kind of Mediterranean prawn, but in the United States it describes any kind of shrimp sautéed in butter, olive oil, white wine, and garlic. Pasta was separate from meatballs in Italy and not inevitably served with tomato sauce, but spaghetti as a single dish in the United States came with both.

As Italian American restaurants grew larger, their menus expanded beyond the Bohemian stage, but kept to the basic premise of offering a considerable amount of food at a low price. A 1935 Fior d'Italia menu mentions American steaks, chops, and shrimp cocktail, but also recognizably Italian specialties such as frittata, veal scallopini, pastas, risotto, and zabaglione. Similar to Mamma Leone's, it featured a prix-fixe dinner. The basic dinner, at 75 cents, boasted a generous five courses, including a pasta selection; the more expensive dinner for $1 featured six courses, an assortment of antipasti to start the meal being the additional offering.[40]

The Italian restaurants of the interwar years profited from changes in Italy's image, as well as the image of Italian Americans. As the radical anarchist association faded, beginning in the 1930s, Italian gangsters such as

Al Capone and movies such as *Scarface* or *Little Caesar* popularized an altogether different sinister idea about Italians. Despite this durable and lurid imagery of criminal families and associations, Italians shed some of their exotic strangeness in the eyes of "regular Americans" without losing their reputation for warmth and culinary proficiency. In the interwar years, the restaurants successfully traded on two favorable images of Italians: their love of family (the notion that Mamma was in back cooking and enjoying it), and their innate artistic temperament. The imagined Italian family, especially its matriarchal side, was as old as the first Bohemian-patronized establishments. The second favorable stereotype, that of a people endowed with a joyfully artistic nature, leveraged the prestige associated with an upper-class idea of Italy as the home of great art from Greek antiquity to the Baroque period. The notion of a refined sensuous and artistic temperament and a love of the beautiful among the upper classes eventually came to be applied to the common people, who were supposedly infused with a Latin joy of life. In 1918, *Good Housekeeping* answered the question of what makes Italian cooking so good by pointing to the "true artist blood in every Italian's veins." Wonderful food requires imagination and a sensitivity to beauty and flavor, and "that is where the Latins have the advantage over us." This astonishingly lyrical encomium continues with an evocation of an Italian family dining outdoors, under an arbor, singing "O Sole Mio" and "Funiculì, Funiculà."[41]

Historians who study the Italian American experience refer to a process of "whitening" that took place after 1920, whereby southern Italians, having been previously considered racially ambiguous at best (an Alabama court in 1922 acquitted a black man of miscegenation since he had married a Sicilian immigrant whose race was thus indeterminate), were now represented as faithful if perhaps loquacious exponents of European culture.[42] The restrictive immigration laws passed by Congress between 1917 and 1924 had been targeted particularly at Mediterranean Italians (the Chinese already having been excluded as of the 1880s), but the enactment of these laws ended the perceived threat that native Anglo-Saxon "stock" of the United States would be overwhelmed by migrants of dubious racial status. The Italians who were already in the country came gradually to be held in affectionate regard and, unlike Germans, immune from direct blame for the rise of fascism.

Rather than the smoky, bare rooms of the Bohemian era, the Italian restaurants of the interwar years were adorned with neoclassical statues and ersatz Old Masters paintings. Strolling musicians or would-be opera singers supplied musical accompaniment. Restaurants established in this era were seldom named after the founding family anymore, but rather for the memorable sights of Italy—the Blue Grotto or Bay of Naples, for example—and were decorated with murals of Venetian gondolas, Mt. Vesuvius, and the Roman Coliseum indiscriminately. They might cater to an Italian American core clientele if they were located in neighborhoods such as Boston's North End or New York's Little Italy, but increasingly the "genuine Italians" were hard to find. A 1930 guide to New York by Rian James observed that although the city's Italian restaurants are owned by Italians and serve what purport to be Italian specialties, "they number scarcely a single Italian among their patrons." Writing about Zucca's (on West Forty-Ninth Street, near Mamma Leone's), James lamented that it presented "exactly what visitors from the middle west expect to find . . ."[43]

A dismissal such as James's may not have been quite fair to the actual diversity of restaurants in New York, but there was certainly a formula for both the menu and the overall cultural package that was being presented to diners. Italian Village in Chicago shows the rapid evolution from artsy hideaway to mass-market spectacle. Established in 1927, its first customers were performers from the Lyric Opera of Chicago. Beginning in the 1930s, the restaurant grew larger and took on the look of an imagined Italian village (cart wheels lying about), and featured a mural of the Rialto Bridge and the Grand Canal, and lots of Italian statues of figures in a state of decorative undress.[44]

Mamma Leone's was the most famous and most successful example of the large, lively Italian restaurants of the mid-twentieth century, providing heaping portions and entertaining ambience, and serving celebrities as well as masses of tourists. After a pause in its expansion during the 1920s, Mamma Leone's bought three adjacent buildings in 1935, tore them down, and built additional space. Ironic though it may seem, the Depression was a far better climate for such restaurants than the Prohibition era that preceded it.

In the 1930s, Leone's took on the aspect it would retain for another fifty years. Until her death in 1944, Luisa Leone, serious but hospitable, presided as if the restaurant were still a neighborhood place with a few tables, and after her death her spirit was still evoked. In fact, the restaurant was cavernous—literally a series of caverns. No reservations were taken and, like Antoine's, another vast and famous restaurant, Leone's not only filled its immense space every night, but customers were crowded together waiting outside. At its postwar peak, 4,000 people were served every day.[45]

The restaurant integrated spectacle and generosity, respecting culinary traditions in accord with Mamma's dictum, "I can cook good Italian food and I'll give the people plenty: they'll come." Accordion players sauntered from table to table; waiters assured the ladies, with a wink and a smile, that the cheesecake had no calories. As was customary at Italian restaurants, there was a set dinner of multiple courses that included cheese, garlic bread, a relish tray of celery and olives, and a choice of pastas (meatballs and spaghetti, lasagna, or gnocchi); then came entrées such as veal dishes, fried calamari, steaks, and chops.[46] This was not the place for anyone eager to lose weight. The à-la-carte menu was large, and the choice of main dishes was also extensive—only later did the restaurant emphasize the prix fixe.

Much as it might seem to fit a pattern, Leone's was innovative and pioneering. Its varied pasta offerings were unusual, as most places offered little more than spaghetti. Leone's lasagna was famous before this became a dish familiar to non-Italians. If it didn't actually invent the multi-plate antipasto, Leone's was probably the first to expand what had been a modest assortment of peppers, anchovies, and salami on one plate into a spectacle of twelve different items, constituting just one course of the fixed dinner. The chaos of dozens of plates on or next to the table catered to Americans' love of choice as well as basic human gluttony.

Fig. 54. Gene Leone, 1898–1986.

As a complement to its mass appeal, Mamma Leone's was an early example of a restaurant powered by association with celebrities. From opera singers like Caruso to film and sports stars like Gene Tunney, W. C. Fields, and Joe Louis, Mamma Leone's deftly combined its everyman appeal with solicitude for an elite clientele. The folksy, Oklahoma-born humorist Will Rogers was a loyal patron, as was the patrician Eleanor Roosevelt. President Dwight Eisenhower was a particular fan. Gene Leone claimed that Eisenhower taught him how to cook steak directly on hot coals. The ex-president even wrote a brief introduction to *Leone's Italian Cookbook* in 1967.[47]

Famous people were often seated in the wine cellar to avoid the kind of scene provoked by a visit from First Lady Eleanor Roosevelt during World War II, an appearance that created such a crush of people that the police had to be called. A meal for the wildly popular piano entertainer Liberace in 1956 was supposed to be served discreetly in the wine cellar, but because he showed up with twice the number of people in his entourage as could be accommodated there, Liberace dined in full view of an entranced public that blew kisses to him, climbed up to the balcony for a better view, and jammed the aisles of the dining room. A line of waiters, like a clutch of defensive tackles protecting the quarterback, encircled the table to keep people at a distance. Gene Leone remembered this incident with exasperation, especially because Liberace seemed to enjoy the chaos and took his time over the meal.[48]

Sardi's, which opened in New York's theatre district as a small Italian restaurant in 1921, also became a favorite haunt of celebrities.[49] It was *the* place to see Broadway stars, and it became the de facto place where playwrights, actors, and producers would await the newspaper reviews on first nights. Patsy's, in Midtown just north of the theatre district, became a favorite of Tony Bennett, Don Rickles, and, above all, Frank Sinatra. Both restaurants are still around.

In 1950, Gene Leone bought the President Theatre, which adjoined his restaurant, and Mamma Leone's expanded to its historic maximum size.

Gene's brothers went on to different enterprises, and Gene became the sole owner in 1952. He would recall the 1950s as the best years ever. Guidebooks listed the restaurant as among the best Italian places in New York, but it simultaneously continued to have mass appeal.[50] On one memorable occasion, 6,000 diners were served after an Army–Notre Dame game at Yankee Stadium, and still some people had to be turned away. Success had a price, however; because of the stress of running the restaurant, and also because Restaurant Associates made him a spectacular offer, Gene Leone sold Mamma Leone's in 1959.[51]

What most people now remember is the Mamma Leone's that was owned by Restaurant Associates. The company got its start running modest concessions and corporate canteens. It then catapulted to fame in the 1950s under Joe Baum, whose projects included Forum of the Twelve Caesars, the Four Seasons, and La Fonda del Sol. Baum largely ignored Mamma Leone's because he was more interested in innovative and elite dining, unsupported by tourism. In the 1970s, however, RA returned to middle- to low-end restaurants. Mamma Leone's flourished consistently in spite of Baum's neglect and the vicissitudes and upheavals at Restaurant Associates.

Under RA management, Mamma Leone's concentrated on a set seven-course dinner, whose immense size, variety, and modest price attracted diners. The à-la-carte options were retained, but, as shown in a menu from about 1960, these were mostly set aside for after-theatre suppers. What the menu calls "Mamma Leone's Famous Dinner" was $5. By 1966, the price rose to $6, and then to $7.50 in the mid-1970s.[52] The meal began with a large portion of mozzarella cheese, along with roasted peppers and the breadsticks that were already placed on the table when patrons were seated. Antipasto consisted of around twelve dishes, some already plated and others brought to the table and served by waiters. Guests then would have a choice of pasta (lasagna and spaghetti with meatballs were consistent favorites), followed by an entrée. Lobster was very popular, as were veal and chicken Parmesan. Customers did not tend to take advantage

Fig. 55. Mamma Leone's menu cover from the 1980s.

of menu options such as beef or duck. Salad and dessert came next, the latter involving a choice among ice cream, cheesecake, zabaglione, pastries, and fruit.[53] As a semi-surprise ending, as if more were needed, fried pastry knots (*bugie*) appeared. The 1960 menu has some supplements, so that ordering Mamma's Whole Stuffed Chicken could bring the price up to $6.25; filet mignon to $8.

The quantity of food and the number of customers necessitated an enormous staff and gargantuan delivery orders. Three thousand pounds of veal were consumed every week. There were seventy waiters and probably more than that number in the kitchen. Dominick Varacalli, who managed the restaurant from 1979 to 1982 and still works for Restaurant Associates, remembers that the restaurant was surprisingly easy to run. He knew it would be full; he knew what people would tend to order, so despite the massive scale, there was little waste. The food cost was between 28 percent and 35 percent of expenses instead of the usual 40 percent for steakhouses and other fancy restaurants. The waitstaff was motivated, professional (that is, not aspiring to some other line of work), and many had been at the restaurant for thirty years or more. One further change under Restaurant Associates was that the restaurant was extensively advertised to out-of-town customers, who were assured that no visit to New York was complete without dinner at Mamma Leone's.[54]

The influx of tourists made Mamma Leone's seem alien to New Yorkers. Craig Claiborne in the first *New York Times* guide to dining, published in 1962, said that the abundant food was most impressive on the first visit. After that, it "may begin to pall," but it was still a good place to bring visitors to the city. Seymour Britchky, another popular restaurant reviewer, in 1976 put Mamma Leone's in a chapter entitled "Tourist Traps" and ridiculed it as "this Disneyland of the restaurant world." He had mild praise for the manicotti, but nearly everything else, he sniffed, was awful. He belittled tourists who not only seemed to enjoy themselves but insisted on getting their photos taken by obliging waiters. Not even the Kodak Instamatic camera, the cell-phone camera of its day, was spared Britchky's contempt.[55] By the 1970s, middle-class values, including former gastronomic virtues such as quantity and predictability, were no longer enough for status in the upper-middle plane of the restaurant hierarchy, let alone the actual high end.

SOPHISTICATION AND STATUS

Beginning in the 1980s, taste became increasingly class-segmented, and Italian restaurants started to be represented in the world of expensive and sophisticated dining. In the chapter on Chez Panisse and the epilogue, we will take a closer look at the decline of the French monopoly on fine dining, a leading phenomenon of recent gastronomic history, and the ways in which Italian foods such as pasta and grilled meat and fish displaced the French aesthetic. Italian cuisine came to be thought of as light and flavorful; rustic yet elegant. It could be found at sleekly decorated restaurants that boasted celebrity chefs, multiple stars in guidebooks, and social prestige.

In place of the more-than-you-can-eat model of Mamma Leone's and its imitators, the new restaurants marketed a version of what was called the "Mediterranean Diet": a supposedly healthful combination of pasta, olive oil–based sauces, grilled fish, and green vegetables— altogether a less buttery, rich, and complex effect than what their French counterparts served. Lightness and simplicity were not cheap—white truffles could add $50 or more to the price of a simple risotto or pasta dish; the ability to charge a price for pasta equivalent to that of meat is one of the enduring reasons for the economic success of Italian restaurants.

That Italian food was able to rise to the restaurant stratosphere is an unusual accomplishment. For nearly a hundred years a seemingly fixed hierarchy placed French cuisine at the top, defining culinary distinction, with Italian, Chinese, and other "ethnic" restaurants considerably lower, providing inexpensive and not particularly prestigious food.

The first signs of a change in how Italian food was regarded came in the lean but innovative 1970s. One curious incident was a review of Rao's, a previously obscure vestige of East Harlem's former Italian neighborhood. In 1977, Mimi Sheraton, the renowned *New York Times* restaurant reviewer, gave Rao's three stars and extolled its Southern Italian food.[56] Her favorites included baked clams with breadcrumbs and oregano, lemon chicken ("the single most unforgettable main course"), and seafood salad. What is significant is not the food in itself, which was hardly unusual, or even its supposed perfection, but the sensation created by the review. With only eight tables and already possessing a near-capacity group of regulars, Rao's became essentially a club whose members received a certain number of table spots per year. Others might be permitted to dine under exceptional circumstances—just enough to fuel a frenzy that has not died down after nearly forty years. There was a perverse incentive to celebrate places that were impossible for ordinary people to experience, but for an Italian restaurant to be in this category in the 1970s was significant.

Most influential for Italian cuisine's image was the popularization of the aforementioned Mediterranean diet. As far back as 1959, Ancel and Margaret Keys had published a book called *Eat Well and Stay Well*, but it had little immediate influence. In 1970, a study of coronary heart disease in seven countries found that the lowest rates were in Greece, Yugoslavia, and Italy. This study's wide diffusion encouraged the Keys' publishers in 1975 to reprint the 1959 book with the title *How to Eat Well and Stay Well the Mediterranean Way*, and it became a bestseller. These authorities identified the Mediterranean diet's components as abundant vegetables; fruit as the most common dessert; olive oil as principal fat source; moderate amounts of fish, poultry, cheese, yogurt, and eggs; slight consumption of meat; and moderate intake of wine. Less than 35 percent of the model diet's calories consisted of fat, and only 8 percent were saturated fats.

There was always some question as to who actually ate this way by custom or habit. The Mediterranean regions do not have anything approaching a unified cuisine, and those who can afford it eat a richer, meatier diet. Only half-jokingly the food historians Massimo Montanari and Alberto Capatti say that the so-called Mediterranean diet most closely resembles the light food served at summer beach resorts in the 1960s— pizzas, salads, antipastos, and the like—food that no one in Italy ever took seriously at any other time of year.[57] Yet despite its absurdity from a strictly factual point of view, UNESCO at the end of 2013 proclaimed the Mediterranean diet part of the world's intangible cultural heritage and apportioned it among Italy, Portugal, Spain, Morocco, Greece, Cyprus, and Croatia.

In the United States, "Mediterranean" generally means Italian with perhaps some Greek touches (yogurt) and a few Spanish tapas. A culinary style associated formerly with huge portions, red sauce, and copious amounts of meat (often breaded and served with cheese) had now transformed into light and healthful.

The Mediterranean diet vogue did not immediately improve the quality of what passed for Italian food in the United States; the 1970s as a culinary decade was something of a nadir on the whole. John Mariani describes a two-week honeymoon automobile trip across the United States in 1977 sampling Italian restaurants everywhere. He and his bride suffered a series of misfortunes at places where al dente pasta was unknown, sauces were overcooked and sugary, the bread was tasteless, and the entrées imperfectly thawed.[58] Also in the 1970s the celebrated *New Yorker* writer Calvin Trillin made fun of pretentious "Continental" (including Italian) restaurants of what he dubbed the "La Maison de la Casa House" type, serving an indifferent and indistinguishable mix of tired and poorly prepared clichés.[59]

Elegant Italian restaurants of the mid-twentieth century featured leatherette banquettes, tuxedoed waiters, and tableside preparation (tossed pasta; Caesar salad; flambéed desserts). There were even some justly acclaimed fancy Italian restaurants such as Romeo Salta and Orsini's in New York or Doro's in San Francisco, but they either served dressed-up versions of the same veal chop or cheesecake featured at Mamma Leone's, or supposedly northern Italian specialties such as carpaccio or tiramisu invented by famous restaurants in Italy but not representative of any tradition of Italian cuisine. High-end Italian restaurants of the 1970s were basically like Mamma Leone's only smaller, more tranquil, carpeted, and perfumed with white truffles. This was the era of Fettucine Alfredo, invented by restaurateur Alfredo Di Lelio in Rome, an extremely simple dish (egg pasta, butter, and Parmesan cheese) prepared dramatically in front of customers and presented as a rare delicacy. Originally popularized in America by movie actors Molly Pickford and Douglas Fairbanks in the late 1920s, Fettucine all'Alfredo as well as other rather plain pasta and risotto preparations in the 1970s were dressed up with Italian truffles, following Craig Claiborne's recommendation in a 1976 column.[60]

Another entrée into the higher echelons grew from Italians running some French or Continental restaurants and adding or retaining Italian touches. Ernie's in San Francisco, for example, was for many years among the most socially prestigious and highly rated restaurants. It opened in 1934 as Il Trovatore, but when Ernie Carlesso sold it to Ambrogio Gotti, one of his waiters, the new owner changed the name to "Ernie's," and turned it into a French restaurant whose specialties included Frogs' Legs Provençal, Tournedos Rossini, and Châteaubriand. Sirio Maccioni, a Tuscan by birth, opened what would become the legendary Le Cirque in 1974. For the next twenty-five years it was one of the leading French restaurants and a favorite of the social, political, and media elite of New York, its patrons defining the upper classes of a slowly recovering city. When Le Cirque was new, Maccioni did not dream of emphasizing Italian food—it was too simple, and his customers equated social distinction with French food. He tried to add a pasta dish or two to the menu, but his French chef refused. In the late 1970s, however, not only was he able to Italianize the restaurant, but this is where Pasta Primavera, another made-up dish that passes for authentically Italian, was invented.[61]

In retrospect, the 1980s are a watershed in the history of American Italian restaurants. Lidia Bastianich opened Felidia in New York in 1983, and the vivid complexity of the food inspired from her native Istria (now mostly in Croatia) came as a kind of revelation of the range of flavors and ingredients. Felidia was modern high-end in décor, neither loud and kitschy nor quiet and stuffy. Five years later, Tony May opened San Domenico on the southern perimeter of Columbus Circle in New York. He had acquired the rights to use the decorative style and menu selections from the San Domenico restaurant in Imola, near Bologna. With its bright-orange walls and linens, terracotta floors, female and well as male servers, and refined northern Italian food, San Domenico too created a gastronomic stir. May presented rustic dishes such as braised tripe along with aristocratic preparations involving lobster and suckling pig. It was one of the first American Italian restaurants to serve rabbit and game; the pastas were dazzling in their artisanal freshness and variety.

Perhaps the most important development of the 1980s, one that radically changed the presentation and perception of Italian food, was the creation in 1985 of the Union Square Café in New York by Danny Meyer. The food was more Italian than anything else, but what truly distinguished it was a combination of stylistic refinement, care for the individual customer, and earthy, delightful, seasonal food. Meyer set out to combine three kinds of restaurants. The first was the informal, locally sourced restaurants of the San Francisco Bay Area, most famously Chez Panisse. The nearby Union Square Greenmarket was the first large farmers' market in New York, and the restaurant emphasized its reliance on the fresh ingredients and seasonal variation afforded by the market's proximity. The cuisine and some of the ambience was inspired by the informal trattoria of Rome, which combined hearty food and warm, personal service. The third influence was that of the great Parisian restaurants. The informality of the American and Italian sort was combined with polished attentiveness of the leading French restaurants.[62]

This remains a difficult blend, what Meyer refers to as an "emulsion," but Union Square Café has nonetheless succeeded in providing a template for a dazzling series of high-end restaurants and changed the setting for serving Italian food. No longer were Italian restaurants faced with a choice between festive, staged informality with large portions of mass-produced food on the one hand, or imposing, elegant restaurants on the French model serving vaguely Continental food on the other. Informality at the Union Square Café was not incompatible with graciousness. Meyer welcomed a publishing and media crowd, particularly at lunch, whose galvanizing effect on the restaurant's soaring popularity was as pronounced as that of the Bohemians on the cozy Italian boites of the early twentieth century. Union Square Café rescued Italian food from both its high- and low-end heaviness and artificiality; from both the spaghetti and meatballs and the double-thick stuffed veal chop.

FINALE

Italian food is so versatile and Italian restaurants in the United States have been so successful that different styles and segments of society can be accommodated at the same time. There are still a few unassuming, small places that have retained their Italian boardinghouse or Bohemian associations, including Ralph's in Philadelphia (established in 1900) or Monte's and Gene's in New York (1918 and 1919, respectively). Private clubs such as Tiro a Segno (founded 1888) in Greenwich Village, or Rao's in East Harlem (founded 1896) today have menus that would not have been out of place a hundred years ago, as well as a marvelous informal atmosphere for those who are admitted. Few Italian restaurants of Mamma Leone's Brobdingnagian size survive, however. Gargiulo's on Coney Island, established in 1907, is cavernous, lively, and Neapolitan-American, and described as a "time warp" in the *Zagat* guide for New York City. Miceli's in Hollywood, founded in 1949, still features waiters singing arias and straw-covered Chianti bottles hanging from the ceiling and staircase. Even if such well-preserved treasures are now rare, most Italian restaurants in the United States, nevertheless, still rely on a formula of abundant food, served with a studied Italian friendliness and informality to people who are not Italian.

"Informality" now means that Italian restaurants can be high-end and yet lively in a way that has nothing to do with strolling minstrels singing "Santa Lucia." Mario Battali's restaurants, for example, beginning with Babbo in Greenwich Village, are part of a personality-driven empire that has popularized a lusty, organ-meat-friendly, and full-flavored Italian cuisine. Formerly modest foods, especially pizza, have now joined hamburgers in being the subject of rankings, artisanal scrutiny, and arguments among foodies. Roberta's, a pizzeria and restaurant in Brooklyn, had such great success in 2011 that *New York* magazine dubbed the fast-gentrifying Bushwick neighborhood "Robertasville."[63]

The energy being put into new kinds of Italian restaurants has even come full circle to a revival of the easily derided "red-sauce" Italian restaurant. Not one but two Frankies Spuntino restaurants in New York serve nostalgic Italian American specialties such as Sunday sauce (tomato and meat "gravy") with meatballs and braciola, or eggplant marinara (with Parmesan and mozzarella). Of course, the ingredients are carefully sourced, the eggplant recipe has half the mozzarella it would have had in the past, and the restaurants feature neither statues nor singing.[64] Restaurants of the Major Food Group, notably Carbone and Parm, the latter with four locations including Yankee Stadium, have also revived and elevated old-fashioned Italian American food, and these venues are wildly popular. The menu at Parm imitates the look of a 1950s place-mat menu and offers baked ziti, hero sandwiches, shrimp scampi, and garlic bread. Italian American red-sauce, checked-tablecloth restaurants have thus become enshrined as classics.

Mamma seems to be making an exuberant return to the kitchen.

THE MANDARIN

"THE BEST CHINESE FOOD
EAST OF THE PACIFIC"

No one needs to be convinced that Chinese food is as American as the proverbial apple pie. There are more than 40,000 Chinese restaurants in the United States—more than there are branches of McDonald's, Burger King, and KFC *combined*.[1] Neither are they limited to large cities with substantial Asian populations. Instead they are spread across the country so that few towns are without at least a Chinese buffet. Their ubiquity makes it difficult to appreciate how unusual it is for one country to adopt so enthusiastically the cuisine of another, especially one whose tastes and food culture are so different.

America was not initially or even consistently infatuated with Chinese cuisine. When Chinese restaurants first appeared in San Francisco and New York in the mid-nineteenth century, the initial reaction was cautiously favorable and curiosity outweighed mistrust and unfamiliarity. This, however, changed, as political and social sentiment shifted and the Chinese were increasingly regarded as a threat. Newspapers called their

IN ORDERING ...

Imagine that you are a Chinese family selecting everything cooked a la carte, just as we do here at The Mandarin. Chinese food is served "family style," with something for everyone, rather than a main entree for each individual.

So for two persons, for instance, a soup and 2 or 3 dishes and rice are enough. For larger groups, order as many dishes as there are persons in the party, plus "one for the table," and a soup. Which would mean for a party of five — a soup, 6 dishes, and rice.

In the case of eight or ten persons, instead of that many dishes, perhaps you will want to select a certain number, and have "double orders," or twice the amount.

In any case, whether you are trying Mandarin Chinese food for the first time, or an epicure wishing to discuss the philosophy of fine food, our entire staff awaits with pleasure to satisfy your pleasure.

MANDARIN SPECIALTIES
(One Day Advance Notice Required)

MANDARIN DUCK $11.00
Ours alone. And yours to relish. Prepared with prideful care from our very own receipe originating from Peking itself!

GOLD COIN CHICKEN 5.50

WHOLE SHARK'S FINS 30.00
The ultimate in luxury for those who dare to scale the epicurean heights in authentic Chinese cuisine.

YUNAN BARBECUED HAM $12.00

BEGGAR'S CHICKEN 6.50
The Mandarin takes great pleasure in being the first and only Chinese restaurant in America, we believe, to serve this chicken which is unusual in name. And in fact, unusual in presentation. A fowl finely flavored, encased in clay, and baked.

WINTER MELON SOUP 6.50

MANDARIN HORS D'OEUVRE PLATE (10 items) . $8.50

MONGOLIAN CHAFING POT 12.00
(Also known as Genghis Khan's Fire Pot)
A charcoal burning chafing pot containing highly flavored chicken broth with thinly sliced meats — chicken, beef, pork, shrimp, vegetables, bean curd and rice noodle

Fig. 56. Menu page from the Mandarin, ca. 1963.

food frightening, dirty, and disgusting, and it was popularly imagined that stray dogs and cats were being rounded up for Chinese kitchens. As early as the 1880s, the Chinese were singled out as undesirable aliens, and legislation cut off immigration and excluded them from many occupations. Given these lurid and unpleasant images of the Chinese, why then did Americans become such passionate devotees of Chinese food?

It is first of all important to recognize that there is little or no relation between openness to culinary experimentation and social acceptance of immigrants. Historically it has been perfectly possible to enjoy the cuisine of people you despise. Many fans of Mexican or Tex-Mex food, or people who vacation in Cancún, nevertheless fret about Mexican immigration. The rise of Indian curry restaurants in Britain during the 1970s and 1980s was accompanied by frequent instances of violence against South Asians. "Lager louts," as young urban tough guys in Britain were termed, adopted hot vindaloo curry as one of their symbols, but that did not prevent them from making a practice of intimidating the owners and waiters at the establishments they frequented.[2]

As was the case with Italian restaurants, the success of Chinese restaurants resulted from shaping the food to suit the American palate—a cultural appropriation best epitomized by chop suey, which swept the nation at the beginning of the twentieth century. Yet even if inauthentic, American Chinese food remains distinctive and, for well over a century, Chinese restaurants have indubitably proliferated and helped to mold popular tastes.

It is daunting, then, to select one Chinese restaurant among thousands, but the story of the Mandarin in San Francisco is both historically significant and intriguing. Opened in 1961 by Cecilia Chiang, sold in 1991, and closed in 2006, the Mandarin was among a small group of high-end Chinese restaurants established after the Second World War that served "Mandarin"—in short, non-Cantonese—dishes. Many Americans had their first pot-stickers, hot-and-sour soup, and other northern or Sichuan dishes at the Mandarin, at New York's Shun Lee, or at Washington's Yenching Palace. The Mandarin was also an early example of an elegant Chinese restaurant. Unlike the few older fancy Chinatown restaurants, it wasn't decorated in exotic pseudo-oriental style, with gilding, dragons, and red lanterns that were supposed to appeal to the American masses, but rather was designed to create an understated ambience, part modernist sleekness, part serene Chinese temple. Cecilia Chiang served as educator and missionary for this most sophisticated of all cuisines. Teacher to a generation of chefs and food writers, she remains to this day, at age ninety-six, as enterprising and charismatic as ever.

Among Chinese restaurants the Mandarin was influential but anomalous. It was significantly not located in Chinatown but on a fairly nondescript block near San Francisco's auto showrooms from 1961 to 1968; then after 1968 it moved to a location overlooking Fisherman's Wharf from Ghirardelli Square, a restored picturesque industrial space housing expensive boutiques. In a restaurant category dogged to this day by an image of cheapness, the Mandarin was a center of elite social life, a place to be seen, yet held fast to Chinese traditions, ingredients, and service. Cecilia Chiang herself, born into a prominent Shanghai family and raised in Peking, does not fit the pattern of Chinese restaurant entrepreneurs, almost all of whom are men from southern coastal China (Guangdong and Fujian Provinces). When she started the Mandarin, Mme. Chiang (as she prefers to be called) had no knowledge of Cantonese, Hokkienese, or any of the other southern languages and was thus ignored by most established restaurant owners.

Cecilia Chiang's life and the history of her restaurant are certainly unusual, but not altogether unique. The fall of Chiang Kai-Shek's Kuomintang government in 1949 to the Communist revolution, save for a redoubt on the island of Taiwan, sent thousands of upper-class Chinese into exile, many eventually to the United States, where their high (often diplomatic) status and at least moderate wealth granted them exemption from the laughably small immigration quota (105 per year!) established by the Magnuson Act of 1943, which actually represented an improvement over the Congressional legislation of 1924 that, in theory, prohibited *any* immigration from Asia. Some postwar Chinese arrivals established themselves by creating restaurants far from traditional Chinatowns, restaurants of soigné appearance, cuisine, and service.[3]

Because of Cecilia Chiang's personality, culinary ambitions, and decades of what might be called outreach, her take on Chinese cuisine, exemplified by her restaurant, has had an immense effect on how Chinese food has been consumed and understood in the United States. Her two autobiographies and her recollections make it possible to appreciate the significance of the Mandarin and the place of Chinese cuisine in American history.[4]

THE CHINESE IN THE UNITED STATES

Chinese restaurants were first established as a result of the 1849 California Gold Rush, an event with immediate global impact that attracted miners from Guangdong Province in southern China. By reasons of its coastal geographic position and local culture, Guangdong has been more open to the outside world than elsewhere in China. The men who came seeking opportunities in California were from the subregions of the Pearl River delta near Canton, and they formed close networks in the new country through their local and kinship connections. In addition to the aspiring miners, many Chinese merchants made the journey across the Pacific and upon arrival set up shops, acting as suppliers, middlemen, or small-scale bankers. These entrepreneurs were typical of generations of South Chinese immigrants who, beginning in the seventeenth century, had already developed towns, plantations, and trade in much of Southeast Asia, notably in the territories of the Dutch East India Company.[5]

In the boomtown environment of San Francisco in the 1850s, Chi-

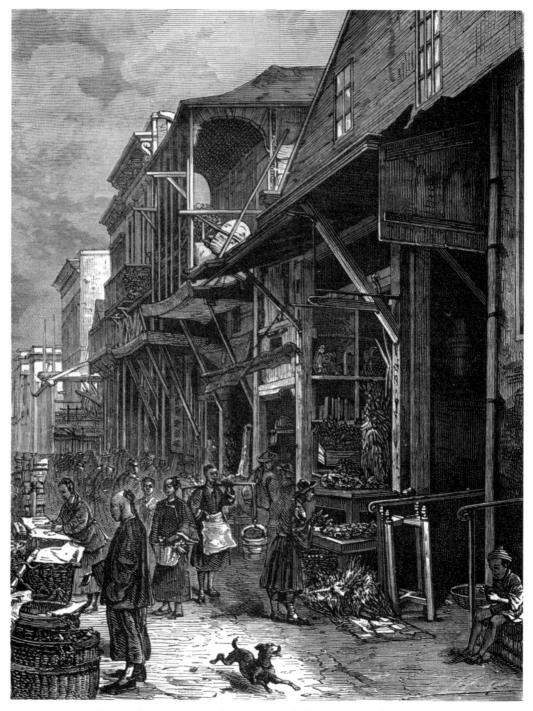

Fig. 57. San Francisco Chinatown in the late nineteenth century.

nese restaurants were appreciated by the community at large, since the alternatives were mostly crude and absurdly expensive. In his account of Gold Rush California, not surprisingly entitled *Eldorado*, Bayard Taylor, a reporter for the *New York Tribune*, described three Chinese restaurants on Dupont Street (later Grant Avenue, the center of post-earthquake Chinatown). According to Taylor, who later became an anti-Chinese agitator, they served Americans who were attracted by the "excellent cookery" and the low price of $1, which bought an all-you-can-eat meal. We have a favorable description of meal at Hong Fa-Lo on Dupont Street, written in 1853 for the *San Francisco Whig*, and a somewhat less enthusiastic account of a Chinese banquet given to Eastern businessmen in 1865 by Chinese merchant leaders at the Hong Hueng restaurant on Dupont.[6] As more Americans came to the region, anti-Chinese sentiment and contempt for the supposedly unhygienic and bizarre cuisine of the Chinese became commonplace.

In 1850 there were perhaps 4,000 Chinese in California, but in 1852 alone something on the order of 20,000 more arrived, attracted by the discovery of gold and the exciting growth of California. After the Civil War, more Chinese workers were brought over to work on the rapidly expanding railroads under formal contracts, but in more menial conditions than before. In 1885 there were still few Chinese involved in the restaurant trade. San Francisco could boast a dozen Chinese restaurants, while New York lagged behind with only six.[7]

As was the case for Italian restaurants, early non-native patrons were drawn from the ranks of Bohemians and their followers. In 1886 the journalist Allan Forman described a visit to Mong Sing Wah on Mott Street in New York's Chinatown. His guide was "a jolly New York lawyer of decidedly Bohemian tendencies." Their first course was a "toothsome stew" called Chow Chop Suey, which Forman termed the national dish of China.[8] The "chop suey craze," which began a decade later in 1896, brought in a much larger mass of would-be sophisticates, followed by tourists and others with no Bohemian pretensions. Groups of friends organized "slumming" expeditions to Chinatown just as the subsequent generation in the 1920s would visit Harlem and also call it "slumming."

By the 1880s, the Chinatowns of San Francisco, New York, and other cities were perceived as dangerous albeit alluring. The Chinese were feared as sinister and alien, requiring official control if not outright repression. Their willingness to work for substandard wages might have conveyed an image of diligence, but it was represented as rejection of basic human rights and priorities. This mistrust commingled with a dislike based on a supposed Chinese affinity for indolent vices such as smoking opium. Out of this set of prejudices, bizarre but widely diffused ideas took hold about the Chinese masterminding sinister global enterprises such as the so-called "white slave trade."

These sentiments of fear became more stridently expressed and were channeled into legislation. The Chinese Exclusion Act of 1882 and the Geary Act of 1892 were the first to target a particular immigrant ethnic group. The Exclusion Act prohibited any immigration by Chinese laborers for ten years. Meanwhile, any Chinese who left the United States could not return unless they obtained proof that they were not laborers. The Geary Act not only renewed the prohibition on Chinese labor but also required that Chinese living in the United States register with the authorities and obtain residence certificates.

These laws had the net effect of banning immigration from China, with some exceptions such as students and merchants, and imposed regulations regarding labor and employment on the Chinese who already lived in the United States. The widespread idea that the Chinese would work for nearly nothing only added to invidious propaganda about oriental depravity and encouraged an extremely discriminatory climate. Chinese men were forced into occupations such as washing and cooking, these being regarded as women's work and thus not desired by American male workers. Chinese laundries and Chinese restaurants—these became stereotypical Asian businesses not because of any particular Chinese propensity for cleaning or cooking but because they provided an opening where ingenuity and persistence could be rewarded. In 1920, according to census records, 11,438 Chinese were employed as restaurant workers, as opposed to the 164 in 1870, but because of the immigration restrictions, there were in fact fewer Chinese working in the country than there had been at the height of the railroad boom after the Civil War.[9] It's interesting to note that between these two dates came the "chop suey craze," which announced a supposedly exotic cuisine adapted to American tastes.

THE CHOP SUEY CRAZE

The year 1896 was a turning point in American culinary history. In that year a Chinese envoy visited the United States, taking the long way home from the coronation of Tsar Nicholas II and a tour of Europe. Li Hongzhang deliberately excluded San Francisco from his itinerary because of its virulent anti-Chinese sentiment. Legend has it that chop suey was introduced in New York by Li Hongzhang's chef, or that it was served for the first time at a reception in his honor at the Waldorf Hotel. An article in the *New York Journal*, "Queer Dishes Served at the Waldorf by Li Hung's Chinese Cook," describes "chow chop suey" as fricasseed giblets. It was at least half right: the distorted English transliteration "chow chop suey" approximates the Cantonese "chao zasui," a dish of stir-fried animal intestines, *chao* essentially meaning "stir-fried," *za* having the sense of "miscellaneous," and *sui* meaning "intestines."[10]

In fact there is no evidence that Li Hongzhang actually ate chop suey on his trip, and regardless, chop suey and other dishes mentioned in the article were already being served in American Chinatowns. As noted, Chow Chop Suey was consumed by the Bohemians who dined at Mong

Fig. 58. Edward Hopper, *Chop Suey*, 1929.

Sing Wah on Mott Street as early as 1886. In 1888, one of the first Chinese Americans to write for an English-speaking readership, Wong Chin Foo, called chow chop suey "a staple dish for the Chinese gourmand," describing it as a mixture of chicken livers and gizzards, fungi, bamboo buds, pig's tripe, and bean sprouts, stewed together with spices and served over rice.[11] Alexander Filippini, a cook at Delmonico's, mentions chop suey as typical of Hong Kong in an appendix on "curious dishes" from around the world at the end of one of his several cookbooks. He doesn't provide a recipe, but significantly, his main ingredient is not entrails but pork.[12]

Li Hongzhang's visit seems to have popularized chop suey, but he had nothing directly to do with its origins. In fact, American chop suey was derived from what we would now call stir-fried dishes in general.[13] The technique of rapid cooking over very high heat was alien to European and American cookery. Wong Chin Foo referred misleadingly to "stewing," which in fact is not the method for making the dish, at least not originally, and indicates, along with Filippini's substitution of pork for intestines, the path of its Americanization. The English term "stir-fry" was introduced long after Chinese food began its rise to popularity—in 1945, to be exact, by a physician named Buwei Yang Chao and her scholarly husband Yuenren Chao in their groundbreaking book *How to Cook and Eat in Chinese*.[14]

Americans liked the combination of meat, vegetables, and Chinese ingredients such as bean sprouts and soy sauce, but preferred these served in thick sauces not characteristic of stir-fried preparations. Among the adaptations made by Chinese restaurants for the American palate were the use of a brown gravy base; the invention of sugary sauces for what were officially called sweet-and-sour dishes; the heavy use of soy sauce (as in Chinese American fried rice); and batter-frying pieces of boneless meat, eschewing innards and bones. These innovations created an ersatz semi-Chinese cuisine that continues to this day.

Chop suey is thus not entirely an American invention, but it was so transformed from its original version that what had once been a stir-fried preparation of viscera became a meat dish with thick gravy and vegetables. Whatever Li Hongzhang actually consumed during his 1896 visit, the fame and popularity of chop suey spread like the contemporary passion for automobiles, along with the reputation of chop suey's lagging cousin chow mein, the latter being served with crisp noodles rather than rice. The craze proved surprisingly durable, and by 1905 there were in New York alone more than 100 chop suey restaurants outside of Chinatown, along Third and Eighth Avenues. This proliferation was accompanied by the first rumors that the dish was not authentic.[15] Other than for a few cranky Bohemian perfectionists, however, authenticity was not, at this point, of great importance.

Nothing stopped the proliferation of Chinese restaurants. Despite the lurid dangers associated with Chinatowns and the fallacious identification of the Chinese with vice, their food became a mainstay of American dining out—not just among Bohemians or sophisticates but also in the most mainstream parts of middle America. There was, to be sure, resistance to normalizing Chinese food, but this was more on a cultural than gustatory basis. According to a story in the *New York Tribune* in 1901, there had been an astounding increase in the number of Chinese restaurants uptown (that is, north of Chinatown), which the author found bewildering because he saw little to like in what such establishments offered. They had "a free and easy atmosphere . . . which attracts many would-be 'Bohemians.' . . . Visitors loll about and talk and laugh loudly. . . . Negroes are in disproportionately large numbers."[16] The same contempt is expressed in a 1904 story in the *Los Angeles Times* that describes the clientele of a late-night chop suey place as consisting of "outcast negroes and white damsels of no reputation" along with "blear-eyed hobos" using chopsticks to eat chop suey, and a "negro girl" in an opium-induced stupor, asking for "so mo' suey."[17] Louche manners, loose morals, opium, racial mixing, poseurs, *and* Chinese food all contributed to these expressions of puzzled rancor.

In 1909 the murder of nineteen-year-old Elsie Sigel, whose decomposing body was found in a trunk in New York City, created a sensation, and encouraged yet another wave of anti-Chinese sentiment. The trunk was found in the apartment of Sigel's lover, Leon Ling, a waiter at a Chinese restaurant on the chop suey corridor of Eighth Avenue. He allegedly murdered Sigel and vanished forever after the police discovered the body. Elsie and her mother regularly had dined at Chinese restaurants and had even decorated their apartment with Chinatown curios. Newspapers, eager to increase circulation, inflamed fears of "white slavery," while references to chop suey and the cruel and devious oriental mind were also featured in press coverage.[18]

All such imaginings notwithstanding, no longer were advanced or Bohemian tastes required to patronize Chinese restaurants. A character in P. G. Wodehouse's 1916 comic play *Uneasy Money* says that chop suey is one of the great things about America, right up there with corn on the cob, New Jersey mosquitos, and the Woolworth Building.[19]

In the 1920s, despite increased xenophobia and the consequent restrictive quotas placed on immigration, Americans well outside artistic and intellectual circles patronized ethnic restaurants, which had by now become integrated into ordinary dining-out options. Chinese restaurants were typically decorated in red and gold, and festooned with iconography of painted or carved dragons and pagodas. The Far Eastern décor contrasted with menus that offered little beyond chop suey and steaks, chops, and other American food. Chop suey had become commonplace without losing any of its popularity. An article in the *New York Times* in 1925 entitled "Chop Suey's New Role" describes the favor accorded to chop suey by female workers seeking lunch. For them Chinatown "is not an intriguing bit of transplanted Orient. It is simply a good place to eat."[20]

During Prohibition, unlike so many other eating places, Chinese restaurants flourished because they were fun, but did not require alcohol to enjoy. Even the Great Depression failed to damage the success of Chinese restaurants, whose exotic but innocuous atmosphere fit in with the American world of Shirley Temple and Busby Berkeley. Some of the Bohemian edge returned in the evenings, however. In the 1920s and 1930s urban chop suey restaurants served as places for young women to meet men, and the establishments were even investigated by vice officers and moral crusaders as likely sites of prostitution.[21] This free-and-easy atmosphere probably had nothing to do with their being Chinese and more to do with the fact they were open late. As we saw in our discussion of Schrafft's, bland, resolutely

Fig. 59. Port Arthur menu cover, 1917.

nonexotic places such as Childs or the Automat attracted a different crowd at night.

Chop suey was so successful from 1900 to 1940 that it tended to draw Chinese restaurants away from variety or complexity. Much as Indian restaurants in London until recently were identified exclusively with curry, Chinese restaurants in the United States were relegated to the status of chop suey joints, offering little else. As chop suey began to gain an unfavorable reputation for being inauthentic, however, menus of Chinese restaurants became a little more varied and complex, dropping the American standard items while breaking up the monopolistic glories of chop suey.

The move away from chop suey began in the 1920s, when the dish was widely suspected to be not really Chinese, but rather something invented

Fig. 60. Postcard showing the interior of the Port Arthur Restaurant,
New York, ca. 1920.

in America to fool Americans. An article in the *New York Times* in January 1928 cited "differing opinions as to whether chop suey . . . is a real Chinese dish or an American's conception of one."[22] Although chop suey actually remained popular into the 1960s, it became an elementary mark of sophistication to disdain it. Chop suey would gradually disappear from menus, not because of the rise of authentic Chinese food but because of changing fashions and preference for other less-than-authentic options. The history of ethnic restaurants reflects a tension between catering to the taste of Americans and a desire for exotic authenticity.

BEYOND CHOP SUEY

In the 1930s, Chinese restaurants started to expand beyond chop suey. The Chinese dishes on the 1938 *New Yorker* cover mentioned in the previous

Fig. 61. John Sloan, *Chinese Restaurant*, 1909.

chapter (see page 177 and Fig. 51 on page 176) are Moo Goo Gai Pan (sautéed chicken with mushrooms and vegetables), Lun Far Chow Mein (lobster chow mein), Duck Yat Garm (duck with noodles), Char Shu Wonton (barbecued-pork wontons), Foo Young (omelet with Chinese vegetables), and Gamgut (probably kumquats). Some of these are surprisingly obscure and no longer found on Chinese menus today, but are hardly derivative of chop suey either.

Chinese, or at least Chinese-style, food broadened its reach in the 1930s, especially with the vogue for pseudo-Polynesian "tiki" restaurants. After the repeal of the Volstead Act in 1933, the return of legal liquor allowed for cocktails to be served in more gracious and gimmicky surroundings than the rough speakeasies of the Prohibition era. South Seas tiki restaurants offered an attractive setting for exotic drinks, but they also featured Chinese food garnished with enough coconut and pineapple to give it a supposedly Polynesian flavor. These places, with their colorful cocktails, familiar but exotically trimmed food, and South Pacific décor spread like lava from an erupting volcano. The legendary Don the Beachcomber, established in Los Angeles in 1934, showed the way.[23] This restaurant and its myriad imitators boasted waterfalls, palm trees, carved idols, and other supposed tropical tropes, serving rum cocktails and Chinese-American food dressed up with tropical touches.

The golden age of the tiki restaurant would come in the two decades following the end of the Second World War. That conflict sent Americans to fight on remote Pacific islands, and although the experience was fatal or nightmarish for many, soldiers who survived brought back stories of remote and beautiful palm-fringed lagoons. Gilded memories and shrewd marketing started to color the image of the Pacific islands, beginning in 1948 with James Michener's Pulitzer Prize–winning *Tales of the South Pacific* and its musical adaptation, featuring hit songs such as "Bali H'ai." Thor Heyerdahl's *Kon Tiki*, an account of a journey by raft across the Pacific, appeared in 1950 and further fed the craze for Polynesian themes. A restaurant genre in its own right, tiki took the unselfconscious inauthenticity of Chinese restaurants a few steps further.

For much of the twentieth century, Chinese food, or what passed for Chinese food, was also marketed as an exotic but easy experiment for the home cook. The 1902 book *Good Housekeeping Hostess* includes chop suey, along with pineapple fish, pineapple chicken, and a kind of crepe flavored with chrysanthemums. There are oriental décor suggestions and a model is given for invitations to ladies' lunches to be composed in accord with what were regarded as amusingly deferential Chinese manners: "Will the most beautiful daughter of the Honorable S_____ accept the solicitation of her humble and unimportant friend . . ."[24] Chinese-themed parties are mentioned in the first Chinese cookbook published in English in 1912.

In Sinclair Lewis's *Main Street*, the frustrated heroine Carol Kennicott tries to bring some culture to the smug and remote Minnesota town of Gopher Prairie. Among her efforts is a party of just this *Good Housekeeping* sort that features chow mein, lychee nuts, and ginger in syrup. No one in Gopher Prairie except one "city-rounder" had ever heard of any Chinese dish except chop suey. Although the party came off, it was not without unease and a sense of trespassing beyond normal expectations.[25]

In the 1920s, companies with faux Chinese names like La Choy and Chun-King began offering canned and bottled Chinese products such as soy sauce, water chestnuts, chow mein noodles, and bean sprouts to mildly ambitious cooks. Exotic home cooking followed in the wake of the rise of Chinese restaurants as Chinese food became a central part of American dining in the interwar and postwar years.

The pattern set for Chinese restaurants before the First World War endured well into the 1960s. An account of Chinese restaurants in New York written by Ling Lew in 1939 shows the continued popularity of chop suey and chow mein. There were 248 Chinese restaurants in the city, 111 in Manhattan alone. About forty of these were in Chinatown, and in general small restaurants fared better than large ones, partly because of the impact of the Depression and partly because the repeal of Prohibition meant that nightclubs, bars, and cabarets drove Chinese restaurants out of certain neighborhoods due to rising rents. The largest Chinese restaurant in New York was Chin's on Broadway north of Times Square. Opened in 1926, it could seat 1,100—almost the same size as Mamma Leone's—and the owner, Chin Lee, as of 1921 also ran an 800-seat restaurant (Chin Lee's) a little farther north on Broadway.[26]

Not all of these restaurants fit a single pattern. In his 1939 study, Ling Lew distinguished within Chinatown a category of restaurants that catered to Americans versus those that had a predominantly Chinese clientele who actually lived in the neighborhood. The latter type were modestly appointed but offered better, more varied, and more authentic food.

At the New Hangchow, with primarily American customers, the menus emphasized varieties of chop suey and chow mein, along with pepper steak, shrimp with tomato, and egg rolls. By contrast, at the Lotus Inn, with a Chinese customer base, the English menu included fried lobster Canton-style, almond roast pork, roast pork with Chinese vegetables, and shrimp with lobster sauce and Chinese vegetables. American customers included African Americans, but Lew noted with regret that they were turned away from many Chinese restaurants because of the white customers' deplorable intolerance.[27]

MID-TWENTIETH-CENTURY CHINESE RESTAURANTS

Menus from the first two postwar decades show little change from this pattern. The Sun Luck restaurant on Forty-Ninth Street in New York was a favorite of theatre-district habitués. A menu from around 1956 includes eight kinds of chop suey, thirteen kinds of chow mein, and seven varieties of egg foo young. Chef's specials include some dishes listed according to the confusing transliteration popular at the time, but with detailed annotation: Fong Gon I Do (scallops sautéed with ham, chicken liver and Chinese vegetables); Hong Shu Har (shrimp with mushrooms, pork, snow-pea pods and scallions); and a classic of that era, War Shew Op (braised boneless duck). This is an ambitious and varied menu, with bird's nest soup, and two kinds of braised whole fish. It is also relentlessly Cantonese.[28]

In 1965 the harshly restrictive immigration laws, dating back nearly half a century (and in the special case of the Chinese, more than eighty years), were radically changed. The Hart-Celler Act, which went into effect as of 1968, kept the general principle of limiting immigrant visas, but lifted the virtual prohibitions on immigrants from East Asia and other "non-white" parts of the world. The impact of this legislation reverberated throughout American life, including the types of restaurants that came to be estab-

Fig. 62. Chinese New Year, *The New Yorker*, 1959.

lished by new immigrants. Calvin Trillin, only half-jesting, likened the Hart-Celler Act to an Emancipation Proclamation for serious eaters.[29]

A second defining event with particular application to the image of Chinese food in the United States was President Nixon's surprise visit to China in 1972. Not only was this an astounding opening to a long-standing enemy, a milestone in American foreign policy, but the spectacle of Nixon and Kissinger deftly manipulating chopsticks at a state banquet in Beijing created a sensation that surpassed even the one provoked by the visit of the Chinese viceroy in 1896. It is hard to believe how unusual it seemed that any non-Chinese person, let alone such very un-Bohemian types as Nixon and Kissinger, should have learned to use chopsticks. But the vogue for the spicy food of Sichuan (or an Americanized version of it) was already under way at the time of Nixon's trip, and it was supplemented by the opening of Hunan restaurants and the fateful introduction of General Tso's chicken.[30]

Most Chinese immigration in the decade or so after 1965 was not from Guangdong directly but rather Hong Kong, Taiwan, and Southeast Asia. Beginning around 1980, as mainland China relaxed its restrictions on travel, the province of Fujian had the most out-migration to the United States. And in the years since 1980, the old urban Chinatowns were supplanted by suburban enclaves—in the San Gabriel Valley east of Los Angeles, for example—or by new urban settlement as in New York's Flushing (Queens) and Sunset Park (Brooklyn). The restaurant industry today is dominated by Fujianese immigrants, their descendants, and their successors.

THE MANDARIN MAKES ITS MARK

The establishment of the Mandarin was accidental, and its success was paradoxical. Cecilia Chiang, a woman of upper-class background, raised in northern rather than southern China, hardly fits the Cantonese or Fuji-anese immigrant pattern. Moreover, she learned to cook only after opening a restaurant. When the original, austerely decorated Mandarin opened its red doors in 1961, Mme. Chiang was already an accomplished woman over forty years of age, with many marvelous as well as harrowing experiences behind her.

After a pampered upbringing, she had endured the devastation of war and had twice taken flight as a refugee, first from the Japanese, and then from the Chinese Communist revolutionaries. She was forced to pull up stakes four times, from wartime Peking to remote Sichuan, then to post-war Shanghai, then to Japan in 1949, and eventually to the United States. The second volume of Cecilia Chiang's 2007 culinary autobiography, *The Seventh Daughter*, takes its name from her position in a wealthy family of twelve children, who lived in a palatial compound in Peking with seven courtyards. Her given name was Sun Yun, but "Cecilia" would be her

Fig. 63. Interior of the Mandarin, 1970s.

name in the Catholic university she attended. The family's fortune came from, among other things, textile factories and newfangled, extremely popular movie theaters. The household had servants who shopped for food under her mother's supervision as well as two chefs, one from Shanghai and the other from Peking. Sun Yun wasn't allowed in the kitchens, much less taught anything about how to prepare food. Her first book, *The Mandarin Way*, which appeared in 1974, is a food memoir of a type that would become almost too popular later: a recollection of childhood oriented around times of the year, festivals, and the foods prepared and served during the annual cycle. It is a tour de force in its power to draw on recollections of early life. *The Mandarin Way* also points out in detail what Mme. Chiang estimates to be her advantage as a late-blooming chef: an excellent memory for specific foods and how they are supposed to taste.

The Mandarin Way evokes a beleaguered but brilliant traditional Chinese culture that the Japanese invasion and occupation, Communist rule, and reckless modernization would largely destroy. It ends with the savage Japanese attack on northern China in 1937 and, in response to the increasing hardship of life in Japanese-occupied Peking, flight to Chungking in the south, the capital of what remained of the Chinese nation. It was a hellish six-month journey in the first part of 1943 for Sun Yun and her Number Five sister. They covered three hundred miles by train and then, from where the line was blocked, walked another thousand miles in a circuitous route across the military front to unoccupied China, then headed west through the mountains to Sichuan. On the way they were robbed by Japanese soldiers. They trudged through mud and through war zones, and passed through every imaginable difficult climate from hyperborean winter near the Yellow River to the obdurately harsh summer heat of the south.

Finally in Chungking the sisters found members of their family and obtained jobs teaching Mandarin to, among others, American embassy personnel. There Sun Yun/Cecilia met her future husband, Chiang Liang, a businessman with advanced training as an economist, and once married, the couple were able to reconstruct some of the comforts of her former life. With the end of the war, they relocated to Shanghai.[31]

They were not to live in comfort for long. In 1949, they fled the advance of the Communist forces and the collapse of the Chiang Kai-Shek regime's control of the mainland. In the apocalyptic atmosphere of the impending Communist victory, they managed to board the last civilian plane out of Shanghai, to Japan. There were only three seats available, and their daughter, May, was taken along. Their son, Philip, later was reunited with his parents in Japan by way of Taiwan, where Chiang Kai-Shek and the Nationalist government had taken refuge. Mme. Chiang says that on the plane she asked her husband why they were relocating to Japan, a country that had arguably ruined their lives. His response was that she would be terribly bored if they had to live in Taipei, the capital of Taiwan, where there was no nightlife.

In the 1940s and early 1950s Japan was under American occupation, and Tokyo, though indeed lively, was still devastated and only slowly rebuilding. Chiang Liang had a diplomatic appointment as a commercial attaché of the Nationalist government now established in Taiwan. This allowed his wife to shop at the American military stores (PX), which had not-particularly-fresh but at least ample, mostly packaged, food.

Mme. Chiang recalls Japan as a turning point for her, a strange and at that time impoverished land where she was accompanied by small children and, at first, no servants. In 1951, motivated by a yearning for Chinese food and a desire to earn money, she and a cousin opened a restaurant near the Meiji Shrine, which they named Forbidden City. As Mme. Chiang recollects, this restaurant experience was partial, but not adequate, preparation for the Mandarin in the United States. The Tokyo enterprise was easy because it was supervised by her cousin and the cooking was entrusted to a series of capable and reliable chefs. While in Tokyo she became familiar in a general way with preparing and cooking food, but her status as a dip-

Fig. 64. Cecilia Chiang in Tokyo, 1950.

lomatic wife allowed her to employ two household cooks, and her official as well as family obligations afforded her only a vague sense of how to run a restaurant.[32]

Forbidden City may not have been a transformational enterprise for Mme. Chiang, but the Tokyo restaurant had an unexpectedly great influence on Chinese food in the United States. Two of its chefs went on to extremely successful American careers. Wang Ching-Ting (later to be known as T. T. "Tiger" Wang) was second in command in the Forbidden City kitchen until 1956, when he left for Washington, DC, to work for Hollington Tong, newly appointed Nationalist Chinese ambassador to the United States. He soon left the ambassador's service and moved to New York after a brief stint at the Peking in Chevy Chase, Maryland—a pioneer northern Chinese establishment. In New York, Wang Ching-Ting worked at Shun Lee, at that time on Broadway and Ninety-First Street, one of a small number of more or less Shanghai-inspired restaurants not far from Columbia University. Along with a partner, Michael Tong, Wang in 1965 bought Shun Lee, relocated it to Midtown, and renamed it Shun Lee Dynasty. a gracious high-end restaurant with expensively designed décor and a largely Western clientele.[33] Shun Lee would expand its franchise and was favored by Craig Claiborne, the powerful restaurant critic of the *New York Times* whose tastes and lyrical as well as carping manner of writing about food would influence a generation. Among other accomplishments, Shun Lee introduced, or at least popularized, General Tso's chicken in the 1970s.[34]

At a somewhat less exalted level, Panda Express, familiar from airports and highway rest stops everywhere, also owes its origin to Mme. Chiang's restaurant in postwar Tokyo. Ming-sai Cherng had been a cook at Forbidden City. His first US restaurant, in Pasadena, California, was called the Panda Inn. It opened in 1973 and, over succeeding decades, his son, Andrew Cherng, turned it into a chain of over 1,700 buffet-style restaurants.

Cecilia Chiang thus had some familiarity with how to run a Chinese restaurant when she came to California, but not in what would be considered a "hands-on" fashion, and certainly not in the peculiar environment of the United States. In 1960 she received a letter from her Number Six sister in San Francisco, informing her of the death of that sister's American-born husband. Through Chiang Liang's diplomatic connections, Mme. Chiang was able to obtain a visa to visit her bereaved sister. In San Francisco she happened upon some friends she had known in Tokyo, who had immigrated to the United States. They proposed to her a partnership to open a Chinese restaurant. They particularly wanted her to invest in the project and to help them negotiate the lease as their English was poor. Although she says her English wasn't all that great either, she put up $10,000 as a deposit and signed the lease. To her dismay, Mme. Chiang learned that her erstwhile partners were withdrawing from the plan. Worse, the landlord refused to give her a refund if she backed out of the long-term lease. Embarrassed to return to Tokyo and have to admit to her husband what had transpired, she determined to make a go of the sixty-five-seat restaurant on Polk Street, a thoroughfare whose main distinction was that it was starting to become a shopping center for gay San Francisco. The signs did not appear auspicious, given that the Mandarin was distant from Chinatown; she—a non-Cantonese woman—was an outsider in the Chinese restaurant business; and her cooking skills were as yet rudimentary.[35]

Mme. Chiang christened her accidental restaurant the Mandarin. From the start she was determined to offer something other than the standard, bland chop suey and egg foo young: "All this Chinatown stuff is a no-no," she said.[36] But how to achieve this goal seemed abstract. Not only was she ignored if not ostracized by most of the Cantonese restaurant community, but she had difficulty obtaining what now seem like basic ingredients, such as sesame oil. One well-established restaurateur, however, did help her. Johnny Kan ran a gracious and sophisticated Chinatown restaurant with the unsurprising name of Kan's, established in 1953.[37] In the 1950s, Kan told patrons who asked for chop suey politely but firmly, "We only serve Chinese food here."[38] He advised Mme. Chiang to make certain simplifying changes, such as trimming her menu and focusing less on Shanghai, but encouraged her to maintain a high standard of service and décor.

Once again, she was able to find skilled chefs, a married couple from Shandong who knew, among other things, how to wrap dumplings and pull noodles. They did not have a complete repertoire of the dishes she wanted to serve, and so she had to reconstruct, with their help, the preparations of her childhood. It was at this point, in the early 1960s, that she not only learned to cook but became proficient, both in her home (with minimal domestic help) and at the restaurant.

Novel and authentic as its food was, the Mandarin would never have succeeded without Mme. Chiang's immense personal charm and her memory for faces as well as tastes. She had a warm, good-humored but authoritative manner of service, a knowledge of her customers, and an ability unobtrusively to educate their palates. She was also adept in enlisting the aid of influential friends. The restaurant would be discovered by the wider world in stages. Her first regular customers were homesick northern Chinese émigrés, Japanese Americans, and executives of Japanese companies. The Japanese have always loved Chinese food, and Mme. Chiang's knowledge of Japanese and experience in Tokyo gave her an in with corporations like Japan Airlines and Sumitomo Bank, which held receptions at the Mandarin and whose individual employees flocked to it.

Local patrons in these first years included the owners of two of the grandest restaurants in San Francisco, Victor Bergeron of Trader Vic's, the most successful exponent of the "Polynesian" restaurant craze, and Alexis Merab, owner of a Nob Hill French/Continental restaurant called Alexis, a Georgian by origin whom Mme. Chiang had known at the university in Peking. Both of these men were well acquainted with Herb Caen, who presided beneficently over San Francisco society through a column in the *San Francisco Chronicle*. Caen started writing what was essentially a daily gossip column in 1938. His contributions had a thoughtful, joyous, and nostalgic angle amounting to something more likable than the malicious tattling of fellow columnists Walter Winchell in New York or Hedda Hopper in Hollywood. Caen had an eye and ear for everything that passed in stylish circles of San Francisco ("Baghdad by the Bay" as he called it), but he was thoroughly at home in less-exalted Bohemian and underground San Francisco as well. Caen's journalistic pertinacity is something of a record, and he had amazingly little trouble flourishing for almost sixty shifting years, his columns devotedly read by beatniks, hippies, and socialites alike. He sailed over cultural chasms, reporting who was dining at old-fashioned, swanky places like Kan's or Omar Khayyam's, or who fell asleep at Parsifal, but in the same column offered sympathetic treatment of anti–Vietnam War agitation and the blossoming of the Flower Children.

In 1963, at the urging of Alexis Merab, Herb Caen came to the Mandarin and subsequently wrote that this "little hole-in-the-wall" restaurant on Polk Street served "the best Chinese food east of the Pacific." Mme. Chiang, who didn't know about the newspaper column, was astounded the next day to see people filling the usually quiet restaurant at opening time, soon followed by others queuing up outside. This single endorsement brought the restaurant fame, and the quality of the food and the warmth of the hostess kept the Mandarin in a position of preeminence thenceforth.

A look at two menus from the early 1960s shows the Mandarin's innovations as well as connections to the Chinese American past, despite Cecilia Chiang's intention to break with Cantonese tradition. Innovative dishes included those with more spice, different textures, and new if not particularly challenging ingredients: sizzling rice soup, hot-and-sour soup (a taste combination previously unknown in Chinese American restaurants), Peking duck, tea-smoked duck, beggar's chicken (stuffed with ham, mushrooms, and water chestnuts and baked in clay), and both grilled and soup dumplings.[39] Luxurious and unusual items such as shark-fin soup and beggar's chicken mixed effortlessly with standard American Cantonese dishes such as wintermelon soup and shrimp toast. Certain regional dishes would

Fig. 65. Menu cover design, 1960s.

never become well known to Americans (fried frog's legs à la Shanghai), but others became famous at the Mandarin and then spread everywhere (prawns in Szechwan sauce). A somewhat surprising imitation of what was then Chinatown orthodoxy is a list of four kinds of chow mein (beef, pork, chicken, and shrimp). The dumplings are, somewhat peculiarly, featured in the chow mein category.

There was a separate menu in Chinese that included dishes not on the English version that were unlikely to have appealed to Westerners at the time—several kinds of tofu, sea cucumber in brown sauce, cold pork

MEATS

MING'S BEEF	$1.95
OYSTER-SAUCED BEEF	1.95
SLICED BEEF WITH CELERY	1.75
GREEN PEPPER BEEF	1.95
BEEF IN THE PAPER	2.00
PEKING SWEET SOUR PORK	1.85
SWEET SOUR MEAT BALLS	1.75

VEGETABLES

CHINESE CABBAGE IN WHITE SAUCE	$1.50
SNOW PEAS WITH MUSHROOMS	1.75
MUSHROOMS AND BAMBOO SHOOTS	2.25
BEAN SPROUTS WITH ONIONS	.95
ASPARAGUS A LA SHANGTUNG	(Seasonal)
FRIED LONG BEANS	(Seasonal)

DESSERTS

FRIED CANDY-COATED APPLE	$2.90
FRIED CANDY-COATED BANANA	2.90
RICE-STUFFED LOTUS ROOT	2.50
ALMOND BEAN-CURD	2.50
EIGHT PRECIOUS RICE PUDDING	3.00
THREE COLORED MASH	2.50

FRIED RICE

SHRIMP FRIED RICE	$.95
HAM FRIED RICE	.75
PORK FRIED RICE	.75

CHOW MEIN

CHICKEN CHOW MEIN (per person)	$1.75
PORK CHOW MEIN (per person)	1.55
BEEF CHOW MEIN (per person)	1.55
SHRIMP CHOW MEIN (per person)	1.75
GRILLED DUMPLING	1.00
SOUP DUMPLING	1.00

SOUP NOODLES

PORK CHOP SOUP NOODLES	$1.25
SMOKED FISH SOUP NOODLES	1.25
CHICKEN SOUP NOODLES	1.25
SHRIMP SOUP NOODLES	1.25

TRADITIONAL SPECIAL FESTIVE DISHES SERVED ON
CHINESE HOLIDAYS

Fig. 66. Mandarin menu, 1960s.

kidney, fish head in casserole—but the Chinese menu also offered chow mein with pork, shrimp, and leek. Some dishes that would later be American favorites were still so outré that they were listed only on the Chinese menu: Kung Pao chicken, twice-cooked pork. These, along with tofu, are now such commonplace menu items that it is hard to believe they seemed too exotic for American consumption in the 1960s.[40]

A mark of high-end Chinese restaurants of the 1970s and 1980s was that they offered desserts other than mere canned pineapple, kumquats, or lychees. The Mandarin's fried, candy-coated banana was widely imitated, and the menu also has "Eight Precious Rice Pudding" (sometimes rendered elsewhere as "Eight Treasures Pudding"), and rice-stuffed lotus root. Another sign of luxury was a wine and cocktail list. During the first years at Polk Street patrons often waited in a nearby bar because the Mandarin didn't yet have a liquor license, something impossible to obtain if a restaurant owner wasn't an American citizen.

The next step, by the mid-1960s, was to find larger quarters. Cecilia Chiang had an ambition to create a restaurant with stunning décor in a conspicuous and beautiful location. She knew that a collection of stores to be dubbed Ghirardelli Square was planned for a chocolate factory of picturesque Victorian vintage, perfectly situated next to Fisherman's Wharf, with panoramic views north to San Francisco Bay and Marin County. The Ghirardelli building's renovation into high-end shops and restaurants was daring at the time, one of the first adaptive reuses of this type. The complex included the original chocolate factory and what was called the Woolen Mill—a former clothing factory that had supplied the military. It was a daunting task for Mme. Chiang to convince Bank of America to make her a loan, especially when they initially informed her they didn't finance Chinese restaurants, and it was equally hard to persuade the owners of Ghirardelli Square that a Chinese restaurant would have sufficient prestige and the appropriate tone for their center. These challenging feats she accomplished through persistence, charm, contacts, and, perhaps most important, by inviting the property owners and bank officers to see and taste what the Mandarin offered.

The Mandarin relocated to the Woolen Mill at Ghirardelli Square in 1968, a year of turmoil in America generally and at UC Berkeley and San Francisco especially, but one that inaugurated a period of fame and prosperity for Cecilia Chiang. The restaurant was favored by San Francisco notables, stars of the rock music firmament like the Jefferson Airplane and John Lennon, as well as representatives of an older era of entertainment such as Danny Kaye and the opera diva Joan Sutherland. At the same time,

Fig. 67. View from the Mandarin, Ghirardelli Square.

the Mandarin was never perceived as the exclusive preserve of celebrities, and its management consistently regarded the quality of the food as paramount. It is hard to overstate the historic significance of this early example of a high-end Chinese restaurant, because, along with a handful of others, Cecilia Chiang challenged American stereotypes of the Chinese American, showing, in her case through food, that the extraordinary cultural heritage of the Chinese could not be reduced to chop suey or amusing Charlie Chan sketches.

The Mandarin in its new home seated three hundred, but Mme. Chiang retained a personal knowledge of her repeat customers when they visited and continued to refine traditional regional dishes and invent new ones, such as minced squab in lettuce cups.[41] The restaurant had views of the city and the bay, several different rooms and levels, and a modern décor with paintings and textiles rather than anything suggestive of traditional Chinese-restaurant kitsch. The wine list was serious and extensive, and the cocktails list did not include Zombies, Blue Hawaiians, or coconut drinks, nor was anything presented with funny little umbrellas. Doris Muscatine, author of the definitive guide *A Cook's Tour of San Francisco*, in the second edition (1969) praised the Mandarin at its new location for its elegant and modern décor as well as its Mongolian barbecue pit with seats built around it. She mentions "Peking or Mandarin duck," and "chao tzui" (what would soon become known in English as pot-stickers).[42]

President Nixon's visit to China in 1972 was a tremendous boon for the Mandarin, as it was for many other Chinese restaurants. It set off restaurant reproductions of the banquet served to the American president in Beijing. Mme. Chiang herself was contemptuous of the lower-class and rudimentary items offered at the Beijing festivities, but nevertheless her restaurant profited from the event. Nixon in China also indirectly stimulated an explosion of interest in non-Cantonese and particularly northern, Sichuan, and Hunan cuisine. What food writer Raymond Sokolov calls a "literal feeding frenzy" ensued.[43] As Americans rebelled against the bland

In Ordering

Imagine that you are a Chinese family selecting everything
cooked à la carte, just as we do here at The Mandarin. Chinese food
is served "family style," with something for everyone, rather than a main
entree for each individual. So for two persons, for instance, a soup and 2 or
3 dishes and rice are enough. For larger groups, order as many dishes as there
are persons in the party, plus "one for the table," and a soup, which would mean,
for a party of five – a soup, 6 dishes, and rice. In the case of eight or ten persons,
instead of that many dishes, perhaps you will want to have fewer selections
but have "double orders," or twice the amount. In any case, whether you
are trying Mandarin Chinese food for the first time, or an epicure
wishing to discuss the philosophy of fine food, our entire
staff awaits with pleasure to satisfy your pleasure.
These are some of my favorite dishes:

□ *Chiao-Tzu* □

Our most popular and famous appetizer: small dumpling turnovers
filled with a delicate meat stuffing, grilled crisp on one side,
served hot and steaming with vinegar and hot pepper oil

□ *Mongolian Lamb (or Beef)* □

Slices of tenderloin of lamb or beef sauteed with scallions
or:
grilled quickly over the Mongolian Fire Pit,
served in hot Mandarin Buns

□ *Mandarin Sweet and Sour Fish* □

Whole fresh rock cod, baked in a special delicate
sweet and sour sauce

□ *Prawns à la Szechwan* □

A traditional Western Chinese dish:
tender young prawns in a spicy, flavorful, hot, red sauce

□ *Smoked Tea Duck* □

Our incomparable version of duck, smoked in special ovens
over burning tea leaves; crispy skin, haunting flavor

□ *Beef à la Szechwan* □

An unusual dish from the West of China. Spicy hot!

□ *Mu Shui Pork* □

Slices of pork lightly sautéed with eggs and mushrooms.
This is especially delicious rolled in paper-thin pancakes with
duck sauce and slivered scallions

□ *Mandarin Crab* □

(In season). Sautéed in the shell, with a pungent sauce
of Chinese rice wine and crushed, fresh ginger

□ *Red-cooked Eggplant* □

Combined with pork in a delicious wine sauce

□ *Spinach Mandarin* □

Fresh spinach leaves and silvery noodles
combined in a light chicken sauce

□ *Asparagus à la Shangtung* □

(In season). Crisply sautéed with a whisper of sesame flavor.
Served cold

□ *Mandarin Glazed Apples (or Bananas)* □

Apples or bananas dipped in batter, glazed with candy syrup
and then plunged into ice water at your table
to crystallize the candied coating

Cecilia Chiang

Fig. 68. Mandarin menu, 1980s.

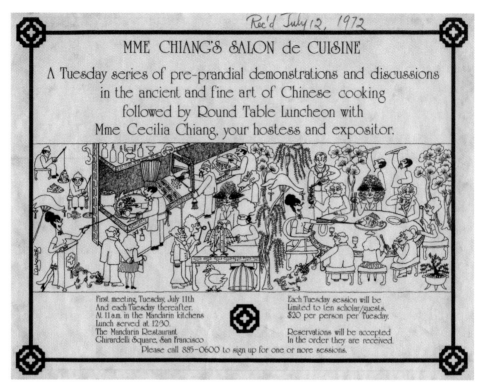

Fig. 69. Promotional flyer for Cecilia Chiang's cooking class, 1972.

culinary landscape of the postwar era, food became more spicy, a trend also visible in Mexican restaurants. The era also saw the initial popularity of Thai restaurants, along with thoroughly American inventions such as blackened redfish and Buffalo chicken wings. Spicy Chinese cuisine proliferated in the 1970s, and Szechwan restaurants opened in shopping malls.

In the same year that President Nixon visited China, Cecilia Chiang started offering cooking classes at the Mandarin, and it was through these classes that non-Chinese chefs such as Julia Child, James Beard, and Alice Waters spread a new way of looking at Chinese food. Waters likens Cecilia Chiang's influence on Americans' appreciation for Chinese food to that of Julia Child's effort for the French.[44] The 1970s were marred, however, by a long labor dispute in which the Mandarin was targeted as an example by the restaurant workers' union. There was intermittent picketing and frequent accusations and threats against Mme. Chiang, who was portrayed as a dragon lady—a persistent stereotype used to denigrate Asian women of strong character.

All this notwithstanding, the Mandarin was so successful that its Southern California fans convinced Mme. Chiang to open a branch on Rodeo Drive in Beverly Hills in 1974. The tastemakers of Hollywood and Beverly Hills were somewhat less adventurous than those of San Francisco, however, and this was reflected in the menu, which also gestures toward dieting, offering bland vegetable dishes, vegetable dumplings, and cold or sautéed tofu. According to Mme. Chiang, people in Los Angeles at that time didn't care for spicy food, nor did they enjoy the textures of noodles in soup.[45]

Running two restaurants proved distracting, particularly with the simmering labor crises in San Francisco, and Mme. Chiang gradually ceded control over the Beverley Hills restaurant to her son, Philip. He built on that foundation to create two inexpensive versions of the master restaurant, both called Mandarette, followed by the tremendously successful moderate-price chain P. F. Chang's, whose first branch opened in Scottsdale, Arizona, in 1993. The "P. F." was for Philip Chiang's business partner, Paul Fleming, and "Chang" was a simplification of "Chiang," which, test marketing apparently showed, made a better graphic impression. This restaurant group now has more than two hundred locations in the United States, Latin America, and the Middle East.[46]

Looking back, Cecilia Chiang remembers the 1980s as the heyday of her restaurant. The economy had improved from the stagnation and inflation of the 1970s. Although Americans' interest in food quality and experimentation with new cuisines seems in retrospect modest compared to the obsessions of today, the prosperity and sophistication of the 1980s created broad demand for high-end restaurants, and Chinese food seemed ready to profit from this trend. Business at the Mandarin was good. The benefits of experience, the end of the labor disputes, and the presence of an excellent management team made things almost easy for a time. The nearly simultaneous death of her manager and accountant, however, induced Mme. Chiang to sell the Mandarin in 1991. It continued to prosper for a time, but the restaurant closed in 2006, ending a remarkable five-decade run and a set of gastronomic innovations that reverberated across the United States.

Uninterested in retirement and energetic as ever, Mme. Chiang in the last twenty-five years has dedicated herself to advising restaurateurs and investing in restaurant projects as well as writing and teaching. She received the James Beard Foundation Lifetime Achievement Award in 2013, a belated mark of her influence and accomplishments. It seemed long overdue, because already by the 1970s, it was obvious that Cecilia Chiang and the Mandarin had significantly transformed American appreciation of Chinese food.

CHINESE FOOD IN AMERICA TODAY

The popularity of Chinese food, of course, continues, despite the passing of the Mandarin and a diminution in the number and visibility of elegant Chinese restaurants. An example of a restaurant that encapsulates historic and current trends is the Lucky Dragon, opened in 2013 on the main street of Garrettsville, Ohio, not far from Hiram College, a small liberal arts institution. Its menu is in some ways typical of those 40,000 Chinese restaurants across the country, but also special as it preserves in several layers almost the entire history of Chinese food in America. Unusually, it is still possible to order chop suey (four kinds) and chow mein (six possibilities). Other evocations of an otherwise vanished era are four kinds of egg foo young, shrimp toast, egg-drop soup, and a pupu platter for two. But this is not just a fossilized 1950s menu, as dishes from the 1970s Szechwan and Hunan boom are also well represented: General Tso's chicken (the chop

Fig. 70. Cecilia Chiang, 2013.

suey of the late twentieth century), kung pao chicken, and hot-and-sour soup. Finally there are a few modern tofu and vegetable dishes. The menu has more than two hundred items, and in case that is insufficient, there is a note that anything not found on the menu can be cooked "within our available ingredients."

How such a restaurant is established, what its business model is, and how its menu is devised, are questions of the sort that until recently were not asked much because Chinese restaurants were simply regarded as part of the landscape. It seemed somehow unremarkable for Chinese immigrants to open restaurants even in the most remote locations. In addition, their owners are themselves not eager to talk about their enterprises. Jennifer 8. Lee and John Jung have recently shown how individuals and families (now almost always from Fujian) establish Chinese restaurants according to a set of effective and reproducible practices.[47] Immigrants begin working in Chinese restaurants, learning to cook food for an American clientele, food that bears little relation to what they eat or prepare for themselves. Eventually they accumulate funds, experience, and sufficient knowledge of English to open their own places. The enterprise is financed by partnership with relatives, loans from relatives, or some other form of community support. Kinship networks, agencies, and advertising provide information about restaurants for sale, or even list promising American zip codes bereft of a Chinese restaurant. The menus are based on standard templates put out by menu-printing companies that the individual proprietor can add to and subtract from.

Village and family ties allow restaurant owners to find out how to prepare dishes their clients ask for or to branch out in new directions. The owner of a restaurant in Morgantown, West Virginia, recalls being asked by several customers if she could serve fried cheese wontons, and so she found out how to make these from a relative. Another restaurateur, in Pell City, Alabama, saw that his customers preferred beef to pork and started serving Mongolian beef (stir-fried beef with vegetables cooked in Hoisin sauce) on the advice of a friend from another state who taught him the recipe— one, needless to say, unknown in Mongolia.[48] The recipes are not generally regarded as secrets within the community at large, and especially not if the inquiry is from far away, beyond all possible competition; furnishing information is part of the collaborative nature of a diaspora network.

The very popularity of Chinese food and its longevity as a favorite American ethnic cuisine has tended to make it predictable, however, and not always the product of attention to quality let alone innovation. Movements to introduce new aspects of Chinese cuisine or to create a more gracious restaurant ambience have not displaced a certain comforting artificiality—the golden dragons and steam-table buffets of so many small towns. In cities, the tendency is for Chinese restaurants to branch out toward serving sushi (which commands a higher price), or an unusual assortment of regional Chinese dishes, Thai, and Vietnamese food. The result is a loss of focus and a lack of innovation for the core Cantonese cuisine.[49]

Some cuisines have moved upward socially to become more prestigious and to command higher prices. This is especially true of Italian food, as discussed in the previous chapter. It used to be associated with cheap spaghetti joints with red-and-white checked tablecloths illuminated by candles stuck into empty Chianti bottles but now includes restaurants offering house-made pastas and cured meats and fabulously expensive dishes prepared with white truffles—places run by chefs who are television personalities. The regional cuisines of Venetia, Emilia-Romagna, Tuscany, or Apulia are recognized by American restaurant-goers.

Japanese food is also segmented. The older, inexpensive "ethnic" cuisine survives, featuring sushi, tempura, miso soup, soba noodles, and the like, but it has been supplemented by some of the most elegant and expensive restaurants in the world. These serve rare, colorful, beautiful delicacies in an austere but perfect way—a kind of model for all modern high-end cuisines. Unlike Italian food's spontaneous ascent, the increasing prestige of Japanese food was influenced, if not orchestrated, by Japanese companies and public-relations campaigns to acquaint the world with high Japanese culture and especially its gastronomic distinction.[50]

Chinese food has not, by contrast, succeeded in gaining visibility for its splendid gourmand side. American customers typically resist the notion of a first-class Chinese establishment in terms of both food and atmosphere. In its prime, however, the Mandarin was something of an exception.

Despite their number and overall economic success, Chinese restaurants, outside of a few enclaves of recent immigration such as Flushing in New York or the Richmond District in San Francisco, have not been able to achieve significant innovations or improvements over the last several decades. Some of the problem is the unshakable bias that Chinese food has to be inexpensive. Customer resistance to anything but bargain-level tabs has meant that Chinese restaurants have only intermittently been able to accomplish what Italian establishments achieved in moving from a low- to high-end image. The twenty-first-century wealth of China has meant that a talented chef can find more lucrative and satisfying employment *outside* the United States. The widespread belief that American Chinese restaurants cannot aspire to much distinction may be because we take Chinese restaurants so much for granted that they seem invisible when so many other sorts of cuisines are being introduced and popularized. Perhaps this is about to change: the Waldorf Astoria Hotel in New York, recently bought by a Chinese company, opened an elegant restaurant in 2015 called La Chine, featuring the food of Zhejiang Province. New regional Chinese restaurants are opening in Pittsburgh to serve a large and eager clientele of Chinese university, business, and medical students and professionals. A recent article in *Saveur* describes the preparation of soup dumplings, eight-treasures duck from Chengdu, and cumin-scented dishes from Xian.[51]

The trajectory of America's love affair with Chinese food has not been consistently upward, but one can hardly fault the joyful and redoubtable Cecilia Chiang for this. In 2012, friends told her she had to "rescue" Chinese food and reopen the sort of restaurant that the Mandarin had once been, so that she might show the way toward appreciating the culinary richness and variety of China. Her response was that, at ninety-three, she was too old, although if she were merely eighty-three, that would be a different story.[52]

SYLVIA'S[1]

THE SOUL OF HARLEM

n August 1962, Sylvia Woods opened her restaurant in New York's Harlem on Lenox Avenue (now also named Malcolm X Boulevard) just north of 126th Street. Fifty years later, her death in 2012 at the age of eighty-six marked the end of her tenure as one of the most venerated restaurateurs in America. For Ms. Woods, these were fifty years of struggle, followed by success, expansion, and eventually fame. Her eponymous restaurant's upward trajectory defied a long decline that seemed to characterize Harlem in the decades after the riots in the summer of 1964.

For most of the late twentieth century, Harlem experienced housing decay and abandonment. The neighborhood was victimized by bank redlining, neglect from an often-indifferent city government, and urban erosion brought about by drugs, violence, and endemic unemployment. Sylvia's was a counterexample to the experience of many businesses in the neighborhood, managing not only to survive but to flourish in the 1970s and 1980s—painful albeit retrospectively picturesque years in the history of New York. As with the Mandarin, Sylvia's owed much of its success to

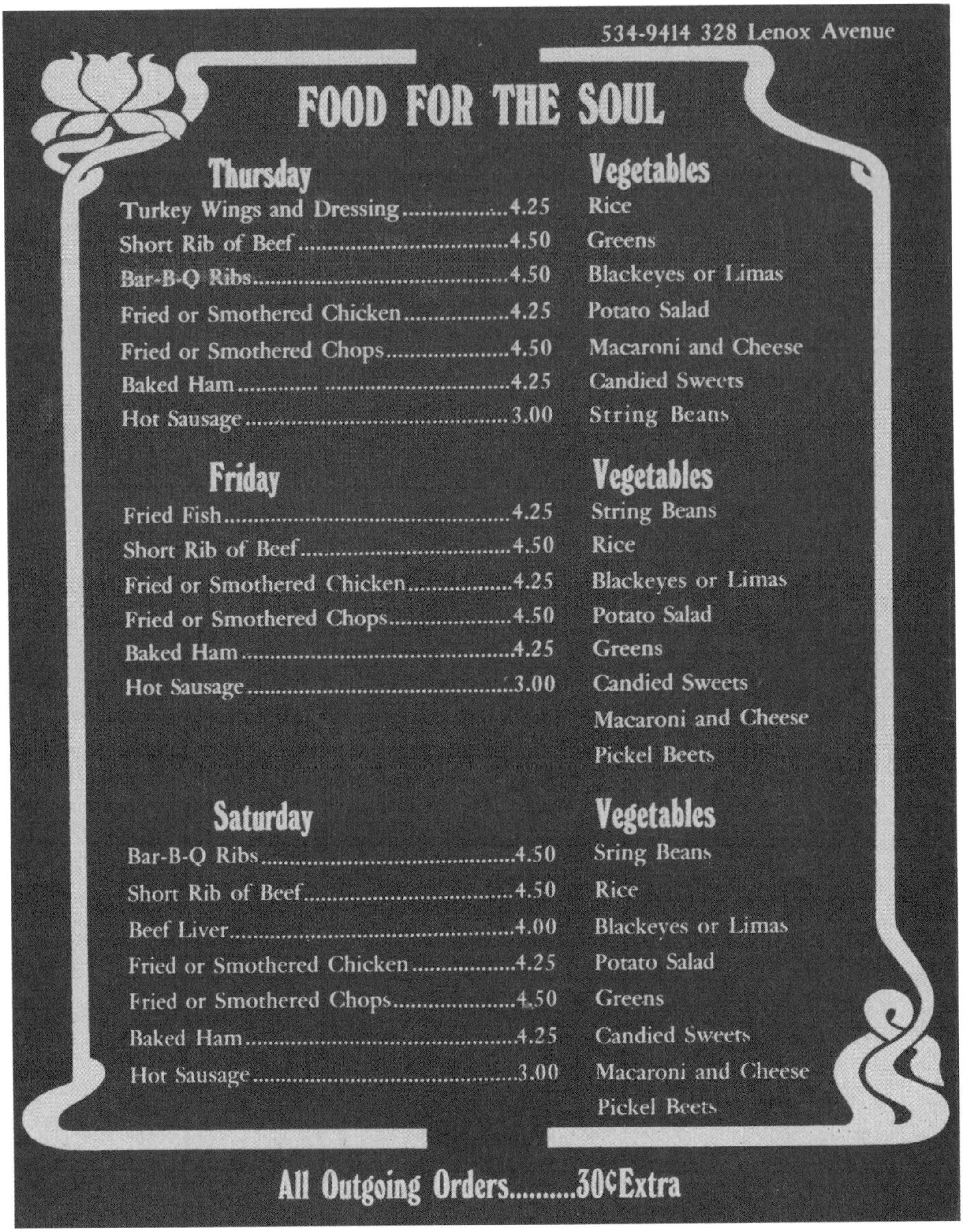

534-9414 328 Lenox Avenue

FOOD FOR THE SOUL

Thursday

Turkey Wings and Dressing..................4.25
Short Rib of Beef..................4.50
Bar-B-Q Ribs..................4.50
Fried or Smothered Chicken..................4.25
Fried or Smothered Chops..................4.50
Baked Ham..................4.25
Hot Sausage..................3.00

Vegetables

Rice
Greens
Blackeyes or Limas
Potato Salad
Macaroni and Cheese
Candied Sweets
String Beans

Friday

Fried Fish..................4.25
Short Rib of Beef..................4.50
Fried or Smothered Chicken..................4.25
Fried or Smothered Chops..................4.50
Baked Ham..................4.25
Hot Sausage..................3.00

Vegetables

String Beans
Rice
Blackeyes or Limas
Potato Salad
Greens
Candied Sweets
Macaroni and Cheese
Pickel Beets

Saturday

Bar-B-Q Ribs..................4.50
Short Rib of Beef..................4.50
Beef Liver..................4.00
Fried or Smothered Chicken..................4.25
Fried or Smothered Chops..................4.50
Baked Ham..................4.25
Hot Sausage..................3.00

Vegetables

Sring Beans
Rice
Blackeyes or Limas
Potato Salad
Greens
Candied Sweets
Macaroni and Cheese
Pickel Beets

All Outgoing Orders..........30¢Extra

Fig. 71. Sylvia's menu, daily specials.

the vivacious personality of its owner. Under her guidance, Sylvia's became a meeting place for political, religious, and community leaders. While retaining that neighborhood focus, Sylvia's also profited from the curiosity of European and Japanese tourists about black America, and beginning in the 1980s lunch at Sylvia's became a required stop on any cultural tour of Harlem.

Most of all, the restaurant's reputation built on a tradition of African American cuisine, a rural, Southern, "down-home" style marketed to a Northern clientele as "soul food." Sylvia Woods adopted the sobriquet "The Queen of Soul Food," and her signature dishes included African American culinary classics such as fried chicken, barbecued spareribs, cornbread, and collard greens. In the late 1960s, "soul food" generally replaced "Southern," "down home," or "country" as the preferred nomenclature for describing the prevailing styles of African American cuisine brought up from the South early in the twentieth century during what is commonly referred to as the Great Migration, when African Americans moved from the South to the cities of the North and Midwest. The gastronomic terms are not mutually exclusive, however. In a 1986 interview, Sylvia Woods, the Queen of Soul Food herself, referred to her cooking as "down-home and family style."[2]

I have chosen to feature Sylvia's here because its story reveals the cultural implications of the movement of black people from the South to the North in the first part of the twentieth century. Beginning before the First World War, black migrants, attracted by economic opportunity and the freer (if hardly egalitarian) North, transformed the spaces and places where they settled and worked. The routes of the railroad lines influenced patterns of settlement so that migrants from Virginia, the Carolinas, Florida, and Georgia relocated to New York, while those from Louisiana and Mississippi tended to favor Chicago. An indicator of this historical shift is the rise in the black population of New York from 91,709 in 1910 to 327,706 in 1930. In 1930, less than one-quarter of the city's black population had been born in New York State. About the same number were foreign-born. One-half came from the South. These figures show the influence of the Southern exodus, and also the less-appreciated presence in Harlem of people from the West Indies and Africa.[3]

African American New Yorkers had long been concentrated in Greenwich Village, but after about 1850 they moved to what was called the Tenderloin, in southern midtown Manhattan. Only around 1900 did Harlem start to be settled by black New Yorkers moving from other neighborhoods. By the time the Southern exodus kicked into high gear around 1910, Harlem was becoming the center of African American life in New York City.

A QUEEN IS BORN

Sylvia Woods's life exemplifies the importance of family ties and enduring cultural contacts between the South and the North. Born Sylvia Pressley in 1926 in the small town of Hemingway, South Carolina, she came from a family of farmers, laundresses, and laborers.[4] Her father, Van Pressley, died just days after her birth, a delayed casualty of gas attacks he suffered during the First World War. As a child, Sylvia once asked her mother why she didn't get a husband to help with work on the farm. Julia Pressley received a monthly government check after her husband's service-related death, payment that would cease if she married again. Showing her daughter the veteran's compensation check, Mrs. Pressley said, "Sylvia, this is my husband."[5]

The family hardly escaped the pernicious consequences of a rigidly segregated and unequal society. In 1906, Sylvia's maternal grandfather was hanged in South Carolina for a murder he did not commit in what amounted to a police-initiated lynching. Her grandmother, a midwife, did not know how to read or write, but managed to buy a farm. Despite the poverty and racial oppression of her childhood, Sylvia Woods remembered Hemingway as a close-knit, peaceful, and mutually supportive community. Her family was entrepreneurial, loyal, and confident that their abilities and labor would reap rewards.

Sylvia Pressley grew up without electricity or running water; almost everything the family ate was from their farm, and they used a mule to plow and to bring back wood from the forest. In her recollections she celebrates the food of her childhood: on Sundays, chicken (fried, roasted, or smothered), ham, pork roast, or beef stew; on Labor Day (the end of the corn, tobacco, and cotton harvests), barbecued venison and raccoon, okra, butter beans, and collard greens; for routine breakfasts, biscuits and syrup, grits, okra, tomatoes, and fried fish; and on normal days, a round of vegetables, baked ham, barbecued ribs, macaroni baked with cheese, and perlou, the Low Country rice specialty made with meat, shrimp, sausage, or vegetables.

When Sylvia was three, her mother moved, temporarily, to New York to take a job as a laundress. After five years she returned to South Carolina, but the attraction of the North—its gritty, cacophonous vibrancy—continued to draw the family in that direction. During the Second World War, Sylvia Pressley went to New York to attend beauty school, and returned home to open a hairdressing parlor. In 1944 she married her childhood sweetheart, Herbert Deward Woods, when he was on a brief leave from the navy. They moved to New York after the war ended, but Herbert Woods reenlisted. In the military, which tended to put many black soldiers into forms of domestic work, he learned baking. He would later bring this skill to the restaurant.

Over the years there was a constant back-and-forth between South Carolina and New York. Sylvia and Herbert's three children were sent to live in Hemingway in 1953. Reflecting on this frequent travel, Sylvia wrote that Hemingway seemed to her a suburb of New York, while New York looked like a big city just down the road from the tiny town.[6] In 1954, the year the

Supreme Court issued its historic *Brown v. Board of Education* desegregation decision, Sylvia Woods quit a job in a factory located inconveniently far away in Brooklyn and started waiting tables at Johnson's Luncheonette, a Harlem restaurant with a counter and just a few booths with tables. She knew a lot about cooking, but not restaurant work. As her memoir makes clear, food in the African American South, and for that matter, the South generally, was associated with homes, families, and communities, not something perfected in restaurants. The only restaurant in Hemingway did not even serve black people; before she started work at Johnson's, Woods had almost never been inside a restaurant.[7] Nevertheless, she was determined to get the job. Mr. Johnson asked her if she had any experience and she replied energetically in the affirmative. He told her, "Get me a cup of coffee," and, unfamiliar with the spigot, she burned herself on the coffee that flowed too fast from it. Despite the mistake, Johnson decided Sylvia Woods was a dedicated and certainly self-confident worker and hired her anyway.[8]

In 1962, at Mr. Johnson's suggestion, Woods bought the luncheonette from him for $20,000, mortgaging the family farm in Hemingway to pay for it. She waited for a year until she had paid off her grandmother, who actually had the title to the farm, and then changed the name of the establishment to Sylvia's. It did not seem different from any of the other small, struggling restaurants in the neighborhood, but it soon became more than merely a place to grab a meal. Sylvia Woods was good at establishing an atmosphere where people felt like talking and lingering, so along with the good food, its attraction was as a place to meet up and be seen. Its food was excellent and evocative. With its six booths and fifteen barstools at a counter, Sylvia's served food that was familiar to folks from the rural South, food that was hard to obtain or cook in the city.

In the Johnson years and in the beginning of Sylvia Woods's ownership, the restaurant was best known for breakfast. It developed a group of regulars, whom Sylvia Woods and her family called by their occupations: "Coca-Cola man," or "Con-Ed man," in the latter case a reference to the local utility, Consolidated Edison.[9] A breakfast menu from the 1980s includes eggs, sausage, salmon cakes, bacon, pork chops, beef liver, chicken, and sardines—all of which could be ordered with grits. Hotcakes round out this menu. The same document shows dinner specials during the week. Some items, such as beef short ribs, fried or smothered chicken, and baked ham, were available most days. Others, such as chicken giblets, oxtails or fried fish, were offered only one day of the week. There was always a wide choice of vegetables, including pickled beets, greens, and candied sweet potatoes, but also standard Southern "vegetable" side dishes such as potato salad and macaroni and cheese.[10]

The menu hasn't changed dramatically in the intervening thirty years or so. New items include a "sassy Angus burger" and chicken and waffles (Harlem or California style). Chicken giblets are gone, but chicken livers with gravy are quite popular. There is more fish, and some of it can be obtained grilled rather than fried. The vegetables are not listed casually as in the past, but rather are carefully described for the uninitiated. Instead of "greens" we have "collard greens," and they can be had traditional or vegetarian (that is, with or without smoked pork). Vegetable gumbo is available on weekdays. Oxtail, meat loaf, roast beef, and other dishes that were as much Middle American as Southern have disappeared.[11]

Sylvia's is near Harlem's main thoroughfare, 125th Street, and around the corner from the Apollo Theater, the neighborhood's leading showplace. The restaurant quickly became known for both its food and the charismatic warmth of Sylvia Woods herself, making it a gathering place for Harlem notables. Sylvia's was by no means unique, for many other well-established Harlem restaurants served Southern food. Copeland's on West 145th Street started as a catering business in 1958 and was rebuilt after a fire in 1981. Wimp's Bakery was famous for its red-velvet cake, but also for smothered chicken, fried and then slow-simmered in gravy. Singleton's continued to serve down-home items like pig ears and hog maws long after Sylvia's and most other places gave them up; and Wells Supper Club (also known simply as Wells) is often credited with inventing chicken with waffles.[12] Sylvia Woods's cousin and adopted sister, Louise Thompson, opened Louise's Family Restaurant in 1964, and it was well regarded for its smothered chicken, fish and grits, and barbecued ribs. Ms. Thompson died in 1977, and her daughter Julia Wilson, along with her husband, Isaac Wilson, ran it until it closed in 2008.[13] Other restaurants were established later, such as Charles' Southern Style Kitchen in the 1980s, famous for fried chicken, and Amy Ruth's in 1998. Manna's Soul Food, a buffet restaurant, was founded by Korean-born Betty Park in 1983 and now has three branches in Harlem.[14]

Sylvia's achieved distinction by the creation of a welcoming atmosphere that managed to attract celebrities without seeming to shut out the people of the neighborhood. The minister, social activist, and television host Al Sharpton recalls that the King of Soul Music, James Brown, used to come uptown to Harlem just to ride around and dine at Sylvia's, where they sat at whatever table was available—no special treatment. "You haven't been to Harlem if you haven't been to Sylvia's," Brown used to say.[15] There were other places with good food and a warm welcome, but Sylvia Woods, an exuberant optimist, truly loved her customers. As she told her eldest son, Van, after he said she ought to act a little more reserved, her motto was "Give Love, Show Love."[16] Unlike some of the other restaurants featured in this book, Sylvia's showed affection to all, and to this day, political and entertainment notables are not singled out for particular seats or flattery.[17]

Sylvia's fame in Harlem did not translate into a citywide reputation, because its founding and prosperity in the 1960s coincided with the increasingly marginalized status of the neighborhood in the mental geography of white New Yorkers. It wasn't just that Harlem was a segregated African American neighborhood, but that it became at once feared and ignored by white outsiders. This invisibility had not always been the rule. Harlem had been the hottest neighborhood in the city for jazz and nightclubbing in the

Fig. 72. Sylvia Woods and her employees outside the restaurant.

1920s and much of the 1930s. Although the "Harlem Renaissance" and the popularity of black-inspired popular culture brought fame and occasionally fortune to musicians like Duke Ellington, writers like Langston Hughes, and singers like Paul Robeson, it also showed the paradoxes and absurdities of deep-seated and seemingly ineradicable discrimination against blacks.[18] Some popular Harlem nightclubs with black jazz and dance entertainment did not admit African Americans as patrons. The blues composer and musician W. C. Handy was turned away from the Cotton Club while his music was being played inside.[19] An English observer during the 1930s remarked that experiencing clubs of this sort allowed the visitor "to see as much of real Harlem as a tourist sees of the African jungle sitting in a cocktail bar in Capetown."[20]

Some of the Harlem spots of the interwar boom period featured Southern food, or at least fried chicken and barbecued spareribs. The food at nightclubs was more eclectic and in any event dining was not the point of the venue, but it was a profitable aspect as wee-hours expensive snacks accompanied overpriced alcohol. The Cotton Club boasted of its Mexican, Chinese, and Southern food.[21] A mid-1920s Cotton Club menu offered varieties of chop suey, chow mein, egg foo young, and fried rice.[22]

After the Second World War, Harlem felt increasingly isolated, more as a consequence of being ignored than by its own insularity. Its citizens traveled all over the city for work and school, but white people ceased coming to Harlem for entertainment. The Velvet Underground's 1967 song "I'm Waiting for my Man," includes lines emblematic of white assumptions about Harlem like "Hey white boy, what you doin' uptown?"

The foreignness of Harlem in the minds of white New Yorkers provided the context for the sensation created by Gael Greene's review of Sylvia's in the March 1979 issue of *New York Magazine*.[23] As she readily admitted, Greene hadn't been to Harlem "since Rosa Parks refused to sit down at the back of that bus in Montgomery, Alabama . . ." (in other words, the 1950s). This review didn't exactly make the fortunes of Sylvia's, for it was already

CHINESE MENU

SOUPS
Chicken 50
Noodle 50
Chicken with Rice 50
Tomato with Eggs 50

CHICKEN CHOP SUEY
Chicken Chop Suey 1.75
Subgum Chicken Chop Suey 2.00
Chicken Chop Suey w. Mushrooms .2.00
Moo Goo Guy Pan 2.25

PORK, BEEF CHOP SUEY
Pork Chop Suey 1.50
Shrimp Chop Suey 1.75
Beef Chop Suey 1.50
Beef and Tomato 1.50
Pepper Steak 1.50
Pepper Steak w. Mushrooms . .1.75

FOO YONG DAN
(Omelettes) Chinese
Meat Foo Yong 1.50
Shrimp Foo Yong 1.75
Chicken Foo Yong 1.75

CHICKEN CHOW MEIN
Chicken Chow Mein 1.50
Chicken Chow Mein w. Mushrooms .1.75
Shrimp Chow Mein 1.75
Roast Pork 1.00

FRIED RICE
Meat Fried Rice 1.25
Shrimp Fried Rice 1.50
Chicken Fried Rice 1.50
Rice, Plain Boiled 25

AMERICAN MENU

RELISHES
Table Celery 50
Queen Olives 50
Stuffed Olives 50

Crabmeat Cocktail 1.25
Lobster Cocktail 1.50
Shrimp Cocktail 1.25

STEAKS, ETC.
Lamb Chops 1.75
Sirloin Steak 2.00
Filet Mignon 2.25
Steak, Minute 1.75
Broiled Ham Steak 1.50
Welsh Rarebit 1.25
Long Island Rarebit 1.50

CHICKEN
½ Broiled Spring Chicken 2.00
Chicken a la King 2.00
Chicken Mexicaine 2.00

COLD MEATS
With Potato Salad
Sliced Cold Chicken 1.75
Smoked Tongue 1.50
Boiled Ham 1.50
Assorted Cold Cuts 1.75

EGGS
Ham or Bacon and Eggs 1.25
Ham Omelette 1.25
Chicken Omelette 1.50
Mushroom Omelette 1.50
Spanish Omelette 1.50

SALADS
Lobster 2.00
Chicken 1.75
Shrimp 1.75
Crabmeat 1.75

POTATOES, ETC.
French Fried 50
Hash Brown 50
Lyonnaise 50
Green Peas 50
Sliced Tomato 50
Hearts of Lettuce 50

SANDWICHES & CAKES
Special Steak 1.75
Club 1.25
Chicken 1.00
Tongue 1.00
Swiss or American Cheese 75
Boiled Ham 75
Raisin or Pound Cake 50
Almond or Marble Cake 50

COFFEE, TEA, ETC.
Tea, Pot 35
Coffee, Pot 35
Milk 50

SPECIALS
Hot Turkey Sandwich 1.50
Steak Sandwich 1.75

Fig. 73. Menu from the Cotton Club, ca. 1925.

quite successful. Greene noted a sign at the restaurant proclaiming Sylvia Woods "The Queen of Soul Food," a self-coronation that no one in the neighborhood openly disputed. Prominent members of the Harlem political and entertainment worlds already routinely dined there, and a 1979 mention in Harlem's newspaper, the *New York Amsterdam News*, extolled the fried or smothered chicken and the meat loaf.[24] Greene's article effectively put the restaurant on the white person's map of the city, however, allowing it to attract new customers while retaining its neighborhood base.[25] Greene was surprised at the homey and friendly ambience, and this white restaurant critic's reassurances and the growing attention Sylvia's received from foreign tourists, started to change outsiders' perceptions of Harlem in the 1980s.

Reading Gael Greene's review today shows how strange the city of thirty-five years ago can seem. Greene's editor at *New York* initially opposed the idea of reporting on Sylvia's because that would encourage readers to do "something dangerous," namely visit Harlem. And Greene recollected that at first she was inclined to agree.[26] In her review she attributes the then odd idea of venturing into Harlem to a friend she calls the "Rocky Mountain Sybarite." Her initial response was to dismiss the Sybarite's plan as romantic nostalgia for the "bad old good old days" of the Cotton Club and Cole Porter. She also wondered if a white group "ribbing and chicken hopping in Harlem" would be welcomed. Once she overcame her doubts, the trip began inauspiciously, as it proved hard to convince a taxi driver to drive to Harlem, but the welcome at the restaurant was just fine, and in fact Sylvia Woods hugged her.[27] The ribs ("they were the why of this exercise") and candied yams ("sugary bliss") were outstanding, and in retrospect Greene remembered the biscuits as well as the ribs as the stars of the show. Not everything took Greene's fancy, however, and the review was not an unalloyed rave. The cornbread was "wishy-washy," Greene reported, and the fried chicken "pedestrian and over-done." The beef stew did not look appealing, but turned out to be full of flavor. The peach cob-

Fig. 74. Sylvia's menu cover.

bler was mediocre, but breakfast was wonderful. One wonders what black readers of *New York* and Sylvia's regular patrons thought of the review and its patronizing tone.

Gael Greene's experiences finished on a positive note—the waitress said, "Thank you and come again," and Greene concludes the article: "you can bet we will." A bit like Mimi Sheraton's 1977 review of Rao's, the secretive Italian restaurant in East Harlem, this account of an adventure uptown caught the imagination of those New Yorkers who not only didn't live in Harlem but, like Greene, had avoided it. Rao's, a white-owned Italian restaurant in what was considered a dicey neighborhood (East Harlem) was besieged by random visitors after Sheraton's review, defending itself by in effect becoming a club, for regulars only, and as such it remains. Sylvia's is larger and in other ways different. It never achieved status comparable to that of Rao's among New Yorkers living outside of Harlem, and it never turned away first-time visitors. It did obtain a unique reputation in the minds of people from outside of Harlem and was the only "soul food" restaurant they could name. Former mayor Ed Koch, not surprisingly, believed it was the only actual restaurant in Harlem.[28]

Still, it was neighborhood reputation that allowed Sylvia's to expand in 1979–1980 by taking over what had been the Uptown Bar next door. It eventually annexed two further store spaces, and currently it seats 450. In the 1980s it flourished as a hangout for political leaders such as borough presidents Percy Sutton and David Dinkins. The latter was New York's only African American mayor, from 1990 to 1994. Al Sharpton recalled that the restaurant was a kind of "neutral space," where opposing views could be peacefully exchanged.[29] The restaurant was a mandatory stop for politicians courting the votes of Harlem residents (hence Koch's impression of its uniqueness). It was also a place where, again according to Sharpton, you had to show up from time to time or else people thought you had retired. Among its regulars were black entertainment and sports stars such as Diana Ross, Quincy Jones, James Brown, and Muhammad Ali.[30]

In the 1980s, Sylvia's became a stop for tourist buses. At a time when most white New Yorkers still avoided Harlem, European and Japanese tourists were fascinated by its Jazz-Age history and its nascent hip-hop culture. Entrepreneurs such as Moroccan-born Lucien Corcos organized escorted tours of churches and historic sites such as Alexander Hamilton's house on Convent Avenue and the Morris Jumel Mansion on 160th Street, Washington's headquarters during the battle for New York. At eleven a.m. on Sundays, tourists were taken to churches such as First Corinthian Baptist on 116th Street and Seventh Avenue (now Adam Clayton Powell Boulevard) to hear Gospel music and a rousing sermon, followed by a meal at Sylvia's that would introduce the legendary "soul food" cuisine.[31]

It's easy to make fun of these visitors who can hardly be said to have obtained an in-depth impression of Harlem, but it is to their credit that they were motivated enough to do something that never occurred to most white Americans. Sylvia's came in for criticism that it was forsaking its regulars in favor of these tourists who, by definition, couldn't be loyal customers.

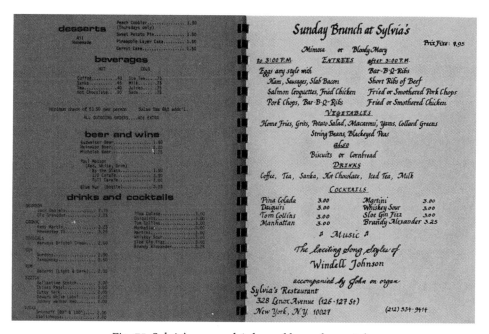

Fig. 75. Sylvia's menu, drinks and brunch specials.

Shortly after Sylvia Woods died, a *New York Times* blog quoted Kelly Smith, a longtime regular, as saying, "It was a neighborhood spot. Then it got so big, locals didn't go there anymore." But this is not literally true—the proportion of tourists may be high, but they have not taken over numerically or radically changed the spirit or food of the place. True, chicken gizzards were removed from the menu, along with calf's liver and onions. There are more grilled dishes, seafood, and salads now. But these changes were in response to local preferences and put in place as Sylvia Woods's children Bedalia Woods, Crizette Woods, and Kenneth Woods took over.

At one time the restaurant seemed so much a reflection of Sylvia Woods's personality that some doubted that it could survive her passing. In fact, it has pursued profitable innovations that did not come from Sylvia herself, such as a catering branch started by Bedalia Woods that now accounts for one-quarter of the business.[32] Not every new idea has worked smoothly, however, and the restaurant has had particular difficulties expanding. A branch in Atlanta opened in 1997, but did not manage to achieve the fame of its Northern parent and closed in 2005. A Sylvia's in St. Petersburg, Florida, opened in 2013 in the former Manhattan Casino, a long-abandoned landmark of African American entertainment where Duke Ellington once performed. The premises are owned by the city of St. Petersburg and the restaurant is run under the Sylvia's name by a nonprofit urban development group.[33]

AFRICAN AMERICAN, SOUTHERN, AND AMERICAN CUISINE

The Woods family's experience of oppression, migration, and enterprise are typical of the history of many African American families. The culinary traditions enshrined in the menus at Sylvia's—fried chicken, spareribs, greens, barbecue, biscuits—are symbols of black culture and

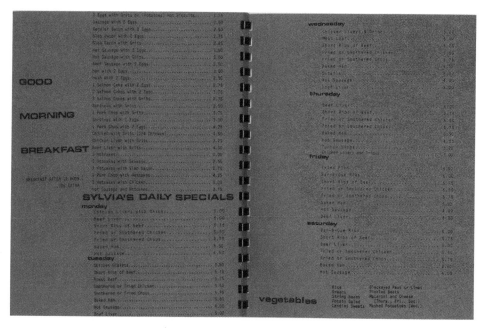

Fig. 76. Sylvia's menu, à la carte and daily specials.

self-understanding encapsulated by that now somewhat passé term "soul food." But even more than being the preserve of a cross-cultural tradition moving among Africa, the South, and the North, the food exemplified by Sylvia's is a basis for the story of American food.

To describe the African American role in the making of American food would require a book longer than this one, and it has been the object of a number of excellent studies. What is worth emphasizing here, besides the story of a particular restaurant, is how artificial categories such as "soul food," or even the broader "Southern food" break up the sweep of American culinary invention and adaptation. African American food has a particular set of characteristics and history, but it affects all aspects of America's culinary evolution, not just those of a so-called minority community. Even in the long years of racial subordination, this overall influence was here-and-there acknowledged by white observers. An article in the *New York Times* on November 10, 1895, for example, stated:

In so far as we have a National cooking it is of African, rather than European origin. Cooking in the U.S. was "treated by slaves and freedmen," in the opinion of many good judges, to results not surpassed by the most sophisticated arts of Gaul.[34]

On one level this is a perfectly conventional statement for its time. In talking about New Orleans we saw how widespread was the idea among white people that black cooks they enslaved or employed had unusual skills and could reproduce and elaborate on the culinary inventions of Europe and America. The author of the *New York Times* article goes further, however, crediting black cooks with inventing American cuisine, not just acting under white instructions.

More conventionally, during at least the first century after Emancipation, white observers limited the role apportioned to black domestic servants and restaurant owners to a creative but passive guardianship of culinary knowledge. The chapter on Antoine's made mention of the first edition of the *Picayune Creole Cookbook* in 1906, which mourned the passing of a generation of African American cooks who kept alive the home-cooking Creole traditions of the families they served and without whom that tradition was endangered.[35]

Black cooks' supposed nurturing of white traditions and white writers' admiration for their abilities were enduring ideas. In the 1920s and 1930s, cookbooks written by whites adopting the voice of a black female cook proliferated. The authors of *Aunt Caroline's Dixieland Recipes* (1922) asserted, "In the art of cooking the 'Old Southern Mammy' has few equals and recognizes no peers."[36] In some of these books, such as *Aunt Priscilla in the Kitchen* (1929), the recipe is given in what purports to be Southern black dialect, as in this conclusion to a recipe for chili con carne made with chicken: "A wall of nice cooked rice round de edge of yo' dish, wid de chicken an' sauce in de middle am mighty fine." As Jennifer Jensen Wallach remarks, this recipe exemplifies the perverse complexity of American ideas about food and race: instructions for making a Mexican American dish, described by a white woman, and voiced in pseudo-black dialect.[37]

An American regional cookbook put together for the New York World's Fair of 1939–1940 is full of racist references to dishes invented by "darkie cooks," "mammies," and the like and then appropriated by white people. Catfish curry, for example, was "a Negro favorite, which by virtue of its goodness was taken up to the big house and there remains." This book complacently acknowledges that African American cooks have certain unique skills—only "darkie mammies can make this wonderful dish" (boneless turkey). Generally, however, the role of household cooks is that of ingenious custodians of essentially white culinary traditions.[38]

In his 1955 *Food Odyssey*, the restaurant evaluator Duncan Hines wrote that almost all famous Southern dishes are the work of "Negro cooks" or show signs of "at least their special touch." Often his observations are coupled with assertions of the instinctual, uneducated nature of this skill, observable especially in the lack of reliance on written texts or precise measurements. Hines condescendingly continues:

They cooked by instinct, these artists of the saucepan and skillet, like a musician who plays by ear, and measured everything as "a smidgen of this and pinch of that"; and their educated hands could tell when bread or pie crust felt just right.[39]

This instinctual manner of cooking, though, has often been a boast of African American cooks themselves. *Vibration Cooking*, the title of Vertamae Smart-Grosvenor's pioneering cookbook and memoir of 1970, refers to preparing food by using nonformulaic knowledge:

And when I cook, I never measure or weigh anything. I cook by vibration. I can tell by the look and smell of it.[40]

In the 1997 film *Soul Food*, directed by George Tillman, the family matriarch Big Mama Jo tells one of her daughters that she never relies on written recipes and doesn't need to measure out ingredients—it's all in her head.[41]

In her two cookbooks, Sylvia Woods, of course, accommodates the home cook who lacks her experience; measurements are precise and steps are spelled out. Cooking is always a skill acquired by experience, in Woods's accounts, not a magical gift, but it is also not something to be followed dutifully according to written instruction either, especially for basic but difficult things like biscuits. It takes some practice to make biscuits, Sylvia Woods asserts, and those made by her longtime Hemingway-born chef Ruth Gully she considered superior to anyone else's. In order to master biscuit making it is important to remember what the dough should feel like. When it comes to pot roast, Woods presents both her recipe and Ruth's, inviting the reader to choose. They are very similar, except that Woods's calls for cooking the meat with A1 and Worcestershire sauce.[42]

For many years the prevailing official (white) consensus was that black people had a talent for cooking, but didn't create anything other than a marginal kind of food of their own—what then became identified as soul food, set apart from anything whites were interested in. Southern food, on the other hand, was deemed white even if, more often than not, it was cooked by African Americans.[43] Arbitrarily barbecue, fried chicken, and biscuits were said to belong to whites while chitterlings (intestines), pigs' ears, poke salat, and paw-paws were marginalized as exclusively black property. Contradicting this orthodoxy, surveys by the South Carolina agricultural experiment station undertaken between 1939 and 1942 showed that African American "dietary habits resembled those of white families in corresponding sections of the state." There were some differences—whites ate shrimp often, while blacks tended to have them only for an occasional breakfast. Hambone with green beans or stewed pears was distinctly white while hominy or cabbage with fat meat gravy and collards boiled with meat was black.[44]

The "ownership" of Southern food remains controversial, as attested by disputes launched in 2013 by allegations that celebrity restaurateur and chef Paula Deen not only made racist remarks, engaged in sexual harassment, and underpaid her kitchen workers but also presented their recipes as her own creations. One of her African American former collaborators, Dora Charles, recently published a cookbook called *A Real Southern Cook in Her Savannah Kitchen*. On the question of differences between black and white Southern cooking, Ms. Charles said recently "Southern country food is pretty much the same for black people and white people, except most black cooks are more concerned with seasoning." African American cooks often make up their own spice mixtures. For example, "Savannah seasoning" is one of Ms. Charles's favorites. It has Lawry's seasoned salt, garlic, black pepper, and table salt and is used with ribs, pork chops, and baked spaghetti.[45]

In the nineteenth and twentieth centuries, African American cooks, especially those living outside the South, referred to their culinary style as "Southern." One of the first cookbooks published by an African American bears the title *What Mrs. Fisher Knows About Old Southern Cooking*, and it dates from 1881. Its author, Abby Fisher, grew up in South Carolina, married and lived in Mobile, and achieved success as a chef in San Francisco.[46]

Beyond the question of how much similarity there is between black and white Southern cuisine is the larger matter of American food and its black origins. As long ago as 1975, the distinguished anthropologist Sidney Mintz pointed out that African influence permeates all of America, and that one way of understanding the African role in areas such as food is to look at what are considered white Southern practices.[47] But this observation, the fruit of academic research, is actually not so different from the offhand *New York Times* observation of 1895 quoted earlier.

The mainstream of African American cuisine begins, of course, with Africa. This may seem obvious, but how African culinary ingredients and techniques were brought to the New World is still a matter of exploration and debate. There is a certain amount of mythology and invented narratives surrounding the African origins of black American cuisine, but there is no question about the significance of these origins. What would be called "soul food" in the 1960s was the result of West African, Western European, and Native American cooking practices. Even before the seventeenth century, when the African slave trade grew exponentially to provide coerced labor for American sugar, tobacco, rice, indigo, and other international cash crops, there was trade and food exchange between Africa and the rest of the world.[48] Before 1600, Native American crops such as corn (maize), cassava, and sweet potatoes were already common in West Africa, as were European breeds of pigs and chickens. Arab and East Asian traders brought bananas and plantains to Africa, while Asian rice introduced by the Portuguese was cultivated alongside native African rice. There were limits to this global exchange, such that, for example, certain West African staple ingredients like palm oil, which was used as the basic cooking medium, were unavailable in the Americas, and so was replaced in this case by pork fat.

The Igbo, Mande, and other peoples of western Africa were thus not completely unfamiliar with the American agricultural environment they were forced to confront. The newly enslaved arrivals introduced African watermelon and okra, but other African food crops such as eggplant and millet were already being grown in the New World. Bananas, plantains, kale, black-eyed peas, and peanuts were common to both Africa and America before 1650, even though their origins were diverse. Many of the spices favored by African cooks had also been well known in medieval Europe as a result of Arab and Persian influence. Africans brought long-grain rice to South Carolina, along with certain ways of preparing one-pot stews.[49] Yams were an entirely African export, but Africans would also become identified with ingredients and dishes that had New World origins or were eaten by whites as well—cornbread, okra, fat back, chitterlings, and collard greens, for example.[50]

This hardly means that European and African cuisines were similar, but rather that the Portuguese and other intermediaries between the continents had already introduced certain European ingredients to Africa and were familiar with what Africans ate when the Transatlantic slave trade began. Slave ships prepared a rough equivalent of the pounded cooked starch known as "fu fu" in West Africa, made with yams, rice, or cassava and garnished with palm oil and pepper.[51]

Those who survived the harrowing journey across the Atlantic were forced into cruel, mostly agricultural, labor. What they consumed depended on several factors, especially climate, which influenced what the staple export crop was, and the lifestyle and business model of the European slave owners.[52] At one extreme was the Caribbean, where slaves were set to work on the harvesting and processing of sugar. Requiring immense numbers of slaves, sugar was nevertheless hugely profitable. Plantation owners were either absentee proprietors (living in England or the northern American colonies), or remained on the islands for a short time. In any event, they generally did not plan to make a life in the New World but rather to spend their riches in the home country. The population of the British islands such as Barbados, Jamaica, and Antigua was 90 percent of African origin since the native inhabitants died out and the colonists were never enthusiastic about staying. Under such circumstances, slaves were allowed to raise their own crops and feed not only themselves but their masters as well. The Caribbean has a distinctive and African-inspired cuisine, though the Spanish and French colonies reflected more European influence than did the English islands.

An opposite culinary extreme for British America was New England, which although hardly uninvolved in slavery, had a small slave population and an economy that did not depend on plantation crops. It was settled by Europeans, many of them religious dissenters determined to build a life in the New World rather than returning to Europe, who were uninterested in making a fortune off export crops. This is not to say that they were permanently sectarian in their way of life, nor that they shunned wealth, but New England made its initial fortunes serving as a broker between the Caribbean and Britain and in various other mercantile ventures. What the rural population grew and ate depended on knowledge obtained from the native inhabitants, so for the first century or so of colonization corn, pumpkins, clams, cranberries, and the like replaced English staples such as wheat bread or cake.

The American South resembled the Caribbean in its slave-intensive production of cash crops, but unlike the Caribbean sugar planters, the American slave owners created a life they regarded as permanent rather than becoming absentee landlords or planning a European retirement. Culinary traditions developed through exchanges between Africans and Europeans rather than Africans possessing entirely separate foodways. A dish like sweet-potato pie, identified with African American cuisine, combines the British American predilection for pies and the African American familiarity with yams and sweet potatoes.[53]

In the nineteenth-century South, cotton was, of course, the great export crop and the economic basis of slavery, but what was referred to as "the peculiar institution" of slavery had not begun as the result of cotton but rather of the profits to be made in sugar, tobacco, indigo, and rice. The coastal regions where these were grown in the late seventeenth and eighteenth centuries were the first to develop cuisines that presented overlapping elements of black and white tastes. Coastal South Carolina was given over to rice and indigo cultivation, and while slaves were harshly controlled and not encouraged to establish their own enterprises, an identifiable cuisine with a strong African influence developed. In North Carolina,

Virginia, and Maryland, there was a somewhat greater European (that is, British) influence on what was grown for food and what was prepared. There tobacco was the most profitable crop, and although slave labor was vital to the industry, production was on a smaller scale without the vast concentrations of slave labor characteristic of plantations, thus strengthening the white culinary influence.

Grudgingly or willingly, Southern landowners allowed their slaves license to dig gardens and feed themselves. These "botanical gardens of the dispossessed" were one source of food.[54] The plantation owner distributed basic items such as cornmeal, salt, bacon, or other lesser cuts of pork. A third source of food for the slaves was what could be foraged or hunted in the woods and fields—opossum, deer, muskrat, squirrel, and also plants such as pokeweed, milkweed, or marsh marigold. Involuntary African migrants retained and adapted their food gathering and preparation customs as well as tastes: a large variety of vegetables flavored with small amounts of meat (often from hunted or trapped animals), fried in oil or grilled. In some cases traditional techniques were applied to new ingredients such as squash, peppers, different kinds of beans, or paw-paws. White Southerners consumed things that slaves (other than house servants) had no access to: coffee, tea, brandy, spices, and imported delicacies such as almonds. Sugar, and therefore desserts, cookies, and sweets were rarely enjoyed by slaves.[55] This was a contrast created by differential wealth and culinary opportunities, however, not a matter of taste.

In most respects the diets of slaves and white Southerners resembled each other. Both populations ate the meat from pigs, though whites tended to keep the better cuts, the chops and pork roasts, while the slaves were given smaller pieces of meat that were made into stews, or they would use organs such as the intestines (chitterlings) that whites threw away. Slaves were more likely to eat wild as well as cultivated greens. Both blacks and whites ate cornbread, hominy, and grits, but the latter were more likely to have white bread as well.[56] The similarity of diet between ordinary white and black people was greater than between master and slave: The poor white population of the nineteenth-century South ate pork from the less prestigious parts of the hog, cornbread, greens, sweet potato pie, candied yams, black-eyed peas, and rice, much like blacks who had largely developed the cultivation and preparation of these staples.[57]

What white plantation owners ate was usually prepared by slaves, and so these African American cooks on occasion became expert in high-end European cookery. Thomas Jefferson's cook, James Hemmings (brother of Jefferson's "companion" Sally Hemmings), traveled with him to Paris, where Jefferson was ambassador from 1784 to 1789. We know Hemmings popularized waffles, bread stuffing, ice cream, and vanilla flavoring.[58] His influence, and that of other African American chefs who worked for wealthy white families, extended to the general American population. Cookbooks written by members of the Jefferson and Randolph families, such as Mary Randolph's widely read *Virginia Housewife*, include recipes for catfish soup, peanut soup, Virginia gumbo, and other originally African American dishes.[59]

In the North, long before the Civil War, blacks established food businesses to serve a more urban society than that of the South. In the North they also organized services such as catering for bachelors and for moderately well-off households of the sort that couldn't afford a large staff of servants. In post-revolutionary Philadelphia, African American street vendors sold pepperpot—a soup made with tripe, potatoes, spinach, and spices that resembled the more expensive turtle soup. It was partly a West African dish and was even served with a kind of fu fu made from West Indian plantains or cornmeal. Pepperpot was also distantly based on Spanish and Portuguese stews, but mostly was an original adaptation to the products available in Philadelphia. There were dozens of varieties of pepperpot, and it is still a local, if now endangered, specialty.[60]

Robert Bogle was the first of a group of African American caterers in Philadelphia who began as servants for temporary jobs ("public butlers").

Bogle started his business on South Eighth Street in 1812, and by 1830 it was so well known for providing celebratory dinners that Nelson Biddle, a member of what is still one of the most prominent families in Philadelphia, wrote a poetic "ode" to the man whose magnificent meals ushered in the newly christened baby, the blushing maiden's wedding, and the memorial of death. African American caterers eventually formed an association that controlled the catering industry throughout the nineteenth century. The eminent black social scientist and political leader W. E. B. Du Bois remarked that the Philadelphia caterers "took complete leadership of a bewildered group of Negroes, and led them steadily to a degree of affluence, culture and respect such as has probably never been surpassed in the history of the Negro in America."[61]

In New York around 1800, as in Philadelphia, African Americans were ubiquitous food street-sellers, particularly offering oysters, which flourished around the islands and marshes of New York Harbor. The most famous vendor was an African American named Thomas Downing, who started harvesting his own oysters to sell and then established a restaurant ("oyster refectory," as it was termed) on the shore so that the oysters could be kept alive in a watery holding tank until needed. Oyster stands were not new, but they tended to be simple to the point of decrepitude, whereas Downing's was gracious and served complex cooked oyster dishes and roasted or raw oysters at elegantly set tables. Thomas's son, George Thomas Downing, opened a full-fledged restaurant in New York in 1842 and a hotel in Newport, Rhode Island, in 1854. After the Civil War, he became the manager of the dining room of the US House of Representatives.[62]

SOUTHERN FOOD TO SOUL FOOD

At the beginning of the twentieth century there was a well-established African American cuisine, or really a series of local food customs in the

South, where the great majority of black people still lived. Black cooking had much in common with that of white Southerners, and although there were particular kinds of dishes exclusively identified with whites or blacks, class and region mattered as much as, if not more than, race. For the North as well, there was an identifiable African American cuisine before 1920, but the predominance of African Americans in the catering and restaurant business serving a white as well as black clientele meant that African Americans were adept at preparing all kinds of European and American foods.

Beginning in the 1920s restaurants serving the new arrivals from the South, as we have seen, opened in Harlem and other urban black neighborhoods in the North and Midwest. Descriptive terms like "Southern" or "down-home" indicated that they were intended to cater to homesick recent arrivals who did not have the ingredients, equipment, or space to prepare the food of their memories. Not all that different from the trajectory of Chinese and Italian restaurants, these places soon started attracting patrons who had not grown up "down home," wherever that was. The difference was that whites, who might patronize nightclubs in Harlem, were not interested in Southern food, especially the Southern food of poor people, white or black. The new clients were urban-born African Americans.

As the proportion of the black urban population became increasingly Southern or the children of Southerners, down-home cooking tended to become a marker of nostalgia and identity. In Ralph Ellison's *Invisible Man*, the unnamed narrator grows up in South Carolina and comes to Harlem after being expelled from college. At first Harlem seems a magical land of opportunity, but he discovers that in the North the oppression of African Americans simply takes different forms. At one point the narrator sees a street vendor selling baked yams and is overcome with longing for home. He buys some yams and suddenly, as he eats them while walking, he feels free. He imagines how shocked his Northern friends would be to see him enjoying simple country food, and he scorns their unwillingness to acknowledge the things they love that make them who they are: yams, chitterlings, or boiled hog's maw.[63]

Repeating a pattern from the nineteenth century, African American food entrepreneurs of the early twentieth century sold their goods on the street. Harlem vendors competed to offer Southern specialties such as fried chicken, roast corn, and chitterlings. Lilian Harris Dean, an early migrant who arrived from Mississippi in 1901, became famous as "Pig Foot Mary," and her specialty was celebrated in 1925 by the writer James Weldon Johnson: "Everybody knows 'Mary' and her stand and has been tempted by the smell of her pigs feet, fried chicken and hot corn . . ."[64] Restaurants followed, but most of them remained simple establishments, a small step up from a street stand. Some of the more successful Harlem restaurants specialized in fried chicken (Tillie's Chicken Shack), or barbecued ribs (the Bon Goo Barbecue), and they cultivated regulars, provided entertainment (at Tillie's there was a piano available for patrons to play), and each had a special atmosphere.[65]

Urban blacks who had grown up in the North gradually came to identify with what had previously been dismissed as "country." Southern rural food, indicated by tags such as "country" or "Southern," eventually became "soul food," denoting a common possession even for those who had not grown up on a farm in the South. A 1960 article in the African American paper the *Philadelphia Tribune* noted that members of the black elite could be seen eating at a place called Dell's, which served traditional Southern food "which ten years ago was frowned on by the masses of the so-called 'elite' Negro society. Now it's considered fashionable to eat 'down home' cooking."[66] Within a decade of that article's publication, traditional food was a mark of identity, excluding whites who did not share its emotional background, and it became as much part of black culture as the blues.

"Soul" was first used in conjunction with "brother" and "sister," terms that had established usage in the black church. In 1903 W. E. B. Du Bois published *The Souls of Black Folk*, which is both a personal and sociological investigation into the lives and outlook of African Americans living under a regime of cultural as well as economic subordination. Among other things it is also one of the earliest accounts of what African Americans ate after Emancipation.[67] It may seem farfetched to attribute an academic origin to a popular-culture usage, but Du Bois's celebrity status makes it at least possible; this particular book discusses how black people have an inner spirit that is veiled (Du Bois's term) when dealing with the demands and contempt of whites. Another effort to separate African American self-conceptions from white categories came in the 1930s when the newspaper the *Chicago Defender* campaigned to get black people to call themselves "Race Men" rather than "Colored" or "Negroes," both of which were white-defined phenotype categories.

None of this proves that "soul" was specifically applied to food before the 1960s, but does suggest there was a context for identifying African American cuisine with a creative tradition independent of white-imposed definitions. By the mid-1960s "soul" started being used as an adjective meaning not just something produced by or resonant with black people, but an expression of ethnic identity. It was applied to music—not so much the traditional music of the South or blues or Gospel, but the commercial songs of popular singers and styles, from James Brown to Motown. Soon "soul" was a marketing term that could include combs, hairdos, and, finally, food.[68]

The emergence of "soul food" to describe what was previously "down-home" or Southern coincided with changes occurring in the civil rights movement. The mid-1960s saw a shift in African American strategies away from alliances with whites to achieve integration and toward the assertion of African American cultural as well as political autonomy, encapsulated by the Black Power movement. Rather than aiming at a world in which race wouldn't matter, advocates of Black Power such as Stokely Carmichael (who later changed his name to Kwame Touré) extolled the culture of African Americans and restricted access to its legitimate appreciation. In an interview with the *New York Times* in 1966, Carmichael expressed what would soon become an African American consensus: that white people who claimed to be part of the movement couldn't embrace what it was to be black. Specifically they "cannot relate to chitterlings, hog's head cheese, pig feet, ham hocks, and cannot relate to slavery, because these things are not part of their experience."[69]

The Black Power movement marks an obvious turning point in race relations and politics. Assertions of African American difference challenged complacent assumptions that everyone would become like white people. In the limited field of food culture, however, cultural nationalism was neither completely successful nor really accurate. As culinary historian Adrian Miller remarks, a four-hundred-year old cuisine blending African, European, and Native American contributions was now black-owned, and that even without any connection to the South, a black person was defined by this food. Carmichael grew up in Trinidad and, apart from his activities as an organizer for the Student Non-Violent Coordinating Committee (SNCC), had no experience living in the American South, so, as Miller goes on to say, he was presumably unaware that rural whites and blacks had a similar diet.[70] An elderly African American observer from Atlanta recently interviewed by Frederick Opie concludes, "I don't know any of those so-called soul food items that southern Euro-Americans particularly did not eat."[71]

Whether or not the term "soul food" adequately describes the range of African American cooking is debatable, and in the twenty-first century its use has waned. In embracing the term, Sylvia Woods simply accepted the prevailing formulation of the late 1960s. Some other prominent female chefs who perfected personal and regional takes on African American food carefully avoided calling their cuisine "soul food." Edna Lewis came from Freetown, Virginia, a community of blacks freed even before the abolition of slavery, and spent much of her career at white-owned restaurants in New York. In a 1996 interview with the magazine *Southern Living* she rejected the term "soul food" to describe her cooking: "That's hard times in Harlem, not true Southern food."[72] Lewis's second cookbook, published in 1976 at the height of the soul food movement, was entitled *The Taste of Country Cooking*, and the last (2003) was called *The Gift of Southern Cooking.*

Other chefs simply ignored "soul" because it obscured their own distinctiveness. Leah Chase, a prominent African American restaurateur from New Orleans, was asked by a BBC television host if she considered her food soul or Creole. Without elaboration she said Creole.[73] These women were authors of cookbooks that have achieved more fame than the two collections of relatively basic recipes that Sylvia Woods published. Edna Lewis's cookbooks, for example, include information about the dishes featured along with reminiscences and culinary history, while Leah Chase's *The Dooky Chase Cookbook* reflects the cooking of her restaurant in New Orleans that, like Sylvia's, was both a culinary landmark and a meeting place for black political and cultural leaders.[74]

Even forceful advocates of black identity did not necessarily accept the importance of soul food, however. Some dismissed it as simply poor people's food. Eldridge Cleaver, author of the 1968 bestseller *Soul on Ice*, said people in the ghettos didn't actually like soul food much: they preferred steaks, just as white people did.[75] The Nation of Islam, a movement that achieved fame and power in the 1960s under the leadership of Elijah Muhammad, denounced what it called the "slave diet" imposed on blacks as part of a conspiracy to undermine their health. Pork (forbidden to Muslims), was especially criticized, but so were black-eyed peas and cornbread. In *How to Eat to Live* (1967) and *How to Eat to Live, Book 2* (1972), Muhammad promoted whole grains, brown rice, and vegetables. A sweet-bean pie was one of the leader's favorites and a feature of Black Muslim bakeries that proliferated in the 1970s.[76]

The famed comedian Dick Gregory became a vegetarian in 1963. In the beginning this was a reaction against cruelty to animals, but gradually

Fig. 77. Leah Chase, 2006.

Gregory felt that black people needed to make a radical change in diet to save them from the bad health effects of what they were eating. Beginning in 1967, Gregory promoted the nutritionist Alvenia M. Fulton's ideas, which advocated what she called "soul food with a mission." They collaborated on *Dick Gregory's Natural Diet for Folks Who Eat: Cookin' with Mother Nature*, which appeared in 1973. In this book soul food is held responsible for the symptoms of ill health suffered by the black community, from baldness (not very likely) to hypertension (certainly correlated with a high-cholesterol diet). According to Gregory, leaders who promoted soul food as a treasured black cultural expression were guilty of undermining, even murdering, their own people.[77]

Is soul food really to blame for African American health problems related to nutrition? Probably not, on two grounds: first is the difference between what people in the rural South and urban North ate, and second is the far greater harmful significance of fast foods, sugared drinks, and other aspects of contemporary life. As with many cuisines that developed in a rural and poor environment, African Americans' diets originally didn't have very much meat, fat, or sugar, emphasizing vegetables instead, and offered a variety of different foodstuffs. What restaurants served (the North being much more restaurant-oriented in the first place) was weighted toward meat courses with vegetables as small supplements, a contrast with the real diet of the Southern countryside, where people grew their own food. Living conditions in Northern cities were hardly ideal, but there was less physical labor than on farms and more sugar, meat fat, and carbohydrates available. This is not to say that Southern or soul food was particularly healthful; no food of real poverty is. What really would cause the problems of obesity, diabetes, and hypertension, however, was the modern diet of fast foods, processed foods, large portion sizes, sodas, and a largely sedentary lifestyle. This is related to class as much as race, and many of the poor areas in the United States with severe health problems such as obesity (South Dakota and Appalachia, for example) have few African American residents.

What undermined soul food was not so much the attacks by nutrition advocates but rather its shriveling historical roots in the South. Agriculture became mechanized, African American farms became rare, and pizza, burgers, doughnuts, and the like took over there, just like everywhere else, as the nation's cuisine became homogenized. There have been efforts to modernize soul food or to make it more healthful. *Soul Food Love*, a recent cookbook by Alice Randall and her daughter Caroline Randall Williams, begins with an absorbing account of one family's food traditions, discussing the health damage inflicted both by these traditions and by modern life and diet. The recipes are innovative—chicken breasts with grapes and mushrooms, broccoli with peanuts and raisins—but greens, sweet potatoes, and shrimp in a stew make appearances even if pork or red meat do not.[78]

Sylvia Woods staked her claim as the Queen of Soul Food not as an assertion of black identity against a hegemonic white culture but as a form of language, a culinary shorthand, to describe what she had always been cooking and what she considered the tradition of her Southern childhood and youth. Despite the legal progress against discrimination, African Americans (then as now) lived apart from whites. For at least the first two decades of her restaurant's history, whatever she called her food, Sylvia Woods was completely dependent on a black clientele. Her customers might have been seeking out the food they had always eaten, or the food of their childhood, but whatever their motives, they were African American. Soul food and Southern food might be quite similar, but until recently blacks and whites shared an interest in minimizing the connections. Ironically, as appreciation of culinary history has grown recently, both Southern and soul cuisines have experienced a gentle, stately fading-away, one that Sylvia's has so far resisted.

The decline of traditional African American food in Harlem is not due entirely to large cultural shifts. Restaurants less agile and famous than Sylvia's have been damaged by the newfound desirability of Harlem as a residential mecca for young, affluent white as well as black people. Waning connections between North and South, the image of African American Southern food as unhealthy, and the gentrification of Harlem are factors in the decline of the traditional Harlem restaurant. Prosperity, rising property values, as well as changes in the perception of what constitutes traditional African American food have destroyed more restaurants than the abandonment and disorder of the late-twentieth century. Copeland's survived the decline of Harlem as well as a fire in 1981, but its curtain finally came down in 2007 and its owner, Calvin Copeland, blamed a lack of business on gentrification.[79] Wilson's, M & G Diner, Pan Pan Restaurant, Wimp's Bakery, Louise's, Singleton's, and the Wells Supper Club are other venerable Harlem institutions that have closed in recent years.[80]

Beginning around 2000, these mainstays were supplemented and, to some extent, supplanted by restaurants offering lighter takes on such things as collard greens, flavored with other vegetables rather than smoked pork, but many of these newcomers—Mobay Café, Raw Soul, Native, or Veg—didn't last.[81] New restaurants open up all the time in Harlem, as everywhere else, but most of them are not particularly African American, at least with regard what has traditionally been understood to be "soul food."[82] A recent list of the "Top Ten" Harlem restaurants includes an Ethiopian restaurant; a branch of Dinosaur, a national barbecue chain; an Italian American holdout (Patsy's); a ramen place; a Puerto Rican cuchifritos specialist; and one traditional neighborhood restaurant, Charles' (now called Charles' Country Pan-Fried Chicken).[83]

Red Rooster, located right down the street from Sylvia's, is a special case that has experienced enviable success. This is partly due to its famous owner, Marcus Samuelsson, but also because it is able to present dishes such as chicken and waffles with a vibe that somehow makes them seem healthful without being particularly different from what people ate at the old-fashioned places. Sylvia's not only managed to survive Harlem's hard decades that followed its opening, but it continued to do well in the first decades of the twenty-first century. According to Lindsey Williams, grandson of Sylvia Woods, Red Rooster has been a positive draw for business, increasing rather than taking away from customers at Sylvia's.[84]

Perhaps Antoine's is closest to Sylvia's when it comes to proudly and persistently upholding a fragile tradition. This is only ironic on the surface—a New Orleans restaurant with a white, upper-class tradition and a black restaurant in the North. Both preserve a past that is widely admired but not emulated—remaining vital, beautiful, and nonetheless endangered.

Le Pavillon

MENU
Diner

Caviar Malossol 8.00	Saumon Fumé 3.00	Anguille Fumée 2.75
Jambon de Bayonne 2.50	Foie Gras Truffé 6.00	Grapefruit 1.00
Little Necks 1.50	Cherrystones 1.50	Melon 1.50
Cocktails: Lobster 5.00	Shrimps 3.00	Crab Meat 4.00

Potages

Petite Marmite Pavillon 2.75	Consommé Double aux Diablotins 2.00	Saint Germain Ambassadeur 2.00
Bisque de Homard 3.00	Soupe à l'Oignon Gratinée 2.50	Ox-Tail Clair 3.00	Billi-Bi 3.00
Madrilène en Gelée 2.00	Tortue Verte au Sherry 3.00	Germiny aux Paillettes Dorées 2.75

Poissons

Délices de Sole Cancalaise 4.50	Homard Newburg 7.50	Moules au Chablis 4.25
Timbale de Crab Meat Thermidor 5.50	Grenouilles Provençale 4.75	Suprême de Striped Bass Normandy 4.50
Goujonnette de Sole, Sauce Tartare 4.50		Truite de Rivière Sautées Grenobloise 4.75
Spécialités: Homard 7.50	Sole Anglaise	Moules 4.25

Entrées

SELLE D'AGNEAU FAVORITE 6.50 — LA POULARDE DERBY, COEUR DE CELERI (Pour 2) 15.00

Le Caneton à l'Orange, Pommes Soufflées (Pour 2) 15.00

Coeur de Filet Bouquetière 8.50		Vol-au-Vent Régence 5.50
Médaillon de Ris de Veau Maréchal 5.25	Côte de Volaille Pojarsky 5.25	Suprême de Pintadon Carlton 5.50
Foie de Veau au Bacon 4.75	Pigeonneau Bresanne 6.00	Grenadin de Veau Beauséjour 5.00
Spécialités: Châteaubriana (Pour 2) 18.00	Volaille (selon grosseur)	Ris de Veau 6.00

Rotis

Poularde	Grain	Canard	Pigeon
Reine	Poussin		Carré d'Agneau
Selle d'Agneau			

Plats Froids

Poularde à la Gelée à l'Estragon 5.50	Langue Givrée 3.25	Jambon d'York 3.50
Terrine de Canard 4.50	Boeuf Mode à la Gelée 5.00	Terrine de Volaille 4.50

Légumes

Petits Pois à la Française 1.75	Haricots Verts Maitre d'Hôtel 1.75	Coeur de Céleris au Beurre 2.00
Epinards à la Crème 1.75	Courgettes Fines Herbes 2.00	Aubergines Bordelaise 2.00
Laitues Braisées au Jus 2.00	Choux-Fleurs, Sauce Hollandaise 2.50	Champignons des Gourmets 3.25

Entremets

Patisserie Pavillon 2.00	Soufflés Tous Parfums 3.25	Crêpes Pavillon 3.25
Désir de Roi 2.50	Cerises Jubilée 3.50	Poire Hélène 3.00
Péche Melba 2.50	Macédoine de Fruits aux Liqueurs 2.50	Coupe aux Marrons 2.50
Glaces: Vanille 1.25 Chocolat (Menier) 1.25	Moka 1.25 Fraise 1.25	Citron 1.25 Framboise 1.25
Café .70	Demi Tasse .60	Bread and Butter 1.00

Fig. 78. Le Pavillon dinner menu from the early 1960s.

LE PAVILLON

MIDCENTURY FRENCH

L e Pavillon, the leading high-end restaurant in America in the mid-twentieth century, was founded by accident. A temporary restaurant created for the New York World's Fair of 1939–1940 was successfully transplanted after the fair closed to more permanent quarters in Midtown Manhattan. That restaurants change their "mission" is not unusual— Delmonico's began as a pastry shop and Antoine's as a boardinghouse, but, in those two cases, transformations into restaurants were logical expansions. Like the Mandarin, however, Le Pavillon came into being through unforeseen circumstances. Henri Soulé, the maître d'hôtel, owner, and soul of Le Pavillon, was the victim, or ironically indirect beneficiary, of a historical calamity—the shocking collapse of France before the Nazi Blitzkrieg in May and early June of 1940.

The French exhibit at the New York World's Fair was centered on what was called officially "Le Restaurant du Pavillon de France," but customers came to refer to it as simply "the French Restaurant." For the United States it was a uniquely authentic display of French gastronomy and in its

Fig. 79. Exterior view of the French Pavilion at the New York World's Fair, 1939.

first season, May 9 to October 31, 1939, the restaurant served more than 136,000 meals to an avid public.[1] The French government had entrusted the project to Jean Drouant, owner of three celebrated Parisian restaurants. Henri Soulé, maître d'hôtel of one of them, the Café de Paris, was asked by Drouant to manage the World's Fair establishment.

By October 1939, when the fair closed for the winter, France was already at war with Germany but despite the conflict, during an initial period when not much was happening on the military front, the French government decided that the French Pavilion and its restaurant should reopen for the second year of the fair. Soulé was duly demobilized from the army and returned to New York at the head of a reduced restaurant team in April 1940. On May 10, the so-called Phony War abruptly ended and the Germans unveiled a war of rapid maneuvering, what later was dubbed the Lightning War (*Blitzkrieg*). As the Luftwaffe bombed civilian as well as military targets, including streams of refugees, German forces led by Panzer tanks mercilessly rolled through Belgium, the Netherlands, Luxembourg, and then France. Encircling the Allied armies, the Germans found themselves masters of the battlefields more easily and suddenly than they had expected. Military strategists as well as the public had anticipated a replay of the terrible attrition of World War I, with tens of thousands of lives sacrificed for a few miles or mere feet of territory. What actually occurred was even worse: a ferocious and fast-moving form of warfare and the rapid collapse of the French Army and its British ally. A virtually unde-fended Paris fell on June 14, just over a month after the real conflict began,

Fig. 80. Menu cover from Le Restaurant Français at
the French Pavilion, New York World's Fair, 1939.

Fig. 81. Menu cover from Le Restaurant Français at
the French Pavilion, New York World's Fair, 1940.

and the government fled to the South, which soon also fell to the Nazi
advance. Marshal Pétain agreed to a collaborationist set of surrender terms
before the end of June.

The shock of the fall of France reverberated as far as New York. The
end of the second and last World's Fair season in the fall of 1940 meant that
the restaurant personnel had to decide whether to return to Nazi-occupied

France or, as stranded refugees, try to make a go of it in America. At first undecided, Drouant started the plan to establish a French restaurant in Manhattan, but he was homesick and returned to Paris, undeterred by the presence of the Germans. Soulé, who had no intention of returning to a humiliated France, organized the French Pavilion veterans who wished to remain in the United States and bravely opened Le Pavillon at 5 East Fifty-Fifth Street, a few steps from Fifth Avenue, in that dire fall of 1941, less than two months before America's own entry into the world war.[2]

Notwithstanding these adversities, Le Pavillon was an immediate success. It weathered the war years without great difficulty, and dominated the New York and national restaurant scene for more than twenty years, restoring French cuisine to the preeminence it had enjoyed before Prohibition and redefining haute cuisine in America as something indisputably French. In 1957 a quarrel with his landlord led Soulé to move Le Pavillon two blocks north, to East Fifty-Seventh Street, but soon there was a reconciliation and in 1958 he opened La Côte Basque at the old location, a restaurant only slightly less formal than Le Pavillon. In 1954, he took over the Hedges in East Hampton to serve as a summer venue for Le Pavillon's clients. It was convenient to Soulé's country retreat on Montauk Point and lasted until 1964, two years before Soulé died.

Unquestionably, Henri Soulé trained an entire generation of French chefs and New York restaurant owners, some of whom departed as refugees from the tyranny of this irritable genius. In 1962 Charles Masson, one of the waiters at Le Pavillon, opened La Grenouille, today the last classic, elegant French restaurant remaining in New York. Robert Treboux, also a Le Pavillon waiter, owned Le Veau d'Or, Le Manoir, Le Clos Normand, and La Rôtisserie Française. La Caravelle was established in 1960 by disaffected chefs and staff members from Le Pavillon. Pierre Franey and Jacques Pépin, two influential chefs, cookbook writers, and media personalities, departed in 1960 to work for Howard Johnson's when Soulé cut the overtime hours of the restaurant workers to save money. Notwithstanding

Soulé's flawed personality, Le Pavillon, in Pierre Franey's words, ran "a culinary university training French cooks and dining room staff for service throughout America."[3]

Le Pavillon and Henri Soulé raised the standards of fine dining, but also adversely affected the reputation of French restaurants. Snobbery, discrimination, and intimidation were majestically deployed by the imperious if often entertaining Soulé, and these imputed characteristics have damaged the reputation of French cuisine in America ever since. French restaurants aspiring to anything higher than bistro steak-and-frites cooking are now exceptionally rare. It is easier to find Indian vegetarian or Ethiopian food in the United States than an actual French restaurant.

One cannot blame this situation entirely on Soulé; favoritism and snobbery were not the principal aim of Le Pavillon's owner but rather by-products of peculiarly American forms of social exclusivity. Americans did not need Soulé to instruct them on how to measure status by where they were seated and how they were received at restaurants, but Soulé adopted and perfected this form of discrimination so well that it eventually became identified with French food, French culture, and French character. The international eclipse of French food in the last thirty years is due to many factors other than perceived snobbery, some of which might be the richness and complexity of French cuisine, a crisis of French culinary traditions, or the rise of Asian and Latin American tastes. Nevertheless, the largely unjustified reputation of the French in general and American French restaurants in particular for hauteur and exclusivity was solidified in the postwar years when French cuisine ruled and the master of the reigning culinary style was Soulé. That style included a limited but well-executed selection of haute-cuisine classics; tableside service (carving, arranging, presenting); a high degree of formality and professionalization; and a hierarchical order in the dining room and kitchen.

Part of the reason for the power and influence of Soulé, a somewhat comical and not intrinsically imposing man, lies in the quality of the food served at Le Pavillon. Jacques Pépin, not an admirer of Soulé by any means, acknowledged that the restaurant surpassed other already-established grand French restaurant venues in New York, such as Le Chambord or Lafayette. Le Pavillon produced extraordinary French classical cuisine, Pépin declared. In its time it was among the best restaurants in the world.[4]

FRENCH TRANSPLANT OR AMERICAN ADAPTATION?

Henri Soulé was from Saubrigues, a small town in Landes in the southwest of France, near the grand Atlantic coastal resort of Biarritz. A man of few

Fig. 82. Henri Soulé inspecting a roast.

pleasures and no interests outside of work—he once said that his hobby was paying his bills on time—Soulé used to retreat for a couple weeks in summer to Landes, where in place of the grande cuisine of restaurants he ate modest dishes such as Brandade de Morue (flaked cod with potatoes) and replied to the occasional Americans who thought they recognized him that they were mistaken. His heart had always remained in Saubrigues, he told an interviewer, and if in a business sense he was perfectly adapted to America, he was also homesick.[5] Joseph Wechsberg, author of an admiring and detailed biography of Soulé, did not know (or at least did not disclose) that Soulé was married and that his wife lived in Bayonne, the metropolis closest to Saubrigues.[6]

Yet this was also a man who, quite unusually for France at the time, set out to learn English in 1926, taking a demotion to work at the Trocadero Restaurant in London's Piccadilly Circus. He obtained American citizenship as soon as possible after opening Le Pavillon. He made his fortune in the United States and found the American part of his double-life quite comfortable.

Henri Soulé stood five feet five inches tall, stout but graceful. His eyes are described by Wechsberg as uniquely expressive, mostly expressing disapproval. Less impressed, longtime *New York Magazine* restaurant critic Gael Greene recalled him as "pasty faced," with "owl eyes."[7] Nevertheless, she added that he was a "flirtatious, five-foot-five cube of amiability," and admired him as a "showman, snob, perfectionist, martinet, con-man, wooer and wooed master of haute cuisine."[8] He always wore a dark-blue suit with a gray tie when presiding over lunch, and a tuxedo at dinner. His English was fluent, but in anger or for effect he would revert to French. When in a good mood, his staff were "my boys"; when not, they were merely "ces types" (something between "these guys" and "these bastards").[9]

Soulé was passionately devoted to his restaurant. He was always present and functioned both as host and carver. Alongside the waiters, he carved and arranged meat, fish, and vegetables at a sideboard. One might think, given Soulé's perfectionism, that his accomplishment was simply to transplant an elegant Parisian restaurant to America, but he was more perceptive than this, and Le Pavillon was more successful than any attempt at literal reproduction would have proven. Wechsberg said that one's first impression on entering Le Pavillon was that it was unmistakably French, and indeed, the original look was created by the designer who had decorated the Café de Paris, where Soulé had worked before coming to the United States.[10] Quite a bit later and thus with the benefit of historical perspective, Adam Gopnik, with characteristic flair, wrote that La Côte Basque (Soulé's second New York City restaurant) possessed a "thorough, even comic Frenchness that had made it so entirely New York." This second restaurant was adorned with murals depicting scenes of the southwest French coast, evoking not so much the soul of France as the fantasies of New Yorkers in 1958 when it opened.[11]

For all its exaggerated and stylized "vie en rose" atmosphere, Le Pavillon never attempted to match the haute cuisine of the Parisian grand restaurants. The food was delicate and relatively simple; it required skill to prepare and serve, but the offerings consisted of a limited dossier of the classic culinary repertoire. In his obituary for Soulé in the *New York Times*, published January 28, 1966, the food columnist Craig Claiborne lovingly recalled Le Pavillon's "Mousse de Sole 'Tout Paris'" with truffles in the center, served with both a Champagne and a lobster sauce; its pilaff of mussels; and Oeufs à la Neige (a dessert of meringue, custard, and caramel). Soups such as Potage Germiny (a consommé) and Billi-Bi (mussel broth) were uncomplicated, but involved last-minute treatment and so required precise timing. A specialty of the restaurant was Poulet Pavillon, a roast chicken served with a sauce of chicken stock, Champagne, cream, and Cognac, with the natural juices of the cooked chicken drizzled over the platter as a final touch.[12] Such dishes may not seem light or simple now,

Fig. 83. Henri Soulé inspecting tins of caviar.

but they were vibrant and unpretentious compared to the elaborate chaud-froids and chartreuses of the grand tradition, dishes that took days to prepare and that Soulé did not attempt.

The kitchen at Le Pavillon was more loosely organized than that of a restaurant in France as well. It had fewer cooks in relation to the number of meals served and its personnel moved among different stations and operations in a way that the more structured, hierarchical tradition in France would not have permitted.[13] The two major differences between Le Pavillon in New York and grand restaurants of France, however, were in the ingredients available to the chef and in the taste of patrons. Soulé lamented the poor quality of the veal in America as compared to France and complained that for all the wealth of his customers he could not provide them with simple delicacies that middle-class Frenchmen routinely enjoyed: Marrenes oysters; young partridge; Mediterranean fish such as red mullet or *loup de mer*; properly aged cheeses; or the first spring vegetables (*primeurs*). Soulé remarked, "Everything [here] is fresh all year round and, naturally, is never quite fresh, if you see what I mean." Soulé also regarded American eggs and butter as inferior. New York regulations prohibited the restaurant from serving Truite au Bleu, which requires keeping the fish alive until the last moment.[14]

Few patrons noticed or cared about these deficiencies. If American vegetables were bland and large, it hardly mattered, as the menu offered only a few creamed and gratin vegetable side dishes. Jacques Pépin noted that at the Plaza Athénée in Paris, where he had trained, there was a *chef de partie* and five *commis* in charge of vegetables, tasks put onto a single assistant cook at Le Pavillon.[15] In the absence of crayfish from Lake Annecy, *rascasse* from Marseille, or ham from the Morvan, Soulé relied on expensive but easy forms of elegance—truffles in profusion, Beluga caviar served from four-pound tins. For favored guests whose tastes he respected, Soulé proffered off-menu bourgeois specialties such as cassoulet (beans, sausage, and duck confit) or tête de veau (calf's-head thinly sliced with a vinaigrette).

There was a small parallel menu that aspired to offer deeper flavors than what was proposed by the sober respectability of the public document. The favored few could make requests in advance for lobster soufflé or beef filet with truffles. A cold omelet with crabmeat was always available to the Duke and Duchess of Windsor or Cole Porter, and occasionally to others by special beneficence.[16]

ON THE MENU

When the restaurant at the French Pavilion opened on May 9, 1939, the *New York Times* declared it "a retreat for epicures." A gathering of 375 guests dined on chicken consommé with cheese sticks, Lobster Pavillon (a version of Homard à l'Américaine), lamb with potato balls and stuffed artichokes, capon in tarragon aspic, lettuce and asparagus vinaigrette, and strawberries with ice cream and petits fours.[17] The popularity of the restaurant was based on its food, but diners were also dazzled by the tableside service that included complicated but seemingly effortless fish-boning operations, elaborate meat carving, and flambéed desserts. Although crêpes suzette, the most famous flamed dessert, weren't actually invented here, the restaurant did much to popularize them.

It wasn't as if New York did not already have French restaurants, but, as observed in previous chapters, the advent of Prohibition had meant the death of an older generation of luxury establishments of the more-or-less French sort. Prohibition had been over for six years by 1939, and restaurants such as Le Voisin, Marguery, La Rue, Passy, and Café Chambord were already doing business in New York City when the World's Fair opened. Of these, Le Voisin was the oldest, founded 1912, having managed somehow to survive both Prohibition and the Great Depression.[18]

Despite their evocative names, these restaurants served American upper-middle class food with only a few French touches. La Rue's specialty was Guinea Hen Smitane (the sauce made with cream, sherry, raisins, and mushrooms).[19] A menu from Le Voisin dated April 5, 1932, features chicken potpie, not unknown at Howard Johnson's, and Terrapin Maryland, once a delicacy at Delmonico's. Pot roast "à la mode bourgeoise" may have resembled pot au feu, but probably was closer to what others were calling Yankee pot roast. Voisin did offer slightly more authentic dishes, such as frogs' legs meunière and broiled sweetbreads en casserole Florentine. At least the French presence was stronger with the desserts: orange soufflé, coupe aux marrons, and pancakes suzette.

A 1937 menu from the same establishment is more ambitious. On Fridays one could order Bouillabaisse à la Marseillaise and on Wednesdays, coulibiac of English sole. Pressed mallard duck was available daily in 1937. In about 1940, the restaurant Passy relied on broiled trout, lamb chops, and filet mignon, but the menu also highlighted Strasbourg foie gras, Sole Marguery, and Frogs Legs Provençale.[20]

Le Pavillon was considerably out in front of this feeble competition. For its opening-night meal on October 15, 1941, there was little advance publicity but nevertheless the street outside was jammed with limousines and the reputation of the fair's French Restaurant ensured a full house. Caviar and smoked salmon introduced the meal; the restaurant's chef Pierre Franey recalled the mousse of sole and beef filet with truffle sauce. Soulé recollected Poulet Braisé au Champagne.[21] A Pavillon regular named Elaine Whitelaw says that although New York had wonderful restaurants before Le Pavillon, "I remember suddenly feeling for the first time an unquestionably great restaurant had opened in America."[22]

By the end of the year the menu had settled into what would be a fairly stable pattern that lasted over the entire life of the restaurant:

December 31, 1941[23]

Jambon de Bayonne $1.10

Melon de Casaba   .70

Saumon fumé $1.25

Cherrystones   .40

Anguille fumé   .90

Blue Points   .45

Cocktail Sauce   .10

Grapefruit   .40

Cocktails: Lobster $1.25   Shrimp .80   Crab Meat .80

POTAGES

Petite Marmite Pavillon   .90

Consommé Celestine   .50

Tortue vert au Sherry   .80

Saint Germain Longchamp   .50

Billy Bee   .75

Bisque au homard   .80

Germiny en tasse pailletes   .80

Soupe à l'oignon au Chablis   .80

POISSONS

Filet de sole au Chablis $1.75

Truite au rivière Georges Sand $2.00

Homard à la Newburg $2.00

Suprême de turbotin Galliera $1.75

Darne de saumon au Champagne $2.00

Moules marinière $1.50

Coquilles de Crabe Thermidor $1.50

Striped Bass grillé au fenouil $1.75

Grenouilles Provençale $2.00

Spécialités: *Homard* $2.00   *Sole* $1.75

Moules $1.75   *Grenouilles* $2.00

ENTRÉES

La poularde farci Périgourdine $2.25

Coeur de filet Mascotte $2.50

Caneton à l'orange (pour 2) $6.00

Noisettes d'agneau des Gourmets $2.00

Poussin grillé Valentinois $2.00

Cotelette de volaille Pojarsky $1.75

Pigeon en compote $2.25

Medaillon de ris de veau Clamart $2.00

Pintadon Régence (pour 2) $5.00

Spécialités: *Châteaubriand (pour 2)* $6.00

Volaille (selon grosseur)

Ris de veau $2.00   *Steak* $3.00

PLATS FROIDS

Boeuf mode à la gelée $1.50

Jambon de York $1.50

Poularde à l'estragon $1.50

Terrine de volaille $ 1.50

Langue $1.25

Roastbeef $1.50

Terrine de Caneton $1.50

LÉGUMES

(a choice among a dozen or so possibilities)

ENTREMETS

Patisserie Pavillon   .30

Soufflés tous parfums $1.25

Crêpes suzette $1.50

Compote de fruits   .75

Poire Hélène   .80

Pêche Melba   .80

Macédoine de fruits frais aux liqueurs   .80

Désir du roi   .75

Coupe aux marrons   .75

Mince Pie Pavillon $1.00

Glaces: Vanille .40   Chocolat .40   Moka .40

Fraise .40   Pistache .40

Café .30   Demitasse .25

Unlike the practice at Antoine's in New Orleans, the client at Le Pavillon ignorant of French was not expected to interrogate the waiter for explanations. Pierre Franey assumed in retrospect that patrons would have been eager enough to avoid embarrassment to forego asking for interpretation.[24] What appears here as "Billy Bee" is a mussel cream soup that in later menus would be adjusted to its French standard, "Billi Bi." Some of the cold dishes such as ham, roast beef, and tongue—were concessions to Anglo-American tastes. Le Pavillon offered mussels, turbot, guinea hen, and pigeon—all rare to unknown at other New York French restaurants— and it did not deign to offer lamb chops, chicken pot pie, or other American standards.

By 1948, in an uneasy but expansive postwar environment, the menu was very similar to that of 1941 except for the entrées and a new course of roast meat and fowl (rotis).[25] Chicken with tarragon, quarter of lamb, Guinea hen en cocotte, kidneys en casserole, calf's liver, and vols-au-vents were new. Roasts included chicken, duck, pigeon, pheasant, and lamb. The most expensive item was Châteaubriand at $12.00 for two people (more than $110 in today's money).

Although the menu at Le Pavillon, as with that of Antoine's, presented consistency over a long period, there were some changes and additions. Despite Soulé's complaints to Wechsberg about not being able to serve Mediterranean loup de mer, there it is, in Champagne sauce on a late-1950s lunch menu, along with six egg dishes, offered notwithstanding Soulé's invidious comparison between French and American eggs.[26]

A pair of menus from about 1970 shows what the restaurant offered four years after Soulé died and shortly before it closed in 1971. Both menus are still written exclusively in French, but the food is on its way to becoming mediocre. The first, a lunch menu, highlights a somewhat international set of daily specials such as beef Stroganoff and chicken livers "Algérienne," and American items on the order of calf's liver with bacon. A course of "Grillades" replaces the roast meat of dinner and includes English mixed grill, minute steak, deviled chicken, as well as the traditional Châteaubriand, now $22.00 for two (upward of $130 today).[27]

The 1970 dinner menu is similar to that of 1948, offering grapefruit and melon as modest appetizers, caviar and shellfish at the high end, and presenting the same array of soups as in 1941. The fish course selection is also little changed with lobster, sole, and mussels listed as specialties just as in 1941. Fourteen entrées are different from the past, but their primary products (calf's liver, guinea hen, duck, sweetbreads, and steak) are the same.[28]

Under Soulé the usual listings at Le Pavillon did not tell the full story, because there were three categories of additional dishes: daily specials (*plats du jour*), specialties of the house, and off-menu dishes whispered to special customers.[29] Soulé estimated that with some prodding, half his guests would order the expensive daily specials, which were the financial mainstays of the restaurant—items such as roast saddle of lamb, Volaille Alexandra (chicken with Mornay sauce over mousselines), or Poulet à l'Archiduc (chicken with quenelles, kidneys, and wine-cream sauce).

The *spécialités de la maison* were more elaborate, such as that aforementioned Mousse de Sole "Tout Paris" (which required four hours to prepare), lobster soufflé, or beef filet smothered in truffles.[30] Finally there were always a few portions of classic but unpretentious bourgeois dishes set aside for patrons of status and discernment, those whom Wechsberg referred to as "members of the club," whom Soulé would inform that he had something just for them: blanquette de veau or sausage with lentils, for example. In the late 1950s when Pierre Franey was head chef, he would meet with Soulé every morning at eleven thirty in the dining room of the restaurant to discuss the plan for the day and especially the eight or ten portions of off-menu dishes.[31]

What distinguished Le Pavillon was the quality of what was prepared, not its vast range. Craig Claiborne remarked in his memoirs that the food at Le Pavillon was "for the gods" and dismissed all other supposedly distinguished restaurants of 1957 when he took over as *New York Times* food editor. Notwithstanding his snobbish tendencies, Claiborne's opinion here is worth paying attention to because of his expertise and objectivity. His enthusiasm did not arise from a cozy relationship with the even more snobbish (as well as irritable) Soulé; no one had such a relationship, and in any event, Claiborne, much as he liked being cosseted, was quite professional with respect to restaurant reviewing. He did have some sybaritic advantages that would be hard, or at least ruinous, to duplicate now: at his first meal at Pavillon Claiborne drank a Montrachet with the rice pilaf with mussels and he finished off a La Tâche with his Tournedos Rossini.[32]

Claiborne quoted with approval a remark of then-famed children's-book author Ludwig Bemelmans, that Le Pavillon was the finest French restaurant in Manhattan, perhaps even in France as well.[33] As can be seen from Henri Soulé's own estimation of the difficulties of duplicating for the richest Americans what ordinary French people could easily acquire, such a statement cannot have been true. Food historian Patric Kuh makes this clear in comparing Soulé with Fernand Point of La Pyramide in Vienne, the most celebrated restaurant proprietor in immediate pre- and postwar France, who respected Soulé and even helped him buy some rare Burgundies. Point acknowledged that Soulé presented French cuisine in a good light to Americans, but asked, rhetorically, how French could any restaurant in America really be? It was a question of authentic ingredients but also of customer expectations. La Pyramide could offer regional and bourgeois dishes such as choucroute, pigs' feet, or Brandade de Morue, while Le Pavillon's clients expected caviar, lobster, and truffles.

Point saw himself as the master of a cherished culinary tradition; Soulé, on the other hand, had to be more than an impeccable representative of grande cuisine. He was required to perform in a particular social context and to master arbitrary but effective forms of social distinction. He was far from reluctant to do this, personal nostalgia for Brandade de Morue notwithstanding, but it made Le Pavillon more a reflection of a peculiarly American snobbery than a close approximation to French manners and customs.

The foolishness of status competition aside, Le Pavillon catered to upper-class American tastes in the 1950s and early 1960s that were, in certain respects, in advance of today's supposed sophistication. This is evident, for example, when it comes to organ meat, which at the moment defines adventurous eating, yet Pavillon menus routinely featured some sort of sweetbreads (Ris de Veau Régence, the sauce made from demi-glace, Rhine wine, and truffle peelings, for example); kidney dishes (Rognons de Veau Grand Mère, kidneys in mustard-cream sauce with diced potatoes, mushrooms and lardons); and also offered calves' brains, liver, and tripe.

HAVES AND HAVE-NOTS

An important difference between Point's La Pyramide and Soulé's Le Pavillon had to do with the competitiveness of American patrons, their desire to be distinguished above others by virtue of the location of their table and other marks of special treatment—a contrast between France and the United States that persists to this day. In fundamental ways, restaurants in France have a more considerate and (it may seem counterintuitive to assert this) more egalitarian view of their customers.

In France, two guiding assumptions are that the visitor is there for a leisurely meal and that a certain standard of well-being should apply to everybody. This does not mean that regulars don't receive special treatment, a basic business practice everywhere in the world, but in France the happiness of the few does not depend on some form of unhappiness imposed on the merely ordinary. In America, and most strongly in New York, however, there have to be bad tables, constituting "Siberia" (a term Soulé probably didn't invent but which suited his purposes perfectly) in order for those at the prime tables to feel the true thrill of privilege.

The French are not unfamiliar with snobbery—any reader of Proust knows with what enthusiasm and assiduity they can cultivate social discrimination—but in France restaurants are not considered a first-rate forum for displaying the perquisites of inequality. In New York, favor and exile have been part of the restaurant scene dating from even before Le

Pavillon was founded. The American fancy restaurant template is the nightclub and it takes its hierarchical form from Broadway and Hollywood. To be seen, and to be seen as favored, started to become important after the First World War. It was not enough that movie stars and other famous and colorful characters were favored patrons, but there had to be ordinary nobodies seeking entry who were rejected or relegated to a table in Siberia (whether or not that term was used).[34] In the late nineteenth century, Delmonico's and Sherry's had their regulars, but holding private dinners (by definition not in the limelight) and just being there in the first place were more important than positioning by reason of which table you were seated at. In a world of relatively stable social elites (aristocracy without celebrities), public appearances as at restaurants were less important than quieter distinctions such as club affiliation, yacht racing, summering in Newport, charitable board membership, or invitations to private parties.

During the interwar years, the Social Register elite was supplemented and even supplanted by sports and movie stars, playboys, the better class of gangsters, and other famous people of undistinguished family background. Their every move was charted by gossip columnists, and restaurants and nightclubs that catered to their need for publicity flourished. Who showed up at El Morocco or the Stork Club would be diligently reported by Louella Parsons or Walter Winchell. As early as the 1920s, Sardi's, was de rigueur for people in the Broadway theatre, but what was more important there than having a specific table was having your caricature on the wall.

The New York restaurant that most successfully adopted the nightclub model was the Colony, beginning in the 1930s. The point was not merely to be seen there, but to be seated at the right tables. When the Duke of Windsor decided to stay at the Colony bar area for a meal rather than go into the dining room ("the bar has such a gay atmosphere"), seats at the few tables there immediately became desirable, while the back part of the spacious main room, beautiful as it was with its red banquettes, mirrors, and crystal chandeliers, was contemptuously dubbed the "doghouse" (in other words, Siberia) and fobbed off on tourists. The alcove banquettes of the Colony's main dining room, at which only two could be seated, were considered nearly equal in status to the bar; even in the bar there were distinctions: the corner tables were the real crème de la crème.[35]

Although its specialties were American items such as chicken hash and soft-shell crabs, the Colony's food was considerably better than the chow mein and minestrone soup at the Stork Club or the cannelloni at Sardi's. Craig Claiborne recalled the Colony with grudging praise.[36] Le Pavillon had authentic French food, and Henri Soulé had different standards for bestowing favor than did Gene Cavallero of the Colony. In his encomium to Le Pavillon and its creator, Joseph Wechsberg claimed in the face of an avalanche of contrary evidence that Henri Soulé was unimpressed by wealth or social prominence. But Wechsberg also admits that Le Pavillon might in future be remembered not so much for its glorious food but as the scene of "epic fights for a good table . . . a symptom of the battle for survival in the status jungles of Manhattan around the middle of the twentieth century."[37]

Le Pavillon was originally located on Fifty-Fifth Street just east of Fifth Avenue, across the street from the grand St. Regis Hotel. Close to the entrance were seven tables in a space dubbed by those in the know as "the Sanctuary" and referred to by Soulé and his staff as "la salle Royale." Despite proximity to the revolving door and consequently the constant comings and going of patrons, the Sanctuary represented the achievement of Nirvana in terms of reputation. Everyone entering the restaurant passed through the Sanctuary, looking at the famous and favored. Soulé professed to find the lust for the entryway absurd, remarking of its habitués "they would rather dine in the telephone booth than in the [regular] *salle*."[38] There were two ordinary dining rooms: first, the *nouvelle salle*, which had been a Western Union until it was taken over by Soulé in the early years of Le Pavillon. This room to the left of La Royale and near the bar was also rather cramped and heavily trafficked. The *vielle salle* (Siberia), was the old main dining room at the rear of the building. Quiet and, despite its large size, rather private, the *vielle salle* might seem to have been perfect for those more interested in good food enjoyed in tranquility than in the social game, but the level of service and deference to the customer's comfort tended to decrease as one was seated farther from the prestigious tables at the front.

Such discrimination among customers would be even more exaggerated at such restaurants as La Côte Basque after Soulé's death, or later and notoriously at Le Cirque, object of two legendary simultaneous reviews in 1993 by Ruth Reichl, who received shabby treatment when disguised as a frumpy lady dining with another woman and obsequious service when she showed up openly as the *New York Times* reviewer ("the King of Spain is waiting at the bar, but your table is ready"). Shabby treatment in this instance meant being seated near the restrooms, a long delay before being able to order, and having the wine list snatched away by a waiter who "needed it" for a more favored table.[39]

In France professionalism and politeness do not countenance open contempt for ordinary patrons. Soulé was bemused by the social habits of his clients but was nevertheless willing to take advantage of their jockeying for favor. He told Wechsberg that at the new Pavillon on Fifty-Seventh Street no one would complain about being seated in its main *salle*, but here too the narrow passage between the entrance foyer and the *salle* became desirable above everywhere else. The ten tables were crowded so closely together that the waiters had to pause in their carving to let people through. This cramped space, nevertheless, became the new Salle Royale.

If Soulé followed rather than led with regard to tables, he perfected other ways of showing favor and disfavor. An example of discrimination among customers was how the bill was paid. Soulé refused to acknowledge the newfangled credit cards (which also levied fees on the merchant) introduced in the 1950s. Favored regulars were offered house accounts. As is still customary for members of private clubs, they left the restaurant when ready, allowing the proprietor make up the bill, add taxes and tips, and mail them a monthly statement. Cash was acceptable, but the object of a rather grudging transaction. Even slower was a kind of improvised second-class method of paying by a house check, a document resembling an IOU, which required identification and enough back and forth from the waiter to signal to all that you were being made to pay in a tedious fashion. Those whom Soulé considered below the mark who nevertheless had the effrontery to ask for a house account were humiliated into giving up the idea.[40]

As with the all-French menu, the special dishes, and the Royale/Siberia seating spectrum, the obvious discrimination between the cosseted and the nobodies became an emblem of the restaurant as an intimidating ordeal of trial by snobbery. This perception has dogged the reputation of French restaurants in the United States ever since, but is unfair since it is hardly as if American high-end restaurants have become that much more democratic now that French restaurants are an endangered species. Although it is customary to begin any account of the modern restaurant boom by conjuring up the bad old days of damask tablecloths, dress codes, leather-covered menus, and haughty maîtres-d'hôtel, restaurants today impose distinctions that would never have occurred to Henri Soulé: near-impossible reservations, no reservations, the speakeasy restaurant type with no visible sign out front, special telephone lines for favored customers, mandatory tasting menus, or forcing clients to pay in advance of their meal. The model is no longer the nightclub of the Copacabana or El Morocco type, but the culinary version of a dance club complete with velvet rope and line of suppliants, lacking only a bouncer. Le Pavillon is not responsible for these contemporary syndromes of distinction that arise out of some fundamental American, not French, need for a competitive individual sense of worth and achievement, but it paved some of the way by not only calibrating privileged treatment with wealth but also discriminating in an affluent society among different kinds of riches or high status.

It bears repeating that it would be foolish to think Soulé was anything other than snobbish, temperamental, and dangerous to cross. He was able to carry off running his restaurant according to capricious and tyrannical rules because he understood how to alternate charm with coldness, devoted himself to his establishment, and served wonderful food. Arrogance, stubbornness, and bad temper meant that he made mistakes in calculating his own interests that would ultimately undermine the continued success of Le Pavillon.

Soulé ruled his kingdom with such authority that it would seem foolhardy to challenge him, but there were some who tried. Even regulars who complained about their table received icy stares and peremptory instructions on the order of "You will sit here, madam, and please stop arguing." A confrontation with a female client ended with Soulé saying, as if delivering a line from a 1940s movie, "Tell me, good woman, did you come to eat at Le Pavillon, or did you come to argue with Soulé."[41] Soulé achieved Pyrrhic victories, but whether through overconfidence or a self-destructive desire to pick fights, he also suffered actual defeats.

The building that housed Le Pavillon at 5 East Fifty-Fifth Street was bought in 1955 by Harry Cohn, owner of Columbia Pictures. A tyrannical figure in his own right, known to some as "King Cohn" and to others as "White Fang," Cohn was furious that he had always been seated in the back of the restaurant and not in the Sanctuary. He reminded Soulé that he controlled the amount of a rent increase, as the lease on the space was due to expire. Soulé, however, was enraged rather than intimidated; he considered Cohn just the sort of vulgarian who, if he couldn't be kept out of the restaurant altogether, must never be admitted into its inner circle. Perhaps this was a manifestation of anti-Semitism or maybe simply an unprejudiced aversion to a genuinely dislikable person. In any event, Soulé was unmoved, and when the lease expired and the rent was raised to an astronomic level, he negotiated a relocation to the Ritz Tower at 111 East Fifty-Seventh Street.[42]

The new Pavillon duly opened in the fall of 1957 at just a slightly northward remove, conveniently near Tiffany's. Cohn died in 1958, and Columbia Pictures offered Soulé the old property at a substantial but not stratospheric rent. Now that his adversary was removed, the actual location of the old Pavillon appeared to Soulé to be too good to pass up, even at $40,000 a year (or was it $75,000 a year?—the sources differ). La Côte Basque was created on the premises of the old Pavillon as a lower-priced alternative with a simpler menu and only one sort of all-purpose wineglass. Soulé expansively likened his two restaurants to the Paris Opéra and Opéra Comique, or the Louvre and the Jeu de Paume: "The Pavillon is elegant and the Côte Basque is amusing." But the spirit of the man and the time is perhaps better summarized by his further observation, uttered in the royal if not Olympian third person as usual: "Some

Fig. 84. Interior of the Fifty-Seventh Street Le Pavillon, ca. 1960.

people may find it quite convenient that Henri Soulé has two restaurants in Manhattan. A man may take his wife to the Côte Basque and the other lady to Pavillon."[43]

The new Pavillon was supposed to be bigger and better, with improved lighting and a perfect arrangement of mirrors and flowers. Some clients, however, found the place less inviting. Limousines couldn't double-park on Fifty-Seventh Street, a main thoroughfare. Several stairs had to be negotiated, an obstacle for elderly patrons; and although the new Salle Royale was cramped and lively, it did not have to be traversed by the less fortunate on their way to Siberia, cutting down on the pleasure derived from the display of privilege.[44]

La Côte Basque opened with great fanfare and immediate success in 1958 and would have a longer life than Le Pavillon. In fact, it started to draw away Pavillon customers as the latter restaurant faltered in the 1960s. Soulé was loyal to Le Pavillon as his unique personal creation and so, a mere four years after it opened, he sold La Côte Basque to a competitor, the Café Chambord. In 1965, shortly before his death Soulé bought it back at a bargain price, the Chambord having been unable to run it profitably. Besieged by various troubles by that time, Soulé was reluctant to abandon the idea of a lighthearted sibling to the solemn Pavillon.[45]

That tussle with Harry Cohn had resulted in at least a partial win for Soulé. The same cannot be said for a gratuitous fight with the Kennedys on the eve of John Kennedy's election as president in 1960. The patriarch, Joseph Kennedy, was a regular in the Royale and may have been one of the original investors in Le Pavillon back in 1941. His son John dined there often and was known for drumming on the Christofle silver serving gueridons as he passed by them. On one occasion, a group of Kennedys was interrupted by an intrusive photographer (the sight of the Democratic candidate dining at the most expensive restaurant in the nation might be considered bad publicity). Soulé, although normally not the sort of restaurateur to invite photographers, regarded the Kennedys' ejection of the intruder as a challenge to his authority and attacked Joseph Kennedy, saying that "his son has not been elected president and already he is acting like a dictator." Thoroughly miffed, the Kennedys walked out and moved their patronage to La Caravelle, one of many establishments run by Pavillon alumni.[46]

There is a deeper history to this affair that goes back before the presidential election to an occasion when Joseph Kennedy loudly asked the maître d'hôtel, Fred Decré, why he as an American was working for "that lousy Frenchman." Shortly after this insulting remark, Soulé, not one to ignore such provocation, opined vocally that with regard to the upcoming presidential race, John Kennedy didn't have a chance of being elected.[47] Of course, he *was* elected, and for a brief time French cuisine flourished in the sophisticated Kennedy White House, whose chef, René Verdon, had trained at La Caravelle before taking on his new job.

Even more unfortunate and ultimately costly were Soulé's confrontations with the restaurant's employees, as briefly mentioned earlier. There had been a forty-two-day walkout in 1945, when waiters demanded to rotate service stations so that the most lavish spenders would not be monopolized. Strikes and lockouts because of wage disputes took place in 1954 and 1956. And difficulties with the restaurant workers' union were part of the reason for the sale of the profitable La Côte Basque in 1962.[48] A man as imperious as Soulé was not suited to labor negotiation.

The quarrel that attracted the most adverse publicity and caused Soulé the loss of his best and most experienced staff arose over the number of hours worked. Le Pavillon, despite Soulé's ambition to serve an aristocracy serenely indifferent to the rise or fall of economic indicators, was in fact sensitive to fluctuations in the financial markets that undergird New York City's vitality. In early 1960, with the stock market and the general economy in the doldrums, Soulé demanded that his head chef, Pierre Franey, reduce the hours of the kitchen staff from forty to the union minimum of thirty-five. Franey refused, feeling he had already made savings in expenses and that morale would drastically deteriorate. Franey had worked for Soulé for more than twenty years by this point, but along with his protégé, Jacques Pépin, and six others he walked out. They would never return, their departure creating a brief but dramatic stir. Among the restaurants founded in the wake of the mass departure was La Caravelle, whose chef was Roger Fessaguet, former chef at the Hedges and sous-chef at Le Pavillon. It became the favored restaurant of the Kennedys as well as other political and entertainment celebrities, and served impeccable French food. Soulé felt compelled to place an advertisement in the *New York Times*, informing readers that "despite what may have been said to the contrary by others, the only restaurants in the city in which HENRI SOULÉ is interested are Le Pavillon and La Côte Basque."[49] A few years after the incident, Franey tried to greet Soulé as they passed on the street, but was ostentatiously ignored.[50]

After the walkout, the restaurant was temporarily closed, and Craig Claiborne, in a *New York Times* article entitled "Le Pavillon Shut in a Gallic Pique," outlined the tragicomic elements of the dispute and accurately depicted the dictatorial willfulness that undergirded Soulé's character and conduct. Despite his knowledge of Soulé's flawed character, and his close friendship with Franey, Claiborne continued to admire Soulé. This did not prevent him from praising La Caravelle, however, writing to Roger Fessaguet to say that since coming to the *New York Times* he had never seen such a well-deserved chorus of praise for a new restaurant and that he should be proud of this achievement.[51]

AU REVOIR

Wechsberg's book about Le Pavillon and Henri Soulé was published in 1962. He presented Soulé as imperturbable in his authority, with all labor disputes set in the past and with no allusion made to the Kennedy fracas.

Despite this optimistic portrayal, there were some trends that Soulé could not control. Le Pavillon was losing clients both to its sister, La Côte Basque, and to competitors run by veterans and refugees from Soulé's restaurants such as La Caravelle and La Grenouille. Soulé announced that La Caravelle, named for a type of sailing ship, would sink. This did not happen, and La Caravelle became the favorite watering hole of the Kennedy White House circle once the clan had renounced Le Pavillon.[52] Julia Child's success as a television chef increased the popularity of French cuisine, but her informality and endearing enthusiasm undermined the angry-deity image cultivated by Soulé.

The opening of the Four Seasons in 1959 as a fancy, non-French restaurant should have provided little if any immediate competition, but nevertheless Soulé was appalled that there should be so much fuss over what he saw as an expensively designed restaurant with dubiously eclectic food. He prohibited his staff, on pain of being fired, from setting foot in it.[53] Yet in 1961 when the owner of the Four Seasons, Restaurant Associates, planned to become a public company, Soulé unsuccessfully sounded them out about joining forces.[54]

None of this meant that Le Pavillon was endangered in any immediate sense, but its worried, meticulous, and overworked proprietor was. He bought back La Côte Basque in 1965, and in an exuberant interview with Gael Greene, expressed withering contempt for the Chambord proprietors he had previously sold it to and promised to restore its grandeur. He boasted that he had both plenty of money and excellent health and then laughingly cautioned Greene against quoting what he had just said about money.[55] Alas, the reopened Côte Basque received an ambiguous and strained review from Craig Claiborne, a great fan of Soulé's but hardly a shill.[56] And Soulé turned out to be wrong about his health—he died the following year of a heart attack at the age of sixty-two. According to one account, he died in the men's room at La Côte

Basque; according to another he was yelling over the phone at a union official when his heart stopped.[57]

At the time of his death there was already a sense that Soulé embodied a unique and probably passing phase of gastronomic distinction and restaurant snobbery. Craig Claiborne's worshipful *New York Times* obituary declared Soulé "the Michelangelo, the Mozart and the Leonardo of the French restaurant in America." Claiborne was frank in his admiration of Soulé's caprice, disdain, and discrimination—all praised, not merely excused, as defending the highest standards. Claiborne concluded "his like may never be known in this country again."[58] Certainly no one has come along who could match Soulé's formidable temperament and authority, but this unique restaurateur would continue to influence high-end American dining for decades after, and even to this day. Restaurants founded and staffed by his former employees defined French cuisine adapted to the United States and offered a setting for rituals of social distinction. Without intending to, Soulé had established a "university," as Pierre Franey put it, not only for training chefs and restaurant managers but for educating and shaping the tastes of clients.[59] His form of snobbery and bullying also endured as a peculiarity of American restaurants, even when they claimed to be rejecting the old formal, haughty, clubby atmosphere. Soulé conformed almost comically to American stereotypes about French arrogance, but in fact he fashioned an American attitude toward dining that did not die with him. We haven't seen his like, exactly, but we have seen many imitators.

SOULÉ'S LEGACY

When Henri Soulé died there were something on the order of twelve restaurants in New York and eight elsewhere in the United States that had been established or whose kitchen had been taken over by Pavillon alumni.[60] The French restaurant along the formidable lines he had perfected represented the highest form of dining out in America for another two decades.

It had been widely assumed that Mme. Henriette Spalter, who had run the coat-check concession at Le Pavillon since the World's Fair, was Soulé's unacknowledged wife, but she was in fact his mistress. That he had a wife living in France came as a posthumous surprise.[61] Following his death, Mme. Olga Soulé arrived in New York to claim her inheritance and sold Le Pavillon to a group of investors led by Claude C. Philippe, banquet manager of the Waldorf Astoria. "Philippe of the Waldorf," as he was known, had briefly and unhappily employed the young Craig Claiborne, who was glad to point out in the press the unfortunate afterlife of Le Pavillon under Philippe's management. The restaurant now featured music, allowed charitable solicitations, and even put out a television set for special occasions. Perhaps worst of all, lemon quarters served with the salmon had not had their seeds removed![62] The restaurant closed ignominiously in 1971.

Mme. Spalter, a beneficiary under Soulé's will, bought La Côte Basque after Soulé's death. "I wish to keep the name of Henri alive," she is reported to have said, and La Côte Basque was a great success.[63] Its offerings were in the tradition of Le Pavillon—lobster bisque, sweetbreads Barrigoule, filet of Sole with mustard sauce, and quenelles de brochet with sauce Nantua. Craig Claiborne approved, awarding it four stars in 1967.[64] Mme. Spalter was also a faithful follower of Soulé with respect to absolute rulership over her domain. She was famous for banning women wearing pants and imposed strict dress codes on men as well. There were conspicuously favored tables, while Siberia was as frozen as ever.

Mme. Spalter was quite happy to go along with one emerging trend that Soulé had not been pleased about—that certain luxury restaurants were becoming monopolized at lunch by wealthy women, characteristic of New York places such as La Grenouille or Sette Mezze to this day. In 1975, Truman Capote famously published a venomous chapter of his never-finished novel *Answered Prayers*, entitled "La Côte Basque, 1965," in which two leisurely luncheon conversations at the restaurant tear down the reputations of at least fifty socially prominent and readily identifiable people, almost all women. So thinly disguised and so scabrous was the series of stories that a real society figure, Anne Woodward (Anna Hopkins in the story), committed suicide shortly before its publication. Within high society, Woodward had been suspected of deliberately shooting and as a result killing her husband in 1955, claiming she mistook him for a burglar, and Capote recounted this tale with grotesque touches and with gusto. This was just one of the many secrets that he revealed in a reckless move that severed his relationships with prominent women whose company and stories he had enjoyed for years.

La Côte Basque, its literary reputation now enriched by scandal, would have its ups and downs over the next three decades. In 1976 it was given only two stars (good) in Seymour Britchky's guide to New York restaurants, but it was awarded four stars by *Forbes* magazine at the end of 1979, and three out of a maximum four stars (excellent) by Mimi Sheraton in 1982.[65] Mme. Spalter sold the restaurant in 1979 and returned to Paris after living forty years in New York, dying there in 1981. The purchaser was the restaurant's chef, Jean-Jacques Rachou, and La Côte Basque continued to prosper until the new century. Victim of both changing fashions and the economic and tourist downturn following the attacks of September 11, 2001, La Côte Basque closed in 2004, reopening as a more casual brasserie, variously named J. J. Rachou Brasserie, Brasserie LCB, and some other combinations of the chef's name, the initials of the old restaurant, and the word "brasserie." None of this worked, and the restaurant closed definitively in 2007.

The end of this last direct legacy of Henri Soulé is one of a number of milestones along the road to the near-disappearance of French cuisine in the United States, a subject to be dealt with further in the epilogue to this book. In 2004, when La Côte Basque was shuttered for the first time, there were only seven elegant, traditional French restaurants left in New York; in 1975, according to *New York Observer*, there had been twenty-five of them.[66] Now (2016), despite a small revival of interest in bistros of the steak-frites sort, only La Grenouille, Le Veau d'Or, and Le Périgord have a clear connection to the elegant French restaurant tradition of the past. French prestige outlasted Henri Soulé, and its decline became visible only twenty years after his demise.

THE FOUR SEASONS
THE EPITOME OF MODERN

T he opening of the Four Seasons on New York's Park Avenue proved to be a sensation. As with everything masterminded by its corporate owner, Restaurant Associates, the event on July 29, 1959, was a *planned* sensation. More than Philip Johnson's architectural design, the marble pool, the art by Picasso and Miró, or the seasonal concept for the food, the sheer expense of putting the restaurant together dominated the headlines. At $4.5 million (the equivalent now of about $35 million) the Four Seasons remains, in constant dollars, among the most expensive American restaurant designs ever put into effect. As a point of comparison, the entire cost of the Guggenheim Museum, which opened the same year and was one of the last buildings designed by Frank Lloyd Wright, was a mere $3 million.[1] Craig Claiborne, the powerful food critic for the *New York Times*, wrote an article on the imminent launch with the headline "$4.5 Million Restaurant to Open Here." *Look* magazine, a mass-circulation weekly, entitled its treatment "New York's New 4½ Million Dollar Restaurant" and pointed out that regardless of whether the Four Seasons was actually worth this figure

Dinner at   The Four Seasons

Cold Appetizers

Salsify in WILD GAME MARINADE 1.10   *Poached* CARP *in Sweet and Sour* ASPIC 2.25
Winter Farmhouse Terrine 2.25   BAGNA CAUDA *of Seedless Avocados* 1.65
Virginia BLUE CRAB *Lump* 2.95   *Little Neck or Cherrystone Clams* 1.35
Blue Point Oysters 1.50   *Mousse of Chicken Livers* 2.25   *Caviar, per serving* 7.50
STONE CRAB CLAWS, *Spiced Mayonnaise* 3.25   ICELAND *Herring, Pommes Vapeur* 1.95
Prosciutto or Smithfield Ham with BOSC PEAR *or Pineapple* 2.65

Snails in POTS 2.25   GREEN CRÊPES *with Prosciutto* 1.85   PAUPIETTE *of Smoked Turkey* 1.65
Our Coquille St. Jacques 2.25; *also with Snail Butter*
Crisped Shrimp Filled with MUSTARD FRUITS 1.85   TERRAPIN à *la Maryland* 5.25
Soufflé of FINNAN HADDIE 2.65   SPICED *Crabmeat Crêpes* 2.45
SNAILS *in Their Shells,* DIJONNAISE 1.85   *Whole Périgord Truffle in Pastry* 8.00

Hot Appetizers

SAUCISSE *en Brioche* 1.95   DEVILED *Oysters on the Half Shell* 2.25   CROMESQUIS *of Game* 1.65
NEW ENGLAND *Lobster Tartlet* 2.50   COCOTTE *of Goose Liver and Apples* 2.50
COULIBIAC *of Salmon* 1.65   QUAIL *Stuffed with* NUTS AND GRAPES 3.75
BEEF MARROW *in Bouillon or Cream* 1.85   *Mussels Poulette* 2.25
DUTCH *Herring Crêpe, Sour Cream* 2.00   *The Four Seasons Mousse of Trout* 2.50

Soups and Broths

Onion Soup with CALVADOS, *Gratiné* 1.25
Double Consommé with Madeira 1.10
Watercress VICHYSSOISE 1.10   COLD *Caraway Squash Bisque* 1.35

Potage Mongole 1.10   *Consommé -* ROSEMARY QUENELLES 1.25
VERMONT *Cheese Soup* 1.35   *A* DECEMBER *Vegetable Potage* 1.10
Beet and Leek MADRILÈNE .95   CELERIAC *Vichyssoise* 1.10

LOBSTER THERMIDOR *with Morels* 7.00   *Crabmeat Casanova* FLAMBÉ 5.65
Barquette of Flounder with Glazed Fruits 4.95   *The* CLASSIC *Truite au Bleu* 5.25
Filet of Sea Bass, AMANDINE 4.50   LOBSTER AROMATIC *Prepared Tableside* 6.50

Sea and Fresh Water Fish

BAKED RED SNAPPER STEAK, *Créole* 4.95   OCEAN TROUT *in Flaming Fennel* 4.85
Broiled MAINE *Lobster* 6.50   *Frog's Legs* PROVENÇALE *or in the* FOUR SEASONS *Style* 5.25
POACHED LOBSTER *in Court-Bouillon* 6.75   *Winter Sole with King Crab, Mornay* 4.85

This Evening's Entrees

Planked WHITEFISH *with Clams and Mussels* 5.25   YOUNG BOAR HAM, *Christmas Dressings* 5.85
TRUFFLED JERSEY CAPON *with Risotto, Sauce Suprême* 5.65

Roast RACK *of* LAMB-OREGANATO, *for Two* 14.00   *Wild* MALLARD DUCK à *la Presse* 8.50
Breast of Chicken in SuSu *Curry,* SAMBALS 5.25   SALMIS *of* PARTRIDGE, *Alsacienne* 6.50
ROAST SUCKLING PIG, *Stewed Crabapples* 5.85

ROAST HOLIDAY GOSLING, *Apple Kraut* 5.75   ROAST SIRLOIN OF BEEF, *Eggplant Stuffed Tomato* 6.50
MEDALLIONS OF VEAL, *Parmesan, Spiced Lentils* 5.50

A Variety of Seasonals

CRISPED *Duckling with Bitter Oranges, Flambé* 5.95   RARE FILET STROGONOFF 6.50
Potted Pigeon, NUTTED WILD RICE 5.85
VENISON STEAK *with Juniper, Sauce Poivrade* 5.25

Steaks, Chops, and Birds

* * * * * * * *
*Calf's Liver-*THICK, *Sage Butter* 5.25   *Amish Ham Steak, Apple Fritter* 4.65
* * * * * * * *
SIRLOIN STEAK *or* FILET MIGNON *Served for One* 7.50; *for Two* 15.00
Sirloin Steak Poivre en PAPILLOTE 7.50
TWIN TOURNEDOS *with Woodland Mushrooms* 7.00
* * * * * * *
Saddle of Venison, WILD GAME SAUCE, *for Two* 14.00   BABY PHEASANT *with Laurel Leaves* 5.50
BROCHETTE OF BEEF AND LAMB, *Sauce of Ripe Olives* 5.25

BROILED OVER CHARCOAL *
Jersey Poularde 4.50   *Two Triple Lamb Chops* 5.75
* * * * * * *
Sirloin VINTNER *Style* 7.75   SKILLET STEAK *with Smothered Onions* 7.50
Beefsteak SCANDINAVIAN 7.25   *Steak with* TINY OYSTERS 7.75
Filet of Beef POIVRE *Flambé* 8.00
SPIT ROASTED WITH HERBS *
LEG OF LITTLE PIG, *Hot Apple Sauce, for Two* 11.00   FATTED SCOTCH GROUSE, *Bar-le-Duc* 8.50
The HEART *of the* PRIME RIB, *Sliced Thin* 5.50

Winter Salads

* * * * * * *
Bouillabaisse Salad 4.75   *Rack of Venison,* CUMBERLAND 5.85
JULIENNE OF *Smoked Turkey and Pineapple* 5.25   *Beef in Burgundy Aspic* 4.75
* AS A DINNER ACCOMPANIMENT *
WINTER *Greens* .95   BELGIAN *Endive and Grapefruit* 1.50
DILLED *Cabbage and Ham* 1.25   *Beefsteak Tomato,* CARVED AT TABLE 1.25
OUR FIELD GREENS ARE SELECTED EACH MORNING AND WILL VARY DAILY

* AS A MAIN COURSE
Glazed Smoked Pork, CELERIAC SALAD 4.85
Lobster and WILD MUSHROOMS 5.50   *Julep of Crabmeat in* SWEET PEPPERONI 5.50
* * * * * * *
NASTURTIUM *Leaves* 1.50   *Raw Mushrooms,* MALABAR *Dressing* 1.65
MARINATED *Bean Sprouts, Soya Dressing* .95
Salad Dressing with ROQUEFORT *or* FETA CHEESE .50 *additional*

Vegetables and Potatoes

Celery or Cauliflower Gratinée 1.25   *Wild Rice* 1.65   *Beignets Varies* 1.25
Soufflé of ARTICHOKE, *for Two* 3.85   *Onions in Onions* .95
Buckwheat, FORESTIÈRE .95   *Beets with* ORANGE 1.25
* * * *
French Fried .95   *Apricot Sweets* .95   *Baked in Jacket* .95

SEASONAL GATHERINGS MAY BE VIEWED IN THEIR BASKETS   *Squash with Toasted Nuts* 1.25
Brussels Sprouts and Bacon CRACKLINGS 1.25
Broccoli FLOWERS, *Hollandaise* 1.95   *Bouquet Platter, per Person* 1.50
* * * *
POTATOES: *Mashed in Cream* .95   *Roesti* .95   *Vapeur* .95

Fig. 85. Four Seasons menu, ca. 1960.

in terms of its culinary offerings, it certainly looked expensive. The avant-garde review *Evergreen* chimed in with an article, "The Most Expensive Restaurant Ever Built."[2]

Restaurant Associates in the 1950s developed concepts of the restaurant as entertainment and as gourmet destination, concepts that endure to this day if not in the same over-the-top form. Unlike some of Restaurant Associates' other lavish realizations, such as the mock-epic Forum of the Twelve Caesars or the pan–Latin American La Fonda del Sol, the Four Seasons, both as an architectural and culinary statement, would be enduring and generally admired, if only fitfully rewarding financially. The Four Seasons was always a prestigious restaurant, but in its first decades it barely earned its very expensive keep. It was a Wagnerian *Gesamtkunstwerk*—not just a restaurant but a painstaking aesthetic project. Nothing was taken for granted and everything, from the flatware to the bathroom faucets, was custom-made. The glasses cost an unheard-of $2 each.[3] Neither was anything installed with any thought as to its maintenance cost. In a city inured to crowding and compression, space was used extravagantly, from a marble lined pool to the ample room provided between tables. Everything changed exuberantly with the seasons—the menus, the waiters' uniforms, the ashtrays, the indoor landscaping, coat-check tags, and even, for fanatical good measure, the typewriter ribbon colors. The building owners, the Seagram Company, contributed most of the initial cost and gave the Four Seasons favorable leasing terms. The bill for an average meal for two in 1960 required about $40, a dizzying sum for that time. Even with these subsidies and prices the restaurant lost money. The extravagance of the setting, the difficulty of filling its tables (it sat 400), and the expense of fulfilling what was promised by its vast menu were near ruinous.[4]

From its inception the Four Seasons was considered a New York landmark and institution, easily meriting that overused word "iconic." In his not-completely-favorable review in the fall of 1959, Craig Claiborne began by saying, "There has never been a restaurant better keyed to the tempo of Manhattan than the Four Seasons," and went on to remark that it was "perhaps the most exciting restaurant to open in New York within the last two decades" (in other words, since the inauguration of Claiborne's cherished Le Pavillon).[5] It would take some time, however, for it to find its identity and for its innovations to inspire ideas about modern food. In terms of atmosphere and probably expense, the Four Seasons was impossible to imitate, and it had few direct followers. Its influence, however, has been immense in three areas: separating fine dining from French style, showing respect for the seasons and the quality of primary ingredients, and reflecting a new kind of social-status ritual to which the term "power lunch" was first specifically applied.

As we have seen, in 1959 and for quite some time after, almost all high-end restaurants in New York were French. Behind the leader, Le Pavillon, which was at or near the zenith of its fame, came a host of epigons: Le Veau d'Or, Passy, Quo Vadis, Café Chambord, Brussels, and many more. The cuisine at the Four Seasons was not exactly American, but rather modern, eclectic, and cosmopolitan—revolutionary for its time and thereby offering a challenge to French preeminence in high-end dining.

The idea of seasonality is now so much part of sophisticated American taste that it is hard to appreciate how startling it seemed in 1959. A long tradition had defined luxury dining as *defiance* of the seasons: importing out-of-season fruit or exotic and expensive products such as truffles or caviar. To be wealthy was to ignore seasonal limitations, to eat hothouse peaches in winter and iced desserts in summer.

"Seasonal" at this point did not necessarily mean local, however, and in this regard Chez Panisse would have a more direct influence on how we dine today than the Four Seasons. Nevertheless, following the changing year, even if conceived as a more decorative than culinary point of departure, demonstrated how to use America's natural riches to vivid effect. It is no accident that one of Alice Waters's favorite restaurants and inspirations has been the Four Seasons, notwithstanding Chez Panisse's radically different look and relation to social and corporate power.[6]

The owners of the Four Seasons have always relished the restaurant's position as a stage for the performance of social distinction. Its lunch regulars used to be literary and creative stars, and now they are predominantly finance plutocrats, but the Bar Room, also known as the Grill Room, continues to show how social power is displayed. In an article published in 1977, Michael Korda, the legendary editor in chief of Simon & Schuster, described the leaders of the publishing world dining in the Grill Room as "power lunchers." He depicted a memorable scene that had little to do with high society and everything to do with business: deals were made, prestige was reinforced, and networks and relationships were created and maintained.[7] Rather than there being one Society, as in the 1880s heyday of Delmonico's, there were now multiple centers of business for which publicity and reputation were important—from real estate to finance; from marketing to book publishing. In 1979, two years after the Korda article, Lee Eisenberg in the pages of *Esquire* coined the specific term "power lunch," so widely used thereafter as to seem retrospectively eternal, but in fact invented in a very particular time and place.[8]

It has been common to say that the Four Seasons' allure has less to do with food and more with atmosphere and service. Even Joe Baum, its charismatic creator, said that people don't go to fancy restaurants because they're hungry, but because they are attracted to the excitement and entertainment.[9] In its early years, in fact, the Four Seasons oscillated uneasily between modernist austerity and vulgar spectacle. The Pool Room was used for fashion shows, and on one occasion the models paraded through the pool itself. For the launching of the soft drink Fresca, the pool was covered with a sheet of ice. Young female dancers garishly and routinely accompanied the service of "Pyramids de boeuf," and wild mushrooms were presented on a silver tray lined with grape leaves before being cooked at the table.[10]

Fig. 86. The Pool Room at the Four Seasons.

For regular customers, the food might be ostentatiously secondary. Once the restaurant's "power lunch" reputation was established, some habitués made a point of ordering absurdly ordinary food as a demonstration of entitled indifference to gourmandise—William Shawn of *The New Yorker* ate cornflakes with milk, and Michael Korda preferred a lunch of creamed spinach, baked potato, and nonalcoholic beer. Warren Buffett asked for a Coke and a Dairy Queen ice-cream cone.[11] The Hollywood agent Irving Paul "Swifty" Lazar asked for a runny omelet but was told, jocularly but firmly, "This isn't a diner," showing that in fact some requests were not met.[12] Notwithstanding all this posturing, food was and remains the great, if quirky, contribution of the Four Seasons to American dining.

The Four Seasons was unusual, given that it was a restaurant put together by a committee, or rather by an uneasy collaboration among architects, designers, and actual restaurateurs. The high-modernist style of the Seagram Building in which it made its home was the idea of Phyllis Bronfman Lambert, the daughter of the company's owner, Samuel Bronfman. An artist and sculptor, the young Phyllis Bronfman also had considerable knowledge about architecture. She was living in Paris in 1954 when her normally remote father sent her preliminary plans for Seagram's new headquarters building on Park Avenue. She responded with an eight-page typed single-spaced letter vividly denouncing the soulless gigantism, cheapness, and empty "sensationalism" that would result from implementing the plan, and insisted that the family create a distinguished monument.[13] Phyllis convinced her father to elevate the architectural ambitions of the building, and he appointed her as the director of planning. Guided by the art

Fig. 87. Philip Johnson, Mies van der Rohe, Phyllis Lambert, ca. 1959.

historian Richard Krautheimer, who had been her teacher at Vassar, she chose Mies van der Rohe as the architect, with Philip Johnson as his associate. They created a building that was immediately recognized as among the greatest examples of twentieth-century architecture.

The dark-topaz glass set in a bronze rectangular tower radiates an internal luminescence and provides a spiritual, not just imposing, presence. It is set back from the street, its plaza allowing passersby to see the building, much as a cathedral or palace has a large public space in front of it. The idea of public plazas would come to be regarded as an unfortunate innovation—windy, treeless, and unwelcoming spaces that the New York City zoning laws encouraged because they could be traded for added building height and bulk, In the 1950s, however, a building at a setback with a plaza seemed to embody a generous urban idea of air and light, as opposed to maximizing the imprint of the building by bringing its façade out to the street.

The design was austere, but called for expensive and beautiful materials. The lower floors sit under the front pillars, forming a podium on which the bulk of the building is raised. The two floors of what came to be the restaurant presented both an opportunity and an obstacle. An entrance on Fifty-Second Street leads into a lower floor, now used as a cloakroom and waiting area, from which an impressive stairway goes up to the restaurant. Originally there was also an entrance to the building lobby, and since Fifty-Second Street slopes downward, this Park Avenue entrance led directly to the restaurant level. Access to the Four Seasons from the Seagram Building lobby has been closed off for some time, however, for reasons of security.

The grand but somewhat awkwardly arranged two-level space might plausibly have sheltered a bank or a luxury automobile showroom. Putting a restaurant in this vast setting was thus daring. Once Mies van der Rohe considered himself done with the task of designing the building, it fell to Philip Johnson to arrange the 22,000-square-foot assemblage as a

Fig. 88. The Seagram Building.

Fig. 89. Staircase at the Four Seasons.

restaurant. Johnson later remarked that he was trying to fill the space and keep his commission while remaining true to van der Rohe's architectural vision. Acknowledging that considerable space was wasted, Johnson observed rather exaggeratedly that such is the case with great cathedrals as well.[14] Of course, cathedrals don't measure success by the same intense profit-driven metrics as restaurants, and the wasted space has been a perpetual challenge.

In designing the interior, Johnson created two rooms measuring sixty feet by sixty feet, with twenty-foot ceilings connected by a corridor. The Pool Room has a square reflecting pool bordered with Carrera marble at the center. The other room, nearer to the staircase, was built with a spacious bar set off on the west side and, consequently, holds fewer tables. This was known as the Bar or Grill Room and had a somewhat more enclosed and clubby feel than the Pool Room.

Among the collaborators on the project were landscape architect Karl

Linn, interior designer William Pahlmann, lighting expert Richard Kelly, and industrial designers L. Garth and Ada Louise Huxtable. Mimi Sheraton, already an acknowledged food expert and later restaurant critic for the *New York Times*, coordinated planning for the menus. The west and north walls of the Pool Room were glass, and covered with a series of thin gold anodized aluminum chains designed by Marie Nichols. They ripple and flow, an effect of the ventilation and temperature, not part of the original plan but charmingly mysterious. The other walls are elegantly paneled in French walnut and rawhide. The main decorative feature of the more severe Bar Room is a hanging sculpture by Richard Lippold made of hundreds of narrow rods suspended by almost invisible wires, an effect "like golden strokes of rain," according to an observer writing in *The New Yorker*.[15]

The restaurant was designed to use some of its extra room to display distinguished artwork. Phyllis Lambert donated a large piece of a stage curtain painted by Picasso in 1919 for Sergei Diaghilev's Ballets Russes. Diaghilev at some point sold the central part of the curtain, forming what was sometimes referred to as a "tapestry." The work came to be known as *Le Tricorne*, and it depicts the aftermath of a bullfight, the horses dragging out a dead bull from a bullring. Until 2014, it was the centerpiece of the passage between the two principal rooms. A Jackson Pollock painting, *Blue Poles*, hung in the private dining room, and a series of tapestries by Joan Miró adorned the Fifty-Second Street lobby.

Even though many people worked on putting together the restaurant, the Four Seasons is really the creation of Joe Baum, the idea man and visionary in the Restaurant Associates organization. Before Baum joined it in 1953 as vice president under Jerome Brody, the company ran nondescript enterprises like Riker's coffee shops, the Corner House restaurants, and the luncheonette and employee cafeteria at Ohrbach's department store. After 1970, when Baum was gone, RA reverted to routine but lucrative services: family and fast-food restaurants, commissaries, and in-flight meals. Baum, though obsessed by details, can't be considered a bottom-line financial genius. His ideas were risky and breathtakingly expensive; he liked planning more than maintenance, the project more than the brand. The consistent moneymaker for Restaurant Associates was the non-glamorous Mamma Leone's, which long antedated Baum's era and which he didn't touch. In the late-1960s, growing tired of daring but expensive concepts, the company would marginalize Baum and diversify, eventually with unfortunate results, into candy (the Barracini company) and lodging (Treadway Inns).

Yet during Restaurant Associates' dozen heady years from 1953 to 1965, Baum put into effect a variety of extraordinary ideas, beginning with one of the most unlikely sites: the airport for Newark, New Jersey. Named after

Fig. 90. Joe Baum (center) with Restaurant Associates colleagues tasting proposals for dishes at La Fonda del Sol, ca. 1960.

what was already one of America's least glamorous cities, the Newarker opened in 1953. Baum wanted to attract customers who were not flying or picking anyone up, but rather willing to dine there as a destination in itself. The Newarker featured attentive service; fine silverware and linens; and gimmicks such as serving "three-clawed lobster," desserts garnished with sparklers, and waiters wielding giant peppermills. Flambéed dishes were prominent: shashlik, scallops, and even (shades of Antoine's), coffee with brandy. Baum loved what we now regard as the kitschy practice of tableside flaming, and couldn't resist bringing it to the supposedly aristo-cratic Four Seasons. As he remarked in a 1964 interview, "The customers like to see things on fire . . . and it doesn't really hurt the food much."[16] The Newarker was a short-lived sensation, but for its moment it achieved astounding success.

There followed the reimagining of the Hawaiian Room at the Hotel Lexington on Forty-Eighth Street, which allowed Baum, who was becom-ing the latter-day restaurant version of P. T. Barnum, to show his ability to carry off a dubious concept with thoroughness and panache. "Aloha!" the menu proclaimed, and went on to present a series of jocular descriptions intended to divert the customer: a drink called Ana Ana—"A sorcerer's brew of gin, rum and brandy, fiendishly blended—not for the sorcerer's apprentice!" or a multicourse dinner dubbed the Beeg Luau, consisting of "Polynesian Pupus on the Fiery Popo! Tournedos of Beef, Saigon; Chicken Momi; Flaming Satés of Steak and Lamb; Mandarin Vegetables"; and a des-sert of "Flaming Snow Mountain."[17]

All over the country there were already plenty of Polynesian-themed establishments, but Baum insisted on the necessity of rethinking the tiki idea on the basis of "research." Baum's constant preoccupation with legiti-mating his restaurant ideas seems hilarious—on the order of the "research" done by Hollywood studios for spectacles like *Ben Hur* or *Cleopatra*. Unfet-tered by historical or anthropological authenticity, Baum profited from his enthusiasms and travels. He attended luaus in Hawaii, coming away with

Fig. 91. Menu cover from the Newarker restaurant, ca. 1958.

ideas for flambéed dishes. His investigations showed him how things were done by West Coast pioneers in the Polynesian genre, such as the owners of Don the Beachcomber and Trader Vic's. The Hawaiian Room succeeded not because it resembled Hawaii but because of its theatricality, just like the Newarker. The spectacle in turn attracted stage, broadcast, and movie personalities like Arthur Godfrey, Elizabeth Taylor, and Laurence Olivier.

It is amazing how one man's singular vision can influence an entire generation, and the potential proliferation of Baum's creative enterprises seemed almost endless. A jolt of energy for his already fervid imagination was a deal for a new restaurant in one of the buildings of Rockefeller Center. The Forum of the Twelve Caesars opened dramatically in 1957, advertised as "the best imperial restaurant in two thousand years." The Forum's interpretation of ancient Roman cuisine bore about as close a relationship to its model as the Hawaiian Room did to Polynesia. Baum was supposedly inspired by the imperial lords of modern business who congregated in Rockefeller Center, or he may have started with a "forum" concept to encourage the exchange of ideas among the bigwigs at media-companies. Maybe the Roman imperial theme was simply the result of his associate William Pahlmann's fortuitous purchase of seventeenth-century portraits of the first twelve Roman emperors (a number hallowed by the Roman historian and biographer Suetonius). In any event, another campaign of research meant trips to Italy to visit archaeological sites, museums, artists, and craftsmen. The entire restaurant staff was ordered to read Suetonius's *Lives of the Twelve Caesars* along with the recipes attributed to Apicius, author of the only extant Roman cookbook. Latin snippets on the menu were checked by a professor of classics at Hunter College, who also lectured to the staff on ancient Rome. At the head of the Forum menu, the equivalent of the Hawaiian Room menu's cheery "Aloha," was the portentous *"Cenabis bene . . . apud me"* from Catullus ("You will dine well ... at my table").[18] The ice buckets for Champagne were modeled on Roman soldiers' helmets. The head of Bacchus, the god of wine, decorated copper and brass service plates (made in Milan), and the waiters were gotten up in imperial-purple and royal-blue outfits that vaguely suggested togas.[19]

The menu at the Forum was endless and full of laughs, with items like "Oysters of Hercules WHICH YOU WITH SWORD WILL CARVE" (that is, big enough for a knife and fork—oversize oysters were already a feature at the Newarker); "Fresh truffles HERCULANEUM—Prepared 'Under the Ashes'"; "Fiddler Crab Lump A LA NERO—Flaming of Course." A salad was anointed as "THE NOBLEST CAESAR OF THEM ALL." A note on the menu invites patrons to special-order flamingo, larks, and thrushes, while peacocks are *always* available.[20] The noted food writer and restaurant reviewer Mimi Sheraton recalls certain dishes with longing: the Caesar salad, fiddler crab, clay-baked chicken, and poached lobster ("Lobster Jupiter"), but adds that the spectacle interfered with any reasoned appreciation of the food.[21]

Baum, ever the showman extraordinaire, acknowledged that the Forum was not to be taken entirely seriously, and its menu puffery now seems reminiscent of roadside attractions or used-car salesmanship. Yet, as real estate and advertising still show, marketing success in America doesn't depend on restrained good taste. During its career, the Forum's prestige location, impressive clientele, and stratospheric prices meant there was no danger of its becoming a mass entertainment venue. The imperial restaurant concept was appropriate for what Baum called "a time of lusty elegance in which the good things of life are presented to the leaders of the world"—a statement with a typically Baumian epigrammatic as well as megalomaniacal quality.[22]

Launched only two years after the Forum of the Twelve Caesars, the Four Seasons was supposed to be a complete contrast, though no less lavish. Once Baum and his associates had convinced Seagram to put in a restaurant, it was clear that the governing concept could not borrow from Hollywood. The menu, setting, and staffing were supposed to convey dig-

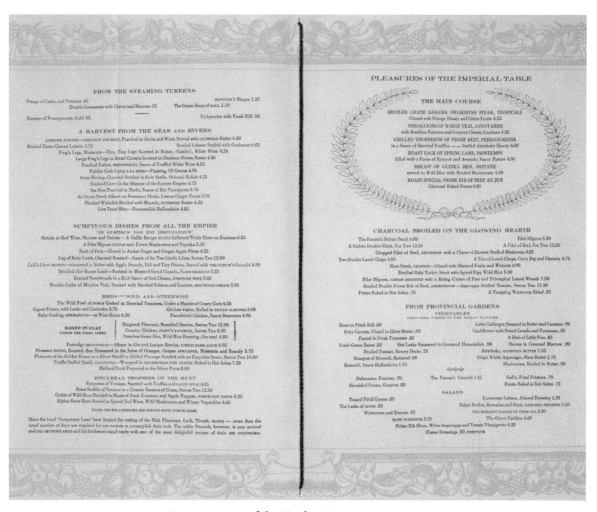

Fig. 92. Forum of the Twelve Caesars menu, 1957.

nity and an understated welcome. Nevertheless, certain Restaurant Associates patterns were repeated at the Four Seasons: locating the establishment in a prestige building and getting the corporation that owned it to pay for most of the installation; rethinking everything, even the height of the tables; buying nothing off the rack but commissioning décor, clothing, and utensils especially for the site; a near-comical attention to detail (all those signs of the changing seasons); and an immense menu with rhetorical flourishes, although in this case not nearly as silly as those at the Forum.

In a conversation with *Restaurants & Institutions* magazine in 1960, Baum emphasized that above all he was looking to create a modern restaurant, and that in keeping with the Seagram Building's status as a great example of contemporary architecture, the restaurant had to have a contemporary look. The interviewer observed that the care exerted in preparing the restaurant must mean something more than mere lavishness. Baum's response was perhaps wrong, but nevertheless intriguing: "We think this country is fast leaving the era in which expense was the chief criterion of quality. People are becoming more discriminating . . . because they have more taste and experience." Rather than try to ride an established trend, a restaurant of the caliber of the Four Seasons needs "to create a distinctive product with its own merit, and then sell it."[23] To do so Baum was able to combine what had previously been two separate kinds of restaurant impresarios: those who appealed to class snobbery and selectivity and those who sold aggressively to all comers. Oscar Tschirky of the Waldorf Astoria, credited with inventing the velvet rope to be lifted for favored customers, exemplifies the payoff for social discrimination, while Dario Toffenetti, whose Times Square restaurant's boisterous menu perfected the "You can't pass up our delicious Spaghetti" genre, represents aggressive salesmanship.

Baum's constant temptation to emphasize populist theatricality was checked by the high-modernist distinctiveness of the Four Seasons. Its severe perfection accounts for the restaurant's ability to outlast the outrageous Forum of the Twelve Caesars or another subsequent Baum experiment, La Fonda del Sol, located in the Time Life Building. For our purposes, however, the most daring and important of Joe Baum's efforts to distinguish the Four Seasons from the pack of luxury restaurant rivals was, first, that it wasn't French, and second, that it followed the changing seasons.

Joe Baum clearly felt that it would be pointless to try to present yet another high-end French restaurant, convinced that his new creation should be contemporary rather than traditional. It was also conceived of as a reflection of the city of New York, not a copy of a style established by Paris. Should it relate to New York by borrowing from the nationalities that made up this city of immigrants? Or try to evoke eighteenth- and nineteenth-century Manhattan? Rejecting these concepts, Baum decided to invoke as his principal inspiration New York's mid-twentieth-century status as a center of government, communications, transportation, art, theatre, and fashion, as well as its "mélange of many peoples."[24] Mimi Sheraton recalls that Baum said he wanted the restaurant to reflect the role of New York as "the crossroads of the world," and that meant an eclectic international menu and a variety of cooking techniques.[25]

The actual name of the restaurant preceded any detailed plan for the menu; that is, the seasonal menu was an outgrowth of, not the inspiration for, the decision to name the restaurant after the seasons. Competing ideas for what to call the restaurant seemed like aching hangovers from planning the Forum (*The Imperator; Restaurant of the Seven Wonders; Plaza of the Twelve Fountains*); or vague ideas referring to time (*The Time Table; Janus; Le Passage du Temps*). Ultimately Baum was partially influenced by the German Vier Jahreszeiten (Four Seasons) hotels in Germany and, more immediately and (given his mercurial temperament, paradoxically), he was entranced by the serene minimalism of Japanese style. Elizabeth Gordon, the editor of *House Beautiful*, had given Baum a collection of Japanese haiku and some poems on the passage of time inspired him to choose the seasons as the theme for his new restaurant. The concept of the rotating seasons would reflect the constantly changing city. The intrinsic theme of movement allowed for the menu to shift with the course of the year, but also resolved the contradictions between the Zen idea of tranquility and the bustle of New York, the desire for stable harmony versus the pursuit of fashion.[26]

It took some time though for the actual name to be selected. It is hard to think that alternatives such as *The Colonnade of the Four Seasons* or *The Four Seasons of the Zodiac* would have worked, let alone *Season-Go-Round*. The simplicity of the name that was ultimately selected focused attention on seasonal dining, the ancestor of today's farm-to-table and foraging aesthetic. There was even an herb garden on the premises. The restaurant contracted with specific farms for their produce and bought wild mushrooms from (among others) the avant-garde composer John Cage. Menus boasted: "OUR FIELD GREENS ARE SELECTED EACH MORNING AND WILL VARY DAILY," and baby vegetables were presented to diners so they could order what they wanted for salads or to accompany the entrées.[27]

"Seasonal," in 1959 however, did not necessarily mean local. The fact that things were in season *somewhere* fulfilled the restaurant's mission, and great effort was expended to fly in delicacies from other parts of the world. The Four Seasons was not the only New York restaurant to fuss about French truffles in the fall, but few also obtained the tiny aromatic forest strawberries, *fraises des bois*, in the spring, nor did they aspire to present European birds such as ortolans during the season for game. Purchasers employed by the restaurant boasted that they imported Dover sole, smoked salmon, and Colchester oysters from England; venison from Norway; and grapes, grape leaves, and peaches from Belgium.[28] Tiny "French" carrots were acquired in Oregon, in this case to fashion a simple dish entitled, Forum-style, "THE YOUNGEST CARROTS in Butter."[29]

The menu was assembled by the French-trained Swiss chef Albert Stockli, the future *New York Times* food critic Mimi Sheraton, and the grand figure of American cooking, James Beard. Joe Baum wanted an eclectic menu of dishes from all over the world, symbolizing New York's position as a (or *the*) global center. This ambition played against his simultaneous and prescient emphasis on seasonal dining. The portly, temperamental, and often-charming Beard was equally eclectic, but less interested than Baum in world cuisines. He advocated high-quality primary American ingredients in an era when such an approach was ignored by both the high and low ends of the culinary spectrum: by Francophile gourmands on the one hand and the marketers of processed and convenience food on the other. Constantly in need of money to support an expensive set of tastes, Beard served as a spokesman for Green Giant frozen foods and made other lucrative compromises with the American food industry, but he remained an effective voice for authentic flavors, for what he called "a homely quality," by which he meant not the suburban hominess of tuna-salad sandwiches and canned peaches, but the memory of his idyllic outdoor boyhood. At the mouth of the Columbia River in Oregon where he grew up, fish, crabs, wild berries, herbs, and oysters abounded.[30] Beard had a grandiose appetite, but unlike most postwar gourmands, he also had an affection for simple pleasures, such as the hash-browned potatoes made at a luncheonette near his townhouse in Greenwich Village by a short-order cook who pressed the potatoes on the grill with a coffee can.[31] Most other chefs and food writers concentrated on the French rules and repertoire—Francophile Craig Claiborne criticized the Four Seasons for not sculpting its vegetables in uniform shapes according to accepted practice.[32] Beard was willing to experiment and valued unshaped, non-Escoffier vegetables such as fiddlehead ferns, a seasonal item at the Four Seasons not seen on other restaurant menus until the 1990s.[33]

The Four Seasons chef, Albert Stockli was considered a difficult character, but he was more amenable to Baum's pyrotechnic tastes and less entranced by simple authenticity than Beard. His personal enthusiasms included curries and herbs, and temperamental though we was, Stockli was not a prima donna but rather quite adaptable, willing to throw himself into all of Baum's projects, amusing as well as bizarre, beginning with the Newarker. Stockli had worked previously for ocean-liner companies and in Atlantic City at the Claridge Hotel, so he had a tolerance for spectacle as well as an ability to organize a kitchen for a large number of customers. Mimi Sheraton performed much of the creative work of researching and trying out dishes from everywhere in the world. A Portuguese *cataplana*, a rounded pot with a hinge, was used for a sausage-and-clams dish; a Japanese wooden steamer was used for rice *kamameshi*. In the two months before the restaurant opened, Baum, Sheraton, and Stockli tried out thirty-five dishes every day. Even the most impractical dishes were prepared if they seemed interesting. Sheraton mentions whole calf's liver braised in Burgundy as memorable, but it didn't make it onto the final menus.[34]

During the early years of the Four Seasons there was an inevitable tension between freshness and special effects. Carving gigantic beefsteak tomatoes at the table managed to combine naturalness with theatrical artifice, but in most cases the desire for simplicity was in conflict with the effort to entertain. There was a "herring cart" to show off pickled fish options and a salami and sausage "tree" for the service of charcuterie. Even though in the planning stages Baum asserted there would be no flambéed dishes at the Four Seasons, in fact, they were all over the menu: French woodcock flamed in Cognac; beef au poivre flambé; ocean trout in flaming fennel. Even beef Stroganoff, which Stockli had said was to be made in authentic Russian style, was flamed at tableside.[35]

The menu was large enough to accommodate a veritable cornucopia of not necessarily harmonious ideas, whose demands on the kitchen must have been nightmarish. In the first years of the restaurant a typical menu had more than twenty hot appetizers; more than twenty cold appetizers; twenty-five possibilities for steak, chops, and poultry; sixteen salads; ten frozen desserts (including Berry Glacier, Flambé); and six soufflé choices (the cappuccino soufflé would become celebrated). There were also off-menu items known to the cognoscenti, such as sweet-and-sour pike in tarragon aspic or piccata piglet in pastry.[36]

Menus included a category entitled "A Variety of Seasonals," but these were often things such as calf's liver with prosciutto or avocados that were not readily identified with a particular season in the way that asparagus or venison would be.[37] Moreover, liver was listed as a seasonal item on spring, summer, and fall menus. Bouillabaisse salad appears as a "summer salad," a "winter salad," a "spring salad," and as an autumn "seasonal." In the 1971 *The Four Seasons Cookbook*, bouillabaisse salad is presented as perfect for a summer luncheon. This dish combined cold red snapper, lobster, and shrimp, served with tomato and lemon in a bowl lined with lettuce. In 1971 it was accompanied by a saffron sauce that Chef Maurice Chantreau, who arrived in 1966, added to Chef Stockli's recipe.[38]

In keeping with James Beard's preferences, the Four Seasons menu emphasized both heartiness and freshness. Although not quite to the same degree as the Forum of the Twelve Caesars, the Four Seasons was intended for a largely male clientele.[39] Freshness or an emphasis on vegetables did not mean light cooking. Respect for basic ingredients was a preliminary requirement, as in James Beard's cookbooks and classes, not an austere goal in itself. Beard was an enemy of distracting sauces and stodgy tradition, but not in any sense a lightly grilled, sauce-on-the-side kind of guy.

Beyond Beard's efforts to restore the integrity of ingredients, the menu designers at the Four Seasons were genuinely, if peculiarly, innovative. As early as the year of its opening, 1959, the food at the Four Seasons was characterized as "New American Cuisine," but it offered a global and eclectic repertoire rather than anything rigorously local or identifiably American.[40] Its chefs and planners reworked or lightly satirized classic dishes such as turning bouillabaisse into a salad, or serving Lobster à l'Américaine with croustades. They developed "signature" dishes that were compatible with prevailing tastes, such as crisped shrimp with mustard fruit (a Stockli invention); chocolate velvet (a sponge cake stuffed with liquor-infused praline paste, chocolate, and whipped cream with chocolate icing); or lobster parfait with mint. Where else in New York around 1960 could you get salsify, a white root vegetable, served here (the menu lapsing again into

Forum of the Twelve Caesars usage), in a WILD GAME MARINADE; or green almonds *en brochette* or as an accompaniment to potted squab?[41]

The menu was so large that it could be used to demonstrate anything—French traditions, riffs on French traditions, American regions (crayfish étoufée), unique dishes, local seasonal specialties (shad and shad roe), European seasonal specialties (whole Périgord truffle and prosciutto in pastry), steaks, spit-roasted dishes, charcoal-broiled dishes, and so forth. The Four Seasons was simultaneously almost comically historical—probably the last restaurant in New York to serve Terrapin à la Maryland, and innovative—the first to offer nasturtium leaves. Under the circumstances it was a challenge to be able to provide a consistent dining experience, let alone to make a profit.

A CRISIS OF CASH AND CONFIDENCE

Some distinguished restaurants, such as Le Pavillon, experience immediate success. Their historical trajectory is a rapidly rising arc and then a slow but consistent decline. In the case of the Four Seasons, as with Chez Panisse, the early fame of the restaurant could not prevent repeated crises or assure balance and predictability. As a financial enterprise, the Four Seasons had a choppy start, followed by near disaster, followed by ups and downs and finally a degree of calm profitability. A restaurant can be admired yet fraught with turmoil. The Four Seasons always had certain inherent difficulties. It is awkwardly large; as a landmark it is impossible to alter but difficult to maintain because much of the décor is irreplaceable; it has immense wasted space (from the point of view of upkeep and profitability)—a first floor devoted to a coat check and small gallery, the pool taking up space in the middle of one dining room.

In the 1960s an immediate problem was the inattention of its creator. As he moved on to planning La Fonda del Sol, the restless Joe Baum withdrew from close supervision of the Four Seasons. La Fonda del Sol was yet another original concept, designed by Alexander Girard with uniforms by Rudi Gernreich, a fashion designer best known for inventing the topless bikini. The planning and furnishing of the new restaurant cost a mere $3 million. Perhaps because of Baum's absence, but certainly because of its large menu and overall eclectic cuisine, the Four Seasons developed a reputation for inconsistency. In 1964, Craig Claiborne, never a total enthusiast, said the food could be excellent on occasion and at other times "pedestrian." Twenty years later, Gael Greene remarked "the kitchen remains wildly uneven."[42]

Although greatly admired in the 1960s, the Four Seasons seldom filled its tables, especially, ironically in the light of later history, at lunch. Until after 1973 and the takeover of the restaurant by Tom Margittai and Paul Kovi, the vast and essentially gloomy Grill or Bar Room languished, while the more obviously romantic Pool Room was the favored destination of both tourists and regulars. George Lois, an advertising designer who thought up ads for the Four Seasons, recalled that sometimes he would wave to the architect Philip Johnson across the somber space of a deserted Grill Room.[43] It may be, as Gael Greene said in 1984, that New Yorkers in 1959 weren't ready for the Four Seasons, preferring French, cozy, and safe.[44]

In a 1960 interview with *Fortune* magazine, Joe Baum claimed the restaurant took only six months to start showing a profit, and that it was grossing $250,000 per month.[45] In 1964, Baum said the Four Seasons and Mamma Leone's did an annual (gross) business of $4 million each.[46] Even if these figures were accurate, the difference was that Leone's was profitable and the Four Seasons remained a net loser. Under a new manager, Stuart Levin, the menu and look of the Four Seasons received loving attention while customers were duly cosseted. In fact, clients probably received too much indulgence as Levin handed out discounts and free meals to well-known guests and corporations. Levin assiduously courted the famous and succeeded in attracting Princess Margaret and her then husband, the photographer Lord Snowden, to host a private dinner. President John F. Kennedy's forty-fifth birthday party on May 19, 1962, was also celebrated there. Guests, who contributed $1,000, dined on a rather modest meal of baked crab, chicken broth with spring wheat, beef medallions, and birthday cake. Kennedy had devoted so much time to chatting with each table, that he was able to have only some cream of asparagus soup and a beer before going off to Madison Square Garden, where Marilyn Monroe sang him a rather suggestive version of "Happy Birthday."[47]

Restaurant Associates prospered during the "go-go" segment of the 1960s, and its stock price raced upward, reaching $47 a share in 1968, but Martin Brody, who came on as president of RA in 1965, instituted a strategy of acquiring low-end restaurant chains and selling off or neglecting the trophy properties. RA management concentrated its attention on enterprises such as Waldorf Systems, which ran cafeterias, pancake houses, and drive-ins. This was followed by a vigorous expansion into catering to captive audiences in airport terminals, amusement parks, turnpike rest stops, and employee cafeterias. The marketing vice president for RA said dismissively that the Four Seasons was great if you wanted just to sit around and gaze at your navel in beautiful surroundings, or (on an equal level of eccentricity, apparently), if you wanted a restaurant that placed "a heavy emphasis on quality food properly prepared and served."[48]

In 1969, RA grossed $110 million but started losing money ($720,560). The losses escalated due to overreach exacerbated by various disasters, ranging from strikes at Ford Motor Company and Baltimore Airport to a speculative bubble in chocolate that ruined the Barracini candy business. By 1970 the stock had plummeted to $4, and the cost-cutting imposed to deal with the crisis showed. In an article from that year entitled "Restaurant Associates: Twilight of the Gods," Gael Greene observed with regret that the carpets at the Four Seasons were dirty and the tablecloths had holes. Wilted flowers sat around without being changed; the menu and the staff were trimmed. In that grim year, 1970, Joe Baum was fired and would go on to a new career developing Windows on the World at the World Trade Center.[49]

Greene mourned the death of elegance and class and believed the social upheaval and the youth revolution meant that budget meals and granola would replace fine dining altogether. Fortunately she was wrong and, as it happened, the seemingly permanently unprofitable Four Seasons would help instill a new kind of restaurant enthusiasm in the unpromising 1970s—one that would flower in the subsequent decade.

MARGITTAI AND KOVI

As the gloom deepened, the first cookbook bearing the Four Seasons name was published in 1971. This volume was in some respects the last sparkler of the Baum era—printed on different-colored paper for each seasonal section and lavishly but oddly illustrated in color. Not one photograph of the restaurant appears, however, and there is a tendency to present brooding, mysterious displays of food—a tureen of soup in the snow, lobster in a vase, an asparagus bunch floating in air over a foggy Hudson River. Despite the surreal pictures, the innovative quality of the food was toned down and French classics were emphasized.[50]

Amidst the corporate bloodlettings at Restaurant Associates in the early 1970s, two executives still cared about the gracious, or at least high-end, legacy of Joe Baum. Tom Margittai had started at RA in 1962, rising to vice president in charge of "tablecloth" restaurants, a position that now seemed ready for elimination. Paul Kovi, like Margittai, of Transylvanian Hungarian origin, was in charge of the Four Seasons, and he too bemoaned the neglect and penny pinching that were afflicting the restaurant. In 1972, Margittai was thinking over an offer to become director of the Playboy Clubs, then at the height of their popularity. James Beard advised him against it and remarked that in fact Margittai would do a good job of running the Four Seasons independently. Much to his surprise, Margittai found that RA was desperate enough to unload the Four Seasons, and the Seagram family was so eager to get rid of RA, that he and Paul Kovi were able to buy the restaurant with just $15,000 of their own money. The catch was that it came with the Forum of the Twelve Caesars, which was losing money even more inexorably than the Four Seasons.

In the depths of the recession brought on by the economic impact of the Vietnam War and the first oil embargo, Kovi and Margittai miraculously energized the fading restaurant. On May 15, 1974, they bravely introduced themselves as the new owners of the Four Seasons in a full-page *New York Times* advertisement. They hired Joseph Renggli, a new Swiss chef, and reoriented their attention to New Yorkers, especially corporate executives. They were prescient enough to decide that, despite the famous *Daily News* headline "Ford [that is, President Ford] to City: Drop Dead," New York would survive its brush with bankruptcy and apparent social disintegration. They perceived that out of the ordeal was emerging a new elite. The once-empty former Grill Room, now officially renamed the Bar Room, suddenly became the city's most important lunch scene. Catering to media and finance leaders who didn't want to spend all afternoon on lunch, but who nevertheless needed to hold court during that meal, the owners made the menu shorter and the meal more convenient while keeping the hushed atmosphere and seasonal emphasis.

New dishes were developed so that the menu remained interesting even if many customers ordered the same thing all the time. Among the novelties were Italian pastas and risottos. It's hard to imagine that, given the immense size of the menu in the early years of the Four Seasons, there had been almost nothing in the way of pasta. As will be seen with regard to Chez Panisse, the shift toward Italian entrées was more than a mere expansion of options but a move toward simpler, less French, and more what would come to be called "Mediterranean" food—a cuisine perceived

Fig. 93. The Bar Room at the Four Seasons.

as light and even healthful, yet hearty and flavorful. The Italianization of not-specifically-Italian restaurants started in the late 1970s and would become a little-noticed but significant trend. Carpaccio, risotto, branzino, farro, and semifreddo are now standard items on the Four Seasons menus, and at most fancy restaurants for that matter. Even more important than the culinary adaptations was a shift in the social behavior of New York City's elites and the ability of the Four Seasons to understand and profit from it.

POWER LUNCHES

Under Margittai and Kovi, aided by their new associates Alex von Bidder and Julian Niccolini, the food became more consistent and well received, even if Mimi Sheraton in 1979 awarded the Four Seasons only two out of a possible four stars in a *New York Times* review, finding the food "uneven."[51] By this time the Bar Room was firmly established as a place for business and publishing insiders to lunch. Although it could feel "clubby," it was not really a club, since the space was public and entry did not require being upper-class or the alumnus of an elite college.

Creating an exclusive circle was not quite the same thing as instituting a literal club. To this day the most exclusive private clubs discourage business discussion over lunch and prohibit diners from referring to documents. The traditional club is supposed to be a refuge from commerce, and although membership might result in contacts and friendships leading to deals and alliances, clubs function informally to link people together, much as do golf games or charity events. Thus for those who actually wanted to discuss business deals and might not have attended Princeton, the Bar Room proved ideal. It even welcomed a few female executives and creative talent. Its quiet combination of luxury and austerity distinguished it from masculine restaurant hangouts in the era of the three-martini lunch, which favored a boisterous, even raucous, English chop-house ambience. In keeping with its International Style architectural modernity, the Four Seasons was cool rather than full of noise; the Bar was less about steaks and whole lobsters than about poached salmon and chicken paillard. Here you didn't get up and table-hop in the Broadway or Hollywood manner, as used to be required at what gossip columnists called "watering holes," like the Stork Club, the Russian Tea Room, the "21" Club, or Sardi's. At the Bar Room everyone saw you dining, knew you were a person of substance and local charisma, and wondered what corporate or cultural maneuvers you were planning.

For leading editors, literary agents, real-estate executives, bankers, and fashion designers it was important to be seen, to carry on negotiations privately but in sight of others. If the curse of the Four Seasons had been its size and unusable space, these features paradoxically became uniquely advantageous in a city where so-called luxury restaurants cram tables next to each other. The Four Seasons Bar patrons could see their neighbors, hear their own confidential conversation without difficulty, and not be overheard—all in a serenely luxurious setting. The Bar at lunch catered to regulars to such an extent that there started to be a form of "negative reservation"—favored customers had a regular table and notified the restaurant when they were *not* going to show up, otherwise they would arrive as usual.

It is interesting that here again the advice of James Beard was crucial. Far from being a corporate titan, he nevertheless understood the sort of food that would entice such people. The Bar Room offered faster preparation and presented simply prepared fish and grilled meat in line with the diet-conscious recipes of the 1980s and the restaurant's tradition of disengaging from French precedent. In 1979 paillards of veal, beef, chicken, and lamb were conspicuous on the menu. A Bar burger with creamed spinach, or a skewer of shrimp and chipolata sausage, or gravlax with dill sauce were other typical entrées. At two p.m., lunch was over for the dealmakers in the Bar. Michael Korda observed, "You can have a simple, fine meal and be back at your desk in two hours."[52]

In the late 1970s, the Bar Room regulars formed a panoply of the leading tastemakers and rebuilders of the struggling metropolis, and were well-known figures from fashion, art, and publishing: people like Calvin Klein; Oscar de la Renta; editor Albert Vitale; literary agent Lynn Nesbit; and writers Truman Capote, Lillian Hellman, and Gay Talese. Among the 1970s regulars was Clay Felker, who had an uncanny sensitivity for trends and gauging minute-by-proverbial-minute who was gaining or losing power and prestige. The founder and editor of *New York* magazine and briefly (1977–1979) owner of *Esquire*, Felker enlisted Lee Eisenberg to write about the scene at the Bar Room, where, it was breathlessly asserted, "our literary, fashion, and oenological tastes of the future are determined." Eisenberg's October 1979 *Esquire* article, "America's Most Powerful Lunch," provided an actual seating chart, showing where luminaries like Calvin

Klein or Lewis Rudin (a real-estate titan) or Michael Korda sat.[53] Eisenberg introduced the term "power lunch," and the popularity of the article ensured at long last the financial success of the Four Seasons.

Eisenberg was hardly the first to write about the elite's restaurant rituals. In the mid-1960s, for example, the luxury lifestyle magazine *Town and Country* presented a diagram of who was seated where at La Caravelle.[54] The older social solidarity, however, was based on fame rather than business or professional success. The aura radiated by the Duke and Duchess of Windsor or Jacqueline Kennedy Onassis was produced by their exalted station and style, mingled with a distinguished if not necessarily likeable personality. The reputation of such restaurant patrons in 1970 was not so different from the status ascribed to those who dined at Delmonico's in the 1880s, when Ward McAllister and Mrs. Astor ruled New York society. Sports figures, presentable gangsters, and above all movie stars were added to old money in the twentieth century, but the elite at the Four Seasons was distinguished by different qualities from those followed by the gossip columns of the time. It was new for a table at a grand restaurant to become the property of a literary agent like Mort Janklow or an editor like Betty Prashker of Doubleday. Lois Wyse, who ran her own advertising agency, was quoted in the *Esquire* article as saying: "They call me the goddess of the Bar Room. The center banquette is always mine—even Jackie O. can't take it away from me. In it I extend my business life. The Bar Room has a *great* business atmosphere, particularly for women. The tables are far apart, and there's no romance possible."[55]

As definitions of glamour changed, a different kind of elite started to draw more attention, a financial elite defined not by old money or even manufacturing but by deal-making and the economic expansion as well as "creative destruction" this entailed. Money tended to displace talent, or perhaps the more purely financial deals came to command more prestige than the arrangements of agents and media companies. A *New York Magazine* article in 1986 and the prologue to Mariani and von Bidder's book about the Four Seasons from 1994 provide lists of prominent lunch guests at the Bar Room, fairly evenly balanced among publishers, media figures, real-estate magnates, and bankers. Sandy Weill, at that time head of Shearson-Lehman, Henry Kissinger, and Frank Zarb, at that time chief executive of Travelers Group are there, but so are writers, advertisers, and producers.[56]

More than two decades later, many publishing offices have moved downtown and expense accounts have been reduced. Its remaining luminaries congregate around Union Square and Gramercy Park, especially at Danny Meyer's Union Square Café. When I asked Alex von Bidder, one of the owners of the Four Seasons, if agents, writers, and publishers were still regular Bar Room lunch patrons, he looked at me pityingly, as if I'd asked for directions to the nearest Automat. Bankers, fund managers, fixed-interest notables, and real-estate leaders have long since vanquished everybody else.

VON BIDDER AND NICCOLINI

The 1980s were good years for the restaurant. New York was again a place to make serious money even if it was still plagued by crime, its subways and highways in ruins, and its racial relations uneasy. The world described in Tom Wolfe's *Bonfire of the Vanities* was one of circumscribed but intense prosperity, surprising given the jarringly fast decline and social disintegration of the 1970s. Many old-line restaurants started to fade or closed their doors altogether as French cuisine, starched linen, and officious maîtres d'hôtel became *vieux jeu*. The timelessness and unstuffy sophistication of the Four Seasons successfully resisted trends toward informality or the expansion of international cuisine options. This is not to say that the Four Seasons was fossilized—it came up with a "spa menu" and the Bar Room started offering pre-theatre dinners. But as it celebrated its twenty-fifth

Fig. 94. The new and former owners of the Four Seasons, 1995: Alex von Bidder, Julian Niccolini, Tom Margittai, and Paul Kovi.

anniversary in 1984 by inviting all its employees to bring a guest to dinner, the restaurant seemed to bask in high modernist permanence, paradoxical given Baum's emphasis on New York's dynamism and modernism's radical rejection of the past.

The unchanging look was deceptive. In 1979 the Seagram Company sold the building to the academic pension fund TIAA-CREF, and although Seagram's retained considerable leased-back office space and attempted to

We Suggest That You Order
The Espresso and Sambuca Soufflé
At The Beginning Of The Meal

SPA CUISINE [R]

APPETIZER: Marinated VEGETABLES and MUSHROOMS with Safron
MAIN COURSE: **Escalope of STURGEON with Tomatillo Sauce, Wild Pecan Rice**

HOT AND COLD APPETIZERS

Smoked Nova Scotia SALMON
ASPARAGUS Vinaigrette
Terrine of CAPON and STURGEON with Piccalilli
FETTUCCINE Primavera
Cherrystone CLAMS
PROSCIUTTO di Parma and Melon
Blue Crab GUMBO
A Spring VEGETABLE Soup

THIS EVENING'S ENTREES
FOR THE FOUR SEASONS THEATRE DINNER

Sautéed Filet of TROUT with Almonds
Stuffed Spring CHICKEN with Watercress and Mushrooms
Médaillons of LAMB with Zucchini and Eggplant
VEAL Pojarski with Vichy Carrots
Grilled ENTRECOTE with Béarnaise and Crisp Potatoes
Spring GREENS

THE DESSERTS

ESPRESSO and SAMBUCA Soufflé
A Parfait of Spring FRUITS
CHOCOLATE and ORANGE Mousse Cake
OUR SHERBETS

THE FOUR SEASONS BEVERAGE SERVICE

FORTY ONE FIFTY

THE FOUR SEASONS

Fig. 95. The Four Seasons "Spa" menu, 1980s.

protect the unique attributes of the building, TIAA was not a culturally enlightened landlord and strongly resisted efforts to designate the Four Seasons interior as a landmark. Between 1988 and 1993 a legal and regulatory struggle took place, with TIAA attempting to preserve the possibility of altering the restaurant space and using it for another purpose. The fund lost, the restaurant was landmarked, and TIAA, claiming it didn't want to pay for bringing the building up to date, sold it to a real-estate investment, development, and management company, RFR Holding LLC, in 2000. By 2013, RFR bought out its partners and the company, and its principals, Aby J. Rosen and Michael Fuchs, became sole owners of the building, along with a lot of other New York real estate.

At the turn of the century, in 2000, the same year RFR took over the building, the French media company Vivendi Universal and Pernod bought the Seagram company's beverage products. Vivendi collapsed in 2002 as a result of spectacular mismanagement, but not before selling Seagram assets and destroying the look and integrity of the company's offices in the building.[57]

In the late 1980s and into the 1990s, the Four Seasons began to experience problems common to many high-end New York establishments: dependence on the fluctuations of the stock market (the crash of 1987 and recession of 1990–1992 were damaging), and federal tax law changes imposed in 1988 that limited business entertainment deductions. By the end of the 1990s, it also suffered from changes in restaurant fashions. If the Four Seasons was not formal in the old French, Le Pavillon manner, it could never be deemed rustic, homey, countrified, or any of the adjectives used over the past twenty years to convey authenticity. Finally, while it had blazed a trail of culinary innovation in the 1960s and 1970s, it defied the trend toward chef-driven restaurants, remaining one of the few places whose image was created and tended by the front-of-the-house team. The current owners, Alex von Bidder and Julian Niccolini, bought out Margittai and Kovi in 1995. Niccolini has been in charge of the food and von

Bidder has attended to the business, but they are both constantly on the floor and interact with or handle their customers flawlessly, the product of experience and innate diplomacy.

Few fine-dining monuments have withstood changes in cuisine and ambience. With the exception of La Grenouille, all the grand Midtown French restaurants that exemplified the glory of midcentury cuisine have closed: Lutèce, La Caravelle, La Côte Basque, Le Cygne. Innovative 1980s restaurants like Chanterelle and the Quilted Giraffe are also gone. The farm-to-table movement created Brooklyn cuisine and encouraged the Brooklynization of Manhattan restaurants. Against some of these trends the Four Seasons managed to maintain itself as an outpost of a different era. In 2015 the power lunch was flourishing and people still dressed up in defiance of a prevailing informal fashion eclecticism. If flaming dishes were rare, tableside service (presenting and then boning fish, for example) remained part of a highly skilled and professional service style. Dover sole, skillet steak, and velvet cake were always featured. The vogue for ingredient-driven dining and local, seasonal cuisine allowed the Four Seasons to come into its own, to realize a potential that derived from the unstable genius of Joe Baum. It is the one traditional elite restaurant in New York that merely had to refine its presentation of seasonality to fit fashions that started in the 1990s rather than create it anew. More than just preserving a certain panache, the restaurant worked to perfect its elegant yet innovative food. In 1999 it won a James Beard Award as the nation's outstanding restaurant, a prize conferred not for décor or ambience but for cuisine.

Mariani and von Bidder end their 1994 book with a reflection that perhaps it had never been the food that drew customers to the restaurant.[58] Certainly the imposing, high-modernist surroundings; the sense that every meal taken there is important; the gracious but unintimidating service; and the hands-on attitude of its managers contributed to the success of the Four Seasons. In the twenty-first century there were few other large restaurants where the owners were so intimately familiar with their guests. According to von Bidder, in 2014, 85 percent of those dining at the Four Seasons on any given day were known to the management—even those who might elsewhere be dismissed as tourists were thought of as people living far away but returning to the restaurant whenever they were in New York.[59] In the end, however, and despite the persistent criticism of the restaurant for its inconsistent food, the actual cuisine put together by the various chefs and owners is what made the Four Seasons stand out as one of the most durably influential yet unique restaurants in America.

CODA

As Joe Baum once observed, New York is defined by dynamism and change, and the proliferation of officially protected landmarks and historic neighborhoods notwithstanding, the destruction and reconstruction of the city has continued and accelerated as Fifty-Seventh Street becomes "billionaire row," the waterfront is reclaimed, and rustic food commands triple-digit restaurant tabs. No restaurant can survive as a historical artifact in New York, even an artifact of modernism, but the end of the Four Seasons in its old home is not an inevitable result of creative destruction but rather of particular circumstances and personalities.

New York is an eternally treacherous place to do business, now not because of violence and crime, even if these are imprinted the popular imagination, but because of the city's unquenchable allure to the world's wealthiest people. This has allowed for the creation of restaurants like the Four Seasons, which Joe Baum intended for globe-spanning leaders of industry, but also undermines anything built on history. And it seems this chapter in history is on the verge of coming to a close. There are a number of ironies in connection with the now inevitable expulsion of the Four Seasons from the Seagram Building. New York's contempt for tradition, as noted by Joe Baum, has caught up with his greatest monument. The scene of so many deals is now doomed by a transaction it can't control and the insatiable appetite of the real-estate industry. A restaurant that survived and even flourished in the dark years of New York City's decline may be extinguished by prosperity.

On February 4, 2014, the *New York Times* reported that Aby J. Rosen, a principal executive of RFR Holding, which owns the Seagram Building, proposed to fix steam leaks from the wall behind Picasso's canvas for the Ballets Russes *Le Tricorne*. These repairs would require removal of the work of art. The New York Landmarks Conservancy, which owns the so-called tapestry, said that such a move would destroy the brittle fabric and denied that there was anything wrong with the wall that would necessitate such a radical step.[60] Although the restaurant's interior was declared a landmark in 1989, the Picasso tapestry was excepted, as it was not a structural part of the layout.

The *Times* article reported that Rosen contemptuously referred to the curtain as "a *schmatte*" (Yiddish for a rag). Provocatively Philistine though this statement is, Rosen is hardly indifferent to art and has assembled a large collection of contemporary works by luminaries such as Damien Hirst and Jeff Koons. The New-York Historical Society agreed to display *Le Tricorne*, resolving that issue, although to the detriment of the restaurant because the Picasso curtain has been identified almost essentially with it since the beginning. In fact, no repair work to the wall took place after *Le Tricorne* was removed.

Behind the aesthetic discussion was maneuvering typical of the New York real-estate scene. The restaurant's lease was set to expire in the summer of 2016, and the building's owners were determined to triple the rent, which would bring it to something on the order of $3 million a year, and to receive a share of the revenue.[61] In the spring of 2015, Rosen and RFR proposed to alter the interior of the restaurant by constructing toilets where the wine cellar now is, enlarging the lobby coat room, opening the top panels of the walnut wall of the Pool Room, and putting in planters where a glass partition now separates the Grill Room bar and dining space. Except for allowing a change in carpeting, the New York Landmarks Commission turned Rosen down, but he made it clear that when the current lease expired, the Four Seasons would be gone and a "cooler" restaurant put in its place.[62] In July 2015, the Major Food Group concluded what Greg Morabito on the New York Eater website termed "the deal of the century" to take over the Four Seasons space in 2016.[63] The "Torrisi wolfpack," (another pithy contribution of Greg Morabito's) runs outstanding and successful Italian and Italian American restaurants such as Parm, Carbone, and Santina, along with Dirty French, a sophisticated but informal French restaurant located on the Lower East Side. Aby Rosen is asking for investors to raise something on the order of $30 million to refurbish the restaurant and turn it into three different "concepts" with separate menus.[64] This is in keeping with the daring original plan and the results, if marking a break with the past, will be exciting.

As this is being written, the Four Seasons owners have announced that they plan to move to a new location on Park Avenue. The restaurant has been so closely identified with its unique, modernist setting that it is hard to imagine a new space could re-create anything resembling it. In a moment of uncharacteristic but understandable pessimism, Julian Niccolini told a party celebrating the fiftieth anniversary of a New York City law protecting historical landmarks that "since we are not going to be here after 2016, the Four Seasons will not exist."[65] That law, and a spring 2015 ruling against plans to alter the Four Seasons interior, assures the preservation of the look of the restaurant, but the new owners, while promising current regulars continuity, have emphasized what must be regarded as inevitable and dramatic changes in food, style, and atmosphere.

A combination of corporate largesse and great architecture, combined with Joe Baum's visionary enthusiasm, created a unique but at the same time historically influential restaurant whose innovations affected everything from farm-to-table dining to the business lunch. This legacy will survive the end of what once seemed, for all its revolutionary beginnings, a timeless New York institution. When the restaurant had just opened, the decorator magazine *Interiors* observed:

> [The design] is not a stage setting; rather it is a theater that is not to date, nor tire the audience but to focus on a perpetually changing mis-en-scene [*sic*], of the world's greatest metropolis, and of the pleasure of being served, eating, drinking and conversing.[66]

:CHEZ:PANISSE:

:CAFE:&:RESTAURANT:

:1517:SHATTUCK:BERKELEY:94709:

:548·5525:

Dinner Menus for the Week of October 5-9, 1976

Tuesday October 5 $11.00	Fresh tuna marinated with olive oil, lemon juice, green peppercorns, and chives --or-- pâté of chicken livers with Cognac Fresh fall vegetables stewed in butter with herbs Roast duckling with a quince puree Cheese Fruit *walnut ice cream*
Wednesday October 6 $11.00	Soup of mussel broth lightly thickened with egg yolks and cream Fresh Eastern mussels with creme Chantilly Roast leg of yearling lamb with a spinach puree and Madeira deglazing juices Salad or cheese *", pears in red wine* Fruit
Thursday October 7 $20.00	Northern California Regional Dinner Spenger's Tomales Bay bluepoint oysters on ice Cream of fresh corn soup Mendocino style, with a crayfish butter Smoked Garrapata trout steamed over California bay leaves Sauteed Monterey Bay prawns Hand Ranch Sebastopol geese cooked and preserved in goose fat Local California cheese Caramelized fresh figs California walnuts, almonds, and pears
Friday October 8 $12.50	Cream soup of tomatoes with a fresh herb butter Garlic sausage with fresh horseradish and cream sauce Fresh Garrapata trout wrapped in bacon, rolled in breadcrumbs, and grilled, with a lemon butter sauce Salad or cheese Fruit *chocolate cake Fanchon*
Saturday October 9 $12.50	Soup of fresh pumpkin pureed in a rich chicken stock with shallots Fresh Eastern oysters sauteed in butter and white wine, with crushed black peppercorns Boned chicken cutlets rolled in breadcrumbs and sauteed in butter; served with a stew of fresh fall vegetables Salad or cheese Fruit

call Penny *order figs on Jackson* *flowers* *order oranges berries*

A word of explanation about our reservation system: Chez:Panisse has two seatings for dinner--early and late. The early seating is from 6:00 through 7:00, and the late seating from 8:30 until 9:30. We do not take reservations for the period between 7:00 and 8:30. We are limited to a total of eighty-five reservations in order to keep the upstairs cafe open all day and through the dinner hours. Cancellations and unkept reservations, unfortunately, do occur, leaving the possibility of calling at the last minute for a table.

Fig. 96. Chez Panisse menu for October 5–9, 1976, with the Northern California Dinner.

CHEZ PANISSE

"THE WAY WE EAT NOW"

ugust 28, 1971, was opening night at Chez Panisse, a new French restaurant in an old two-story house of vaguely Victorian origin in Berkeley, California. Chez Panisse was the creation of Alice Waters—today a household name, but then a twenty-seven-year-old political activist, former Montessori schoolteacher, and enthusiast of French provincial cuisine. Her friends and neighbors knew her to be an excellent cook and a warmhearted hostess, but these would not, at first glance, seem to have qualified her as a restaurateur, especially as Waters was determined to run the restaurant informally, as if it were her own home. Moreover, the location seemed unpromising: it was a former student residence and, not surprisingly, rather run-down. Although Chez Panisse has for several decades anchored a neighborhood full of food enterprises sometimes called the "Gourmet Ghetto," its main street, Shattuck Avenue, still features shabby houses, 1950s commercial buildings, and lots of traffic.

Rock music journalist Greil Marcus, an original investor in Chez Panisse, was in attendance at that first dinner.[1] He and his wife arrived at nine for the second seating and were immediately presented with a delicious pâté en croûte. Others at their big table had come at six, and while the pâté had been promptly served, the first shift had to wait more than two hours for their entrée. Once the disgruntled early arrivals tasted what was finally placed in front of them, however, Marcus recalls, there was a palpable change in mood. The duck with olives evoked a feeling of incredulous delight that anything could taste so marvelous, and all impatient discontent was forgotten. The sense of extraordinary excitement was sustained as the meal concluded with a plum tart.

The set menu cost $3.95, the laughable equivalent of $23 today. The price would gradually increase, but the combination of uniquely delicious food and barely controlled chaos would remain a constant for decades. The restaurant was unique among American French restaurants for its informal and improvisatory air. No one in the kitchen had professional cooking experience; Alice Waters and her associates relied on cookbooks and untried recipes in the manner of weekend cooks. Her first chef, Victoria Kroyer, had been a philosophy graduate student.

The first surviving menu (one that was printed, not written on a blackboard) is from Halloween 1971. It offered hors d'oeuvres including homemade terrine, boeuf en daube Provençal, salad, and fruit tart, and the charge had been upped to $4.50.[2] Early regulars discovered the charm of showing up and seeing what happened. The menu offered little or no choice on any single occasion, but because it changed every day, it was always new. Some dishes didn't work, but more often they were nothing short of sparkling. When things came together, the freshness and intensity of each course made the meal something of a Platonic ideal of French cuisine that was on the one hand familiar, and on the other better than had been imaginable.

Even on the first night, word that Chez Panisse would be special had spread, and a line of people outside waited to get in; the restaurant only began accepting reservations six months later. Special though it was, there were more employees than customers, a bad sign from a business perspective. Another often-repeated refrain was financial difficulty, starting just two weeks after opening when the payroll could not be met. Famous restaurants like Delmonico's and Le Pavillon found a successful formula immediately. Others, such as the Four Seasons and Chez Panisse, were admired for their food but required years, even decades, to figure out how to make a profit.

In those post-hippie days of the early 1970s, there were plenty of French restaurants in the Bay Area, but this one was quickly perceived as being unusual. In May 1972, the Bay Area restaurant critic, Jack Shelton, gave Chez Panisse a favorable review, and his enthusiasm set a pattern for subsequent food writers' reactions. He lauded the restaurant as an exciting experiment; not everything succeeded, but the food was always thought-provoking and sometimes exhilarating. Shelton used words such as "adventuresome," "delightful," "daring," and "courageous," which would be repeated in years to come by other reviewers.[3] Only a little over three years later Chez Panisse and Alice Waters had become nationally renowned. In its October 1975 issue, the authoritative magazine *Gourmet* compared the tired American French restaurant formula—"the unholy trinity" of onion soup, duckling à l'orange, and crème caramel—with the "joyous exploration" at Chez Panisse of French cuisine in all its "vigor, freshness and variety."[4] Yet in the spring of 1976, the frustration and fatigue of dealing with financial turmoil and staff discontent induced Alice Waters to put Chez Panisse up for sale. That plan, however, was withdrawn for want of buyer interest, and the combination of success and instability would continue. By 1980, Chez Panisse was more than an innovative French restaurant; it had become the most famous restaurant in the country. It was also, hesitantly, inconsistently, and unselfconsciously, on the way to pioneering a new American cuisine that would supplant obeisance to France.

Fig. 97. Alice Waters.

THE PARADOXES OF CHEZ PANISSE

The most influential of Alice Waters's ideas can be summed up as a few interlocking precepts:

Primary ingredients must be of high quality.
Quality must be defined in terms of freshness and naturalness.
Freshness and naturalness are to be thought of in terms of seasonality,
location, and small-scale, non-industrial agricultural practices.

These principles are now taken for granted as restaurants vie to satisfy "locavores" and follow the seasons. In the 1970s, however, they were not only new but peculiar, virtually unheard-of. There is another aspect intrinsic to Chez Panisse that was equally revolutionary but less obvious: viewing naturalness as something that enhances sensual pleasure, not as a form of penance. In other words, it's not enough to have environmentally virtuous food if the food is boring. The taste had to be better, deeper, and more delightful than either mass-produced supermarket products or unpalatable health food. The aesthetic promoted by Chez Panisse contrasted with the bland, thawed-out offerings of most supposedly elegant restaurants of the 1960s, and it also equally took issue with the austere macrobiotic diet of the counterculture. The latter movement, for all its communal intensity, was never going to gain a significant number of adherents because it considered gustatory pleasure bourgeois and materialistic, as opposed to the fun of sex, drugs, or rock-and-roll. The counterculture may not have had much power nationally, but it did in Berkeley. For an advocate of social change like Alice Waters to establish a French restaurant there— and an earnestly authentic, even fussy French restaurant at that—seemed to a some a betrayal according to the moralistic streak among the right-thinking people of the West Coast, for whom being a "gourmet" was as bad as driving a Cadillac.[5]

This is one of several paradoxes in the story of Alice Waters and Chez Panisse: that she could effectively put forward plans for radical social change while creating a top-ranked restaurant; that such a restaurant could emerge from the prevailing brown-rice-and-granola food culture of the Bay Area; and that serving only one no-choice lineup of dishes could ultimately produce the greatest variety of any restaurant's total repertoire.

The central paradox is that a restaurant with exacting standards for preparing the traditional food of provincial France would become instrumental in creating a new American cuisine. The California characteristics of this cuisine, identified by the mid-1980s, include innovations in sourcing (local, organic, seasonal) and preparation (open-fire cooking and open kitchens); fusion of different culinary traditions; eclectic menus and specific products such as goat cheese, gathered salad greens, pizza, or salsa.[6] All of these were attributes of Chez Panisse, some from the start, some as a result of the transformation of its original French identity. Today Alice Waters rejects the term "California cuisine" to describe what supplanted French cuisine at Chez Panisse, and seems to prefer (maybe) "Mediterranean," because there is no historical background to California cuisine.[7] "New American," rather than "California," is more neutral, but perhaps too broad a term for what Alice Waters and other chefs pioneered in the 1970s. "New American" describes a *series* of movements and styles that have as a common element the primacy of regional or local ingredients rather than imported products and styles.

Two ordinary meals at Chez Panisse demonstrate the change over time: one served on August 26, 1975, began with marinated shrimp and mushrooms grilled on a skewer with shrimp butter sauce, followed by fresh trout sautéed in brown butter with lemon juice.[8] The main course was chicken stuffed under the skin with ham and fennel, poached in stock, and served with Béarnaise sauce. Salad or cheese and then fruit finished a meal full of different tastes (particularly lots of sauces), but simple, creative; French in spirit, but not overly literal. In January 1992 the menu was not French at all: a salad of Chioggia beets, new potatoes, red endive, and black truffles; tagliolini with Dungeness crab, Meyer lemon, and chervil; charcoal-grilled Niman-Schell Ranch top sirloin with anchoiade (grilled crushed anchovies served on toast), grilled leeks, and turnips; and chocolate torte with noyeau (walnut liqueur) ice cream.[9] The latter meal was as ambitious as the Francophile dinner in 1975, but with no French sauces, more attention to local ingredients, the presence of Mediterranean items (pasta), and a grilled entrée.

Between 1992 and the present, the change has been less dramatic, the pattern having been set by the 1990s. The menu for November 14, 2014, consists of butternut-squash galette with sage, chestnuts, and endive salad, followed by Gulf shrimp and bay scallop raviolini in an herb broth. The entrée is grilled BN Ranch beef rib-eye with black-pepper sauce, turnip gratin, onion rings, and watercress. The dessert is a hazelnut stracciatella and mocha ice-cream bombe.[10]

Menus from the more casual upstairs Café at Chez Panisse, introduced in 1980, tend to provide more elaborate descriptions of locally sourced items and no hint of French influence. A menu dated July 26, 2007, identifies three specific farms on the list of eight appetizers. For the entrées two farms are specified: Laughing Stock Farm (grilled pork) and James Ranch (lamb shoulder). Desserts include Ram Das Orchard (plum tart), a bowl of Raye Byrne's mulberries, and a Frog Hollow Farm Fantasia nectarine. Pizza, local salmon, and baked goat cheese with lettuce are also featured. The only sauces are tomato and salsa rossa (made with sun-dried tomato and peppers).

The standard narrative about Chez Panisse is this: it began as a French restaurant, but sometime in the 1970s Alice Waters, with or without inspiration from Chef Jeremiah Tower, moved away from imported culinary traditions in favor of local, seasonal ingredients, more simply and vividly prepared than allowed for by French orthodoxy.[11] A larger context for the

$ $

same narrative is that a group of American chefs and food experts ranging over several generations redirected their love of French cuisine to something more appropriate to their own origins. James Beard, Julia Child, and M.F.K. Fisher, according to this interpretation, discovered in postwar France the beauty of a cuisine rooted in local culture and small-scale agriculture, but at some point (the year 1970 has recently been suggested) they realized that they could no longer be subservient to French definitions of cuisine. They resolved to fight the mediocrity of American food, not by substituting an impossible French provincial authenticity but by creating a new American style.[12]

As it turns out, there is an even more interesting story that complicates this reductionist and self-congratulatory tale. Some of the additional elements are: the persistence of Chez Panisse as a French restaurant beyond 1980, the role of other chefs and food experts, several waves and false starts of what has been called the "California Food

Fig. 98. Exterior view of Chez Panisse.

Revolution," and the way in which the decline of French and the rise of American food are not the same story, but two independent if interacting phenomena.

Certainly a food revolution did occur, and the transformation received its initial impetus in California. Retrospective responsibility for the revolution is related to controversies about who should get credit for innovation. Joyce Goldstein, at one time the chef for the Café at Chez Panisse, has written an entire book to support the argument that the "California Food Revolution" was not solely due to Chez Panisse. Nevertheless, her opinion of Alice Waters is summarized in grudgingly favorable terms:

> I did not set out to write an encomium to Alice, but I've got to hand it to her, she drove the train of the ingredient revolution. I cannot tell you how many times her name came up while I was interviewing farmers, artisans, and chefs whom she supported and pushed to do more and better. We all have profited from her persistence and passion. She's stuck to her guns despite criticism that she's overly idealistic and elitist.[13]

David Kamp remarked that Chez Panisse "has some legitimate claim to being the most influential dining establishment in America since Le Pavillon," praise all the more significant because, as with Goldstein, this evaluation is given reluctantly.[14] Kamp, author of the wry history of high-end food *The United States of Arugula*, finds the restaurant, its acolytes, and its guardians altogether too self-satisfied. A third reluctant encomium comes from Jeremiah Tower, chef at Chez Panisse in the 1970s, who has directly taken issue with Alice Waters over the question of who really fomented the revolution:

> Her vision was incredibly strong and has never wavered, really, so she deserves credit for sticking by it. To have never given up that vision, and not to have done it another way, like Wolfgang Puck, with a $378 mil-

lion a year gross income—it's almost unique in this part of our culinary history.[15]

That "vision" has a number of elements, some of which are now found all over the American restaurant scene, such as the seasonal, locavore emphasis on prime ingredients. But there are other aspects particular to Alice Waters that are not shared by most successful American chefs, yet they are profoundly influential on public attitudes. Prime among these is the belief that food is a way to change society and to bring attention to the endangered natural environment. This idea of food being at the center of social change is particularly cherished by Alice Waters, but only partially shared by other restaurateurs. Her specific agenda has shifted from sweeping political transformation in the 1970s to protecting small farms and then to advancing sustainable agriculture, radically improving what children eat in school, and attacking global warming. Her commitment as a food activist has remained consistent and, in fact, has grown over the last two decades.

To the degree that Chez Panisse arose as a counterintuitive result of 1960s Berkeley political radicalism, it has been easy to make fun of political radicals' gourmet tastes and the curious idea of bringing about social justice through food. Right from the start, many politically dedicated Berkeley people saw Chez Panisse as a self-indulgent retreat from the barricades. Even other social activists who had gone into high-quality food enterprises, such as the collective of the Cheese Board (a store in North Berkeley), regarded Chez Panisse as aggressively capitalist and at one point refused to supply the restaurant and its "bourgeois clientele." In fact, from its creation and through the diffusion of its practices, Chez Panisse has represented a powerful force against corporate-led homogenization of taste as well as a break with the culinary puritanism of the counterculture of the late-1960s.[16]

Throughout it all, and despite criticism for supposed bourgeois leanings, Waters has adhered to her original vision and its components. There are no branches or spin-offs of Chez Panisse in Las Vegas, New York, Hong Kong, London, or anywhere, in fact. The single restaurant remains at its original location. The atmosphere is still informal and spontaneous, if calmer and more professional than in its first decades. Alice Waters originally saw the restaurant as a collaborative effort, a place of warmth for staff and friends to gather. This now seems normal, as whole territories from Brooklyn to Portland subscribe to these restaurant goals, but Chez Panisse was a radical break from the established model of a dual dictatorship: that of the chef in the kitchen and the maître d'hôtel in the front.

About the only major physical change to the restaurant since 1971 was the addition in 1980 of the Café on the second floor of the building, a more casual place not in terms of dress (since Chez Panisse was never formal) but in terms of menu choice and the ability to vary the size of a meal. One can order à la carte at the Café, but the main restaurant has always had a set menu. Of course, the food has changed dramatically since 1971. While remaining true to the original mission of quality ingredients, experimentation, and freshness, the restaurant has shed its former carefully shaped French identity. Alice Waters remarked in 2001 how at the start, "all I ever wanted was to be like a little Michelin one-star restaurant."[17] Although the restaurant now can hardly be considered French, it has not abandoned that ideal. In ambience and philosophy Chez Panisse resembles not so much a current one-star restaurant in France (which would be more elegant), but an example from provincial France of the postwar decades. In terms of cuisine, it bears only a tenuous relationship to France, except it can be said to retain some connection to the food of Provence.

Even if Alice Waters's image of a particular moment in French culinary history is not widely shared (most chefs are too young anyway), the ideas about food, cooking, and aesthetics derived from that image are ubiquitous. Before Chez Panisse, the perfection of primary ingredients was not a mainstream American aspiration. Quite the contrary—for most of the twentieth century, the definition of prestige in dining ignored freshness and simplicity in favor of novelty, obtainable through variety (thirty-two kinds of ice cream!) or foreign ingredients defined as chic precisely because they *weren't* of local origin (French foie gras; Dover sole; tropical fruit; "new" imports such as water chestnuts or kiwi fruit). In a system of industrial agriculture and large-scale food processing, it was and remains hard to furnish really fresh food. John and Karen Hess's 1970s diatribe, *The Taste of America*, showed how the hegemony of the food industry caused even professional gourmets to forget what food is supposed to taste like.[18] *Forgetfulness* has always been of great concern to Alice Waters—that we have become oblivious to the real taste of peaches, tomatoes, shrimp, or chicken and so cheerfully accept flavorless substitutes: fruit bred for durability or tasteless poultry from factory-farms. Combatting corporate-induced forgetfulness and restoring the memory of what food should be is not just a question of choosing correctly and in season, but also involves a struggle to change the way food is grown, processed, purchased, and appreciated. Alice Waters and her several campaigns have affected the way Americans eat and think about food, including people who don't patronize trendy restaurants, so much so that even recalcitrant behemoths such as the fast-food industry, school systems, and the various levels of government have had to pay attention.[19]

THE "HISTORIOGRAPHY" OF CHEZ PANISSE

Chez Panisse was named after Honoré Panisse, the kindly, elderly sail maker in Marcel Pagnol's cinematic trilogy (*Marius*, *Fanny*, *César*), produced between 1929 and 1936. The films depict the fellowship at César's Bar de la Marine in the port of Marseilles, the model for the conviviality of Chez Panisse. Alice Waters named her daughter, Fanny, after the lovely if feckless female protagonist in the series. Waters was also inspired by her experiences as a college student, spending time on a program in France in 1965. As was the case with James Beard, Craig Claiborne, Julia Child, and so many other Americans, Waters discovered the beauty of food in France. She adored the mussels at Honfleur and Steak Bercy in Paris, but her moment of gastronomic revelation was at a restaurant in an old stone house in Brittany, where she was served a perfect meal of cured ham with melon, trout with almonds, and a raspberry tart. The fish had just been taken from the stream in back of the restaurant, and the berries from the garden.[20] During its first decade, Chez Panisse tried to replicate the culinary experience of a rural French auberge. The great change came gradually in the 1980s: first a lighter Mediterranean aesthetic (especially Provençal and northern Italian), and then, through experimentation and persistence, the creation of a new American cuisine.

Unlike other restaurants presented in this book, Chez Panisse has had a daunting amount written about it. In some ways, this makes it easier to discuss because the history seems so well documented. Food historians have at times deemphasized Chez Panisse precisely because it is so well known, and they have presented the California "food revolution" as a complicated story involving many characters and ideas.[21] In other ways, it is difficult to consider the trajectory of Chez Panisse because of what we think we know. In particular, the changes are usually dealt with in terms of the retrospectively inevitable advent of locavore California cuisine. We know the outcome, therefore the past is structured according to what we are familiar with, but it was in fact *not* inevitable that Chez Panisse should have become the originator of a national food upheaval.

Certain controversies that feature in histories of the California culinary scene won't detain us much here: for example, should Jeremiah Tower or other associates of Alice Waters receive more credit for the restaurant's innovations? Is Waters really a chef or a rather a promoter of ideas and a composer of salads? Should Linda Guenzel be regarded as the real author of the *Chez Panisse Menu Cookbook* of 1982? Such problems of credit and attribution are considered with exemplary fairness in Thomas McNamee's *Alice Waters and Chez Panisse.*[22]

In addition to biographies and other accounts of Alice Waters, we have works by those once associated with her. Jeremiah Tower is the author of a fascinating autobiography entitled *California Dish.* Joyce Goldstein wrote a book about the emergence of California cuisine. Many of the beautiful special-occasion menus by Patricia Curtain have been collected together in *Menus for Chez Panisse.*[23] Researching the culinary history of Chez Panisse is aided by the preservation of a complete run of menus from 1971 to 1991, painstakingly assembled by Linda Guenzel and Joyce McGillis in bound volumes entitled *Beyond Tears* and *Way Beyond Tears.*[24] Immersion in this massive series gives one a sense of what it meant to produce a different meal every day. The collection shows the shifts in menu language from French to bilingual to English, the growing importance of local food and farmers, the influences of Italy and Asia, and the emergence of a creative Mediterranean/New American cuisine.

CALIFORNIA CUISINE BEFORE CHEZ PANISSE

French provincial restaurants serve the cuisine of their provinces; Italian regional restaurants produce the same specialties that local people cook in home kitchens. The California food shifts, however much they emphasized seasonal ingredients, took place in restaurants that only obliquely reflected a deeper culinary culture of home cooking practices.[25] What Californians ate at Chez Panisse and in restaurants calling themselves "New American" or "Californian" beginning in the 1970s seems radically different from suburban 1960s cooking, and certainly the revolution was not based on years of culinary folk wisdom. Yet restaurant innovations of the 1970s and 1980s were not completely divorced from earlier styles of cooking and dining. Even as Chez Panisse opposed the bland conformity of tract-home

California, its success was based on preexisting attempts at gastronomic distinction and California's particular mix of informality, eclecticism, and poolside socializing.

All revolutions have to create a grim image of the past or the status quo against which they are revolting. Every "Renaissance" has to manufacture its own "Gothic" period or "Dark Ages," that came before it, and the American food transformation that began in the early 1970s is no exception. Especially in the world of food writing, an awful and homogenized past has to serve as the insipid prologue for the glorious revelation that leads to how we eat in an enlightened manner today.

Food historians disagree about when the culinary renaissance in the United States is supposed to have begun. In his account of "the reinvention of American taste" in *Provence, 1970*, Luke Barr says the 1950s were dreadful, but he likes the late 1960s, which he views as a time of promise and rapid innovation. For Raymond Sokolov, on the other hand, the 1960s were no better than the preceding decade. The food eaten by the majority of the American population was processed and tasteless, while at the high end of so-called gourmet dining, the tyrant Henri Soulé imposed pretentious mediocrity from his fortress at Le Pavillon.[26]

And yet in those supposedly dark days, people of discernment thought they were living in an age of unparalleled food enthusiasm and sophistication. The success of *Gourmet* magazine, founded in 1941, signaled a widespread appreciation for the finer gastronomic things in life. A *New Yorker* cartoon of 1958 shows an office door with *Gourmet's* name and a sign reading "Out to lunch, back at 5."[27] *Gourmet* perfectly combined aspirational snobbery with engaging informality. Its features about vacations in castles and color photographs of elaborate table settings were difficult to live up to, but columns like "You Asked For It" (extracting secret recipes from restaurant chefs) and "Sugar and Spice" (recipes from readers and answers to various questions) were chatty, amusing, and personal. Correspondence came from everywhere in the United States, not just the coastal cultural capitals. More cooking and entertaining at home went on in the 1950s and 1960s than is the case now. James Beard was a revered authority, and Julia Child made French cuisine accessible with the publication of *Mastering the Art of French Cooking* in 1961, followed by her transformational television cooking show, which began in 1963.

Experiencing life in France and its culinary philosophy changed Alice Waters as it had Julia Child previously. Waters's early customers, however, were more influenced by California's prevailing food styles: bland, colorful, casual, eclectic, and not entirely the stereotypical "TV Dinner by the pool."[28] To paraphrase the title of historian David Strauss's book about the background to the gourmet explosion of the 1960s, *Setting the Table for Julia Child*, there were precursors to the revolution catalyzed by Chez Panisse who, in effect, set the table for Alice Waters.[29]

Cooking and entertaining were more creative and interesting in twentieth-century California than in other parts of the United States. Californians have traditionally emphasized outdoor cooking, Chinese and Mexican influences, tropical and subtropical dishes, and salads. Some of these tendencies either spread to other parts of the country or were simply slight intensifications of national trends, but there was a distinctive postwar California style notable in the recipes featured in *Sunset* magazine and the cookbooks put out by this publication. *Sunset* is the oldest American regional lifestyle magazine, originating in 1898 as a vehicle for the Southern Pacific Railroad to market the western United States. Taken over by the Lane family in 1929, *Sunset* subsequently addressed itself to people already living in California, not tourists or those who might be enticed to move there. So distinct was the magazine's regional identity that until the 1980s, it did not accept subscribers from outside the Western states.[30] *Sunset* published articles about home improvements appropriate to California's climate, gardening adapted to milder and drier conditions than those prevailing in most of the rest of the country, and recipes for an informal, vaguely multinational type of food.

It's easy to make fun of *Sunset's* bland, suburban cooking: grilling, Mexican food with the spices left out, Chinese food using canned ingredients. Yet *The Sunset Cook Book of Favorite Recipes*, first published in 1949, was distinctive for its Asian aspects and its focus on West Coast ingredients such as abalone and Dungeness crab. True, by the 1969 edition, it included recipes based on cream-of-mushroom soup, bizarre concoctions such as "Hamburger Soup" or "Green Beans Supreme" (made with canned string beans, mushroom soup, and canned French-fried onions), or a ham, cheese, water chestnut, and mushroom soup casserole called "Bruncho Relaxo."[31] Still, the same collection has recipes for squid, Armenian chicken, boraks, and moussaka.[32] Not all of its recipes called for canned chow mien noodles and lychee nuts or tacos sprinkled with cheddar cheese. *Adventures in Food*, an international cookbook put out by *Sunset* in 1964, includes directions for making Italian pasta from scratch, for killing lobster with a knife and mallet before preparing Homard à l'Americaine, and recipes for ceviche, escebeche, and couscous.[33]

Self-satisfied though it was, *Sunset* prepared the way for the changes advanced by Chez Panisse. *Sunset* offered recipes free from the French or English culinary traditions featured in other aspirational magazines and cookbooks. Many basic products in California, especially vegetables and salad ingredients, were already of better quality than elsewhere, even under the agribusiness regime, and *Sunset* promoted a stylish informality that would come to define California's aesthetic.

Cosmopolitan San Francisco was more dignified than the California norm, and its prestigious restaurants tended to be French. Alice Waters remembers La Bourgogne with affection, and a few other vanished restaurants such as Jack's or the Blue Fox are worth shedding a tear for. Berkeley had its own food scene, including one of the largest fish restaurants in the country, Spenger's, which served hundreds of customers every night at a time when local fish, crabs, and abalone still abounded. But in the pre–Chez Panisse era, East Bay cognoscenti preferred a group of French restaurants that were not as mass-market as Spenger's, but were less formal than the socialite and opera-goers' San Francisco restaurants. The Pot Luck in Berkeley, for example, was locally famous and tried to provide an earthy, convivial version of semi-French cuisine with lots of cream and wine sauces: sweetbreads sauce Madère, kidneys sauté à la crème, crabe amandine, and pot roast Bordelaise were featured, along with continental specialties such as beef Stroganoff and Hungarian stuffed cabbage.[34] In its original incarnation (it opened in 1954) the restaurant, as its name implied, had a single menu and the diner had to accept what was on offer. It was bought in 1962 by Hank Rubin, a veteran of both the Spanish Civil War and the Second World War. Rubin was committed to left-wing causes and claimed to be the first Bay Area proprietor of an establishment with predominantly white customers to hire African American waiters. He created a menu that offered considerable choice and experimented with international cuisine, especially when it came to soups. His major interest, however, was wine.[35] The Pot Luck was boisterous and disorganized and its food was not particularly distinguished. The restaurant's former manager, Narsai David, recalls an all-too-typical proclivity for cost-saving over respect for ingredients: its kitchen went through drums of prepared chicken-soup base and crates of dehydrated onions and garlic. Thawed, diced vegetables were cooked in margarine.[36]

In the spring and summer of 1967, Alice Waters, then twenty-three years old, became a waitress at Quest, another aspirational Berkeley French restaurant. Unlike the Pot Luck, it had a limited menu choice of three entrées on any given night. The job was unpleasant and the food seems to have been poor. Waters told Thomas McNamee that she already cooked better than they did at Quest and that she didn't learn anything from the kitchen, but in an interview with a Berkeley student in 2006, she credited Quest with giving her the idea of a set-menu format.[37] Besides that, even great restaurant visionaries can benefit from once having been a waiter or waitress, learning about the orchestration of a restaurant from the bottom up.

The California regional setting for Chez Panisse when it opened was not as obviously important as was the influence of French cuisine. Direct inspiration for Chez Panisse came from Alice Waters's experiences in France, but also through interpretations of European provincial authenticity by the English writer Elizabeth David. David had the quixotic idea of writing about marvelous food in postwar England, where rationing remained in place until 1954 and the basic diet was even worse than during the actual war. *Mediterranean Food* (1950), *French Country Cooking* (1951), and *Italian Food* (1954) were intended to bring to benighted English kitchens something of the flavor of what David called "those blessed lands of sun and sea and olive trees." The beauty of the food of these blessed lands was best appreciated not at the grand restaurants of Paris, Rome, or Venice but in the countryside, where barge workers, fishermen, and farmers were pictured as dining with knowledgeable but and unpretentious gusto.[38]

In the summer of 1966, Alice Waters was still under the enchantment of her time in France and cooked her way through Elizabeth David's *French Provincial Cooking*. Waters was also involved in the Berkeley antiwar movement, whose high tide was the campaign to elect Robert Scheer, an editor of the radical magazine *Ramparts*, in the Democratic primary for an East Bay congressional seat. That close but unsuccessful contest in 1966 and the reversal of leftist hopes represented by the election of Ronald Reagan as governor of California may have encouraged Waters to see food as a more productive activity than direct political action.

Another French cookbook by a foreign enthusiast exerted an influence equal to that of Elizabeth David's works: Richard Olney's *The French Menu Cookbook*, which appeared in 1970. Olney was an American painter who came to France in the 1950s and discovered the delights of French country life and cuisine that were fading away but still sufficiently intact to learn from. Of the decline of French rural life, the great historian Fernand Braudel has said that the greatest social change of the twentieth century was the virtual extinction of the peasant in Europe. The domination of agriculture over every other form of economic activity and the need to employ vast numbers of people in gaining subsistence came to a close. This was particularly sudden in France, which up until the Second World War was still a land of regional, small-scale, labor-intensive agriculture.[39] Evoking a France of "farmhouse kitchens—rustic tables laid by mothers, grandmothers or old retainers" Olney was re-creating a world that was slipping through his fingers—evanescent, but substantial enough to give him the opportunity to enjoy a lot of wonderful meals. He learned from the last of the old retainers how to do everything with traditional tools and materials, not only in the kitchen but on the farm as well.[40]

From Olney, Alice Waters obtained an appreciation of French provincial (and especially Provençal) food rooted in a local culture, the techniques of outdoor cookery not traditionally associated with French restaurants, and the idea of having a single menu without offering patrons a choice. This last restriction might seem more appropriate to Olney, who entertained at his home, than to a restaurant, but it fit in with the desire of Chez Panisse's owner to run it as if it were a house. Although a devotee of France and its cuisine, Olney also provided the seed of a later idea that a French spirit could animate a menu consisting of food from other lands. Beyond faithfully reproducing an Occitan cassoulet or Burgundian jambon persillé in as literal a fashion as possible, one might approach other cuisines, even that of the United States, with the "sensuous and aesthetic concept that differentiates a French meal from all others."[41]

Two great advocates of cooking reform in America were less important to Chez Panisse than one might have expected. James Beard and Julia Child are rightly considered to have rescued, or at least attempted to rescue, America from its infatuation with bland convenience. Beard was enamored of both European grand tradition and American cuisine of a less-centralized and more rural social era. Although, as we have seen,

Beard was instrumental in molding the Four Seasons, his greatest influence was as a cookbook writer, and he particularly dominated American outdoor cooking. Beard admired Chez Panisse, though with a few petty reservations. A review written in 1974 complained about green peppercorns floating in a sauce—they should have been crushed—but he was impressed by what seemed more like a home where you had to pay than a real restaurant.[42]

Through her television broadcast *The French Chef*, Julia Child showed every step in the complex but perfectly feasible process of making French dishes. Her confidence-inspiring personality reassured timid cooks and raised the level of countless dinner parties. She is deservedly revered as a founding mother of the modern American gourmet movement. One thing she was not, however, was a dedicated advocate of using the best possible ingredients. Her success as a popularizer of French cuisine was premised on the ability of the American home cook to turn out wonderful French cuisine. Child insisted that shopping at the supermarket was fine—there was no need to live in Normandy or Burgundy, or even to patronize farmers' markets. Her television performance would have been undermined had she said that ordinary, mass-produced ingredients would produce inferior results. In 1981 Child took Waters to task for saying that restaurants should deal directly with small-scale and environmentally responsible farmers:

> You have an unduly doleful point of view about the way people shop for food. Visit any supermarket and you'll see plenty of fresh fruits and vegetables. And if you don't like the looks of what you see displayed at the market, complain to the produce manager. That's what I do, and it always gets results.[43]

As one can imagine, the two chefs' philosophies clashed. It may be that Child felt as if she were being superseded.

It becomes obvious that many things went into creating Chez Panisse and achieving its success, but amidst the incredible variety of food served, the financial and personal upheavals, and the constantly changing cast of characters, the personality and vision of Alice Waters was consistent—always surrounded by friends, lovers, and associates. She was easily drawn to projects or directions, not all of which worked out, but preserved her original notion of Chez Panisse as a producer of beautiful food and a gathering place for a happier and more spontaneous society.

THE EARLY YEARS

Within a relatively short time Waters and Chez Panisse had created a new and influential form of American high-end dining. The restaurant was unusual by virtue of its informality and its founder's passion for finding the best ingredients, but it was a French restaurant and thus within the tradition set by Delmonico's and recalibrated by Le Pavillon. The dramatic change would be its shift from a provincial French establishment to something more individual but also more American, not only in terms of primary products but in taste and inspiration. A dramatic change indeed, but hard to date to any particular year or event. In stages, and fits and starts, the transition to an American aesthetic was accomplished between 1975 and 1985.

The food writer and cookbook author Colman Andrews remarked that the most innovative aspect of Alice Waters's plan for Chez Panisse was the determination to base the menu on what food could be obtained that actually tasted good. Everyone else at the time planned a menu and then bought the ingredients, and there were some basic financial reasons for this practice.[44] Fanatical attention to primary products as well as the amateur nature of the Chez Panisse project meant that more labor and more money were devoted to acquiring and preparing food than other, more professionally-run, establishments would have countenanced. In a 1977 *Oakland Tribune* interview, Waters said that from the first, Chez Panisse "served fresh food and didn't care how much it cost to do it. So I used as much olive oil as I wanted . . . Most restaurant people aren't willing to be extravagant like me, and that makes a difference."[45] Great effort was made to find the best ingredients and to avoid relying on flavorless if convenient agribusiness produce. Fresh ducks were obtained in Chinatown, shellfish from fishermen north of the Bay Area; friends grew tiny, fragrant French strawberries (*fraises des bois*), and foraging for mushrooms and wild greens began early in the restaurant's career. Waters expected everyone in the kitchen to be directly involved in appreciating the basic products and cooking them, so there was none of the hierarchical (and efficient) apportioning out of offices such as garde manger or saucier. Devotion to the food meant financial crises; spontaneity meant difficulty in tracking expenses and encouraged wastage, free meals for employees' friends, and even theft.

There seems little doubt about whether Alice Waters is a chef, if not in the conventional mold. She herself has expressed ambivalence about this question, however. In the same intriguing 1977 *Tribune* interview she said that she was an anomaly in a male-dominated business and consequently people "still don't believe I'm the chef."[46] She compared herself favorably to top chefs in the Bay Area, most of whom produced reliable French clichés. But she then went on to state that actually she didn't think of herself as a chef, because she didn't consider it a career or a way to make serious money. In short (and this couldn't have pleased professionals), she said, "I feel it's a hobby."

Chef or not, Waters never wanted to be confined to the kitchen. Arranging the flowers, talking to guests, interacting with the entire staff, and having a public presence were necessary to her well-being and sense of purpose. Her authority did not stem from single-minded supervision of the kitchen but rather from a fine palate and a personal charisma that attracted talented people. She sought everyone's reaction to new dishes, and since the menu was changing all the time, innovations were constantly presented. Nevertheless, her opinion was the one that prevailed.

The founding principles and style of Chez Panisse were based on the rustic outlook preached by Elizabeth David. A meal on January 28, 1972, started with fennel soup, followed by fresh grilled trout, salad, and orange custard. Another menu from the summer of 1972 is an early example of the Provençal themes that would become ever more important—pissaladière (a tart typical of Nice with caramelized onions, tomatoes, and anchovies); soupe au pistou (a vegetable, bean, and pasta soup); saumon aioli (salmon, not typical of the Mediterranean but rather of the Pacific, accompanied by a garlic mayonnaise found in Provence and Catalonia); salad; fruit; and cheese.

Victoria Kroyer, Chez Panisse's first chef, departed in May 1972, and Waters took over the cooking for a few months. Kroyer returned in October from an unsuccessful love affair that had taken her to Montreal, but she quit definitively at the end of the year because her friend and sous-chef Barbara Rosenblum was being let go. This ushered in the era of Jeremiah Tower, whose tenure was from 1973 to 1976, as well as a few months in late 1978. This period can be regarded either as an interlude in the restaurant's history (fancier and more ambitious cuisine than either before or after), or as crucial in building the national reputation of Chez Panisse and setting it on its future, American course.

JEREMIAH TOWER

Almost every aspect of Tower's career at Chez Panisse is controversial, and the subject of conflicting stories, beginning from the moment he first walked into the restaurant. He responded to an advertisement in a San Francisco newspaper asking for a chef who could cook according to the

Fig. 99. Jeremiah Tower, 1985.

teachings of Elizabeth David and Fernand Point, the latter the chef and proprietor of La Pyramide in Vienne, one of the greatest restaurants in France.
According to his own account, Tower showed his merit by single-handedly
saving a soup that was simmering on the stove. Others on the scene recollect that Tower submitted an impressive list of menus and cooked a trial
meal for the staff.[47] Whatever the circumstances, the successful audition
launched a wildly creative few years of the Waters-Tower partnership.
Alice Waters remembers "I, of course immediately fell in love with him . . .
Yes he was gay, but that never stopped me from trying. He was incredibly
handsome and had taste."[48] In addition to his heroic appetites and exuberance, Tower was a tireless chef. And insofar as he wasn't literally tireless,
he found that cocaine extended his energies as well as sharpening his confidence and braggadocio.[49]

As was the norm at Chez Panisse at that time, Jeremiah Tower had
no previous professional experience. He did possess massive knowledge

acquired from voracious reading and restaurant-going. He had studied to be an architect, but he was broke in 1973 when starting at Chez Panisse and had not succeeded in finding his real métier.

His lack of restaurant experience notwithstanding, Tower had great skills and a pitch-perfect palate. Exhaustive study of cookbooks and recipes gave him an unusual intellectual and theoretical background in culinary culture. Tower recalls that he was puzzled and amused by the peculiar juxtaposition of Elizabeth David and Fernand Point in the newspaper advertisement.[50] Elizabeth David's fresh, simple dishes were perhaps appropriate, he thought, for penurious postwar English housewives, but Chez Panisse had not yet ventured beyond this easy level even to glimpse the Parnassian heights of Fernand Point's *Ma cuisine*, the antithesis of David's simplicity. Vienne might be in the French provinces, but La Pyramide produced food as elaborate and difficult as anything found in Paris. Tower brought to Chez Panisse an improvisatory ability to reproduce the classic haute cuisine of the top restaurants as well as the specialties of every province of France. He could devise menus with the most complicated dishes from the French repertoire, post them in front of Chez Panisse without ever having tried cooking any of them, and yet pull off what no one else in America could envisage attempting.

This was not Alice Waters's homey French style, which Tower tends to recollect patronizingly as beef bourguignon, nice little salads, and fruit tarts. There is no doubt that the restaurant that gained accolades from *Gourmet* in 1975 was not solely the manifestation of Alice Waters's original vision. Eventually Waters and Tower would come to a parting of the ways, but for three crucial years they were collaborators. It wasn't just a segmented alliance in which Waters foraged greens and put together salads while Tower produced elaborate braised ducklings with Rouennaise sauce (Bordelaise with duck liver), or wild boar soup with saffron, or sweetbreads in brioche with Champagne sauce. Together they developed a passion for the best ingredients and found them not by flying in Dover sole or Beluga caviar but by seeking them out literally in their own backyard. Their motives for this quest were not the same, however: Waters wanted the ingredients for their own sake, while Tower needed unusual products not sold in ordinary stores in order to try out his experiments. Wild fennel was required for a certain way of grilling pork loin and game. It might be impossible to make authentic bouillabaisse without specific fish from the Mediterranean waters off Marseille, but Tower brought a six-foot conger eel purchased in Chinatown in order to give it a try.[51]

It is hard to imagine how difficult it was to obtain what now would be considered basic, even banal, ingredients. Tower drew up a fascinating list of things that were tricky or impossible to find in America before the late 1970s: extra-virgin olive oil, nut and grape-seed oil, Bündnerfleisch (dry-cured beef), gravlax, snap peas, radicchio, Sherry vinegar, yellow bell peppers, and fresh pasta.[52] Fresh fish and ducks had to be purchased in Chinatown. Fresh herbs or baby vegetables were not commercially available, Tower recalls, and they therefore either had to be grown at the restaurant or brought to the kitchen door by hippies, foragers, hobbyists, and part-time farmers. Wild berries, wild mushrooms, trout from Big Sur kept alive to make *truite au bleu*, wild boar, and fruit from old trees in vacant lots all showed up at the back door of Chez Panisse.

Tower's ambitions ranged from a "vacation" tour of virtually every French regional cuisine, to homages to Escoffier's classic recipes of the late-nineteenth and early twentieth century, to preparing Salvador Dalí's sinister surrealistic dinners. One of the Dalí erotically themed menus calls for a "drugged and sodomized between-course service," which came out as leg of lamb injected with Madeira and brandy, roasted with garlic and herbs. Another included an "aphrodisiac course" of lobsters cooked in court-bouillon, flamed in brandy, and served on a bed of spinach and pistachio nuts with a white cream sauce. A "sado-masochistic soup" consisted of onions, beef marrow, ginger, beef ribs, pork meatballs, leeks, cabbage, chickpeas, semolina, and turnips with red pepper.[53] Tower also developed his own over-the-top menus that no one else ever had thought of, such as a dinner in June 1975 of six courses, accompanied by eight different Sauternes, including a 1922, 1955, and 1967 Château d'Yquem. The cost, a mere $20 ($78 in 2015) would today buy perhaps a single glass of one of the wines.[54]

Among the restaurants that inspired Jeremiah Tower was the Four Seasons. He was fascinated by the range of the menu, the "staggering cost" involved, the restaurant's fanatical attention to fresh vegetables, the beefsteak tomatoes carved like roast meat at the table, the unheard-of items like nasturtium leaves and broccoli flowers . . . "they were obviously mad," he said, meaning it as a high compliment.[55] In considering new ways to think about ingredients, Tower was also influenced by fellow bon vivant James Villas, who wrote on food for *Town and Country* and who speculated on the possibility of developing an American cuisine based on its regional products.

The plan to try a California regional dinner came from an elaborate Four Seasons menu in March 1976 that accompanied a California wine tasting, the Four Seasons being one of the few Eastern restaurants to consider California wines as meriting attention. Although this particular Four Seasons menu was, in fact, French (Duck Bigarade; veal and morels in cream, fish quenelles), it emphasized American ingredients, such as shad used for the quenelles. Another inspiration for Tower was, strangely enough, the 1893 cookbook by Delmonico's Charles Ranhofer, *The Epicurean*, which has a recipe for cream of green corn soup à la Mendocino served with crayfish butter.[56] Strange because, as Tower remarks, it is a mystery how a French chef at the top restaurant in New York came to hear about an obscure and distant California county. Ranhofer was a French chef by training and preference, happy to adapt recipes for American game, terrapin, oysters, and the like, but completely uninterested in regional specialties and so hardly a plausible source for the rediscovery of America's native culinary potential.

On October 7, 1976, after Jeremiah Tower had already announced he was leaving Chez Panisse, a "Northern California Regional Dinner" was served. The menu shows not only a break with the French tradition, but the impetus to demonstrate local sourcing (my remarks are in brackets). A slightly different version of the menu (probably an earlier draft) is pictured at the opening of this chapter.

Spenger's Tomales Bay bluepoint oysters on ice [The immediate source being the Berkeley fish restaurant's retail store, the provenance from a coastal inlet of Marin County.]

Cream of fresh corn soup, Mendocino style with crayfish butter [Ranhofer's recipe, with no discernible connection with Mendocino, a place known neither for corn nor crayfish.]

Big Sur Garrapata Creek smoked trout steamed over California bay leaves [The restaurant had been using Garrapata Creek trout for all manner of difficult French dishes requiring live trout. This was a simple and robust preparation. Wild bay trees grow all along the central California coast hills and canyons.]

Monterey Bay prawns sautéed with garlic, parsley and butter [The only thing distinguishing the dish is the relatively local origin of the shrimp.]

Preserved California geese from Sebastopol [In the first version of the menu, the geese are specified as coming from Hand Ranch. "Preserved" to avoid the French "confit." In the earlier version "cooked and preserved in goose fat."]

Vela dry Monterey Jack cheese from Sonoma [Here not only is point of origin important but the adjective "dry" distinguishes a hard cheese with the consistency of aged Gouda from the gummy supermarket Monterey Jack. The earlier menu simply promised local California cheeses.]

Fresh caramelized figs

Walnuts, almonds, and mountain pears from the San Francisco Farmers' Market

Historians of the California or American food revolution consider this meal a turning point in emancipating what became known as New American cuisine from tutelage to France. "The switch had been thrown," Patric Kuh writes, "one should now treat California with the same seriousness as Alsace or Brittany.[57] Tower himself denies any intent to change the course of American dining with this meal. It was simply part of his exit from Chez Panisse and his determination to enjoy himself in the process.[58] Alice Waters says, with the benefit of hindsight, that the restaurant was finding its style: "This could be a menu from last week as easily as thirty years ago."[59] The meal is made to bear more weight than it can support, however. Important as it was, Chez Panisse did not invent "California Cuisine" or "New American Cuisine" in one night, nor as the result of one epiphany.

A CRUCIAL TRANSITION, 1977–1983

When Jeremiah Tower departed at the end of 1976, Waters once again became the chef, although her French sous chef Jean-Pierre Moullé did much of the work. Moullé arrived in 1975, during the height of the Tower regime, and brought a corrective dose of professional training. He would stay for thirty-five years, avoiding the limelight and providing continuity as well as a culinary philosophy compatible with that of Alice Waters. He had grown up in Franche Comté near the Swiss border and the Jura Mountains, where he had learned how to hunt, fish, dress, and cook whatever he wanted. Moullé's devotion to locality, desire for simplicity, and his complete and unflustered French skill set helped him put into effect what Waters had thus far sketched out.

Initially Moullé and Waters had a contentious as well a cooperative relationship, and some of this back-and-forth is discernible in the uncertainty of menu language. In June 1977 the menus, which had been in French and

English (or in French with English explanations) became English-only.[60] By the summer of 1978, however, French had regained ground, the menu was bilingual, and the cuisine was firmly French again. The Mendocino corn soup dinner had been an experiment, not a transformation. There were recipes from the Troisgros brothers' restaurant in Burgundy and menus of Occitan regional specialties. Some forays into Mexican cuisine provided a change of pace, and a week of tropical dinners in mid-August 1978 featured Mexican-style charcoal-grilled fish marinated in spices with garlic and chilies, and curried leg of lamb with Indian condiments. More common was the menu for October 4, 1978: bourride (fish stew thickened with eggs), fish with vegetables, grilled quail, salad, cheese, and fruit. More than two years later, the menu is French and the influence of Jeremiah Tower is still palpable—the Jeremiah Tower of inventive but traditional haute cuisine. New Year's Eve 1980–1981 was marked by soufflé d'huîtres au caviar (oyster soufflé with caviar), foie gras en gelée de poivre (foie gras in pepper aspic), timbale de fruits de mer (seafood timbale), rôti d'oie aux truffes (roasted goose with truffles), salade de mâche, cheese, and a Bavarois rubané (a layered dessert of crème anglaise, whipped cream, and cake).

Other restaurateurs, some of them veterans of Chez Panisse, would move more quickly and self-consciously to reject France and pioneer a novel American style. Mark Miller, who had come to Chez Panisse as sous-chef in 1977, felt hemmed in by what he referred to as the prevailing nostalgia for "French Provençal 1928" and in 1979 opened the Fourth Street Grill, cooking Southwestern food in what was still a desolate warehouse neighborhood known as the Berkeley Flats. Judy Rodgers, who also started at Chez Panisse during the post-Tower year 1977, would go on to turn the Union Hotel in Benicia into a shrine to New American cuisine, and then find even greater success at the Zuni Café in San Francisco.[61] Jeremiah Tower opened Stars in San Francisco in 1984, offering an elegant take on traditional American as well as French and Italian cuisine (Tower recalls being inspired particularly by Delmonico's) and an influential multiplication of options in terms of cuisine, size of meal, and level of formality ("from blue jeans to black tie").[62]

At Chez Panisse, change would come not in an abrupt discovery of California cuisine but through the influence of Italy, Provence, and other Mediterranean regions. The introduction of pasta, previously unknown on the Chez Panisse menu, pizza, goat-cheese salads, meat and fish grilled with herbs and olive oil, and other dishes now so characteristic of a certain kind of Mediterranean, elegant-casual, "California" restaurant menu did not happen all at once. It is hard to remember that they had to be invented or brought out of low-end Italian categories. This sort of food was served at the upstairs Café at Chez Panisse, which opened with its own wood-burning oven that could, among other things, turn out an unusually satisfying pizza.[63] The Café had an actual menu with choices, offering seasonal and changing dishes, but setting aside the foie gras and truffles of the main restaurant. At its initiation in 1980, the Café was intended to attract the old regular customers priced out by the now expensive main restaurant and to bring back some of the conviviality and informality that had waned in the more cliquish atmosphere of the mid-1970s.

The measure of the Café's success is its gradual influence over the main restaurant. On October 4, 1979, before the installation of the special pizza oven, "Pizza Provençale" was listed as an appetizer. "Pizza aux saucisses Niçoises" (pizza with Nice sausage) was on the main restaurant menu on March 29, 1980. Pasta first appears in 1979, still in French: homemade noodles served with Piedmontese sauce ("pâtes à ma façon," November 17, 1979); fish tortellini ("tortellini de poisson," March 13, 1980); capellini with seafood ("capellini fruits de mer," May 14, 1980); noodles with basil, shallots, garlic, and green beans from Chino Ranch ("nouilles au basilic et haricots verts," June 6, 1981). Italian started to replace French on the menus in 1982, "pasta Siciliana" on February 17, 1982, for example. These Italian or California-Italian dishes went from being occasional to ubiquitous in the early 1980s.

CHEZ PANISSE CAFE   NEW YEAR'S EVE 1991

Oysters on the half shell, $9.00

Bagna Cauda with white truffle oil, $8.50

Frutti di mare al forno with focaccia and aïoli, $10.75

Leek soufflé pudding with truffle fennel butter, $9.00

Foie gras terrine with pain de mie toast & bronze lettuces, $11.50

Winter greens with focaccia, $6.50

•

Wild mushroom pasta gratin al forno, $16.00

Roast lamb loin with winter vegetable cakes
& truffled wine sauce, $19.00

Grilled duck breast with two purées, sour cherries,
& Cognac sauce, $17.50

DESSERTS

Pear, walnuts, & Roquefort cheese, $5.50

Ginger cake with warm pears and whipped cream, $6.00

Apple & mince tarte Tatin with crème fraîche, $6.50

New Year's eve sundae, $6.50

Black bottom pie, $6.00

Fig. 100. Menu from the Café at Chez Panisse, 1991.

Provençal dinners became frequent in the early 1980s, featuring such things as grilled leeks, tomato soup, or crepinettes (small sausages) made of suckling pig (October 3, 1981). Ratatouille made from a recipe of the restaurant Mas des Serres in Provence appeared on the menu on July 8, 1981.

Baked goat cheese salad, first served February 13, 1982, was a Chez Panisse invention based on Provençal ingredients, and it would become an American culinary cliché. Waters adopted Provençal and Italian techniques of grilling—simpler methods of preparation than those standard for classic French cuisine. As Patric Kuh has noted, a great advantage of the new simplicity was that it required less skill and expense to produce. This was true for Provençal, Italian, and California cuisines, all of which shaded into one another in America.[64]

Another would-be turning point was a Northern California Regional Dinner served on December 8, 1980. For some reason it is less celebrated than the 1976 Jeremiah Tower meal, partly because it didn't lead to anything and was not associated with Tower's outsized ambitions and personality. It began with Pigeon Point oysters, grilled and served with butter and caviar, followed by pasta with Monterey shrimp and garden vegetables. The main course was roast leg of suckling pig from Dal Porto Ranch, served with wild mushrooms. Salad with Sonoma goat cheese preceded a dessert of kiwi, persimmon, pomegranate, and pear sherbets. This didn't gain much attention, and soon the menu at Chez Panisse reverted to French classics.

The early 1980s, specifically 1982–1984, were crucial. A new chef, Paul Bertolli, enchanted Waters with Italian food, a culinary novelty she recalls as "a breath of fresh air for me."[65] She also benefited from the skills and reliability of David Tanis, who started at the Café in 1983. From 1982 the menus were in English, except for occasional dinners in honor of Richard Olney or other notables. And after thirteen years in business, the restaurant started to make money in 1984, thanks in part to the administrative discipline imposed by Alice's father, Pat Waters. A 1984 cookbook offered recipes for the new, casual Italian pizza, calzones, and pasta dishes. Waters's daughter Fanny was born in 1983 and in that same year Alice started the Farm Restaurant Project to bring farmers and restaurateurs into direct contact, beginning a public effort to relate the pleasure of good food with

:CHEZ:PANISSE:

1517 SHATTUCK AVENUE, BERKELEY, CALIFORNIA 94709 :: 548-5525

MENUS FOR THE WEEK OF FEBRUARY 28–MARCH 3, 1984.

Tuesday
February 28
$40.00

Asparagus, pea, leek, & sorrel velouté
Baked oysters with osetra caviar, cucumbers, and
    Champagne sabayon sauce
Grilled veal loin with red onion purée
Garden salad
Apricot & walnut puff pastry tart

Wednesday
February 29
$40.00

Horn of plenty soufflé (wild black chanterelles)
Clear pigeon soup with anise noodles & vegetable
    julienne
Medallions of beef with foie gras sauce and scalloped
    potatoes
Garden salad
Tangerine, Lavender Gem, & grapefruit sherbets

Thursday
March 1
$40.00

Raw beef filet sliced thin; with shallots, capers,
    anchovies, & sun-dried tomatoes
Fish soup with roasted red peppers & croûtons
Fried lamb chops with waffle potatoes and fennel
    and artichoke gratin
Garden salad
Espresso ice cream, winter fruit compote, & biscotti

Friday
March 2
$40.00

Spicy crab pizza with roasted peppers
Turnip & turnip green soup with croûtons and mustard
    blossoms
Grilled baby pheasants with sautéed apples
Garden salad
Sweet potato & pecan pie

Saturday
March 3
$40.00

Mussels ravigote
Pasta with grilled artichokes
Grilled quail al mattone
Potatoes sautéed in goose fat, with bacon
Kale, beet greens, & baby mustard greens with shallots
    and vinegar
Garden salad
Warm chocolate torte with chocolate sauce

We do not accept credit cards. Wine corkage, $10.00. Signed copies
of the Chez Panisse Menu Cookbook are sold upstairs at the bar.

Fig. 101. Menu from Chez Panisse, 1984.

social responsibility. According to Waters, having a child increased her desire to make the future habitable and worthwhile.[66] The restaurant was steadier than it had ever been in terms of staff continuity and reliability, cash flow, and overall management. It was also coming up with ideas to teach and agitate for changes in food cultivation and distribution.

Bertolli simplified the cuisine and turned it slowly, but permanently, in a Mediterranean and primarily Italian direction. His menus show a confident but hard-to-grasp eclecticism but surprisingly little in the way of local source indication. One meal in 1984 begins with Provençal grilled Baja shrimp and fennel with aioli, proceeds to northern Italian risotto with braised chicken, then moves on to French sautéed sweetbreads with Sauternes and truffles. Two of the menus begin with a complicated salad, and all of them have "garden salad" as a fourth course. Pasta appears on two days. Sautéed foie gras, pheasant and yellow cabbage soup, and deep-fried filet mignon with watercress sauce show a certain Tower-esque spirit, but the overall trend was toward lighter, simpler Mediterranean-inspired California cuisine.

NOUVELLE CUISINE, NEW AMERICAN, CALIFORNIA

The decade of the 1980s was a turning point in culinary history with the emergence of a new American cuisine, centered in and inspired by California, but spread everywhere, even as far as New York, until then a faithful disciple of France. Cooks like Judy Rodgers and Mark Miller in California, and Larry Forgione in New York, built on Chez Panisse's example by establishing relationships with farmers and searching for seasonal and local ingredients, their explorations extending to neglected American cookbooks of the past and regional specialties. As mentioned earlier, the Café at Chez Panisse also inspired a signature item of the new cuisine: pizza, now a sophisticated and carefully crafted dish rather than a messy, street-food staple. In 1981, Wolfgang Puck installed a brick, oak-burning pizza oven at his new restaurant, Spago, in Los Angeles, built to the same specifications as the one constructed a year earlier for the Chez

Fig. 102. Chez Panisse menu cover, November 14, 2014.

Panisse Café. Spago was designed differently from Chez Panisse. The pizza oven formed part of an open kitchen, and it produced pizzas with toppings unrecognizable to purists, or even Alice Waters in the 1980s, toppings ranging from prawns to prosciutto, scallops, or zucchini flowers. Indeed, Spago became famous for a truly eccentric "lox-and-bagels pizza" with smoked salmon, caviar, red onions, and crème fraîche.[67] Enthusiasm for pizza spread rapidly beyond Spago. As early as the spring of 1982, it was obvious that, to quote *Gourmet* reviewer Caroline Bates, "pizza, the bread of peasants, has become chic."[68]

An indirect impetus toward energizing American cuisine came from developments in France. The movement that the French gastronomic authorities Henri Gault and Christian Millau dubbed "La Nouvelle Cuisine" in 1970 undermined the orthodoxy of French gastronomy first established by Marie-Antoine Carême in the early nineteenth century and perfected by Auguste Escoffier at the beginning of the twentieth. Nouvelle cuisine made France accessible to outside influences (Japanese in particular), but also opened the way to innovation elsewhere by ending the unquestioned French definitions of haute cuisine. The epilogue to this book will take up the unintended effects of Nouvelle Cuisine on the French position in the world of gastronomy. By undermining and setting aside tradition, the movement inadvertently made it possible to develop other sources of culinary authority. It assuredly contributed to the weakening of French self-confidence, and so encouraged trends originating from outside France, from Asian fusion to molecular gastronomy; from locavore regionalism to slow food.

Initially the Nouvelle Cuisine innovations must have seemed unwelcome to Alice Waters, as Chez Panisse in the 1970s was trying to re-create the traditions of French rural cuisine that the new movement condemned or ignored. The last thing Waters wanted to hear was that France's culinary traditions had to be radically altered. Other restaurants, however, such as Puck's Spago or Forgione's American Place, simply moved beyond France and explicitly took on the identity of "California" or "New American." By the end of the 1980s, many aspects of the current American food scene had been established: the waning of French authority, the mixture of casual surroundings and demanding food, and a restaurant culture that imitated the star system established by the entertainment industry.

Despite (or perhaps because of) the fact that the restaurant finally was profitable, Alice Waters told her staff at a 1986 retreat that the primary goal was not to make money but to rather "to educate ourselves and the public" and to be conscious of "our responsibility to the rest of the world."[69] Beginning roughly at this juncture, the story of the actual restaurant is eclipsed by the career of Alice Waters. Up until the mid-1980s, the paths of Chez Panisse and its founder were parallel, but as Waters became involved with causes such as AIDS relief and agricultural sustainability, her mission and personality extended beyond the restaurant.

The Farm Restaurant Project was started in 1983, an effort to engage chefs directly with the farmers who supplied them. In 1994, Waters established the Edible Schoolyard to try to bring gardens and real food to Martin Luther King Jr. Middle School in Berkeley and from there to schools across America. She attempted to enlist President Clinton and later President Obama in the cause of better food and nutrition, in schools in particular, but with only partial success. In 1999, Waters became closely involved with the Slow Food movement, begun in Italy as a protest against the fast-food influence of McDonald's and in favor of preserving and restoring cooking at home, paying attention to food, and saving threatened local culinary traditions.

Waters's vision and persistence prevailed on another front. When her daughter Fanny started her undergraduate career at Yale University in 2001, Waters managed to convince the university's administration to change the buying and cooking practices of its twelve undergraduate college dining halls, moving them away from institutional food-service contracts to seek out their own suppliers and even developing relationships with local farmers. At Waters's instigation, the university set up a demonstration farm that involved students, most of whom had no experience with gardens, let alone agriculture. One of the first things established at the small farm was a brick pizza oven.

All of these projects derived some of their strength from the reputation of Chez Panisse and shared with it a mission to show that food tasted better when it was locally and carefully cultivated. Waters's increasing commitment to the wider world and social responsibility, however, meant that feuds and management problems at the restaurant flared up constantly. In 1990, serious thought was given once again to closing Chez Panisse, as Waters felt sufficiently torn among her various obligations to contemplate "quitting while we were ahead."[70] She resisted this temptation, but the twentieth-anniversary celebration in 1991 provoked angry letters to the San Francisco newspapers about the restaurant's alleged elitism. Paul Bertolli, frustrated at being in the shadows, departed in 1992 after a ten-year stint. Yet, unexpectedly, the restaurant flourished in the 1990s. In 1993, Lindsey Shere won the James Beard Foundation award as best pastry chef, while in 2001 *Gourmet* named Chez Panisse the best restaurant in the United States. It is still going strong today.

Overall trends of the last thirty years will be discussed at greater length in the epilogue, but to give an idea of Chez Panisse in terms of both its heritage and its current incarnation, one can look at menus for a typical week. Those for the week of August 28, 2014, show a few vestiges of classic French cuisine, especially among the desserts, including peach Melba (an invention of Escoffier's), a bombe glacée, and a raspberry soufflé with crème anglaise. Most of the first courses are salads, often with seafood (shrimp, squid, tuna confit, salmon carpaccio). Italian cuisine is represented by herb tagliatelle and wild greens agnolotti along with Arista alla Fiorentina (pork loin grilled with wild fennel). Two Moroccan-inspired dishes appear on August 27: hairia, a bean soup with saffron, and grilled quail stuffed with couscous, served with preserved lemon and zucchini fritters.

None of this is particularly Californian insofar as one can identify such a thing, but ten specific farms and ranches of origin are named over the six-day period, along with geographic descriptors such as Monterey Bay squid and Bolinas black cod. Not everything is local—there are Gulf (of

CHEZ PANISSE

An aperitif

Butternut squash galette with sage,
chestnuts, and endive salad

∾

Gulf shrimp and bay scallop raviolini
in herb brodo

∾

Grilled BN Ranch beef rib-eye
with black pepper sauce, golden turnip and savory
gratin, onion rings, and watercress

∾

Hazelnut, stracciatella,
and mocha ice cream bombe

Friday, November 14, 2014

Fig. 103. Chez Panisse menu, November 14, 2014.

Mexico) shrimp and soft-shell crabs from farther east. Taken together, the menus are varied but harmonious. What they share is attention to the primary ingredients and in particular careful sourcing. The cost has risen to $85 per person for weekdays and $100 on weekends. If these prices are no longer absurdly inexpensive as in the 1970s and 1980s, they are still well below the high-end, prix-fixe norm for California.

Waters has a presence in any discussion about the present and future of food that transcends one relatively modest establishment, but she has not renounced the care of the restaurant, which is the springboard for her reputation on other food-related areas. Ferran Adrià serves as something of a counterexample. After closing his internationally renowned restaurant elBulli in 2011, at a time when more than 1 million people were trying to reserve a table, he struggled to retain his oracular status in the food world. Revered though he remains, Adrià, no longer a chef, has not found an effective vehicle for his opinions and experiments. Waters has achieved a position as one of the most influential authorities on food, society, and change without abandoning her original vision of a particular restaurant and its ambience. Back in 1993, Michael Bauer of the *San Francisco Chronicle* gave Chez Panisse four stars, proclaiming it a "temple of gastronomy," the birthplace of the California Cuisine movement, a place that met even the exalted expectations it now evoked. He added that Alice Waters had inspired just about every chef in the country.[71] All of this is true today, if anything more intensely. We might simply say "American cuisine movement" in place of "California cuisine," and extend her influence and inspiration beyond chefs to include anyone who thinks seriously about food. How chefs cook, the look of restaurants, and the ways in which owners of food businesses talk about their social and environmental responsibilities are all inconceivable without the imaginative and practical accomplishments of the former schoolteacher and political activist turned late-twentieth-century culinary pioneer.

The foregoing chapters have told ten stories about influential American restaurants and the lives of those who created and shaped them. While it is important to appreciate their individuality, these restaurants collectively provide an account of American food over the past two hundred years and reveal a way to explore how American cuisine has changed. Certain aspects of taste and restaurant fashion in the United States are associated with particular historical moments: the lavish ostentation of Victorian fourteen-course dinners at Delmonico's; the early-twentieth-century combination of blandness, convenience, and middle-class respectability worked out by the likes of Schrafft's and Howard Johnson's; or the Bohemian atmosphere of the first generation of "ethnic" restaurants. But there are also obvious continuities underlying shifts in taste and the mosaic of different American restaurant types. Diversity of culinary choices is an American phenomenon, especially in the proliferation of restaurants serving foreign foods. This started in the late nineteenth century and is still growing today as Peruvian, Ethiopian, and Korean restaurants have been added to the already extensive mix.

Another long-term characteristic, recently extinguished but traceable as an unbroken line from the founding of Delmonico's through the first years of Chez Panisse, is the hegemony of French cuisine. While so-called ethnic restaurants and convenient places such as Howard Johnson's flourished without reference to any international gastronomic standard, high-end dining was synonymous with French food during the first 150 years of American restaurant history. To be sure, luxury dining included cooking American products. We have seen that terrapin, wild duck, and oysters were not only prestigious and consumed constantly by the upper class, but also that there was an extensive and place-specific repertoire of game and fish and, well into the twentieth century, regional specialties, persisting most notably in New Orleans. All this local abundance and variety notwithstanding, the standard for upper-class dining was set by Paris and imitated, with greater or lesser fidelity, not only by New York and San Francisco but, until just recently, throughout the country.

A final item of American culinary continuity is not so much a question of cuisine specifics as of attitude. For all of its history, the United States has been a country of hearty appetites and widespread access to inexpensive food, yet also widespread indifference to culinary diversity and quality. This does not mean putting up with bad food, although it has often been surprisingly easy to find it even at high prices. But until recently it was considered un- American to fuss about food—to talk about it, to encourage culinary traditions or innovations, or even to linger at the table. It is not that Americans don't enjoy eating but rather, as we've seen in a number of contexts, they don't think it is worth a lot of discussion or time. Upper-class gourmandise is seen as slightly decadent and effeminate. Long lunches or complicated recipes are regarded as a waste of time better spent in work or some more vigorous form of leisure. Immigrants have received criticism for excessive attention to shopping, cooking, and uneconomical expenditure of money and time that could go to more "American" priorities of efficiency and work.

This set of attitudes comes down to overeating but underthinking, and has affected not only the general population but the elite as well. For every Delmonico's or Pavillon aficionado, there have always been many others in the moneyed classes who regarded food as merely instrumental, as a biological need. The image of the hard-charging entrepreneur does not allow room for leisurely meals or wine connoisseurship. Intellectuals and academics are a little more contradictory in their attitudes, divided between those who do spend a certain amount of time and energy on cuisine (most college towns will have a greater variety of restaurants than the surrounding area) and others like the great philosopher Ludwig Wittgenstein, who exemplifies an attitude most commonly found among natural scientists—namely that he didn't care what he ate as long as it was the same thing every day. This does not necessarily mean an absence of enjoyment, at least after a fashion. Wittgenstein greeted the arrival of his regular bread and cheese with expressions like "hot ziggity," a manifestation of enthusiasm he learned from his Kansas-born American colleague Norman Malcolm. It wasn't, therefore, that eating was a waste of time in his mind; rather, he was relieved not to have to think about food, even to the extent of deciding what to order in a café or restaurant.[1] Wittgenstein may provide an extreme or more articulate example of a widespread attitude, but his limited range is not dissimilar to ordering a fast-food burger from the drive-through every day. Such a customer is neither puritanical nor devoid of appetite, but speed and a repeatable form of gratification are paramount. He, or she, is eager to be doing something other than eating, and as quickly as possible. The contemporary era has started to change this ethos dramatically. The delicious revolution ushered in by Chez Panisse and its allies at the creation of New American food in the 1980s is notable for the mass extension of what had previously been almost alien: animated interest in, discussion of, and even academic respectability accorded to food and cuisine.

The purpose of this final chapter is to look at the recent scene, to describe what has happened to change not only American attitudes toward dining but many of the patterns set by the ten restaurants already considered. It also offers an opportunity speculate on dining out in America in the near-term future.

THE END OF FRENCH RULE

Unquestionably the most significant shift in recent gastronomic history has been the end of French authority to define haute cuisine. The chapter on Chez Panisse described how American chefs from the 1940s to 1960s were inspired by France and its culinary culture, and how they used the French teachings about food to revive and introduce American ingredients and traditions. The ability to imagine an American haute cuisine that did not hew to French dictates has a number of earlier anticipations—for example, the founding philosophy of the Four Seasons in 1959. One must understand this shift not merely as the changing of the guard from France to America, or as a mere alteration of fashion, but rather as an effect of a global weakening in the influence of French cuisine. For three hundred years France had defined the repertoire, vocabulary, and style of prestigious food. The end of that power may be as significant in its own way as the fall of the Berlin Wall.

Historically France achieved its culinary hegemony without an especially aggressive foreign policy. No one from France ever set out to impose a gastronomic empire on a reluctant world. Upper-class American tastes, along with that of all European countries and the elite of many other parts of the world, embraced Paris as the holy city of cuisine. The universally acknowledged leader among American restaurants for most of the nineteenth century was Delmonico's, which presented itself as a French restaurant. In the mid-twentieth century the standard-bearer was the impeccably French Le Pavillon. So pervasive and unquestioned was the dominance of French cuisine that Alice Waters established her restaurant in hopes of re-creating a certain kind of French gastronomic experience and she even gave it a French name.

By contrast, the only French restaurants that remain in the top forty restaurants as ranked by the New York *Zagat Guide* for 2015 are La Grenouille, Bouley, Daniel, and Picholine.[2] The 2015 San Pellegrino world restaurant ranking has no entry from France in the top ten, although Mirazur on the Riviera and L'Arpège in Paris come close at numbers 11 and 12.[3] El Celler de Can Roca in Catalonia has the top spot, and it has been fighting out this distinction with Noma in Copenhagen for the last few years. No fewer than five restaurants in the Spanish Basque country place among the San Pellegrino top twenty, and the list is geographically quite diverse, as Brazil, Thailand, and Peru are represented.

The San Pellegrino list is a rather opinionated survey that exalts avant-garde, experimental restaurants, but its ranking shows how French gastronomy has been marginalized in the eyes of global opinion and, unfortunately, this has affected France as well. The fact that France recently campaigned to have "the French gastronomic meal" designated in the UNESCO intangible world heritage list shows a distressing lack of self-confidence. It is hard to imagine any of the great chefs and gastronomes of the past seeking out international bureaucratic validation for what they considered a self-evident distinction. The awkward construction of the UNESCO award—"French gastronomic meal" instead of simply "French cuisine"—was required because UNESCO did not want to imply French superiority to Chinese, Mexican, Japanese, Italian, or any other food culture.

It wasn't all that long ago that French superiority was serenely enjoyed and universally recognized. A charming relic of French hegemony are the musings of French food-guide celebrities Henri Gault and Christian Millau on the subject of what might be the world's greatest restaurant in the travel magazine *Holiday*.[4] A large-format color monthly that was a lifestyle magazine before such a term was coined, *Holiday* in its June 1969 issue asked Gault and Millau to consider this question. The two mulled it over, acknowledging at the outset their preconceptions and responding *"tant pis"* (too bad) to hypothetical accusations of chauvinism. They then proceeded to eliminate most of the globe from further consideration: the Soviet Union and China had deliberately wiped out whatever culinary heritage they had. According to Gault, the best Chinese food was not to be found in Hong Kong or Singapore, let alone China, but at San Francisco's Imperial Palace. The Middle East, save Francophile Lebanon, Latin America, and eastern Europe were deemed "gastronomically under privileged." Africa was a total loss, except for Senegal and Morocco, both former French colonies. As for the "Anglo-Saxon" world, it suffered from pretentiousness and inauthenticity. True, there were some good, maybe even great, restaurants in London, Montreal, and New York, but the chefs of these places were French.

Once safely ensconced within the borders of Europe, the pair were relieved, but still contemptuous. The foods of Spain and Portugal were "ordinary and heavy." The experts disagreed about Italy, Gault complaining, "I don't have a single exciting memory except for the scampi at Harry's Bar in Venice." Millau defended at least a few restaurants: Dodici Apostoli in Verona, Sabatini in Florence, and Giannino in Milan, but he did not offer an energetic defense of Italian food. Danish food is of good quality, Millau remarked, and "children like it very much," but "obviously this is not great cuisine." Belgium is full of honorable but not quite top restaurants; the Swiss were said to cook "in the French manner, adequately, but without spark."

Finally, they turned to France for which a good twenty-five restaurants were discussed. Most of them were in Paris, but the final competition came down to Troisgros and Bocuse, both near Lyon. Troisgros was regarded as traditional, intimate, and familial, while Chef Paul Bocuse was praised as a master of grandeur and creativity. The dishes at Bocuse extolled by Gault and Millau were light, playful, and original: mussel soup with fresh saffron; partridge with cabbage. Ultimately, though, the contrast drawn is one of personality and philosophy: the Troisgros brothers are character-ized as working purely for the sake of art while Bocuse is depicted as work-ing for fame; the brothers represent wisdom, the other glory. Of course, innovation à la Bocuse was to be the path to celebrity status for chefs.

In retrospect it may be that French gastronomic authority was unsus-tainable in a world that was, if not exactly more democratic, at least less deferential to Europe. The rise of Asian cuisines, a clear manifestation of new origins for global trends, will be treated below. Some of the waning of French power was caused by developments within France itself, a crisis of traditions and self-confidence. Michael Steinberger, author of *Au Revoir to All That,* subtitled his book "Food, Wine, and the End of France."[5] This is a lament for French inability to maintain culinary rule. Steinberger points to overregulation, economic dislocation, and sclerotic administra-tion as among the contexts for French culinary decline. This may be a general European problem, although other countries such as Spain and Italy have these economic and administrative difficulties as well, yet their food reputations are flourishing.

The French culinary crisis began with what seemed like a Renaissance, just after Gault and Millau's *Holiday* article. As already noted, the move-ment known as La Nouvelle Cuisine dominated the 1970s and, despite its immediate success, amounts to the beginning of the end rather than a lasting renewal. Nouvelle Cuisine certainly garnered attention for its distinguished chef-advocates such as Alain Chapel, Roger Vergé, Michel Guérard, Paul Bocuse, and the food critics Gault and Millau. Although, as just noted, Gault and Millau were as oriented to France's gastronomic leadership as anyone, they were also publicists for a new turn in France's creative journey.

Nouvelle Cuisine dismantled the chef's modest role as custodian or at best reinventor of tradition and transformed the chef into a creative lumi-nary. In the *Holiday* article in which Bocuse was identified as running one of the two greatest restaurants, he is credited with an originality and creativity that in fact set much of the tone and path for Nouvelle Cuisine. The Troisgros brothers were later transformed from guardians of tradition to stars of the new orthodoxy of innovation. In the Bocuse model, the chef was an original artistic genius, a master of classic techniques to be sure, but no more attached to the past than Picasso had been.

For Steinberger in *Au Revoir to All That*, Nouvelle Cuisine was a missed opportunity to save French culinary culture. I think of it as a failed reform on the order of Mikhail Gorbachev's attempt in the 1980s to salvage the Soviet regime—a fateful crack in the facade of the established order that revealed its weakness and accelerated its collapse. Nouvelle Cuisine presented itself as a reformation, a return to authenticity and simplicity against the tired artifices of what passed for classic cuisine in which ingredients were ignored in favor of overelaborate effects. It was only partially a revolution, and its principles included an injunction against embracing "systematic modernism." The Ten Commandments of Nouvelle Cuisine pronounced by Gault and Millau in 1973 were:

Thou shall not overcook
Thou shall use fresh, quality products
Thou shall lighten thy menu
Thou shall not be systematically modernistic
Thou shall seek out what the new techniques can bring you
Thou shall eliminate brown and white sauces
Thou shall not ignore dietetics
Thou shall not cheat on thy presentation
Thou shall be inventive
Thou shall not be prejudiced[6]

The commandments constituted a call to arms against what Gault and Millau referred to as *les horreurs de la cuisine*: gelatinous quenelles, tasteless farmed fish, sauces made from recycled Espagnole base, too much use of herbes de Provence, dishes presented without enough truffles (and truffles from jars, at that). Meals prepared according to the culinary reformation were light rather than rich ("away with rich sauces that have murdered so many livers and concealed so much tasteless fish," Gault and Millau wrote). Cooking time was reduced, as was portion size and the length of the menu. Attention was paid to the beauty of the basic ingredients rather than to offering a range of poorly executed exotica. "Inventive" as laid down in the commandments was interpreted according to an Asian, particularly Japanese aesthetic. Small, beautiful, colorful courses were presented on large dishes in imitation of Japanese minimalism. Asian flavors and ingredients such as star anise, fish sauce, and soy sauce were introduced. Above all, in Nouvelle Cuisine the chef was an *auteur*, the master of invention, surprise, change, and artistry.[7]

Laying down a series of commandments in this exuberant fashion seems quintessentially French: the desire for order imposed with a certain esprit. Nouvelle Cuisine encouraged chefs to follow their unique inspiration, though still within a framework of rules. The chef as creative genius rather than as expert artisan would be a lasting result of Nouvelle Cuisine long after the "commandments" were forgotten. Nouvelle Cuisine of the 1970s thus had two missions that have since gone separate ways: to exalt primary ingredients simply prepared, and to advocate variety resulting from breaking with tradition—new combinations such as Asian fusion. Nouvelle Cuisine's emphasis on freshness and intrinsic quality contributed to the American rediscovery of local, seasonal food, while the push to innovate was later taken up by "molecular," "modernist" cuisine with its new tastes, textures, and technologies.

Nouvelle Cuisine was by no means universally accepted among French chefs. In 1975 Roger Fessaguet of La Caravelle (previously at Le Pavillon) clarified for an *Esquire* magazine fact-checker that indeed, he could be described as a traditionalist when it came to cooking, and not only that: "I am against this so-called 'New French Cooking' which is too often against common sense."[8] Nouvelle Cuisine also came in for a certain amount of ridicule for its high prices and small portions, its reliance on strange combinations (vanilla and maple syrup flavoring sweetbreads or fish), and its lack of sensuality (chefs such as Michel Guérard pioneered spa cuisine). In the long run, Nouvelle Cuisine did change French cooking, but it also had the character of a peculiar, short-lived fad. Its fall from favor by 1990 left France not only separated from the tradition of classic grande-cuisine but also deprived of cutting-edge innovation or even a sense of what such innovation might look like. The innovators of the 1990s were being nourished in other pastures, especially in Catalonia and the Basque country.

Still, Nouvelle Cuisine did have influence beyond the term of its sway over French gastronomy, especially by releasing chefs from tutelage to a craft tradition, and in creating room for Asian and other influences. Interviewed by Mitchell Davis, the eminent New York restaurant critic and food writer Mimi Sheraton observed that French Nouvelle Cuisine gave American chefs the confidence to dispense with rules and experiment. "I was not a big advocate of the Nouvelle Cuisine," Sheraton notes. "I think it was done to such an extent, like an ideologue, that it cost the French their reputation for food for a long time, but I do think the signal was there that there is not only one classic way to do it."[9]

FIVE TRENDS

The vacuum opened up by the brief triumph of Nouvelle Cuisine and the longer-term decline of French authority was not the only source of creativity and change in American cuisine, but rather the movement created preconditions for the transformation of restaurant dining in the United States since 1980. The five trends outlined here are by no means exhaustive or definitive, but amount to long-term developments, not just fashions on the order of seared foie gras one year followed by pickled ramps the next.

I. Farm-to-Table

The most important trend in American restaurant dining over the past thirty years is undoubtedly the "farm-to-table" movement that emphasizes freshness, local sourcing, and seasonality. As discussed in the chapter on Chez Panisse, the farm-to-table philosophy defines food ingredients by taste, season, and freshness rather than by how hard they are to acquire or their expense: real local peaches rather than cloudberries flown in from Scandinavia; foraged mushrooms rather than French truffles in cans or jars; Niman Ranch bacon rather than thawed-out filet mignon. As far back as 1834, when the Delmonico brothers bought their Williamsburg farm, restaurant chefs have tried to obtain fresher produce, but success and prestige were seldom defined by simplicity and quality, and instead were more often the result of piling up ingredients (ice-cream sundaes; pizza with dozens of toppings choices); the ability to obtain out-of-season items (berries in the winter); or creating a spectacle (flambéed dishes). The most revolutionary aspect of the farm-to-table movement, then, is attention to the taste of fundamental ingredients and the definition of quality in terms of taste. Since most of American gastronomic history has been based not on taste but rather on variety, technology, and convenience, this represents a real change. Critics' jibes notwithstanding, the new standard is not confined to a few elite preserves; rather, it has taken over restaurants' ambitions across the United States, even affecting the fast-casual and fast-food markets.

II. Molecular/Modernist Gastronomy

The other major restaurant trend besides farm-to-table emphasizes technology and innovation rather than a revival of lost arts. Molecular or modernist gastronomy—the drive to transform food and to expand tastes and textures beyond the familiar—is more important globally than farm-to-table, in part because unlike the United Sates, much of the world still *has* small farms and local cuisine. The winners in the annual San Pellegrino list of the world's top fifty restaurants are almost entirely in the modernist category, a style of cooking that became celebrated in the 1990s. If we were embarking on a "ten chefs that changed the world" project instead of ten restaurants that changed America, the most prominent personage of the late twentieth and early twenty-first century would be Ferran Adrià of elBulli. What used to be called "molecular gastronomy" is infatuated with special effects, technology, and things that have never been seen before. The chef is a creator, an artist, even a culinary alchemist, but not a curator.

With pardonable exaggeration, Lisa Abend entitled her book about working at Ferran Adrià's restaurant *The Sorcerer's Apprentices*.[10] He and his associates were trying to create a new language of food and to show its properties and possibilities with little reference to precedents. Certain techniques were rejected—grilling, butter-based sauces—not from a sense of virtue but rather as an American pioneer might leave the well-watered landscape of the East Coast for alluring if more dangerous western horizons. Newness at elBulli consisted of: the application of technique to gastronomy (transformations of texture and intensity); shock (seemingly conflicting ingredients); solids into liquids and vice-versa; trompe l'oeil; and other forms of surprise. The old was sometimes affectionately referred to, but in almost unrecognizable form, thus the beloved Catalan pa amb tomàquet (grilled bread with olive oil, garlic, and tomato smeared on it) was transformed into a liquid.

The Catalan avant-garde cuisine has been particularly subversive. The antecedents of elBulli are from the interwar period and include Surrealism, the Futurist Cookbook, and Salvador Dalí's culinary and pseudo-culinary escapades. The path of elBulli traces a microhistory of cuisine since the 1980s. Founded in 1961 by a German couple as a mini-golf course, elBulli evolved gradually from a snack bar into a restaurant serving typical Costa Brava tourist cuisine. By the late 1970s, it had adopted a more serious, essentially French menu. When Ferran Adrià arrived in 1985, it was still French. His goal was to restore Catalan cuisine and to innovate on the basis of that tradition. At some point in the 1990s, however, elBulli metamorphosed and adopted a vastly more experimental, creative, and research-oriented mission, leaving Catalonia behind and developing a dossier of exactly 1,846 culinary inventions based on techniques such as caramelization, foaming, spherification, single dishes with multiple temperatures, and in general a transformative alchemy.[11]

Ferran Adrià's fame was intense but, in the United States, not all that long-lasting. In Anthony Bourdain's *Kitchen Confidential*, a memoir and reflection on restaurant cooking that launched an extraordinary media career, one of Bourdain's friends dismisses Ferran Adrià as "that foam guy," as in "that foam guy is bogus."[12] In 2000 when the book was published, American chefs could easily dismiss Adrià. On the other end, after the closure of elBulli at the height of its fame in 2011, Adrià has faded from public memory and obsession.

Noma in Copenhagen, the restaurant that displaced elBulli in 2010 as the world's preeminent restaurant in the San Pellegrino rankings, combines attention to a specific locale on the one hand with shockingly new ingredients and techniques on the other. Chef René Redzepi has taken locavore to a new degree of intensity, all the more impressive because of the austere climate and (seemingly) limited natural abundance of the European north. Noma's menu is based not just on Scandinavian farm-to-table but on foraging—beach- or forest-to-table.

Located in a semi-abandoned neighborhood of shipyards and warehouses, Noma began as an effort to bring to Scandinavia some of the techniques and deconstructive approaches pioneered at elBulli, where Redzepi served a term as a *stagier*. Traditional Danish garnished cod was served with beetroot sauce instead of butter; biksemad, normally a kind of hash, was made from scratch instead of leftovers and with lobster as its principal ingredient. Not content with what seemed like rather timid adjustments to a limited repertoire, Redzepi launched a more radical way forward, emphasizing Scandinavian time and place—especially season and habitat. Variety would come not from adding sea buckthorn to crème brûlée but from dishes in which this weed was the star, or from experimenting with dozens of different varieties of horseradish, or from learning about fermentation in order to have intriguing food during the long winter. Redzepi thus paid attention to the sourcing and attention to farmers, foragers, and locale characteristic in America of Chez Panisse, but also embraced the experimentation and daring of elBulli. The ingredients are in keeping with their natural habitat, so in some sense extremely unpretentious—raw carrots, for example. But it is a complicated habitat as well—a dish that Noma calls "Blueberries Surrounded by Their Natural Environment" involves not only blueberry sorbet and fresh blueberries, but spruce granita, spruce ice cream, and brioche, as well as wild ingredients such as wood sorrel and heather.[13]

Redzepi's cuisine is built on the Scandinavian natural environment but is dependent as much on the wild habitat as on the cultivated. Foraging brings in new ingredients like beach weeds reminiscent of capers, or variations such as hundreds of types of edible fungi, but at the same time the cuisine requires advanced techniques: the blueberry dessert is made with xanthan gum and is processed at various stages using a Thermomix (a superprocessor), a Pacojet (to purée frozen foods), and a Superbag (a sieve in bag form for consommés). Redzepi writes of shedding the influence of elBulli in the matter of ingredients and deconstruction in favor of an orientation toward the seasonal and local, but he does not reject creativity or the application of technology. Redzepi is both an earnest conservator of the local food tradition and a charismatic scout—a figure in the landscape and an alchemist.

Beyond the restaurant's ability to combine shock and terroir, as it were, Noma may be seen as the logical outcome of an essential similarity between modernist and farm-to-table cuisines—they both require more resources than middlebrow (or middle-income) cuisine. They also demand more effort on the part of the chef or restaurateur: both for the locavore in contracting with local farmers or cultivating or foraging, as well as for the modernist in machinery and the cost of creativity.

Returning to America, the overwhelming preference is for the farm-to-table movement's emphasis on the seasonal, local, and traditional. US restaurants are less interested in transformation by technological intervention. Revolutionary though it is, the farm-to-table movement represents an effort to revive historical, "heirloom," or "artisanal" practices. Even if traditional cooking has been enfeebled by more than a century of standardization, technological manipulation, and homogenization of national tastes, the movement presents itself as restoring a pastoral American landscape of small farms and a rich and diverse natural environment. Modernist cuisine, on the other hand, is based on innovation. The new is sacred and the past has no particular authority except as a series of experiments or references. Innovative and disruptive though the United States is in various areas, the principal dynamic in its cooking is more reformation than revolution.

Most American restaurants that receive significant attention these days are involved in restoring tradition— local farms, "heirloom" breeds, free-range hens, small-batch Bourbon whiskey—and few follow modernist innovation. In all historical periods, tradition and innovation characterize fashionable dining, but in the contemporary United States, tradition is stronger. Restaurants of the elBulli sort, based entirely on creativity and originality, are not common. The traditional foods are, of course, presented in a different manner from their original models: lighter, spicier, influenced by Asian flavors and techniques. What we are seeing in the twenty-first century is fidelity not to reenactment, but to *ingredients*. Thus,

Sean Brock's Husk in Charleston, South Carolina, bans ingredients that come from outside the South (such as olive oil), gearing the restaurant's philosophy toward "exploring the reality of Southern food."[14] For the single region of the South Carolina Low Country, a revival described in a recent book by David S. Shields emphasizes the rediscovery of neglected ingredients such as sorghum and forgotten local varieties such as Carolina gold rice. Common grains milled in traditional ways are available (cornmeal), and knowledge of wild plants and endangered cooking techniques has been revived.[15]

For all their many contrasts, both the farm-to-table and modernist movements share an opposition to industrial and corporate food-industry products and ways of doing business. Whether this represents merely an elitist sideshow or something that will influence eating at a more popular level is up for debate. My opinion is that widespread concern for where food actually comes from is changing the cultivation, processing, buying, and serving of food in America. Mass-market influence for molecular gastronomy may seem to be minimal, given the small number of modernist restaurants, their high price, and somewhat oracular philosophies. On the other hand, the American food industry has for ages been dedicated to the transformative scientific manipulation of food. Pringles or cornflakes are in their way as startling as any of those 1,846 dishes invented by elBulli. One reason the United States may not have embraced molecular gastronomy is that we already eat lots of peculiar, non-natural, scientifically manipulated products—they just aren't crafted, complex, or trendy.

III. Celebrity Chefs

It is hardly as if there were no famous chefs before 1980. The first European chef we know about whose renown qualifies him as a genuine celebrity is Guillaume Tirel, known as "Taillevent," a French chef who lived from about 1310 to 1395. King Charles V of France bestowed on him a knighthood and a coat of arms whose main feature is three stewpots. His tomb survives at Hennemont Priory in Lorraine, showing Taillevent in sculpted relief dressed as an armored knight with a sword and a shield bearing his heraldic device. He is flanked not only by his first and second wife, but also by his dog at his feet. What has changed since Taillevent is not so much that chefs are famous whereas before they were anonymous but that restaurants are known especially for their chefs. In our world, the chef is often the founder and owner, while the front-of-the-house manager has become less prominent. At the high end, restaurants are chef-driven, while much of the lower end is managed by corporate chains. The idea of the chef as creative genius and vivid personality reflects the dominant culture of American celebrity, complete with accolades, scandal, failure, and rapid change.

The invention of the European restaurant well over two hundred years ago did not immediately end the association of great chefs with royal or other grand private patrons. There were plenty of restaurants in the Paris of the early nineteenth century, but the most famous chef of that era, Marie-Antoine Carême (1784–1833), worked only for private notables such as the Prince Talleyrand, the English prince regent (the future king George IV), and Baron James Meyer Rothschild.[16] Auguste Escoffier (1846–1935), the greatest chef of the late nineteenth and early twentieth centuries, had a very different trajectory.[17] He codified and simplified what Carême had established as the immense catalogue of French techniques, sauces, and presentations, but unlike his earlier compatriot, Escoffier spent his career at hotel restaurants: the National in Lucerne; the Savoy in London, where he collaborated with celebrity manager César Ritz; and later the Carlton Hotel, also in London.

Carême and Escoffier attained their celebrity positions by writing, engaging in appropriate but energetic self-promotion, and setting themselves up as arbiters of the rules of cuisine. Well before the beginning of the twentieth century, the restaurant was clearly the place to achieve fame as a chef, and whatever the advantages of cooking for a private employer

Fig. 104. Marie-Antoine (Antonin) Carême (1784–1833), the leading chef
of the early nineteenth century.

(better hours, less stress), public notice was not among them. Nevertheless, until recently restaurant managers and not the chefs were the real
celebrities. Oscar Tschirsky of New York's Waldorf Astoria, a discrimi-

nating social observer, was far more famous than whoever was in the hotel's kitchens. Henri Soulé at Le Pavillon is also a model of the fame and authority of the front of the house (in this case, the restaurant owner as well). Although his chefs such as Pierre Franey and Jacques Pépin went on to considerable fame, they were clearly and uncomfortably subordinate during their time at Le Pavillon.

The rise of the chef in status, independence, and renown has much to do with the Food Network, which began in 1993, its imitators, and spin-offs. Not only do many chefs present colorful personalities that play well on television, but they can be seen to create and manage (or mismanage) high-pressure situations. Chefs, often more important than the food on their shows, provide entertainment, which is the point of television and visual media generally. No maître d'hôtel can compete with chefs yelling, cooking, and competing.[18] Kissing the hands of countesses, snubbing ordinary people, or gliding from table to table only goes so far.

In their *Holiday* magazine interview, Gault and Millau were prescient in one observation at least—the difference between the Troisgros brothers, who in 1969 were masters of an established tradition, and Paul Bocuse, a creator of lighter, more playful dishes that referred to the past but in a jesting homage. Bocuse presented partridge chartreuse at his restaurant, a classic dish, but using juice from pressed partridges rather than the meat of the bird, thus creating something new.

This is not to say that chefs suddenly discovered innovation whereas before they had merely followed precedent. Great chefs of the seventeenth to nineteenth centuries on the order of Scappi, La Varenne, Carême, and Escoffier made drastic changes in haute cuisine, but they replaced one authoritative system with another. What has happened dramatically since 1980 is the fragmentation of authority and the elimination of agreed-upon codes, old *or* new. Chefs still influence one another, especially with regard to technique—Ferran Adrià and foam, for example—but not in defining canonical dishes.

In the foreword to *Mastering the Art of French Cooking*, Julia Child observed that the Frenchman looks for a "well-known dish impeccably cooked and served." Even in France this is no longer the rule and certainly in the United States has a quaint, archaic feel. The downfall of French authority and the rise the creative chef have meant an impetus in the direction of "endless reinvention," in the words of Daniel Humm, chef of New York's Eleven Madison Park.[19] For better or worse (and there is a downside), the top chefs are no longer masters of a craft but artists.

IV. The Influence of Asia

No longer can Asian food in America be defined by invented adaptations such as chop suey, or ersatz iconography like little umbrellas on faux-Polynesian cocktails. Asian tastes and ingredients have become vital to the international culinary style, and within the United States, the expansion of Asian restaurants, and not just Chinese ones, has been relentless. The international trend can be traced back to Nouvelle Cuisine, which embraced tropical products like kiwi, vanilla, or Indian spices as well as a Japanese-inspired simplicity and eye for perfection. "Asian fusion" encompasses a lot of failed experiments or gimmicks. It can be another way of appearing hip while adding enough ingredients to distract the diner from noticing the actual quality of the food. It has, however, greatly influenced the high-end dining experience.

Even though Nouvelle Cuisine opened the door to Asia, it did so as a series of gestures rather than the result of any systematic study. Jean-Georges Vongerichten became one of the most articulate exponents of incorporating Asian tastes, but in order to accomplish this, he had to escape Europe. His Asian journey was eccentric in its time because, the openness of Nouvelle Cuisine to Asia notwithstanding, French training was still considered the only path to culinary distinction. Another example of early experimentation with blending European and Asian tastes was the Fischerzunft hotel and restaurant in Schaffhausen, Switzerland. In the 1980s André Jaeger and his Chinese wife, Doreen Jaeger-Soong, developed a Chinese-French style there based on Jaeger's experience at the Peninsula Hotel in Hong Kong and Soong's upbringing, also in Hong Kong. Curry, Chinese five-spice blend, sesame, mangoes, and Chinese noodles—all barely known in Europe—were ubiquitous on the Fischerzunft menu.[20]

The Asian inflection at fine restaurants in the United States is from Japan more than any other part of Asia, but Thailand, Indochina, and of course China are important as well. At Vongerichten's New York restaurant Jean-Georges, the menu has more Japanese and Indochinese shadings than Chinese. Yuzu, lemongrass, and Kaffir lime are favorite ingredients, and Hamachi sashimi avocado (with yuzu and radish) is one of Vongerichten's signature dishes. At Le Bernardin, a seafood restaurant and one of the most acclaimed establishments in New York, Japanese sashimi is evoked, yuzu is in a vinaigrette and a custard, a lemongrass *nage* accompanies crab salad, and a cardamom-ginger vinaigrette comes with the cured salmon.[21] It's worth noting that the *Zagat* guide identifies both Jean-Georges and Le Bernardin as "French," when in fact they are something quite different, albeit hard to describe.

Below this exalted level, the ethnic restaurant scene, once dominated by Chinese and Italian, has expanded both in terms of number of restaurants and types of cuisine. While Chinese food has in certain respects stagnated, neither sought out by food adventurers nor catering to the expensive market, Japanese food has developed an upscale representation. Thai restaurants are everywhere, not just in hip enclaves. There is also more variety among Indian restaurants than the curry houses of old. Some of this is simply an expansion of what was already under way before 1980. The effects of the liberalizing of immigration quotas after 1965 include the establishment of new immigrant communities and the opening of new types of restaurants.

Expansion of ethnic restaurants, however, is not completely or proportionately related to immigration. Many immigrant groups are still underrepresented, or their restaurants cater to the community rather than to a general public. There are 60,000 Filipinos in New York City, for example, but a scant seven or eight Filipino restaurants. Either because of American tastes or lack of opportunity, the food of the Philippines has not established itself in the way that Thai has.[22]

It is surprising that Asian food, although so well represented and so profoundly influential on the fanciest restaurants, has had limited success in fashioning its own high-end cuisines. This reflects old tropes and fixed American ideas of what level of price is expected at "ethnic "restaurants. Certain Japanese restaurants, of course, are among the most expensive in the United States, and indeed Japan itself is arguably the leading culinary destination of the world if measured by such criteria as number of Michelin-starred restaurants. One can easily spend upward of $200 per person at superb restaurants like Masa, Nobu, or Rosanjin in New York. There are, however, no Chinese, Thai, or Indian restaurants at this price point, at least none commonly recognized by ordinary diners. There were fancy Chinese and Indian restaurants in the 1980s and 1990s, although never at the stratospheric level of contemporary Japanese leaders, but even such elegant places as Darbar, Monsoon, or Uncle Tai's in New York have closed and have not been imitated or replaced.

Asian influence in the United States is doubtlessly related to the growth of Asian economies in the past decades; the extraordinary modernization of China; and the rapid development of Taiwan, South Korea, and Singapore, followed more recently by India. Certain Asian inventions, such as bubble tea or banh mi, have become global retail commodities. There is still a selectivity about this success and impact, though, and not only Filipino but also Indonesian and Malaysian cuisine remain underrepresented.

Insofar as there is a new cuisine fashion, it is decidedly for Latin America. Peru is the standard-bearer at the moment, offering not only great restaurants but cooking classes, gastronomic holidays, and outposts of established Peruvian restaurants in the United States. Two Peruvian restaurants appear in the San Pellegrino top twenty, and the country is able to promote both inexpensive and fancy restaurants in its own cities and abroad. At the same time, Brazilian food is stuck in a certain carnivorous all-you-can-eat niche. Despite massive immigration from Colombia to the United States, its cuisine is little known outside immigrant circles. Mexican food is everywhere, but its small haute category is dominated by chefs who are not from Mexico—Rick Bayless, for example.

V. The New Informality of the Dining Experience

Contemporary fine dining is characterized by what Alison Pearlman has defined as "smart casual," a term similar to Priscilla Ferguson's "haute food," as distinguished from "haute cuisine."[23] Haute food and smart casual are based on novelty and eclecticism, not tradition; authenticity rather than elegance. Informality is evident in décor, the dress and style of the waitstaff, and in an overall attitude that reflects the priorities of chefs and a younger population rather than of restaurant managers and older, dressy clients. A nonexhaustive checklist of smart-casual attributes might include: open kitchens and open fires; unusual industrial, found, or designed space; artisanal beer and whiskey lists; comfort food; eclectic and even metacultural food (that is, riffs on rather than imitations of foreign cuisine); tasting menus; small plates (based perhaps on a combination of low-end Spanish tapas and high-end Japanese *kaiseki*); and a blurring of high and low cuisine—the inclusion of low-end favorites like burgers or fried chicken alongside forgotten ingredients like salsify or fiddlehead ferns and, on the same menu with the burgers, lobster, and foie gras (local if possible).[24]

There was a time not so long ago when restaurant décor was directly related to price. Expensive restaurants required men to wear a jacket and tie, and featured starched table linens, a maître d'hôtel wearing a tuxedo,

Fig. 105. Beer Tasting ("High Hops"), *The New Yorker*, 2014.

and a hushed, almost reverent atmosphere. That atmosphere is disappearing now for reasons of cost, and because chefs and their often effusive personalities surpass the front-of-the-house managers. The food triumphs over décor. Informality has the advantage of costing less, and in addition is thought to convey authenticity. The restaurant does not depend on opulence to distract attention from the mediocrity of the food, as was (supposedly) characteristic of a benighted past. Thus bare wood tables crowded together and friendly waitstaff are found in most new restaurants, whatever their price or pretensions.

Chefs create the sort of spaces they want, perhaps with loud music (as with Mario Batali), special tables in the kitchen, or no choices from a menu. The patrons' preferences are not ignored—a nice innovation is seats at a bar for singles or those without a reservation—but it is a mistake to think that just because restaurants don't have a dress code they are less intimidating than in the bad old days. As mentioned in the chapter on Le Pavillon, the most sought-after restaurants now practice any number of user-unfriendly policies: no-choice menus, requiring prepayment (in effect a ticket system), or deliberately creating a difficult reservation procedure. If chefs got their way, the restaurant patron would be a pilgrim who arrived at the shrine after overcoming many obstacles, and some chefs have indeed succeeded in imposing near-religious forms of obeisance.

Informality today is more than a question of décor; it extends to the food, well crafted and fanatically sourced though it may very likely be. At the fancy restaurant of yore, with its elaborately folded napkins and soft lighting, you would not expect pizza or burgers on the menu any more than you would anticipate sitting on a barstool at a counter eating foie gras or morels.

The Union Square Café, for many years voted the favorite restaurant of New Yorkers by contributors to the *Zagat* guide, listed hamburgers on the menu from the time it opened in 1985, as did Jeremiah Tower's Balboa Café in 1983, but the real inventor of the gourmet, or at least expensive, hamburger was the exclusive and old-line 21 Club in New York, which has offered it since 1950. Such a possibility certainly never occurred to Henri Soulé, and only in the twenty-first century have French restaurants in the United States discovered burgers in a big way. In 2002, Daniel Boulud at db Bistro Moderne created a hamburger made with slow-cooked short ribs of beef and several other beef cuts, with foie gras in the middle of the patty. A few years later Andy d'Amico, owner of three Provençal restaurants, put a "5 Napkin Burger" on the menu of Nizza and found it so successful that he started a chain dedicated to burgers, also so named.

The informal ethos defines social selectivity not by obvious or outdated signs of upper-class status (dress-code, facility with French) but rather through an array non-French knowledge—for example, not having to ask what *is* yuzu anyway? It is possible to have only a hazy idea of wine lore if you know what seasonal craft beers to order, and to be cognizant of the differences between Bangkok and Isarn regional cuisines is as impressive as knowledge of the food of Burgundy or Périgord. Discrimination is not gone, and neither is the use of the restaurant as a means of social positioning, but there are many separate contests, not one or two based on French or English guidelines.

These five, then, seem to be the major recent and current trends, all of which emphasize innovation in terms of composition and service of dishes, but also traditions of agriculture, foraging, fishing, and raising livestock and poultry. This tension between innovation and tradition, when it works, provides an exciting experience, a wonderful sensuality, and unexpected thrills. The only way to predict the future is to extrapolate from what is happening now, and of course it's impossible to imagine something one doesn't yet notice. In his 1991 book, the food critic John Mariani was confident that the cult of the celebrity chef was in decline, that America was turning away from burgers, and that the growth of fast-food outlets was slowing. Against these mistaken predictions, he also presciently noted the growth of concern among restaurateurs about the social and environmental implications of food.[25]

Rather than try to divine the future, it might be useful to close with some thoughts about America's restaurant heritage. If this book has had a forward-looking orientation to assess influence and change, the totality of the restaurants considered, nevertheless, communicates something about the history of American food and our expectations for it. Historical study should lead to wisdom and modesty, specifically intelligent diffidence about predicting the future and assuming nothing ever existed in the past that resembles our world. A book about food, however important the subject, cannot pretend to instill an appropriate philosophy of life, but part of my purpose has been to show that the past is both beautiful and important. Food and cuisine reflect the culture at large, something historians have not always sufficiently been aware of. Thus, as we have seen, in the nineteenth century, Delmonico's, its provisioners, its customers, and imitators were busy depleting the United States of its ecological riches and heritage—wild ducks, turtles, prairie chicken and passenger pigeons, and other high-end delicacies that would either become extinct or endangered by the beginning of the twentieth century. Diners at elegant restaurants must certainly have enjoyed their pleasures, while they lasted. Attributes of food that we boast about and pay extra for (grass-fed beef, "heirloom" tomatoes, Long Island bay scallops) were then taken for granted. All chickens in this vanished America were free range, not out of deliberate virtue but rather because the unhealthful and inhumane industrialized model of chicken farming did not yet exist. It would have been hard to find Vietnamese phở or pad Thai in any restaurant in 1850 or 1900, but even Asian favorites such as abalone, now astronomically expensive, were laughably commonplace.

Food is always affected by the condition of the natural environment, and in 1900, there simply were fewer people—one-quarter of our current global population. It is not just the need to feed everyone (which is done poorly, given the resources that do exist) but also the ways in which development has taken place that have changed food. We are actually fortunate that the cheerful scenarios of *The Jetsons*, futurologists, and frozen-food-industry leaders in the 1950s and 1960s have not come true: that by the year 2000 everyone would be eating nutritious pills that dispensed with the need for meals, or they would be reconstituting meals instantly from frozen or dried ingredients. Not that microwaves haven't come close to fulfilling the latter prediction since their introduction in the early 1970s, but nonetheless real food has managed to survive.

Another way of dismissing the past is to recall its bad food and to assume that no one cared about what they ate, maybe because they smoked all the time, drank constantly, or were too busy, too puritanical, or too ignorant to care. And yet social critics and analysts periodically observe a wave of previously unheard-of gourmandise sweeping the nation. In 1950, David Riesman's *The Lonely Crowd*, a classic sociological study of postwar prosperity and its discontents, observed that "many people are and many more felt they must be gourmets." The taste for "tossed salads and garlic, elaborate sauces, dishes en casserole, *Gourmet* magazine, wine and liquors" was being disseminated throughout the hinterland from New York and San Francisco.[26]

In 1968, the screenwriter and social critic Nora Ephron believed she was in the midst of an extraordinary, even ridiculous, food boom. Its origins, she posited, were the 1950s, when postwar sophistication meant that "everyone" started serving curry and learned not only to use garlic but to mince it rather than shoving it through a press. Rumaki—marinated chicken livers or water chestnuts wrapped in bacon and sprinkled with soy sauce—rocketed to prominence and then became a hopeless cliché.[27]

The enthusiasm of people like Ephron doesn't really mean that postwar food was particularly good. Riesman's supposedly prestigious "en casserole" would degenerate into the notorious casseroles of the 1950s, featuring canned cream of mushroom soup added to canned tuna fish, leftover macaroni, or turkey. Claims to sophistication for both home and restaurant cooking would not impress modern food enthusiasts: Swedish meatballs, fondue, shish-kebab, beef Stroganoff, and crêpes suzette—all now either laughable or "retro," were touchstones of the 1960s. The same decade saw the triumph of restaurants with flocked velvet wallpaper, immense leatherette-covered menus, and waiters in tuxedos. They served what was described as "continental food," an indeterminate style mocked by Calvin Trillin as pretentious and belittled by John and Karen Hess as faux luxurious when it came to the actual food. Such places relied on processed and frozen ingredients for supposedly elegant or creative dishes such as Chicken Kiev (chicken stuffed with ham and cheese), Tournedos Mexicana (steak with chili sauce), or Beef Wellington (steak with foie gras in pastry). The immense pepper grinder wielded by the waiter was de rigueur; a lot of desserts as well as specialties such as Steak Diane were flamed at the table.[28]

Even in this benighted era people weren't simply foolish or walking in gastronomic darkness. In the not-too-distant future food critics and even historians will deride our foie-gras burgers and cronuts. In fact, it has already started. Simply looking at New York magazine's yearly "Where to Eat" issue, especially Adam Platt's "Ten Trends We're Done With" sidebars, reveals the tragically ephemeral nature of food fashion. Some recent entries include $70 chicken dinners for two, Mexican Coca-Cola, pre-appetizer snacks, and gourmet pickle plates. Since 2010, Brooklyn restaurants as depicted in New York have gone from not-really-serious to huge, to "the Brooklynization of Manhattan" to "Brooklyn sells out tastefully."

Above or beneath the waves of fad and change appear some very basic American facts: the appetite for change itself, a love of experimentation, a preference for variety over canonical dishes and preparations, and eclectic if not omnivorous interest in foreign cuisine. What has not yet been fully realized, although there are promising signs, is the restoration of regions, ecologies, and cooking traditions. The greatest cuisine can involve wild experiments, but in Catalonia, Japan, and France there are intact traditions underlying them. The chronicle of American cuisine is in part the destruction of a rich heritage in favor of convenience, uniformity, and blandness. The results are still visible in poverty statistics and related findings about obesity, malnutrition, and hunger.

A country that has started to care about the taste of food and how it is produced can surely do better not only at its high-end restaurants but in the real choices offered to everyone.

APPENDIX

CLASSIC RECIPES FROM THE TEN RESTAURANTS THAT CHANGED AMERICA

The following recipes are taken from cookbooks created by the restaurants featured in this book. They represent a range of courses, and have been chosen to show the particular style of each restaurant—elaborate, bland, rich, hearty, simple, and occasionally peculiar.

Delmonico's

From Charles Ranhofer, *The Epicurean* (New York: Charles Ranhofer, 1893), 1007, 932–33.

What came to be known as Baked Alaska, an ice-cream dessert covered with a hot meringue, was invented by Delmonico's chef Charles Ranhofer on the occasion of the US purchase of Alaska from the Russian Empire in 1867. Because of its extremes of temperature, this dessert was originally dubbed "Alaska, Florida" by Ranhofer and it appears under that name in his 1893 cookbook.

ALASKA, FLORIDA
Note: Ranhofer usually did not specify amounts, nor did he list the ingredients before the cooking instructions.

Prepare a very fine vanilla-flavored Savoy biscuit paste.* Butter some plain molds two and three-quarter inches in diameter by one and a half inches in depth; dip them in fecula [*i.e. cornstarch or other plant starch*] or flour, and fill two-thirds full with the paste. Cook, turn them out and make an incision all around the bottom; hollow out the cakes and mask the empty space with apricot marmalade.

Have some conical-shaped ice cream molds, fill them half with uncooked banana ice cream and half with uncooked vanilla ice cream; freeze, unmold, and lay them in the hollow of the prepared biscuits; keep in a freezing box or cave.

Prepare also a meringue with twelve egg-whites and one pound of sugar. A few minutes before serving, place each biscuit with its ice on a small lace paper and cover one after the other with the meringue pushed through a pocket furnished with a channel socket, beginning at the bottom and diminishing the thickness until the top is reached; color this meringue for two minutes in a hot oven, and when a light golden brown, remove and serve at once.

*SAVOY BISCUIT

Note: The Alaska, Florida recipe calls for using the uncooked paste, but this recipe to which Ranhofer refers shows what is meant in the above instructions by the terse words "cook, turn them out."

Grease a high biscuit mold with melted prepared veal kidney suet; drain off any surplus fat by reversing the mold, then glaze with sugar icing and fecula, half of each. Pour into a vessel one pound of powdered sugar flavored with vanilla and a pinch of salt, and fourteen egg-yolks one at a time and beat the whole forcibly to have it get quite frothy; whip fourteen egg-whites to a stiff froth, and put a fourth part into the yolks, also six ounces of potato fecula and six ounces of flour, the two later to be sifted together.

As soon as the whole is thoroughly combined, add the remainder of the beaten whites. With this fill the mold three-quarters full and stand it on a baking pan; fix it so that the mold will not fall; place it carefully in the mildest spot in the oven.

In order to bake this biscuit properly, it is essential that the oven be first thoroughly heated, then allowed to fall to a mild temperature; leave it for two and a quarter to two and a half hours. When done to perfection unmold on a grate, cool.

Antoine's

From Roy F. Guste Jr., *Antoine's Restaurant Since 1840 Cookbook* (New York: W. W. Norton, 1980), 30, 119,120, 125.

Oysters Foch was named after Gen. Ferdinand Foch, commander of the French Army during the First World War, who visited New Orleans in 1919. Oysters Foch, Bienville, and Rockefeller are three original cooked oyster dishes, the latter made according to a still-secret recipe invented in 1899. The Colbert Sauce served over the fried oysters in this recipe is made from a base of tomato and Hollandaise sauces.

HUÎTRES FOCH (serves 3)

> 6 slices toast, trimmed of crust
> 6 Tb canned pâté de foie gras
> 3 dozen raw oysters
> 1 cup finely ground yellow cornmeal
> 2 tsp salt
> ½ tsp ground white pepper
> 2 cups Colbert Sauce*

Spread each toast with 1 tablespoon of foie gras. Mix the cornmeal with the salt and pepper and roll the oysters in the mixture. Fry them in deep fat until they are cooked and drain on absorbent paper. Place six on each toast and cover the oysters with Colbert Sauce.

*COLBERT SAUCE

> ⅔ cup Tomato Sauce**
> ⅓ cup Sherry
> ¾ cup warm Hollandaise Sauce***
> caramel food color

Put the Tomato Sauce and the Sherry in a saucepan and reduce to about ⅔ cup. Let cool slightly and blend with the Hollandaise. Add enough caramel color to give the sauce a nice brown color.

**TOMATO SAUCE

> 3 Tb butter
> ¾ cup chopped onion
> 2 Tb flour
> 2 cups chicken stock
> 1½ cups chopped tomato pulp
> ¼ tsp dried thyme
> 2 cloves garlic, minced
> ½ stalk celery, chopped
> 2 sprigs parsley, chopped
> 1 bay leaf
> Salt and ground white pepper

Melt 2 tablespoons of the butter in a saucepan and add the chopped onion. Cook until they begin to color, add the remaining tablespoon butter, the flour and cook until golden brown. Stir often to be sure nothing sticks to the pan. Now add all remaining ingredients and season to taste. Simmer for 30 minutes. Pass sauce through a strainer.

***HOLLANDAISE SAUCE

> 2 cups melted butter, warm
> 8 egg yolks
> 2 Tb lemon juice
> 2 Tb tarragon vinegar
> ¾ tsp paprika
> Salt and cayenne pepper to taste

Beat the egg yolks together with the lemon juice and vinegar and pour the mixture into the top of a double boiler. Cook on a low heat stirring constantly, never letting the water in the double boiler come to a boil. Continue cooking until the mixture thickens. Remove from the fire and beat in the warm melted butter, a little at a time. Add the paprika and the salt and pepper.

Schrafft's

From Joan Kanel Slomanson, *When Everybody Ate at Schrafft's* (Fort Lee, NJ: Barricade Books, 2006), 27.

Chicken à la King was among the most popular main courses at Schrafft's beginning in the 1930s. Invented around 1900, the dish was considered dainty and elegant in its original context. Perhaps for today's tastes it seems simultaneously bland, hearty, and fattening.

SCHRAFFT'S CHICKEN À LA KING (serves 4)

> ½ cup (1 stick) unsalted butter
> ½ cup flour
> 2 cups chicken broth
> ½ cup heavy cream
> ¼ cup milk
> 2 egg yolks, slightly beaten
> 2 cups cooked chicken, skinned, boned and cut into strips
> 1 cup sliced mushrooms, sautéed in butter
> Salt and pepper to taste
> ½ cup pimento, thin-sliced in strips

Melt butter in a large saucepan. Add flour, blending the mixture.

Heat broth. Slowly add it and the cream and milk to the flour mixture, stirring constantly. Cook for 5 minutes on low heat.

Stir in the other ingredients and cook for 2 minutes.

Serve on toast or in patty [pastry] shells.

Howard Johnson's

From Anthony Mitchell Sammarco, *A History of Howard Johnson's: How a Massachusetts Soda Fountain Became an American Icon* (Charleston, SC: The History Press, 2013), 104.

As a large restaurant chain, Howard Johnson's relied on a commissary system of centralized kitchens. The clams would have been prepared as strips by the supplier, but here the whole clam body is fried. Individual recipes of this size were adaptations for family cooks, but nevertheless, the result is an authentic evocation of the chain's most famous dish.

FRIED CLAMS (also known as "Clams as Sweet as a Nut") (serves 4)

> 1 cup evaporated milk
> 1 cup milk
> 1 egg
> ¼ teaspoon vanilla
> Dash salt and pepper
> 4 dozen freshly shucked clams
> 1 cup cake flour
> 1 cup yellow cornmeal
> oil for frying

Combine evaporated milk and whole milk, egg, vanilla, salt and pepper. Soak clams in liquid and then dredge in combination of cake flour and cornmeal, fluffing them in the flour mixture for light but thorough coverage. Shake off excess flour and fry in oil.

   Serve with French-fried potatoes, tartar sauce, homemade rolls and butter.

Mamma Leone's

From Gene Leone, *Leone's Italian Cookbook* (New York: Harper and Row, 1967), 75.

Leone describes his friend Alfredo di Lelio as a master showman and perfect host. Di Lelio's restaurant, Alfredo's of Rome, has been famous for more than a century for a deceptively simple dish that Gene Leone compared to his mother's shrimp sauce in that it is impossible for anyone else to imitate perfectly.

FETTUCINI AL'ALFREDO OF ROME (serves 4)

> 2 cups sifted all-purpose flour
> 3 eggs
> ¼ tsp salt
> 2 Tb cold water
> Cornmeal
> ¾ cup butter
> 6 Tb grated Parmesan cheese

Place the flour on a pastry board, make a well in the center, and add eggs, salt and 1 table-spoon of the water. Knead until the dough forms a ball and comes away from your hands clean. Cover and let stand for 1 hour.

Cut dough into 4 pieces. Roll out paper thin, as thin as possible. Place on a towel to dry for 20 minutes. Now roll each sheet into a scroll about 2 and ½ inches wide. Place on a board and cut into ¼ inch strips. Pick up with both hands and lightly shake loose, spreading the strips on wax paper. Sprinkle a little cornmeal over the fettucini.

Cook the fettucini in salted boiling water for 10 minutes. Check to see if it is cooked the way you like it. When ready, drain well and place back in hot pot. Add about half the butter; mix well. Add half of the cheese and mix again. Place in a warm bowl. Add the rest of the cheese and butter and mix well. Place the bowl in a hot oven for 2 minutes. Remove, and serve from bowl onto hot plates at table.

The Mandarin

From Cecilia Chiang, *The Seventh Daughter: My Culinary Journey from Beijing to San Francisco* (Berkeley: Ten Speed Press, 2007), 124.

Cecilia Chiang fled from Japanese-occupied Peking in 1943 and, accompanied by one of her sisters, embarked on a journey to seek refuge with the Nationalist forces in southern China. After a nightmarish series of adventures they arrived in Chungking, where they were helped by a wealthy and influential uncle. This Szechwan (Sichuan) specialty, which Cecilia Chiang had for the first time at her uncle's house, was popularized by the Mandarin and spread across the country with the wave of Szechwan restaurants that opened during the 1970s.

SICHUAN TWICE-COOKED PORK (serves 6)

> 1 and ½ lb piece pork belly, skin-on or off, as lean as possible
> 2-in. piece unpeeled fresh ginger, lightly smashed
> 2 Tb peanut oil
> 4 thinly sliced garlic cloves
> 2 green onions, green part only, halved lengthwise and cut into 2-inch pieces
> 1 Tb black bean sauce
> ¼ tsp chili oil
> ¼ tsp soy sauce
> 1 and ½ leeks, white part only, quartered lengthwise and cut crosswise into 2-inch pieces
> 1 red bell pepper, seeded and cut in 1-inch squares

Put the pork in a medium saucepan and add water to cover it by 1 inch. Bring to a boil over high heat and cook about 2 minutes. Transfer the pork to a sieve or colander and rinse well with cold water.

Rinse out the pan and add the pork, ginger and enough cold water to cover by 1 inch.

Return the pan to the burner and simmer over medium-low heat 45 minutes. Remove from the heat and let the pork sit in the liquid for 15 minutes.

Remove the pork from the pan, transfer to a bowl and discard the liquid. Refrigerate the pork, covered, until firm and thoroughly chilled. Using a sharp knife, halve the pork crosswise, slice it into thin (about ⅛ in.) pieces.

Heat a large wok over high heat until a bead of water dances on the surface and then evaporates. Add the peanut oil, swirl and add the sliced pork. Stir constantly for 1 minute to coat with oil. Toss in the garlic, green onions, black bean sauce, chili oil and soy sauce. Stir to combine well and stir-fry 1 minute more. Add the leeks, cook for 1 and ½ minutes and then toss in the red bell pepper and cook for 30 seconds. Serve immediately.

Sylvia's

From Sylvia Woods and Christopher Styler, *Sylvia's Soul Food: Recipes from Harlem's World-Famous Restaurant* (New York: William Morrow and Company, 1992), 95.

Sylvia Woods complains in this book that vegetables today are not cooked enough—it is as if they were just dipped in boiling water. These beans, simmered in ham broth, are not al dente.

BOILED STRING BEANS WITH HAM (serves 8)

    1 bone from a smoked ham or 8 pig tails
    2 to 3 lbs fresh string beans
    1 Tb salt
    1 tsp freshly ground black pepper
    1 tsp sugar

Put the ham bone in a 6-quart pot with enough water to fill halfway. Heat to boiling. Lower the heat to a simmer, and cover. Simmer 45 minutes.

Prepare the beans while the bone is simmering. Snap the stem end from each bean and pull gently along the length of the bean to remove the string. Rinse the beans in a colander under cold running water. Drain and add to the pot along with the salt, pepper and sugar. Simmer the beans until very tender, up to 30 minutes for old, tough beans or around 15 minutes for very tender string beans. Check the seasoning halfway through the cooking and adjust if necessary. Remove and drain the beans. Serve hot.

Le Pavillon

From Pierre Franey, *The New York Times 60-Minute Gourmet* (New York: Times Books, 1979), 308–9.

A recipe for an off-menu cold omelet that Franey used to prepare when he was chef at Le Pavillon. As Franey remarks, "Such unadvertised dishes offer the owner or maître d'hôtel the opportunity to whisper into a favored customer's ear, 'I have something created especially for you and I think you'll like it.'"

OMELETTES FROIDES AU CRABE

> 8 large eggs
> 2 Tb finely chopped parsley
> 1 Tb freshly chopped tarragon
> ¼ cup heavy cream
> ¾ cup peeled, red, ripe tomatoes cut into ½-inch cubes
> Salt and freshly ground pepper to taste
> 4 Tb butter
> Crab dressing*
> Tomato mayonnaise left over from crab dressing (see recipe)
> Parsley sprigs for garnish

Break the eggs into a mixing bowl. Beat lightly. Add the parsley, tarragon, cream, tomatoes, salt and pepper to taste. Beat well.

Use a small omelet pan or preferably a 7-inch Teflon pan. Heat about ½ teaspoon of butter in the pan. Add about ½ cup of egg mixture. Let cook until firm and lightly browned on the bottom, stirring quickly with a fork until the omelet starts to set. When set, slip a large pancake turner under the omelet and turn it quickly to the other side. Let cook about 5 seconds. Remember, you want to produce a flat omelet, not a typical folded omelet. Turn the omelet out flat onto a sheet of waxed paper. Continue making the omelets until all the egg mixture is used.

When ready to serve, add equal portions of the crab dressing to the center of each omelet. Fold over. Garnish with parsley sprigs. Serve with the leftover tomato mayonnaise.

*GARNITURE DE CRABE

> 1 whole egg
> 1 tsp imported mustard
> ½ tsp Worcestershire sauce
> Salt and freshly ground pepper to taste
> 1 cup peanut, vegetable or corn oil
> 2 Tb bottled chili sauce
> 2 Tb fresh parsley
> 1 Tb finely chopped shallots
> 1 tsp cognac
> 1 lb crabmeat, preferably lump crab
> Juice of half a lemon

Break the egg into a mixing bowl and add the mustard, Worcestershire sauce, salt and pepper. Beat with a whisk.

Gradually add the oil, beating constantly until thickened. Add the chili sauce, parsley, shallots and cognac to blend. Set aside.

Add the crabmeat to a mixing bowl. Add half the sauce. There should be just enough to bind.

The Four Seasons

From Charlotte Adams, *The Four Seasons Cookbook* (New York: Holt, Rinehart and Winston, 1971), 151, 282.

Among the many experiments undertaken by the Four Seasons in its early years was Crisped Shrimp with Mustard Fruit. The sauce is based on a very old traditional dish (Mostarda Cremonese) from Cremona in Lombardy and here is paired with shrimp by Chef Albert Stockli. It was a long-lasting success. In this cookbook, arranged by seasons, the Crisped Shrimp is considered a spring dish. Mostarda Cremonese is essentially preserved fruit in sugar and mustard oil. Traditionally served with meat dishes and sometimes as an accompaniment to cheese, here it is mixed with Béchamel sauce to go with shrimp. The recipe calls for using prepared imported mostarda, sold in jars at specialty food stores, but it is not impossible to prepare at home.

CRISPED SHRIMP WITH MUSTARD FRUIT

2 and ½ lbs. shrimp (= about 24 large shrimp)
3 cups court-bouillon
1 cup Cremonese mustard fruit with liquid
4 cups flour
2 Tb oil
1 tsp baking powder
3 cups water
2 egg yolks
Salt to taste
Flour for dipping
2 cups sauce Béchamel*
2 Tb dry mustard
6 Tb mustard fruit in chunks

Poach shrimp in court-bouillon until they turn pink (about four minutes). Drain. Shell and de-vein. Mince the cup of mustard fruit in their liquid. Slit shrimp halfway through and stuff with the minced fruit. Pat firmly so that stuffing remains in shrimp.

Make a thick batter by mixing flour, oil, baking powder, water, egg yolks and salt. Roll shrimp in flour, dip into batter, and deep-fry in 400-degree oil until brown (4–6 minutes). Drain. Mix Béchamel with mustard and the 6 additional tablespoons of mustard fruit. Heat to piping. Serve in a separate dish as a sauce for the shrimp.

*SAUCE BÉCHAMEL

¼ cup (½ stick) butter
½ cup flour
1 qt milk, heated
1 carrot, sliced
½ onion, stuck with 4 cloves
Bouquet garni: parsley, bay leaf and celery

Melt butter and stir in flour until smooth. Cook over low heat a few minutes and add milk. Stir until thickened. Add carrot, onion and bouquet garni. Simmer 10 minutes and strain.

Chez Panisse

From Alice Waters, *Chez Panisse Vegetables* (New York: HarperCollins, 1996), 107–8.

Chez Panisse always emphasized seasonal dining, and Alice Waters has presented many deceptively simple recipes that depend on products of quality and freshness. Chez Panisse paid particular attention to salads as more than a mere accompaniment. This one is appropriate for autumn, as chicories such as curly endive and radicchio are best at that time. The late fall is also the season for persimmons.

CURLY ENDIVE, RADICCHIO, AND FUYU PERSIMMON SALAD
(serves 6)

1 shallot
1 Tb red wine vinegar
A splash of sherry vinegar
Salt and pepper
1 radicchio
3 small heads curly endive
6 ripe fuyu persimmons
6 Tb olive oil

Peel and finely dice the shallot and put it in a salad bowl with the vinegars and a pinch of salt.

While the shallot is macerating, fill up the sink or a large bowl with cold water. Peel the radicchio, discarding the outer leaves; tear the remaining leaves into bite-size pieces and toss them into the water. Remove the outer leaves of the curly endive, saving only the pale green and white, tender hearts. (Reserve the outer leaves for cooking greens.) Cut out the tough core and add the leaves to the sink. Gently agitate the greens and let them sit in the water for a few minutes. Scoop out the leaves from the water with your hands without disturbing the sand and dirt at the bottom of the sink. Dry the leaves in a salad spinner.

Peel and slice the persimmons into ¼-inch wedges. Whisk the olive oil into the shallot and vinegar and taste for acidity, adjusting as necessary. Add the persimmon slices to the bowl, season with salt and pepper and toss. Add the chicories, season with salt and pepper, and gently toss again, mixing all the ingredients. Taste the salad and adjust the seasoning if necessary. Serve on a platter or chilled plates.

ACKNOWLEDGMENTS

I've accumulated many debts in researching and writing this book. I have tried to mention in the text and notes specific people and institutions who have helped me. Here I'd like to record my gratitude to those who encouraged my work on food and restaurant history, areas that, for all my enthusiasm, I had a lot to learn about.

Danny Meyer, an inspiration to many besides me, was kind enough to write an introduction to this book and to introduce me to people in the restaurant world.

I owe the idea for this book, a different kind of project for someone who has studied medieval European history, to my experiences during the academic year 2002–2003 when I had a fellowship at the New York Public Library's Dorothy and Lewis Cullman Center for Scholars and Writers. I was supported both by the Center and by the American Council of Learned Societies. I spent most of the time working on a book about spices in the Middle Ages, but an exhibition of selections from the library's superlative menu collection organized by William Grimes of the *New York Times* fascinated me and made me wonder why American food was so different in the nineteenth century. I am not a skilled museum-goer, being slow to assimilate images behind glass, and must have spent dozens of lunch breaks looking at these menus. At the Cullman Center I received a lot of good advice from the late Peter Gay, then its director, a man of astonishing range and intellect, uninterested in cuisine as an aesthetic experience, but astute about cultural historical subjects. I am grateful to the current director of the Cullman Center, Jean Strouse, who has followed up on my slow progress after the magical year spent there. Jeremy Treglown, a Cullman Fellow in my year, and his wife, the late Holly Eley, first started me on writing about modern food topics. At the New York Public Library I am especially obliged to Rebecca Federman for showing me the hidden corners of the menu collection and for advice with all aspects of the history of American food.

Yale University afforded me time and resources to undertake research on a subject I was not exactly hired to teach. I am grateful to my colleagues in History and the Yale administration for the benefits of their collegiality.

Bob Weil of Liveright encouraged me to try this project and has been a source of guidance and good-humored support throughout. I have been privileged to work with him and his colleagues at Liveright/Norton, including Maria Guarnaschelli, Will Menaker, and Peter Miller. I benefited greatly from the careful work of Rachelle Mandik, my copyeditor at Norton.

The images in this book were collected by the meticulous, patient, and knowledgeable picture-researcher Brian Meyer. For archival and library research I relied on Spencer Weinreich, a former Yale student now at Oxford University; Alex Serebransky, a Pelham High School student now at Duke University; and James Warlick, a Yale student now a US Marine. Raleigh Cavero, a recent Yale graduate, carefully read the manuscript and found more errors than I believed possible and made many helpful suggestions. Agnieszka Rec, who recently received her PhD in medieval history at Yale, researched and edited several chapters of this book. Ashley Young, a Yale student now studying at Duke University, assisted me with New Orleans culinary history. Liz Williams, director of the Southern Food and Beverage Museum in New Orleans, has been of key importance in my work on New Orleans and Southern food, and the museum she leads is a vital resource for all of American cultural history. Jay Stiefel of Philadelphia introduced me to many people whom I have learned from and has informed me about Philadelphia and nineteenth-century America.

The indefatigable menu collector Henry Voigt of Wilmington, Delaware, generously shared not only his archive but also his extensive knowledge of the historical context of American dining. Andrew Coe and Anne Mendelson helped me with Chinese restaurant information. Professors Frederick Douglass Opie and Harold Forsythe read and gave me valuable comments on the Sylvia's chapter. Richard Gutman and Erin Williams at Johnson & Wales University Library showed me their menu collection and materials recently bequeathed by Chef Roger Fessaguet of Le Pavillon and La Caravelle. Richard Gutman is also the great authority on diners and I benefited from his knowledge more than is apparent from their scant mention in this book. Cara De Silva has found many intriguing articles and pieces of information that she has generously shared with me. Janet Steinmeyer, President of Mitchell College, shared her knowledge of the food business and introduced me to others with experience in the restaurant world.

Many scholars of food, history, and culture have given me the benefit of their research and I would especially like to thank Krishnendu Ray, Frederick Kaufman, and Laura Shapiro, without whose work I would have been unable to think seriously about food in America.

Restaurateurs have been of tremendous importance in my undertaking and completing this project and in telling me about the real world of running a restaurant day after day. I am extremely grateful to Alice Waters of Chez Panisse; Rick Blount and Yvonne Alciatore of Antoine's; Alex von Bidder of the Four Seasons; Lindsey Williams, grandson of Sylvia Woods; and Nick Valenti and Dominick Varacalli, whose long and distinguished restaurant careers included supervising Mamma Leone's.

Cecilia Chiang, owner of the Mandarin, has been an enthusiastic and inspiring supporter of my work since I first interviewed her four years ago.

My wife, Bonnie Roe, read and corrected the manuscript, but much more than that, she has been my affectionate companion and guide during this project and for many years during which we've shared some wonderful meals.

My parents, Alfred and Marcia Freedman, died in 2011 shortly after I started work on this book. I miss them and recall meals we had together when I was growing up in New York City, at home (my mother was an excellent cook) and in favorite restaurants such as Tien Tsin on 125th Street and Amsterdam Avenue and Mon Paris on East Twenty-Ninth Street.

NOTES

TEN RESTAURANTS AND AMERICAN CUISINE

1. A depressingly meticulous account of a Maine lobster festival is provided by David Foster Wallace in "Consider the Lobster," *Gourmet*, August 2004, 50–64. While most of the article deals with the inhumane practice of cooking lobsters while they are still alive, there is also a catalogue of the "irksome little downers" associated with culinary mass spectacles.

2. Alexandre Dumas, *Grand dictionnaire de cuisine* (Paris: Phébus, 2000; originally published 1873), 34. He goes on, however, to repeat the calumny that the Chinese restaurant staples are cats, dogs, and rats.

3. Andrew Haley, *Turning the Tables: Restaurants and the Rise of the American Middle Class, 1880–1920* (Chapel Hill: University of North Carolina Press, 2011), 112–13.

4. Ibid., 101, 111–12.

5. I am grateful to Holly Schaffer of Yale University for her fascinating discussion of shirmal and two other Indian items of Persian origin, described in a paper entitled "Breads and Sweets from Iran to India," presented at a conference on Asian food at the University of Copenhagen, June 2015.

6. Rice-A-Roni, "Our Founding Family," www.ricearoni.com/About/Our_Founding _Family.

7. TV Toy Memories, "Vintage 1962 Rice-A-Roni Commercial," https://www.youtube .com/watch?v=yzOR_Fal_SY.

8. Sidney W. Mintz, *Tasting Food, Tasting Freedom: Excursions into Eating, Culture, and the Past* (Boston: Beacon Press, 1996), 104–5.

9. James W. Parkinson, *American Dishes at the Centennial* (Philadelphia: King & Baird, 1874), 2–17.

10. Charles Ranhofer, *The Epicurean* (New York: Charles Ranhofer, 1893), 1092.

11. Andrew Beahrs, *Twain's Feast: Searching for America's Lost Foods in the Footsteps of Samuel Clemens* (New York: Penguin, 2010). See also Raymond Sokolov, *Fading Feast: A Compendium of Disappearing American Regional Foods* (New York: Farrar, Straus and Giroux, 1981); Jane and Michael Stern, *500 Things to Eat Before It's Too Late and the Very Best Places to Eat Them* (Boston: Houghton Mifflin Harcourt, 2009).

12. Rex Stout, *Too Many Cooks* (New York: Murray Hill Books, 1938).

13. Henri Gault and Christian Millau, "Which Is the World's Greatest Restaurant?" *Holiday*, June 1969, 32–33, 76–79. This will be discussed more fully in the Epilogue, pages 411–13.

14. John F. Mariani, *How Italian Food Conquered the World* (New York: Palgrave Macmillan, 2011).

15. Steven J. R. Ellis, "Eating and Drinking Out," in *A Cultural History of Food in Antiquity*, ed. Paul Erkamp (London: Berg, 2012), 101–8.

16. Peter Scholliers, "Eating Out," in *A Cultural History of Food in the Age of Empire*, ed. Martin Bruegel (London: Berg, 2012), 109.

17. Priscilla Parkhurst Ferguson, "Eating Out, Going Out, Staying In," in *A Cultural History of Food in the Modern Ages*, ed. Amy Bentley (London: Berg, 2012), 112.

18. Ellis, "Eating and Drinking Out," 108–12.

19. Michael Freeman, "Sung," in *Food in Chinese Culture: Anthropological and Historical Perspectives*, ed. K. C. Chang (New Haven: Yale University Press, 1977), 158; Andrew Coe, *Chop Suey: A Cultural History of Food in the United States* (Oxford: Oxford University Press, 2009), 224–40.

20. Rebecca L. Spang, *The Invention of the Restaurant: Paris and Modern Gastronomic Culture* (Cambridge, MA: Harvard University Press, 2000).

21. See Rachel Eden Black, "Dining Out: Bourgeois Anxiety in Nineteenth-Century Paris," MA thesis, History, University of British Columbia (1999).

22. Spang, *Invention of the Restaurant*, 174; Edward Planta, *A New Picture of Paris or the Stranger's Guide to the French Metropolis . . .* (London: Leigh, 1837), 100–106

23. Ralph Rylance, *The Epicure's Almanack: Eating and Drinking in Regency London: The Original 1815 Guidebook* (London: British Library, 2012).

24. Colleen Taylor Sen, *Curry, A Global History* (London: Reaktion, 2009), 38; Ruth Cowan, *Relish: The Extraordinary Life of Alexis Soyer, Victorian Celebrity Chef* (London: Weidenfeld and Nicholson, 2006); Ruth Brandon, *The People's Chef: The Culinary Revolution of Alexis Soyer* (New York: Walker, 2005).

25. William Grimes, *Appetite City: A Culinary History of New York* (New York: North Point Press, 2009), 4.

26. Ibid., 5–8, 12–13.

27. Ibid., 9–11.

28. Lately Thomas, *Delmonico's: A Century of Splendor* (Boston: Houghton Mifflin, 1967), 8–18.

1. Cindy R. Lobel, *Urban Appetites: Food and Culture in Nineteenth-Century New York* (Chicago: University of Chicago Press, 2014), 106.

2. Michael Batterberry and Ariane Batterberry, *On the Town in New York: The Landmark History of Eating, Drinking and Entertainments from the American Revolution to the Food Revolution* (New York and London: Routledge, 1999), 46–47.

3. Edward Henry Durell, writing under the pseudonym H. Didimus, *New Orleans as I Found It* (New York: Harper and Brothers, 1845), 21.

4. Menu in the Library of the Museum of the City of New York, reproduced in the front matter [i–xii] of Lately Thomas, *Delmonico's: A Century of Splendor* (Boston: Houghton Mifflin, 1967).

5. Robert Shaplan, "Delmonico: The Rich New Gravy Faith" (part one of a two-part article), *The New Yorker*, November 10, 1956, 202.

6. New York Public Library, Manuscripts, Samuel Ward Papers, Box 5, "History of Delmonico's," typescript copy (early twentieth century) made by J. T., 1. On Ward, see Kathryn Allamong Jacob, *King of the Lobby: The Life and Times of Sam Ward, Man-About Washington in the Gilded Age* (Baltimore: Johns Hopkins University Press, 2010).

7. See especially Mark McWilliams, "Distant Tables: Food and the Novel in Early America," *Early American Literature* 38 (2003): 365–93.

8. Waverley Root and Richard de Rochemont, *Eating in America: A History* (Hopewell, NJ: The Ecco Press 1995), 113; Harvey Levenstein, *Revolution at the Table: The Transformation of the American Diet* (Berkeley and Los Angeles: University of California Press, 2003), 11; John Mariani, *America Eats Out* (New York: William Morrow and Company, 1991), 37.

9. Shaplan, "Delmonico," part 1, 189.

10. *Pall Mall Gazette* 41, no. 6236 (March 7, 1885): 3. I am grateful to Mr. William Helfand for this citation.

11. Marie Kimball, *Thomas Jefferson's Cookbook* (Charlottesville: University of Virginia Press, 1976), vii; Corby Kummer, "Pasta," *Atlantic Monthly*, July 1986, theatlantic.com/magazine/archive/1986/07/306226/, accessed September 28, 2015.

12. "A Salon of Saracenic Splendor," taken from the title of the second part of Shaplan's article on Delmonico's in *The New Yorker* for November 17, 1956, 105–37.

13. Anthony Trollope, *North America* (Philadelphia: Lippincott, 1862), chapter 13, 334–35. Terrapin was also associated with Philadelphia as, for example, by Colonel John W. Forney, who wrote in *The Epicure* in 1879 that while Baltimore, Washington, and New York take pleasure in terrapin, only in Philadelphia is it a crime not to have a passionate attachment to the turtles. See Susan Williams, *Food in the United States*, ca. 1820–1890 (Westport, CT Greenwood, 2006), 119–20. But this is more a question of taste and styles of preparation than habitat. See also Andrew Beahrs, *Twain's Feast: Searching for America's Lost Foods in the Footsteps of Samuel Clemens* (New York: Penguin, 2010), 148–82, especially 161.

14. Thomas, *Delmonico's: A Century of Splendor*, 65–66.

15. Edith Wharton, *The Age of Innocence* (New York: D. Appleton & Co., 1920), chapters 5 and 33.

16. Cited in Mark McWilliams, *Food and the Novel in Nineteenth-Century America* (Lanham, MD: Rowman & Littlefield, 2012), 113, 125.

17. Thomas, *Delmonico's: A Century of Splendor*, 3–28.

18. Ibid., 29–53.

19. Leopold Rimmer, *A History of Old New York Life and the House of the Delmonico's* (New York: n.p., 1898), 13–14.

20. Thomas, *Delmonico's: A Century of Splendor*, 220–22. The 1873 menu is in the Henry Voigt Collection of American Menus, Wilmington, Delaware, and posted on Mr. Voigt's blog, *The American Menu*, on February 26, 2014, www.theamericanmenu .com/2014/02/life-times-of-antonio-sivori-part-ii.html#more, accessed July 17, 2015.

21. Shaplan, "Delmonico," part 1, 201–2.

22. Thomas, *Delmonico's: A Century of Splendor*, 64–65.

23. Thomas, *Delmonico's: A Century of Splendor*, 65–72; Shaplan, "Delmonico," part 1, 204–5.

24. Ward, "History of Delmonico's," 5–7.

25. Thomas, *Delmonico's: A Century of Splendor*, 93–97.

26. Janet Clarkson, *Menus from History: Historic Meals and Recipes for Every Day of the Year*, vol. 2 (Santa Barbara: Greenwood, 2009), 675–77.

27. Thomas, *Delmonico's: A Century of Splendor*, 120.

28. See Ward McAllister, *Society as I Have Found It* (New York: Cassell, 1890).

29. Thomas, *Delmonico's: A Century of Splendor*, 161.

30. William Grimes, *Appetite City: A Culinary History of New York* (New York: North Point Press, 2009), 106–8; Thomas, *Delmonico's: A Century of Splendor*, 156–63

31. Richard L. Bushman, *The Refinement of America: Persons, Houses, Cities* (New York: Knopf, 1992), 358–59.

32. Jerome Mushkat, "Delmonico, Lorenzo," *American National Biography*, vol. 6 (New York: Oxford University Press, 2000), 396–97.

33. Thomas, *Delmonico's: A Century of Splendor*, 170–73.

34. Charles Ranhofer, *The Epicurean* (New York: Charles Ranhofer, 1893).

35. Grimes, *Appetite City*, 57–58.

36. Alexander Filippini, *The Table: How to Buy Food, How to Cook It and How to Serve It* (New York: Charles L. Webster & Co., 1889).

37. Ranhofer, *The Epicurean*, 392–98.

38. Ranhofer, *The Epicurean*, 420–25. An excellent, exhaustively detailed description of cooking terrapins is provided by Becky Libourel Diamond, in *The Thousand Dollar Dinner: America's First Great Cookery Challenge* (Yardley: PA: Westholme, 2015), 115–19.

39. Quoted in Henry Voigt's blog, *The American Menu*, May 25, 2014, www .theamericanmenu.com/2014/05/a-wonderful-machine.html, accessed July 10, 2014.

40. Ranhofer, *The Epicurean*, 256–57; Jeremiah Tower, *California Dish: What I Saw (and Cooked) at the American Culinary Revolution* (New York: Simon & Schuster, 2003), 107; Joyce Goldstein, *Inside the California Food Revolution: Thirty Years That Changed Our Culinary Consciousness* (Berkeley and Los Angeles: University of California Press, 2013), 137.

41. Filippini, *The Table*, 414, 417.

42. Actually he first called it "Baked Florida-Alaska" because of its being both warm and cold. See Judith Choate and James Canora, *Dining at Delmonico's: The Story of America's Oldest Restaurant* (New York: Stewart, Tabori and Chang, 2008), 200.

43. Rimmer, *History of Old New York Life*, 24–25.

44. Thomas, *Delmonico's: A Century of Splendor*, 234–36.

45. Michael Lesy and Lisa Stoffer, *Repast: Dining Out at the Dawn of the New American Century, 1900–1910* (New York: W. W. Norton, 2013), 181–82.

46. Grimes, *Appetite City*, 147–49.

47. Caleb Carr, *The Alienist* (New York: Random House, 1994), 119–34. The meal is based on one of Ranhofer's menus, *The Epicurean*, 1137. "Sorbet Elsinore," whatever that was, appears on this menu but not in the cookbook.

48. On Rector's and its menus, see Henry Voigt's blog, *The American Menu*, August 22, 2015, www.theamericanmenu.com/2015/08/rectors.html, accessed August 29, 2015.

49. H. Barbara Wenberg et al., *American Impressionism and Realism: The Painting of Modern Life, 1885–1915* (New York: Metropolitan Museum of Art, 1994), 220–22.

50. Menu in Grimes, *Appetite City*, 135, and a 1900 menu in the New York Public Library, Rare Books Division, Buttolph Collection.

51. New York Public Library, Buttolph Collection, menu from April 18, 1899. Handwritten at bottom, "Delmonico's, Beaver Street."

52. Thomas, *Delmonico's: A Century of Splendor*, 326–27.

53. A menu from October 25, 1917, in the New York Public Library, Buttolph Collection. Terrapin Maryland, Salmi of Plover, and other elegant dishes were available to order.

54. Quoted by Mariani, *America Eats Out*, 59.

55. New York Public Library, Buttolph Collection and in the Henry Voigt Collection. Posted on "The American Menu," www.theamericanmenu.com/2015/06/west-meets-east.html#more, accessed July 15, 2015.

56. For this I'm very grateful to David Cecelski, an expert on the people and food of the "Downeast" section of the North Carolina coast.

57. Owen Wister, *The Virginian: A Horseman of the Plains* (New York: Macmillan, 1919; originally published 1904), 123 (chapter 13).

58. Paul Freedman, "American Restaurants and Cuisine in the Mid-Nineteenth Century," *New England Quarterly* 84 (2011), 12–15.

59. Ibid., 22.

60. Harvard University, Radcliffe Institute for Advanced Study, Schlesinger Library, Menus, Box 1, menu from December 19, 1844. Two Tremont menus from 1847 are in the Library of Congress, one is reproduced in Mariani, *America Eats Out*, 28.

61. James W. Parkinson, *American Dishes at the Centennial* (Philadelphia: King & Baird, 1874), 26–32. These pages reprint a reminiscence by one of the New Yorkers who attended the dinner, Mr. R. B. Valentine, in the *Philadelphia Press* newspaper, published September 4, 1874. The meal is lovingly described in Diamond, *The Thousand Dollar Dinner*.

ANTOINE'S

1. I am greatly indebted to Rick Blount, owner of Antoine's; his mother, Mme. Yvonne Alciatore; and his cousin Roy F. Guste Jr. for giving me access to materials related to the history of Antoine's, for their recollections, and for their many kindnesses to me. My former Yale student Ashley Young (now a graduate student at Duke) and Liz Williams, director of the Southern Food and Beverage Museum in New Orleans, helped me greatly with information on Antoine's and its historical context.

2. New Orleans, Historic New Orleans Collection, Williams Library, MS 632, Erin Greenwald, "Antoine's Restaurant History," Working Files, Folder 17, genealogy of the Alciatore family. I express my gratitude to Erin Greenwald for letting me see these files and showing me so much about the history of Antoine's.

3. From a booklet commemorating the restaurant's centennial, *Souvenir du restaurant Antoine*, ca. 1940, 5, copies at Tulane University, Howard Tilton Memorial Library, Special Collections, Louisiana Research Collection, and in books and ephemera assembled at Antoine's Restaurant. The collection at Antoine's also includes menus that allow one to follow the changes and continuities in what has been served there.

4. Meigs O. Frost, "Gourmet's Shrine," *New Orleans Times-Picayune*, April 3, 1940, 15 of a 16-page special section commemorating the hundredth anniversary of Antoine's; Clem Hearsey, column from October 8, 1911, reprinted in this same commemorative newspaper section, 5.

5. Harnett T. Kane, *Queen New Orleans: City by the River* (New York: William Morrow and Company, 1949), 325.

6. Frost, "Gourmet's Shrine," 2; menus from 1885, 1887, 1890, 1891, and 1892 owned by Antoine's.

7. Roy F. Guste Jr., *Antoine's Restaurant Since 1840 Cookbook* (New York: W. W. Norton, 1980), 35, 126.

8. Both menus are in the Antoine's collection. By 1961, the author of a Brennan's cookbook gingerly mentioned Creole food as really a form of French provincial cuisine, there being no such thing as a definitive French cuisine, Hermann B. Deutsch, *Brennan's New Orleans Cookbook* (New Orleans: Crager, 1961), 39–40.

9. Kane, *Queen New Orleans*, 127–43.

10. Frost, "Gourmet's Shrine," 2.

11. J. H. Ingraham, *The South-West, by a Yankee*, vol. 1 (New York: Harper and Brothers, 1835), 118–19.

12. On roux, see Tom Fitzmorris, *Hungry Town: A Culinary History of New Orleans, the City Where Food Is Almost Everything* (New York: Stewart, Tabori and Chang, 2010), 80–81. Before the twentieth century, roux was not as dominant. Early recipes for gumbo, for example, don't always start with making a roux.

13. Elizabeth Williams, *New Orleans: A Food Biography* (Lanham, MD: Rowman & Littlefield, 2013), 139; C. C. Robin, *Voyages to Louisiana 1803–1805*, trans. Stuart O. Landry Jr. (New Orleans: Pelican Publishing Company, 1966), 155.

14. Pierre Clément de Laussat, *Memoirs of My Life to My Son During the Years 1803 and After, Which I Spent in the Public Service in Louisiana as Commissioner of the French Government for the Retrocession to France of that Colony and its Transfer to the United*

States, trans. Agnes-Josephine Pastwa (Baton Rouge: Louisiana State University Press, 1978), 86.

15. The bar is described, rather contemptuously, by the journalist A. Oakley Hall, *The Manhattaner in New Orleans, or Phases of Crescent-City Life* (New York: J. S. Redfeld, 1851), 10. The typical fare of the dining room is presented in Robert C. Reinders, *End of an Era: New Orleans 1850–1860* (New Orleans: Pelican Publishing Company, 1964), 152.

16. It retains this meaning in the *Larousse Gastronomique*.

17. John Greaves Nall, *Great Yarmouth and Lowestoft: A Handbook for Visitors and Residents* (London: Longmans, Green, Reader and Dyer, 1866), 376.

18. New York Public Library, Rare Books, Menus from the Fifth Avenue Hotel and from the Revere House Hotel (Boston); from the Windsor Hotel, Jacksonville (Digital Gallery ID 40000000254). Charles Ranhofer, *The Epicurean* (New York: Charles Ranhofer, 1893), 889.

19. *Historical Sketch Book and Guide to New Orleans and Environs* (New York: W. H. Coleman, 1985), 91.

20. On tourism and the vicissitudes of the French Quarter, see Anthony J. Stanonis, *Creating the Big Easy: New Orleans and the Emergence of Modern Tourism, 1918–1945* (Athens, GA: University of Georgia Press, 2006), especially 141–69.

21. *The Picayune's Creole Cook Book*, 2nd ed. (New Orleans: The Picayune, 1901; repr. New York, 1971), 5–6. In its fifth edition the title was slightly adjusted to the name it is generally known under, *The Picayune Creole Cookbook*. On the history of this cookbook and the changes in its racial mise-en-scène, see Rien Fertel, "'Everyone Seemed Willing to Help': *The Picayune Creole Cookbook* as Battleground, 1900–2008," in *The Larder: Food Studies Methods from the American South*, ed. John T. Edge et al. (Athens, GA: University of Georgia Press, 2013), 10–31.

22. As noted by Theresa McCulla, "Representing Modern New Orleans: Food and the Evolution of the Multiethnic City," (PhD dissertation, in progress, Harvard University), citing a 1951 publication.

23. From "Cook Who Is Known for 'Dream Melon' to Teach Creole Cuisine," *Times-Picayune*, May 15, 1938, also pointed out to me by Theresa McCulla.

24. Nathaniel Burton and Rudy Lombard, *Creole Feast: Fifteen Master Chefs of New Orleans Reveal Their Secrets* (New York: Random House, 1978), especially the introductory pages xviii–xx. See also Carol Allen, *Leah Chase: Listen, I Say Like This* (Gretna, LA: Pelican Publishing Company 2002); Austin Leslie and Marie Rudd Posey, *Austin Leslie's Creole Soul: New Orleans Cooking with a Soulful Twist* (New Orleans: De Simonin Publications, 2000).

25. Greenwald, "Antoine's Restaurant History," folder 17, which includes a carefully researched family genealogy; Guste, *Antoine's Restaurant*, 9–12.

26. On the history of Mme. Bégué's, see Poppy Tooker's introduction to *Mme. Bégué's Recipes of Old New Orleans Creole Cookery* (Gretna, LA: Pelican Publishing Company, 2012), 18–28.

27. "Bohemian" is an important term in the history of American restaurants from about 1880 to 1920. It denotes unconventional urban people of artistic temperament,

though not necessarily artists. Bohemians patronized new sorts of restaurants, such as Italian and Chinese places. They are discussed more fully in the chapter devoted to Mamma Leone's.

28. Historical New Orleans Collection, a menu dated April 2, 1958.

29. Menus for Grunewald's and Fabacher's in the Historical New Orleans Collection. A copy of the Grunewald booklet, entitled *Recipes of Famous Creole Dishes Served at the Dinner Tendered to Hon. Wm. A. Rodenberg and the House Committee on Industrial Arts and Expositions* (New Orleans: Grunewald Hotel, 1911) is in the Historical Library of the Louisiana State Museum in New Orleans.

30. Frost, "Gourmet's Shrine," 15.

31. From a booklet entitled "Antoine's Restaurant Since 1840," dating from between 1923 and 1934 (Roy Alciatore is stated as being the proprietor, but Jules is still alive and involved in the restaurant's management), 6.

32. The system still exists, although not with its former marks of exclusivity. Mary Lee Burke, "Who's Your Waiter?" *New Orleans* (August 1969), 14–17, gives an account of how this used to work.

33. Clementine Paddleford, *Recipes from Antoine's Kitchen*, a booklet made from an article originally appearing in the syndicated Sunday supplement "This Week" (New York, 1948), 20–21. A better approximation is given in Fitzmorris, *Hungry Town*, 87–88.

34. Guste, *Antoine's Restaurant Cookbook*, 32.

35. From the Henry Voigt Collection of American Menus, Wilmington, DE.

36. New York Academy of Medicine, Rare Books Library, Margaret B. Wilson Menu Collection.

37. A menu reprinted in Guste, *Antoine's Restaurant Cookbook*, 17–19, has the same violinist "Allons Chez Antoine" cover as that of the 1920s but must be from just after 1934 because Roy Alciatore is listed as the proprietor, Jules died in 1934, and the prices are nearly the same as those in a similar menu in the Antoine's collection still listing Jules as proprietor. These menus have dispensed with the roast fowl, but added salads.

38. Described by Henry Litchfield West, "Breakfast at Antoine's," *Wine and Food*, Autumn 1939, 236–42, a fervid homage to the restaurant's bouillabaisse. There is a recipe for "Bouillabaisse, Antoine's Recipe" in the WPA Guide, *New Orleans City Guide* (Boston: Houghton Mifflin, 1938), 165–66.

39. Antoine's advertisement in the *New Orleans Times-Picayune*, January 25, 1937.

40. His collection of menus is in the restaurant's library/archive.

41. This was emphasized by his daughter, Yvonne Alciatore, in a conversation with me, March 13, 2013.

42. Frances Parkinson Keyes, *Dinner at Antoine's* (New York: Julian Messner, 1948).

43. Menu at Antoine's.

44. Greenwald, "Antoine's Restaurant History," Folder 19.

45. The room couldn't just have been renamed ("Victory Room," for example), because its elaborate décor was obviously Japanese.

46. *New Orleans: Its Unique Viands. Where to Get Them. A Word of Advice to the Passenger Man* (New Orleans?: n.p., dated October 13–14, 1903), 2. A copy of this booklet is in

Tulane University, Howard Tilton Memorial Library, Special Collections, Louisiana Research Collection.

47. A guidebook entitled simply *New Orleans* (New Orleans?: n.p., ca. 1919). A copy in Yale University, Sterling Memorial Library, has the call number Egk40 N4.

48. Cited in Frost, "Gourmet's Shrine," 15.

49. Lucius Beebe, "The Miracle at Antoine's," *Holiday* (January, 1953), 57–59.

50. A menu from the early 1940s (judging by prices) in the collection at Antoine's; the 1980 menu from Guste, *Antoine's Restaurant Cookbook*, 20–22. The earlier (ca. 1910–1940) menu is in the same book, 17–19, and there are also several copies at Antoine's itself.

51. A point made in an account of Etienne's Cuisine Français in Peggy Scott Laborde and Tom Fitzmorris, *Lost Restaurants of New Orleans and the Recipes that Made Them Famous* (Gretna, LA: Pelican Publishing Company, 2012), 104–6.

52. Fitzmorris, *Hungry Town*, 119–210.

53. Ibid., 44–54.

54. Ibid., 135–36.

55. Ibid., 210–11.

SCHRAFFT'S

1. See Andrew Haley, *Turning the Tables: Restaurants and the Rise of the American Middle Class, 1880–1920* (Chapel Hill: University of North Carolina Press, 2011) and, for a geographically focused example, Jessica Ellen Sewell, *Women and the Everyday City: Public Space in San Francisco, 1890–1915* (Minneapolis: University of Minnesota Press, 2011), 67–94.

2. Shattuck is quoted in a profile by Oliver H. Garrett, "Without Benefit of Tin Foil," which appeared in *The New Yorker*, May 19, 1928, 31.

3. "Overheard at Schrafft's," *The New Yorker*, January 28, 1950, 19.

4. "Overheard at Schrafft's," *The New Yorker*, January 26, 1946, 19.

5. William Grimes, *Appetite City: A Culinary History of New York* (New York: North Point Press, 2009), 216.

6. I have discussed the ways in which restaurants did and did not accommodate female customers, Paul Freedman, "Women and Restaurants in the Nineteenth-Century United States," *Journal of Social History* 48 (2014), 1–19.

7. Martha Ann Peters, "The St. Charles Hotel: New Orleans Social Center," *Louisiana History* 1 (1960), 206–7.

8. Junius Browne, *The Great Metropolis: A Mirror of New York* (Hartford: American Publishing Company, 1869), 265–66.

9. Cindy R. Lobel, *Urban Appetites: Food and Culture in Nineteenth-Century New York* (Chicago: University of Chicago Press, 2014), 126.

10. *The Albion*, September 28, 1833. I am grateful to Jan Whitaker, author of the matchless blog *Restaurant-ing Through History*, for showing this to me.

11. George G. Foster, *New York by Gas-Light and Other Urban Sketches*, ed. Stuart M. Blumin (Berkeley: University of California Press, 1990), 73.

12. George Ellington (pseudonym), *The Women of New York or Social Life in the Great City* (New York: The New York Book Company, 1870), 272–77. Later, toward the end of the century, fancy brothels provided refined meals. The Henry Voigt Collection of American Menus (Wilmington, DE) includes an elaborate menu of the 1890s from the notorious "Palette Hotel" on West Fifty-Second Street in New York. Described in a posting for January 1, 2013, on Mr. Voigt's blog, *The American Menu*, www.theamericanmenu .com/2013/01/dining-at-love-hotel-in-gilded-age.html#more, accessed July 17, 2015.

13. Joe O'Connell, "History of Delmonico's Restaurant and Business Operations in New York," posted 2001 at www.steakperfection.com/delmonico/History.html, accessed May 2013; Lately Thomas, *Delmonico's: A Century of Splendor* (Boston: Houghton Mifflin, 1967), 121, 131–32; Grimes, *Appetite City*, 104.

14. On the dinner and its exclusion of women see "Mrs. Croly," *Sorosis: Its Origins and History* (New York: J. J. Little, 1886), 5–15; Thomas, *Delmonico's*, 104–18, 138–40.

15. *Harper's Weekly*, December 5, 1891, 982.

16. Examples from Michael Lesy and Lisa Stoffer, *Repast: Dining Out at the Dawn of the New American Century* (New York: W. W. Norton, 2013), 127–29.

17. Haley, *Turning the Tables*, 159–61.

18. The first menu is from the University of Houston, Conrad N. Hilton College of Hotel and Restaurant Management, Hospitality Industry Archives (Digital Menu Collection, no. 201007_091). The second is in the American Antiquarian Society collection in Worcester, MA (digitally available through American Broadsides and Ephemera, no. 16827).

19. Lobel, *Urban Appetites*, 126–27.

20. Quoted in Grimes, *Appetite City*, 210.

21. George G. Foster, *New York in Slices, by an Experienced Carver: Being the Original Slices Published in the N.Y. Tribune* (New York: W. F. Burgess, 1849), 72, refers to the ice-cream saloons on Broadway that served women on their way home from Stewart's. On department-store restaurants, see Jan Whitaker, *Service and Style: How the American Department Store Fashioned the Middle Class* (New York: Macmillan, 2006), 225–31.

22. Michael Batterberry and Ariane Batterberry, *On the Town in New York: The Landmark History of Eating, Drinking, and Entertainments from the American Revolution to the Food Revolution* (New York and London: Routledge, 1999), 92.

23. Foster, *New York by Gas-Light*, 72.

24. Lobel, *Urban Appetites*, 128.

25. In the Henry Voigt Collection there are two such menus, datable to 1861–62, that seem to have been in use for some time as a few advertisements have been cut out and replaced.

26. Garrett, "Without Benefit of Tinfoil," 29–30.

27. Jan Whitaker, "When Ladies Lunched: Schrafft's," *Restaurant-ing Through History* (blog), August 27, 2008,restaurant-ingthroughhistory.com/2008/08/27/when-ladies -lunched-schrafft%E2%80%99s/, accessed July 18, 2015.

28. Article in *Drug Store Merchandising* 9, no. 12 (1921), 26.

29. Whitaker, "When Ladies Lunched"; Jane Kanel Slomanson, *When Everybody Ate at*

Schrafft's: Memories, Pictures and Recipes from a Very Special Restaurant Empire (Fort Lee: Barricade Books, NJ, 2006), 8–11.

30. Slomanson, *When Everybody Ate at Schrafft's*, 8.

31. Ibid., 19.

32. Ibid., 161–69; Christopher Gray, "Streetscapes: Schrafft's. Midday Haven, Lost to a Faster-Paced City," *New York Times*, June 29, 2008.

33. On Childs, see Lesy and Stoffer, *Repast*, 84–91; Grimes, *Appetite City*, 183–86.

34. Quoted in Lesy and Stoffer, *Repast*, 91.

35. George Chauncey, *Gay New York: Gender, Urban Culture and the Making of the Gay Male World, 1890–1940* (New York: Basic Books, 1994), 164–66.

36. I am grateful to Laura Shapiro for this information, which comes from letters in the Library of Congress.

37. "Overheard at Schrafft's," *The New Yorker*, September 24, 1966, 55.

38. On men's versus women's preferences, see Jessamyn Neuhaus, *Manly Meals and Mom's Home Cooking: Cookbooks and Gender in Modern America* (Baltimore: Johns Hopkins University Press, 2003); Sherrie A. Inness, *Dinner Roles: American Women and Culinary Culture* (Iowa City: University of Iowa Press, 2001), 17–36.

39. Henry Voigt Collection of American Menus, Wilmington, DE, one menu dated September 10, 1919, the other February 27, 1920.

40. Both screenplays were written by Nora Ephron, a connoisseur of, among other things, food-related social comedy.

41. J. C. Croly, *Jennie June's American Cookery Book* (New York: American News Company, 1866), 306.

42. Mary F. Henderson, *Practical Cooking and Dinner Giving* (New York: Harper and Brothers, 1878), 36–39.

43. Tom Wolfe, "Honks and Wonks," in *Mauve Gloves and Madmen, Clutter and Vine and Other Stories, Sketches and Essays* (New York: Macmillan, 1976), 226–27. The essay is about class and accents in New York.

44. "Overheard at Schrafft's," *The New Yorker*, November 18, 1933, 19.

45. New-York Historical Society (NYHS), Menus S38.6.2, from January 21, 1932, at the West Fifty-Seventh Street branch includes corned-beef hash with homemade chili sauce.

46. From the same January 21, 1932, menu as above, a NYHS Menu S92.2.19, dated October 29, 1936, from 13 East Forty-Second Street, and the February 27, 1920, menu in the Voigt Collection (no location mentioned).

47. Henry Voigt Collection (February 27, 1920); NYHS, menus S 38.6.2 (January 21, 1932); S133.4.12 (August 4, 1952); S136.6.2 (late 1956; before Halloween); S136.6.3 (November 1959).

48. NYHS S136.6.2 (late 1956).

49. NYHS, S38.6.2 (January 21, 1932); S95.2.19 (October 29, 1935).

50. Avocado and orange: NYHS, S88.2.7 (June 21, 1932); Orange and grapefruit: S60.1.5 (undated—1920s?) and a Voigt menu dated May 10, 1931 for the branch at 141 W. Forty-Second Street. The Voigt menus from 1919–1920 include a stuffed banana salad (1919) and a banana nut salad (1920).

51. Slomanson, *When Everybody Ate at Schrafft's*, 71, 171. I have not been able to find a video of either commercial on the Internet.
52. Whitaker, "When Ladies Lunched."
53. Slomanson, *When Everybody Ate at Schrafft's*, 170.
54. Joan Fisher, conversation with me, August 24, 2015.

HOWARD JOHNSON'S

1. Anthony Mitchell Sammarco, *A History of Howard Johnson's: How a Massachusetts Soda Fountain Became an American Icon* (Charleston: The History Press, 2013), 90. A history of Howard Johnson's and its cultural context is given by Warren J. Belasco, "Toward a Culinary Common Denominator: The Rise of Howard Johnson's, 1925–1949," *Journal of American Culture* 2 (1979), 502–18.
2. Brian Miller, "Howard Deering Johnson: The Man Under the Orange Roof," *Journal of Hospitality and Tourism Education* 17, issue 4 (2006), 8.
3. Victor Nelson, introduction to a panel discussion "Howard Johnson Merchandising 'Tools,'" in *Howard Johnson's Second Annual Agents' Seminar at Cornell University, Ithaca, New York* (bound typescript, 1958), 3. Copy in Cornell University Library. Mr. Nelson was vice president and general manager of the company.
4. Max Apple, "The Oranging of America," in Apple, *The Oranging of America and Other Stories* (New York: Grossman Publishers, 1976), 1–19.
5. *The Story of Howard Johnson's*, a 1938 pamphlet published by the company, reproduced by the Milton (Massachusetts) Historical Society, www.miltonhistoricalsociety.org/Sampler/HowardJohnson.html, accessed December 21, 2014.
6. Sammarco, *History of Howard Johnson's*, 25–28
7. *The Story of Howard Johnson's*.
8. Sammarco, *History of Howard Johnson's*, 43–47.
9. *The Story of Howard Johnson's*.
10. Bruce Kraig, "Duncan Hines," in *The Oxford Encyclopedia of Food and Drink in America*, ed. Andrew F. Smith (Oxford: Oxford University Press, 2004), vol. 1, 613–14. On Duncan Hines's life and career, Louis Hatchett, *Duncan Hines: How a Traveling Salesman Became the Most Trusted Name in Food* (Lexington KY: University of Kentucky Press, 2014).
11. Harvey Levenstein, *Paradox of Plenty: A Social History of Eating in Modern America*, 2nd ed. (Berkeley: University of California Press, 2003), 48. DeVoto's wife, Avis, was a cookbook editor and a close friend and mentor of Julia Child.
12. Ilya Ilf and Eugene Petrov, *Little Golden America: Two Famous Soviet Humorists Survey These United States*, trans. Charles Malamuth (New York and Toronto: Farrar & Rinehart, 1937). See Jan Whittaker, "Restaurant-ing With Soviet Humorists," *Restaurant-ing Through History* (blog), May 5, 2013, restaurant-ingthroughhistory.com/2015/05/13/restaurant-ing-with-soviet-humorists/, accessed June 10, 2015.
13. The definitive history of the diner is by Richard J. S. Gutman, *American Diner Then and Now* (Baltimore: Johns Hopkins University Press, 2000).
14. Gutman, *American Diner*, 58.

15. Levenstein, *Paradox of Plenty*, 48.
16. Belasco, "Toward a Culinary Common Denominator," 504.
17. Sammarco, *History of Howard Johnson's*, 50–53.
18. Ibid., 53.
19. Paul Broten, "Pay Off Equipment with a Payroll Dollar," in *Howard Johnson's First Annual Management Seminar, School of Hotel Administration, Cornell University, Ithaca, New York* (bound typescript, 1957), part 4, 12. Copy at Cornell University. Broten was a Professor of Hotel Engineering at Cornell's School of Hotel Administration.
20. Nelson, introduction to "Howard Johnson Merchandising 'Tools,'" 12–13.
21. Broten, "Pay Off Equipment with a Payroll Dollar," part 1, 1–26.
22. Sammarco, *History of Howard Johnson's*, 70–72.
23. Ibid., 72–82.
24. Philip Langdon, *Orange Roofs, Golden Arches: The Architecture of American Chain Restaurants* (New York: Knopf, 1986), 47–51.
25. Charles Alexander, "Mr. Johnson in Your Town," in *Howard Johnson's First Annual Management Seminar,* part 1, 4. Alexander was Franchise Manager for Howard Johnson's and he says here that many branches closed during the war unnecessarily, "through sheer funk" and "disloyalty" to the company.
26. Sammarco, *History of Howard Johnson's*, 54–57.
27. Langdon, *Orange Roofs, Golden Arches*, 53–54.
28. See "HoJo's Lost Mojo," Web Urbanist, December 29, 2013, weburbanist.com/2013/12/29/hojos-lost-mojo-10-abandoned-howard-johnsons, accessed December 23, 2014.
29. Miller, "Howard Deering Johnson: The Man Under the Orange Roof," 5–8.
30. Adam Gopnik, *The Table Comes First: Family, France and the Meaning of Food* (New York: Random House, 2011), 16.
31. "Howard Johnson's," Roadside Fans website, www.roadsidefans.com/features/howard-johnsons, accessed December 23, 2014.
32. C. K. Dwinell, General Manager of the Motor Lodge Division, remarks at a 1957 panel discussion in *Howard Johnson's First Annual Management Seminar*, part 8, 16–17.
33. Theresa Howard, "Howard Johnson," *Nation's Restaurant News* 85 (1996).
34. Ibid.
35. "Howard Johnson International," Reference for Business, www.referenceforbusiness.com/history/He-Ja/Howard-Johnson-International-Inc.html, accessed December 23, 2014.
36. Sammarco, *History of Howard Johnson's*, 90.
37. Pierre Franey, *A Chef's Tale: A Memoir of Food, France and America at Table* (New York: Knopf, 1994), 117–19; Jacques Pépin, *The Apprentice: My Life in the Kitchen* (Boston: Houghton Mifflin:, 2003), 144–45.
38. Pépin, *The Apprentice*, 162–63, 210–11.
39. Sammarco, *History of Howard Johnson's*, 91.
40. Roadside Fans website.
41. *From Maine to Florida with Howard Johnson's* (n.p., 1939).
42. Belasco, "Toward a Culinary Common Denominator," 514.

43. Sammarco, *History of Howard Johnson's*, 63–65, 134–36.

44. New York Public Library, Rare Books, Buttolph Menu Collection. A similar menu in terms of list and prices is at coolculinaria.com/products/howard-johnsons-new -england-1940s-1950s, accessed December 24, 2014. It probably dates from around 1938 or 1939. Eighty branches of Howard Johnson's from Maine to New York are listed on the menu.

45. Recipe in Sammarco, *History of Howard Johnson's*, 96–97.

46. From the Henry Voigt Collection of American Menus, Wilmington, DE.

47. Three menus, one dated 1950 (www.mhodistributors.com/hojo-orange-b, accessed December 24, 2014), and two others that must come from the late 1940s, judging from the prices, one in the author's possession, the other at 1.np.blogspot.com/ _FfgGLTCpfMQ/SqgZ9kowzgI/AAAAAA, accessed December 24, 2014.

48. Two menus, 1962 and (probably) 1963, at www.mhodistributors.com/hojo-3 and www.mhodistributors.com/hojo-4, accessed December 22, 2014.

49. John Sherry, "Legal Aspects of the Restaurant Business," in *Howard Johnson's First Annual Management Seminar*, part 2, 9–10.

50. "Students Picket Howard Johnson's to Protest Discrimination in South," *Harvard Crimson*, October 8, 1962.

51. "And Justice for All" website of Durham County Library, andjusticeforall.dconc.gov/ gallery_images/civil-rights-demonstrations, accessed December 24, 2014.

52. Benjamin Houston, *The Nashville Way: Racial Etiquette and the Struggle for Social Justice in a Southern City* (Athens, GA: University of Georgia Press, 2012), 191; *The New Georgia Encyclopedia*, "Lester Maddox."

53. John F. Love, *McDonald's: Behind the Arches* (Toronto: Bantam Books, 1986), 117.

54. Sammarco, *History of Howard Johnson's*, 90

55. Ibid., 138.

56. Belasco, "Toward a Culinary Common Denominator," 513–14. On Chipotle, Sarah Nassauer, "What's Made from Scratch?" *Wall Street Journal*, February 25, 2015, D1–D2.

57. What follows is based on Sammarco, *History of Howard Johnson's*, 140–46, and Miller, "Howard Deering Johnson," 8.

58. Josh Ozersky, *Colonel Sanders and the American Dream* (Austin: University of Texas Press, 2012).

59. Ray Kroc, *Grinding it Out: The Making of McDonald's* (Chicago: Contemporary Books, 1977), 6–11.

60. Love, *McDonald's: Behind the Arches*, 113–50

61. Langdon, *Orange Roofs, Golden Arches*, 101–3.

62. David Gerard Hughes, *Selling 'Em by the Sack: White Castle and the Creation of American Food* (New York and London: New York University Press, 1997), 287–88.

63. Jennifer Jensen Wallach, *How America Eats: A Social History of U.S. Food and Culture* (Lanham, MD: Rowman & Littlefield, 2013), 170.

64. Hughes, *Selling 'Em by the Sack*; Josh Ozersky, *The Hamburger: A History* (New Haven: Yale University Press, 2008), 21–53.

65. Ozersky, *The Hamburger: A History*, 34–35.

66. True, Nathan's Famous serves hot dogs at 238 establishments in the United States, including its original Coney Island store, and 43 abroad (including one in Afghanistan). Wienerschnitzel is another hot-dog chain with more than 320 branches in mostly Western states. Founded in 1961 as Der Wienerschnitzel, the definite article was later dropped, perhaps because in German it's actually Das Wienerschnitzel, but this would seem an excessively scrupulous correction compared to the fact that Wienerschnitzel is a sautéed breaded veal cutlet, not a hot dog. The reach of these chains is almost negligible in the fast-food scale of things.

67. Julie Jargon, "How to Revive McDonalds: Ideas from Four Experts," *Wall Street Journal*, December 23, 2014.

68. Gopnik, *The Table Comes First*, 16.

MAMMA LEONE'S

1. Krishnendu Ray, "Topographies of Taste; American Cities and Gustatory Hierarchies," unpublished paper given at the American Historical Association, January 2013.

2. In a *Washington Post* article on July 12, 2015, Lavanya Ramanathan says we should stop calling immigrant restaurants "ethnic" because it implies a picturesque kind of poverty, www.washingtonpost.com/lifestyle/food/why-everyone-should-stop -calling-immigrant-food-ethnic/2015/07/20/0, accessed September 5, 2015.

3. Jennifer 8. Lee, *The Fortune Cookie Chronicles: Adventures in the World of Chinese Food* (New York: Twelve, 2008), 9; "Guess How Many Pizza and Italian Restaurants There Are in the United States," www.visualizing.org/visualizations/guess-how-many -pizza-and-italian-restaurants-there-are-united-states, accessed June 9, 2015.

4. "Restaurant Life in San Francisco," *Overland Monthly and Out West Magazine* 1, no. 5 (November, 1868), 471–73.

5. Andrew Haley, *Turning the Tables: Restaurants and the Rise of the American Middle Class, 1880–1920* (Chapel Hill: University of North Carolina Press, 2011), 111.

6. Cindy L. Lobel, *Urban Appetites: Food and Culture in Nineteenth-Century New York* (Chicago: University of Chicago Press, 1914), 187–88.

7. Haley, *Turning the Tables*, 98–99.

8. Rachel Laudan, *Cuisine and Empire: Cooking in World History* (Berkeley: University of California Press, 2013), 263–64; Richard Pillsbury, *From Boarding House to Bistro: The American Restaurant Then and Now* (Boston: Unwin Hyman, 1990), 145.

9. John F. Mariani, *How Italian Food Conquered the World* (New York: Palgrave Macmillan, 2011).

10. Jennifer Jensen Wallach, *How America Eats: A Social History of U.S. Food and Culture* (Lanham, MD: Rowman & Littlefield, 2013), 78.

11. Harvey Levenstein, *Revolution at the Table: The Transformation of the American Diet* (Berkeley: University of California Press, 2003), 104–5.

12. Interview with Nick Valenti, December 11, 2013. I am grateful to Mr. Valenti for talking with me about the restaurant's history.

13. Lobel, *Urban Appetites*, 181–82.

14. Hasia R. Diner, *Hungering for America: Italian, Irish and Jewish Foodways in the Age of Migration* (Cambridge, MA: Harvard University Press, 2001), 48–61.

15. Mariani, *How Italian Food Conquered the World*, 51.

16. Haley, *Turning the Tables*, 100–101.

17. On twentieth-century American Bohemianism see Christine Stansell, *American Moderns: Bohemian New York and the Creation of a New Century* (Princeton: Princeton University Press, 2000). Bohemians and restaurants, Luc Sante, *Low Life: Lures and Snares of Old New York* (New York: Farrar, Straus and Giroux, 1991), 320–38; George Chauncey, *Gay New York: Gender, Culture, and the Making of the Gay Male World, 1890–1940* (New York: Basic Books, 1994), 33–46.

18. Judith R. Walkowitz, *Nights Out: Life in Cosmopolitan London* (New Haven and London: Yale University Press, 2012), 114–17.

19. Clarence E. Edwards, *Bohemian San Francisco, Its Restaurants and Their Most Famous Recipes: The Elegant Art of Dining* (San Francisco: Paul Elder and Co., 1914), 6–7.

20. Ruth L. Bohan, "Whitman and the 'Picture-Makers,'" in *Whitman Among the Bohemians*, ed. Joanne Levin and Edward Whitely (Iowa City: University of Iowa Press), 132,

21. Gene Leone, *Leone's Italian Cookbook* (New York: Harper & Row, 1967), 1–5.

22. The menu is photographed in Francine Brevetti, *The Fabulous Fior: Over 100 Years of an Italian Kitchen*, 2nd ed. (Nevada City, CA: San Francisco Bay Books, 2004), 17.

23. Brevetti, *Fabulous Fior*, 23–26. Caruso, a great restaurant aficionado, invested in Mori's, a Greenwich Village restaurant. See Simone Cinotto, *The Italian American Table: Food, Family and Community in New York City* (Urbana, IL: University of Illinois Press, 2013), 199.

24. Brevetti, *Fabulous Fior*, 18–19; Edwards, *Bohemian San Francisco*, 24–25.

25. Maria Sermolino, *Papa's Table d'Hôte* (Philadelphia and New York: J. B. Lippincott Co., 1952).

26. Sermolino, *Papa's Table d'Hôte*, 41–42; William Grimes, *Appetite City: A Culinary History of New York* (New York: North Point Press, 2009), 127–29; Donna Gabaccia, *We Are What We Eat: Ethnic Food and the Making of Americans* (Cambridge, MA: Harvard University Press, 1998), 99–101.

27. Sermolino, *Papa's Table d'Hôte*, 125–26, 130, 134.

28. Grimes, *Appetite City*, 200; Sermolino, *Papa's Table d'Hôte*, 41; Brevetti, *Fabulous Fior*, 15.

29. From the Henry Voigt Collection of American Menus, Wilmington, DE, featured on his blog, *The American Menu*, September 13, 2011, www.theamericanmenu .com/2011/09/italian-well-sort-of.html#more, accessed July 18, 2015.

30. Nick Mount, *When Canadian Literature Moved to New York* (Toronto: University of Toronto Press, 2005), 67–68.

31. Grimes, *Appetite City*, 126; *Where and How to Dine in New York* (New York: Lewis Scribner and Co., 1903; repr. London, 2013), 106–7 of reprint; "Where Gotham Eats: Bohemian Resorts that Are Popular in New York," *The Day*, June 20, 1904, 7.

32. Beth Thompson and Louis Hanges, *Eating Around San Francisco* (San Francisco: Suttonhouse Limited, 1936), 51; Mariani, *How Italian Food Conquered the World*, 50.

33. According to the noted art collector Judith Hernstadt, some of the statues at Mamma Leone's that were sold after the restaurant's demise were valuable works by noted nineteenth-century American sculptors such as Hiram Powers and Chauncey Bradley Ives. As stated in a conversation with me, December 18, 2015.

34. Leone, *Leone's Italian Cookbook*, 6–7.

35. Cinotto, *Italian American Table*, 189–93.

36. Brevetti, *Fabulous Fior*, 37–42.

37. Cinotto, *Italian American Table*, 182.

38. Diner, *Hungering for America*, 54.

39. Walkowitz, *Nights Out*, 119.

40. Reproduced in Brevetti, *Fabulous Fior*, 54–55.

41. Cinotto, *Italian American Table*, 200.

42. Ibid., 78–79.

43. Ibid., 204–5.

44. Mariani, *How Italian Food Conquered the World*, 55.

45. Conversation with Dominick Varacalli, former manager of Mamma Leone's, January 19, 2014. I thank Mr. Varacalli for giving me a vivid impression of Mamma Leone's.

46. Mariani, *How Italian Food Conquered the World*, 55–56; Lawton Mackall, *Knife and Fork in New York: Where to Eat and What to Order*, 2nd ed. (Garden City, NY: Doubleday, 1949), 70–71.

47. Leone, *Leone's Italian Cookbook*, 11. On Eisenhower's recipe and its tricky logistics, see Matt Lee and Ted Lee, "For a Better Steak, Cook Directly on Charcoal," *New York Times*, June 25, 2015.

48. Leone, *Leone's Italian Cookbook*, 10–11.

49. Vincent Sardi Sr. and Richard Gehman, *Sardi's: The Story of a Famous Restaurant* (New York: Henry Holt and Company, 1953). Here Sardi described the restaurant's food as "Italian-French-American," but it began by serving Italian food from Piemonte, where Sardi and his wife grew up (207).

50. For example, Maria Lo Pinto, *New York Cookbook*, including a restaurant guide (New York: A. A. Wyn, 1952), 228.

51. Leone, *Leone's Italian Cookbook*, 12.

52. As indicated on a menu from the 1970s in the New York Public Library, Rare Books and Manuscripts Dept., Joe Baum Papers, Box 40.

53. Conversations with Nick Valenti and Dominick Varacalli.

54. Conversation with Dominick Varacalli.

55. *The New York Times Guide to Dining Out in New York,* ed. Craig Claiborne (New York: Athenaeum, 1964), 80; Seymour Britchky, *Seymour Britchky's New and Revised Guide to the Restaurants of New York* (New York: Random House, 1976), 317–19.

56. Mimi Sheraton, "The Pleasant Avenue Food Connection," *New York Times,* August 19, 1977. The title of the article refers not only to the restaurant's location but also implicitly to the 1971 movie *The French Connection.*

57. Alberto Capatti and Massimo Montanari, *Italian Cuisine: A Cultural History*, trans. Aine O'Healy (New York: Columbia University Press, 2003), 33.

58. Mariani, *How Italian Food Conquered the World*, 115–16.

59. Calvin Trillin, *American Fried: Adventures of a Happy Eater* (New York: Doubleday, 1974), 5.

60. Mariani, *How Italian Food Conquered the World*, 78–79, 146–47.

61. Alison Pearlman, *Smart Casual: The Transformation of Gourmet Restaurant Style in America* (Chicago: University of Chicago Press, 2013), 33.

62. Danny Meyer, *Setting the Table: The Transforming Power of Hospitality in Business* (New York: Harper, 2006), 61.

63. Ashlea Halpern, "Robertasville," in a section on "Next Great Neighborhoods," *New York*, April 3, 2011.

64. The cookbook, Frank Falcinelli et al., *The Frankies Spuntino Kitchen Companion and Cooking Manual* (New York: Artisan, 2010), is a compendium of recipes for dishes served at the restaurants before 2010. See especially 137, 151–54.

THE MANDARIN

1. Jennifer 8. Lee, *The Fortune Cookie Chronicles: Adventures in the World of Chinese Food* (New York: Twelve, 2008), 8.

2. On ethnic restaurants and attitudes of intolerance and discrimination generally, see Vicki I. Ruiz, "Citizen Restaurant: American Imaginaries, American Communities," *American Quarterly* 60 (2008), 1–21. For the case of Indian food in Britain, Elizabeth Buettner, "Going for an Indian: South Asian Restaurants and the Limits of Multiculturalism in Britain," *Journal of Modern History* 80 (2008), 865–901.

3. On the importance of what she refers to as the "Taiwan Connection," see Anne Mendelson, *Chow Chop Suey: Food and the Chinese American Journey* (New York: Columbia University Press, forthcoming).

4. Cecilia Sun Yun Chiang, *The Mandarin Way* (Boston and Toronto: Little, Brown and Company, 1974); Cecilia Chiang, *The Seventh Daughter: My Culinary Journey from Beijing to San Francisco* (Berkeley and Toronto: Ten Speed Press, 2007). I take this opportunity to thank Cecilia Chiang for speaking with me about her experiences and impressions on several occasions from 2012 to 2015.

5. Jean Gelman Taylor, *Indonesia: Peoples and Histories* (New Haven: Yale University Press, 2003), 121–31.

6. Andrew Coe, *Chop Suey: A Cultural History of Chinese Food in the United States* (New York: Oxford University Press, 2009), 103–7, 123.

7. Coe, *Chop Suey*, 112–25; William Grimes, *Appetite City: A Culinary History of New York* (New York: North Point Press, 2009), 130. In 1903 there were still only a small number of restaurants in New York's Chinatown, Harley Spiller, "Chow Fun City: Three Centuries of Chinese Cuisine in New York City," in *Gastropolis: Food and New York City*, ed. Annie Hauck-Lawson and Jonathan Deutsch (New York: Columbia University Press, 2009), 135.

8. Coe, *Chop Suey*, 157–59.

9. Lee, *Fortune Cookie Chronicles*, 56–57.

10. Haiming Liu, "Chop Suey as Imagined Authentic Chinese Food: The Culinary Iden-

tity of Chinese Restaurants in the United States," *Journal of Transnational American Studies* 1 (2005), 5–6. Liu's entire article (pages 4–18) and Renqiu Yu, "Chop Suey: From Chinese Food to Chinese American Food," *Chinese America: History and Perspectives* 1 (1987), 87–100, describe the origins and diffusion of American chop suey.

11. Wong Chin Foo, "The Chinese in New York," *The Cosmopolitan: A Monthly Illustrated Magazine*, June 1888, 304. I'm grateful to Professor John Eng-Wong of Brown University for this reference

12. Alexander Filippini, *The Table: How to Buy Food, How to Cook It and How to Serve It* (New York: Charles L. Webster and Company, 1889), 414.

13. Mendelson, *Chow Chop Suey.*

14. Buwei Yang Chao, *How to Cook and Eat in Chinese* (New York: John Day, 1945).

15. Arthur Bonner, *Alas! What Brought Thee Hither? The Chinese in New York, 1800–1950* (Madison, NJ: Fairleigh Dickinson University Press, 1997), 97–105; Coe, *Chop Suey*, 161–68, 176–77.

16. Bonner, *Alas! What Brought Thee Hither?*, 105.

17. Josh Kun, *To Live and Dine in L.A.: Menus and the Making of the Modern City* (Santa Monica: Angel City Press, 2015), 114.

18. Mary Ting Yi Lui, *The Chinatown Trunk Mystery: Murder, Miscegenation and Other Dangerous Encounters in Turn-of-the-Century New York City* (Princeton: Princeton University Press, 2005).

19. Coe, *Chop Suey*, 191.

20. Bertram Reinitz, "Chop Suey's New Role," *New York Times*, December 27, 1925. My former Yale student Margaret Tung found this in researching her paper "From Chinese to Chinese-American: The American Appropriation of Chinese Food in New York City During the Jazz Age" (2010).

21. Heather Lee, "Chop Suey for Two," paper presented at the American Historical Association, New York, January 5, 2015.

22. "Origins of Chop Suey Remain a Mystery," *New York Times*, January 8, 1928.

23. Sven A. Kristen, *The Book of Tiki* (Cologne: Taschen, 2000).

24. *The Good Housekeeping Hostess* (Springfield, MA: Phelps Publishing Company, 1904), 71–77.

25. Coe, *Chop Suey*, 185–94.

26. Ling Lew, *The Chinese in North America: A Guide to Their Life and Progress* (Los Angeles: East-West Culture Publishing Association, 1949), 221. I am grateful to Professor John Eng-Wong for this reference and for translating its key Chinese texts for me. See also Louis H. Chu, "The Chinese Restaurant in New York City," MA thesis, New York University, February 1939 (I thank Krishnendu Ray for showing me this paper), 21, 33–36, 40, 61.

27. Chu, "The Chinese Restaurant," 47, 61–67.

28. Menu in the Henry Voigt Collection of American Menus, Wilmington, DE. Featured in Mr. Voigt's blog, *The American Menu*, December 18, 2010, www.theamericanmenu.com/2010/12/god-bless-america.html#more, accessed July 19, 2015.

29. Calvin Trillin, *Feeding a Yen: Savoring Local Specialties, from Kansas City to Cuzco* (New York: Random House, 2003), 71.

30. Coe, *Chop Suey*, 219–40; Lee, *Fortune Cookie Chronicles*, 66–83.

31. In addition to the recollections contained in *The Mandarin Way*, Cecilia Chiang described her early life in interviews with Victor Geraci in August and September, 2005, "Cecilia Chiang: An Oral History" in the regional Oral History Office of the Bancroft Library, University of California, audio files 1 and 2 (transcript pages 1–56). A more detailed account of the long walk to Chungking is in *Seventh Daughter*, 133–36, 139–57.

32. My interview, October 25, 2012; "Cecilia Chiang: An Oral History," 60–62. In general see Mendelson, *Chow Chop Suey*.

33. My conversations with Cecilia Chiang, October 26, 2014, and April 17, 2015. She says she in effect made a gift of the sous-chef to the ambassador. I am indebted to Michael Tong, owner of Shun Lee, for information about the founding and early years of his restaurant in an interview, November 24, 2014.

34. The movie *The Search for General Tso* (2014, directed by Ian Cheney), shows definitively how this dish was named, invented, appropriated, and diffused.

35. Chiang, *Seventh Daughter*, 7–12; "Cecilia Chiang: An Oral History," 65–68.

36. "Cecilia Chiang: An Oral History," 67.

37. On Johnny Kan and his restaurant, see Madeline Y. Hsu, "From Chop Suey to Mandarin Cuisine: Fine Dining and the Refashioning of Chinese Ethnicity During the Cold War Era," in *Chinese Americans and the Politics of Race and Culture*, ed. Sucheng Chan and Madeline Y. Hsu (Philadelphia: Temple University Press, 2008), 173–93. There is also a Kan's cookbook: Johnny Kan with Charles L. Leong, *Eight Immortal Flavors* (Berkeley: Howell-North Books, 1963).

38. As described by columnist Herb Caen in a eulogy for Johnny Kan at his funeral, quoted by Hsu, "From Chop Suey to Mandarin Cuisine," 180.

39. I thank Cecilia Chiang for two menus, which date probably from between 1962 and 1964.

40. I'm grateful to Yiwen Li, a graduate student at Yale University, for translating the Chinese menu into English.

41. "Cecilia Chiang: An Oral History," 70. Also mentioned in my interview, October 25, 2012.

42. Mendelson, *Chow Chop Suey*.

43. Raymond Sokolov, *Steal the Menu: A Memoir of Forty Years in Food* (New York: Knopf, 2013), 92.

44. Meredith Brody, "Local Heavies to Celebrate Cecilia Chiang, the Julia Child of Chinese Cooking," *SF Weekly*, September 16, 2009, sfweekly.com/foodie/2009/09/16/local-heavies-to-celebrate-cecilia-chiang-the-julia-child-of-chinese-cooking.

45. Interview, October 25, 2012.

46. John Heckathorn, "An Interview with Philip Chiang, Founder of P. F. Chang's," *Honolulu Magazine*, October 11, 2011.

47. Lee, *Fortune Cookie Chronicles*, 179–208; John Jung, *Sweet and Sour: Life in Chinese Family Restaurants* (n.p.: Yin and Yang Press, 2010).

48. These examples come from the work of another former student of mine, Mary Zou, who wrote a paper about Fujianese immigrants and Chinese restaurants in 2011.

49. Robert Sietsema, *New York in a Dozen Dishes* (Boston: Houghton Mifflin Harcourt, 2015), 48–50.

50. Acceptance of sushi was a first step, undertaken by companies such as Japan Airlines beginning in the 1960s, Esther Hahn (yet another former Yale undergraduate student), "The Acceptance and Assimilation of Sushi in Post–World War II White America," senior essay, Yale University, April 2008, 15, 27. See also Anne Mendelson, "A Fish Story," *Gourmet*, October 2002, 176–83.

51. Melissa McCart, "America's Next Great Chinatown Takes Root in Pittsburgh," *Saveur* (online), www.saveur.com/how-pittsburgh-is-growing-americas-next-chinatown -chinese-restaurants, accessed October 24, 2015.

52. As she described in an interview with me, October 24, 2012.

SYLVIA'S

1. I am very grateful to Professor Harold Forsythe of Fairfield University and Professor Frederick Douglass Opie of Babson College for their comments on this chapter.

2. Caren Pratt, "Sylvia's Is Not Just Any Eatery: It's Down Home and Family Style," *New York Amsterdam News*, December 6, 1986.

3. Isabel Wilkerson, *The Warmth of Other Suns: The Epic Story of America's Great Migration* (New York: Random House, 2010); Nicolas Lemann, *The Promised Land: The Great Black Migration and How It Changed America* (New York: Knopf, 1991). On the migration as it affected the uptown culinary scene, see Damian M. Mosley, "Cooking Up Heritage in Harlem," in *Gastropolis: Food in New York City*, ed. Annie Hauck-Lawson and Jonathan Deutsch (New York: Columbia University Press, 2009), 274–92. On its overall culinary influence, including some fascinating case studies, Frederick Douglass Opie, *Hog and Hominy: Soul Food from Africa to America* (New York: Columbia University Press, 2008), 54–82.

4. She provides an autobiographical introduction to *Sylvia's Family Soul Food Cookbook: From Hemingway, South Carolina, to Harlem* (New York: William Morrow and Company, 1999), 7–66.

5. Woods, *Sylvia's Family Soul Food Cookbook*, 11.

6. Ibid., 34–35.

7. Ibid., 36–37. That doesn't mean there were no African American–owned restaurants in the South. See Opie, *Hog and Hominy*, 102–11.

8. Eric Spitznagel, "Sylvia Woods," in the *New York Times Magazine* feature "The Lives They Lived," July 19, 2012, B10, quoting from remarks by her son Kenneth Woods and a friend, Terry Frishman.

9. Conversation with Lindsey Williams, grandson of Sylvia Woods, April 17, 2014.

10. New York Public Library, Schomburg Center for Research in Black Culture, Menu Collection.

11. From the restaurant's website, sylviasrestaurant.com/menus, accessed January 30, 2015.

12. Wells might have introduced this combination to New York in the 1930s, but its roots go back much further, to the nineteenth-century "Pennsylvania Dutch." See

Adrian Miller, *Soul Food: The Surprising Story of an American Cuisine One Plate at a Time* (Chapel Hill: University of North Carolina Press, 2013), 59. It is mentioned as a specialty of Joe Wells's in Maria Lo Pinto, *New York Cookbook* (New York: A. A. Wyn, Inc., 1952), 232. Chicken with waffles appears on a 1949 menu, otherwise generic American, for the Hotel Theresa, a former Harlem landmark at 125th Street and Seventh Avenue, Henry Voigt Collection of American Menus, Wilmington, DE.

13. Timothy Williams, "In Changing Harlem, Soul Food Struggles," *New York Times*, August 5, 2008. There is a brief mention of this older sister in Sylvia Woods's account of her life and restaurant and a picture of Sylvia with Louise as teenagers in *Sylvia's Family Soul Cookbook*, 9–10.

14. Jason Tomassini, "Manna's: As Soul Food Dwindles in Harlem, an Unlikely Champion Survives," *The Uptowner*, December 27, 2010.

15. Spitznagel, "Sylvia Woods," remarks by Al Sharpton.

16. Spitznagel, "Sylvia Woods," remarks by Van Woods.

17. Robin D. Stone, "Sylvia Woods Left Behind a Legacy of Love in Harlem—and Beyond," *Ebony*, July 1, 2015.

18. Before achieving fame as a singer and actor, Robeson had been a football star at Rutgers University. Although he had a law degree from Columbia University, he found it difficult to practice law in the racial climate of the 1920s. On his life, see Martin Baumi Duberman, *Paul Robeson: A Biography* (New York: Knopf, 1988).

19. David Levering Lewis, *When Harlem Was in Vogue* (New York: Knopf, 1981), 209.

20. John A. Jakle, *The Tourist: Travel in Twentieth-Century North America* (Lincoln: University of Nebraska Press, 1985), 261.

21. Jim Haskins, *The Cotton Club* (New York: Plume, 1984), 33, 102–3. While preserving its Harlem accouterments, the Cotton Club moved from Harlem to midtown Manhattan in 1936.

22. New York Public Library, Schomburg Collection, a menu from the late 1920s.

23. Gael Greene, "Harlem on My Mind," *New York Magazine*, March 12, 1979.

24. See the column "The World of Dining," in the *New York Amsterdam News* for May 5, 1979.

25. In Sylvia Woods's obituary in the *New York Times* by Margalit Fox (July 19, 2012, B10), Greene's review is said to have had the effect of "sealing the restaurant's success," but this underestimates Sylvia's already-established popularity and by implication exaggerates subsequent white patronage.

26. Sophia Hollander, "As Sylvia's Endured, Harlem Changed," *Wall Street Journal*, July 20, 2012.

27. In recalling that first visit to the restaurant after Sylvia's death, Greene says some "extremely white, blonde friends" proposed the trip, they went first for breakfast, there were derelicts and bars everywhere, and that it was wonderful. Spitznagel, "Sylvia Woods."

28. Spitznagel, "Sylvia Woods," remarks by Ed Koch.

29. Hollander, "As Sylvia's Endured."

30. Comments accompanying Spitznagel, "Sylvia Woods."

31. Andrew L. Yarrow, "A Bus Tour That Shows Harlem's Many Sides," *New York Times*,

September 9, 1983, C11. The dining section of the *New York Amsterdam News* on May 19, 1984, says the brunch was served at three p.m. and gives particular accolades to the short ribs of beef, along with eggs and ham or sausage, salmon croquettes, and barbecued ribs.

32. Conversation with Lindsey Williams, April 17, 2014.

33. Sylvia's Restaurant, St. Petersburg, www.sylviasstpete.com.

34. Cited in Anthony Stanonis, "The Triumph of Epicure: A Global History of New Orleans Culinary Tourism," *Southern Quarterly* 46 (2009), 148–49.

35. On black cooks in Southern white kitchens generally, see Rebecca Sharpless, *Cooking in Other Women's Kitchens: Domestic Workers in the South, 1865–1960* (Chapel Hill: University of North Carolina Press, 2010).

36. Jennifer Jensen Wallach, *How America Eats: A Social History of U.S. Food and Culture* (Lanham, MD: Rowman & Littlefield, 2013), 186.

37. Ibid., 187.

38. Crosby Gaige, *New York World's Fair Cook Book: The American Kitchen* (New York: Doubleday, Doran & Company,1939), 46, 62.

39. Duncan Hines, *Duncan Hines' Food Odyssey* (New York: Crowell, 1955), 105.

40. Vertamae Smart-Grosvenor, *Vibration Cooking: Or, the Travel Notes of a Geechee Girl* (New York: Doubleday, 1970; repr. Athens, GA: University of Georgia Press, 2011), xxxvii (of reprint).

41. Pointed out by Anne L. Bower, "Introduction: Watching Soul Food," in *African American Foodways: Explorations of History and Culture*, ed. Anne L. Bower (Urbana, IL: University of Illinois Press, 2007), 3.

42. Sylvia Woods and Christopher Styler, *Sylvia's Soul Food: Recipes from Harlem's World-Famous Restaurant* (New York: William Morrow and Company, 1992), 2, 24–27.

43. John Egerton, *Southern Food: At Home, On the Road, in History* (New York: Knopf, 1987), 16.

44. Opie, *Hog and Hominy*, 60–62.

45. Dora Charles, *A Real Southern Cook in Her Savannah Kitchen* (Boston: Houghton Mifflin Harcourt, 2015). Ms. Charles was interviewed by Kim Severson, "It's All in the Seasoning," *New York Times*, September 2, 2015, D1, D7.

46. [Abby Fisher], *What Mrs. Fisher Knows About Old Southern Cooking* (San Francisco: Women's Cooperative Printing Office, 1881; repr. Bedford, MA: Applewood Books, 1995). The reprint includes an excellent commentary by Karen Hess, 73–94.

47. Sidney Mintz, "History and Anthropology A Brief Reprise," in *Race and Slavery in the Western Hemisphere*, ed. Stanley Engerman and Eugene D. Genovese (Princeton: Princeton University Press, 1975), 483–84, n. 18.

48. A point emphasized by Opie, *Hog and Hominy*, 3–15.

49. On Africans and rice in the New World, Judith A. Carney, *Black Rice: The African Origins of Rice Cultivation in the Americas* (Cambridge, MA: Harvard University Press, 2001); Karen Hess, *The Carolina Rice Kitchen: The African Connection* (Columbia, SC: University of South Carolina Press, 1992).

50. Jessica B. Harris, *High on the Hog: A Culinary Journey from Africa to America* (New York:

Bloomsbury Publishing, 2011), 7–19; Robert L. Hall, "Food Crops, Medicinal Plants, and the Atlantic Slave Trade," in *African American Foodways,* 17–44.

51. Opie, *Hog and Hominy,* 28. See also Wallach, *How America Eats,* 37–38.

52. Much of what follows is based on the work of James E. McWilliams, *A Revolution in Eating: How the Quest for Food Shaped America* (New York: Columbia University Press, 2005).

53. Opie, *Hog and Hominy,* 33.

54. Carney, *Black Rice,* 156.

55. Anne Yentsch, "Excavating the South's African-American Food History," in *African American Foodways* (as above, note 41), 65–71.

56. William C. Whit, "Soul Food as Cultural Creation," in *African American Foodways,* 47–53.

57. Opie, *Hog and Hominy,* 38.

58. James Hemmings asked Jefferson for his freedom, and this was granted in 1796, on condition that he train his younger brother Peter and two female slaves, Edith Fossett and Frances Hern, to succeed him, Miller, *Soul Food,* 131.

59. Harris, *High on the Hog,* 77–82.

60. Mary Anne Hines et al., *The Larder Invaded: Reflections on Three Centuries of Philadelphia Food and Drink* (Philadelphia: Library Company of Philadelphia and the Pennsylvania Historical Society, 1987), 22–23, 26.

61. Ibid., 64; Harris, *High on the Hog,* 118–21.

62. Mark Kurlansky, *The Big Oyster: History on the Half Shell* (New York: Random House, 2006), 165–69; Harris, *High on the Hog,* 122–25.

63. As described by Harris, *High on the Hog,* 176–77.

64. Ibid., 177–78.

65. Opie, *Hog and Hominy,* 111–13.

66. Miller, *Soul Food,* 41.

67. A point made by Frederick Douglass Opie, "Influence, Sources, and African Diaspora Foodways," in *Food in Time and Place: The American Historical Association Companion to Food History,* ed. Paul Freedman, Joyce Chaplin, and Ken Albala (Berkeley and Los Angeles: University of California Press, 2014), 197.

68. Opie, *Hog and Hominy,* 127–33; Harris, *High on the Hog,* 206–8.

69. Miller, *Soul Food,* 44–45.

70. Ibid., 45–48.

71. Opie, *Hog and Hominy,* 130.

72. Quoted in Miller, *Soul Food,* 6.

73. Carol Allen, *Leah Chase: Listen, I Say Like This* (Gretna, LA: Pelican Publishing Company, 2002), 63.

74. Edna Lewis, *The Taste of Country Cooking* (New York: Knopf, 1976); Leah Chase, *The Dooky Chase Cookbook* (Gretna, LA: Pelican Publishing Company, 1990).

75. Eldridge Cleaver, *Soul on Ice* (New York: Dell, 1968), 29.

76. Opie, *Hog and Hominy,* 159–65; Harris, *High on the Hog,* 209–11.

77. Opie, *Hog and Hominy,* 165–68.

78. Alice Randall and Caroline Randall Williams, *Soul Food Love: Healthy Recipes Inspired*

by One Hundred Years of Cooking in a Black Family (New York: Penguin Random House, 2015).

79. Fernanda Santos, "Harlem Mainstay Survived Riots, but Falls to Renewal," *New York Times*, July 23, 2007.

80. Valerie Kinloch, *Harlem on Our Mind: Place, Race and the Literacies of Urban Youth* (New York: Teachers College Press, 2010), 27.

81. Williams, "In Changing Harlem, Soul Food Struggles." Louise's family restaurant was described in this article as "endangered," and indeed it would close later in 2008.

82. John Freeman Gill, "Frederick Douglass Boulevard: Newly Revived," *New York Times*, December 31, 2013.

83. Zachery Feldman, "The Ten Best Restaurants in Harlem," *Village Voice* blogs, November 12, 2013, blogs.villagevoice.com/forkintheroad/2013/11/the_10_best_restaurants_in_harlem.php, accessed January 2, 2015.

84. Conversation with Lindsey Williams, April 17, 2014.

LE PAVILLON

1. Joseph Wechsberg, *Dining at the Pavillon* (Boston and Toronto: Little, Brown and Company, 1962), 23.

2. William Grimes, *Appetite City: A Culinary History of New York* (New York: North Point Press, 2009), 252–56.

3. Pierre Franey, *A Chef's Tale: A Memoir of Food, France, and America* (New York: Knopf, 1994), 96.

4. Jacques Pépin, *The Apprentice: My Life in the Kitchen* (Boston: Houghton Mifflin, 2003), 137.

5. Patric Kuh, *The Last Days of Haute Cuisine: The Coming of Age of American Restaurants* (New York: Viking, 2001), 37.

6. Gael Greene, "Quintessential Soulé Food" (a review of La Côte Basque), *New York*, November 25, 1968.

7. Wechsberg, *Dining at the Pavillon*, 10–11; Greene, "Quintessential Soulé Food."

8. Cited in David Kamp, *The United States of Arugula: The Sun-Dried, Cold-Pressed, Dark-Roasted, Extra Virgin Story of the American Food Revolution* (New York: Broadway Books, 2006), 37–38.

9. Wechsberg, *Dining at the Pavillon*, 37.

10. Ibid., 45.

11. Adam Gopnik, "Aftertaste," *The New Yorker*, March 22, 2004, written just after the closing of La Côte Basque.

12. Descriptions of dishes from Craig Claiborne, "In Classic Tradition Henri Soulé Set Towering Standards in Search of Gastronomic Perfection," *New York Times*, January 28, 1966; Pépin, *The Apprentice*, 138–39; and Kuh, *The Last Days of Haute Cuisine*, 32.

13. Pépin, *The Apprentice*, 138.

14. Wechsberg, *Dining at the Pavillon*, 182–84.

15. Pépin, *The Apprentice*, 138.

16. Kuh, *The Last Days of Haute Cuisine*, 40–41; Amy Azzarito, "Haute Cuisine: New York

Style," written for a New York Public Library blog, November 19, 2007, exhibitions. nypl.org/biblion/worldsfair/fashion-food-famous-faces-pop-culture-fair/essay/essay-azzarito-french-food, accessed July 20, 2015; Pierre Franey, *The New York Times 60–Minute Gourmet* (New York: Times Books, 1979), 308–9 (reproducing and commenting on the recipe for the crab-meat omelets).

17. Franey, *A Chef's Tale*, 80.

18. John Mariani, *America Eats Out* (New York: William Morrow and Company, 1991), 143–44.

19. Michael Batterberry and Ariane Batterberry, *On the Town in New York: The Landmark History of Eating, Drinking and Entertainments from the American Revolution to the Food Revolution* (New York and London: Routledge, 1999), 252–53.

20. Menus from the Henry Voigt Collection of American Menus in Wilmington, DE.

21. Wechsberg, *Dining at the Pavillon,* 28–29; Franey, *A Chef's Tale*, 92.

22. Mariani, *America Eats Out*, 147.

23. From the Henry Voigt Collection.

24. Franey, *A Chef's Tale*, 92.

25. Menu from April 21, 1948, Providence, RI, Johnson & Wales University, Culinary Arts Museum Library, Louis Szathmary Menu Collection.

26. Johnson & Wales, Culinary Arts Museum Library, Roger Fessaguet Collection, menu no. 2001.075.0605.

27. From Mariani, *America Eats Out*, 148.

28. From Batterberry and Batterberry, *On the Town in New York*, 291–93.

29. Wechsberg, *Dining at the Pavillon*, 51–54.

30. Wechsberg, *Dining at the Pavillon*, 163, offers the recipe with the notation "amateurs are cautioned not to try it."

31. Craig Claiborne, *A Feast Made for Laughter* (Garden City: Doubleday, 1982), 157–58.

32. Ibid., 139–46.

33. Ibid., 140.

34. Mrs. Joan Fisher, quoted at the end of chapter 3 with regard to Schrafft's, recalls the El Morocco Club's "Siberia" in the 1950s as well defined, and far from the entrance and the center stage. Conversation with me, August 24, 2015.

35. Batterberry and Batterberry, *On the Town in New York*, 257–58.

36. Claiborne, *A Feast Made for Laughter*, 121–22.

37. Wechsberg, *Dining at the Pavillon*, 59.

38. Ibid., 89.

39. Ruth Reichl, *Garlic and Sapphires: The Secret Life of a Critic in Disguise* (New York: Penguin, 2005), 34–49.

40. Kuh, *The Last Days of Haute Cuisine*, 49–50.

41. Wechsberg, *Dining at the Pavillon*, 95; Franey, *A Chef's Tale*, 93.

42. Franey, *A Chef's Tale*, 110–11; Kamp, *The United States of Arugula*, 75–76.

43. Wechsberg, *Dining at the Pavillon*, 36.

44. Ibid., 34; Franey, *A Chef's Tale*, 111.

45. Grimes, *Appetite City*, 257–58.

46. Ibid., 257.

47. Kuh, *The Last Days of Haute Cuisine*, 93–94.

48. Wechsberg, *Dinner at the Pavillon*, 80–83.

49. *New York Times*, January 21, 1961, Clipping from Johnson & Wales, Culinary Arts Museum Library, Fessaguet Collection, 2011.075.2323.

50. Kuh, *The Last Days of Haute Cuisine*, 92–93; Franey, *A Chef's Tale*, 116–17; Pépin, *The Apprentice*, 144–45.

51. The article about the dispute: Thomas McNamee, *The Man Who Changed the Way We Eat: Craig Claiborne and the American Food Renaissance* (New York: Free Press, 2012), 86–89, 127–29, 130–31; Claiborne's letter in Johnson & Wales, Culinary Arts Museum Library, Fessaguet Collection, 2011.075.2323, dated January 21, 1961.

52. Kamp, *The United States of Arugula*, 80.

53. John Mariani and Alex von Bidder, *The Four Seasons: A History of America's Premier Restaurant* (New York: Crown Publishers, 1994), 42.

54. Kuh, *The Last Days of Haute Cuisine*, 95–96.

55. Gael Greene, "Papa Soulé Loves You," *New York Herald Tribune*, June 13, 1965 (Sunday supplement).

56. McNamee, *The Man Who Changed the Way We Eat*, 128.

57. Ibid., 130.

58. Claiborne, "In Classic Tradition Henri Soulé Set Towering Standards," 44.

59. Franey, *A Chef's Tale*, 96.

60. Craig Claiborne, "La Mistral Is the Newest Offshoot of Pavillon Tree," *New York Times*, December 1, 1964.

61. Greene, "Quintessential Soulé Food"; Batterberry and Batterberry, *On the Town in New York*, 315–16.

62. Claiborne, *A Feast Made for Laughter*, 161; McNamee, *The Man Who Changed the Way We Eat*, 134–35.

63. Greene, "Quintessential Soulé Food."

64. McNamee, *The Man Who Changed the Way We Eat*, 136.

65. *Seymour Britchky's New, Revised Guide to the Restaurants of New York* (New York: Random House, 1976), 200–201; *Forbes*, December 24, 1979, 22; *Mimi Sheraton's The New York Times Guide to New York Restaurants* (New York: Times Books, 1982), 204–6.

66. Joseph Berger, "Côte Basque, a Society Temple, Is Closing," *New York Times*, September 8, 2003.

THE FOUR SEASONS

1. A point made in John Mariani and Alex von Bidder, *The Four Seasons: A History of America's Premier Restaurant* (New York: Crown Publishers, 1994), 36

2. *New York Times,* July 16, 1959; *Look*, October 13, 1959, 58–60; B. H. Friedman, "The Most Expensive Restaurant Ever Built," *Evergreen Review* 10 (1959): 11–12.

3. Phyllis Lambert, *Building Seagram* (New Haven: Yale University Press, 2013), 136–49.

4. Mariani and von Bidder, *The Four Seasons*, 35–36; Geoffrey T. Hellman, "Directed to the Product," *The New Yorker,* October 17, 1964, 106.

5. Craig Claiborne, "Food News: Dining in Elegant Manner," *New York Times*, October 2, 1959.

6. Mentioned by Alice Waters in an interview with me, July 25, 2013. The importance of the Four Seasons for Jeremiah Tower, chef at Chez Panisse from 1973 to 1975, is noted in Thomas McNamee, *Alice Waters and Chez Panisse* (New York: Penguin, 2007), 122.

7. Michael Korda, "Le Plat du Jour Is Power," *New York Times*, January 26, 1977.

8. Lee Eisenberg, "America's Most Powerful Lunch: How the Books You Read, the Clothes You Wear, the Wines You Drink Begin at the Four Seasons," *Esquire*, October 1979, 34–41.

9. Hellman, "Directed to the Product," 68–69.

10. Mariani and von Bidder, *The Four Seasons*, 50; Robert Misch, "New York," *Wine and Food,* Autumn 1963, 159–60.

11. Mariani and von Bidder, *The Four Seasons*, 156–57. Warren Buffett's partially unsuccessful request is mentioned on the restaurant's Facebook page for April 2014. Accessed July 1, 2014. Korda, "Le Plat du Jour," said that the more powerful the individual, the fewer calories in his or her meal.

12. Conversation with Michael Korda, October 7, 2015.

13. The letter is reproduced in Lambert, *Building Seagram*, 240–47.

14. From the website "Untapped Cities," March 12, 2014, untappedcities.com/2014/03/12/inside-the-four-seasons-restaurant-in-the-seagram-building-photos, accessed July 3, 2015.

15. Cited in Robert A. M. Stern et al., *New York 1960: Architecture and Urbanism Between the Second World War and the Bicentennial* (New York: Monacelli Press, 1995), 350.

16. Hellman, "Directed to the Product," 80–81.

17. Ibid., 91–92.

18. Patric Kuh, *The Last Days of Haute Cuisine: The Coming of Age of American Restaurants* (New York: Viking, 2001), 55–57; Michael Batterberry and Ariane Batterberry, *On the Town in New York: The Landmark History of Eating, Drinking and Entertainments from the American Revolution to the Food Revolution* (New York and London: Routledge, 1999), 297–98.

19. Mariani and von Bidder, *The Four Seasons,* 17–19; Hellman, "Directed to the Product," 72–74.

20. A 1957 menu in the New York Public Library, Rare Books Division, Miss Frank Buttolph Collection and an undated menu in Antoine's Restaurant papers.

21. Mimi Sheraton, *Eating My Words: An Appetite for Life* (New York: William Morrow, 2004), 141.

22. Hellman, "Directed to the Product," 70.

23. "What Makes a Classic?," *Restaurants & Institutions*, January, 1960, 189–93. In the New York Public Library, Joe Baum Papers, Box 28, Folder 11.

24. Ibid., 193.

25. Mimi Sheraton, "Seasons in the Sun," *Vanity Fair*, August 1999.

26. Mariani and von Bidder, *The Four Seasons*, 27–29; Batterberry, *On the Town in New*

York, 296–97; William Grimes, *Appetite City: A Culinary History of New York* (New York: North Point Press, 2009), 276.

27. New York Public Library, Joe Baum Papers, Box 28, Box 40, five menus from ca. 1960–63 (judging from the prices), from every season.

28. Robert Sheehan, "Four Seasons: A Flourish of Food," *Fortune,* February 1960, 214; Hellman, "Directed to the Product," 102; James A. Beard, foreword to Charlotte Adams, *The Four Seasons Cookbook* (New York: Holt, Rinehart and Winston, 1971), 12–13.

29. NYPL Joe Baum Papers, Box 28, summer menu (1960–1963).

30. Robert Clark, *James Beard: A Biography* (New York: Harper Collins,1993), 42–48.

31. David Kamp, *The United States of Arugula* (New York: Broadway Books, 2006), 62; Kuh, *Last Days of Haute Cuisine*, 60–61.

32. Claiborne, "Dining in Elegant Manner," 22.

33. James A. Beard, "Fresh from the 4 Seasons to Your Table." This undated press clipping is in the NYPL, Joe Baum Papers, Box 28, Folder 11.

34. Sheraton, *Eating My Words*, 144.

35. The herring and salami/sausage service was mentioned to me by Mimi Sheraton. "No more flaming tournedos," Baum, as quoted by Peter Hellman, "Power House; How the Four Seasons Does It," *New York,* November 3, 1986, 47; "we wouldn't flame dishes," Baum, as quoted by Mariani and von Bidder, *The Four Seasons*, 26. References to flamed dishes are in a summer menu and four winter menus, 1960–1963, all in Box 28 of the Joe Baum Papers. Beef Stroganoff: Stockli as quoted in Sheehan, "A Flourish of Food," 213; Claiborne, "Dining in Elegant Manner," 22.

36. Sheehan, "A Flourish of Food," 213.

37. The following observations are taken from the collection of menus from the early years of the restaurant in Boxes 28 and 40 of the NYPL, Joe Baum Papers.

38. Adams, *The Four Seasons Cookbook*, 254.

39. Baum planned the Forum as a "gutsy, masculine restaurant," Mariani and von Bidder, *The Four Seasons*, 18. Later (page 49) Mariani and von Bidder remark: "Romantic as The Four Seasons was, there was never any question that the restaurant had been planned, in fact, as a masculine haunt."

40. Silas Spitzer in *Holiday* magazine, cited by Sheraton, "Seasons in the Sun."

41. NYPL, Joe Baum Papers, Box 28, winter menu; Box 40, spring menu.

42. *The New York Times Guide to Dining Out in New York*, ed. Craig Claiborne (New York: Athenaeum, 1964), 139; Gael Greene, "The Four Seasons at 25," *New York*, June 18, 1984, 48.

43. Mariani and von Bidder, *The Four Seasons*, 53.

44. Greene, "The Four Seasons at 25," 51.

45. Sheehan, "A Flourish of Food," 214.

46. Hellman, "Directed to the Product," 74–75.

47. Mariani and von Bidder, *The Four Seasons*, 65–70; "Happy Birthday JFK and Wow Marilyn Monroe," *Cool Culinaraia* (blog), March 13, 2014, coolculinaria.com/blogs/news/7982863–happy-birthday-jfk-and-wow-marilyn-monroe, accessed December 9, 2015.

48. Mariani and von Bidder, *The Four Seasons*, 81–82.

49. Gael Greene, "Restaurant Associates: Twilight of the Gods," *New York*, November 2, 1970.

50. Adams, *The Four Seasons Cookbook*.

51. Mimi Sheraton, "Seasons in the Sun."

52. Eisenberg, "America's Most Powerful Lunch, 41.

53. Ibid., 39–40.

54. An issue of *Town and Country* from about 1964 includes an article about La Côte Basque that gives seating plans and favored tables for La Côte Basque, the Colony, 21 Club, El Morocco, and La Caravelle. See George Christy, "Côte Basque: Nothing But the Best," clipping in Johnson & Wales University, Culinary Arts Museum Library, Roger Fessaguet Collection, red unnumbered folder "Valuable Old Letters."

55. Eisenberg, "America's Most Powerful Lunch," 36.

56. Mariani and von Bidder, *The Four Seasons*, vii–xii; Peter Hellman, "Power House," 47–51.

57. Lambert, *Building Seagram*, 206–38.

58. Mariani and von Bidder, *The Four Seasons*, 191.

59. As Alex von Bidder told me in an interview, October 25, 2013.

60. David Segal, "At Four Seasons, Picasso Tapestry Hangs on the Edge of Eviction," *New York Times*, February 4, 2014.

61. Charles V. Bagli and James Barron, "Four Seasons on Shaky Ground at Park Avenue Home," *New York Times*, February 7, 2014, A13.

62. Phyllis Lambert, "Save New York's Four Seasons," *New York Times*, May 16, 2015, A21; Robin Pogrebin, "Landmarks Commission Rejects Plan to Change Four Seasons Restaurant," *New York Times*, May 20, 2015.

63. Greg Morabito, "The Deal of the Century Wouldn't Have Happened Without Vito Schnabel," *NY Eater*, July 30, 2015, ny.eater.com/2015/7/30/9074697/four-seasons-vito, accessed October 3, 2015; Greg Morabito, "Unstoppable Torrisi Wolfpack to Revamp the Four Seasons Space in 2016," *NY Eater*, July 24, 2015, ny.eater.com/2015/7/24/9035879/unstoppable-torrisi-wolfpack-to-revamp-the-four-seasons-in-2016, accessed October 3, 2015.

64. As reported by Daniel Geiger, "Seagram Building Owner Seeks 30 Million for Upscale Restaurant That Will Replace Four Seasons," *Crain's New York Business*, December 8, 2015, crainsnewyork.com/article/20151208/REAL_ESTATE/151209884/aby-rosen-seeks-30-million-for-upscale-restaurant-at-seagram.

65. James Barron, "Power Lunch Proceeds as Usual at Restaurant," *New York Times*, June 5, 2015.

66. Cited in Stern, *New York 1960*, 350.

CHEZ PANISSE

1. Greil Marcus, "1971: Berkeley," *Lapham's Quarterly* 4, no. 3 (Summer, 2011), 94–95.

2. Thomas McNamee, *Alice Waters and Chez Panisse: The Romantic, Impractical, Often Eccentric, Ultimately Brilliant Making of a Food Revolution* (New York: Penguin, 2007), 51.

3. Ibid., 68.

4. Caroline Bates, "Spécialités de la Maison—California," *Gourmet*, October, 1975, 11–12.

5. On the health-food movement and its occasional intersections with slow, artisanal cooking and taste, see Warren Belasco, *Appetite for Change: How the Counterculture Took On the Food Industry* (New York: Pantheon Books, 1989: 2nd ed. Ithaca: Cornell University Press, 2007).

6. Joyce Goldstein, *Inside the California Food Revolution: Thirty Years That Changed Our Culinary Consciousness* (Berkeley: University of California Press, 2013), 2.

7. Interview with Alice Waters, July 24, 2013.

8. Menu from Alice Waters's personal collection, Berkeley, entitled "Beyond Tears: The First Eight Years," compiled by Linda Parker Guenzel, vol. 1.

9. Menu in the author's possession.

10. Menu in the author's possession.

11. David Kamp, *The United States of Arugula: The Sun-Dried, Cold-Pressed, Dark-Roasted, Extra Virgin Story of the American Food Revolution* (New York: Clarkson Potter Publishers, 2006), 129–93; Patric Kuh, *The Last Days of Haute Cuisine: The Coming of Age of American Restaurants* (New York: Viking, 2001), 133–57.

12. Luke Barr, *Provence, 1970: M.F.K. Fisher, Julia Child, James Beard, and the Reinvention of American Taste* (New York: Clarkson Potter Publishers, 2013).

13. Goldstein, *Inside the California Food Revolution*, 43.

14. Kamp, *United States of Arugula*, 123.

15. Quoted in ibid., 164.

16. Ibid., 141–42.

17. McNamee, *Alice Waters and Chez Panisse*, 308.

18. John L. Hess and Karen Hess, *The Taste of America* (New York: Grossman, 1977).

19. Emphasized in a conversation with me, July 24, 2013. Of course, Alice Waters is part of a larger movement that combines sustainability, social justice, and the better distribution of food. The history and political context of such efforts in California is the subject of Sally K. Fairfax et al., *California Cuisine and Just Food* (Cambridge, MA, and London: Harvard University Press, 2012).

20. Recollected in the introduction to Alice Waters, *The Chez Panisse Menu Cookbook* (New York: Random House, 1982), ix–x.

21. The point of Goldstein, *Inside the California Food Revolution*.

22. McNamee, *Alice Waters and Chez Panisse*.

23. Jeremiah Tower, *California Dish: What I Saw (and Cooked) at the American Culinary Revolution* (New York: Free Press, 2003); Goldstein, *Inside the California Food Revolution*; Patricia Curtain, *Menus for Chez Panisse* (New York: Princeton Architectural Press, 2011).

24. I thank Alice Waters for showing me these volumes.

25. Goldstein, *Inside the California Food Revolution*, 3.

26. Barr, *Provence, 1970*, 13–19; Raymond Sokolov, *Steal the Menu: A Memoir of Forty Years in Food* (New York: Knopf, 2013), 47–64.

27. David Strauss, *Setting the Table for Julia Child: Gourmet Dining in America, 1934–1961* (Baltimore: Johns Hopkins University Press, 2011), 134–37.

28. From Frank Zappa's "Brown Shoes Don't Make It," on the Mothers of Invention album *Absolutely Free*, 1967: "TV Dinner by the pool; I'm so glad I'm through with school."

29. Strauss, *Setting the Table*.

30. L. W. "Bill" Lane Jr., "Sunset Magazine: A Century of Western Living," sunset-magazine .stanford.edu/html/magazine.html.

31. *Sunset Cookbook of Favorite Recipes* (Menlo Park: Lane Publishing, 1975; eleventh printing of the 1969 edition), 12, 31, 50.

32. Ibid., 33, 42, 49.

33. *Adventures in Food* (Menlo Park: Lane Publishing, 1964), 60–61, 82–83, 90, 124–26.

34. Pot Luck menu from 1969, Los Angeles Public Library, menu collection.

35. Barry Glassner, "The Only Place to Eat in Berkeley' Hank Rubin and the Pot Luck," *Gastronomica* 2, no. 4 (Fall 2002), 26–31.

36. Goldstein, *Inside the California Food Revolution*, 19–20.

37. McNamee, *Alice Waters and Chez Panisse*; Hannah Hoffman, "An Interview with Alice Waters, Berkeley Restaurateur," *Chronicle of the University of California* 8 (Fall 2006), 89.

38. Kuh, *The Last Days of Haute Cuisine,* 128–32. On David's life and cooking ideals, see Lisa Chaney, *Elizabeth David: A Biography* (London: Macmillan, 1998).

39. Fernand Braudel, *The Identity of France*, trans. Siân Reynolds, vol. 2 (London: Collins, 1990), 674–75: "To my mind the spectacle that overshadows all others, in the France of the past and even today, is the collapse of a peasant society . . . An ancient peasant France, a France of bourgs, villages, hamlets, and scattered houses survived more or less unchanged until at least 1914, and some would say 1945."

40. Olney's life and ideas are discussed throughout Barr, *Provence, 1970*.

41. McNamee, *Alice Waters and Chez Panisse*, 45.

42. Ibid., 98. In 1978, Beard said he made a point of dining at Chez Panisse when he was in San Francisco, that he'd never had a dull meal there, and that many people think it serves the finest French and Continental food in the Bay Area, *Los Angeles Times*, April 6, 1978.

43. McNamee, *Alice Waters and Chez Panisse*, 162.

44. Goldstein, *Inside the California Food Revolution*, 134.

45. *Oakland Tribune*, July 17, 1977, 15.

46. Ibid. As we've seen, the founders and chefs of Mamma Leone's, the Mandarin, and Sylvia's were female, but within the world of high-end and French restaurants, Waters was, of course, anomalous.

47. Tower, *California Dish*, 67–70; Kamp, *The United States of Arugula*, 149–50.

48. McNamee, *Alice Waters and Chez Panisse*, 78.

49. Tower, *California Dish*, 92–93.

50. Ibid., 67–68. See also his later recollections in Kamp, *United States of Arugula*, 151.

51. Kamp, *United States of Arugula*, 152, 155.

52. Tower, *California Dish*, 133.

53. Menus from September 30–October 4 and October 7–11, 1975. Dalí's *Les diners de Gala* was published in Paris and in English in New York in 1973.

54. Menu (in English) in Waters, *Chez Panisse Menu Cookbook*, 265; the original French in McNamee, *Alice Waters and Chez Panisse*, 105–6, and Tower, *California Dish*, 94–95.

55. Tower, *California Dish*, 103.

56. Charles Ranhofer, *The Epicurean* (New York: Charles Ranhofer, 1893), 256–57.

57. Kuh, *The Last Days of Haute Cuisine*, 147. See also Andrew F. Smith, *Eating History: 30 Turning Points in the Making of American Cuisine* (New York: Columbia University Press, 2009), 257–62.

58. Tower, *California Dish*, 111.

59. McNamee, *Alice Waters and Chez Panisse*, 127.

60. Ibid., 135.

61. Kamp, *United States of Arugula*, 298–99.

62. Tower, *California Dish*, 165–94; conversation with Jeremiah Tower, August 23, 2014.

63. According to McNamee, *Alice Waters and Chez Panisse*, 148, Alice Waters, Jeremiah Tower, Bob Waks (of the Cheese Board shop in Berkeley), and the vintner Jay Heminway discovered wood-fired pizza in Turin. Jeremiah Tower says they got the idea from a pizzeria in San Francisco called Tomasso's (in conversation with me, August 25, 2014), and Jean-Pierre Moullé too remembers it this way. See Goldstein, *Inside the California Food Revolution*, 182.

64. Kuh, *Last Days of Haute Cuisine*, 171–72.

65. McNamee, *Alice Waters and Chez Panisse*, 182.

66. Ibid., 190–91.

67. Kamp, *United States of Arugula*, 246–50, 298. Puck did not invent the open or glass-enclosed visible kitchen. It was already a feature of Kan's in San Francisco, an elegant Chinese restaurant founded in the 1950s. See Johnny Kan with Charles L. Leong, *Eight Immortal Flavors* (Berkeley: Howell-North Books, 1963), 15–16. According to Alison Pearlman, *Smart Casual: The Transformation of Gourmet Restaurant Style in America* (Chicago: University of Chicago Press, 2013), 72, the first open kitchen displayed to customers for reasons other than reassurance about hygiene was John N. Novi's Depuy Canal House in High Falls, New York, in 1974.

68. Pearlman, *Smart Casual*, 22.

69. McNamee, *Alice Waters and Chez Panisse*, 227.

70. Ibid., 244–46.

71. Michael Bauer, *San Francisco Chronicle*, March 17, 1993, quoting McNamee, *Alice Waters and Chez Panisse*, 256.

EPILOGUE

1. Wittgenstein said this to the Cornell philosopher Norman Malcolm, his host for a visit to Ithaca in 1949. See Norman Malcolm, *Ludwig Wittgenstein: A Memoir*, 2nd ed. (Oxford: Oxford University Press, 2001), 69. On the academic intellectual's contempt for food, Steven Shapin, "The Philosopher and the Chicken: On the Dietaries of Disembodied Knowledge," in *Science Incarnate: Historical Embodiments of Natural Knowledge*, eds. Christopher Lawrence and Steven Shapin (Chicago: University of Chicago Press, 1998), 21–50.

2. Le Bernardin, Per Se, and Jean Georges are only in the vaguest sense French—they are more individual creations.

3. "The World's 50 Best Restaurants," www.theworlds50best.com/list/1–50 –winners#t1–10, accessed July 10, 2015.

4. Henri Gault and Christian Millau, "Which Is the World's Greatest Restaurant?" *Holiday*, June 1969, 32–33, 76–79.

5. Michael Steinberger, *Au Revoir to All That: Food, Wine, and the End of France* (New York: Bloomsbury USA, 2010).

6. As given in Steinberger, *Au Revoir to All That*, 31–34.

7. Patrick Rambourg, *Histoire de la cuisine et la gastronomie françaises* (Paris: Editions Perrin, 2010), 283–99.

8. Letter of October 13, 1975, Providence, Johnson & Wales University, Culinary Arts Museum Library, Roger Fessaguet Collection, red unnumbered folder "Valuable Old Letters."

9. Quoted in Mitchell Davis, "A Taste for New York: Restaurant Reviews, Food Discourse, and the Field of Gastronomy in America," doctoral dissertation, food studies, New York University, 1999, 152.

10. Lisa Abend, *The Sorcerer's Apprentices: A Season in the Kitchen at Ferran Adrià's elBulli* (New York: Free Press, 2011).

11. Sam Borden, "Ferran Adria Feeds the Hungry Mind," *New York Times*, January 15, 2015.

12. Anthony Bourdain, *Kitchen Confidential: Adventures in the Culinary Underbelly* (New York: Bloomsbury, 2000), 266. Here Bourdain describes elBulli as the "restaurant of the minute." Bourdain later changed his mind, admitting that he first visited the restaurant with a "hostile attitude." See Coleman Andrews, *Ferran: The Inside Story of El Bulli and the Man Who Reinvented Food* (New York: Gotham Books, 2010), 47–48.

13. René Redzepi, *Time and Place in Nordic Cuisine* (London and New York: Phaidon Press, 2010), 1–17, 289.

14. Husk Restaurant, www.huskrestaurant.com/about/, accessed July 25, 2015.

15. David S. Shields, *Southern Provisions: The Creation and Revival of a Cuisine* (Chicago: University of Chicago Press, 2015).

16. On his career, see Ian Kelly, *Cooking for Kings: The Life of Antonin Carême, the First Celebrity Chef* (New York; Walker & Company, 2004).

17. His *Memoires of My Life* was translated by Laurence Escoffier (New York: Van Nostrand Reinhold, 1997). See also Timothy Shaw, *The World of Escoffier* (New York: Vendome Press, 1995); Kenneth James, *Escoffier: The King of Chefs* (Hambledon and London: Bloomsbury, 2002).

18. On the front-of-the-house side currently, see Nicholas Lander, *The Art of the Restaurateur* (London and New York: Phaidon Press, 2012).

19. Julia Child and Daniel Humm quoted in Priscilla Parkhurst Ferguson, *Word of Mouth: What We Talk About When We Talk About Food* (Berkeley: University of California Press, 2014), 170, 177.

20. Richard Condon, "A Swiss Inn on the Rhine," *Gourmet*, September 1986, 44–48, 73–75.

21. Ferguson, *Word of Mouth*, 156–58, 171–72.

22. Krishnendu Ray, *The Ethnic Restaurateur* (London: Bloomsbury, 2016). I'm grateful to Professor Ray for discussing this with me.

23. Alison Pearlman, *Smart Casual: The Transformation of Gourmet Restaurant Style in America* (Chicago: University of Chicago Press, 2013); Ferguson, *Word of Mouth*, 170–96.

24. Ferguson, *Word of Mouth*, 170–96.

25. John Mariani, *America Eats Out* (New York: William Morrow and Co., 1991), 262–65.

26. David Strauss, *Setting the Table for Julia Child: Gourmet Dining in America, 1934–1961* (Baltimore: Johns Hopkins University Press, 2011), 134.

27. Nora Ephron, "The Food Establishment: Life in the Land of the Rising Soufflé (Or Is It the Rising Meringue?)," in *The Most of Nora Ephron* (New York: Knopf, 2013), 408–11.

28. Sylvia Lovegren, *Fashionable Food: Seven Decades of Food Fads* (New York: Macmillan, 1995), 175–207; Jane and Michael Stern, *American Gourmet: Classic Recipes, Deluxe Delights, Flamboyant Favorites, and Swank "Company" Food from the '50s and '60s* (New York: HarperCollins, 1991), 145–54. Peter Moruzzi, *Classic Dining: Discovering America's Finest Mid-Century Restaurants* (Layton, UT: Gibbs Smith, 2012) is primarily an inventory of surviving restaurants of this type rather than a history, but it has an authoritative list of their culinary and atmospheric attributes.

SELECTED BIBLIOGRAPHY

Abend, Lisa. *The Sorcerer's Apprentices: A Season in the Kitchen at Ferran Adrià's elBulli.* New York: Free Press, 2011.

Adams, Charlotte. *The Four Seasons Cookbook.* New York: Holt, Rinehart and Winston, 1971.

Adventures in Food. Menlo Park, CA: Lane Book Company, 1964.

Alexander, Charles. "Mr. Johnson in Your Town." In *Howard Johnson's First Annual Management Seminar.* March 6–8, 1957. School of Hotel Administration, Cornell University Library.

Allen, Carol. *Leah Chase: Listen, I Say Like This.* Gretna, LA: Pelican Publishing Company, 2002.

Andrews, Coleman. *Ferran: The Inside Story of El Bulli and the Man Who Reinvented Food.* New York: Gotham Books, 2010.

Apple, Max. "The Oranging of America." In *The Oranging of America and Other Stories,* 1–19. New York: Grossman Publishers, 1976.

Auden, W. H. "In Schrafft's." *The New Yorker,* February 12, 1949.

Azzarito, Amy. "Haute Cuisine: New York Style." *New York Public Library* (blog). November 19, 2007, exhibitions.nypl.org/biblion/worldsfair/fashion-food-famous -faces-pop-culture-fair/essay/essay-azzarito-french-food.

Bagli, Charles V., and James Barron. "Four Seasons on Shaky Ground at Park Avenue Home." *New York Times,* February 7, 2014.

Barr, Luke. *Provence, 1970: M. F. K. Fisher, Julia Child, James Beard, and the Reinvention of American Taste.* New York: Clarkson Potter Publishers, 2013.

Barron, James. "Power Lunch Proceeds as Usual at Restaurant." *New York Times*, June 5, 2015.

Bates, Caroline. "Spécialités de la Maison—California." *Gourmet*, October 1975.

Batterberry, Michael and Ariane. *On the Town in New York: The Landmark History of Eating, Drinking and Entertainments from the American Revolution to the Food Revolution.* New York and London: Routledge, 1999.

Beahrs, Andrew. *Twain's Feast: Searching for America's Lost Foods in the Footsteps of Samuel Clemens.* New York: Penguin Press, 2010.

Beebe, Lucius. "The Miracle at Antoine's." *Holiday,* January 1953.

Bégué, Elizabeth Kettenring Dutry, and Poppy Tooker. *Bégué's Recipes of Old New Orleans Creole Cookery.* Gretna, LA: Pelican Publishing Company, 2012.

Belasco, Warren. *Appetite for Change: How the Counterculture Took On the Food Industry.* New York: Pantheon Books, 1989; 2nd ed. Ithaca: Cornell University Press, 2007.

————. "Toward a Culinary Common Denominator: The Rise of Howard Johnson's, 1925–1949." *Journal of American Culture* 2 (1979): 502–18.

Berger, Joseph. "Côte Basque, a Society Temple, Is Closing." *New York Times*, September 8, 2003.

Bohun, Ruth L. "Whitman and the 'Picture-Makers.'" In *Whitman Among the Bohemians*, edited by Joanna Levin and Edward Whitely, 132–54, Iowa City: University of Iowa Press, 2014.

Bonner, Arthur. *Alas! What Brought Thee Hither? The Chinese in New York, 1800–1950.* Madison, NJ: Fairleigh Dickinson University Press, 1997.

Borden, Sam. "Ferran Adria Feeds the Hungry Mind." *New York Times*, January 15, 2015.

Bourdain, Anthony. *Kitchen Confidential: Adventures in the Culinary Underbelly.* New York: Bloomsbury, 2000.

Bower, Anne L. "Introduction: Watching Soul Food." In *African American Foodways: Explorations of History and Culture*, edited by Anne L. Bower, 1–16. Urbana, IL: University of Illinois Press, 2007.

Braudel, Fernand. *The Identity of France.* Vol. 2. Translated by Siân Reynolds. London: Collins, 1990.

Brevetti, Francine. *The Fabulous Fior: Over 100 Years of an Italian Kitchen.* 2nd ed. Nevada City, CA: San Francisco Bay Books, 2004.

Britchky, Seymour. *Seymour Britchky's New, Revised Guide to the Restaurants of New York.* New York: Random House, 1976.

Brody, Meredith. "Local Heavies to Celebrate Cecilia Chiang, the Julia Child of Chinese Cooking." *SF Weekly Blog*, September 16, 2009, sfweekly.com/foodie/2009/09/16/local-heavies-to-celebrate-cecilia-chiang-the-julia-child-of-chinese-cooking.

Browne, Junius. *The Great Metropolis: A Mirror of New York.* Hartford, CT: American Publishing Company, 1869.

Buettner, Elizabeth. "Going for an Indian: South Asian Restaurants and the Limits of Multiculturalism in Britain." *Journal of Modern History* 80 (2008): 865–901.

Burke, Mary Lee. "Who's Your Waiter?" *New Orleans*, August 1969.

Burton, Nathaniel, and Rudy Lombard. *Creole Feast: Fifteen Master Chefs of New Orleans Reveal Their Secrets.* New York: Random House, 1978.

Bushman, Richard L. *The Refinement of America: Persons, Houses, Cities.* New York: Knopf, 1992.

Carney, Judith A. *Black Rice: The African Origins of Rice Cultivation in the Americas.* Cambridge, MA: Harvard University Press, 2001.

Capatti, Alberto, and Massimo Montanari. *Italian Cuisine, A Cultural History.* Translated by Aine O'Healy. New York: Columbia University Press, 2003.

Chaney, Lisa. *Elizabeth David: A Biography.* London: Macmillan, 1998.

Chao, Buwei Yang. *How to Cook and Eat in Chinese.* New York: John Day, 1945.

Charles, Dora. *A Real Southern Cook in Her Savannah Kitchen.* Boston: Houghton Mifflin Harcourt, 2015.

Chase, Leah. *The Dooky Chase Cookbook.* Gretna, LA: Pelican Publishing Company, 1990.

Chauncey, George. *Gay New York: Gender, Urban Culture, and the Making of the Gay Male World, 1890–1940.* New York: Basic Books, 1994.

Chiang, Cecilia. *The Seventh Daughter: My Culinary Journey from Beijing to San Francisco.* Berkeley and Toronto: Ten Speed Press, 2007.

Chiang, Cecilia Sun Yun. *The Mandarin Way.* Boston and Toronto: Little, Brown and Company, 1974.

Choate, Judith, and James Canora. *Dining at Delmonico's: The Story of America's Oldest Restaurant.* New York: Stewart, Tabori, and Chang, 2008.

Chu, Louis H. "The Chinese Restaurant in New York City." MA thesis, New York University, February 1939.

Cinotto, Simone. *The Italian American Table: Food, Family, and Community in New York City.* Urbana, IL: University of Illinois Press, 2013.

Claiborne, Craig. "$4.5 Million Restaurant to Open Here." *New York Times,* July 16, 1959.

————. "In Classic Tradition Henri Soulé Set Towering Standards in Search of Gastronomic Perfection." *New York Times,* January 28, 1966.

————. *A Feast Made for Laughter.* Garden City: Doubleday, 1982.

————. "Food News: Dining in Elegant Manner." *New York Times,* October 2, 1959.

————. "La Mistral Is the Newest Offshoot of Pavillon Tree." *New York Times,* December 1, 1964.

Clark, Robert. *James Beard: A Biography.* New York: Harper Collins, 1993.

Clarkson, Janet. *Menus from History: Historic Meals and Recipes for Every Day of the Year.* Vol. 2. Santa Barbara: Greenwood Press, 2009.

Cleaver, Eldridge. *Soul on Ice.* New York: Dell, 1968.

Coe, Andrew. *Chop Suey: A Cultural History of Chinese Food in the United States.* New York: Oxford University Press, 2009.

Condon, Richard. "A Swiss Inn on the Rhine." *Gourmet,* September 1986.

"Cook Who Is Known for 'Dream Melon' to Teach Creole Cuisine." *Times-Picayune,* May 15, 1938.

Croly, J. C. *Jennie June's American Cookery Book.* New York: American News Company, 1866.

Dalí, Salvador. *Les diners de Gala,* Paris: Draeget, 1978, and in English trans. J. Peter Moore. New York: Felicie Schumsky, 1973.

Davis, Mitchell. "A Taste for New York: Restaurant Reviews, Food Discourse, and the Field of Gastronomy in America." Doctoral dissertation, New York University, 1999.

Deutsch, Hermann B. *Brennan's New Orleans Cookbook.* New Orleans: Crager, 1961.

Diamond, Becky Libourel. *The Thousand Dollar Dinner: America's First Great Cooking Challenge*. Yardley, PA: Westholme, 2015.

Diner, Hasia R. *Hungering for America: Italian, Irish, and Jewish Foodways in the Age of Migration*. Cambridge, MA: Harvard University Press, 2001.

Duberman, Martin Baumi. *Paul Robeson: A Biography*. New York: Knopf, 1988.

Durell, Edward Henry. Writing under the pseudonym H. Didimus. *New Orleans as I Found It*. New York: Harper and Brothers, 1845.

Dwinell, C. K. 1957 panel discussion. In *Howard Johnson's First Annual Management Seminar*. March 6–8, 1957. School of Hotel Administration, Cornell University Library.

Edwards, Clarence E. *Bohemian San Francisco, Its Restaurants and Their Most Famous Recipes: The Elegant Art of Dining*. San Francisco: Paul Elder and Company, 1914.

Egerton, John. *Southern Food: At Home, On the Road, in History*. New York: Knopf, 1987.

Eisenberg, Lee. "America's Most Powerful Lunch." *Esquire,* October 1979.

Ellington, George (pseudonym). *The Women of New York or Social Life in the Great City*. New York: The New York Book Company, 1870.

Ephron, Nora. "The Food Establishment: Life in the Land of the Rising Soufflé." In *The Most of Nora Ephron*, by Nora Ephron, 408–20. New York: Knopf, 2013.

Escoffier, Auguste. *Memoirs of My Life*. Translated by Laurence Escoffier. New York: Van Nostrand Reinhold, 1997.

Fairfax, Sally K. et al. *California Cuisine and Just Food*. Cambridge, MA, and London: Massachusetts Institute of Technology Press, 2012.

Falcinelli, Frank et al. *The Frankies Spuntino Kitchen Companion and Cooking Manual*. New York: Artisan, 2010.

Feldman, Zachery. "The Ten Best Restaurants in Harlem." *Village Voice Blog*, November 12, 2013, blogs.villagevoice.com/forkintheroad/2013/11/the_10_best_restaurants_in_harlem.php.

Ferguson, Priscilla Parkhurst. *Word of Mouth: What We Talk About When We Talk About Food*. Berkeley: University of California Press, 2014.

Fertel, Rien. "'Everyone Seemed Willing to Help': *The Picayune Creole Cookbook* as Battleground, 1900–2008." In *The Larder: Food Studies Methods from the American South*, edited by John T. Edge et al., 10–31. Athens, GA: University of Georgia Press, 2013.

Filippini, Alexander. *The Table: How to Buy Food, How to Cook It, and How to Serve It*. New York: Charles L. Webster and Company, 1891.

Fisher, Abby. *What Mrs. Fisher Knows About Old Southern Cooking*. San Francisco: Women's Cooperative Printing Office, 1881; reprinted Bedford, MA: Applewood Books, 1995.

Fitzmorris, Tom. *Hungry Town: A Culinary History of New Orleans, the City Where Food Is Almost Everything*. New York: Stewart, Tabori, and Chang, 2010.

Fitzmorris, Tom, and Peggy Scott Laborde. *Lost Restaurants of New Orleans and the Recipes that Made Them Famous*. Gretna, LA: Pelican Publishing Company, 2012.

Foster, George G. *New York by Gas-Light and Other Urban Sketches*. Edited by Stuart M. Blumin. Berkeley: University of California Press, 1990.

————. *New York in Slices, by an Experienced Carver: Being the Original Slices Published in the N.Y. Tribune*. New York: W. F. Burgess, 1849.

Fox, Margalit. "Sylvia Woods, Soul-Food Restaurateur, Is Dead at 86." *New York Times,*

July 19, 2012. www.nytimes.com/2012/07/20/dining/sylvia-woods-soul-food -restaurateur-is-dead-at-86.html?_r=0.

Franey, Pierre. *A Chef's Tale: A Memoir of Food, France and America at Table.* New York: Knopf, 1994.

————. *The New York Times 60-Minute Gourmet.* New York: Times Books, 1979.

Freedman, Paul. "American Restaurants and Cuisine in the Mid-Nineteenth Century." *New England Quarterly* 84 (2011): 1–55.

————. "Women and Restaurants in the Nineteenth-Century United States." *Journal of Social History* 48 (2014): 1–19.

Friedman, B. H. "The Most Expensive Restaurant Ever Built." *Evergreen Review* 10 (1959).

From Maine to Florida with Howard Johnson's. Howard Johnson's Company, 1939.

Gabaccia, Donna. *We Are What We Eat: Ethnic Food and the Making of Americans.* Cambridge, MA: Harvard University Press, 1998.

Gaige, Crosby. *New York World's Fair Cook Book: The American Kitchen.* New York: Doubleday, Doran & Company, 1939.

Garrett, Oliver H. P. "Without Benefit of Tin Foil." *The New Yorker,* May 19, 1928.

Gault, Henri, and Christian Millau. "Which Is the World's Greatest Restaurant?" *Holiday,* June 1969.

Gill, John Freeman. "Frederick Douglass Boulevard: Newly Revived." *New York Times,* December 31, 2013.

Glassner, Barry. "'The Only Place to Eat in Berkeley': Hank Rubin and the Pot Luck." *Gastronomica* 2, no. 4 (Fall 2002): 26–31.

Goldstein, Joyce. *Inside the California Food Revolution: Thirty Years That Changed Our Culinary Consciousness.* Berkeley: University of California Press, 2013.

The Good Housekeeping Hostess. Springfield, MA, and New York: Phelps Publishing Company, 1904.

Gopnik, Adam. "Aftertaste." *The New Yorker,* March 22, 2004.

————. *The Table Comes First: Family, France, and the Meaning of Food.* New York: Random House, 2011.

Gray, Christopher. "Streetscapes: Schrafft's. Midday Haven, Lost to a Faster-Paced City." *New York Times,* June 29, 2008.

Greene, Gael. "The Four Seasons at 25." *New York Magazine,* June 18, 1984.

————. "Harlem on My Mind." *New York Magazine,* March 12, 1979.

————. "Papa Soulé Loves You." *New York Herald Tribune,* June 13, 1965 (Sunday supplement).

————. "Quintessential Soulé Food." *New York Magazine,* November 25, 1968.

————. "Restaurant Associates: Twilight of the Gods." *New York Magazine,* November 2, 1970.

Grimes, William. *Appetite City: A Culinary History of New York.* New York: North Point Press, 2009.

Guste, Roy F. Jr. *Antoine's Restaurant Since 1840 Cookbook.* New York: W. W. Norton and Company, 1980.

Gutman, Richard J. S. *American Diner Then and Now.* Baltimore: Johns Hopkins University Press, 2000.

Haley, Andrew P. *Turning the Tables: Restaurants and the Rise of the American Middle Class, 1880–1920*. Chapel Hill: University of North Carolina Press, 2011.

Hall, A. Oakley. *The Manhattaner in New Orleans, or Phases of Crescent-City Life*. New York: J. S. Redfeld, 1851.

Hall, Robert L. "Food Crops, Medicinal Plants, and the Atlantic Slave Trade." In *African American Foodways: Explorations of History and Culture*, edited by Anne L. Bower, 17–44. Urbana, IL: University of Illinois Press, 2007.

Halpern, Ashlea. "Robertasville." *New York Magazine*, April 3, 2011.

Harris, Jessica B. *High on the Hog: A Culinary Journey from Africa to America*. New York: Bloomsbury Publishing, 2011.

Haskins, Jim. *The Cotton Club*. New York: Plume, 1984.

Hatchett, Louis. *Duncan Hines: How a Traveling Salesman Became the Most Trusted Name in Food*. Lexington, KY: University Press of Kentucky, 2014.

Hauck-Lawson, Annie, and Jonathan Deutsch, eds. *Gastropolis: Food and New York City*. New York: Columbia University Press, 2009.

Hellman, Geoffrey T. "Directed to the Product." *The New Yorker,* October 17, 1964.

Hellman, Peter. "Power House: How the Four Seasons Does It." *New York Magazine,* November 3, 1986.

Henderson, Mary F. *Practical Cooking and Dinner Giving*. New York: Harper and Brothers, 1878.

Hess, John L., and Karen Hess. *The Taste of America*. New York: Grossman Publishers, 1977.

Hess, Karen. *The Carolina Rice Kitchen: The African Connection*. Columbia, SC: University of South Carolina Press, 1992.

Hines, Duncan. *Duncan Hines' Food Odyssey*. New York: Crowell, 1955.

Hines, Mary Anne et al. *The Larder Invaded: Reflections on Three Centuries of Philadelphia Food and Drink*. Philadelphia: Library Company of Philadelphia and the Historical Society of Pennsylvania, 1987.

Historical Sketch Book and Guide to New Orleans and Environs. New York: W. H. Coleman, 1885.

Hoffman, Hannah. "An Interview with Alice Waters, Berkeley Restaurateur." *Chronicle of the University of California* 8 (Fall 2006): 87–90.

Hogan, David Gerard. *Selling 'Em by the Sack: White Castle and the Creation of American Food*. New York and London: New York University Press, 1997.

Hollander, Sophia. "As Sylvia's Endured, Harlem Changed." *Wall Street Journal*, July 20, 2012.

Houston, Benjamin. *The Nashville Way: Racial Etiquette and the Struggle for Social Justice in a Southern City*. Athens, GA: University of Georgia Press, 2012.

Hsu, Madeline Y. "From Chop Suey to Mandarin Cuisine: Fine Dining and the Refashioning of Chinese Ethnicity During the Cold War Era." In *Chinese Americans and the Politics of Race and Culture*, edited by Suchen Chan and Madeline Y. Hsu, 173–93. Philadelphia: Temple University Press, 2008.

Ilf, Ilya, and Eugene Petrov. *Little Golden America: Two Famous Soviet Humorists Survey These United States*. Translated by Charles Malamuth. New York and Toronto: Farrar & Rinehart, 1937.

Ingraham, J. H. *The South-West, by a Yankee.* Vol. 1. New York: Harper and Brothers, 1835.

Inness, Sherrie A. *Dinner Roles: American Women and Culinary Culture.* Iowa City: University of Iowa Press, 2001.

Jacob, Kathryn Allamong. *King of the Lobby: The Life and Times of Sam Ward, Man-About-Washington in the Gilded Age.* Baltimore: Johns Hopkins University Press, 2010.

Jakle, John A. *The Tourist: Travel in Twentieth-Century North America.* Lincoln, NE: University of Nebraska Press, 1985.

James, Kenneth. *Escoffier: The King of Chefs.* Hambledon and London: Bloomsbury, 2002.

Jung, John. *Sweet and Sour: Life in Chinese Family Restaurants.* n.p.: Yin and Yang Press, 2010.

Kamp, David. *The United States of Arugula: The Sun-Dried, Cold-Pressed, Dark-Roasted, Extra Virgin Story of the American Food Revolution.* New York: Broadway Books, 2006.

Kan, Johnny, and Charles L. Leong. *Eight Immortal Flavors.* Berkeley: Howell-North Books, 1963.

Kane, Harnett T. *Queen New Orleans: City by the River.* New York: William Morrow and Company, 1949.

Kelly, Ian. *Cooking for Kings: The Life of Antonin Carême, the First Celebrity Chef.* New York: Walker & Company, 2004.

Keyes, Frances Parkinson. *Dinner at Antoine's.* New York: Julian Messner, 1948.

Kimball, Marie. *Thomas Jefferson's Cookbook.* Charlottesville: University of Virginia Press, 1976.

Kinloch, Valerie. *Harlem on Our Mind: Place, Race, and the Literacies of Urban Youth.* New York: Teachers College Press, 2010.

Kraig, Bruce. "Duncan Hines." In *The Oxford Encyclopedia of Food and Drink in America,* edited by Andrew F. Smith, 613–14. Vol. 1. Oxford: Oxford University Press, 2004.

Kristen, Sven A. *The Book of Tiki.* Cologne: Taschen, 2000.

Kroc, Ray. *Grinding It Out: The Making of McDonald's.* Chicago: Contemporary Books, 1977.

Kuh, Patric. *The Last Days of Haute Cuisine: The Coming of Age of American Restaurants.* New York: Viking, 2001.

Kummer, Corby. "Pasta." *Atlantic Monthly,* July 1986.

Kun, Josh. *To Live and Dine in L.A.: Menus and the Making of the Modern City.* Santa Monica, CA: Angel City Press, 2015.

Kurlansky, Mark. *The Big Oyster: History on the Half Shell.* New York: Ballantine Books, 2006.

Lambert, Phyllis. *Building Seagram.* New Haven: Yale University Press, 2013.

Lander, Nicholas. *The Art of the Restaurateur.* London and New York: Phaidon, 2012.

Langdon, Philip. *Orange Roofs, Golden Arches: The Architecture of American Chain Restaurants.* New York: Knopf, 1986.

Laudan, Rachel. *Cuisine and Empire: Cooking in World History.* Berkeley: University of California Press, 2013.

Laussat, Pierre Clément de. *Memoirs of My Life to My Son During the Years 1803 and After, Which I Spent in the Public Service in Louisiana as Commissioner of the French Government for the Retrocession to France of that Colony and Its Transfer to the United States.* Translated by Agnes-Josephine Pastwa. Baton Rouge: Louisiana State University Press, 1978.

Lawton, Mackall. *Knife and Fork in New York: Where to Eat and What to Order*. 2nd ed. Garden City, NY: Doubleday, 1949.

Lee, Jennifer 8. *The Fortune Cookie Chronicles: Adventures in the World of Chinese Food*. New York: Twelve, 2008.

Lee, Matt, and Ted Lee. "For a Better Steak, Cook Directly on Charcoal." *New York Times*, June 25, 2015.

Lemann, Nicolas. *The Promised Land: The Great Black Migration and How It Changed America*. New York: Knopf, 1991.

Leone, Gene. *Leone's Italian Cookbook*. New York: Harper and Row, 1967.

Leslie, Austin, and Marie Rudd Posey. *Austin Leslie's Creole-Soul: New Orleans' Cooking with a Soulful Twist*. New Orleans: De Simonin Publications, 2000.

Lesy, Michael, and Lisa Stoffer. *Repast: Dining Out at the Dawn of the New American Century, 1900–1910*. New York: W. W. Norton and Company, 2013.

Levenstein, Harvey. *Paradox of Plenty: A Social History of Eating in Modern America*. 2nd ed. Berkeley: University of California Press, 2003.

————. *Revolution at the Table: The Transformation of the American Diet*. Berkeley and Los Angeles: University of California Press, 2003.

Lew, Ling. *The Chinese in North America: A Guide to Their Life and Progress*. Los Angeles: East-West Culture Publishing Association, 1949.

Lewis, David Levering. *When Harlem was in Vogue*. New York: Knopf, 1981.

Lewis, Edna. *The Taste of Country Cooking*. New York: Knopf, 1976.

Liu, Haiming. "Chop Suey as Imagined Authentic Chinese Food: The Culinary Identity of Chinese Restaurants in the United States." *Journal of Transnational American Studies* 1 (2005): 5–6.

Lo Pinto, Maria. *New York Cookbook*. New York: A. A. Wyn, Inc., 1952.

Lobel, Cindy R. *Urban Appetites: Food and Culture in Nineteenth-Century New York*. Chicago: University of Chicago Press, 2014.

Love, John F. *McDonald's: Behind the Arches*. Toronto: Bantam Books, 1986.

Lovegren, Sylvia. *Fashionable Food: Seven Decades of Food Fads*. New York: Macmillan, 1995.

Lui, Mary Ting Yi. *The Chinatown Trunk Mystery: Murder, Miscegenation, and Other Dangerous Encounters in Turn-of-the-Century New York City*. Princeton: Princeton University Press, 2005.

Marcus, Greil. "1971: Berkeley." *Lapham's Quarterly* 4, no. 3 (Summer, 2011): 94–95.

Mariani, John F. *America Eats Out*. New York: William Morrow and Company, 1991.

————. *How Italian Food Conquered the World*. New York: Palgrave Macmillan, 2011.

Mariani, John F., and Alex von Bidder. *The Four Seasons: A History of America's Premier Restaurant*. New York: Crown Publishers, 1994.

McAllister, Ward. *Society as I Have Found It*. New York: Cassell Publishing Company, 1890.

McNamee, Thomas. *Alice Waters and Chez Panisse: The Romantic, Impractical, Often Eccentric, Ultimately Brilliant Making of a Food Revolution*. New York: Penguin, 2007.

————. *The Man Who Changed the Way We Eat: Craig Claiborne and the American Food Renaissance*. New York: Free Press, 2012.

McWilliams, James E. *A Revolution in Eating: How the Quest for Food Shaped America*. New York: Columbia University Press, 2005.

McWilliams, Mark. "Distant Tables: Food and the Novel in Early America." *Early American Literature* 38 (2003): 365–93.

——— . *Food and the Novel in Nineteenth-Century America.* Lanham, MD: Rowman & Littlefield, 2012.

Mendelson, Anne. *Chow Chop Suey: Food and the Chinese American Journey.* New York: Columbia University Press, forthcoming.

——— . "A Fish Story." *Gourmet,* October 2002.

Meyer, Danny. *Setting the Table: The Transforming Power of Hospitality in Business.* New York: Harper, 2006.

Miller, Adrian. *Soul Food: The Surprising Story of an American Cuisine One Plate at a Time.* Chapel Hill: University of North Carolina, 2013.

Miller, Brian. "Howard Deering Johnson: The Man Under the Orange Roof." *Journal of Hospitality and Tourism Education* 17, no. 4 (2006): 8.

Mintz, Sidney. "History and Anthropology: A Brief Reprise." In *Race and Slavery in the Western Hemisphere,* edited by Stanley Engerman and Eugene D. Genovese, 477–94. Princeton: Princeton University Press, 1975.

Moruzzi, Peter. *Classic Dining: Discovering America's Finest Mid-Century Restaurants* Layton, UT: Gibbs Smith, 2012.

Mosley, Damian M. "Cooking Up Heritage in Harlem." In *Gastropolis: Food and New York City,* edited by Annie Hauck-Lawson and Jonathan Deutsch, 274–92. New York: Columbia University Press, 2009.

Mount, Nick. *When Canadian Literature Moved to New York.* Toronto: University of Toronto Press, 2005.

Mushkat, Jerome. "Delmonico, Lorenzo." In *American National Biography,* edited by John A. Garraty and Mark C. Carnes, vol. 6, 396–97. New York: Oxford University Press, 2000.

Nall, John Greaves. *Great Yarmouth and Lowestoft: A Handbook for Visitors and Residents.* London: Longmans, Green, Reader and Dyer, 1866.

Nassauer, Sarah. "What's Made from Scratch?" *Wall Street Journal,* February 25, 2015.

Nelson, Victor. Introduction to a panel discussion, "Howard Johnson Merchandising 'Tools.'" In *Howard Johnson's Second Annual Agents' Seminar at Cornell University, Ithaca, New York.* March 19–21, 1958. Cornell University Library.

Neuhaus, Jessamyn. *Manly Meals and Mom's Home Cooking: Cookbooks and Gender in Modern America.* Baltimore: Johns Hopkins University Press, 2003.

"New York's New 4½ Million Dollar Restaurant." *Look,* October 13, 1959.

The New York Times Guide to Dining Out in New York. Edited by Craig Claiborne. New York: Athenaeum, 1964.

O'Connell, Joe. "History of Delmonico's Restaurant and Business Operations in New York." *SteakPerfection,* www.steakperfection.com/delmonico/History.html. Updated 2001.

Opie, Frederick Douglass. *Hog and Hominy: Soul Food from Africa to America.* New York: Columbia University Press, 2008.

——— . "Influence, Sources, and African Diaspora Foodways." In *Food in Time and Place: The American Historical Association Companion to Food History,* edited by Paul

Freedman, Joyce Chaplin, and Ken Albala, 188–208. Berkeley and Los Angeles: University of California Press, 2014.

Ozersky, Josh. *Colonel Sanders and the American Dream*. Austin: University of Texas Press, 2012.

—————. *The Hamburger: A History*. New Haven: Yale University Press, 2008.

Paddleford, Clementine. *Recipes from Antoine's Kitchen*. In the syndicated Sunday supplement "This Week." New York: United Newspapers Magazine Corporation, 1948.

Parkinson, James W. *American Dishes at the Centennial*. Philadelphia: King & Baird, 1874.

Pearlman, Alison. *Smart Casual: The Transformation of Gourmet Restaurant Style in America*. Chicago: University of Chicago Press, 2013.

Pépin, Jacques. *The Apprentice: My Life in the Kitchen*. Boston: Houghton Mifflin, 2003.

Peters, Martha Ann. "The St. Charles Hotel: New Orleans Social Center." *Louisiana History* 1 (1960): 206–7.

The Picayune's Creole Cook Book. 2nd ed. New Orleans: The Picayune, 1901; reprinted New York: Dover Publications, 1971.

Pillsbury, Richard. *From Boarding House to Bistro: The American Restaurant Then and Now*. Boston: Unwin Hyman, 1990.

Pratt, Caren. "Sylvia's Is Not Just Any Eatery: It's Down Home and Family Style." *New York Amsterdam News*, December 6, 1986.

Ramanathan, Lavanya. "Why Everyone Should Stop Calling Immigrant Food 'Ethnic.'" *Washington Post*, July 21, 2015.

Rambourg, Patrick. *Histoire de la cuisine et la gastronomie françaises*. Paris: Editions Perrin, 2010.

Randall, Alice, and Caroline Randall Williams. *Soul Food Love: Healthy Recipes Inspired by One Hundred Years of Cooking in a Black Family*. New York: Clarkson Potter Publishers, 2015.

Ranhofer, Charles. *The Epicurean*. New York: Charles Ranhofer, 1893.

Ray, Krishnendu. *The Ethnic Restaurateur*. London: Bloomsbury, 2016

Recipes of Famous Creole Dishes Served at the Dinner Tendered to Hon. Wm. A. Rodenberg and the House Committee on Industrial Arts and Expositions. New Orleans: Grunewald Hotel, 1911..

Redzepi, René. *Time and Place in Nordic Cuisine*. London and New York: Phaidon Press, 2010.

Reichl, Ruth. *Garlic and Sapphires: The Secret Life of a Critic in Disguise*. New York: The Penguin Press, 2005.

Reinders, Robert C. *End of an Era: New Orleans 1850–1860*. New Orleans: Pelican Publishing Company, 1964.

Reinitz, Bertram. "Chop Suey's New Role." *New York Times*, December 27, 1925.

"Restaurant Life in San Francisco." *Overland Monthly and Out West Magazine* 1, no. 5. (November 1868): 471–73.

Rimmer, Leopold. *A History of Old New York Life and the House of the Delmonicos*. New York: n.p., 1898.

Robin, C. C. *Voyage to Louisiana 1803–1805*. Translated by Stuart O. Landry Jr., New Orleans: Pelican Publishing Company, 1966.

Root, Waverley, and Richard de Rochemont. *Eating in America: A History*. Hopewell, NJ: The Ecco Press, 1995.

Ruiz, Vicki I. "Citizen Restaurant: American Imaginaries, American Communities." *American Quarterly* 60 (2008): 1–21.

Sammarco, Anthony Mitchell. *A History of Howard Johnson's: How a Massachusetts Soda Fountain Became an American Icon*. Charleston, SC: The History Press, 2013.

Sante, Luc. *Low Life: Lures and Snares of Old New York*. New York: Farrar Straus Giroux, 1991.

Santos, Fernanda. "Harlem Mainstay Survived Riots, but Falls to Renewal." *New York Times*, July 23, 2007.

Sardi, Vincent Sr., and Richard Gehman. *Sardi's: The Story of a Famous Restaurant*. New York: Henry Holt and Company, 1953.

Segal, David. "At Four Seasons, Picasso Tapestry Hangs on the Edge of Eviction." *New York Times*, February 4, 2014.

Sermolino, Maria. *Papa's Table d'Hôte*. Philadelphia and New York: J. B. Lippincott Co., 1952.

Severson, Kim. "It's All in the Seasoning." *New York Times*, September 2, 2015.

Sewell, Jessica Ellen. *Women and the Everyday City: Public Space in San Francisco, 1890–1915*. Minneapolis: University of Minnesota Press, 2011.

Shaplan, Robert. "Delmonico: The Rich New Gravy Faith." Part 1 in *The New Yorker*, November 10, 1956. Part 2 in *The New Yorker*, November 17, 1956.

Sharpless, Rebecca. *Cooking in Other Women's Kitchens: Domestic Workers in the South, 1865–1960*. Chapel Hill: University of North Carolina Press, 2010.

Shaw, Timothy. *The World of Escoffier*. New York: Vendome Press, 1995.

Sheehan, Robert. "Four Seasons: A Flourish of Food." *Fortune*, February 1960.

Sheraton, Mimi. *Eating My Words: An Appetite for Life*. New York: William Morrow, 2004.

———. *Mimi Sheraton's The New York Times Guide to New York Restaurants*. New York: Times Books, 1982.

———. "The Pleasant Avenue Food Connection." *New York Times,* August 19, 1977.

———. "Seasons in the Sun." *Vanity Fair*, August 1999.

Sherry, John. "Legal Aspects of the Restaurant Business." In *Howard Johnson's First Annual Management Seminar*. March 6–8, 1957. School of Hotel Administration, Cornell University Library.

Shields, David S. *Southern Provisions: The Creation and Revival of a Cuisine*. Chicago: University of Chicago Press, 2015.

Sietsema, Robert. *New York in a Dozen Dishes*. Boston: Houghton Mifflin Harcourt, 2015.

Slomanson, Jane Kanel. *When Everybody Ate at Schrafft's: Memories, Pictures and Recipes from a Very Special Restaurant Empire*. Fort Lee, NJ: Barricade Books, 2006.

Smart-Grosvenor, Vertamae. *Vibration Cooking: Or, the Travel Notes of a Geechee Girl*. New York: Doubleday, 1970; reprinted Athens, GA: University of Georgia Press, 2011.

Smith, Andrew F. *Eating History: 30 Turning Points in the Making of American Cuisine*. New York: Columbia University Press, 2009.

Sokolov, Raymond. *Steal the Menu: A Memoir of Forty Years in Food*. New York: Knopf, 2013.

Spitznagel, Eric. "Sylvia Woods." In the *New York Times Magazine* feature, "The Lives They Lived," July 19, 2012.

Stanonis, Anthony J. *Creating the Big Easy: New Orleans and the Emergence of Modern Tourism, 1918–1945*. Athens, GA: University of Georgia Press, 2006.

——. "The Triumph of Epicure: A Global History of New Orleans Culinary Tourism." *Southern Quarterly* 46 (2009): 148–49.

Stansell, Christine. *American Moderns: Bohemian New York and the Creation of a New Century*. Princeton: Princeton University Press, 2000.

Steinberger, Michael. *Au Revoir to All That: Food, Wine, and the End of France*. New York: Bloomsbury USA, 2010.

Stern, Jane, and Michael. *American Gourmet: Classic Recipes, Deluxe Delights, Flamboyant Favorites, and Swank "Company" Food from the '50s and '60s*. New York: HarperCollins, 1991.

Stern, Robert A. M. et al. *New York 1960: Architecture and Urbanism Between the Second World War and the Bicentennial*. New York: Monacelli Press, 1995.

Stone, Robin D. "Sylvia Woods Left Behind a Legacy of Love in Harlem—and Beyond." *Ebony*, July 1, 2015.

Strauss, David. *Setting the Table for Julia Child: Gourmet Dining in America, 1934–1961*. Baltimore: Johns Hopkins University Press, 2011.

Sunset Cookbook of Favorite Recipes. Edited by M. R. Piper. Menlo Park, CA: Lane Publishing, 1975.

Taylor, Jean Gelman. *Indonesia: Peoples and Histories*. New Haven: Yale University Press, 2003.

Thomas, Lately. *Delmonico's: A Century of Splendor*. Boston: Houghton Mifflin, 1967.

Thompson, Beth, and Louis Hanges. *Eating Around San Francisco*. San Francisco: Suttonhouse Limited, 1936.

Tomassini, Jason. "Manna's: As Soul Food Dwindles in Harlem, an Unlikely Champion Survives." *The Uptowner*, December 27, 2010.

Tower, Jeremiah. *California Dish: What I Saw (and Cooked) at the American Culinary Revolution*. New York: Free Press, 2003.

Trillin, Calvin. *American Fried: Adventures of a Happy Eater*. New York: Doubleday, 1974 .

——. *Feeding a Yen: Savoring Local Specialties, from Kansas City to Cuzco*. New York: Random House, 2003.

Trollope, Anthony. *North America*. Philadelphia: Lippincott, 1862.

Walkowitz, Judith R. *Nights Out: Life in Cosmopolitan London*. New Haven and London: Yale University Press, 2012.

Wallach, Jennifer Jensen. *How America Eats: A Social History of U.S. Food and Culture*. Lanham, MD: Rowman and Littlefield, 2013.

Waters, Alice. *The Chez Panisse Menu Cookbook*. New York: Random House, 1982.

Wechsberg, Joseph. *Dining at the Pavillon*. Boston and Toronto: Little, Brown and Company, 1962.

Weinberg, Barbara H. et al. *American Impressionism and Realism: The Painting of Modern Life, 1885–1915*. New York: Metropolitan Museum of Art, 1994.

West, Henry Litchfield. "Breakfast at Antoine's." *Wine and Food*, Autumn, 1939.

Wharton, Edith. *The Age of Innocence*. New York: D. Appleton, & Co., 1920.

Where and How to Dine in New York. New York: Lewis, Scribner, & Co., 1903; reprinted London: Forgotten Books, 2013.

"Where Gotham Eats: Bohemian Resorts that Are Popular in New York." *The Day,* June 20, 1904.

Whit, William C. "Soul Food as Cultural Creation." In *African American Foodways: Explorations of History and Culture,* edited by Anne L. Bower, 45–58. Urbana, IL: University of Illinois Press, 2007.

Whitaker, Jan. *Service and Style: How the American Department Store Fashioned the Middle Class.* New York: Macmillan, 2006.

———. "When Ladies Lunched: Schrafft's." *Restaurant-ing Through History* (blog), restaurant-ingthroughhistory.com/2008/08/27/when-ladies-lunched-schrafft%E2%80%99s/.

Wilkerson, Isabel. *The Warmth of Other Suns: The Epic Story of America's Great Migration.* New York: Random House, 2010.

Williams, Elizabeth. *New Orleans: A Food Biography.* Lanham, MD: AltaMira Press, 2013.

Williams, Susan. *Food in the United States, 1820s–1890.* Westport, CT: Greenwood Publishing Group, 2006.

Williams, Timothy. "In Changing Harlem, Soul Food Struggles." *New York Times,* August 5, 2008.

Wister, Owen. *The Virginian: A Horseman of the Plains.* New York: Macmillan, 1919; originally published London: Macmillan, 1904.

Wolfe, Tom. "Honks and Wonks." In *Mauve Gloves and Madmen, Clutter and Vine and Other Stories, Sketches, and Essays.* New York: Macmillan, 1976.

Woods, Sylvia. *Sylvia's Family Soul Food Cookbook: From Hemingway, South Carolina, to Harlem.* New York: William Morrow and Company, 1999.

Woods, Sylvia, and Christopher Styler. *Sylvia's Soul Food: Recipes from Harlem's World-Famous Restaurant.* New York: William Morrow and Company, 1992.

"The World of Dining," *New York Amsterdam News,* May 5, 1979.

Yarrow, Andrew L. "A Bus Tour That Shows Harlem's Many Sides." *New York Times,* September 9, 1983.

Yentsch, Anne. "Excavating the South's African-American Food History." In *African American Foodways: Explorations of History and Culture,* edited by Anne L. Bower, 59–100. Urbana, IL: University of Illinois Press, 2007.

Yu, Renqiu. "Chop Suey: From Chinese Food to Chinese American Food." *Chinese America: History and Perspectives* 1 (1987): 87–100.

INDEX

Page numbers in *italics* refer to illustrations.

Auden, W. H., 91
Aunt Caroline's Dixieland Recipes, 268
Aunt Priscilla in the Kitchen, 268–69
Au Revoir to All That (Steinberger), 413, 414
Au Rocher de Cancale, Paris, xlii
Automats, 95, 106, 112–14, *113*, 125, 190
automobile culture:
    Depression and, 139
    Howard Johnson's and, 129, 131, 132, 136, 160
avocados, 74

Babbo, New York, 208
Baked Alaska, 32
Balboa Café, San Francisco, 431
Ball, Bradley Martin, 34–35
Bank Coffee House, New York, xliv
Bank of America, 240
Barr, Luke, 379
bars, free-lunch, 95, 97
Bastianich, Lidia, 205–6
Bates, Caroline, 402
Battali, Mario, 208, 431
Bauer, Michael, 406
Baum, Joe, xxiii, 199, *333–35*, *334*, 337–44, 346–47, 349, 356, 359, 360–61, 362
Bayless, Rick, 429
Beard, James, 244, 342–43, 349–50, 353, 372, 380, 384–85, 484*n*
Beebe, Lucius, 81
Beef Robespierre, 51–52, 83
Bégué, Elizabeth, 68–70
Bégué, Hippolyte, 69, 70
Bégué's Restaurant, New Orleans, 68–70, *71*
Bemelmans, Ludwig, 307
Benicia, Calif., 395
Bergeron, Victor, 236
Berkeley, Calif.:
    antiwar movement in, 383
    "Gourmet Ghetto" of, *365*, 381–82
Bertolli, Paul, 398, 400, 404
Bice Group, 44

Biddle, Nelson, 277
Big Night (film), 191–92
Bird, Isabella, 104–5
Black Power movement, 280–81
Blackstone Capital Partners, 163
Blake, Curtis, 145–46
Blatch, Harriet Stanton, 100–101
Blitzkrieg (Lightning War), 290–91
Blount, Rick, 59, 88, 89–90
Blount, Yvonne Alciatore, 88
Blue Poles (Pollock), 333
Bluestein, Louis, 65
Bocuse, Collonges-au-Mont-d'Or, France, xxxiv, 412–13
Bocuse, Paul, 412–14, 425
Boeuf Robespierre, 72
Bogle, Robert, 276–77
Bohemian, use of term, 182–83, 459*n*–60*n*
Bohemian San Francisco (Edwards), 182–83
Boiled String Beans with Ham (Sylvia's), 443
Bonfire of the Vanities (Wolfe), 355
Boston, Mass., North End of, 195
Bostonians, The (James), 10
Bouley, New York, 411
Boulud, Daniel, 432
Bourdain, Anthony, 89, 419, 486*n*
Braudel, Fernand, 383–84, 484*n*
Brennan, Ella and Dick, 86, 87
Brennan's, New Orleans, 54, 65
Britchky, Seymour, 201–2, 321
Brock, Sean, 421–22
Brody, Jerome, 333
Brody, Martin, 348
Bronfman, Samuel, 329
Brooklyn, N.Y., restaurants in, xlvi, 359
Brown, James, 258
Browne, Junius, 96
Brown v. Board of Education, 255–56
brunch, invention of, 68–69
Buffett, Warren, 328, 480*n*
Bugs Bunny (char.), 80

Downing, Thomas, 277
Dreiser, Theodore, 34, 188
Drouant, Jean, 290, 293
Du Bois, W. E. B., 277, 279–80
Ducasse, Alain, 15
Dumas, Alexandre, xxvii
Durham, N.C., 159
Durrell, Edward Henry, 4
Dutch East India Company, 213
Dutreuil, Louis, 69

East India Club, xliii
Eat Well and Stay Well (Keys), 203
Edible Schoolyard, 403
Edwards, Clarence, 182–83
Eggs Sardou, 75, 77, 83, 90
Eisenberg, Lee, 327, 353–54
Eisenhower, Dwight, 198
elBulli, Roses, Catalonia, 406, 418–19,
    486n
El Celler de Can Roca, Girona, Catalonia,
    411
Eldorado (Taylor), 215
Eleven Madison Park, New York, 426
Ellison, Ralph, 278
El Morocco, New York, 478n, 482n
environment, food and, 433–34
Ephron, Nora, 117, 434
Epicure, 455n
Epicurean, The (Ranhofer), 24, 26, 27,
    29–33, 63, 392
Erie Canal, 8, 57
Ernie's, San Francisco, 205
Escoffier, Auguste, 391, 402, 423
Esquire, 327, 353–54
ethnic restaurants and cuisines, xxxvii,
    176, 407, 408, 467n
  authenticity of, xxx
  convenience and predictability of, xxxv
  expansion of cuisine types in, 427–29
  Filippini and, 31–32
  history of, 173–75, 177
  mass appeal of, xxxvi, 173–74, 179–80,
    435

middle-class patrons of, xxvi, 93, 95,
    175, 221
  proliferation of, xxvii–xxviii, xxx
  see also Mamma Leone's; Mandarin;
    specific cuisines
Evergreen, 325
excess, premium on, 30–31

Fairbanks, Douglas, 205
Fanny (film), 376
farmers' markets, 206
Farm Restaurant Project, 398–99, 403
farm-to-table movement, 359, 363, 398–
    99, 400, 403, 417, 419, 421–22
  see also food, locally sourced; locavore
    movement
fast-food chains, xxxv, xl–xli, 125–26, 130,
    141, 285, 403
  as competition for Howard Johnson's,
    159–60, 168
  franchising and, 131
  hamburgers and, 164–65
  Howard Johnson's as precursor of, 133,
    164, 165
  proliferation of, xxvii
  rise of, 164–65
  supersizing and, 168
fast foods, health risks of, 284–85
Felidia, New York, 205–6
Felker, Clay, 353
Feltman, Charles, 166
Feltman's German Gardens, Coney
    Island, 166
Ferguson, Priscilla, 429
Fessaguet, Roger, 317, 415–16
Fettucine Alfredo, 205
Fettucini al'Alfredo of Rome (Mamma
    Leone's), 441–42
Fifth Avenue Hotel, New York, 22
Filipino cuisine, 428
Filippini, Alexander, 27, 218
  ethnic recipes of, 31–32
Fior d'Italia, San Francisco, 184, 186, 189,
    191, 193

Soulé, Henri (*continued*)
    Kennedy family's feud with, 315–16,
        317–18
    labor disputes and, 316–17
    perfectionism of, 297
    poor quality of American ingredients
        lamented by, 299, 305, 307
    snobbery and favoritism of, 294, 306,
        310, 311–12, 313, 319
    tyrannical character of, 293, 313, 317,
        319
Soulé, Olga, 320
"soul," use of term, 279–80
soul food:
    civil rights movement and, 280–81
    health issues and, 284
    in relation to Southern food, 279, 280
    waning of, 281–82, 284–85
    see also African American cuisine
Soul Food (film), 270
Soul Food Love (Randall and Williams),
    285
Soul on Ice (Cleaver), 282
Souls of Black Folk, The (Du Bois), 279–80
South:
    cash crops in, 272, 274–75
    racism in, 254–55
    segregation in, 158–59, 254
    slavery in, 274–75
    white and black diets compared in,
        275–76, 281
South Carolina, xlv, 254
    traditional cuisine of, 274
Southeast Asia, 229
    Chinese entrepreneurs in, 213
Southern food, 267
    nostalgia and, 278–79
    urban blacks' attraction to, 279
    "white" vs. "black" foods in, 270–71
    see also African American cuisine; soul
        food
Southern Living, 282
South Pacific (Rodgers and Hammerstein),
    225

Soyer, Alexis, xliii
Spago, Los Angeles, 400–402
Spalter, Henriette, 320–21
Spenger's, Berkeley, 381–82
Sprague, Reginald, 139
standardization, 136, 157, 167
Starbucks, 167–68
Stars, San Francisco, 395–96
Statesville, N.C., 159
Steinberger, Michael, 413, 414
Steward, xxviii
Stewart, A. T., 16
stir-fried dishes, 219
Stockli, Albert, 342, 343–44
Stork Club, New York, 134, *135*, 310
Strange Interlude (O'Neill), 135–36
Strauss, David, 380
Streetcar Named Desire, A (Williams), 63
Student Non-Violent Coordinating
    Committee (SNCC), 281
Suetonius, 337
sugar, 272, 273, 274
Sun Luck, New York, 227
Sunset, 380–81
Sunset Cook Book of Favorite Recipes, The,
    381
supersizing, 168
Supreme Court, U.S., *Brown v. Board of
    Education* decision of, 255–56
Surrealism, 391, 418
Sutton, Percy, 264
Sylvia's, Harlem, xxiii, xxv, xxxvi–xxxvii,
    xlv, 184, 251–87, *259*, 443
    Atlanta branch of, 266
    beginnings of, 256
    breakfasts as specialty of, 256–57, 264
    expansion of, 264
    Gael Greene's review of, 260, 262, 264
    menus of, *252, 257, 263, 265, 266, 267*
    regulars at, 256–57, 264–66
    St. Petersburg branch of, 266
    as tourist destination, 265–66
    welcoming atmosphere of, 256, 258,
        262

Paul Freedman is Chester D. Tripp Professor of History at Yale University, where he has taught since 1997. From 1979 until 1997 he taught at Vanderbilt University. He has written on topics related to medieval Europe, especially Catalonia, the Church, and peasants. In 2007 Freedman edited *Food: The History of Taste*, which won a book award from the International Association of Culinary Professionals and was nominated for a James Beard Award. It has been translated into ten languages. His book *Out of the East: Spices and the Medieval Imagination* (2008) is about the desire for spices in the Middle Ages and how it led to European efforts to explore and conquer. *Food in Time and Place* (2014), a volume co-edited with Joyce Chaplin and Ken Albala, appeared under the auspices of the American Historical Association.

Ten Restaurants
That Changed
America